WRITING WITHOUT FORMULAS

Updated Edition

William H. Thelin

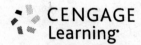
CENGAGE
Learning·

Australia • Brazil • Japan • Korea • Mexico • Singapore • Spain • United Kingdom • United States

CENGAGE
Learning·

Writing Without Formulas:
Updated Edition

Writing Without Formulas
William H. Thelin

© 2008 Cengage Learning. All rights reserved.

Senior Manager, Student
Engagement:

Linda deStefano

Janey Moeller

Manager, Student
Engagement:

Julie Dierig

Marketing Manager:

Rachael Kloos

Manager, Production
Editorial:

Kim Fry

Manager, Intellectual
Property Project Manager:

Brian Methe

Senior Manager, Production
and Manufacturing:

Donna M. Brown

Manager, Production:

Terri Daley

For product information and technology assistance, contact us at
Cengage Learning Customer & Sales Support, 1-800-354-9706

For permission to use material from this text or product,
submit all requests online at **cengage.com/permissions**
Further permissions questions can be emailed to
permissionrequest@cengage.com

This book contains select works from existing Cengage Learning resources and was produced by Cengage Learning Custom Solutions for collegiate use. As such, those adopting and/or contributing to this work are responsible for editorial content accuracy, continuity and completeness.

Compilation © 2014 Cengage Learning.

ISBN-13: 9781285901916

ISBN-10: 1285901916

WCN: 01-100-101

Cengage Learning

5191 Natorp Boulevard
Mason, Ohio 45040
USA

Cengage Learning is a leading provider of customized learning solutions with office locations around the globe, including Singapore, the United Kingdom, Australia, Mexico, Brazil, and Japan. Locate your local office at:

international.cengage.com/region.

Cengage Learning products are represented in Canada by Nelson Education, Ltd.

For your lifelong learning solutions, visit **www.cengage.com/custom.**
Visit our corporate website at **www.cengage.com.**

Printed in the United States
of America

· CONTENTS ·

· PREFACE ·

I have taught first-year college composition courses in five different schools for close to twenty years. In many ways, I have been composing *Writing Without Formulas* ever since I started teaching. In every class, my students taught me something about teaching and writing that I pondered. Keeping a teaching journal and saving successful class plans, I amassed quite a bit of material, and a pattern emerged about the effective teaching of composition. Students needed to learn conceptually to incorporate skills and knowledge into their writing processes. They needed to see a purpose behind the writing task, decide how best to explore the topic, and then figure out the best way to revise their drafts for their intended audience. Although many compelling new approaches to teaching composition are published every year, I could not find a textbook that complemented what I was discovering in my own teaching and learning; so I decided to write one. *Writing Without Formulas* represents the best ideas, exercises, and assignments that I sifted from my experiences with hundreds of students and colleagues.

The underlying ethos of *Writing Without Formulas* is that when accomplished writers first examine a topic, they pose problems and uncover the critical matters that make for intriguing essays. Eschewing assignments and exercises that put structure before content, *Writing Without Formulas* invites students to make decisions about writing within the context of audience awareness and critical analysis. In *Writing Without Formulas,* arranging or organizing a piece of writing comes after the student has generated important ideas about the subject and knows the needs and concerns of the targeted audience. Each chapter emphasizes that a writer learns about and modifies the initial thesis by thoroughly understanding the rhetorical situation of the writing task. While much of value resides in the pages of books that structure themselves around the modes of discourse or genres, I intentionally diverged from that model to encourage students to understand important rhetorical concepts and arrive at effective ways to approach and arrange their writing.

Part I focuses on five concepts that successful student writers need to know and practice: determining the reason or purpose for writing, critically analyzing a topic, responding to audience needs and concerns, organizing an essay, and using language effectively. Each chapter guides students through a new concept, stimulating their interest with examples from both student and professional writing, and gives students ample opportunity to practice their understanding of the concept within rhetorical situations. Students will have many opportunities to apply the five concepts effectively in their formal essays.

Part II continues to help students develop effective writing and reading processes and introduces them to rhetorical situations encountered in collaboration, writing with evidence, and research. Students will discover practical advice on honing the processes they have begun to develop and will find ways to work through the challenges of group assignments, essays focusing on argument, and tasks requiring the use of sources. Diverse readings and compelling examples clarify important points, helping students understand the necessity of developing processes, establishing a writer's voice while working with peers and professional texts, and handling particular rhetorical situations.

Part III encourages students to apply the knowledge learned in Parts I and II. Students need to see a problem in order to revise effectively. Many students are interested in subjects that surround them daily. When we give them choices, they often gravitate toward their own experiences with our culture's and subculture's values, habits, and idiosyncrasies. Students who write about what they know often produce competent prose, but their theses tend to lack originality. Students resist revising the content of their essays because the material feels too close and comfortable. The lessons they learn about audience awareness and language choices during revision are too limited because they cannot see problems with their drafts.

I developed topics that interest students from varying regions and backgrounds and chose readings to help them defamiliarize their ideas. Defamiliarization makes ordinary experiences, customs, and feelings seem extraordinary or strange, provoking curiosity and stimulating interest, and thus allows students to critically locate their views within a larger framework. The process of defamiliarization creates rhetorical problems that open up students to revision.

Writing Without Formulas anticipates students' interest with chapters revolving around humor, the supernatural, and honesty and deception, among other topics. Part III defamiliarizes these topics with challenging questions and approaches. The readings and apparatus do not let students settle on pat conclusions; instead, their creative capacities are stimulated. This is accomplished in part through prompts that intensely question the details and language use of what students otherwise might perceive as common sense. The readings themselves pose problems by giving little-known facts and introducing marginalized ideologies. Students are gently urged to new levels of awareness, which creates cognitive openings for new knowledge about writing to enter. Further, the apparatus in Part III reminds students to integrate the rhetorical knowledge from earlier in the book into their writing, thus tying previous lessons into their actual writing activities.

Through this focus on content-driven writing assignments, students learn on a deeper level than when we give them formulas or rules to follow. They see the purpose for adding detail, for example, and they draft and revise to respond to their audience's needs, or to incorporate an insight derived from a critical analysis, or to nurture an idea springing from a particular choice of words. *Writing Without Formulas* gives sound advice about rhetorical concepts that lets students know *why* they are doing what they do. In keeping with the aphorism that still rings true, *Writing Without Formulas* shows students how to write instead of telling them.

Features

Detailed Discussion of Rhetorical Concepts

The first part of *Writing Without Formulas* focuses students on purposes for writing, critical analysis, audience awareness, organization of ideas, and language usage. Each concept is introduced by an actual classroom situation that lends itself to key questions about the rhetorical concept. The text answers these questions in a thorough review of how writers understand, respond to, and use the concept and introduces students to the necessity of weaving these understandings into writing tasks. It also provides readings and classroom activities to illuminate the concepts.

Writing Without Formulas does not ignore the skills instructors expect students to learn and use. In Part II, students learn about brainstorming and other activities associated with the writing process, investigate the best strategies for effective reading, see practical approaches to collaboration, and develop strategies for finding and using outside resources. As in Part I, the concepts that writers need to know are explained in great detail and are supported by concrete examples.

Critical Approach to Topics

Throughout *Writing Without Formulas*, materials and readings stimulate student thinking. In Part III, thematic chapters help students question the assumptions and practices of our culture. Each chapter begins with an overview of the topic that raises questions about our values, our relationship to one another, and the effects of our actions. Students are encouraged to do brainstorming and freewriting about critical areas and key terminology before turning to professional readings on the topic. Suggested assignments lead students toward situating their experiences or observations within the problems and debates brought up by the readings. Each chapter contains one assignment explicitly designed for groups of students. Finally, any easily drawn conclusions are countered by supplemental readings that seek to broaden the boundaries of the original set of readings. The multiple layers aid in development of students' critical thinking skills.

Creative Classroom Activities

Under the headings "Discussion," "Writing," "Collaborating," "Openings for Writers," "Language," and "Assignment Ideas," instructors will find multiple classroom activities that help students learn and practice the important concepts in the first two parts of *Writing Without Formulas*. These activities encourage the conceptual learning important to this text's foundation. Students are not asked to locate the thesis sentence of a reading or to do any other exercise that caters to formulaic understandings of writing. Instead, the activities ignite students' imaginations, placing them in hypothetical rhetorical situations or calling on their knowledge of contemporary culture to draw parallels to concepts crucial to good writing and communication. Sometimes students are asked to follow up on ideas introduced in student or professional readings; other times, they analyze the slang expressions they use; and still other times, they introduce people in their peer groups the way contestants on *Jeopardy* are introduced. Each activity strengthens student understanding of a concept and leads to the integration of the concept into student processes.

Readings

Throughout *Writing Without Formulas*, readers will find diverse selections that examine many different aspects of our culture. My vision of a classroom is a place of democratic, progressive goals in which students may challenge the status quo and investigate alternative perspectives and sources of information. Many of the readings, while not specifically aligned with a political party's platform, explore social issues from a variety of critical, personal, and political perspectives. Mainstream voices are prominent, but readers will also find marginalized social critics such as animal activists, Marxists, and paranormal investigators. I also have included several student essays. Perhaps more important are the many vignettes throughout the book; my experiences with students are crucial to understanding how I arrived at my conclusions about writing. Students will enjoy seeing how an instructor learned from his students.

Sustained Focus on Collaboration

Writing Without Formulas contains an informative chapter on student collaboration, but the emphasis on collaboration does not stop there. Collaborative activities and assignments can be found throughout the book. "Collaborating" and "Discussion" activities in Parts I and II invite students to work together to come to consensual understandings. The use of peer groups for sharing student writing is similarly explored.

Each chapter in Part III has a separate assignment designed specifically for collaborative writing. Each of these assignments incorporates enough work to ensure that students will want to collaborate rather than work individually. Yet, the assignments do not overwhelm students or ask them to do more than they are capable of doing. Instead, students will surmise that some writing activities need to be done together in order to accomplish the desired goal.

Flexible Organization

Instructors can enter *Writing Without Formulas* at just about any point and succeed in teaching their students how to write. They do not need to feel bound to a particular order or approach. The book can be followed chronologically, but instructors might want to dive right into one of the topics in Part III and incorporate lessons from the first two parts of the book as they assess student need. Instructors may also move to the concepts of writing they find most important and skip chapters without losing coherence. Clear illustrations of rhetorical concepts in Parts I and II through references to the selections in Part III give instructors opportunities to link rhetorical lessons to Part III topics. In addition, instructors can teach a Part III topic and refer to particular points in Part I or II as necessary to facilitate student learning.

Additional Resources

Instructor's Resource Manual

The Instructor's Resource Manual contains in-depth explanations on incorporating *Writing Without Formulas* into the classroom. Along with suggesting ways to use the classroom activities and assignments, the manual discusses ways to respond to student work that will help maintain consistency with the text. Instructors need not worry about student responses that seem to have gone awry. The activities and assignments have been tested in actual classrooms, and the manual demonstrates how to deal with student misunderstandings of the text's ideas.

Website

The website accompanying this text includes links to appropriate online sources that can supplement the readings. It also contains additional classroom activities to reinforce the important rhetorical concepts in each chapter. Additionally, apparatus from Cengage Learning is available through links, including important support for students' syntactical and grammatical difficulties. Both students and instructors can benefit from this website.

Acknowledgements

Every book is a collaboration. Too often, behind-the-scenes people are not given enough credit for the encouragement they supplied, the sacrifices they made, and the insights they provided. Some of these people might be obvious to those who have read such acknowledgement pages before, as it takes many employees of a publisher to produce a book. *Writing Without Formulas* would not have been completed without Meg Botteon, my development editor, who made me wise to the world of textbooks and kept me on a steady enough of a path to finish this. Thanks for putting up with me, Meg. Suzanne Phelps Weir was also instrumental to this project. As editor in chief at the time, she believed in my different approach to teaching composition and never lost faith in my abilities, even when I did. After Suzanne left Houghton Mifflin, I had the pleasure of working with senior sponsoring editor Lisa Kimball, who has been equally encouraging. In the final stages of this project, Samantha Ross, the senior project editor, and Sarah Truax, the editorial associate, were extremely helpful and, like poor Meg, had to put up with my idiosyncrasies and complicated life. Let me also mention Mary Wilkinson, the sales representative when I started at the University of Akron, who first heard my ideas for a textbook and passed them along, and Heather McMaster, Joanne DeLapa, and Tom Ziolkowski, whose enthusiasm in talking about possible adoptions renewed my zeal for the project when my spirits had temporarily waned.

As much as I am in the debt of the above named people, it is those who contributed in other ways, sometimes directly, sometimes indirectly, who I would most like to acknowledge. Chief among these people are, of course, my past and present students, who enabled me to learn how to reach them and figure out what I was doing. I have forgotten many of the names and even some of the faces have faded over time, but I cannot thank them enough. I only wish I could acknowledge each of them personally. And where would I have been as a professor if enthusiastic professors had not piqued my interest as a student? There are far too many, but Dr. Arthur Lane's wit and wisdom sticks out in my memory, as does the initial mentoring of Dr. Thia Wolf, who led me into the field of composition studies. Dr. Cherryl Smith was the first of many who had to put up with me for a long project, as she directed my Master's thesis and was quite kind and brilliant in helping me toward completion. Dr. Michael Williamson survived the task of directing my doctoral dissertation, giving me much direction and focus. I thank you all, as I feel your work with me has found its way into these pages. Since becoming a professor, many colleagues have given me similar guidance. John Tassoni, who has co-authored the Instructor's Resource Manual, continues to amaze me with his insights, and his advocacy of what I do humbles me. Ira Shor has influenced me perhaps more than any other colleague and has been a patient, good friend over the years. My colleagues in Rhetoricians for Peace and Working-Class Culture and Pedagogy have similarly given me many ideas to ponder that have shaped my thoughts and theories. I owe you all.

Perhaps most important are those who support me on a daily basis. On the top of this list are my wife, Leann, and my daughter, Katrina. They had to do without me many evenings and weekends so I could meet deadlines or brainstorm ideas. My father and mother, Howard and Vivien Thelin, have offered much encouragement and have helped out my family in many ways. Dr. Diana Reep and Dr. Tom Dukes from the University of Akron have been supportive in good times as well as bad and picked up the slack on occasion to allow me to work on the book. My workout partner and friend Bacari Brown always pushed me in the gym, letting me release stress and stay sane. And I cannot overlook the staff at Max McQ's. Lora Long and Nick Pulos lead the list of a lot of servers who poured my scotch just right while listening with a compassionate ear during those moments when I was discouraged or feeling overwhelmed. To all, you have no idea how important you have been to the completion of this book.

Finally, I would like to thank the many reviewers who read either the proposal or a draft and gave suggestions toward making *Writing Without Formulas* a successful book: Jennifer Beech, University of Tennessee at Chattanooga; Mary Ann Bretzlauf, College of Lake County; Avon G. Crismore, Indiana–Purdue University, Fort Wayne; Debra Dew, University of Colorado, Colorado Springs; Christina Fisanick, Xavier University; Shu-Huei Henrickson, Rock Valley College; Julie C. Kearney, Penn State, Harrisburg; Sophia Kowalski, University of Central Florida; Robert Lamm, Arkansas State University; Robert Lamphear, Oakland University; Nicole Montoya, University of Texas at El Paso; Kathleen Snow White, Pima Community College; Wayne Stein, University of Central Oklahoma; Theresa Trela, West Texas A&M University; and Kelly Wonder, University of Wisconsin–Eau Claire.

·INTRODUCTION·

The title of this textbook might strike you as strange. *Writing Without Formulas?* What does that mean? You are used to formulas in chemistry classes, I imagine, but not in courses about English. Writing does not involve calculations or memorizing steps in a process. It is not objective the way many other disciplines are. Naturally, then, you will be writing without a formula. Why state the obvious?

If these sentiments resemble your feelings, we are in agreement. A textbook should not need to declare itself formula-free. But it is necessary to make this statement about the title of my textbook. It reveals concerns I have had as a professor of English about how students have been taught writing. Too many textbooks and too many classrooms rely on formulaic methods to teach writing. But writing does not boil down to formulas.

This textbook avoids some of the formulaic strategies used by textbook writers. It does not discuss types of papers, such as expository essays or descriptive narrations. To do so puts structure ahead of the topic and limits your creativity as a writer. While published and student essays are used to illuminate points and stimulate your thinking, I do not talk about modeling your essays on them. Instead of copying the styles of professional and student writers, you will develop a style and a voice of your own.

The book does not instruct you to follow a set process for writing. Each writer must discover his or her own best approach to a writing task or situation. This book does not dictate what an "essay" should look like or how to go about writing a "paper." Such instruction regresses into formulas. I prefer that you discover knowledge about writing on your own, and I hope that you generate completely unique ideas, structures, and processes.

Instead of showing you formulaic techniques for replicating stale, stagnant models of prose, this textbook introduces important concepts about writing—such as "twisting clichés" and creating reality through language—that will breathe life into your work. Each chapter discusses how these concepts influence the decisions you make as a writer. Making decisions and anticipating reader response are what writing is about. To develop into a better writer, you must take chances. Through trial and error, you will see how to integrate these key concepts into your writing. My hope is that you will learn how to develop and express your thoughts and experience the excitement in writing.

Writing Without Formulas has been organized in three parts. Part I discusses the key concepts behind writing. Once you understand the reasons for writing and know how to develop a critical analysis, what audience concerns to keep in mind, what options to consider in structuring an essay, and why paying attention to language is important, you can begin exploring the next two parts. Part II discusses approaching a writing task, group work, overcoming resistance to reading, writing with evidence, and research. Each chapter in Part II integrates the key concepts into a discussion of common concerns students have about aspects of writing. Part III presents diverse readings on topics not seen in many composition textbooks, such as the supernatural, humor, and honesty and deception. Each chapter in Part III introduces issues within the topic, presents readings from which you can extract information or simply ponder in relation to the topic, and offers possible assignments.

You can write papers based on the chapters in Part III while you are learning the key concepts in Part I or are studying the common elements of writing addressed in Part II. The text has been designed to allow you and your instructor to jump back and forth. The questions and issues raised by the topics in Part III reinforce the understandings you will gain from Parts I and II, but you will become equally adept at writing if you work on assignments in Part III and refer back to the first two parts when you reach stumbling blocks.

Few students look forward to reading a required textbook, but I do hope you will find this one enjoyable and stimulating. I love to write, but I understand that not everyone does. My goal in *Writing Without Formulas* is not to try to convert you into a lover of writing. Rather, I want you to build confidence so that you can use writing effectively in your college courses, your activities as a citizen, and your career—and even for those times when you record your experiences and insights for no one other than yourself.

· PART I ·

KEY CONCEPTS OF WRITING

Good writing transcends formulas. As you have experienced in your own reading, good writing pleases, stimulates, coaxes, and consoles. A thoughtful author understands key concepts of writing rather than following a preset structure or copying someone else's style. In eliminating the common formulas of writing instruction (some of which are discussed in Chapter 1), this book invites a legitimate question: "What will be taught in their place?" This first part of *Writing Without Formulas* should answer that question. You will learn about the purposes of writing, about performing a critical analysis, about understanding the relationship between your writing and the audience, about structuring your writing, and about scrutinizing language choices. These key concepts form the basis of Part I. If you grasp them and try to implement them in all your reading and writing tasks, you will be able to make informed decisions that produce good writing.

The first chapter reviews the reasons that we write. Often, students do not see the purpose of learning to write. Many students perceive their first-year writing course as a requirement, a hoop to jump through. Chapter 1 focuses on the diverse situations where knowing how to write enhances your personal life, your responsibilities as a citizen, your college experiences, and your chosen career.

The second chapter explores the role of critical analysis in developing a meaningful thesis. Many student writers can tell good stories or relay information, but their essays fall short because they do not integrate a thesis into their writing. Chapter 2 shows the many different ways that a writer can approach and interpret a situation, an event, or a fact to reach a fresh, insightful point.

The third chapter explains the critical role that audience plays in writing. Over the years, many students have been told to add detail to their paper, to look at a topic from another perspective, or to clarify the ideas. All this advice stems from concerns about audience. Chapter 3 discusses how to understand the needs of potential readers and respond to their questions or objections to convey your ideas as clearly as possible.

The fourth chapter shifts to the matter of an essay's arrangement. A writer must take the audience into consideration when putting a paper in order, especially when a thesis challenges tenets of the status quo, as discussed in Chapter 2. Yet, the specific ways to tie together the introduction, body, and conclusion of an essay have been the main area in which formulaic instruction has misled student writers. Chapter 4 covers the structuring of writing independently, showing how to make organizational decisions.

The fifth chapter focuses on the use of language. Its concern is not so much with correct usage and grammar as it is with helping you understand the complexities of language as both a writer and a reader. Chapter 5 scrutinizes the way we construct information in our writing and shows the power of language in framing reality.

These concepts appear throughout *Writing Without Formulas*, as they are the basis behind making strong rhetorical choices when you write and producing effective essays, reports, and researched papers. Activities in each chapter will help you understand and implement the concepts in Part I.

While writing is rarely easy, the goal of this book is to empower you to make thoughtful, informed decisions as you write. Understanding the purposes of writing and grasping the key concepts presented here will allow access to that power. Making informed decisions will start you on the path toward becoming an effective writer.

CHAPTER 1

REASONS FOR WRITING

Last semester, an eighteen-year-old student sat in my office, listlessly gazing at the floor. Maria had hoped to learn the formula for revision so she could earn an A on her paper about her relationship with her ex-boyfriend. Unfortunately, I had no formulas to diagram for her. I discussed essential concepts, such as awareness of her audience and producing a thesis from an analysis, but she seemed to resist applying them to her writing. Finally, she let out an exasperated sigh and looked at me. "I just want to know how to fix this essay. I don't want to know this other stuff. I'm going to be an accountant. Why do I need to know how to write?"

Students like Maria often have limited experience with the various uses of writing. In fact, they dread the thought of writing because they connect it with tasks assigned in school and perhaps with unpleasant evaluations and comments from teachers. I talked to Maria about how interesting writing a paper could be and linked writing to objectives of our university, such as cultural literacy, critical thinking, and effective communication. I also mentioned that while papers for her classes did compel her to write, they comprise only one of the many reasons a person takes pen in hand or composes on a keyboard. Writing is a combination of thinking, communicating, and reflecting, I told her. As such, it offers a unique form of learning and allows for active participation in the world by accountants and everyone else.

Maria rolled her eyes. As in accounting, she wanted a step-by-step procedure that would work not just for this assignment but also for others. Perhaps you had the same reaction as Maria did to my explanation about the

 **Online Study Center**

This icon will direct you to web links and additional resources on the website http://college.cengage.com/english/thelin/ writing_without_formulas/1e/student_home.html

5

uses of writing. You might have groaned or shaken your head, since you have either heard it all before or think it sounds corny. The very words *learning* and *participation* hearken back to the rituals of school, even though I was trying to show the real-world application of writing. Let's face it; few people enjoy school. But there are legitimate reasons to write in the college classroom and elsewhere, and I would like you to share this belief. To try to convince you, I start with this premise: School is a game; education is not.

As I talked with Maria, I started to see that the rules she had learned about writing had more to do with formulas for school than with anything else. Writing had become a game of figuring out how to please her teacher through neatness and presentation. She had been rewarded for having correct margins, skipping exactly three lines between her title and her first paragraph, having a thesis statement in the first paragraph, and spelling correctly. She was also a well-behaved student who attended all of her classes and did not miss deadlines, and she received points for these accomplishments in her high school English classes. With this as her view of writing, no wonder she did not see its relevance to the world outside the classroom! Like other students, she had confused the *processes* of school with the *substance* of education. She had learned how to play a game, not to write effectively. When she recognized this distinction, she was able to start developing skills and applying knowledge. Writing began to have a real purpose for her.

I would like to help you see the relevance of writing to your life. I want to get past the games of school. Of course, I'm taking an awkward first step: You're reading a textbook, a staple of the schooling process, and you're doing it for a class, another familiar part of the process. I also cannot deny that I designed the techniques and topics you will find in this book to be taught in a course on composition in an educational institution. Like you and your previous teachers, I seem to be firmly embedded in the schooling process.

However, the most confining situations still let you learn if you allow for it. Malcolm X, the famous civil rights activist of the 1950s and 1960s, honed his reading and writing skills in prison. If he was able to increase his level of literacy and improve his eloquence while behind bars, the rest of us can learn despite the rules and prescriptive formulas that might get in our way.

MALCOLM X

Learning to Read

In reading this excerpt from his autobiography, notice how Malcolm X motivated himself to learn and then became consumed by knowledge. Broadening his literacy shaped his identity.

It was because of my letters that I happened to stumble upon starting to acquire some kind of a homemade education.

I became increasingly frustrated at not being able to express what I wanted to convey in letters that I wrote, especially those to Mr. Elijah Muhammad.

In the street, I had been the most articulate hustler out there—I had commanded attention when I said something. But now, trying to write simple English, I not only wasn't articulate, I wasn't even functional. How would I sound writing in slang, the way I would *say* it, something such as, "Look, daddy, let me pull your coat about a cat, Elijah Muhammad—"

Many who today hear me somewhere in person, or on television, or those who read something I've said, will think I went to school far beyond the eighth grade. This impression is due entirely to my prison studies.

It had really begun back in the Charlestown Prison, when Bimbi first made me feel envy of his stock of knowledge. Bimbi had always taken charge of any conversations he was in, and I had tried to emulate him. But every book I picked up had few sentences which didn't contain anywhere from one to nearly all of the words that might as well have been in Chinese. When I just skipped those words, of course, I really ended up with little idea of what the book said. So I had come to the Norfolk Prison Colony still going through only book-reading motions. Pretty soon, I would have quit even these motions, unless I had received the motivation that I did.

I saw that the best thing I could do was get hold of a dictionary—to study, 5 to learn some words. I was lucky enough to reason also that I should try to improve my penmanship. It was sad. I couldn't even write in a straight line. It was both ideas together that moved me to request a dictionary along with some tablets and pencils from the Norfolk Prison Colony school.

I spent two days just riffling uncertainly through the dictionary's pages. I'd never realized so many words existed! I didn't know *which* words I needed to learn. Finally, just to start some kind of action, I began copying.

In my slow, painstaking, ragged handwriting, I copied into my tablet everything printed on that first page, down to the punctuation marks.

I believe it took me a day. Then, aloud, I read back, to myself, everything I'd written on the tablet. Over and over, aloud, to myself, I read my own handwriting.

I woke up the next morning, thinking about those words—immensely proud to realize that not only had I written so much at one time, but I'd written words that I never knew were in the world. Moreover, with a little effort, I also could remember what many of these words meant. I reviewed the words whose meanings I didn't remember. Funny thing, from the dictionary's first page right now, that "aardvark" springs to my mind. The dictionary had a picture of it, a long-tailed, long-eared, burrowing African mammal, which lives off termites caught by sticking out its tongue as an anteater does for ants.

I was so fascinated that I went on—I copied the dictionary's next page. 10 And the same experience came when I studied that. With every succeeding page, I also learned of people and places and events from history. Actually the dictionary is like a miniature encyclopedia. Finally the dictionary's A section had filled a whole tablet—and I went on into the B's. That was the way I started copying what eventually became the entire dictionary. It went a lot faster after so much practice helped me to pick up handwriting speed. Between what I wrote in my tablet, and writing letters, during the rest of my time in prison I would guess I wrote a million words.

I suppose it was inevitable that as my word-base broadened, I could for the first time pick up a book and read and now begin to understand what the book was saying. Anyone who has read a great deal can imagine the new world that opened. Let me tell you something: from then until I left that prison, in every free moment I had, if I was not reading in the library, I was reading on my bunk. You couldn't have gotten me out of books with a wedge. Between Mr. Muhammad's teachings, my correspondence, my visitors, . . . and my reading of books, months passed without my even thinking about being imprisoned. In fact, up to then, I never had been so truly free in my life.

The Norfolk Prison Colony's library was in the school building. A variety of classes was taught there by instructors who came from such places as Harvard and Boston universities. The weekly debates between inmate teams were also held in the school building. You would be astonished to know how worked up convict debaters and audiences would get over subjects like "Should Babies Be Fed Milk?"

Available on the prison library's shelves were books on just about every general subject. Much of the big private collection that Parkhurst had willed to the prison was still in crates and boxes in the back of the library—thousands of old books. Some of them looked ancient: covers faded, old-time parchment-looking binding. Parkhurst . . . seemed to have been principally interested in history and religion. He had the money and the special interest to have a lot of books that you wouldn't have in a general circulation. Any college library would have been lucky to get that collection.

As you can imagine, especially in a prison where there was heavy emphasis on rehabilitation, an inmate was smiled upon if he demonstrated an unusually intense interest in books. There was a sizable number of well-read inmates, especially the popular debaters. Some were said by many to be practically walking encyclopedias. They were almost celebrities. No university would ask any student to devour literature as I did when this new world opened to me, of being able to read and *understand*.

15   I read more in my room than in the library itself. An inmate who was known to read a lot could check out more than the permitted maximum number of books. I preferred reading in the total isolation of my own room.

When I had progressed to really serious reading, every night at about ten P.M. I would be outraged with the "lights out." It always seemed to catch me right in the middle of something engrossing.

Fortunately, right outside my door was a corridor light that cast a glow into my room. The glow was enough to read by, once my eyes adjusted to it. So when "lights out" came, I would sit on the floor where I could continue reading in that glow.

At one-hour intervals at night guards paced past every room. Each time I heard the approaching footsteps, I jumped into bed and feigned sleep. And as soon as the guard passed, I got back out of bed onto the floor area of that light-glow, where I would read for another fifty-eight minutes until the guard approached again. That went on until three or four every morning. Three or four hours of sleep a night was enough for me. Often in the years in the streets I had slept less than that. [. . .]

I have often reflected upon the new vistas that reading opened to me. I knew right there in prison that reading had changed forever the course of my life. As I see it today, the ability to read awoke inside me some long dormant craving to be mentally alive. I certainly wasn't seeking any degree, the way a college confers a status symbol upon its students. My homemade education gave me, with every additional book that I read, a little bit more sensitivity to the deafness, dumbness, and blindness that was afflicting the black race in America. Not long ago, an English writer telephoned me from London, asking questions. One was, "What's your alma mater?" I told him. "Books." You will never catch me with a free fifteen minutes in which I'm not studying something I feel might be able to help the black man.

Yesterday I spoke in London, and both ways on the plane across the Atlantic I was studying a document about how the United Nations proposes to insure the human rights of the oppressed minorities of the world. The American black man is the world's most shameful case of minority oppression. What makes the black man think of himself as only an internal United States issue is just a catch-phrase, two words, "civil rights." How is the black man going to get "civil rights" before first he wins his *human* rights? If the American black man will start thinking about his *human* rights, and then start thinking of himself as part of one of the world's great peoples, he will see he has a case for the United Nations.

I can't think of a better case! Four hundred years of black blood and sweat invested here in America, and the white man still has the black man begging for what every immigrant fresh off the ship can take for granted the minute he walks down the gangplank.

But I'm digressing. I told the Englishman that my alma mater was books, a good library. Everytime I catch a plane, I have with me a book that I want to read—and that's a lot of books these days. If I weren't out here every day battling the white man, I could spend the rest of my life reading, just satisfying my curiosity—because you can hardly mention anything I'm not curious about. I don't think anybody ever got more out of going to prison than I did. In fact, prison enabled me to study far more intensively than I would have if my life had gone differently and I had attended some college. I imagine that one of the biggest troubles with colleges is there are too many distractions, too much panty-raiding, fraternities, and boola-boola and all of that. Where else but in a prison could I have attacked my ignorance by being able to study intensely sometimes as much as fifteen hours a day?

You must extract the substance of your education from the process of going to school. Only then will you see the importance of writing outside the context of college in order to understand its importance inside. My take on formulas about writing you might have learned in school, such as the five-paragraph essay, emphasis on grammar, and other issues, appears later in this chapter. For now, the following example should clarify my point about extracting substance.

Just about every child draws, colors, and paints. At an early age, we gravitate to reproducing or creating our world through art. Most parents do not initially interfere with their children's creative impulses, even if the children hold crayons awkwardly or make messes with glue. As we get older, producing scribbling and rough images no longer satisfies our needs. We want to improve so that our art captures our intentions more precisely. To make this transformation, we need to follow some rules.

Some parents purchase art kits for their children to begin the integration of rules and processes into the children's art. Other parents interact directly with their children, explaining that color must stay within the lines of a coloring book or that using pencil to outline a picture before using crayons or paint will let them correct mistakes. Computer programs allow for experimentation with the blending of colors and the structure of a drawing.

Art teachers in elementary school build on these lessons and introduce more complicated lessons, such as perspective, shading, and three-dimensional crafts. Children must learn the proper order for tasks within an art project and adhere to conventions in size and shape as well as behaviors such as neatness. As students, children receive grades for their finished products and might even have to compete against other students in school fairs and other contests. Eventually, children learn many rules and processes that seem to confine their freedom of expression, and they may start resenting the loss of fun in artistic endeavors. Like my student Maria, these children might not see the relevance of following rules for art, since they do not plan on being artists in the future.

But art lessons provide much needed information if children can extract the substance from the process. It is not always necessary to follow a strict order of idea, pencil outline, inking, coloring, and lettering when you are drawing a comic strip, for example, but having an image in mind before you start and understanding viewers' needs for clarity are important. These concepts will help later in the presentation of business reports, in the design of banners for parties or community carnivals, and in the creation of posters for political activism, such as for a protest march. You will want to produce something inspiring or provocative. You still have the trappings of school processes. Someone is going to assign you a task, and you must meet a deadline. You must obtain approval from someone above you, even if you are not receiving a grade, and your project will have requirements. Viewers will judge your final project. The difference is that you see the *purpose* for making something pleasing and you have extracted the substance from the processes taught to you. You do not look at these art projects as just another game in school.

The strategies you developed for coping with rules that accompany otherwise enjoyable activities are not as far removed from school and writing as you may think. The only difference comes from your understanding of the

---

DISCUSSION

Think of some concepts and skills that you apply frequently in your life. They can be anything—cooking, rapping, carpentry, etiquette—as long as you feel that you use these concepts or skills effectively in life outside of school. Where did you learn them? Were there rules you had to follow? How did you get past the parts of the process you did not like? Talk with your classmates about the parts of the learning experience that benefited you and the strategies you learned for coping with rules or processes that bothered you.

---

immediate applicability of the skills or concepts you know. Similarly, you need to see the purpose behind your education and understand how the application of concepts can help you beyond college. The grade on your transcript for this class, your diploma in four years, or other rewards (or fear of punishment) should not substitute for the substance of education. These motivators constitute external pressure for doing well. Authentic, purposeful writing involves a genuine reason for doing the task and a sense of self-satisfaction—not mere relief—on completion. Within the conventions of the schooling process, you can find the type of purpose—and, therefore, motivation—that you discovered for other activities you enjoy.

The first concept revolves around the reasons for writing. If you do not see writing as more than a vehicle of schooling, you will be back within a meaningless process. There are four main reasons to engage in writing: personal inspiration, the responsibilities of citizenship, the requirements of college, and the demands of the workplace. Yes, one of these reasons involves your college courses, but you may be surprised by the flexibility and creativity encouraged in this book. Throughout, we discuss concepts, techniques, and strategies for you to experiment with and apply when you are compelled by one of these reasons to write.

Writing from Personal Inspiration

On occasion, we want to record what we have experienced. Other times, we want to communicate an idea to a friend. Still other times, we need to vent to release pent-up anger or frustration, maybe to better understand its source. In these moments, our desires do not differ greatly from those of professional writers. Something has inspired us. We are writing because we want to.

Observation   Sensual stimulation can cause us to want to remember something or to share it with others. The very act of writing commits an observation to memory and allows us to recall it. On a hike, maybe we came across a doe and a fawn, and our observation inspires us to think about the gracefulness of their motions or the subtlety of the maternal protective instinct. Wanting to share this observation, we re-create the scene in an email to a friend, or we jot a few notes on a piece of paper so as not to forget to tell our coworkers about it the next day. A professional writer takes this type of inspiration one step farther. He or she forms a thesis, perhaps comparing the scene to previous observations, and structures an essay around the encounter. We might think that professional writers are more talented than we are or that they have centered their careers on writing, but the truth is that published writers spring from all walks of life, starting with nothing more than the need to capture an inspiring moment and say something about it to a group of interested people.

Complaints   Inspiration also comes when we're angry about experiences we have had as consumers. We write letters of complaint to credit card companies, businesses, and consumer agencies. These experiences have taught us the importance of knowing how much detail to include, what part of an incident to highlight, and why asking for a refund or other forms of redress is correct. You might be surprised by the results a well-written letter can get. Anger serves as fuel for hard-hitting writing, as long as it does not get out of hand, and writing can prevent retailers or others from taking advantage of us. When we tactfully word our frustration so that we communicate without insulting or alienating the audience (we discuss the audience in Chapter 3), a letter of complaint accomplishes much. The following example is a different sort of complaint in which a customer acted on behalf of a server at a local restaurant.

Letter to a Restaurant Manager

Dear Manager of LaLond's:

While I rarely write letters of complaint, my experience at LaLond's this past Wednesday night became very unpleasant due to the actions of the assistant manager on duty. My friends and I felt that he berated a server for no reason, and we hope the server will not be punished for a situation that was not her fault.

The server in question is named Sherry, and she served us promptly and professionally throughout the evening. However, a table of men across from us continually demanded her attention when she was serving us and other customers in the area. While they appeared at first to have a legitimate complaint about the temperature of their food, they hounded Sherry throughout the evening. She tried to be courteous and to respond to their requests, but the men became belligerent and made many hurtful comments to her that had nothing to do with the service she provided or the quality of the food. Sherry called over the assistant manager. Without listening at all to Sherry, he apologized to the men, bought them a round of drinks, and scolded Sherry. After they left, we could see and hear the assistant manager yelling at her in front of all patrons, telling her that she had to shape up or find another job.

Sherry has been our server many times, and we find her quite pleasant and highly competent. The men in question subjected Sherry to personal abuse, and the assistant manager should have sought out the facts before humiliating her. My friends and I regularly dine together on Wednesdays and will spend up to a hundred dollars on food and refreshments. I cannot see us returning to LaLond's for one of these nights unless we can be assured that servers will receive the respect they deserve from management.

Thank you,

Donna Sheffield

Donna Sheffield

Reflection   People are also inspired to keep journals or blogs. A journal or a blog, like a trusted friend, can help you solve relationship, work, and other problems by reflecting on the experience through writing. Writing involves discovery. The act of writing pushes us to more complex understandings of ourselves and our world. Writing down a series of events casts it in a new light. The very words we choose help shape the reality of the situation, as is discussed in Chapter 5. Trying to precisely describe our emotions and experiences lets us understand smaller, hidden feelings and observations that come to light only through vocabulary choices. Most of the time, such entries go no farther than our own eyes, and they do not need to. Other times, journal entries can be the source of writing to be shared, such as a blog that allows reader comments and feedback.

Gratitude and Good Cheer   Making people feel better is another reason to write. We might feel warmth in our hearts that inspires the desire to communicate special feelings, such as with a lover or a cherished relative. Receiving a gift makes us want to show our gratitude to the sender. Sorrow also might need to be expressed when someone suffers a loss. We want to express our connection to a specific person at such a time, letting him or her know our sentiments and hoping that we can demonstrate our love, offer comfort, or raise spirits. A phone conversation might be awkward or intrusive, depending on the circumstance. A personal note, though, gives you a chance to think through your message and choose the very best words to express your gratitude, joy, or remorse. The person on the other end can read your note at his or her leisure.

While greeting cards can send holiday and birthday wishes, the verses and messages often seem contrived when you want to express your sincere thanks, your emotion at an accomplishment such as a birth or graduation, or your support at a time of need. E-cards allow you to personalize your message by writing your own words in the section devoted to personal notes. You can use nicknames in personalized notes, refer to special times that only you and the other person know about, and say exactly how you feel. Even people who are strangers can benefit from words of commendation that lift their spirits. Workers appreciate your sending letters or email to their supervisors or to the corporate office when they have done something well. We often want to recognize a clerk or a staff person who has taken care of a problem or has performed a favor. Writing a note or email makes others feel better and gives us a feeling of accomplishment for recognizing the worth in others.

What does personal inspiration have to do with you as a college student? Simply put, you are more than just a student. You are a person with feelings and ideas. You already write all the time. Why else do you check your email and return messages with updates on your life? Why do you leave notes for your parents or write birthday cards to your grandmothers? Why do you participate in websites like Facebook and MySpace? Writing beyond the rules for school assignments is not remote from your everyday life.

The opportunity for reflection and personal growth attracts many people to writing. Writing what you like—writing to suit your needs—lets you apply lessons from education in a meaningful way. What better way to start than to use words to create meaning from something that matters to you?

[handwritten margin note: think of writing we do as school]

WRITING

Have you ever been inspired to write for any of the reasons discussed above? Did you ever wish you had written to somebody or about something? Write about one of those moments when you wish you had shared an observation or idea with another person, had taken the time to complain to a person or an organization about a problem you experienced, or had written to yourself to sort through your feelings.

Writing as a Citizen

The letters to the editor sections in daily newspapers and online news sites show how engaged citizens communicate through writing. In a democracy, responsible people make their voices heard. Otherwise, as the saying goes, we have no one to blame but ourselves for laws, ordinances, and rulings that we do not like. At its best, effective writing increases public awareness and brings about change. When the stakes are high, the ineffective communication of ideas can undermine a whole platform.

Letters to the Editor   Daily newspapers and online news services offer citizens the chance to publish counterarguments to editorials or to reveal the slant of articles. Citizens correct facts, show the personal effect of governmental actions, and share anger or distress about public events. Because letters to the editor are short and meaty, many government officials peruse them daily to get a sense of the community's reaction to events. Letters that get to the point, engage in critical analysis, or use humor have a better chance of getting published than those that repeat clichés or meander endlessly. Published letters have a chance of being read by someone in power, and that person can start remedying the situation. Even letters that go unheeded still remind other citizens of alternative ways of thinking, which can indirectly affect registering and voting practices.

Political Action Citizens committed to change also can start or work for nonprofit or special interest groups to get their messages heard. These groups use persuasive pamphlets, letters, websites, and email to ask for financial support, to lobby elected officials, and to educate voters. Writing that merely lists facts without clearly connecting them persuades no one. Writing that documents ineffectively or does not distinguish between credible and unreliable sources strains the patience of readers. Writing that rants and has no control over voice delegitimizes the entire agenda, causing group members to be dismissed as fanatics. Public officials and voters cannot afford to waste their time on absurdities.

Further, your name and email address are likely to be available, particularly when you contribute to a public listserv. Although electronic ethics suggest that posts or synchronous messages not be forwarded to nonsubscribers without the permission of the author, too often they are forwarded anyway. If you write something that is reactionary and that is not well thought out, your words could be circulated to thousands of people who do not share the sentiments of those on the listserv, which could damage your reputation and the reputation of the group you represent. Ultimately, the presentation of written materials can make the difference between a community's future being enhanced or jeopardized, depending on the severity of the problem under consideration.

TRUEMAJORITY

"Computer Ate My Vote" Scores Coast to Coast Wins

Here's an example of political advocacy from the political action group True-Majority. Notice the upbeat tone in which the facts are presented. As a citizen, would this information influence you in any way?

Friends:

We're making waves and the tide is turning. The last week has been a big one for the Computer Ate My Vote campaign, and I wanted to share with you some of the progress we've been making.

In California, 50 TrueMajority members filled a Sacramento sidewalk last week calling for accountability from paperless electronic voting terminals. It was a fun event—our "hungry computer" prowled around for votes to eat and TrueMajority balladeer Laramie Crocker sang his ode to paperless voting, "Little Black Box," while the crowd urged state officials to dump California's unverified voting machines. The very next day California's Voting Systems and Procedures Panel said that's exactly what should be done. The panel recommended to California Secretary of State Kevin Shelley that he revoke the certification of the model TSx paperless electronic voting machine, made by Diebold Election Systems.

This is big news. California is the biggest market for election equipment in America. A rejection of paperless electronic voting terminals there will have ripple effects throughout the country, and we expect California Secretary of State Kevin Shelley to issue that decertification any day. We continue to work in California to extend the decertification of the Diebold TSx machines to *all* paperless electronic voting machines.

> On the day of the California announcement, TrueMajority members in Canton, Ohio, gathered outside the annual shareholders' meeting of Diebold Corporation. Ironically, Ohio is considering buying the very same Diebold TSx machines recommended for decertification in California.

A banner reading "Diebold Devours Democracy" floated from three helium-filled weather balloons outside the auditorium where Diebold CEO Walden O'Dell addressed shareholders and media. Activists gathered around a smoking, flashing mock-up of a malfunctioning Diebold voting terminal as True-Majority organizers detailed the long list of failures by Diebold's machines in states across the nation. The event made news not only in Ohio newspapers and on Ohio television and radio but also throughout the country due to coverage by the national wire services.

Our work continues in Ohio, where the legislature is still debating a bill to require a paper trail (a TrueMajority organizer testified in favor of it). The bill doesn't go as far as we'd like—some counties would still be able to purchase paperless machines this year, and retrofit them later—but it's still a turnaround for a state which had been on the verge of locking *every* county into paperless voting for the foreseeable future. Diebold, meanwhile, seems to be changing its tune. Instead of claiming that paper trails are difficult to produce, as they did at the beginning of our campaign, company spokespeople said last week they'd be happy to make paper-capable machines for states that want them.

We reported to you earlier that eight states have required paper trails for their electronic voting terminals. Here's more good news—Maine just joined the club April 22, when Governor Baldacci signed LD1759 into law. State Rep. Hannah Pingree, the chief sponsor of the Maine bill, tells us that your messages to the secretary of state there softened the ground and were important in getting the law passed.

We're not stopping there, though. In addition to pushing on in Ohio and California, we'll soon be taking on the new federal Election Assistance Commission. That's the new board tasked with writing the standards for electronic voting machines. We'll be asking them to write "voter verified paper trail" into the federal standards, so all those states who are waiting until next year to buy voting machines will buy the right ones. Look for an alert soon on that topic.

More and more news outlets are waking up to this nationwide movement, and elected officials are listening. I'm glad to be able to work with all of you to protect our democracy.

Ben

Ben Cohen

President, TrueMajority.org

PS: For more information about our campaign, check out www.truemajority
.org/voting.cfm. For more information about computer voting systems,
check out www.verifiedvoting.org or www.calvoter.org/votingtechnology
.html#resources.

Public Presentations
Citizens who are rebutting government proposals, making statements to the press, or presenting at town hall meetings also use writing. Many people read their speeches verbatim from cue cards or notes, partly because extemporaneous public speaking terrifies individuals, but also partly because writing helps people find the best word choices. Speakers who have not prepared presentations often stumble in their delivery, even when they think they know what they want to say, losing the opportunity to deliver hard-hitting blows for their positions. In other cases, the heat of the moment will cause individuals to forget the tightly constructed phrases they put together. Even the best orators write down what they want to say and go through several drafts before committing a speech to memory.

COLLABORATING

Make a list of issues that concern you, even if you do not know many of the details. Feel free to list community concerns, concerns about things you heard on the radio, or concerns about global situations. Share this list with a group of three or four classmates, and pinpoint similar sentiments. What forum would be best to express these sentiments? Work together to write a paragraph to voice your collective views to that forum.

Writing in College

You may have noticed that you write more fluently and for longer stretches when you write about what you know. But if you were to write only about subjects that already interest you or that you understand thoroughly, you would never extend yourself as a writer. You need to extend yourself to improve your writing and to learn new concepts and ideas. Until you confront a problem while writing, you will not be able to respond effectively to assignments in other college courses, not to mention to civic writing or business writing tasks.

Putting an end to the game of giving teachers what they want will let you see that college writing assignments are opportunities to communicate what you have understood, developed, implemented, and discovered. You cannot change your assignments, but you can look at writing in your courses through a new lens. Your professors are interested in reading your work. They no more want you to adhere to formulaic conventions that stifle your thoughts and voice than you do. Certainly, you have to follow formats for particular types of college writing, such as lab reports and research proposals, and some professors do ask you to follow conventions to aid in careful reading of your work. But if you did not enjoy writing your paper, your professor is unlikely to enjoy reading it.

Many myths and fallacies about professors' standards have circulated throughout college campuses. You may have heard some of these mistaken notions about academic writing in high school or college classrooms. Let's review and critique some of the myths and fallacies and explore the reasons you should not follow these conventions in the classroom or in other types of writing:

The Five-Paragraph Theme   In the five-paragraph theme, all points are presented in the introduction; the conclusion repeats the introduction; paragraphs are limited to five sentences each; and exactly three points are used in support of a thesis. While some essays are five paragraphs long, professional writing rarely uses the formulas found in this structure. The repetition bores readers, and the tight structure limits the author's voice.

The Modes of Discourse   Although you might not be familiar with this term, you are familiar with assignments based on the modes, such as comparison and contrast, definition, cause and effect, and argument. The problem is that the modes favor structure over content, forcing you to look for a topic that fits the mode instead of for a mode that fits the topic. Most college assignments give students a subject or a choice of subjects and rely on the students to find the best ways to explore and present the topic. Beyond page limits, special formats, or other parameters set by your professor, you do not have to fit your writing into a particular structure if you choose to compare, describe, define, or argue something.

Emphasis on Grammar Surface-level correctness ensures that your reader can understand you. Too many mistakes can distract a reader from your point. However, a grammatically correct paper is not necessarily an effective paper. Without strong content, which is drawn from critical analysis, awareness of audience, and language choices, an error-free paper will not engage a reader. You need to focus on more areas of the writing process than just surface-level correction.

still important

Formal Thesis Statements Starting your prewriting or drafts with a thesis statement restricts opportunities for exploration of your topic. A thesis should emerge from an essay, not be imposed on it. Once developed, the thesis does not have to be stated explicitly in the introduction. Some of the sciences do not like surprises coming at the conclusion of a paper, but a thesis implied elsewhere in an essay can be just as effective as a thesis statement in the introduction. When formal thesis statements are used in professional writing, they can be found in various places in an essay. Look at "The Insufficiency of Honesty" by Stephen Carter on page 417, Chapter 15. Where is his thesis statement?

You might still wonder how to generate excitement about topics and assignment requirements selected for you in college writing. The real lesson, however, revolves around your understanding of audience needs, your awareness of language usage, your decisions about organization, and your ability to critically analyze. If you can grasp these concepts in the different contexts in which they are presented in future chapters, you will find real-world applications to college writing.

what comp is!

But college writing also has the real purpose of communicating to your professors what you have understood, developed, implemented, and discovered. This communication allows professors across the curriculum to assess your knowledge more accurately. Poor writing can lead to grades that do not reflect how much you actually learned about a subject. Professors give advice and make recommendations based on what they believe students know and can contribute. Their judgments of you, especially within your major, can influence their decisions to invite you to participate in research, to write letters of recommendation for you, and to help you make contacts in the field, all of which will affect your career options.

DISCUSSION

List some rules or guidelines you acquired through your previous experiences with writing. Given what has been said in this chapter, how many of those rules or guidelines might be myths or fallacies? Why? Can you extract important concepts from your lists—ideas that might have been lost in your haste to conform to the rules or guidelines?

Writing in the Workplace

You might already have experience in the workplace. If so, you have a good idea of how valued strong writing skills are. Through email, memos, manuals, and reports, workers at many levels develop ideas and communicate them to people above and below them on the corporate ladder. Lack of clarity in a memo can lead to confusion about responsibilities and delegation of duties. Consumers can injure themselves or misuse products when manuals convey inconsistent or vague instructions. Innovations can be ignored if reports do not grab the attention of an executive. Carelessly written email messages can be used against individuals and corporations in lawsuits.

Much business or technical writing might seem dry when compared with opportunities for expression found in personal, civic, and even academic writing. Some businesses train executives to keep memos short and to avoid revealing too much of the reasoning behind decisions to workers. Some projects involve monotonous or bland research, making written reports dull. When dealing with consumers, many businesses resort to jargon or slogans and do not directly answer questions. However, examples of poor business writing reinforce the need to learn important concepts.

Cautious, Not Skimpy   Little in this world is dull by nature, and new employees in a business do not have to reproduce dry writing. No rule keeps memos short and to the point, other than the fear of writing something that might get you or your business in trouble. Careful writing, not sparse writing, is the answer. Memos that can build the esteem of the recipient while giving clear information and instructions will succeed best.

BILL THELIN

Norming Groups

In the following office memo, you will notice that necessary details are available to the recipients who are addressed directly and to those copied on the memo. To help employees who may have forgotten the purpose for the venture, paragraph 2 outlines why faculty members are to meet for the norming sessions.

TO:	Composition Faculty
FROM:	Bill Thelin Director of Composition
DATE:	April 6, 2004

SUBJECT: Norming Groups

I am very pleased with the progress we have made in implementing our new system of portfolio assessment. I appreciate the effort and skill you are bringing to this project. Please continue to give me your input as we approach the end of the semester.

It is time again to form norming groups for Week 15. As you know, to ensure consistency in the program, we have instructors share a designated number of portfolios and calibrate grades together, producing a norm that we all follow. I have posted a schedule of times when you can meet for a norming session. Sign your name for the date and time that is most convenient for you. All faculty members are required to attend one session and bring at least three portfolios with them to share with other participants.

As always, feel free to come to me with any problems. I will again make myself available during all times listed to answer questions that come up, review particularly troublesome portfolios, or help in any other way.

Please sign up for a date and time by **Friday, April 16.**

CC: Diana Reep, Chair, Department of English
       Thomas Dukes, Assistant Chair, Department of English

Finding Importance   Before starting job-related writing, first determine why the writing is important—what purpose it will serve—and then find a way to make reading it compelling to the higher-ups who are its intended audience. Job-related writing is not busy work. Something is riding on it. Your research could be the basis of a request or a grant for funding, or you might be asked to write a request or grant yourself. Without the resources you are requesting, a product line might not be established. Assessment reports about personnel could be the basis for giving an employee a bonus or for terminating the employee. A productivity report might lead to downsizing or upgrading. Under such circumstances, you would not want to submit an inaccurate analysis of your company.

While this type of writing might seem tedious, it matters. Searching for the crucial details through critical analysis will enliven your writing strategies (see Chapter 2). By looking for a particular angle or finding something that is not obvious, you can motivate yourself to write a report that is both accurate and engaging.

Avoiding Deception   Different perspectives and agendas cause many consumer complaints. Explaining your company's position clearly while showing that you understand the consumer's difficulty not only creates goodwill but

---

WRITING

Pretend that you are a member of a student committee. Your job is to write a portion of a request for a grant for new and/or updated computer labs. Your portion is the rationale. Rationales must persuade decision makers to release funds. In this case, you should show that the equipment requested will significantly add to student learning.

To gain an understanding of the importance of updated technology, visit the campus computer labs to assess their strengths and weaknesses or consult an instructor or lab technician about technology she or he would like to have available in the labs. Remember to give enough information to make the need clear. Do not gloss over your reasoning. At the same time, avoid deception. Do not overstate or understate the condition of the current equipment or make false claims.

---

can also lead to solutions. Straight answers when your business has erred—even when the truth might cost the business money—produce repeat business. Who would you rather deal with: a business that responds to questions with gobbledygook or a business that takes care of the problem? Of course, if your manager encourages you to shade the truth, it is up to you to make an ethical decision. Is this the type of company you want to work for? It is hard to label deliberate dishonesty or obfuscation "good writing." Just as with personal, civic, and college writing, the best prose cannot overcome weak content.

Summary

Good writing involves much more than applying formats and prescriptions. Learning to write means understanding concepts that you call on when occasions to write occur. While the classroom might seem like an artificial setting in which to hone writing skills, much can be accomplished that will have direct relevance to your future. As a student, you must separate the process of schooling from the substance of learning effective writing strategies. These strategies will aid you when occasions arise to write, whether those occasions involve communicating about personal inspiration, acting as a citizen, demonstrating knowledge in a college classroom, or performing duties in a business.

CHAPTER 2

CRITICAL ANALYSIS FOR WRITING

Sam wrote a pretty interesting account of a car accident in which he had been involved and presented it to a peer group workshop. The group members asked him for details in certain spots and prodded him to admit what he eventually did—that he had been drinking before the accident. They discussed organization, focused on some word choices, and seemed to be satisfied that they had critiqued Sam's paper thoroughly. But one woman, Jerusha, finally asked this question: "What is the thesis?"

Sam looked to the others and said, "Car accidents, right?" Indeed, his paper was about a particular car accident. But a thesis involves asserting or questioning something about the subject. An essay needs to have a thesis or a main point. If it does not, the essay is simply a story or a set of observations. What did Sam want to say about car accidents?

SAM ROBINSON

The Car Accident (draft)

When I started driving, I promised myself I would be very careful. But as I got more used to getting behind the wheel, I guess I got too confident. I didn't watch out for myself and what I was doing. I figured I knew how to drive so what was to worry. I can handle sharp corners. I know how long it takes to brake.

I went to a party last summer and drove my folks' car. I was with my friend Jimmy. We had a great time dancing, drinking, and laughing,

Online Study Center

This icon will direct you to web links and additional resources on the website http://college.cengage.com/english/thelin/writing_without_formulas/1e/student_home.html

but it got time to go. I'd never been to this house before, so the road started looking unfamiliar. Jimmy and me wondered which turn to take and how to get back to the main road.

He would point one way and I would say another, so we would go far in one direction until nothing looked familiar and then head back the other way. We kept looking for signs, as Jimmy thought he remembered the name of a street, but we couldn't read the street signs when we saw them. We even drove back to Carol's house just to see if we started out fresh from the beginning, could we make it? I was tired and getting madder and madder, and I jackrabbited the car at every stop sign. When I bothered to stop at them.

Well, after traveling down another road we didn't recognize, I told Jimmy I think I remember this side street name, as I got out of the car and looked at the sign. He said it sounds right, so we started hauling down that street. I was driving too fast, I know, but I swear there was no sign that said we were on an "S." I only saw it under sunlight when I went back next week. I started swerving to stay on the road, but as I went left, then right, I couldn't control the car. We hit the barrier and came to a stop with the front two tires off the road. There was only a cliff beneath it. We could have been killed!

We were able to get out of the car. Jimmy had a tough time as his side didn't have any roadway under it, as we had skidded right before hitting, but he made it out with my help. We walked until we found a house with a light on it, and the people were nice enough to let us in. We called my folks, who were hopping mad, and they called a tow truck and drove out there themselves to pick us up.

The car's front end was all messed up, and we decided to total it. We didn't have collision insurance, so we got nothing for the car. Accidents are really scary and I'm just glad I got out of this one alive!

→ just a story, no real purpose

Sam studied his essay. "I guess I could say that you shouldn't drive drunk," he murmured.

"But if you were drunk, why did you leave that out?" Jerusha asked. "If that's the thesis of the essay, you would have mentioned it right away."

← this if something is big packed at it should be looked

Jerusha was claiming that Sam was copping out, turning to the easy and obvious cliché about drunk driving that he thought would fit. Details that pop up later can add to or alter a thesis, but in this case, Sam avoided mentioning the drinking intentionally. The group felt compelled to explore why Sam would cop out if the drinking was important for his thesis. Jerusha and the others speculated that his avoidance could be a reaction to public scorn for drunk drivers. Maybe Sam wanted to avoid that label or avoid the responsibility it involves.

"But I wasn't really drunk," Sam contended. "I had only three beers." He explained that he did not want readers to think that drunkenness was the cause of the accident, because it wasn't. He talked about the darkness of the road he had been on and the sharp curves. As he answered his peer group's questions, an initial thesis took form: Drivers are only as good as the roads on which they drive.

Should Sam have avoided the details of drinking before driving? No. But to have used his easy thesis of not driving drunk would have shut off other possible avenues of exploration. Developing his thesis involved accounting for the social perception revealed in his peer group. By studying the ideas and reactions of his fellow students carefully, he better understood why he initially rejected the dominant social perception. Still, Sam needed to include the details of how much he drank and why he thought it was acceptable to drive. Otherwise, he would have little to examine in trying to find a relevant thesis. He needed the details to engage in the most essential activity in writing: critical analysis. A critical analysis of this draft would expose his assumptions to scrutiny, would make him see where they came from, would test their validity, and would let him form a generalization from the conflict between common societal values and his experience.

Such a process prevents writers from succumbing to clichés in their theses. Sometimes when we use the term *cliché*, we are referring to language that is repeated often and seems trite or bland. The expression "It was raining cats and dogs" is a cliché for this reason. It does not communicate precise detail, and it fails to evoke emotion in the reader.

In this chapter, however, we are interested in clichéd thinking and how to avoid it. Clichéd thinking occurs when a person applies a common societal belief to a situation too quickly. You might be tempted to use clichés because they seem to speak truth. In many ways, they are safe. But clichés fail to account for the variables in any given situation. A cliché needs to be modified or extended to convey a logical, meaningful thesis.

In Sam's case, the popular slogan "Don't drink and drive" would have functioned like a cliché because it mirrored what he and his peers had probably heard in alcohol awareness campaigns and driver's education seminars instead of resulting from careful analytic thought. Choosing "Don't drink and drive" or "Friends don't let friends drive drunk" as a thesis would have conveyed a clichéd attitude about the subject and would have undermined a legitimate warning about driving while under the influence. Fortunately, Sam worked through ideas—the possibility that alcohol consumption deludes us into thinking we are more "okay" than we think, the contention that even slight impairment of judgment renders a person unable to drive a car—before arriving at a thesis about the many factors that must coincide for an accident to occur. He believed that the driver's ability, whether impeded by alcohol, a natural lack of coordination, anger, or fatigue, is part of a much larger equation and that the societal focus on a driver's sobriety blinds us to other dangers on the road that could be more easily fixed.

↳ though this is true, this would have been a cop out thesis writing what he thinks he should say rather than what he wants the essay to do

SAM ROBINSON

The Car Accident

When I started driving, I promised myself I would be very careful. But as I got more used to getting behind the wheel, I guess I got too confident. I didn't take matters into consideration like I should have, such as road conditions, darkness, and fatigue. I figured I knew how to drive so what was to worry. I can handle sharp corners. I know how long it takes to bring my car to a full stop.

I went to a party last summer and drove my folks' car. I was with my friend Jimmy, and the house was located in the mountains, up some windy roads. We had a great time dancing and joking around with our friends. Alcohol was served at the party, and I drank three beers during the three hours we were at the party. When it was time to go, I quickly checked myself to make sure I was not impaired, as I never want to drive drunk. A person my weight, according to my driver's ed class, can consume one drink every hour without losing coordination. So I was safe.

I'd never been to this house before, so the road started looking unfamiliar. Jimmy and I wondered which turn to take and how to get back to the main road. He would point one way and I would say another, so we would go far in one direction until nothing looked familiar and then head back the other way. We kept looking for signs, as Jimmy thought he remembered the name of a street, but we couldn't read the street signs when we saw them, as it was so dark. We found our way back to Carol's house, and although I was frustrated, I sensed that I could figure out the directions better if we came back to our starting place. We should have just gone inside and asked for directions, but we didn't want to look like dweebs. We started back down the hill. I was tired and getting madder and madder. I jackrabbited the car at every stop sign, when I even bothered to stop at them.

After traveling down another road we didn't recognize, I told Jimmy I thought I remembered the name of a side street we had passed, but the moonlight was not enough for me to be sure, so I got out of the car and looked at the sign. He said it sounded right when I told him the name, so we started hauling down that street. I was driving too fast, I know, but I swear there was no sign on that next block that said we were coming to an "S" road—one that winds sharply like a snake. I started swerving to stay on the road, but as I went left, then right, I couldn't control the car. We hit the barrier and came to a stop with the front two tires off the road. There was only a cliff beneath them. We could have been killed!

We were able to get out of the car. Jimmy had a tough time as his side didn't have any roadway under it, as we had skidded to the right before hitting, so the passenger's side was practically hanging over the side of the mountain. He made it out with my help, as I made sure I didn't unbalance the car by exiting before he did. We walked until we found a house with a light on it, and the people were nice enough to let us in. We called my folks, who were hopping mad. They called a tow truck and drove out there themselves to pick us up.

The car's front end was all messed up, and we decided to total it. We didn't have collision insurance, so we got nothing for the car. I

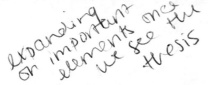
expanding on important once we see the thesis elements

argued with my parents, who figured they had gotten me off a drunk driving charge by waiting until the next day to inform the police about the damage to the barrier. I insisted that I was not drunk, and I got the mother of the girl whose house it was to call my mom and tell her that I had been sober. We drove out there the next week in my mom's car, and although we saw the warning sign about an "S" curve, they agreed it would be hard to see in the dark. It was old and did not reflect well when headlights were on it. There were no street lights anywhere on that block and the lanes were very narrow. I didn't feel it at the time, but there were several deep potholes we noticed right around the place where my car hit the barrier. My ability to handle the car could have been affected by one of those potholes if I hit one. Jimmy said he did remember us hitting one.

A lot of factors go into a car accident occurring. Our society likes to blame the individual and tries to find reasons that place the fault squarely on him. A driver's ability only contributes so much to an accident. Everyone cannot be a safe driver all the time, as mistakes are human. We get into cars when we're tired, angry, and distracted, and all drivers get lost some time, which reduces our natural caution when we're trying to find our way. Local and state governments can help to protect individuals against these moments by ensuring that roadways are safe. Street signs should be able to be seen in the dark. Street lights need to be installed in places that have a hazard potential. Roads need to be fixed. I'm a good driver, but some drivers start with coordination that is less than perfect, and some drivers do get drunk. We can protect them and any pedestrian or other vehicle they might run into by having better road conditions. So much focus on preventing drunk driving, while definitely something to avoid, blinds us to easier solutions towards road safety.

BIG PICTURE

true, not cliché.

Sam engaged in critical analysis to reach his conclusion. Perhaps we would be more comfortable as readers if he had admitted more responsibility, but the point of critical analysis is not to reach a thesis that everyone agrees with. Rather, it is to reach a thesis that challenges preconceptions and can lead us toward fruitful paths of action. As much as we do not want people to drive after drinking, Sam's thesis offers a new perspective that can help reduce automobile accidents.

DISCUSSION

Writing that does not stir passion, that remains safe in clichés, offers little to the reader. Sam takes a risk with his ideas. Do you think that Sam's thesis is a denial of his own responsibility in the accident? What other conclusions could he have reached to avoid clichés?

You might be wondering how to engage in critical analysis. What is the process? How can you do it? While no exact formula exists, the following sections give you the basic concepts behind critical analysis and let you practice this method of thinking.

Interrogating the Obvious

One way to engage in critical analysis and develop a unique, provocative thesis relies on intensive questioning of surface explanations for incidents. In other words, do not settle on your first instinct when searching for a thesis. Your first instinct might be correct, of course, or might be as close to accurate as possible, but the time you spend interrogating the obvious will remove nagging doubts from your mind and your readers' minds about the conclusions you have drawn from your subject. At its best, interrogating the obvious helps you take the significant parts of an incident into account and allows you to focus on the most relevant aspects of information or data. It might reaffirm some key tenets of what you first thought while adding or subtracting new elements for you to ponder. Developing the habit of interrogating the obvious also will aid you beyond the classroom in understanding world events, personal relationships, and the mechanisms of corporations.

Twisting the Cliché   If you start with the most apparent explanation in your process of thinking, you are probably echoing a societal cliché. Try turning the cliché on its head. For instance, if you are thinking about the value of honesty, you may come up with the cliché "Honesty is the best policy." What if you were to seriously consider its opposite, "Honesty is the worst policy" or "Dishonesty is the best policy"? Can somebody think this way? What would motivate them to do so? How do those motivations differ from those of someone who advocates honesty?

This type of questioning of a common belief will produce an array of options for you to consider—in this case, perhaps places in the middle of the extremes of best and worst. The reasons most people shy away from complete truth-telling might help you produce an insight about honesty and be able to apply it to your subject. Instead of using the pat conclusion about honesty being the best policy, you can put a twist on the cliché, perhaps suggesting limitations to the use of honesty. Chapter 15 includes a reading by Stephen Carter called "The Insufficiency of Honesty" in which the author has wrestled with this issue and has decided that integrity is a better policy than honesty. You do not need to subscribe to the exact opposite of a cliché to make this exercise valuable. The exact opposite is simply a starting point for further questioning.

WRITING

Look at the chapter topics for Part III in the table of contents. Choose one of the topics, and write a statement about it that you would consider to be the most obvious. More than likely, this statement will contain clichéd language or attitudes. Write about the statement, using the method of twisting the cliché to question its legitimacy or accuracy.

Focusing on Interrelatedness of Key Elements Many explanations, whether clichés or not, isolate the key element or the triggering device in a subject. Interrogating the obvious asks you to find many variables and see how they connect to produce the results. You might have heard a chef or a cook discuss the secret ingredient that makes the difference between a mediocre entrée and a superb one. Yet, most cooks will tell you that no one ingredient makes the difference. The combination of subtle variations in preparation, such as cooking temperatures and the amounts of ingredients, produces the difference.

Thus, you should look in your subject for the interrelatedness of key elements and see how they connect. You can ask yourself how many of them you could tweak to produce a difference. While at times you might find one element that seems to be crucial, searching for more than one element will often let you notice subtleties that went unnoticed the first time around, subtleties that are worth mentioning when you form your thesis.

LYNNE LUCIANO

Male Body Image in America

Examine how this article ties together several factors in American society that have led to an obsession with appearance. It does not isolate one variable only but shows the interconnectedness of elements.

American men spent $3 billion on grooming aids and fragrances in 1997. They also spent nearly $800 million on hair transplants and $400 million on hairpieces. Sales of exercise equipment and health-club memberships raked in $4 billion. An estimated eighty-five million Americans, mostly male, are doing some kind of weight training. Even serious bodybuilding, once a fringe activity largely relegated to the lower classes, has gained middle-class status as upwardly mobile men of all ages grunt and strain for the blood-vessel-constricting high known as the pump. For men who have more fat than muscle, a lucrative foundation-garment industry offers Butt-Busters and Man-Bands to flatten bulges. Men are dieting in unprecedented numbers, and an estimated one million of them suffer from eating disorders commonly thought to afflict only women.

Also surprising is men's pursuit of beauty through the scalpel: in 1996, the bill for male cosmetic surgery was $500 million. Just under $200 million was spent on the two most popular surgeries, liposuction and rhinoplasty (nose jobs), with the rest going for esoteric surgeries like pectoral implants and the creation of cleft chins, not to mention the ultimate male surgery, penis enlargement. We are clearly witnessing the evolution of an obsession with body image, especially among middle-class men, and a corresponding male appropriation of, in the words of the feminist Barbara Ehrenreich, "status-seeking activities . . . once seen as feminine."

What, then, does it mean to be a man at the dawn of the twenty-first century? The historian and philosopher Elisabeth Badinter has concluded that models of masculinity haven't changed much over the centuries. She points to four "imperatives" for today's men: first and foremost, men must be men—"no sissy stuff"; second, they must be competitive, constantly demonstrating their success and superiority; third, they must be "detached and impassive"; and, finally, they must be willing to take risks and confront danger, even to the point of violence. These four imperatives have two qualities in common: they are diametrically opposed to what is generally regarded as feminine behavior, and they say nothing about how a man is supposed to *look*.

Until World War II, it is true, male attractiveness was derived from activity; how a man behaved and what he achieved were the true measures of his worth. In the immediate aftermath of World War II, it seemed these ideals would continue along their accustomed track. The American male would provide for his family, succeed at his job, and be strong, rugged, and virile. While women labored at self-beautification, men devoted themselves to more important matters. Men were not exactly indifferent to their bodies, but any man who overly emphasized his physical appearance risked being accused of vanity. Men who wore toupees aroused amused derision at best. Although obesity among Americans had reached alarming proportions by mid-century, men shied away from dieting, despite warnings about heart disease. Exercise, which at least had the cachet of being "masculine" because it was associated with action, didn't get much more strenuous than golf and gardening. Workouts that raised serious sweat had few middle-class adherents, and cosmetic surgery was regarded as the exclusive preserve of women. As for the body's most intimate parts, a cloud of secrecy shrouded them, as well as their function (and dysfunction), from public debate and public view.

5   What has caused American men to fall into the beauty trap so long assumed to be the special burden of women? Does men's concern about their

bodies mean they've become feminized? Have they been so addled by the women's movement that they are responding by becoming more like women? There is no simple, single answer. Rather, a confluence of social, economic, and cultural changes has been instrumental in shaping the new cult of male body image in postwar America.

The changing status of women brought about by second-wave feminism has radically reshaped how women view the male body. As long as men controlled economic resources, their looks were of secondary importance. Though feminism would have many, often conflicting, objectives, the liberal feminism that emerged mainly among professional and upper-middle-class women focused on social and legal constraints that denied women equal access to the workplace. As the role of breadwinner became a shared one, men's economic power and sense of uniqueness would be undermined.

The impetus behind the rising number of college-educated wives entering the workplace came less from the need to contribute to the family income, however, than from the diminishing attractions of the home. Avid middle-class pursuit of higher education, especially at graduate and professional levels, deterred growing numbers of young men and women from early marriage. At the same time, greater latitude for sexual experimentation made it less likely that women would marry just to legitimize sexual relations. An emphasis on the importance of self-fulfillment also undermined marriage as a priority for many young Americans. It was during the 1960s that the term *lifestyle* was first used in reference to being single: its significance lay in its suggestion of choice. Marriage was no longer expected but a matter of personal taste, as were its alternatives, divorce and cohabitation, which became ever more common.

By the end of the decade, the average age at first marriage had risen, and the marriage rate had begun to drop, and continued to drop through the 1970s. A survey of college students at that time showed that 82 percent of the women rated a career as important to self-fulfillment, whereas only 67 percent believed this was true of marriage. The *Cosmopolitan* editor Helen Gurley Brown, who had spent most of the 1960s trying to create an image of the *Cosmo* girl as mirror image of the sexually uninhibited *Playboy* man, emphatically agreed: marriage, she told her legions of female readers, was nothing more than "insurance for the worst years of your life."

Try as she might to turn men into sex objects, Brown was ahead of her time in 1962. For most women, being single was still stigmatizing rather than stimulating. And as Brown herself was quick to point out, sexual liberation didn't work without economic liberation, and that hadn't arrived yet. But as the decade progressed, single life took on new legitimacy and had wide-ranging social and economic effects. One of the most significant was that in the dating marketplace, single women were as likely to be doing the choosing—and rejecting—as men, elevating the importance of male looks to a whole new level. Why, demands the woman who works out rigorously to keep her body lean and fit, should I put up with a man who spends his leisure time sitting on a couch watching television? Or, as the feminist Germaine Greer inquired with some acerbity in 1971, was it too much to ask that women be spared "the daily struggle for superhuman beauty in order to offer it to the caresses of a subhuman ugly mate"?

10   Economic change wasn't limited to women's more substantial paychecks. World War II catapulted America into unprecedented power and prosperity. Lavish government spending, corporate expansion, and the development of a vast complex of technological industries based on the postwar symbiosis of military, government, and science created thousands of secure, well-paying white-collar jobs. As union wages rose, stimulated by cost-of-living increases and buffered by national prosperity, millions of working-class Americans could afford middle-class lifestyles and the accoutrements that defined them.

For nearly a quarter century, expectations of continued affluence and material progress were undimmed. But in the 1970s, America's virtually unchallenged global economic preeminence, as well as its internal prosperity, would confront foreign competition, inflation, declining corporate profits, and unemployment. In the ensuing downsizing that persisted well into the 1990s, hardest hit would be those most accustomed to job success and security—white males. To maintain an edge, it became important not just to be qualified for a job but to look as if one were; and that meant looking dynamic, successful, and, above all, young.

These changes are related to a more complex and extremely significant alteration in American life since midcentury: the rise of a culture increasingly based on self-fulfillment and the cultivation of self-esteem. Though many factors brought about this sea change, one of the most compelling was the proliferation of consumerism and its emphasis on the importance of self-image.

America's transformation from a culture of production to one of consumption was well under way by the turn of the nineteenth century. At that time, the basic needs of most middle-class Americans were being met, and manufacturers therefore sought to create desire in place of necessity. They were aided by advertisers who set out to convince consumers that their very identities depended on owning the right products, that they could be whatever they wished, as long as they purchased enough goods.

Advertising agencies appeared on the American landscape as early as the 1850s but remained on a small scale until World War I, when technological and cultural factors converged to create the modern advertising industry. New technologies like arc and neon lighting allowed ads to be displayed in more interesting and enticing ways, while advanced printing methods like lithography made it possible to copy images less expensively and more attractively. During the war, advertising and public relations joined forces with the U.S. government to generate propaganda and unifying symbols as a means of mobilizing support for the war among a fragmented and diverse population—an effort devoted more to popularizing and legitimizing the war than to disseminating real information. Afterward, products poured off booming American assembly lines, and advertisers mobilized consumer enthusiasm in much the same way. Ad agencies created personalities for their products, which were sold not on the basis of what they could do but on the basis of the image they projected—as one advertising mogul put it, they sold the sizzle, not the steak.

Advertising was helped in its crusade by the emergent popularity of psy- 15
chology. Terms like *ego* and *repression* were bandied about in everyday conversation, and by the 1920s, the idea of complexes had moved out of medical
circles and into the lives of ordinary people. Americans, buffeted by changes
brought about by industrialization and the new public life of cities, had fallen
prey to feelings of anxiety and insecurity. Magazines and self-help books
asked, "Do you have an inferiority complex?" and emphasized the importance
of self-scrutiny. Advertisers seized on the connection between the psychological and the physical, urging consumers to buy their products to overcome deficiencies ranging from dandruff to bad breath.

Well into the twentieth century, women were advertisers' main targets. Consumption—that is, shopping—was defined as women's work. Single
women were encouraged to compete for men by buying commodities to make
themselves more beautiful, and married women were encouraged to demonstrate their husbands' success by their purchasing power. But as commodities
became increasingly central to defining self-worth, men, too, would be pulled
into the vortex of consumerism, warned by advertisers that the wrong "look"
posed a threat to career, love life, and self-esteem.

In its early days, advertising had been simply a means of linking buyer
and seller by presenting basic information about a product—how big it was,
for example, or how much it cost. But in an urbanizing and modernizing culture, advertising evolved from selling mere products to selling their benefits.
Advertising is about image, self-esteem, and display of the self. It is *not* about
what the psychologist Erik Erikson calls, in his studies of human psychological development, "the mature person's developing sense of the importance of
giving something back to community and society." In a consumer society, a
sense of responsibility to the larger community doesn't develop. As the soci-
ologist Diane Barthel points out, every advertiser knows that the critical attribute of any product is "What will it do for *me*?" The line between commodity
and individual has become blurred, so that we *are* what we buy. Americans
have been beguiled by marketing acumen, and the body has become the ultimate commodity.

The importance of self-presentation originated early in the century,
though initially it was more subtle than it is today. As early as the second
decade, social critics were noting that America was shifting from a culture
of character to a culture of personality. Character implies self-discipline and
a sense of inner direction, whereas personality revolves around the ability to
please others—not necessarily through real accomplishment but by winning
friends and influencing people. While character is its own reward, personality
demands external validation and appreciation.

By midcentury, the ethos of personality had almost entirely displaced
older notions of character. Image is described by the historian Daniel Boorstin
as "a studiously crafted personality profile of an individual . . . a value caricature, shaped in three dimensions, of synthetic materials." Like the right personality, it relies on external indicators to proclaim our personal worth and
determine how others see and evaluate us. The right clothes, the right car, and
even the right body and face—all can be purchased rather than cultivated.

20   The 1960s brought not only social upheaval but an emphasis on sexuality, self-expression, and youth. Commercial packaging of youth actually began in the 1950s, when marketers recognized teenagers' "purchasing power," a term first used after World War II. By 1959, teenagers controlled ten billion dollars in discretionary income, more than the total sales of General Motors. Teen society was grounded in a sense of acute difference from adult society and was primarily defined in terms of consumer choices, especially in fashion and music. Yet in other respects, adolescents in the 1950s appeared to want the same things as their parents: a mate, a family, a home in the suburbs. They spent a great deal of time practicing for their future by playing courtship games like going steady and getting pinned. Most girls looked forward to taking on the responsibilities of motherhood, and boys wanted to become men. As for adults, though they wanted to look attractive and have that elusive quality known as "sex appeal," they generally didn't wish to look, or behave, like teenagers. The culture of youth was distinctive *because* it was reserved for the young.

The cultural importance of youth surged in the 1970s, as prosperity continued to allow teenagers to pursue their distinctive consumerism and because so many defining aspects of the 1960s—fashion, hair, music, radicalism—had centered on young people, especially those of college age. Even the soldiers who fought in the Vietnam War were younger than those of any previous American war: their average age was nineteen, compared with twenty-four for soldiers in World War II. Although the end of the 1960s was marked by disillusionment over the decade's social and political turmoil, the desirability of being (and looking) young remained undimmed. Growing numbers of Americans, confronting the prospect of turning thirty, became determined never to leave adolescence—at least, not physically. Youth was no longer a stage of life to be passed through but one to be clung to tenaciously.

In the 1970s, the obsession with youthfulness combined with the emphasis on self-expression and acquisitiveness to create an entirely new culture grounded in the importance of self-esteem. Narcissism, identified in the 1960s by Erikson as a modern form of neurosis, was recast by the historian and cultural theorist Christopher Lasch into a theory of modern social history. According to Lasch, the bewildering array of images to which the average American was subjected led to a preoccupation with projecting the "right" image of oneself in order to confirm one's very existence. If the 1950s had been defined by conformity, the 1970s were characterized by a sense of selfhood "hopelessly dependent on the consumption of images" and consequently on relentless self-scrutiny. The marketing of commodities, Lasch cautioned, created a world of insubstantial images difficult to distinguish from reality. Within this world, images were incorporated into Americans' visions of themselves, with important implications for body image for both genders. Advertising and mass marketing held out the promise of self-fulfillment and eternal youth through consumerism—for everyone. Finally, as the historian Margaret Morganroth Gullette has observed, "the system that sells products based on fears of aging . . . turned its giant voracious maw toward that next great big juicy market, men."

In the 1990s, that "big juicy market" was the largest it had ever been—the baby boomers were entering middle age. These thirty-one million people—12 percent of the population—were beginning to experience the trauma of midlife crisis. In 1993, the National Men's Resource Center declared that all men undergo a midlife crisis and that a major manifestation of this was growing concern about the loss of physical appeal.

It's tempting to surmise that men's interest in body image, and their relatively recent concerns about physical attractiveness, along with sexualization of the male body, means they are becoming feminized. This, however, is decidedly not the case. Looking good is part of a quintessential male strategy whose ultimate aim is to make men more successful, competitive, and powerful. The means of achieving this goal may be new, but the objective is not.

Millions of American men have been transformed into body-conscious 25 consumers of revealing fashions, seductive perfumes, and the services of hairstylists, personal trainers, and plastic surgeons. Due credit for this transformation must be given to advertisers, marketers, and self-esteem gurus, who have sold men—and all of us—a message of self-transfiguration through self-commodification. The traditional image of women as sexual objects has simply been expanded: *everyone* has become an object to be seen.

Finding What's Not There   Essential components of a subject often are initially missed by a writer, sometimes because they seem obvious or not particularly relevant. Yet, readers will wonder about these components, just as Jerusha and the other group members wondered about the issue of drinking in Sam's essay about the car accident. Interrogating the obvious means reexamining what we have written and looking for elements that are not there. Traditional questions we can ask involve who, what, where, when, why, and how. You might not need to incorporate the answers to these questions into the final version of your essay, but you might find that one or two of the details can shed some light on your thesis.

NOREENA HERTZ

from The Silent Takeover

In this excerpt from The Silent Takeover, *Noreena Hertz questions what the public is not hearing in the official version of the success of the free market. Notice that she asks why, how, and what, then reveals missing details that lead her to believe that corporate behemoths are engaging in a "silent takeover" of the world.*

Benetton provides an apt metaphor for politics today. Over the last eighteen years this Italian fashion company has run the most provocative advertising campaigns ever seen. Twenty-foot billboards with the picture of a starving black baby; the AIDS victim at his moment of death; the bloodied uniform of a dead Bosnian soldier; the "United Killers of Benetton" campaign, a ninety-six-page magazine insert with photograph after photograph of condemned prisoners languishing on America's death rows. Benetton shocked us to attention, but shock is all it provided. It didn't rally us into action. Nor did it try and address these issues itself. Their advertising provided no exploration of the morality of war, there was no attempt to relieve poverty or cure AIDS. The only goal was to increase sales, not to start a discussion of the issues behind capital punishment. And if it profited from others' misery, so what?

We are living in a Benetton bubble. We are presented with shocking images by politicians who try to win our favor by demonizing their opponents and highlighting the dangers of the "wrong" representation. They speak of making a difference and changing our lives. Mainstream parties offer us supposedly different solutions and choices: Democrats tout liberal virtues, Republicans tout conservatism, all in an attempt to secure our votes.

But the rhetoric is not matched by reality. The solutions our politicians offer are as bogus as those of Benetton: a Chinese girl standing next to an American boy, a black woman holding hands with a white woman. Models with unusual faces, strong faces, sometimes beautiful, sometimes not. Multicolored people in multicolored clothes.

Political answers have become as illusory as the rows and rows of homogenized clothes, standard T-shirts, and cardigans folded in your local Benetton store. Commercialized conservatism and conformity par excellence. Politicians offer only one solution: a system based on laissez-faire economics, the culture of consumerism, the power of finance and free trade. They try and sell it in varying shades of blue, red, or yellow, but it is still a system in which the corporation is king, the state its subject, its citizens consumers. A silent nullification of the social contract.

5   But, I will argue, the system is undeniably failing. Behind the ideological consensus and supposed triumph of capitalism, cracks are appearing. If everything is so wonderful, why . . . are people ignoring the ballot box and taking to the streets and shopping malls instead? How meaningful is democracy if only half the people turn out to vote, as in the Bush–Gore presidential election, even though everyone knew it was going to be a close race? What is the worth of representation if . . . our politicians now jump to the commands of corporations rather than those of their own citizens?

It took time for people to rise up in protest, to see that the weightless state was unlikely to deliver the clean, safe world that they wanted their children to grow up in. For a long time people didn't question the one-ideology, homogeneous world. Why should they? For many, life was good and getting better. For most of the past twenty years the stock market has risen and interest rates fallen. More people than ever before own their own homes. Two thirds of us, in the developed world, have television sets of our own. Most of us, in the West that is, have cars. Our children wear Nike and Baby Gap. The middle class has grown and grown.

We are drip-fed images that reinforce this capitalist dream. Studios and networks beatify the very essence of capitalism. Prevailing norms and mainstream thoughts are recorded, replayed, and reinforced in Technicolor, while any criticism of the orthodoxy is consciously quashed. . . .

Such is our legacy. A world in which consumerism is equated with economic policy, where corporate interests reign, where corporations spew their jargon on to the airwaves and stifle nations with their imperial rule. Corporations have become behemoths, huge global giants that wield immense political power.

Propelled by government policies of privatization, deregulation, and trade liberalization, and the technological developments of the past twenty years, a power shift has taken place. The hundred largest multinational corporations now control about 20 percent of global foreign assets, and fifty-one of the one hundred biggest economies in the world are now corporations. The sales of General Motors and Ford are greater than the GDP of the whole of sub-Saharan Africa; the assets of IBM, BP, and General Electric outstrip the economic capabilities of most small nations; and Wal-Mart, the supermarket retailer, has higher revenues than most Central and Eastern Europe states.

The size of corporations is increasing. In the first year of the new millennium, Vodafone merged with Mannesmann (a purchase worth $183 billion), Chrysler with Daimler (the merged company now employs over 400,000 people), Smith Kline Beecham with Glaxo Wellcome (now reporting pretax profits of $7.6 billion as GlaxoSmithKline), and AOL with Time Warner in a merger worth $350 billion—five thousand mergers in total in 2000, and double the level of a decade earlier. These megamergers mock the M&A activity of the 1980s. Each new merger is bigger than the one before, and governments rarely stand in the way. Each new merger gives corporations even more power. All the goods we buy or use—our gasoline, the drugs our doctors prescribe, essentials like water, transport, health, and education, even the new school computers and the crops growing in the fields around our communities—are in the grip of corporations which may, at their whim, nurture, support, or strangle us. 10

This is the world of the Silent Takeover, the world at the dawn of the new millennium. Governments' hands appear tied and we are increasingly dependent on corporations. Business is in the driver's seat, corporations determine the rules of the game, and governments have become referees, enforcing rules laid down by others. Portable corporations are now movable feasts and governments go to great lengths to attract or retain them on their shores. Blind eyes are turned to tax loopholes. Business moguls use sophisticated tax dodges to keep their bounty offshore. Rupert Murdoch's News Corporation pays only 6 percent tax worldwide; and in the U.K., up to the end of 1998, it paid no net British corporation tax at all, despite having made £1.4 billion profit there since June 1987. This is a world in which, although we already see the signs of the eroding tax base in our crumbling public services and infrastructure, our elected representatives kowtow to business, afraid not to dance to the piper's tune.

Governments once battled for physical territory; today they fight in the main for market share. One of their primary jobs has become that of ensuring an environment in which business can prosper, and which is attractive to business. The role of nation states has become to a large extent simply that of providing the public goods and infrastructure that business needs at the lowest costs while protecting the world's free trade system. . . .

Never before in modern times has the gap between the haves and the have-nots been so wide, never have so many been excluded or so championless. Forty-five million Americans have no health insurance. In Manhattan, people fish empty drink cans and bottles from trash cans to claim their five cents' redemption value, while in London, car windshield washers armed with squeegees and pails of dirty water ambush drivers at traffic lights. Americans spend $8 billion a year on cosmetics while the world cannot find the $9 billion the UN reckons is needed to give all people access to clean drinking water and sanitation. The British Labour party has gone on record as saying that wealth creation is now more important than wealth redistribution.

In America, during the ten years after 1988, income for the poorest families rose less than 1 percent, while it jumped 15 percent for the richest fifth. In New York City the poorest 20 percent earn an annual average of $10,700 while the wealthiest 20 percent earn $152,350. Wages for those at the bottom are so low that, despite the country's low unemployment figures, millions of employed Americans and one in five American children are now living in poverty. Never since the 1920s has the gap between rich and poor been so great. Bill Gates's net worth alone at the end of the last century, for example, equaled the total net worth of the bottom 50 percent of American families.

15   Capitalism has triumphed, but its spoils are not shared by all. Its failings are ignored by governments which, thanks to the very policy measures they introduced, are increasingly unable to deal with the consequences of their system.

COLLABORATING

Read the following simple story and determine its thesis. Next, by using one of the methods of interrogating the obvious, see if you can arrive at alternative theses or at least at questions that might lead you to a different thesis.

A large male lion lorded over his terrain in a remote savannah in Africa. However, a drought dried up the watering holes that supplied his pride, so all of the lions had to migrate to a new area. As he had done in the old territory, the male lion established one watering hole that belonged exclusively to him. The pride drank from a separate watering hole that at first seemed sufficient. However, the lionesses came to feel that the male lion was hiding something from them. They started complaining about the bizarre behavior of the male lion, saying that his decisions were crazy and his actions outrageous. The rumor spread quickly that the male lion had gone insane. The pride would no longer hunt for him and wanted to know what had happened to its wise, beloved leader.

The male lion could not understand the problem. He felt that he was acting the same as he ever had and thought that the pride had turned lazy and sloth-ful. As his hunger grew, he planned to flee and hunt for himself. On the way out of the new territory, he stopped at the lionesses' watering hole to quench his thirst. He thought the water tasted particularly refreshing and drank for a long time. He did not feel like leaving any more, and his hunger seemed to wane. He strolled over to some of the lionesses and roared how much he had missed them. He agreed with them that hunting was not necessary and started questioning some of the decisions he had made since moving to the new territory. The pride rejoiced. Its leader had regained his sanity.

Investigating Assumptions

You have assumptions about how the world operates. Many of these assumptions seem like common sense. For example, eggs, cereal, and pancakes are commonsense options when you decide on breakfast. On a larger scale, the merits of competition are so ingrained in us that not only does our economic system depend on it but many leisure activities—playing cards, participating in sports, engaging in trivia challenges—also rely on it. Common sense relates to a value system constructed on cultural preferences about harmless matters like breakfast and more complex issues like competition.

When we extend these preferences to assumptions about individuals or groups of people, we create stereotypes, or unfair representations. The use of stereotypes in a thesis can alienate readers. Unexamined adherence to cultural assumptions or personal ones can do even more harm; they interfere with our understanding of our own actions and of how others react to us. Therefore, we must strive to investigate the assumptions behind our subjects as well as behind our lives.

Stereotypes as clichés

Race, Class, and Gender   Assumptions about race, class, and gender abound in society. People growing up in previous generations used to find a color in a typical box of crayons called "flesh tone." The color resembled Caucasian skin, not African American, Hispanic, or any other group's skin. Airlines unabashedly segment members of differing social classes in "first class," "business class," and "tourist" seating. Golf courses around the nation still use the term "women's tees" for the starting spot for players who do not hit for long distances. All these instances show institutions adhering to assumptions about what is normal viewed through a lens of racial superiority, class privilege, or sexism.

When looking for the assumptions within a subject, ask questions about race, class, and gender. A white person who is trying to find a thesis for an essay based in personal experience might ask herself how her narrative might have been different if she or any of the people involved had been Korean, Navajo, or Caribbean. When arguing a point, another person might wonder what conditions of upper-class, middle-class, or working-class life factor into his position on an issue. In finishing a research component of a paper, he might check whether the likes and dislikes expressed in the library materials reflect a gender preference. The differences uncovered might be minimal or insignificant. But a combination of factors might enable these students to work toward theses that critique the influence of one or more of the assumptions on the subject.

WRITING

Many people do not like to write about racial, gender, or class privilege; they believe that such discourse divides us rather than unites us. Some prominent critics of political correctness say that we are all just people and that complaints based on race, gender, and class serve as an excuse for people not to succeed. While social class is important, let's stick to race and gender for now. To investigate the assumption that race and gender don't matter, freewrite in response to the following prompt, adapted from bell hooks's *Teaching Community*: If you were to die and could choose to come back as a white male, a white female, a black female, or a black male, which identity would you choose? Explain your choice, and decide whether your explanation refutes or supports the contention that race and gender matter.

Unearthing Agendas   We often wonder about another person's true agenda, the genuine reasons the person reacts or feels a certain way. In sorting through the logic and evidence of an argument (discussed in Chapter 9), we sense that something has been left out, perhaps even buried so we won't find it. You might agree with Noreena Hertz's arguments (pages 35–38) about the concentration of wealth and its effects on justice and equity, but you might not believe that the capitalist system is "undeniably failing," as Hertz contends, and wonder why she has expressed such passion. You might start digging to unearth and bring to light her agenda. You speculate on her past experiences, and an Internet search reveals that she worked for International Finance Corporation before becoming a prominent academic. Might this color her view of the system?

You need also to examine your own reaction and interpretation. Why do you want to defend the system? Is there a reason you want to question or ignore the startling statistics Hertz presents? It is more difficult to dig deeply to unearth our own agendas than it is to critique those of others. Sometimes we find that a certain perspective, such as Hertz's, threatens our beliefs or our dreams. But if we start our investigation of assumptions with ourselves, we can clearly convey to readers what our agendas are and why facts or claims have not convinced us.

By unearthing our agendas, we avoid the appearance of deception and also learn about the legitimacy of our assumptions. What if our support for an English-only movement stems from our own insecurity about not speaking a second language? What if our belief in stereotypes about gang members fuels our distaste for rap music? These discoveries beg for self-reflection and change, both of which can start when we write about our feelings and bring our assumptions to the surface.

Seeing Patterns

While we are all individuals existing in space separate from other people, our backgrounds, opportunities, belief systems, and actual experiences have more in common with other people's than we often believe. Frequently, we focus on the small matters that distinguish us from others rather than looking at commonalities. We want to be unique. And we are in many ways. You were born on a specific date and time, grew up in a certain locale, and participated in particular games and activities. No one else has experienced life precisely the way you have. In writing, however, focusing on such differences does not always amount to much. By settling on the uniqueness of a situation as part of a thesis, we can shut off critical analysis altogether.

While not ignoring the differences among the experiences we are comparing, we have to question how unique our personal experiences really are. People worry that a lack of uniqueness brings about conformity, a dull cooperation with popular trends, so they often want to stress features that set them apart from the crowd. For the purpose of critical analysis and building toward a theme, think of this type of uniqueness as a variable within similarity, something crucial to our sense of identity, perhaps, but not essential in generating an understanding of a person, place, or event. Following are ways to work toward finding patterns.

Facts and Events as Examples   As a writer, look at any set of facts or description of events as an example of a larger trend in society. The September 11, 2001, attacks on New York City and Washington D.C., for instance, stand out as unique in the minds of many Americans; they appear to have no precursor. But when we probe the details, we find valid comparisons to previous events that did not immediately come to mind.

For instance, the pilots of the hijacked planes committed suicide for their political cause. Twentieth-century history provides many examples of suicide for political purposes, such as Japan's kamikaze pilots in World War II and the Buddhist monks who set themselves on fire to protest the policies of the Ngo Dinh Diem regime in South Vietnam. From here, a writer can look for other connections. Another detail of the September 11 attacks concerns the reaction of our government, such as the creation of the USA Patriot Act. At other times, have Americans curtailed civil rights in favor of national security? Examples abound. Woodrow Wilson and Abraham Lincoln, for example, both placed restrictions on citizens in ways similar to the Patriot Act. Once we see these similarities, others might surface.

The purpose of seeing seemingly unique occurrences as examples is that placing an event or set of facts into a context allows us to better understand it. We can think more clearly about what to do when we know that others have been in similar situations, and we can propose solutions that worked previously or raise objections to those that failed. When we spot a trend, we can evaluate it to see whether it affects our society positively or negatively. For example, knowing that our freedoms have been limited in the past could be either disturbing or comforting. We might notice a pattern of restrictions on individual pursuits of liberty that have gradually eroded our rights. On the other side, we might see a pattern of restoration of rights after temporary restrictions or increased safety as a result of permanent restrictions. Such critiques require first studying patterns by looking at the event as an example of something larger than just the unique occurrence it initially appears to be.

Who Profits?   Sometimes the most penetrating critical analysis begins with the question, "Who stands to benefit the most if a situation remains the same?" Depending on the topic, we may be able to pinpoint specific individuals. But even profiles of the type of person who might profit can yield important insights, as long as we do not succumb to stereotyping or innuendo. Keep in mind that people profit in many different ways besides monetarily, such as by gaining power, earning acclaim, and maintaining their sense of respect or dignity. At times, you might shrug your shoulders over what you uncover using this analytic method; no one seems to be harmed when one person or a group profits. But when you see profiting disguised as taste, preference, or culture, you have to question why a person or group avoids being forthcoming about the profit element. Too often, many or the majority of people suffer when a small number profit.

RICHARD MEYER

Curriculum Is a Political Statement

Like many scholars who have researched how children learn to read, Richard Meyer believes that the widely taught phonics approach has tremendous flaws. In this passage, Meyer talks about decisions made regarding curriculum for reading classrooms. He has conducted research in a classroom taught by a woman named Karen, who was mandated to use a phonics curriculum. Notice that Meyer discusses both who wins and who loses when phonics are taught in the classroom.

As a scholar in education, Meyer uses the widely accepted American Psychological Association (APA) documentation style. You're probably already familiar with internal citations within a text. When an author quotes or paraphrases someone else's words, the author gives the specific page number on which those words first appeared. In academic writing, scholars such as Meyer also often refer to the works of other scholars to grant credence to their own ideas. Text is followed by the last name of another scholar plus the year of publication of the work that contains the idea in parentheses. So in the following excerpt, "(Wilson, 2000)" means that Meyer is building his ideas from previous scholarship, thus placing his ideas within an acceptable context in the field. If readers look at the reference list of the article (not reprinted here), they will find the article or book in question and can consult it if they so choose.

Curriculum is more than a set of materials. Curriculum, in Karen's case, signifies many decisions that were made. Karen was not included in those decisions, but she and her students must live with them—a view made clear to her by her administrators in the school and district.

Curriculum is political because it comes from some *place* and that place is a place (position) of influence and power. The claims that children can't read, aren't learning to read, schools must be bigger (read: more economical), and that all children must experience the same curricular materials (Wilson, 2000) are all serving someone. They are serving curriculum manufacturers, politicians who are serving individuals who want to do away with public schools (Ohanian, 2000), religious groups (Spring, 1997), and legislators who answer to industry (which supports their election). This is what Wilson (2000) called the "Emperor's new education". However, "unlike the small child who exposed the Emperor's nudity, in a related folk tale, no one has succeeded in exposing the Emperor's new education".

But I'm trying to expose it—its undemocratic views, its deprofessionalizing stances toward teachers, and its inhumane treatment of children. Paul (2000) reminded teachers to think about books like *The Giver* (Lowry, 1993), in which culture, differences, and even color are bleached away. Paul explained that "These are worlds uninhabitable to real people *who retain cultural memory* and who *recognize social conflict and complexity*"; italics added). The phonics curriculum that Karen is using is creating uninhabitable literacy worlds for children. Any time we influence the worlds of children, we are making a political statement and engaging in political activity. The curriculum that is enacted is a political document because it touches children's and teachers' worlds. Karen "retain(s) cultural memory" and "recognizes social conflict and complexity" and this causes her pain—pain that I refer to as *curricular heartache*. It is a heartache born of the consciousness of a teacher knowing she can do better than the curriculum that is binding and limiting her and her students.

When a curriculum is enacted, it answers this question: What is a curriculum supposed to do? Perrone (1998) reminded us that "the content of schools seldom relates to what people in a particular community are worried about or care deeply about" (p. 55). He explained that much of what happens in schools is disconnected from the community and that the "disconnectedness trivializes much of what students are asked to learn" (p. 55). In previous school years, Karen saw her children become increasingly phonemically aware with the use of language activities that were relevant to the children. Now she and her students live with imposed irrelevance that ignores bodies of reading research.

5   When an approach to teaching reading discounts or dismisses huge bodies of research, such as the research on miscue analysis (Brown, Marek, & Goodman, 1996), *that* is a political act. Texas and California, two high-population states, influence the rest of the country when decisions are made in those states about the teaching of reading. They influence the rest of the country because publishers cater to high-population states, adjusting what is available for sale to meet the desire of those states' curriculum decision makers. The more publishers match the demands of the high-population states, the more money they make. Texas and California are known for statewide adoptions, meaning millions of dollars are at stake. When those two states became interested in more phonics instruction, publishers were quick to present programs to them (see Taylor, 1998). Those states made adoptions. Their adoptions were analyzed by Dressman (1999), who found that they "disregard or avoid . . . any research findings of the intervening 30 years that refute or adjust traditional beliefs about the efficacy of traditional practices" (p. 257). Dressman went on to say that:

> . . . these programs pay little if any attention to the communicative function of language, to the complex interrelations of the subcomponents of literacy, or to the agency of children as learners or adults as teachers. Instead, they prescribe programs of explicit, systematic instruction in the traditional subcomponents of reading and writing plus prerequisite screening and intervention via phonemic/phonological awareness activities . . . . They tacitly maintain that literacy is a cognitive issue that demands an almost exclusively cognitive approach to its instruction. (p. 257)

Dressman went on to describe the tediousness of these programs, referring to "reading a story aloud occasionally to break the monotonous labor of learning to read as an *unnatural* act" (p. 258; italics added).

Who gains when learning to read is a monotonous unnatural act? The children who rarely experience reading in other contexts aside from school lose; those that hear excited family members read to them outside of school also lose, just not as severely. When a curriculum teaches that reading is unnatural, it is making a political statement because those who have little power, who send their children to school with dreams of accessing power in the form of a better quality of life, are forced to stay marginalized. Their children are being edged out, pushed out, turned off, and disenfranchised from reading. They learn that reading is dull, unnatural, irrelevant, and dismissive of their lives outside of school. This is political work. It is political work that sounds like it would take place in a part of the world in which human rights are ignored, violated, or abused. It is happening here.

DISCUSSION

Can you think of ways that our culture demonstrates the value of individuality or uniqueness? Under what circumstances does our culture value conformity? Think of a time you witnessed or experienced a situation in which one person asserted the uniqueness of a person, place, or event while another person tried to show that the person, place, or event was not unique. What was at stake? Did anyone stand to lose or gain by the outcome? Compare your example with the examples of other students in class. Is there a discernible pattern to your experiences?

Avoiding Poor Reasoning

Critical analysis leads us toward challenging dominant thought in society. Often, we can fulfill a rebellious need through these types of critiques and build much enthusiasm when writing. However, we have to be careful to avoid confusing critical analysis and poor reasoning. Even intelligent people sometimes mistake the two.

Reasonable or rational thinking requires us to adhere to conventions of logic as well as ethics. Poor reasoning seeps into our ideas or arguments when we worry about persuading or convincing an audience or reader that we are correct. We reach for tactics that undermine our thinking and play on the emotions of others. In Part II, we examine the appropriate ways to work with evidence and to avoid lapses in logic, such as those that occur when writers succumb to the bandwagon mentality or straw-person arguments.

For now, we should monitor ourselves for any of the logical fallacies that often occur when a writer is trying to construct a powerful thesis. If you find that you are using any of the strategies discussed below to persuade an audience—whether that audience consists of other students, instructors, or a general readership—rethink your approach and revise accordingly.

Attacks Against Others   We are frequently tempted to discredit an idea or belief on the basis of who introduces it to us. We ignore logic and evidence in favor of the popularity of the person presenting an idea or belief to us. Generally, we attack a person's intellect by making such remarks as "Well, what does he know?" or by bringing up unfavorable characteristics, such as "She's a nerd, so of course she thinks that."

When we find ourselves using such devices, which are called ad hominem attacks, we are really making excuses to avoid pondering a position that threatens some aspect of ourselves. Aside from involving a lack of reflection, the ad hominem attack derives its strength from our hope that nobody we admire adheres to the belief under attack. What would happen if the nerd we degraded believes the same thing as our favorite musician or an admired intellectual or moral figure, such as Albert Einstein or Mahatma Gandhi? That would take us back to where we started, which is with the evidence and logic behind the idea.

Reasonable thinking demands not taking such detours. Questioning the credibility of a source is fine. For example, if a student in your class diagnoses your flulike symptoms as pneumonia, you would be reasonable in doubting her assertion because she is not a doctor. It would be unwise, in fact, to act as if you had pneumonia without getting a second opinion from somebody with a medical degree. Your classmate could be missing something essential in her diagnosis because of her lack of expertise and experience. You seek verification under such circumstances.

When wondering about the validity of facts that someone supplies, it is also perfectly acceptable to ask for verification. People have been known to misread books or to frame the results of a study to favor their own position. When examining eyewitness testimony or the truth behind a story someone tells you, consider the person's background, beliefs, and agenda before deciding about the person's reliability.

But when we dismiss an idea simply because of who says it, we are no longer being reasonable. In writing, it might appear easier to construct a thesis on the basis of an attack on an unpopular person or even to associate opposing viewpoints with unpopular terms you have heard. Radio commentator Rush Limbaugh frequently avoids critical analysis by labeling opponents "liberals" or "feminazis" and excoriating people who agitate for change on the basis of liberal or feminist ideology. The ideas of these opponents persist, though, precisely because they have not been defeated through a reasonable approach. Attacking others does not work because the substance of an idea is separate from the person who holds the idea.

Diversions   While critical analysis calls for making connections that might not be apparent at first, writers have to be careful not to confuse an issue. Some professional writers, whether intentionally or unintentionally, divert an audience from the issue at hand to talk about another situation. This logical fallacy is called a "red herring."

A person, for instance, might want to argue that opening up federal land for oil exploration is necessary because of upcoming shortages. He might say, "If we do not get more oil, we will face higher prices and gasoline rationing, just as happened during the energy crisis of the 1970s. We all remember how bad that was." If the person continues to discuss the hardships brought on by the energy crisis thirty years ago without making direct comparisons to the current situation, he will be diverting the audience in unethical ways, trying to garner support by evoking deprivation. In so doing, he is not explaining anything about the current situation, why he thinks there will be shortages, or how opening up federal lands to exploration will prevent shortages.

A comparison might yield a pattern, as discussed in the previous section, but the focus should be on the pattern, not on the situation thirty years ago. In avoiding the facts of the current situation, the person is not critically analyzing the situation; he is avoiding analysis of the crucial facts and not supporting his position. Alert readers uncover such tactics quickly, which undermines the credibility of the writer's position and brings the writer's integrity into question.

Overgeneralizing   Writers forming generalizations from analyses need to adhere to certain constraints so that they do not apply their conclusions too broadly. Critical analysis uncovers insights and generates theories. However, the insights and theories are not proof. Rather, they suggest possible applications to other situations or point in directions where some ideas can be applied. When we claim that a conclusion applies to all situations, we are overgeneralizing.

For instance, you might write an essay about holidays and reach the conclusion that people have changed the purpose of holiday celebrations from commemoration to simply having fun. This thesis, though perhaps tied to a great deal of evidence about our culture's habits of celebration, cannot account for the somber commemorations on national holidays such as Memorial Day, when many people grieve for the dead at cemeteries. A more accurate thesis might be that many people have distorted the purpose of holidays to having fun. The qualification "many," instead of the implied "all" in the original statement, makes the difference.

Mistakes can also be made when we take one or two incidents, ignore important specifics from those situations, and reach a general conclusion. In the essay about holidays, you might decide that, based on the past two Fourth of July parties you attended, people no longer enjoy fireworks on Independence Day. Two parties supply very little evidence for such a sweeping statement. You might have overlooked the specifics of the situations, such as the age group of the partygoers, the region of the country, or the type of people. A more accurate thesis would limit this conclusion, saying perhaps that you have noticed a decline in the popularity of Independence Day fireworks among people of your age group. The key word *might*, combined with the detail about your age group, keeps you clear of overgeneralizations.

WRITING

Go to the website of your local newspaper, and read several days' worth of op-ed columns, which you will find on the editorial or opinion pages. How do the columnists support their ideas? Do the columnists appear to be reasonable? Did you notice any attacks on others, diversions, or overgeneralizations?

Choose one editorial that you agree with and another that you do not agree with. Write a one-paragraph summary of each editorial, then look again at the editorials to determine how the columnists dealt with people in opposition to them, comparisons to other situations, and generalizing from the evidence they presented. Write down your evaluation of the columnists' ideas, noting places where they might have succumbed to poor reasoning.

Summary

All essays must have a thesis that logically derives from their content. The best way to avoid clichés in a thesis and to assert ideas that strike you as true is to engage in critical analysis. Critical analysis digs deep, looking at the content from several different perspectives and uncovering insights that lead to a strong thesis.

Critical analysis takes many forms: interrogating the obvious, questioning assumptions, and reconceiving uniqueness. When you employ any of these methods, you may discover ideas that you had not considered before. In conveying these ideas, however, you have to be careful to avoid poor reasoning; you can be perceived as illogical and unethical if you attack others, use diversions, or overgeneralize.

CHAPTER 3

AWARENESS OF AUDIENCE

Good writers use critical analysis to reach bold ideas. In expressing these ideas, writers have to be aware of their readers. These actual and imagined readers comprise what we will term the audience. The audience affects what a writer does in everything from how much detail to supply to where to place opposing points of view. An audience also determines the success of any piece of writing.

An audience judges writing on what writers compose. If the audience does not know the writer, either personally or through reputation, all judgments will come from the words the writer uses to establish his or her ethos on the subject. *Ethos* can be loosely defined as the ethical credibility of the writer. Writers demonstrate ethos through words. Authorial intention, or what a writer means to say through writing, does not control the reaction of an audience and cannot be relied on to clarify ambiguity or defend a point of view. A writer must be aware that she or he is constructing a writerly self or a persona that an audience will respond to either positively or negatively.

Anna, who took a course in English composition from me several years ago, wrote a paper about the social issues surrounding gays and lesbians on campus. She focused on the method of tolerance for alternative sexual lifestyles apparently advocated during a freshmen orientation seminar. She was having difficulty living up to this method's expectations, saying that being around people of the same gender who acted in ways indicative of same-sex relationships made her uncomfortable. In the draft of her paper that Anna presented in a whole-class workshop, she concluded that no one should force anyone else to be tolerant.

 **Online Study Center**

This icon will direct you to web links and additional resources on the website http://college.cengage.com/english/thelin/ writing_without_formulas/1e/student_home.html

ANNA BANKS

Sexuality Orientation

I do not like when other people's views are forced onto me. I think that the Freshman Orientation here at _____ does not orient people to being able to live on campus. It brainwashes them into wanting to accept ideas that make them sick.

I try to keep an open mind about everything. The Freshman Orientation started out okay in this respect. I was told there might be some people born elsewhere who could be staying in my dorms, and I said to myself that I would tolerate their ways. I listened to advice on how to communicate when their English was not that good and thought I could offer help if needed.

After the Orientation people reviewed things on campus like speakers and activities, I thought I had heard all I wanted to. I really wanted to know how to find classes and to make sure I didn't get raped by some inbred wandering around. But I found out that the theme for the Orientation was diversity and tolerance. All of a sudden, they bring to the stage some gay and lesbian people.

The guy started by saying that about 10% of the population on the campus is gay and that some sort of research said that as many as 30% of the population could have hidden feelings like that. He then said that if you had ever noticed how well dressed a person of the same sex was or noticed the good figure on a girl or for guys, their muscles, you were displaying normal tendencies that involve homosexual feelings. Fortunately, he didn't say that made us lesbians, because I've noticed when friends are pretty and I know I don't go for chicks! But I felt pretty insulted anyway, as he wanted us to be like them.

A dyke took the stage and I thought she would have a really deep voice and act like a man, but she seemed pretty nice. She didn't try to tell us we were all lesbians, but instead talked about ways to respect gays and lesbians. She said that you shouldn't be uncomfortable around gay couples because they did not pose any threat to you. She said that most gay people did not get passionate in front of heteros, I didn't like how she termed all us that, and that the most you would probably notice would be hand holding or putting arms around each other. The same rules apply, as a "hetero" couple makes people uncomfortable with "public displays of affection" too.

The final guy talked about stereotypes of gays and claimed that some of them were very athletic and manly while lesbians could be feminine and have traditional values. He gave examples of friends of his who did mountain climbing and worked as an ambulance driver. He finished by saying we shouldn't assume we couldn't be friends with gays just because we weren't gays. He said we could still share interests and form friendships.

> I came back home and was thoroughly disgusted. I couldn't believe that people wanted me to tolerate gays and lesbians. When I think of them kissing and stuff like that, it makes me want to throw up. I don't feel right when I am around someone who acts gay or lesbian and don't want someone to force me to pretend to be comfortable. I don't think school should expect me to accept people I don't like. I definitely don't want to be friends with them because then people will think I'm a lesbo. I guess people can do what they like when they're alone, but they cannot expect normal people to agree with it and want to be around it. That's asking too much.

In the workshop, many of Anna's peers could not get past the thesis and what they considered to be her hostility toward gays and lesbians. While some members of the class agreed with her to an extent, the dominant sentiment seemed to be that gays and lesbians should be left alone, that as long as their lifestyle did not affect anyone else, other members of the campus should be tolerant. The students kept asking Anna to investigate her assumptions and unearth her agenda. It seemed that the students saw potential in her paper for self-reflection that would allow her to establish a stronger ethos for her audience. Several asked Anna if she had heard antigay sentiments in her household or among her peers. Anna became frustrated.

"I want to make this paper better," she said. "Give me some ideas I can use."

The students were momentarily stunned. A class leader named Jim broke the silence. "But that's what we're doing," he said. "You haven't given any reasons for not wanting to be around gays and lesbians. You described the seminar but that's about it."

A student named Sandra chipped in. "Yeah, you talk about all the good things said in orientation but not about why they didn't affect you."

"But this is my paper," Anna said. "I don't want it to explain everything."

"But if you want your readers to understand you," I said, "you have to give them your reasons." *Spell it out even more than you feel you have to*

"Right now," Jim said, "it sounds like you hate gays and lesbians and just want us to accept that."

Indeed, Anna's paper was expressing a strong opinion that lacked the forms of critical analysis discussed in Chapter 2. The only person who could read it and take her views seriously would be someone who shared Anna's feelings or experiences. Anna had failed to communicate the logical reasoning or personal convictions that would allow readers to receive her paper more sympathetically.

Anna kept her head down through most of this conversation, but she looked at me after Jim spoke. "So I have to change what I say to make this a good paper?" she asked.

In unison everyone said that wasn't the point. "People do not have to agree with me for me to listen to them," Jim said. "But they have to understand where I'm coming from if I'm going to listen."

"I can't take your ideas seriously," Sandra said, "because you haven't taken my ideas seriously." Sandra was referring to the persona Anna had created. While her fellow students knew a little about Anna through classroom activities, she could not rely on that information to establish ethos with them as readers.

Ultimately, Anna had failed to take the possible reactions of her audience into consideration when she had written this draft. The process of drafting acts as a time of discovery, as is discussed later in Chapter 6, and does not necessarily need to accomplish more than express thoughts and attempt to support them. In revising, however, writers need to consider who will be reading their words, what those readers already know and do not know, what they might believe, and where they might object to a position or statement. Writers also need to look within themselves and reflect on their ideas to build and maintain an ethos that will secure an audience's willingness to listen. Anna did not seem to feel that her audience mattered. Yet, words have no effect if they are not heard. In dismissing the importance of audience, Anna dismissed the communicative function of writing. She felt that her ideas and reasoning should be apparent, and she rejected notions that the experiences she described were a result of her prejudice.

Unfortunately, Anna never submitted a revision of that paper. Had she continued to revise, she may have decided to reflect and examine the prejudice in her thinking. She might have considered religious or moral views that made her oppose gay and lesbian lifestyles and attempted to explain those beliefs more clearly for an audience that she knew did not share these views. She could have revised her paper to critique the orientation seminar through logical means and possibly have found holes in its assumptions, reinforcing

---

DISCUSSION

What do you immediately see when you look at this drawing? Did other students see the same thing immediately? If not, why? Can you perceive the picture differently on a second look? Think about how valuable the audience (in this case, viewers rather than readers) is in interpretation. Does this picture have a definite, precise interpretation not constructed by the audience?

Old Woman . . . or Young Girl?
Hint: The old woman's nose is the young girl's chin.

beliefs she had learned while growing up. A successful revision could have considered the views of an opponent of her beliefs, someone who found that the freshmen orientation gave him or her a refreshing perspective on gays and lesbians. In her first draft, Anna might have intended to sound sympathetic to gays and lesbians and might have meant to say only that the lifestyle was not for her. In the end, we cannot know her intentions. Until she could establish her own ethos by explaining the assumptions on which her arguments rested, she could not hope to accommodate or understand her audience.

An audience constructs meaning from a piece of writing. The best opportunity for feedback between writers and potential readers is during a draft workshop or something like it. Once a piece of writing is published, submitted to a instructor for a grade, given to an executive board to act on, or sent over the Internet to readers, the writer has little control over interpretation. An audience will be puzzled, angered, dismayed, or unaffected if the writer did not anticipate the differing needs, backgrounds, and opinions of its members. Two people can look at the same object and see differing images.

Understanding the audience does not mean altering your intended meaning or disguising your intentions. If you establish a strong or consistent ethos, your audience will be more likely to listen, even if its members do not agree. You do not need to pander to readers in order to communicate. Yet, you do have to understand the diverse views of society and prepare for them. You also need to realize that what is perfectly clear to you might not be clear to someone else; a member of an audience probably has not experienced life the way you have, especially when it comes to specific experiences or other factors that have influenced your beliefs. The guidelines that follow should help you take the audience into account when you write.

Targeting Potential Readers

Not every possible reader warrants consideration when you write. If you were to write about the virtues of Ty Cobb as the greatest baseball player ever, for instance, you would have already targeted people who care about baseball. Someone who has no interest in the game will read no farther, so you do not have to worry about that person as a potential reader. Since baseball is not an obscure sport, you could assume that most potential readers do not need an overview of how the game is played (unlike an extreme sport such as wakeboarding), but you do face a decision about readers' knowledge of baseball history and the finer points of the game. For most writing, you need to factor in common knowledge, cultural considerations, and vocabulary to make decisions about how much information to provide. The following guidelines also determine the amount of research and evidence you need for academic writing.

Common Knowledge   If you learned something in high school or before, you can consider that information to be common knowledge—that is, generally acknowledged to be true. For example, the capitals of states, the dates of major historical events, and the basic components of a cell are all common knowledge. In academic writing, you would not need to cite sources for these facts.

You also do not need to recount common knowledge in setting up your essay. If you provide too much remedial information, you risk insulting or boring your readers. Of course, people's experiences in high school differ, so what counts as common knowledge varies.

If you are worried that an audience will not recollect information important for the acceptance of your thesis, preface your overview with a brief summary of the key points, making it clear that you are supplying a review for the sake of convenience. Avoid condescending remarks or statements indicating that the information is obvious. Sometimes it is frustrating to include information that is second nature to you. You may wish that the audience can be counted on to know more so you can get right to the point. Keep in mind, though, that a condescending tone does not win friends. You probably develop a negative impression when someone implies that you are stupid because you do not already know something. Writing works the same way. If you do not strike a balance regarding common and specialized knowledge, you can lose your audience.

Cultural Considerations   Writers have to understand that the culture in which they live might be unfamiliar to a larger audience. In fact, an audience might hold stereotypical beliefs about particular subcultures. Thus, what is second nature to us might confuse readers or be misunderstood. Consider the following passage from "Bloody Footprints" by Roxanne A. Dunbar.

> The poor whites (white trash) I come from, Okies and their descendents, were those who formed the popular base for the post–World War II rise of the hard right in Orange County, California. Richard Nixon the anti-Communist was their man. They were the "little people" and "silent majority" addressed by Richard Nixon as President, then by Ronald Reagan. They were among the bigots, including my father, who supported George Wallace. During the 1980s, they helped swell the ranks of the Christian Coalition, promoting anti-abortion and anti-gay initiatives.

Dunbar adds much detail to describe "poor whites" or "Okies" because she has anticipated that these terms might evoke another image for her

---

WRITING

In her effort to define the term *poor whites* for her audience, Roxanne Dunbar uses terms like *silent majority* and makes references to American historical figures like George Wallace. What cultural knowledge is needed to make sense of her description? Did you have trouble understanding her point about her family's background? Write an explanation of both the common knowledge and the cultural considerations needed to comprehend this passage fully.

audience. Writers need to examine their topics when revising and ponder whether examples, references, or points rely on specialized cultural or ethnic knowledge that needs further explanation. Weaving in short explanations keeps the audience within the targeted readership and might even pique interest in your particular culture, thus helping to deflate stereotypes.

Vocabulary   Practically nothing alienates a reader more than the use of words and phrases that he or she does not understand. Writers need to use plain, clear English to communicate their ideas. A writer's sophistication, though, can evaporate if he or she tries to "dumb down" his or her vocabulary, and the writer might be perceived as condescending.

To reach your audience effectively, avoid jargon and imply the meaning of uncommon vocabulary words in the context of the sentence. Jargon consists of words and phrases that have developed in a workplace or culture to substitute for longer explanations of events, theories, or procedures. Sometimes jargon users invent words that are not in the dictionary. Other times, jargon is comprised of words already in general usage to mean something slightly or altogether different from the dictionary definitions.

Writers should also avoid unnatural, elevated vocabulary, which occurs when writers try to find too obscure of a synonym to express an ordinary word. To avoid repetition, inexperienced writers sometimes fall prey to using a thesaurus and end up writing sentences with words that they do not ordinarily use and that readers do not know (more on thesaurus usage in Chapter 5). Other times, writers with advanced knowledge or expertise unintentionally use words familiar to people like them but unfamiliar to a general audience. To target readers beyond the small circles where jargon and elevated vocabulary are appropriate, you must take steps to be inclusive. Small efforts to reach a targeted audience will keep its members reading and comprehending.

MARIAH BLAKE

Voices: The Damage Done
Crack babies talk back

Analyze how well this author targeted potential readers. Has she given enough background information, too much, or too little? What do you need to know about the media hype surrounding crack babies to understand the thesis? Is the vocabulary too elevated or full of jargon? Decide who the intended audience was.

Antwaun Garcia was a shy boy whose tattered clothes reeked of cat piss. Everyone knew his father peddled drugs and his mother smoked rock, so they called him a "crack baby."

It started in fourth grade when his teacher asked him to read aloud. Antwaun stammered, then went silent. "He can't read because he's a crack baby," jeered a classmate. In the cafeteria that day no one would sit near him. The kids pointed and chanted, "crack baby, crack baby." Antwaun sat sipping his milk and staring down at his tray. After that, the taunting never stopped. Unable to take it, Antawun quit school and started hanging out at a local drug dealer's apartment, where at age nine he learned to cut cocaine and scoop it into little glass vials. "*Crack baby*," he says. "Those two words almost cost me my education."

Antwaun finally returned to school and began learning to read a year later, after he was plucked from his parent's home and placed in foster care. Now twenty, he's studying journalism at LaGuardia Community College in New York City and writing for *Represent,* a magazine for and by foster children. In a recent special issue he and other young writers, many of them born to crack addicts, took aim at a media myth built on wobbly, outdated science: crack babies. Their words are helping expose the myth and the damage it has done.

Crack hit the streets in 1984, and by 1987 the press had run more than 1,000 stories about it, many focusing on the plight of so-called crack babies. The handwringing over these children started in September 1985, when the media got hold of Dr. Ira Chasnoff's *New England Journal of Medicine* article suggesting that prenatal cocaine exposure could have a devastating effect on infants. Only twenty-three cocaine-using women participated in the study, and Chasnoff warned in the report that more research was needed. But the media paid no heed. Within days of the first story, CBS News found a social worker who claimed that an eighteen-month-old crack-exposed baby she was treating would grow up to have "an IQ of perhaps fifty" and be "barely able to dress herself."

5   Soon, images of the crack epidemic's "tiniest victims"—scrawny, trembling infants—were flooding television screens. Stories about their bleak future abounded. One psychologist told the *New York Times* that crack was "interfering with the central core of what it is to be human." Charles Krauthammer, a columnist for the the *Washington Post,* wrote that crack babies were doomed to "a life of certain suffering, of probable deviance, of permanent inferiority." The public braced for the day when this "biological underclass" would cripple our schools, fill our jails, and drain our social programs.

But the day never came. Crack babies, it turns out, were a media myth, not a medical reality. This is not to say that crack is harmless. Infants exposed to cocaine in the womb, including the crystallized version known as crack, weigh an average of 200 grams below normal at birth, according to a massive, ongoing National Institutes of Health study. "For a healthy, ten-pound Gerber baby this is no big deal," explains Barry Lester, the principal investigator. But it can make things worse for small, sickly infants.

Lester has also found that the IQs of cocaine-exposed seven-year-olds are four and a half points lower on average, and some researchers have documented other subtle problems. Perhaps more damaging than being exposed to cocaine itself is growing up with addicts, who are often incapable of providing a stable, nurturing home. But so-called crack babies are by no means ruined. Most fare far better, in fact, than children whose mothers drink heavily while pregnant.

Nevertheless, in the midst of the drug-war hysteria, crack babies became an emblem of the havoc drugs wreak and a pretext for draconian drug laws. Hospitals began secretly testing pregnant women for cocaine, and jailing them or taking their children. Tens of thousands of kids were swept into foster care, where many languish to this day.

Represent magazine was founded at the height of the crack epidemic to give voice to the swelling ranks of children trapped in the foster-care system. Its editors knew that many of their writers were born to addicts. But it wasn't until late last year, when a handful expressed interest in writing about how crack ravaged their families, that the picture snapped into focus. "I remember hearing about crack babies and how they were doomed,'" says editor Kendra Hurley. "I suddenly realized these were those kids."

Hurley and her co-editor, Nora McCarthy, had worked with many of the 10 writers for years, and had nudged and coddled most through the process of writing about agonizing personal experiences. But nothing compared to the shame their young scribes expressed when discussing their mothers' crack use. Even the most talented believed it had left them "slow," "retarded," or "damaged." The editors decided to publish a special crack issue to help break the stigma and asked the writers to appear on the cover, under the headline "'Crack Babies'—All Grown Up." Initially, only Antwaun agreed. He eventually convinced three others to join him. "I said, 'Why shouldn't we stand up and show our faces?'" he recalls. "We rose above the labels. I wanted to reach other kids who had been labeled and let them know it doesn't mean you can't succeed."

As it happens, when the crack issue went to press, a group of doctors and scientists was already lobbying the *New York Times* to drop terms like "crack baby" from its pages. The group included the majority of American researchers investigating the effects of prenatal cocaine exposure or drug addiction. They were spurred to action by the paper's coverage of a New Jersey couple found to be starving their four foster children in late 2003. For years the couple had explained the children's stunted growth to neighbors and friends by saying, among other things, that they were "crack babies." The *Times* not only failed to inform readers that crack babies don't exist, but reinforced the myth by reporting, without attribution, that "the youngest [of the children] was born a crack baby."

Assistant Managing Editor Allan Siegal refused to meet with the researchers, saying via email that the paper simply couldn't open a dialogue with all the "advocacy groups who wish to influence terminology." After some haggling, he did agree to publish a short letter to the editor from the researchers. While the paper hasn't used "crack baby" in the last several months, it has referred to babies being "addicted" to crack, which, as the researchers told the editors, is scientifically inaccurate, since babies cannot be born addicted to cocaine.

The researchers later circulated a more general letter urging all media to drop the term "crack baby." But the phrase continues to turn up. Of the more than 100 news stories that have used it in the last year, some thirty were published after the letter was distributed in late February.

Represent's writers made a more resounding splash. National Public Radio and AP both featured them in stories on crack's legacy. Inspired by their words, the columnist E. R. Shipp called on New York *Daily News* readers to consider the damage the crack-baby myth has done. A July *Newsday* op-ed made a similar plea, and also urged readers to avoid rushing to judgment on the growing number of babies being born to mothers who use methamphetamines.

15   Still, a number of recent "meth baby" stories echo the early crack-baby coverage. A July AP article cautioned, for instance, that an "epidemic" of meth-exposed children in Iowa is stunting infants' growth, damaging their brains, and leaving them predisposed to delinquency. In May, one Fox News station warned that meth babies "could make the crack baby look like a walk in the nursery." Research is stacking up against such claims. But, then, scientific evidence isn't always enough to kill a good story.

COLLABORATING

Spend time writing a three- or four-paragraph description of an activity you enjoy doing with your family or with a group of close friends. Assume you are writing for a general audience. Discuss what you do and why you like it.

Share your descriptions with your group. Look closely at each description to see where common knowledge has been considered, where cultural assumptions have been explained, and where jargon and elevated language have been avoided. Are there places where too much or too little background information is given? Has the writer failed to communicate something essential about his or her culture? Do any vocabulary choices confuse or alienate you? As a group, form a consensus about the type of reader who would understand and enjoy each paper, and discuss changes that could increase the number of readers.

Anticipating Reader Needs

Once we know our audience, we want to establish our ethos so that readers can relate to us and value our perspective as worthy of consideration. Writing is generally a matter of persuasion. We want readers to believe that the way we communicate a story is the way events actually transpired. We want readers to see our position on an important issue as the most correct and logical position. We want readers to feel so strongly about our thesis that they will respond to a call for action. Anna's draft from earlier in the chapter failed to target her audience, and her problems continued with not anticipating her readers' needs. She wanted to have her perspective valued and understood, but she did not seem to be concerned enough about her readers' needs to try to persuade them.

Persuasion begins with understanding that readers may have different values and experiences than you do. Allowing them to relate to you involves showing them the commonalities between your and their experiences or perspectives. The relationship you want to establish in every piece of writing will be determined by your purpose. Some forms of persuasion are almost invisible and might not be an overt part of your intentions. If you always keep possible differences between you and your audience in mind, you will be able to incorporate responses to your readers' needs in subtle ways.

Value Systems   All of us believe in certain principles. If we feel that a particular set of ideas is beyond question, we have reached a conviction. Most readers have convictions that lead them to develop a system of values that guide their decisions in life. While we cannot possibly anticipate every reader's system, we can and should be aware of the dominant value systems of our community and society. Some of these systems conflict, as we see in the efforts at persuasion by members of opposing value systems in debates over social issues, such as abortion and capital punishment, and in elections, where representatives with differing value systems apply their convictions to foreign and domestic issues. If we are to do serious critical analysis, as advocated in the previous chapter, we need to persuade our audience to consider possibilities beyond its value system. To do this, we have to make a list of where our ideas might conflict with dominant systems and grasp common values that might bring the audience closer to our side.

For example, if you believe that children should take dancing lessons to develop grace and the ability to express themselves, you should anticipate that these ideas will conflict with some value systems. Listing the reasons that people might disagree with you is a good starting point toward finding common values. One such value might involve masculinity. Some fathers would shudder at sending their boys to dance lessons, thinking that such lessons might jeopardize the boys' development into masculine men. If you dismiss such sentiments as a knee-jerk reaction and ignore the need to relate to them in your writing, you will be appealing only to those who are predisposed to agree with you, which might be a very narrow readership. To relate to and even persuade an audience of concerned fathers who value masculinity, you would have to think about how dancing could help a young boy develop a sense of masculinity. Thus, you might talk about the physical strength needed by male ballet dancers. You might mention that Arnold Schwarzenegger, winner of multiple body-building competitions, took dance instruction. Finally, you might observe that good dancing skills in young men lead to attention from young women, which would be in keeping with a value of masculinity.

Knowing in advance what an audience will think and showing the similarities between your goals and theirs will help readers consider your point of view more thoroughly. You will also learn from comparing your ideas to dominant value systems and can either strengthen your position or understand its weaknesses, which perhaps might lead you to tailor what could be construed as an extreme position.

↳ must see the weaknesses in your argument in order to fix them

WRITING

Make a list of your values, and focus on one that you believe most conflicts with a dominant value in society. Narrate a specific experience or observation in which your value influenced the way you interpreted or described an event. Write down the ways you might be able to find common ground with people who did or might have disagreed with your interpretation of the incident.

Life Experiences   Experience is a great teacher for most of us, and we often wonder about the experiences of others. Nothing piques a reader's interest more than hearing about the writer's experience with a topic. When writing, though, we have to remember that readers have not lived our lives and do not have access to our minds.

Details about life experiences help readers conjure up a sense of who you are and how much they can relate to you. As a writer, do not shy away from explaining the situations that led you to believe a certain way or find the importance in a certain subject. Use specific and concrete words so that your audience can envision a description of a personal experience as clearly as possible. Your words should evoke sight, sound, smell, touch, and taste in ways that are precise and vivid. It is one thing to be told that a forest is beautiful and full of life. It is another to experience a writer describing the rich and various shades of green as she treks through a damp, secluded section of Yosemite National Park, glimpsing deer bounding through a meadow and shuddering at the howl of coyotes at night. Readers will stay with you, even if they sense they disagree with your overall point, simply because they are interested in what happened to you.

Readers need to be invested in your writing and perhaps see their own life experiences reflected in it. Thus, life experiences can be used as a brief introduction to a topic, as examples to support a position, or as the basis from which to generalize. Remember again the example of Anna at the beginning of the chapter. The students in her class wanted to know more about her to understand her position on gays and lesbians. She could have included details from her upbringing or her young adult experiences to help her audience understand the development of her beliefs. In so doing, she might also have come to understand her ideas much better, which would have allowed her to establish her ethos much better. Anticipating the needs of an audience helps you develop as a writer.

BARBARA MELLIX

From Outside, In

Barbara Mellix uses her life as an example from which to generalize about African American language usage. While some readers might not share her values, the personal experiences she discusses compel readers to continue reading. While Chapter 5 will discuss the power of words in more detail, look at this selection to see how the author's language choices help the audience better understand her situation and thesis.

Two years ago, when I started writing this paper, trying to bring order out of chaos, my ten-year-old daughter was suffering from an acute attack of boredom. She drifted in and out of the room complaining that she had nothing to do, no one to "be with" because none of her friends were at home. Patiently I explained that I was working on something special and needed peace and quiet, and I suggested that she paint, read, or work with her computer. None of these interested her. Finally, she pulled up a chair to my desk and watched me, now and then heaving long, loud sighs. After two or three minutes (nine or ten sighs), I lost my patience. "Looka here, Allie," I said, "you too old for this kinda carryin' on. I done told you this is important. You wronger than dirt to be in here haggin' me like this and you know it. Now git on outta here and leave me off before I put my foot all the way down."

I was at home, alone with my family, and my daughter understood that this way of speaking was appropriate in that context. She knew, as a matter of fact, that it was almost inevitable; when I get angry at home, I speak some of my finest, most cherished black English. Had I been speaking to my daughter in this manner in certain other environments, she would have been shocked and probably worried that I had taken leave of my sense of propriety.

Like my children, I grew up speaking what I considered two distinctly different languages—black English and standard English (or as I thought of them then, the ordinary everyday speech of "country" coloreds and "proper" English)—and in the process of acquiring these languages, I developed an understanding of when, where, and how to use them. But unlike my children, I grew up in a world that was primarily black. My friends, neighbors, minister, teachers—almost everybody I associated with every day—were black. And we spoke to one another in our own special languages: *That sho is a pretty dress you got on. If she don' soon leave me off I'm gon tell her head a mess. I was so mad I could' a pissed a blue nail. He all the time trying to low-rate somebody. Ain't that just about the nastiest thing you ever set ears on?*

Then there were the "others," the "proper" blacks, transplanted relatives and one-time friends who came home from the city for weddings, funerals, and vacations. And the whites. To these we spoke standard English. "Ain't?" my mother would yell at me when I used the term in the presence of "others." "You *know* better than that." And I would hang my head in shame and say the "proper" word.

I remember one summer sitting in my grandmother's house in Greeleyville, South Carolina, when it was full of the chatter of city relatives who were home on vacation. My parents sat quietly, only now and then volunteering a comment or answering a question. My mother's face took on a strained expression when she spoke. I could see that she was being careful to say just the right words in just the right way. Her voice sounded thick, muffled. And when she finished speaking, she would lapse into silence, her proper smile on her face. My father was more articulate, more aggressive. He spoke quickly, his words sharp and clear. But he held his proud head higher, a signal that he, too, was uncomfortable. My sisters and brothers and I stared at our aunts, uncles, and cousins, speaking only when prompted. Even then, we hesitated, formed our sentences in our minds, then spoke softly, shyly.

My parents looked small and anxious during those occasions, and I waited impatiently for our leave-taking when we would mock our relatives the moment we were out of their hearing. "Reeely," we would say to one another, flexing our wrists and rolling our eyes, "how dooo you stan' this heat? Chile, it just tooo hy*ooo*-mid for words." Our relatives had made us feel "country," and this was our way of regaining pride in ourselves while getting a little revenge in the bargain. The words bubbled in our throats and rolled across our tongues, a balming.

As a child I felt this same doubleness in uptown Greeleyville where the whites lived. "Ain't that a pretty dress you're wearing!" Toby, the town policeman, said to me one day when I was fifteen. "Thank you very much," I replied, my voice barely audible in my own ears. The words felt wrong in my mouth, rigid, foreign. It was not that I had never spoken that phrase before—it was common in black English, too—but I was extremely conscious that this was an occasion for proper English. I had taken out my English and put it on as I did my church clothes, and I felt as if I were wearing my Sunday best in the middle of the week. It did not matter that Toby had not spoken grammatically correct English. He was white and could speak as he wished. I had something to prove. Toby did not.

Speaking standard English to whites was our way of demonstrating that we knew their language and could use it. Speaking it to standard-English-speaking blacks was our way of showing them that we, as well as they, could "put on airs." But when we spoke standard English, we acknowledged (to ourselves and to others—but primarily to ourselves) that our customary way of speaking was inferior. We felt foolish, embarrassed, somehow diminished because we were ashamed to be our real selves. We were reserved, shy in the presence of those who owned and/or spoke *the* language.

My parents never set aside time to drill us in standard English. Their forms of instruction were less formal. When my father was feeling particularly expansive, he would regale us with tales of his exploits in the outside world. In almost flawless English, complete with dialogue and flavored with gestures and embellishment, he told us about his attempt to get a haircut at a white barbershop; his refusal to acknowledge one of the town merchants until the man addressed him a "Mister"; the time he refused to step off the sidewalk uptown to let some whites pass; his airplane trip to New York City (to visit a sick relative) during which the stewardesses and porters—recognizing that he was a "gentleman"—addressed him as "Sir." I did not realize then—nor, I think, did my father—that he was teaching us, among other things, standard English and the relationship between language and power.

10   My mother's approach was different. Often, when one of us said, "I'm gon wash off my feet," she would say, "And what will you walk on if you wash them off!" Everyone would laugh at the victim of my mother's "proper" mood. But it was different when one of us children was in a proper mood. "You think you are so superior," I said to my oldest sister one day when we were arguing and she was winning. "Superior!" my sister mocked. "You mean I am acting 'biggidy'?" My sisters and brothers sniggered, then joined in teasing me. Finally, my mother said, "Leave your sister alone. There's nothing wrong

if you can articulate well, people will think highly of you.

with using proper English." There was a half-smile on her face. I had gotten "uppity," had "put on airs" for no good reason. I was at home, alone with the family, and I hadn't been prompted by one of my mother's proper moods. But there was also a proud light in my mother's eyes; her children were learning English very well.

Not until years later, as a college student, did I begin to understand our ambivalence toward English, our scorn of it, our need to master it, to own and be owned by it—ambivalence that extended to the public-school classroom. In our school, where there were no whites, my teachers taught standard English but used black English to do it. When my grammar-school teachers wanted us to write, for example, they usually said something like, "I want y'all to write five sentences that make a statement. Anybody git done before the rest can color." It was probably almost those exact words that led me to write these sentences in 1953 when I was in the second grade:

> The white clouds are pretty.
> There are only 15 people in our room.
> We will go to gym.
> We have a new poster.
> We may go out doors.

Second grade came after "Little First" and "Big First," so by then I knew the implied rules that accompanied all writing assignments. Writing was an occasion for proper English. I was not to write in the way we spoke to one another: The white clouds pretty; There ain't but 15 people in our room; We going to gym; We got a new poster; We can go out in the yard. Rather I was to use the language of "other": clouds *are*, there *are*, we *will*, we *have*, we *may*.

My sentences were short, rigid, perfunctory, like the letters my mother wrote to relatives:

> Dear Papa,
> How are you? How is Mattie? Fine I hope. We are fine. We will come
> to see you Sunday. Cousin Ned will give us a ride.
> > Love,
> > Daughter

The language was not ours. It was something from outside us, something we used for special occasions.

But my coloring on the other side of that second-grade paper is different. I drew three hearts and a sun. The sun has a smiling face that radiates and envelops everything it touches. And although the sun and its world are enclosed in a circle, the colors I used—red, blue, green, purple, orange, yellow, black— indicate that I was less restricted with drawing and coloring than I was with writing standard English. My valentines were not just red. My sun was not just a yellow ball in the sky.

By the time I reached the twelfth grade, speaking and writing standard English had taken on new importance. Each year, about half of the newly graduated seniors of our school moved to large cities—particularly in the North—to live with relatives and find work. Our English teacher constantly corrected our grammar: "Not 'ain't,' but 'isn't.'" We seldom wrote papers, and even those few were usually plot summaries of short stories. When our teacher returned the papers, she usually lectured on the importance of using standard English: "I *am;* you *are;* he, she, or it *is,*" she would say, writing on the chalkboard as she spoke. "How you gon git a job talking about 'I is,' or 'I isn't' or 'I ain't'?"

15 In Pittsburgh, where I moved after graduation, I watched my aunt and uncle—who had always spoken standard English when in Greeleyville—switch from black English to standard English to a mixture of the two, according to where they were or who they were with. At home and with certain close relatives, friends, and neighbors, they spoke black English. With those less close, they spoke a mixture. In public and with strangers, they generally spoke standard English.

In time, I learned to speak standard English with ease and to switch smoothly from black to standard or a mixture, and back again. But no matter where I was, no matter what the situation or occasion, I continued to write as I had in school:

> Dear Mommie,
> How are you? How is everybody else? Fine I hope. I am fine. So are
> Aunt and Uncle. Tell everyone I said hello. I will write again soon.
> > Love,
> > Barbara

At work, at a health insurance company, I learned to write letters to customers. I studied form letters and letters written by co-workers, memorizing the phrases and the ways in which they were used. I dictated:

> Thank you for your letter of January 5. We have made the changes in
> your coverage you requested. Your new premium will be $150 every
> three months. We are pleased to have been of service to you.

In a sense, I was proud of the letters I wrote for the company: they were proof of my ability to survive in the city, the outside world—an indication of my growing mastery of English. But they also indicate that writing was still mechanical for me, something that didn't require much thought.

Reading also became a more significant part of my life during those early years in Pittsburgh. I had always liked reading, but now I devoted more and more of my spare time to it. I read romances, popular novels. Looking back, I realize that the books I liked best were simple, unambiguous: good versus bad and right versus wrong with right rewarded and wrong punished, mysteries unraveled and all set right in the end. It was how I remembered life in Greeleyville.

Of course I was romanticizing. Life in Greeleyville had not been so very uncomplicated. Back there I had been—first as a child, then as a young woman with limited experience in the outside world—living in a relatively closed-in society. But there were implicit and explicit principles that guided our way of life and shaped our relationships with one another and the people outside—principles that a newcomer would find elusive and baffling. In Pittsburgh, I had matured, become more experienced: I had worked at three different jobs, associated with a wider range of people, married, had children. This new environment with different prescripts for living required that I speak standard English much of the time, and slowly, imperceptibly, I had ceased seeing a sharp distinction between myself and "others." Reading romances and mysteries, characterized by dichotomy, was a way of shying away from change, from the person I was becoming.

But that other part of me—that part which took great pride in my ability to hold a job writing business letters—was increasingly drawn to the new developments in my life and the attending possibilities, opportunities for even greater change. If I could write letters for a nationally known business, could I not also do something better, more challenging, more important? Could I not, perhaps, go to college and become a school teacher? For years, afraid and a little embarrassed, I did no more than imagine this different me, this possible me. But sixteen years after coming north, when my younger daughter entered kindergarten, I found myself unable—or unwilling—to resist the lure of possibility. I enrolled in my first college course: Basic Writing, at the University of Pittsburgh.

For the first time in my life, I was required to write extensively about 20 myself. Using the most formal English at my command, I wrote these sentences near the beginning of the term:

> One of my duties as a homemaker is simply picking up after others. A day seldom passes that I don't search for a mislaid toy, book, or gym shoe, etc. I change the Ty-D-Bol, fight "ring around the collar," and keep our laundry smelling "April fresh." Occasionally, I settle arguments between my children and suggest things to do when they're bored. Taking telephone messages for my oldest daughter is my newest (and sometimes most aggravating) chore. Hanging the toilet paper roll is my most insignificant.

My concern was to use "appropriate" language, to sound as if I belonged in a college classroom. But I felt separate from the language—as if it did not and could not belong to me. I couldn't think and feel genuinely in that language, couldn't make it express what I thought and felt about being a housewife. A part of me resented, among other things, being judged by such things as the appearance of my family's laundry and toilet bowl, but in that language I could only imagine and write about a conventional housewife.

For the most part, the remainder of the term was a period of adjustment, a time of trying to find my bearing as a student in college composition class, to learn to shut out my black English whenever I composed, and to prevent it from creeping into my formulations; a time for trying to grasp the language of the classroom and reproduce it in my prose; for trying to talk about myself in that language, reach others through it. Each experience of writing was like standing naked and revealing my imperfection, my "otherness." And each new assignment was another chance to make myself over in language, reshape myself, make myself "better" in my rapidly changing image of a student in a college composition class.

But writing became increasingly unmanageable as the term progressed, and by the end of the semester, my sentences sounded like this:

> My excitement was soon dampened, however, by what seemed like a small voice in the back of my head saying that I should be careful with my long awaited opportunity. I felt frustrated and this seemed to make it difficult to concentrate.

There is a poverty of language in these sentences. By this point, I knew that the clichéd language of my Housewife essay was unacceptable, and I generally recognized trite expressions. At the same time, I hadn't yet mastered the language of the classroom, hadn't yet come to see it as belonging to me. Most notable is the lifelessness of the prose, the apparent absence of a person behind the words. I wanted those sentences—and the rest of the essay—to convey the anguish of yearning to, at once, become something more and yet remain the same. I had the sensation of being split in two, part of me going into a future the other part didn't believe possible. As that person, the student writer at that moment, I was essentially mute. I could not—in the process of composing—use the language of the old me, yet I couldn't imagine myself in the language of "others."

I found this particularly discouraging because at midsemester I had been writing in a much different way. Note the language of this introduction to an essay I had written then, near the middle of the term:

> Pain is a constant companion to the people in "Footwork." Their jobs are physically damaging. Employers are insensitive to their feelings and in many cases add to their problems. The general public wounds them further by treating them with disgrace because of what they do for a living. Although the workers are as diverse as they are similar, there is a definite link between them. They suffer a great deal of abuse.

The voice here is stronger, more confident, appropriating terms like "physically damaging," "wounds them further," "insensitive," "diverse"—terms I couldn't have imagined using when writing about my own experience—and shaping them into sentences like "Although the workers are as diverse as they are similar, there is a definite link between them." And there is the sense of a personality behind the prose, someone who sympathizes with the workers. "The general public wounds them further by treating them with disgrace because of what they do for a living."

25   What caused these differences? I was, I believed, explaining other people's thoughts and feelings, and I was free to move about in the language of "others" so long as I was speaking of others. I was unaware that I was transforming into my best classroom language my own thoughts and feelings about people whose experiences and ways of speaking were in many ways similar to mine.

The following year, unable to turn back or to let go of what had become something of an obsession with language (and hoping to catch and hold the sense of control that had eluded me in Basic Writing), I enrolled in a research writing course. I spent most of the term learning how to prepare for and write a research paper. I chose sex education as my subject and spent hours in libraries, searching for information, reading, taking notes. Then (not without messiness and often-demoralizing frustration) I organized my information into categories, wrote a thesis statement, and composed my paper—a series of paraphrases and quotations spaced between carefully constructed transitions. The process and results felt artificial, but as I would later come to realize I was passing through a necessary stage. My sentences sounded like this:

> This reserve becomes understandable with examination of who the abusers are. In an overwhelming number of cases, they are people the victims know and trust. Family members, relatives, neighbors and close family friends commit seventy-five percent of all reported sex crimes against children, and parents, parent substitutes and relatives are the offenders in thirty to eighty percent of all reported cases.[12] While assault by strangers does occur, it is less common, and is usually a single episode.[13] But abuse by family members, relatives and acquaintances may continue for an extended period of time. In cases of incest, for example, children are abused repeatedly for an average of eight years.[14] In such cases, "the use of physical force is rarely necessary because of the child's trusting, dependent relationship with the offender. The child's cooperation is often facilitated by the adult's position of dominance, an offer of material goods, a threat of physical violence, or a misrepresentation of moral standards."[15]

The completed paper gave me a sense of profound satisfaction, and I read it often after my professor returned it. I know now that what I was pleased with was the language I used and the professional voice it helped me maintain. "Use better words," my teacher had snapped at me one day after reading the notes I'd begun accumulating from my research, and slowly I began taking on the language of my sources. In my next set of notes, I used the word "vacillating"; my professor applauded. And by the time I composed the final draft, I felt at ease with terms like "overwhelming number of cases," "single episode," and "reserve," and I shaped them into sentences similar to those of my "expert" sources.

If I were writing the paper today, I would of course do some things differently. Rather than open with an anecdote—as my teacher suggested—I would begin simply with a quotation that caught my interest as I was researching my paper (and which I scribbled, without its source, in the margin of my notebook): "Truth does not do so much good in the world as the semblance of truth does evil." The quotation felt right because it captured what was for me the central idea of my paper—and expressed it in a way I would like to have said it. The anecdote, a hypothetical situation I invented to conform to the information in the paper, felt forced and insincere because it represented—to a great degree—my teacher's understanding of the essay, her idea of what in it was most significant. Improving upon my previous experiences with writing, I was beginning to think and feel in the language I used, to find my own voice in it, to sense that how one speaks influences how one means. But I was not yet secure enough, comfortable enough with the language to trust my intuition.

Now that I know that to seek knowledge, freedom, and autonomy means always to be in the concentrated process of becoming—always to be venturing into new territory, feeling one's way at first, then getting one's balance, negotiating, accommodating, discovering one's self in ways that previously defined "others"—I sometimes get tired. And I ask myself why I keep on participating in this highbrow form of violence, this slamming against perplexity. But there is no real futility in the question, no hint of that part the old me who stood outside standard English, hugging to herself a disabling mistrust of language she thought could not represent a person with her history and experience. Rather, the question represents a person who feels the consequence of her education, the weight of her possibilities as a teacher and writer and human being, a voice in society. And I would not change that person, would not give back the good burden that accompanies my growing expertise, my increasing power to shape myself in language and share that self with "others."

"To speak," says Frantz Fanon, "means to be in a position to use a certain syntax, to grasp the morphology of this or that language, but it means above all to assume a culture, to support the weight of a civilization." To write means to do the same, but in a more profound sense. However, Fanon also says that to achieve mastery means to "get" in a position of power, to "grasp," to "assume." This, I have learned both as a student and subsequently as a teacher, can involve tremendous emotional and psychological conflict for those attempting to master academic discourse. Although as a beginning student writer I had a fairly good grasp of ordinary spoken English and was proficient at what Labov calls "code-switching" (and what John Baugh in *Black Street Speech* terms "style shifting"), when I came face to face with the demands of academic writing, I grew increasingly self-conscious, constantly aware of my status as a black and a speaker of one of the many black English vernaculars—a traditional outsider. For the first time, I experienced my sense of doubleness as something menacing, a built-in enemy. Whenever I turned inward for salvation, the balm so available during my childhood, I found instead this new fragmentation which spoke to me in many voices. It was the voice of my desire to prosper, but at the same time it spoke of what I had relinquished and could not regain: a safe way of being, a state of powerlessness which exempted me from responsibility for who I was and might be. And it accused me of betrayal, of turning away from blackness. To recover balance, I had to take on the language of the academy, the language of "others." And to do that, I had to learn to imagine myself a part of the culture of that language, and therefore someone free to manage that language, to take liberties with it. Writing and rewriting, practicing, experimenting, I came to comprehend more fully the generative power of language. I discovered—with the help of some especially sensitive teachers—that through writing one can continually bring new selves into being, each with new responsibilities and difficulties, but also with new possibilities. Remarkable power, indeed. I write and continually give birth to myself.

Allusions   Sometimes, college or workplace writing assignments discourage the use of personal life experiences. Your readers still want something to grasp onto, some way to relate to a situation, something that makes your topic and your perspective matter. When the writing situation calls for more detachment, you might consider using allusions to popular culture or well-known events to connect the topic to the reader. Many writers, for instance, use verses from poems or songs to spring into their topics. If the audience knows the song or poem, it responds with interest. The same holds true for allusions to television shows or movies and to human-interest cases, such as publicized jury trials, tragedies, acts of courage, and criminal activity.

While some allusions can be used as support for a position, their most important function is to meet audience needs. Eric Dezenhall makes use of allusion in his essay, "We Like Our Bad Guys to Be Honest About It," in Chapter 15 (page 436). He mentions *The Sopranos* television show, and the movies *Analyze This* and the cult classic *Animal House,* among other allusions. Authors do not have to state that an allusion is coming. Take this example from Dezenhall's piece: "It's no coincidence that Butch and Sundance are lionized just as Don Corleone's Godfather is—though all are violent criminals." The smooth integration into his essay of these allusions builds his ethos in the mind of the audience; readers see Dezenhall as someone just like them. The thesis has relevance to television shows and movies they and Dezenhall have seen, so they can envision his main point better. While some audience members might not be familiar with your allusions, summaries and specific details will work the same way specific, concrete descriptions work. The audience's needs to be shown rather than simply told will be met.

COLLABORATING

Choose a topic for your group from among the following: knitting, gaining the trust of parents, choosing a car to buy, or behaving in an obnoxious way at a party. After you have chosen a topic, list these three specific audiences: a group of department store salespeople, members of an environmentalist organization, and fifteen-year-old girls. Decide what you want to say about your topic, and anticipate the needs of each audience. How can you get each to relate to you? What differences among these audiences will you have to respond to? What techniques will you have to use to get your point across? Write two paragraphs to each group that demonstrate your ability to make the same point while relating to the audience and possibly persuading its members to accept your point of view.

Responding to Possible Objections

Considering possible objections to your point of view differs slightly, but significantly, from anticipating readers' needs. While allowing the audience to relate to you is the desired outcome of anticipating their needs, responding to their objections means formulating specific strategies. You need to acknowledge differences of opinion and counter the beliefs and evidence of a reader on the opposite side of the political or social spectrum.

When you engage in this type of writing, your purpose is generally argument. Argument engages readers' minds, hearts, and agendas in an attempt to persuade them to take action, adopt a viewpoint, or arrive at a negotiated solution. Chapter 2 examined the critical analysis that can lead to effective argument. Chapter 9 covers the strategies you need to support an argument. We now examine what to do when you take a position that has strong advocates from different perspectives. You cannot ignore audience concerns that stem from objections to your points.

Self-Reflection   At the beginning of the chapter, Anna asked whether she needed to change her position on gays and lesbians to improve her paper. Many student writers have asked their instructors similar questions or have felt that it would be best to give the instructor what she or he wants by taking a different point of view. It cannot be emphasized enough that changing your position does not make a paper better. Insincerity impresses no one, and you might lose the ethos you were beginning to develop in your draft. When your instructor challenges your positions, her or his goal in presenting opposite points of view might differ considerably from her or his political or social perspectives on the world. Yes, instructors hold strong positions on issues, and these positions are often well-formulated, making some instructors reluctant to accept the viewpoint of a student writer. But look at that position for just what it is—a well-formulated counterargument to what you believe. If you are not persuaded by the counterargument, you need to reflect on your own values to see what is at their root.

Often we find that our identity influences our positions more than we would like to believe. Other times, we have emotional responses about an issue due to a life event. Sincerely considering the opposite perspective and modifying our beliefs mean changing who we are and coming to new understandings of our experiences. Such changes are opportunities for growth. You cannot become educated without changing. But your instructor does not expect your opinions to do a complete flip. Just as politicians are criticized for waffling to attract the greatest number of votes, writers who lack the courage of their convictions are difficult to trust. Change should come gradually. You need to reflect in order to check what you think and to make sure that you have not gotten so caught up in trying to win an argument that you have ignored crucial pieces of evidence on your side or the other side.

WRITING

Write about a time when you were directly challenged in class or when you witnessed such a challenge. How did you feel? Did you eventually grow or change? What resistance did you feel? Also consider the effects on other students in the classroom. Did any of them grow as a result of the experience?

Tone   The method in which we convey our position to potential readers goes a long way toward securing understanding. While we need to support our points, expressing uncertainty—the possibility that we could be wrong—often produces positive effects on an audience. A writer whose voice takes a conciliatory stance, offering to examine the evidence and revealing a slight amount of doubt, might at first appear to be foregoing power. However, audiences tend to tune out the know-it-all who is too firm in her or his position. The purpose of persuasion becomes too blatant, and people in general resist overbearing attempts at being persuaded.

Think of your response to telemarketers. They act as if they know all about your needs and that their products are without doubt the best solution. Like most consumers, you may start to feel pressured and become defensive when they attempt to persuade you to try their products. This defensiveness turns into annoyance, and you resent the intrusion. You do not buy what they are selling, and you hang up more quickly when the next telemarketer calls. The tone that conveys a sense that no other way of thinking can be right carries a similar obvious attempt at persuasion, and it will produce similar reactions in readers.

Therefore, writers need to find a reasonable tone. To do so, they acknowledge multiple perspectives about an issue and phrase each perspective in a way that its proponents will agree is accurate. Writers find many ways to appear agreeable. Humor can be effective, as can concern or anguish. Try the approach of uncertainty. Not only will you avoid a combative, off-putting tone, but you will also keep your own mind open to possibilities, which can lead to the discovery of commonalities with your perceived opponents as well as fresh ideas on a subject.

Curse of the Ouija Board

"Curse of the Ouija Board" was written by a student who prefers to stay anonymous. While the story keeps most readers interested, pay attention to how the student weaves uncertainty into her analysis and conclusion. She does not force the reader to agree with her, and she admits to not really knowing whether her perspective is correct. Do you think this method is effective in helping an audience keep an open mind about what amounts to a pretty incredible story?

I never believed in anything being able to predict the future, but an event that happened when I was sixteen years old made me wonder. It all started when my friend Michelle brought out a Ouija board at her party. Only a few of us were left and some of the guys were pretty buzzed. This Ouija board was not the new kind that you can find in a store, but a really old, creepy one. It was bound in a velvet cloth, and Michelle had to dust it off to even reveal the contents.

"My grandmother forbidded me from ever going near this board," Michelle said. "She claimed it was not like an ordinary Ouija board, but was cursed to deliver bad news to the most vulnerable person who plays it."

Everyone starting snorting, telling her to get off it, but she persisted. "She claimed this board predicted her death." Michelle's grandmother had died three or four months before, so the room fell silent. "She knew she was going to die when she was 73 and knew it would be from respiratory disease." I didn't know how old Mrs. Houston was when she died, but I did know it was from emphysema. I felt a little chill go down my back.

"She was only sixteen when she played it the first time," Michelle continued. "The board was given to her by a group of gypsies passing through town. The fortune teller who gave it to her told her that the board was not to be taken lightly, that the spirit within it, named Nazuela, preyed on unwary souls who could not confront their own mortality. She said the spirit demanded a blood sacrifice for every time it was played and could manipulate the future to accommodate its demands. 'Play with care and wisdom,' the fortune teller warned her.

"My grandmother tried to speak to Nazuela while playing, telling the spirit to not bring harm to anyone else and only to speak about her fate. Nazuela apparently granted her wish, because he spelled out her name, the word 'breath,' and the year 1998. My grandmother automatically knew what it meant, but could not stop playing the game. She remembered the gypsy woman's warning about a blood sacrifice, so she pricked her finger with a safety pin and forced out several drops of blood on the board. She wrapped the board up in a velvet cloth and meant to destroy it the next day, but she had a dream that night that said not to destroy the board or risk losing her life prematurely. So she instead bound the board up and hid it in her closet.

"One time when I was eleven or twelve, I found the board and was about to open it. But my grandmother stopped me and told me the story. Even though I was afraid for grandma, I felt compelled to open it. Grandma muttered something about fate eventually winning over, but demanded I swear an oath never to use it until after she was dead. She felt she could protect me if she were on the other side."

No one was laughing at all as Michelle opened the board. It resisted a little bit, as the cloth clung to the board, but it eventually popped open, revealing some dried crusty spots that looked like blood. Some people were saying to stop it, that they knew Michelle was kidding, but she just said no one had to play who didn't want to. The guys were too in to being men to admit they were afraid, but some of my girlfriends crept away, saying it was the devil's work. I felt drawn to the board even though I was doubtful and sat down across from Michelle. We started moving across the board and I swear I could not control where my hands were going. We spelled a "T," then an "A," followed by an "M." My girlfriend Tami started screaming, as she wasn't playing and didn't want to be involved. Michelle and I were focused on each other, but my friends later told me that Tami was about to interrupt the game, when all of a sudden the electricity went out.

Everyone started screaming and I could feel the board still drawing Michelle and I back and forth. A guy had a lighter and Michelle's best friend, Jody, found a flashlight somewhere. My hands and Michelle's had stopped four times while the lights were out. We were finishing when the flashlight came on the board. The final letter was "D." Tami was sure her name had been spelled out and that it meant she was dead. I was shaken by the whole incident and got up from the board. Michelle looked pale and seemed like she was in a trance. One of the guys wrapped the velvet cloth back around the board. Tami was crying and left. None of us knew what to think.

The next morning, my boyfriend called. Tami's brakes had gone out and she had been hit by a truck. She was dead upon impact. I started crying and felt I was responsible. I wanted to go back to Michelle's house and destroy that board, but for some reason, I never even called her. In fact, I've never seen her since, even though she still lives in Anderson and hasn't moved.

I talked to my parents about it, and they said it was just coincidence, to forget about spirits and fortune tellers. They said there was no proof that the board even belonged to Michelle's grandmother and that Michelle probably made up the story about the gypsies and the bad luck following the board. But what about the drops of blood on the board? Maybe they weren't really blood at all, and Michelle had just put some paint in there to fool us. But the dust on the velvet had accumulated over years, so Michelle couldn't have been playing a prank. She would have really had to have been telling a whopper to come up with the name of the spirit, Nazuela, and not mispronounce it at least once. The big thing, though, is that I felt the pull of the Ouija board. Maybe Michelle was really guiding our hands and the power of suggestion overtook me, but I could swear I even heard whispers in my ear, faint but definitely there, spelling out "Tami" and "Dead." Nonetheless, my parents kept insisting, even forcing me to believe, that Tami's car accident was just an unfortunate coincidence and nothing more.

I met the priest at Tami's funeral, but was afraid to ask him about Ouija boards at the time. But later in the week, I went to his parish residence and talked to him, crying about how I thought I was responsible. I thought he would be comforting, but deep inside, I knew why I had to see him, so I wasn't surprised when he met me with a stare and a shake of his head. "There are some things not of this world," he said. "Scripture is full of demons and foul, evil beings." He didn't accuse me of doing anything, nor did he say I was responsible, but he felt a cleansing was necessary. He blessed me, pulled out some prayer book and chanted in Latin. Then he encouraged me to pray every night and to read the Bible. "And never," he said, "fool with the supernatural."

Now I have accepted at this point that I am responsible, or partly at least, for Tami's death. Even if the story behind the Ouija board was not true, Tami thought it was and her hysteria made her unfit to drive. I heard later that she knew her brakes were bad, so it wasn't like a master cylinder went out all of a sudden. But she would have been driving slower and more carefully if her mind hadn't been clouded by stories of her own death. I'm not sure the priest performed a real ritual on me or if he was just helping me get over my grief, but I felt better (and I've never missed a Sunday mass since!). But everything coming together the way it did makes me believe that this story was not a string of coincidences. It seems to me more logical to believe in a spirit guiding fate than in a whimsical world where my friend could be killed just because she thought she was going to die. I'll never really know, but I've grown up a lot since then and feel that the world has some order. Rivers flow in one direction. The sun rises every morning. Trees take in carbon dioxide. Water gives off oxygen. Everything has a reason and a purpose. Writing off any tragedy to coincidence is a way of avoiding responsibility. And I won't live in a world where people can't admit their guilt and move on to make the world a better place.

Refuting or Conceding   In keeping with our discussion on tone, we must constantly remind ourselves that readers whose opinions differ from our own have valid points and evidence to support their perspective. As a writer, you should not avoid discussing evidence that supports the opposition if you want to impress those readers with your points. You will seem uninformed or deceitful if you do not address facts or logical reasoning that points in the other direction. Therefore, you need to present that evidence and either refute it or concede its validity. Refuting means disproving an account of something. If you happen to know that recent scientific inquiries have disproved long-held facts, your task is easy. But evidence often is based on logic or lore. You have to show holes in thinking to get your point across.

As an example, let's suppose that you were writing an article about capital punishment. Advocates of the death penalty often claim that it acts as a deterrent. If you were to try to refute this claim, you would have to ask what evidence has been offered in support of the death penalty as a deterrent. You could easily determine that no one can directly track such information. If a crime has not been committed—in other words, if a would-be murderer has been deterred from killing out of fear of the death penalty—how would a person know that deterrence occurred or find out why it occurred? Generally speaking, people do not confess in public to murderous desires they have seriously considered acting on. Researchers do not know where to find such people, nor are they able to isolate capital punishment as the reason a murder was not committed. By scrutinizing this claim, you can refute the argument that capital punishment acts as a deterrent, as no one on either side really knows whether or not it does.

But you also need to consider conceding a point when a particular piece of evidence stands up to scrutiny. You strengthen your case by admitting that evidence on the other side has legitimacy. Readers do not necessarily like to be shown that everything they have relied on in deciding their thinking on an issue is wrong. Their egos can be damaged, and they will revert to the emotional pull of their original position. A writer can be much more effective in establishing ethos by conceding that elements of the opposing position warrant consideration, but that after careful deliberation, those elements do not match the evidence for the writer's position.

Your position might be 100 percent correct, but if your reader will not listen, being right doesn't really matter. Conceding something to the opposition bestows dignity on proponents of that side and makes them more willing to consider opposing positions, even to the point of changing their minds.

WRITING

Think of a dispute you have had with friends, parents, teachers, or others. Make a list of the reasons you believed you were right. Then list the reasons your opponents disagreed with you. You might have already attempted to repair these differences, but look at the dispute as still active and assume that you want to resolve it. Why do you feel that your reasons are stronger than those of your opponents? What do you not believe about their perspective? Determine what elements are at the crux of the matter (facts, reasoning, agendas, morals), and write to the opponent, using a reasonable tone to assert your position while responding to the objections you listed.

Using Real Readers in Peer Groups

While an audience can consist of a group of imagined readers, feedback from real readers lets you test your ideas on an actual audience. Chapter 7 discusses writing as collaboration—the joint authorship of a piece of writing. Most writers of reports and business documents collaborate with others involved in a project or decision and work to make the prose as fluid and clear as possible. For now, let's look at peer feedback or workshopping. Peer feedback consists of sharing writing with people equally invested in similar writing activities who provide ideas for revision and a sense of the potential of a piece of writing. Peer feedback is not evaluation; it does not involve saying, "This is good" or "I can't stand this." Nor is it sentence-level editing, wherein a reader merely corrects mistakes. Rather, peer feedback involves recognizing an audience and the way a piece of writing affects that audience.

Peer feedback should give a writer suggestions to consider not only to improve the paper through greater clarity and description, but also to anticipate reader needs and respond to their objections. Actual readers' reactions to your stance and approach can be used to modify tone, add necessary introductory material, replace jargon, and make many other revision choices. Peer feedback can also be used to ensure that critical analysis has taken place and that the requirements of an assignment have been met.

A draft, by its very nature, is a first attempt at a writing task, and it needs further work to reach an acceptable level. Keep in mind that the main responsibility in securing strong feedback rests with the writer. The peer review writer's discussion guide should help you fulfill these responsibilities.

PEER REVIEW WRITER'S DISCUSSION GUIDE

- Prepare properly by first doing a self-evaluation of your own essay. Keep a blank piece of paper next to you, and read through the essay. For every concern you have, list the problem on the blank paper. If you're worried, for example, that your critical analysis does not make sense or is not leading to a strong thesis, make note of it. If you doubt that your introduction grabs your audience, write it down so that you do not forget. Whatever comes up when you're reading your own essay, write it down.
- Students often worry that they will hurt someone's feelings with negative comments, so invite your peers to discuss your writing seriously. Explain that you want genuine reactions that will help in revision. Show your seriousness by writing down what your peers say. If you're working online, make sure that you will have access to the dialogue for later use.
- Guide readers to the problem areas you isolated in your self-evaluation. If you do not know whether you have given too much or too little description, lead your readers toward this area. If you're worried that your thesis complicates an issue too much, talk about it with your peers. Do not let a peer group avoid or overlook issues.
- Read through the assignment sheet and have your peers show you the areas where you have fulfilled all of the listed criteria for the assignment.
- Review the instructions on critical analysis on pages 28–45 in Chapter 2, and allow your readers to engage in one or more types of analysis to see if the same conclusions are reached as in your thesis. When you show willingness to seek and take advice, your group members will respond.

As a reader in a peer group, you will learn a great deal by critiquing someone else's paper. If you recognize strengths and weaknesses in the writing of your peers, you gain confidence and start to bring that critical eye to your own writing. You should find this peer review reader's discussion guide helpful in committing yourself to being an effective reader in a peer group.

PEER REVIEW READER'S DISCUSSION GUIDE

- While you want to have a dialogue with the writer, write comments to him or her. If you are allowed to make notes in the margins of the writer's paper, do that. Otherwise, have a separate sheet of paper available to jot down your thoughts. Some online programs allow readers to write comments in a draft, so if you are working in an online environment, consider this option.
- Take your role seriously, and curb any instinct to say or write that a piece of writing is "great," "fine," or "nice." These evaluations do not help the writer, nor do they help you develop your critical skills.
- Write down the specific elements that, as a reader, keep your attention. This will let you see other elements that need refining or rethinking. If your initial impression is mostly favorable, find particular places that strike you as lively, amusing,

or intriguing, and write what the author has done to produce this effect. Starting with compliments almost always allows more penetrating critiques to be considered constructively.

- Do not give insincere compliments, as they mislead a writer and damage your credibility. If your initial impression is unfavorable, look for the potential in the draft and start your commenting there. In the opening example in this chapter, the students in Anna's class attempted to find places in her writing that she could develop, trying to unearth the potential in a paper that offended many. You should try this method as well.
- Think about how the writer can get an audience to relate to his or her point, and write and/or talk about where you see attempts at targeting a particular readership.
- Write about the kernel of critical analysis that is trying to find its way out. From there, you can bring up your more negative reactions, such as confusion because of vague descriptions, a letdown due to clichés, or anger generated by a condescending tone. In all cases, be specific, and treat the writer as you would like to be treated.

Revision

After sharing your draft with a peer group, what do you do? Within just one peer group, you might receive differing reactions and conflicting advice. As a writer, you must understand that revision means more than "fixing" a paper. The insertion or deletion of a few details constitutes editing, not revision. Almost all drafts need revision—to be rethought, restructured, and rewritten. In using real readers, you have a chance to look at both global and local concerns in your draft before submitting the finished version for a grade.

Make Decisions   Peer groups, your instructor, and the process of drafting will present you with options as a writer. You must decide what direction to pursue. The first step in making that decision comes during the peer review. At the end of the session, take out a separate piece of paper, think about the options you can see in your peers' comments, and summarize the major points made. Write fully your initial impressions of the dominant comments, especially those that contradict each other or otherwise send conflicting messages on how to revise. You might forget what was said if you do not record the conversation, and your initial reactions are important as well.

As the writer, you must make decisions about which, if any, of the choices to use in a revision. You do not need to bend to the will of the majority. Rather, listen to how your peers' reactions developed. Find patterns in their thoughts. If you guided your fellow students' responses as suggested above, your concerns or worries will be confirmed or alleviated, and you will have been alerted to other matters you had not thought of.

Look at the patterns to see what demands they are making on you as a writer. You can add detail or explanation, for instance, if readers have pointed out a need to do so, and that detail might open up possibilities regarding your thesis or main point. Perhaps your main point is really more complicated than you allowed for in your draft. If so, not only do you have to add details, but you also need to rethink your thesis. That might mean restructuring your introduction to prepare readers for a new thesis.

Peer feedback does not create a set of instructions for you to follow. Instead, it delivers options to explore. The writer must make the connection between the suggestions and the possible effect on the paper.

Receive Peer Feedback More Than Once You may disagree with the dominant sentiments springing from a session of peer feedback or feel uncomfortable about relying on them. You may understand the feedback but be uncertain about how well you can use it for revising. The solution is to have the peer group—or some members—read your revised draft. This has three benefits. First, you will see whether you understood the feedback. Second, you can test how readers react to your revision—whether you made the best decision based on the options in front of you. Third, you can look for signs of improvement and see if the direction of this revision is worth pursuing.

Discomfort or uncertainty can transform into excitement when you receive the approval of peers, and you will be able to start editing and polishing a paper with confidence. Nagging doubts can also be affirmed, which will send you in a more appropriate direction and help you avoid a bad grade. When you make changes to your paper that you disagree with, strange things can happen. Sometimes we disagree with the suggestions we most need to hear and act on. Every once in a while, it does not hurt to try an approach that we object to. In writing, acting on advice that we initially think is wrong can reap dividends.

COLLABORATING

Review the table of contents for Part III of this book, and select one topic that seems interesting. Freewrite on that topic for approximately twenty minutes, relating an experience or observation associated with it or a perspective you have. (Freewriting here means writing without stopping to check for correctness, clarity, or organization.)

In the time remaining in class, practice giving peer feedback on your freewrites to one another. While your in-class draft will not be as developed as most drafts you submit for peer feedback, it could lead to the eventual development of a paper for this course. Follow the instructions given for discussing writing in small groups, and be sure to take notes and write down summaries of your reactions to peer comments. Next, talk to each other about these reactions, concentrating on your sense of the advice you received. Be as honest as possible about how helpful your peers' comments could be when you revise this in-class draft. Make sure you explain to a writer if she or he misunderstood your comments, and find out if you have been too harsh, too nice, or not careful enough when responding to others' comments. You may be working with this group again, so work through the procedures, and find out what you need to do to improve the quality of your feedback.

Summary

Writing an essay, article, or report results in little if your audience does not understand you, cannot relate to you, or will not listen to you. As a writer, strive to keep both imagined and real readers in mind when constructing a draft and understand that establishing ethos or a credible writerly persona is crucial. You must recognize the type of person who is most likely to be interested in your subject and tailor the writing to fit that targeted reader. Your writing must also consider the audience's needs, especially the likely values and experiences of its members, and show commonalities that will allow readers to see differing perspectives. Establishing a coherent ethos gives you the authority to show those commonalities. If audience members might object to a point of view, the writer needs to respond to those objections and convey understanding and sympathy for opposing positions in order to avoid alienating the audience.

The best method to gauge possible audience reaction is to seek feedback from peers. While you need to listen to all suggestions and understand conflicting reactions, steering peer readers toward areas where you suspect problems or want more information or perspective will open up honest dialogue between writer and readers. You should expect to have difficulty in responding to some suggestions, but attempting revision in response to audience concerns often leads to deeper insights about your writing process, your topic, and yourself.

CHAPTER 4

STRATEGIES FOR ORGANIZING YOUR IDEAS

Every topic you consider as a subject for your paper presents a number of options for approaching it. Each approach leads to decisions about the arrangement of your paper, the organization or order in which you place sentences and paragraphs so that an audience can follow your train of thought. Many students have misconceptions about how to arrange writing and want to impose a preestablished structure onto their papers. This dilemma faced a student named Steve, who I was teaching in a writing class. While Steve put sentences together well, his essays lacked development, and each paragraph seemed like a separate idea, albeit on the same topic. I spoke with him about adding more detail to his first draft and exploring his thesis in greater depth. Steve's second draft contained incredibly long paragraphs where he had added details and ideas, and he expanded on his thesis statement in his introduction and conclusion. I still could not follow his train of thought.

I asked to see him after class, hoping to better understand his strategy for organization. Steve was an affable fellow and approached me with genuine willingness to learn. We sat at my desk and reviewed his introduction. Here's a copy of Steve's draft.

STEVE WINDHORST

Humor in Society

Humor is all around us in society. People like to laugh at other people, which is why comedians talk about well known politicians and actors. Slapstick humor is cruel, as it teases people for physical problems or for tragedies that occur. Jokes often are not funny when you are the one who is being targeted. People need humor to let off some steam, even if the jokes are mean-spirited, as they can avoid examining themselves for unpleasant characteristics they might have.

People like to laugh at other people, which is why comedians talk about well known politicians and actors. Every comedian I have seen talks about figures in society who everyone has heard of, like Michael Jackson or President Bush, and exaggerates their personalities. But comedians talk about all sorts of things other than politicians and actors. They also use stereotypes to talk about situations. There's a joke about the dumb blonde who is supposed to paint the porch for a guy. The guy is trying to rip her off, not telling her that the porch extends all the way around the house and having her do the job for a small amount of money. The blonde starts working and the guy goes back inside. After 10 minutes, she comes back inside and says she is finished. The guy knows she cannot have gotten the whole porch done. But before he says anything, she says, "I feel kinda guilty for just doing the Porsche. I have paint leftover. Do you want the SUV painted too?" We know nobody can be that stupid and the blonde is just a stereotype. It keeps us from worrying about really dumb things that people do. The same can be said about the redneck jokes that go around on the Internet or jokes about gays. Comedians want people to laugh, so they have to refer to something that everyone understands. Laughter is good for the soul. Everyone needs to laugh. Otherwise, we would always be feeling miserable and who wants a society of depressed people? I think comedians serve an important function in our society.

Slapstick humor is cruel, as it teases people for physical problems or for tragedies that occur. People laugh at other people all the time. If someone trips and falls, someone who sees it is bound to laugh. It's like with a food fight in the cafeteria. A lot of people think it is funny if they hit someone with a plate of spaghetti or throw a hard-boiled egg at someone. One time, this really heavy guy in our school named Kevin was minding his own business. He was walking with a tray of food. Some guy stuck out his foot and tripped him. Kevin fell face forward. The food ended up on the floor and Kevin's face and shirt were covered with it. People were laughing but that wasn't good enough. Some people from another table ran by and dumped milk and desserts on him. Everyone started throwing food at each other and laughing. No one knew that Kevin had hurt his knee. He twisted it or something and had to use crutches for about a week. Even then, people made fun of him for trying to get around on crutches. Here he was suffering, unable to walk well, and people were laughing at him! What really got me was all the fat jokes I heard. Some guy was saying that his knee couldn't support all of his lard and blamed him for the accident. I mean, this was cruel. There's all sorts of jokes and teasing you'll hear in high school about people. Then there was this one guy. I guess you would call him a midget, even though he wasn't that small. I guess he was about 5 feet tall in our senior year. He was an all right guy, but people found it so funny to constantly point out how short he was. One guy, who really wasn't all the much taller than him, used to put his elbow on the little guy's head and say, "A leaning post. Perfect height." They would scrunch down in their desks and wave their hand like they had an answer to a question, telling everyone they were like Watson, who was the little guy. We had some dances and most of the girls were taller than him. He still managed to get a few of them to dance with him, though, so the next Monday at school, guys were faking slow dances, commenting about where Watson's head would end up. I won't go into the details. People laughed. I think anything that mimics the physical problems of other people should not be used for jokes. Like some people don't have the normal speaking voices. Why do others think it is so funny to try to copy those voices? Is there a perfect way to sound? Then a lot of people will walk around, pretending to be walking like somebody else. I have seen people bust out laughing at people imitating swaggers, stiffness, and limps. This is just cruelty. More has to be done on high schools to prevent this type of slapstick humor. It's just not funny.

 Jokes often are not funny when you are the one who is being targeted. Lots of jokes deal with people's race or gender or religion. For the most part, if you're the object of the joke, you're not going to laugh at it. Obviously, if something is making fun of your religion, you are going to get mad. Some jokes cannot be told in mixed company. But then there are people who make fun of themselves, talking about their religion or gender or even race! How can that be? I figured that these people make the jokes before somebody else can. That way, they are not the target. Or maybe they're really secure and don't have to worry about what people think. But it's weird how the same joke can be laughed at one time and won't be funny the next. I have heard a lot of girls make PMS jokes. They will laugh, sometimes too much. But if a guy repeats the joke elsewhere to a bunch of girls, he will be greeted with silence. It's like some jokes are permitted to be told by some people and others aren't. I guess you're not a target if you're making fun of yourself. My dad will always talk about his ugly ol' mug or his bald head. But I've noticed that if someone else makes a joke about his hairline, my dad doesn't share in the laugh. Maybe that's why we make jokes about others. If we feel we have been targeted one time, we have to make sure we're not the target the next time. I wish there was a better way. Laughing at real people doesn't help anyone.

 Everyone likes to laugh, and it makes us feel better about ourselves. Comedians exaggerate things about well known people to take our minds off real problems. Slapstick humor makes people laugh at victims of pranks instead of with them and focuses on anything physical that seems odd. Some jokes can only be told by certain people for certain people or they won't be funny. Humor keeps people from examining themselves, which isn't bad, but we should try to avoid the mean-spiritedness that happens when we talk about people we know.

"You definitely have expanded on the thesis here," I said, pointing to the last sentence in his introduction. "But it doesn't seem to be woven into your essay very well. The body of your essay goes in so many directions."

"Yeah, I know," he said. "But each topic sentence comes from the introduction. Doesn't that make it okay?"

I reviewed the introduction and saw what he had done. He had taken a different phrase from his introduction to start each of the three body paragraphs he had used. I asked him why he had done this.

"That's what I was taught," he shrugged. "Isn't that right?" *STOP THINKING*

"Well, look at your paragraphs," I said. "Don't you think you should *ABOUT* break these down?" *WHAT*

"But I couldn't do that without breaking the structure," he countered. *RIGHT*

"What structure?" I asked.

"You know," he said. "One paragraph of intro, three body paragraphs, and a conclusion."

I talked with Steve about some of the professional essays we had read during the semester and asked him if he could remember one that used that exact structure. He could not, so I wondered aloud why he was adhering to rules in his writing that professional writers did not follow.

"But what should I do, then?" Steve asked. "At least I know where to put everything when I follow this rule." *easy! like a cliche!*

"The structure you are trying to follow takes away all of your natural tendencies to organize your ideas," I said. "You have things misplaced here and aren't considering the needs of your audience at all."

"What do you mean?" he asked.

"When you read," I responded. "What happens when you come to a paragraph that takes up a full page?"

Steve thought for a moment, trying to remember, I assumed, a book he had read with such paragraphs. He smiled. "I stop reading," he said. "I'm not getting a break so I tune out. Maybe I try it again later."

"And what happens when you have to go back to the introduction of an article to figure out why one paragraph follows the other?"

He didn't hesitate. "I stop reading."

"Then you can see why this structure might be alienating your audience," I said.

He nodded. Steve took his essay home to try to reorganize it. But like many students, he needed help in figuring out how to grab an audience with his introduction, how to make each paragraph flow into the next, and how to conclude without merely repeating what he had already said.

DISCUSSION

As a class, select one of the essays in Part III of this book. Have one student read the first paragraph aloud, then switch readers, and continue switching to new readers until you have read the whole article. What methods does the writer use to hold the essay together? How does each paragraph connect to the next? Where is the thesis statement in the text, or is it implied more than stated? What happens in the introduction? What happens in the conclusion? Discuss some of the strategies about arrangement that you can infer from this professional essay. What other options were there?

The above exercise should help you glean some basic ideas about the ways essays can look and be shaped. These discoveries must be placed within the understanding of an important concept: Content determines structure. Starting an essay with a structure limits your ability to develop your ideas and confuses your audience, just like Steve's essay did. The structure of a polished essay springs from a careful understanding of arrangement in relation to the content. But that structure applies to that essay and only that essay. Of course, you can repeat some of the strategies and concepts in different writing tasks, but you cannot reuse the same structure. Structure is not a pie tin that can be recycled for any number of pies. Rather, writing grows in different directions, and the writer must connect the ideas and shape them in some order to keep an audience interested and focused. Although there is no one formula for organizing essays, you can use some of the strategies discussed in this chapter to further your understanding of arranging and connecting different parts of an essay.

PETER SINGER

Tools for Research

The following two excerpts are written by activists for animal rights. Both Peter Singer and Peter Wise feel that animal experimentation is wrong. Even though their topics are similar, the two writers take considerably different paths to reach their points.

Anthony Hopkins of the Institute of Neurology, London, poisoned twelve adult and three infant baboons by injecting them with lead in varying doses for periods up to one year. Because earlier experiments on cats had shown that absorption of lead is more complete through the lungs, the doses were injected directly into the trachea, or windpipe, of each baboon, which was then held in an upright position so that the poison could "trickle" into its lungs. Before death occurred, loss of weight was "striking," five of the twelve adults losing 40 percent or more of their initial weight. Eight baboons had convulsive fits, thirty-four convulsive fits being observed, although "it is likely that others occurred when no observer was present."

In one baboon, seizures began with "twitching around the right eye, spreading to the rest of the right side of the face. During the next fifteen seconds the right arm became involved, and then seizures became generalized." Seizures were "occasionally preceded by a cry" and were sometimes "precipitated by a sudden movement of the animal as it tried to avoid transfer from one cage to another or whilst reaching up to take a banana." Other symptoms included bloody diarrhea, pneumonia, inflamed and bloody intestines, and liver degeneration. One baboon became so weak it could not stand up, and its left fingers could not grasp orange segments. For three weeks before it died this baboon was partially blind; it "groped for proffered fruit and on occasions appeared not to see it." Five of the baboons died in seizures; seven were found dead in their cages; the remaining three were "sacrificed."

[handwritten: begin with a horrifying story to get you riled up]

[handwritten: rhetorical question]

When are experiments on animals justifiable? Upon learning of the nature of many contemporary experiments, many people react by saying that all experiments on animals should be prohibited immediately. But if we make our demands as absolute as this, the experimenters have a ready reply: Would we be prepared to let thousands of humans die if they could be saved by a single experiment on a single animal?

This question is, of course, purely hypothetical. There never has been and there never could be a single experiment that saves thousands of lives. The way to reply to this hypothetical question is to pose another: Would the experimenter be prepared to carry out his experiment on a human orphan under six months old if that were the only way to save thousands of lives?

If the experimenter would not be prepared to use a human infant then   5 his readiness to use nonhuman animals reveals an unjustifiable form of discrimination on the basis of species, since adult apes, monkeys, dogs, cats, rats, and other mammals are more aware of what is happening to them, more self-directing, and, so far as we can tell, at least as sensitive to pain as a human infant. (I specified that the human infant be an orphan to avoid the complications of the feelings of parents, although in so doing I am being overfair to the experimenter, since the nonhuman animals used in experiments are not orphans and in many species the separation of mother and young clearly causes distress for both.)

There is no characteristic that human infants possess to a higher degree than adult nonhuman animals, unless we are to count the infant's potential as a characteristic that makes it wrong to experiment on him. Whether this characteristic should count is controversial—if we count it, we shall have to condemn abortion along with experiments on infants, since the potential of the infant and the fetus is the same. To avoid the complexities of this issue, however, we can alter our original question a little and assume that the infant is one with severe and irreversible brain damage that makes it impossible for him ever to develop beyond the level of a six-month-old infant. There are, unfortunately, many such human beings, locked away in special wards throughout the country, many of them long since abandoned by their parents. Despite their mental deficiencies, their anatomy and physiology is in nearly all respects identical with that of normal humans. If, therefore, we were to force-feed them with large quantities of floor polish, or drip concentrated solutions of cosmetics into their eyes, we would have a much more reliable indication of the safety of these products for other humans than we now get by attempting to extrapolate the results of tests on a variety of other species. The radiation experiments, the heatstroke experiments, and many other experiments described . . . could also have told us more about human reactions to the experimental situation if they had been carried out on retarded humans instead of dogs and rabbits.

So whenever an experimenter claims that his experiment is important enough to justify the use of an animal, we should ask him whether he would be prepared to use a retarded human at a similar mental level to the animal he is planning to use. If his reply is negative, we can assume that he is willing to use a nonhuman animal only because he gives less consideration to the interests of members of other species than he gives to members of his own—and this bias is no more defensible than racism or any other form of arbitrary discrimination.

Of course, no one would seriously propose carrying out the experiments described . . . on retarded humans. Occasionally it has become known that some medical experiments have been performed on humans without their consent, and sometimes on retarded humans; but the consequences of these experiments for the human subjects are almost always trivial by comparison with what is standard practice for nonhuman animals. Still, these experiments on humans usually lead to an outcry against the experimenters, and rightly so. They are, very often, a further example of the arrogance of the research worker who justifies everything on the grounds of increasing knowledge. If experimenting on retarded, orphaned humans would be wrong, why isn't experimenting on nonhuman animals wrong? What difference is there between the two, except for the mere fact that, biologically, one is a member of our species and the other is not? But *that*, surely, is not a morally relevant difference, any more than the fact that a being is not a member of our race is a morally relevant difference.

Actually the analogy between speciesism and racism applies in practice as well as in theory in the area of experimentation. Blatant speciesism leads to painful experiments on other species, defended on the grounds of its contribution to knowledge and possible usefulness for our species. Blatant racism has led to painful experiments on other races, defended on the grounds of its contribution to knowledge and possible usefulness for the experimenting race. Under the Nazi regime in Germany, nearly 200 doctors, some of them eminent in the world of medicine, took part in experiments on Jews and Russian and Polish prisoners. Thousands of other physicians knew of these experiments, some of which were the subject of lectures at medical academies. Yet the records show that the doctors sat through medical reports of the infliction of horrible injuries on these "lesser races" and then proceeded to discuss the medical lessons to be learned from them without anyone making even a mild protest about the nature of the experiments. The parallels between this attitude and that of experimenters today toward animals are striking. Then, as now, the subjects were frozen, heated, and put in decompression chambers. Then, as now, these events were written up in a dispassionate scientific jargon. The following paragraph is taken from a report by a Nazi scientist of an experiment on a human being, placed in a decompression chamber; it could equally have been taken from accounts of recent experiments in this country on animals:

> After five minutes spasms appeared; between the sixth and tenth minute respiration increased in frequency, the TP [test person] losing consciousness. From the eleventh to the thirtieth minute respiration slowed down to three inhalations per minute, only to cease entirely at the end of that period . . . about half an hour after breathing had ceased, an autopsy was begun.

Then, as now, the ethic of pursuing knowledge was considered sufficient justification for inflicting agony on those who are placed beyond the limits of genuine moral concern. Our sphere of moral concern is far wider than that of the Nazis; but so long as there are sentient beings outside it, it is not wide enough.

To return to the question of when an experiment might be justifiable. It 10 will not do to say: "Never!" In extreme circumstances, absolutist answers always break down. Torturing a human being is almost always wrong, but it is not absolutely wrong. If torture were the only way in which we could discover the location of a nuclear time bomb hidden in a New York City basement, then torture would be justifiable. Similarly, if a single experiment could cure a major disease, that experiment would be justifiable. But in actual life the benefits are always much, much more remote, and more often than not they are nonexistent. So how do we decide when an experiment is justifiable?

We have seen that the experimenter reveals a bias in favor of his own species whenever he carries out an experiment on a nonhuman for a purpose that he would not think justified him in using a human being, even a retarded human being. This principle gives us a guide toward an answer to our question. Since a speciesist bias, like a racist bias, is unjustifiable, an experiment cannot be justifiable unless the experiment is so important that the use of a retarded human being would also be justifiable.

This is not an absolutist principle. I do not believe that it could *never* be justifiable to experiment on a retarded human. If it really were possible to save many lives by an experiment that would take just one life, and there were *no other way* those lives could be saved, it might be right to do the experiment. But this would be an extremely rare case. Not one tenth of one percent of the experiments now being performed on animals would fall into this category.

↳ some audience consideration

PETER WISE

The Problem with Being a Thing

> It is difficult, to handle simply as property, a creature possessing
> human passions and human feelings . . . while on the other
> hand, the absolute necessity of dealing with property as a thing,
> greatly embarrasses a man in any attempt to treat it as a
> person.
>
> —Frederick Law Olmsted, traveling in
> the American South before the Civil War

Jerom's Story

Jerom died on February 13, 1996, ten days shy of his fourteenth birthday. The teenager was dull, bloated, depressed, sapped, anemic, and plagued by diarrhea. He had not played in fresh air for eleven years. As a thirty-month-old infant, he had been intentionally infected with HIV virus SF2. At the age of four, he had been infected with another HIV strain, LAV-1. A month short of five, he was infected with yet a third strain, NDK. Throughout the Iran-Contra hearings, almost to the brink of the Gulf War, he sat in the small, windowless, cinder-block Infectious Disease Building. Then he was moved a short distance to a large, windowless, gray concrete box, one of eleven bleak steel-and-concrete cells 9 feet by 11 feet by 8.5 feet. Throughout the war and into Bill Clinton's campaign for a second term as president, he languished in his cell. This was the Chimpanzee Infectious Disease Building. It stood in the Yerkes Regional Primate Research Center near grassy tree-lined Emory University, minutes from the bustle of downtown Atlanta, Georgia.

Entrance to the chimpanzee cell room was through a tiny, cramped, and dirty anteroom bursting with supplies from ceiling to floor. Inside, five cells lined the left wall of the cell room, six lined the right. The front and ceiling of each cell were a checkerboard of steel bars, criss-crossed in three-inch squares. The rear wall was the same gray concrete. A sliding door was set into the eight-inch-thick concrete side walls. Each door was punctured by a one-half-inch hole, through which a chimpanzee could catch glimpses of his neighbors. Each cell was flushed by a red rubber fire hose twice a day and was regularly scrubbed with deck brushes and disinfected with chemicals. Incandescent bulbs hanging from the dropped ceiling provided the only light. Sometimes the cold overstrained the box's inadequate heating units, and the temperature would sink below 50°F.

Although Jerom lived alone in his cell for the last four months of his life, others were nearby. Twelve other chimpanzees—Buster, Manuel, Arctica, Betsie, Joye, Sara, Nathan, Marc, Jonah, Roberta, Hallie, and Tika—filled the bleak cells, living in twos and threes, each with access to two of the cells. But none of them had any regular sense of changes in weather or the turn of the seasons. None of them knew whether it was day or night. Each slowly rotted in that humid and sunless gray concrete box. Nearly all had been intentionally infected with HIV. Just five months before Jerom died of AIDS born of an amalgam of two of the three HIV strains injected into his blood, Nathan was injected with 40 ml of Jerom's HIV-infested blood. Nathan's level of CD4 cells, the white blood cells that HIV destroys, has plummeted. He will probably sicken and die.

Sales Tax for Loulis

The biologist Vincent Sarich has pointed out that from the standpoint of immunology, humans and chimpanzees are as similar as "two subspecies of gophers living on opposite sides of the Colorado River." Rachel Weiss, a young Yerkes "care-tech" who watched Nathan being injected with Jerom's dirty blood and saw Jerom himself waste away and die, wrote about what she had seen. During the time she cared for the chimpanzees of the Yerkes Chimpanzee Infectious Disease Building, Rachel learned firsthand that chimpanzees possess "passions" and "feelings" that, if not human, are certainly humanlike. It made them no less "difficult to handle simply as property." She stopped thinking of them as "property" and resigned from Yerkes shortly after Jerom's death.

Seventeen years before Jerom's death, the primatologist Roger Fouts encountered Loulis staring at him through the bars of another Yerkes cage. Loulis's mother was huddled in a corner. Four metal bolts jutted from her head. Fouts doubted that the brain research she had endured allowed her even to know that Loulis was her son. He plucked up the ten-month-old, signed the necessary loan papers, then drove Loulis halfway across the United States to his adopted mother.

Washoe was a signing chimpanzee who lived on an island in a pond at the Institute for Primate Studies in Norman, Oklahoma. Loulis did not want to sleep in Washoe's arms that first night and curled up instead on a metal bench. At four o'clock in the morning, Washoe suddenly awakened and loudly signed *"Come, baby."* The sound jerked Loulis awake, and he jumped into Washoe's arms. Within eight days, he had learned his first sign. Eight weeks later, he was signing to humans and to the other chimpanzees in Washoe's family. In five months, Loulis, by now an accepted family member, was using combinations of signs. At the end of five years, he was regularly using fifty-one signs; he had initiated thousands of chimpanzee conversations and had participated in thousands more. He had learned everything he knew from the other chimpanzees, for no human ever signed to him.

As years passed, Fouts realized that Yerkes could call in its loan and put Loulis to the knife, as his mother had been. When Loulis was seventeen years old, Fouts sought to buy him outright. Yerkes agreed to sell for $10,000, which Fouts didn't have. After strenuous efforts, he raised that amount. But at the last second, a hitch developed. Ten thousand dollars was Loulis's purchase price. As if Yerkes were selling Fouts a desk or chair, Fouts was charged another 7.5 percent in Georgia sales tax.

The scientists who injected Jerom and Nathan kept the baker's dozen chimps imprisoned in a dungeon and invaded the brain of Loulis's mother, and the administrators who collected sales tax for Loulis believed that chimpanzees are things. But they didn't know why. Rachel Weiss and Roger Fouts show that we can come to believe—as they do—that chimpanzees are persons and not just things.

Demolishing a Wall

For four thousand years, a thick and impenetrable legal wall has separated all human from all nonhuman animals. On one side, even the most trivial interests of a single species—ours—are jealously guarded. We have assigned ourselves, alone among the million animal species, the status of "legal persons." On the other side of that wall lies the legal refuse of an entire kingdom, not just chimpanzees and bonobos but also gorillas, orangutans, and monkeys, dogs, elephants, and dolphins. They are "legal things." Their most basic and fundamental interests—their pains, their lives, their freedoms—are intentionally ignored, often maliciously trampled, and routinely abused. Ancient philosophers claimed that all nonhuman animals had been designed and placed on this earth just for human beings. Ancient jurists declared that law had been created just for human beings. Although philosophy and science have long since recanted, the law has not.

10 Legal personhood establishes one's legal right to be "recognized as a potential bearer of legal rights." That is why the Universal Declaration of Human Rights, the International Covenant on Civil and Political Rights, and the American Convention on Human Rights nearly identically state that "[e]veryone has the right to recognition everywhere as a person before the law." Intended to prevent a recurrence of one of the worst excesses of Nazi law, this guarantee is "often deemed to be rather trivial and self-evident" because no state today denies legal personhood to human beings. But its importance cannot be overemphasized. Without legal personhood, one is invisible to civil law. One has no civil rights. One might as well be dead.

Throngs of Romans scoot past the gaping Coliseum every day without giving it a glance. Athenians rarely squint up at their Parthenon perched high on its Acropolis. In the same way, when we encounter this legal wall, it is so tall, its stones are so thick, and it has been standing for so long that we do not see it. Even after litigating for many years on behalf of nonhuman animals, I did not see it. I saved a handful from death or misery, but for most, there was nothing I could do. I was powerless to represent them directly. They were things, not persons, ignored by judges. But I was butting into something. Finally I saw that wall.

> **WRITING**
>
> Look at the different ways Peter Singer and Peter Wise structure their writing after similar beginnings, especially the way they weave in their support and the way they conclude their pieces. Write about the structural differences you see, such as the position of the thesis statements, the places you find evidence, and the flow from paragraph to paragraph. How do you think the content affected the authors' structural decisions? What do you believe was the effect of audience awareness (see Chapter 3) on how the authors organized the information?

Introducing Your Subject

The opening section of most pieces of writing is called an introduction. Its task is to capture readers' attention and orient them toward the subject. While some introductions contain thesis statements, these statements are not necessary components of introductions. Instead, introductions create interest by hinting at the thesis or suggesting the direction in which the essay might head. An introduction can be longer than one paragraph, especially if the author uses stark images or pivotal scenes to entice readers.

An introduction might be thought of as writing's version of a movie trailer. A good preview excites viewers and makes them want to see the whole movie. Audiences may know something about the plot, but if the preview gives away the surprise ending or explains everything that is going to happen, audience members will be less inclined to pay money to see the film when it is released. Previews, therefore, remain brief and hint at movies' highlights. While an introduction to a piece of writing cannot be as disjointed as a movie trailer or merely slap together snippets of scenes from the body, an introduction achieves a similar effect by creating the desire to read more.

Following are some suggestions to help you begin your essays. While many of them might be called "tricks of the trade," remember that the content of your essay should dictate what you do. Find the right type of introduction for your essay, keeping your audience's needs in mind.

Introductions Come Last   Since a paper does not exist before you write it, you really do not know what you are introducing until you have established your paper's thesis. Many writers can put together a coherent introduction without first knowing what the content of the paper will be, but they run into trouble when the body of the paper leads in unanticipated directions. Equally troubling is a thesis that emerges from a critical analysis. The writer's discovery makes for a better paper for all the reasons discussed in Chapter 2, but the introduction might be preparing the audience for something much more pedestrian. In such cases, introductions have to be scrapped or at least reconceived. Therefore, writing the introduction last makes more sense than trying to write it first. You will know what your paper conveys and can think of the best ways to introduce it.

→ write your intro after everything else

Finding Common Ground   An introduction gives you an immediate opportunity to forge a relationship with your audience, in keeping with the discussion about ethos in Chapter 3. After developing the thesis, you can review your ideas and anticipate what your audience will need in order to understand your perspective and relate to you. You need to find common ground, in other words. You can display this common ground in your introduction with a quick reference to a popular icon of modern culture or a brief parallel to a famous occurrence that has relevance to your ideas. Sometimes you can spin a cliché to capture your audience's attention.

For Steve's topic of humor, for instance, we might come up with a variation of "Laugh with people, not at them." Steve's thesis concerned the uses of stereotypes in humor, concluding that people need to ridicule caricatures in order to distance themselves from annoying traits they themselves might embody. You can see that the first sentence of an introduction to this paper might use the cliché like this: "Many people believe that we need to laugh with people, not at them, since we reduce others to objects or stereotypes when we make them the butt of our jokes." The thesis could then be hinted at in the other sentences in the introduction; the introduction would move slowly away from the cliché to suggest something like "If we use caricatures instead of actual people as the butt of our jokes, we might reduce the harm of objectifying people while maintaining humor."

Another way to forge common ground is to ask the audience a question. When you ask a question, readers assume that you are addressing a person or a group of persons, which makes them see themselves as real entities whom you have considered when constructing your essay. Even if the question is rhetorical in nature and is answered by the writer, a good question has anticipated a genuine concern of an audience. Audience members feel that they have been addressed. Peter Singer makes use of this technique in "Tools for Research." While he grabs his audience's attention with the opening vignette of the poisoned baboons, the actual introduction starts with the question, "When are experiments on animals justifiable?"

General to Specific   Starting with interesting information about the subject matter not only gives the audience clues about the topic, but could also be enough to hook audience members. This type of introduction begins with a general statement about the topic and gets more specific by adding facts or increasingly narrow ideas, usually culminating in something provocative. This type of introduction might reveal your thesis more than other types; in moving toward specifics, you draw closer to your actual points. Still, you do not want the information presented here to be repeated in the body of your essay. You are trying to attract readers with your introduction, not tell them the exact points you will make. Therefore, the information will create general interest. On page 111, Gloria Naylor uses this technique to introduce her essay. She starts with a description of the general subject of language, moves to the influence of language on reality, and narrows the topic toward one of her points—the power that societal consensus gives words.

She orients readers without giving away too many details, and readers want to read more.

Pivotal Scene   Many forms of writing include the narration of experience, whether the author's own or someone else's. Some pieces focus on a single event in the life of the writer or of a person he or she has interviewed; the story encompasses the body of the essay, with analysis woven throughout. There is nothing wrong with starting such a paper with an introduction that utilizes methods discussed above. However, consider Scott McMillion's essay, "Treat It Right," in Chapter 16 (page 461). McMillion starts with a pivotal scene from the story he tells about Buck Wilde, who comes on the remains of a mauled hiker. Instead of starting with Wilde's trip into the national park and telling everything he saw and heard before finding the injured man, McMillion puts the reader into Wilde's shoes, using a technique called the imperative voice to affect the reader as much as possible. McMillion continues with this pivotal scene, giving more and more details about what Wilde did to get help and protect other hikers, before going back to the beginning of the story in the first body paragraph, the one that starts "Wilde is an unusual man."

Narrative accounts like this allow a writer to grab the audience's attention by teasing the audience with a portion of the pivotal scene. The same technique can be used in recounting the details of a historical event or in relating case studies of actual human experience. Choosing an exciting part, one where an outcome hinges on the results, and giving the audience a taste of it will make people want to read more. Just make sure that you hint at the thesis or at least provide a clue that you will return to this key moment after recapping how you got there. Otherwise, you might confuse your audience instead of enticing it. Notice that McMillion asks a question early in his introduction: "Put yourself in Buck Wilde's shoes. What are you going to do?" This question hints about the point McMillion is driving toward.

COLLABORATING

Choose two people from your group and introduce them to the class by reading an introduction written collaboratively by the group. First find out some key details about each person. You will have a very boring introduction if you simply say, "This is Sandra, and she attends all the same classes I do." Conduct a brief interview if you are not familiar with the group members, or use the *Jeopardy* technique of having the people tell you a couple of unusual facts about themselves. With this information, use one of the strategies discussed above for introducing the first person and a different strategy for the second person. Each introduction should be no shorter than four sentences. When you present the introductions to the class, take note of what intrigues your peers and of what seems to create clarity for them. Do they want to hear more? Are they confused about anything? Get feedback and think of ways to rewrite the introductions to make them even stronger.

Transitioning from Ideas

The body of a piece of writing, whether a business report, a letter to a friend, or a project for college, constitutes its bulk. Unless the body consists mostly of a chronological retelling of a personal experience or observation, you will need to signal the relationship between each piece of information, especially from paragraph to paragraph. Such signals are called transitions, and they help the writer maintain order in a paper. They connect ideas and examples, allowing writers to construct a path that the audience can follow.

While writers sometimes use rhetorical devices as transitions, the best transitions come from logical sequencing. In other words, one idea naturally progresses into the next in response to audience needs. Again, writers do not conform to a preestablished structure to forge this relationship; instead, they try to arrange elements in their papers so that the audience can understand their train of thought. ↳*always awareness*

No writer can predict what a finished essay will look like. The thesis will determine the audience's needs. Organization comes from coherence within thoughts and a sense of direction, meaning that every idea works toward a goal and each example illuminates those ideas. So when a writer speaks about the organization of an essay, he or she is really speaking of the way the text's ideas have been connected through transitions. The following methods of transition suggest ways to organize your writing.

Increasing Levels of Specificity

Some writing tasks involve a high degree of explanation and support. When they do, you do not want to lose your audience's attention, so you can try the technique of slowly increasing the level of specificity to make sure your essay flows logically. The body of your essay can start with a general and familiar point and transition toward more specific explanations or forms of support.

Contrast, Addition, Summary, and Exemplification

Rhetorical devices of transition help writers and readers locate the purpose of a piece of information quickly. While you do not want to overuse these devices, they can be helpful. The following table lists the most common rhetorical devices. A transition of contrast prepares the audience for a qualifier to a statement or for the presentation of the difference between one set of ideas and another. A transition of addition signals that you will make another point about the same subject. A transition of summary alerts the audience that you are concluding an idea or tying it together. A transition of exemplification lets you smoothly move into an example to support your idea.

Rhetorical devices can be placed at the beginning of a sentence or between the subject and predicate. They must occur early enough in the sentence for an audience to pick up on the relationship between the sentence and the next one or one paragraph and the next.

Contrast	Addition	Summary	Exemplification
However	And	Therefore	For example
But	Also	Then	For instance
Yet	Too	So	Specifically
Instead	Futhermore	Thus	In other words
Even though	In addition	Consequently	That is
On the other hand	Besides	As a result	Particularly
Nevertheless	Moreover	Accordingly	Namely
Although	Next	Hence	
Though	Finally		
Still	Similarly		
Despite	Likewise		
On the contrary			
In contrast			

Repeating Keywords   You definitely want to avoid needless repetition in your paper. However, you can transition from one paragraph to the next by dropping a keyword from the previous paragraph into the first sentence of the next paragraph. You can repeat the word directly, use a different form of the word, substitute a synonym, or use a pronoun. Whatever shape it takes, this repetition provides a direct link from the previous paragraph to the next. So if the end of one paragraph reads, "The degree to which we react to fear limits our ability to confront our insecurities," the first sentence in the next paragraph could read, "Reactions vary in people." The same root word, *react*, appears in both sentences. The subtle shift from a verb to a noun helps prevent direct repetition, which allows for a better flow. Such links will keep your audience aboard, especially when material is complicated. You should use this technique sparingly however, to avoid redundancy.

↳ all "tricks" should be used sparingly to avoid habits/reliance →writing is situational

✶ **Time and Place**   Weaving in your critical analysis is crucial. In writing that uses elongated personal experiences within the body, however, the critical analysis can disrupt the chronological flow. You do not want your readers to be confused about where they left off, but a transition such as "As I was saying" is awkward and too talky; it seems like you have strayed from your point or are disorganized. ✓

Instead, orient your audience to time or place in subtle ways. If a scene that has been interrupted takes place at night, show the continuation of the events with something like "Midnight drew near" or "My bedtime had passed three hours earlier." If a story involves a setting such as a barn, remind the audience where they are with a detail like "I noticed hay stuck in the cuff of my jeans."

↳ carefully placed specific details

Do not underestimate an audience's propensity to get lost. In "Me Talk Pretty One Day" (Chapter 14, page 396), David Sedaris disrupts his narrative of a French classroom to talk about his mother:

> I recalled my mother, flushed with wine, pounding the tabletop late one night, saying, "Love? I love a good steak cooked rare. I love my cat, and I love . . ." My sisters and I leaned forward, waiting to hear our names. "Tums," our mother said. "I love Tums."

Even though Sedaris's analysis and the vignette about his mother take only one paragraph, Sedaris makes sure the reader does not get lost by referring to the teacher and his own notepad in the opening sentence of the next paragraph, clearly placing the narrative in a classroom.

Remember that your readers did not experience the event you're writing about, so they do not know the sequence of events in advance. If your critical analysis is penetrating and you lingered on pertinent details appropriately or, like Sedaris, you included a relevant memory, your readers will be focused on those aspects and will need to have their memories jogged to get back into the narrative. Subtle hints can work wonders in ensuring that chronological organization does not get compromised.

in terms of character sketch especially

Subheadings   Reports often use subheadings as organizational tools. When a writer switches from one idea to the next, she or he inserts a heading, usually in a bold font, that prepares the reader for a shift in focus. This type of transition reduces the reliance on rhetorical devices of transition and on repetition of keywords. Subheadings also allow a reader to scan a document to locate desired information easily.

The subheading should summarize the focus of the next idea in a phrase or a single word. It should never be a full sentence. Look at Peter Wise's "The Problem with Being a Thing" on pages 88–90. Wise uses three subheadings: "Jerom's Story," "Sales Tax for Loulis," and "Demolishing a Wall." All three are phrases, not sentences.

WRITING

Use your current essay assignment to practice your use of transitions. Print your revision, and circle every rhetorical device of transition you have used in the body of the essay. Look at sentences or paragraphs where you have not used rhetorical devices. How are the sentences and paragraphs fitting together? Are ideas progressing from general to specific? Have you repeated keywords and phrases? If your piece is a narrative, have you stuck to chronological order? If you have disrupted that order, how have you transitioned back into the narrative? Did you try subheadings? Be able to identify how each sentence and paragraph connects to the next and how all parts of the body move toward the same goal. If sentences or paragraphs cannot be linked to what comes before and after, you will need to revise to find the proper place for them or make a decision about their worth for this paper.

Placing Your Thesis

Many myths revolve around the placement of the thesis in an essay. As Steve discovered, writers are not obligated to place a thesis statement in the introduction, much less as the last sentence in the introduction. A thesis also does not have to be directly repeated elsewhere in the essay once it is stated. In fact, a thesis does not really have to be stated, although an audience must come away from a piece of writing knowing what the point was.

A thesis is an idea that emerges from a critical analysis, as discussed in Chapter 2. The introduction should hint at it. The conclusion should build on it. Where should it go? You must consider the magnitude of your thesis and gauge possible reactions from your audience. Below are suggestions for determining the most effective placement.

Putting a New Twist on an Old Idea

If your critical analysis has produced a variation of or wrinkle on a well-accepted idea, your strategy for placement will be different than if you are turning a societal norm upside down. You will not puzzle or alienate your audience by stating a new twist to an old idea immediately; in fact, you might intrigue readers, depending on how closely your thesis aligns to the norm. People tend to react well to the tweaking of things they are used to; their comfort level is unaffected, and the hope that your ideas might solve problems or contradictions in the old idea appeals to them. Thus, you can weave the thesis into the introduction or at least state it early in the paper without losing your readers.

Make sure you have assessed your audience correctly. While a group of retired people might welcome ideas to improve their health coverage, for instance, a group of upwardly mobile executives might see your slight changes to established procedures as an attempt at socialized medicine that would increase the tax burden and reduce treatment options. While you cannot always account for extreme reactions, you must guard against certain possibilities. That same group of executives might listen more attentively and be drawn into your argument if you do not reveal your thesis too quickly. You must judge any writing situation appropriately and evaluate the risks before deciding on the placement of the thesis.

WRITING

Look at Elizabeth Pleck's essay, "Festivals, Rites, and Presents," in Chapter 11. Pleck clearly is putting a new twist on old ideas through her look at sentimentality and postsentimentality. What audience has she targeted for this essay? How have her structural choices helped or hindered her in preparing the audience for her thesis?

Using the Oreo Cookie Method

Some writers rely on shock value to keep audiences listening. In other words, audience members cannot believe what they are hearing, so they pay closer attention than they normally would.

Critical analysis can lead to harsh criticism of the status quo, producing a thesis that strongly challenges preconceived notions or shocks an audience. If your goal is to shake an audience out of its complacency, think about putting your thesis in the first sentence in the introduction.

Generally, readers will want to hear an explanation right away; if they do not, they may dismiss you. Therefore, the last sentence of the introduction does not work as well as the first sentence, since your audience will need assurance that your proposal has been thought through. Squeezing your thesis between some catchy opening ideas and an explanation or qualifier to ensure a sense of logic ensures that the audience absorbs the jolt but does not kill its interest. This placement is called the "Oreo cookie method," because it parallels the way an Oreo cookie surrounds the delicious cream with two otherwise bland chocolate cookies. It allows you to soften the blow without compromising what you have to say.

You have probably used a similar strategy in delicate social situations. You have news to deliver that you know your friend will not like, but you have to tell it anyway. You cannot wait to tell your friend until you are leaving; he or she needs time to get used to the news and might want you to spell out the positives as well as the negatives. Thus, you say, "I know how much you really like Ron, but he's not the guy you think he is. He just got arrested for dealing drugs. I know you find this hard to believe, but he has been living a double life for a long time." You then relate the details. The shocking statement is that Ron got arrested. The qualifier, "he's not the guy you think he is," prepares the friend for the news, and the statement about the double life leads to an explanation. Blurting out the news right away could cause panic and hysteria. Saving it until the end of the story would be cruel.

While a critical analysis cannot be accurately compared to bad news, a thesis springing from a critical analysis can have a similar effect on readers comfortable within the status quo. You must proceed cautiously when you have arrived at such a thesis.

AMY WANG

The Same Difference

Amy Wang grabs the attention of her audience early in this essay by recounting a childhood memory of racism. Her introduction hints at her thesis, but she builds sympathy with her audience before detailing her anger at white men and her thesis about the impossibility of white people understanding the worldview of people of color. She concludes with a conciliatory statement. Does the conclusion succeed in softening the blow without compromising Wang's position?

Pivotal scene

It was on my way home that the moment of truth swept by—again. There we were, a friend and I, heading north on the Pennsylvania Turnpike to central New York to visit my parents. Somehow our conversation had parted the curtains before my childhood memories, and before I knew it, I was telling him about an incident I have never quite forgotten.

As I spoke, it was almost as if my adult self were back in Pittsburgh, watching; strange how in my memory the sun is always glinting through a bright haze on that day. The trees are bare, or nearly so, with dark branches that reach out to splinter the sun's rays. I am walking alone, down a white concrete sidewalk littered with leaves, twigs, buckeyes. School is out for the day, and everyone is going home.

From behind come shouts, and I turn to see a group of children from school. A moment passes, and I realize they are shouting at me. I listen for several seconds before the words whip into clarity:

Chink! Hey, chink! Chinky chinky chink!

They are running. I am frozen, my heart the only part of me moving, and it is pounding. Then one of them stoops, picks up a twig and hurls it at me. It lands short, a foot away on the sidewalk. Then I turn, still blocks from home, and run. The twigs keep coming, clattering close behind as the others shout and follow. As I run, I think of the steep steps to the front door and despair.

But when I reach the steps and turn around, only silence follows. And when my mother answers the doorbell's ring, she sees only her daughter, cheeks a little flushed, waiting to be let in. Almost instinctively, I know I must not tell her. It would only hurt her, and there is nothing she can do. Besides, it is nothing I want to discuss.

"Wow," he said. "And you were in sixth grade when this happened?"

"Six," I said. "I was 6 when this happened. I was in first grade."

He was clearly appalled, his eyes in far focus as he tried to understand how such a thing could happen to a small child. I was concentrating on the road, but even a sidelong glance showed he did not, could not, quite understand. And it was then that I felt the familiar stab of disappointment: the realization that no matter how long we traveled together, we would always be on parallel roads, moving on either side of a great divide. I would never know his assurance as he made his way through a world where his skin color was an assumption, and he would never know my anxiety as I made my way through a world where my skin color was an anguish.

We were silent, and after a while he fell asleep. "Wake me up when we get to Allentown," he had said as he drifted off, and we both smiled, remembering a classmate who had once padded an expense account for profit by driving from New York to Allentown and back twice in two days.

The thought of the old mill town triggered memories of another old mill town, where I had gotten my first job out of college. It was at the local newspaper, working nights on the copy desk. Our shifts ended at 1 A.M., and I often drove home through deserted streets, the hush broken only by the whir of an occasional street-cleaning machine or the clanking of a distant garbage truck. The other drivers on the streets at that hour seemed just as weary, just as intent on getting to bed.

In such an atmosphere I often dream, and so to this day a shadowy, slowed-down quality suffuses the memory of turning my head and looking out the side window one night just in time to see an old red Dodge draw up in the next lane at a traffic light. Inside, four young white crewcut men dressed in denim and flannel strain toward me, their faces distorted with hate, their mouths twisted with invective. Our windows are closed, so I am spared their actual words, but their frenzied pantomime leaves little to be imagined.

When the light turns green I pull away hastily, but they cruise alongside for the next few blocks. By the time they tire of me and swing into a left turn, I am seething with fear and rage. I wait until they are committed to the turn, then raise my middle finger. One of them looks back for a final insult, sees my gesture, and gapes—but only for a moment. He turns, and I know he is screaming at the driver to turn back. I gun it.

They never come after me, and I make it home alive. Numb, I crawl into bed. It is only after I lie down that I realize how they might have hurt me, the four of them with their huge Dodge against my tiny Nissan, and I begin to shake. As my mind tumbles, the phone rings. For a moment I think it is them, and then logic returns. I answer, and it is my boyfriend, calling from Boston. I tell him what happened, melting into tears. He is sympathetic, but then he asks: "How do you know they weren't yelling at you because you were a woman?"

15   I don't, of course, but that is not the point. His whiteness rushes through the line with the very question. "It doesn't matter," I tell him, and suddenly I can't stand to hear his voice. I tell him I don't want to discuss it anymore, and hang up.

Somewhere along Route 79 in New York he said, "This is beautiful." I smiled, remembering the years I spent in Finger Lakes country: middle school, high school, college. Here were trees I had climbed, hills I had sledded down, malls I knew by heart; here were roads that led to memories and people who knew my history.

And it was because I had to come back here that another He was able to betray me. It was during the first summer I spent away from home, working at a magazine in New York. Picture now a pavilion on the grounds of a quiet country club where the staff is enjoying the annual company picnic, and there I am by the jukebox, hovering over the glassed-in 45s as a light mist dampens the grass. As the Contours wail "Do You Love Me," I sway to the beat, attracting a stranger's eyes. In a moment he is introducing himself; in an hour he is sitting by me in the bus taking us back to the city; in a week he is asking me out to dinner.

I am no longer thinking clearly. On my last day at the magazine, he watches as I clean out my desk, then asks me, in a low but urgent tone, not to forget him. He tells me he wants my address, and a sudden foreboding chill nearly stuns me with its iciness, sending shivers through my hand as I write out the address and phone number. Then I ask for his address and phone number. I do not think to ask him not to forget me.

Weeks go by without a word, and then one night, I know. The chill comes back: For days I hate white men, all of them, they all bear the blame for his misdeed. But I have known too many good ones for my fury to last, and finally I am forced to admit that I have been a fool, and that this time, at least, it had nothing to do with race.

20   "It could have happened to anyone," a (white male) friend tells me. "It happens to everyone."

I am not immediately consoled. But time goes on, and finally, so do I.

By the time we pulled into my parents' driveway, it was nearly dinnertime. I sprang out, glad to stretch, and bounded into the house, but he was slow to follow, and I had discarded my shoulder bag and greeted everyone by the time he finally appeared in the doorway. I went to introduce him, wondering why he was hanging back. Then he raised his eyes to mine as he came up the stairs, and I realized he was nervous: He was in my world now, and he was finally getting an inkling of what I went through every day.

Payback time. At last.

Then my mother was there, smiling and shaking his hand, and my father was right behind her, also smiling.

25   "Welcome," he said.

For a moment, I could see the horizon, where parallel lines sometimes seem to meet.

Building Toward Consensus   If your thesis does not necessarily shock anyone but still diverges from the societal norm, you might choose to place it toward the end of your essay. This way, you can take audience members along for the ride, giving them hints in the introduction and through the woven-in analysis, but not explicitly stating your thesis until you have completed your review of the salient points.

In a court of law, a judge uses this method to announce a decision on the admissibility of evidence, on a sentence, or on a verdict in small claims courts or nonjuried cases. If you have not seen an actual court case, you probably have seen dramas involving courtrooms or perhaps have watched *Judge Judy* and others on daytime television. A savvy listener will note where the judge lingers on evidence and will have a good notion of where he or she is headed, although that listener may not know exactly what the judgment will be. While you might disagree with the final judgment, you have listened the whole way. Sometimes your opinion and those of others might change, since the judge has built a consensus in the courtroom or in the homes of television viewers. More than likely, you will understand and respect the judgment.

An essay has to conclude, while the verdict in the courtroom is often the last or nearly the last thing said. But a thesis can work if placed toward the end and might grant more consideration from your audience than if you announced it immediately. Note the difference, though, between leading your audience toward a thesis you have developed through critical analysis and slapping a thesis onto the end of a paper to meet an assignment requirement. The former is based on audience awareness; the latter does not attempt the necessary critical analysis and the weaving of that analysis into the body. This distinction could not be more crucial.

COLLABORATING

Have each group member bring a news article from the local paper. Make sure it is a straightforward piece of reporting such as would be found on the front page, not an editorial or analysis. Because many readers only glance at headlines or read the first few paragraphs, news articles generally give the facts right away. As a group, decide what the thesis of each article is. Next, revise the articles, experimenting with different locations for the thesis. How does the content affect your choices in placing the thesis? What changes in arrangement are necessitated by different placement? Besides the ideas listed above, what strategies can you come up with in placing a thesis so that readers' expectations are fulfilled?

Finishing Your Thoughts

Writers may have more trouble with conclusions than with any other part of a paper. Some formulaic advice often given is to restate the thesis, rewrite the introduction, or end with a bang. The first two suggestions do not take into account how a paper progresses after the introduction and what strategies for arrangement are used. The last suggestion, though seemingly powerful, is vague. Introducing a surprise at the end of your paper might puzzle your audience. Even if you like the idea, how do you find a "bang"? How does it spring from an essay? The formulas do not help you figure out how to wrap up ideas, which is the purpose of the conclusion.

→ hard to do but powerful when done well

SHIRLEY JACKSON

The Lottery

This classic short story by Shirley Jackson does not reveal all the important details until the conclusion. Yet, the ending is plausible. When a reader reviews the story, he or she will see how Jackson makes the shock consistent with the body of the story. Jackson ends with a bang, but the details of the story support it.

The morning of June 27th was clear and sunny, with the fresh warmth of a full-summer day; the flowers were blossoming profusely and the grass was richly green. The people of the village began to gather in the square, between the post office and the bank, around ten o'clock; in some towns there were so many people that the lottery took two days and had to be started on June 26th, but in this village, where there were only about three hundred people, the whole lottery took less than two hours, so it could begin at ten o'clock in the morning and still be through in time to allow the villagers to get home for noon dinner.

The children assembled first, of course. School was recently over for the summer, and the feeling of liberty sat uneasily on most of them; they tended to gather together quietly for a while before they broke into boisterous play, and their talk was still of the classroom and the teacher, of books and repri-mands. Bobby Martin had already stuffed his pockets full of stones, and the other boys soon followed his example, selecting the smoothest and round-est stones; Bobby and Harry Jones and Dickie Delacroix—the villagers pro-nounced this name "Delacroy"—eventually made a great pile of stones in one corner of the square and guarded it against the raids of the other boys. The girls stood aside, talking among themselves, looking over their shoulders at the boys, and the very small children rolled in the dust or clung to the hands of their older brothers or sisters.

Soon the men began to gather, surveying their own children, speaking of planting and rain, tractors and taxes. They stood together, away from the pile of stones in the corner, and their jokes were quiet and they smiled rather than laughed. The women, wearing faded house dresses and sweaters, came shortly after their men-folk. They greeted one another and exchanged bits of gossip as they went to join their husbands. Soon the women, standing by their hus-bands, began to call to their children, and the children came reluctantly, hav-ing to be called four or five times. Bobby Martin ducked under his mother's grasping hand and ran, laughing, back to the pile of stones. His father spoke up sharply, and Bobby came quickly and took his place between his father and his oldest brother.

The lottery was conducted—as were the square dances, the teen-age club, the Halloween program—by Mr. Summers, who had time and energy to devote to civic activities. He was a round-faced, jovial man and he ran the coal business, and people were sorry for him, because he had no children and his wife was a scold. When he arrived in the square, carrying the black wooden box, there was a murmur of conversation among the villagers, and he waved and called, "Little late today, folks." The postmaster, Mr. Graves, followed him, carrying a three-legged stool, and the stool was put in the center of the square and Mr. Summers set the black box down on it. The villagers kept their distance, leaving a space between themselves and the stool, and when Mr. Summers said, "Some of you fellows want to give me a hand?" there was a hesitation before two men, Mr. Martin and his oldest son, Baxter, came for-ward to hold the box steady on the stool while Mr. Summers stirred up the papers inside it.

The original paraphernalia for the lottery had been lost long ago, and the black box now resting on the stool had been put into use even before Old Man Warner, the oldest man in town, was born. Mr. Summers spoke frequently to the villagers about making a new box, but no one liked to upset even as much tradition as was represented by the black box. There was a story that the pres-ent box had been made with some pieces of the box that had preceded it, the one that had been constructed when the first people settled down to make a village here. Every year, after the lottery, Mr. Summers began talking again about a new box, but every year the subject was allowed to fade off without anything's being done. The black box grew shabbier each year; by now it was no longer completely black but splintered badly along one side to show the original wood color, and in some places faded or stained.

Mr. Martin and his oldest son, Baxter, held the black box securely on the stool until Mr. Summers had stirred the papers thoroughly with his hand. Because so much of the ritual had been forgotten or discarded, Mr. Summers had been successful in having slips of paper substituted for the chips of wood that had been used for generations. Chips of wood, Mr. Summers had argued, had been all very well when the village was tiny, but now that the population was more than three hundred and likely to keep on growing, it was necessary to use something that would fit more easily into the black box. The night before the lottery, Mr. Summers and Mr. Graves made up the slips of paper and put them in the box, and it was then taken to the safe of Mr. Summers' coal company and locked up until Mr. Summers was ready to take it to the square next morning. The rest of the year, the box was put away, sometimes one place, sometimes another; it had spent one year in Mr. Graves's barn and another year underfoot in the post office, and sometimes it was set on a shelf in the Martin grocery and left there.

There was a great deal of fussing to be done before Mr. Summers declared the lottery open. There were the lists to make up—of heads of families, heads of households in each family, members of each household in each family. There was the proper swearing-in of Mr. Summers by the postmaster, as the official of the lottery; at one time, some people remembered, there had been a recital of some sort, performed by the official of the lottery, a perfunctory, tuneless chant that had been rattled off duly each year; some people believed that the official of the lottery used to stand just so when he said or sang it, others believed that he was supposed to walk among the people, but years and years ago this part of the ritual had been allowed to lapse. There had been, also, a ritual salute, which the official of the lottery had had to use in addressing each person who came up to draw from the box, but this also had changed with time, until now it was felt necessary only for the official to speak to each person approaching. Mr. Summers was very good at all this; in his clean white shirt and blue jeans, with one hand resting carelessly on the black box, he seemed very proper and important as he talked interminably to Mr. Graves and the Martins.

Just as Mr. Summers finally left off talking and turned to the assembled villagers, Mrs. Hutchinson came hurriedly along the path to the square, her sweater thrown over her shoulders, and slid into place in the back of the crowd. "Clean forgot what day it was," she said to Mrs. Delacroix, who stood next to her, and they both laughed softly. "Thought my old man was out back stacking wood," Mrs. Hutchinson went on, "and then I looked out the window and the kids was gone, and then I remembered it was the twenty-seventh and came a-running." She dried her hands on her apron, and Mrs. Delacroix said, "You're in time, though. They're still talking away up there."

Mrs. Hutchinson craned her neck to see through the crowd and found her husband and children standing near the front. She tapped Mrs. Delacroix on the arm as a farewell and began to make her way through the crowd. The people separated good-humoredly to let her through; two or three people said, in voices just loud enough to be heard across the crowd, "Here comes your

Missus, Hutchinson," and "Bill, she made it after all." Mrs. Hutchinson reached her husband, and Mr. Summers, who had been waiting, said cheerfully, "Thought we were going to have to get on without you, Tessie." Mrs. Hutchinson said, grinning, "Wouldn't have me leave m'dishes in the sink, now, would you, Joe?" and soft laughter ran through the crowd as the people stirred back into position after Mrs. Hutchinson's arrival.

"Well, now," Mr. Summers said soberly, "guess we better get started, get this over with, so's we can go back to work. Anybody ain't here?"   10

"Dunbar," several people said. "Dunbar, Dunbar."

Mr. Summers consulted his list. "Clyde Dunbar," he said. "That's right. He's broke his leg, hasn't he? Who's drawing for him?"

"Me, I guess," a woman said, and Mr. Summers turned to look at her. "Wife draws for her husband," Mr. Summers said. "Don't you have a grown boy to do it for you, Janey?" Although Mr. Summers and everyone else in the village knew the answer perfectly well, it was the business of the official of the lottery to ask such questions formally. Mr. Summers waited with an expression of polite interest while Mrs. Dunbar answered.

"Horace's not but sixteen yet," Mrs. Dunbar said regretfully. "Guess I gotta fill in for the old man this year."

"Right," Mr. Summers said. He made a note on the list he was holding.   15
Then he asked, "Watson boy drawing this year?"

A tall boy in the crowd raised his hand. "Here," he said. "I'm drawing for m'mother and me." He blinked his eyes nervously and ducked his head as several voices in the crowd said things like "Good fellow, Jack," and "Glad to see your mother's got a man to do it."

"Well," Mr. Summers said, "guess that's everyone. Old Man Warner make it?"

"Here," a voice said, and Mr. Summers nodded.

A sudden hush fell on the crowd as Mr. Summers cleared his throat and looked at the list. "All ready?" he called. "Now, I'll read the names—heads of families first—and the men come up and take a paper out of the box. Keep the paper folded in your hand without looking at it until everyone has had a turn. Everything clear?"

The people had done it so many times that they only half listened to the   20
directions; most of them were quiet, wetting their lips, not looking around. Then Mr. Summers raised one hand high and said, "Adams." A man disengaged himself from the crowd and came forward. "Hi, Steve," Mr. Summers said, and Mr. Adams said, "Hi, Joe." They grinned at one another humorlessly and nervously. Then Mr. Adams reached into the black box and took out a folded paper. He held it firmly by one corner as he turned and went hastily back to his place in the crowd, where he stood a little apart from his family, not looking down at his hand.

"Allen," Mr. Summers said. "Anderson. . . . Bentham."

"Seems like there's no time at all between lotteries any more," Mrs. Delacroix said to Mrs. Graves in the back row. "Seems like we got through with the last one only last week."

"Time sure goes fast," Mrs. Graves said.

"Clark. . . . Delacroix."

25   "There goes my old man," Mrs. Delacroix said. She held her breath while her husband went forward.

"Dunbar," Mr. Summers said, and Mrs. Dunbar went steadily to the box while one of the women said, "Go on, Janey," and another said, "There she goes."

"We're next," Mrs. Graves said. She watched while Mr. Graves came around from the side of the box, greeted Mr. Summers gravely, and selected a slip of paper from the box. By now, all through the crowd there were men holding the small folded papers in their large hands, turning them over and over nervously. Mrs. Dunbar and her two sons stood together, Mrs. Dunbar holding the slip of paper.

"Harburt. . . . Hutchinson."

"Get up there, Bill," Mrs. Hutchinson said, and the people near her laughed.

30   "Jones."

"They do say," Mr. Adams said to Old Man Warner, who stood next to him, "that over in the north village they're talking of giving up the lottery."

Old Man Warner snorted. "Pack of crazy fools," he said. "Listening to the young folks, nothing's good enough for *them*. Next thing you know, they'll be wanting to go back to living in caves, nobody work any more, live *that* way for a while. Used to be a saying about 'Lottery in June, Corn be heavy soon.' First thing you know, we'd all be eating stewed chickweed and acorns. There's *always* been a lottery," he added petulantly. "Bad enough to see young Joe Summers up there joking with everybody."

"Some places have already quit lotteries," Mrs. Adams said.

"Nothing but trouble in *that*," Old Man Warner said stoutly. "Pack of young fools."

35   "Martin." And Bobby Martin watched his father go forward. "Overdyke. . . . Percy."

"I wish they'd hurry," Mrs. Dunbar said to her older son. "I wish they'd hurry."

"They're almost through," her son said.

"You get ready to run tell Dad," Mrs. Dunbar said.

Mr. Summers called his own name and then stepped forward precisely and selected a slip from the box. Then he called, "Warner."

40   "Seventy-seventh year I been in the lottery," Old Man Warner said as he went through the crowd. "Seventy-seventh time."

"Watson." The tall boy came awkwardly through the crowd. Someone said, "Don't be nervous, Jack," and Mr. Summers said, "Take your time, son."

"Zanini."

After that, there was a long pause, a breathless pause, until Mr. Summers, holding his slip of paper in the air, said, "All right, fellows." For a minute, no one moved, and then all the slips of paper were opened. Suddenly, all the women began to speak at once, saying, "Who is it?" "Who's got it?"

"Is it the Dunbars?" "Is it the Watsons?" Then the voices began to say, "It's Hutchinson. It's Bill," "Bill Hutchinson's got it."

"Go tell your father," Mrs. Dunbar said to her older son.

People began to look around to see the Hutchinsons. Bill Hutchinson 45 was standing quiet, staring down at the paper in his hand. Suddenly, Tessie Hutchinson shouted to Mr. Summers, "You didn't give him time enough to take any paper he wanted. I saw you. It wasn't fair!"

"Be a good sport, Tessie," Mrs. Delacroix called, and Mrs. Graves said, "All of us took the same chance."

"Shut up, Tessie," Bill Hutchinson said.

"Well, everyone," Mr. Summers said, "that was done pretty fast, and now we've got to be hurrying a little more to get done in time." He consulted his next list. "Bill," he said, "you draw for the Hutchinson family. You got any other households in the Hutchinsons?"

"There's Don and Eva," Mrs. Hutchinson yelled. "Make *them* take their chance!"

"Daughters draw with their husbands' families, Tessie," Mr. Summers 50 said gently. "You know that as well as anyone else."

"It wasn't *fair*," Tessie said.

"I guess not, Joe," Bill Hutchinson said regretfully. "My daughter draws with her husband's family, that's only fair. And I've got no other family except the kids."

"Then, as far as drawing for families is concerned, it's you," Mr. Summers said in explanation, "and as far as drawing for households is concerned, that's you, too. Right?"

"Right," Bill Hutchinson said.   55

"How many kids, Bill?" Mr. Summers asked formally.

"Three," Bill Hutchinson said. "There's Bill, Jr., and Nancy, and little Dave. And Tessie and me."

"All right, then," Mr. Summers said. "Harry, you got their tickets back?"

Mr. Graves nodded and held up the slips of paper. "Put them in the box, then," Mr. Summers directed. "Take Bill's and put it in."

"I think we ought to start over," Mrs. Hutchinson said, as quietly as she could. "I tell you it wasn't *fair*. You didn't give him time enough to choose. *Everybody* saw that."

Mr. Graves had selected the five slips and put them in the box, and he 60 dropped all the papers but those onto the ground, where the breeze caught them and lifted them off.

"Listen, everybody," Mrs. Hutchinson was saying to the people around her.

"Ready, Bill?" Mr. Summers asked, and Bill Hutchinson, with one quick glance around at his wife and children, nodded.

"Remember," Mr. Summers said, "take the slips and keep them folded until each person has taken one. Harry, you help little Dave." Mr. Graves took the hand of the little boy, who came willingly with him up to the box. "Take a paper out of the box, Davy," Mr. Summers said. Davy put his hand into the box and laughed. "Take just *one* paper," Mr. Summers said. "Harry, you hold it for him." Mr. Graves took the child's hand and removed the folded paper from the tight fist and held it while little Dave stood next to him and looked up at him wonderingly.

"Nancy next," Mr. Summers said. Nancy was twelve, and her school friends breathed heavily as she went forward, switching her skirt, and took a slip daintily from the box. "Bill, Jr.," Mr. Summers said, and Billy, his face red and his feet over-large, nearly knocked the box over as he got a paper out. "Tessie," Mr. Summers said. She hesitated for a minute, looking around defiantly, and then set her lips and went up to the box. She snatched a paper out and held it behind her.

65   "Bill," Mr. Summers said, and Bill Hutchinson reached into the box and felt around, bringing his hand out at last with the slip of paper in it.

The crowd was quiet. A girl whispered, "I hope it's not Nancy," and the sound of the whisper reached the edges of the crowd.

"It's not the way it used to be," Old Man Warner said clearly. "People ain't the way they used to be."

"All right," Mr. Summers said. "Open the papers. Harry, you open little Dave's."

Mr. Graves opened the slip of paper and there was a general sigh through the crowd as he held it up and everyone could see that it was blank. Nancy and Bill, Jr., opened theirs at the same time, and both beamed and laughed, turning around to the crowd and holding their slips of paper above their heads.

70   "Tessie," Mr. Summers said. There was a pause, and then Mr. Summers looked at Bill Hutchinson, and Bill unfolded his paper and showed it. It was blank.

"It's Tessie," Mr. Summers said, and his voice was hushed. "Show us her paper, Bill."

Bill Hutchinson went over to his wife and forced the slip of paper out of her hand. It had a black spot on it, the black spot Mr. Summers had made the night before with the heavy pencil in the coal-company office. Bill Hutchinson held it up, and there was a stir in the crowd.

"All right, folks," Mr. Summers said. "Let's finish quickly."

Although the villagers had forgotten the ritual and lost the original black box, they still remembered to use stones. The pile of stones the boys had made earlier was ready; there were stones on the ground with the blowing scraps of paper that had come out of the box. Mrs. Delacroix selected a stone so large she had to pick it up with both hands and turned to Mrs. Dunbar. "Come on," she said. "Hurry up."

75   Mrs. Dunbar had small stones in both hands, and she said, gasping for breath, "I can't run at all. You'll have to go ahead and I'll catch up with you."

The children had stones already, and someone gave little Davy Hutchinson a few pebbles.

Tessie Hutchinson was in the center of a cleared space by now, and she held her hands out desperately as the villagers moved in on her. "It isn't fair," she said. A stone hit her on the side of the head.

Old Man Warner was saying, "Come on, come on, everyone." Steve Adams was in the front of the crowd of villagers, with Mrs. Graves beside him.

"It isn't fair, it isn't right," Mrs. Hutchinson screamed, and then they were upon her. *→ differences between "fair" and "right"*

As with many aspects of writing, your thesis and the content will determine your approach to the conclusion. One size does not fit all. In wrapping up a paper, you must consider the emotional effect you have generated in readers so far and the feelings you want them to leave with. You have to ask questions such as these: Do I need to heighten the emotional pull? Do I need to bring them down from a fevered pitch? Do I want to direct them toward thinking or acting a certain way? Do I want to remind them of a particular point by leaving a certain image in their minds? Do I simply want to reinforce the points I made, or do I want to save my most powerful point to send a knockout punch in the conclusion? *don't want to have a formula, like using cliché's.*

In answering these questions, you might see whether any of the techniques below can aid you in developing the most effective conclusion.

Tying Points Together   When a paper has been proceeding at a fairly even, pleasant pace, you do not want to change your tone dramatically to end with a bang. You need, instead, to make sure that your point is clear by reminding the audience of your goal and stating its implications. In tying points together, you might specifically state your thesis for the first time in your essay, following with its ramifications. With such a strategy, you would want to ease concerns about your point by reminding the audience of a lack of alternatives, given the evidence you have presented, and downplaying controversy.

Reread the last three paragraphs in Peter Singer's "Tools for Research" on page 87. His proposal to conduct no research on animals that we are unwilling to conduct on retarded humans might alarm some readers. However, he uses an even tone when he ties his points together, reminding his audience of the dangers of species bias but distancing himself from absolutist thinking.

Singer is advocating change, so he shows the logical progression toward his thesis before asserting it. Tying points together does not mean repeating points that you have already made verbatim. Repetition bogs down a conclusion, giving it a slow, plodding feeling. When you tie points together, you are creating something new from separate, perhaps disparate, parts. This new thing might reinforce old values; critical analysis does not necessarily guarantee fresh insights but rather lets you study the status quo closely. The conclusion that old values have merit brings together the points your analysis produced, so you can state that how intense study of the issue has brought you full circle to the original idea and then discuss what this discovery means to your readers.

might have two thesis, for a good case to some you... the end that you won't reinforce them at... without summarizing... or their come away ideas

Call to Action   A strong critique of an existing situation often leads the writer to want to move his or her audience toward application of the ideas. Calls for action effectively conclude essays by giving audience members options to pursue. A call for action can be as obvious as explaining how to contact a U.S. senator to voice concerns about environmental policy or as subtle as suggesting that every person pick up one piece of trash a day to help in the battle against littering.

However, you cannot slap a call to action onto any essay. The body of your essay must build toward the need for action, and the thesis should closely align with the call. You also want to make sure that your call for action does not depart too radically from reasonable judgment. Demanding that citizens overthrow the government will leave your audience with questions about your credibility. Suggesting ways that voters can put more responsive candidates into office will be met with much less skepticism.

Most of all, a call for action must be sincere. If you do not want to lead the charge, you should not be advising others to do so, no matter how effective such an ending might be.

Last Moment of a Narrative   Papers that use extended narratives in the body can use the last part of the narrative as the conclusion. If you have woven critical analysis into the body and did not announce the thesis in the introduction, you can stop short of completing the story and instead discuss your thesis and end the paper by concluding the story.

For instance, if you had a story about the conflicting perceptions of the causes of an argument between you and your friend, you could narrate the events up to the final point of significance, then launch into your thesis. Your conclusion could pick up the story where you left off, or explain whether you ever came to terms with your friend, or describe what you do now when your perception differs from someone else's.

As long as you do not have more points of significance to analyze, you can wrap up the story with the narration, much like the final scene in a television drama. The climax has passed. Except for shows leaving viewers with a cliffhanger, the last few moments linger on one or two of the main characters, showing what they did or are doing after the fact. An essay with a narrative can end similarly.

Selecting a Powerful Image   If you have used strong imagery in conveying a point, your conclusion can look again at a particularly strong image. Papers that describe the plight of the poor, for instance, may focus on a specific person, leaving an image for people to think about—a homeless person, perhaps, or a child going to bed hungry. If you have incorporated a case study in your paper, you can return to the case study in a manner similar to the strategy for the last moment of a narrative described above. What has happened to this person? Is his or her life continuing in the same way?

Lingering images can be effective when they leave the audience with something to ponder. Images personalize arguments, even if the images are of past events or inanimate objects, such as a mountain or a deserted street. Again, these images will not be effective if they have not been preceded by a discussion of your thesis so that your main point is clear to the audience.

GLORIA NAYLOR

"Mommy, What Does 'Nigger' Mean?"

Gloria Naylor analyzes the word nigger *in the following essay. She ends with an image that, while calm in tone, is emotionally disturbing to the reader.*

Language is the subject. It is the written form with which I've managed to keep the wolf away from the door and, in diaries, to keep my sanity. In spite of this, I consider the written word inferior to the spoken, and much of the frustration experienced by novelists is the awareness that whatever we manage to capture in even the most transcendent passages falls far short of the richness of life. Dialogue achieves its power in the dynamics of a fleeting moment of sight, sound, smell and touch.

I'm not going to enter the debate here about whether it is language that shapes reality or vice versa. That battle is doomed to be waged whenever we seek intermittent reprieve from the chicken and egg dispute. I will simply take the position that the spoken word, like the written word, amounts to a nonsensical arrangement of sounds or letters without a consensus that assigns "meaning." And building from the meanings of what we hear, we order reality. Words themselves are innocuous; it is the consensus that gives them true power.

I remember the first time I heard the word "nigger." In my third-grade class, our math tests were being passed down the rows, and as I handed the papers to a little boy in back of me, I remarked that once again he had received a much lower mark than I did. He snatched his test from me and spit out that word. Had he called me a nymphomaniac or a necrophiliac, I couldn't have been more puzzled. I didn't know what a nigger was, but I knew that whatever it meant, it was something he shouldn't have called me. This was verified when I raised my hand, and in a loud voice repeated what he had said and watched the teacher scold him for using a "bad" word. I was later to go home and ask the inevitable question that every black parent must face—"Mommy, what does 'nigger' mean?"

And what exactly did it mean? Thinking back, I realize that this could not have been the first time the word was used in my presence. I was part of a large extended family that had migrated from the rural South after World War II and formed a close-knit network that gravitated around my maternal grandparents. Their ground-floor apartment in one of the buildings they owned in Harlem was a weekend mecca for my immediate family, along with countless aunts, uncles and cousins who brought along assorted friends. It was a bustling and open house with assorted neighbors and tenants popping in and out to exchange bits of gossip, pick up an old quarrel or referee the ongoing checkers game in which my grandmother cheated shamelessly. They were all there to let down their hair and put up their feet after a week of labor in the factories, laundries and shipyards of New York.

5   Amid the clamor, which could reach deafening proportions—two or three conversations going on simultaneously, punctuated by the sound of a baby's crying somewhere in the back rooms or out on the street—there was still a rigid set of rules about what was said and how. Older children were sent out of the living room when it was time to get into the juicy details about "you-know-who" up on the third floor who had gone and gotten herself "p-r-e-g-n-a-n-t!" But my parents, knowing that I could spell well beyond my years, always demanded that I follow the others out to play. Beyond sexual misconduct and death, everything else was considered harmless for our young ears. And so among the anecdotes of the triumphs and disappointments in the various workings of their lives, the word "nigger" was used in my presence, but it was set within contexts and inflections that caused it to register in my mind as something else.

In the singular, the word was always applied to a man who had distinguished himself in some situation that brought their approval for his strength, intelligence or drive:

"Did Johnny really do that?"

"I'm telling you, that nigger pulled in $6,000 of overtime last year. Said he got enough for a down payment on a house."

When used with a possessive adjective by a woman—"my nigger"—it became a term of endearment for husband or boyfriend. But it could be more than just a term applied to a man. In their mouths it became the pure essence of manhood—a disembodied force that channeled their past history of struggle and present survival against the odds into a victorious statement of being: "Yeah, that old foreman found out quick enough—you don't mess with a nigger."

10   In the plural, it became a description of some group within the community that had overstepped the bounds of decency as my family defined it: Parents who neglected their children, a drunken couple who fought in public, people who simply refused to look for work, those with excessively dirty mouths or unkempt households were all "trifling niggers." This particular circle could forgive hard times, unemployment, the occasional bout of depression—they had gone through all of that themselves—but the unforgivable sin was lack of self-respect.

A woman could never be a "nigger" in the singular, with its connotation of confirming worth. The noun "girl" was its closest equivalent in that sense, but only when used in direct address and regardless of the gender doing the addressing. "Girl" was a token of respect for a woman. The one-syllable word was drawn out to sound like three in recognition of the extra ounce of wit, nerve or daring that the woman had shown in the situation under discussion.

"G-i-r-l, stop. You mean you said that to his face?"

But if the word was used in a third-person reference or shortened so that it almost snapped out of the mouth, it always involved some element of communal disapproval. And age became an important factor in these exchanges. It was only between individuals of the same generation, or from an older person to a younger (but never the other way around), that "girl" would be considered a compliment.

I don't agree with the argument that use of the word "nigger" at this social stratum of the black community was an internalization of racism. The dynamics were the exact opposite: the people in my grandmother's living room took a word that whites used to signify worthlessness or degradation and rendered it impotent. Gathering there together, they transformed "nigger" to signify the varied and complex human beings they knew themselves to be. If the word was to disappear totally from the mouths of even the most racist of white society, no one in that room was naïve enough to believe it would disappear from white minds. Meeting the word head-on, they proved it had absolutely nothing to do with the way they were determined to live their lives.

So there must have been dozens of times that the word "nigger" was spoken in front of me before I reached the third grade. But I didn't "hear" it until it was said by a small pair of lips that had already learned it could be a way to humiliate me. That was the word I went home and asked my mother about. And since she knew that I had to grow up in America, she took me in her lap and explained.

COLLABORATING

Pretend that each member of your group will be honored with an achievement award as a result of accomplishments in school, work, or life. Write three or four paragraphs about your own achievements, then pass that writing to the group member on your left. Each group member is responsible for crossing out all the personal pronouns in the writing they receive so that your writing is now in the third person. Next, group members should write conclusions for the papers in front of them, imagining that the papers will be read at an awards banquet. Group members should share their conclusions with the group and discuss their effectiveness. Which type of conclusion seemed to be the most appropriate? Why? Could more than one type of conclusion have been used? What revisions of the descriptions of accomplishments would have been necessary?

Summary

As a writer, know that your work need not conform to a predetermined structure. Instead, consider the purpose of the writing task, the needs you anticipate from your audience, and the effect of your thesis. The content dictates the strategies for arrangement of your ideas, although organization relies on an introduction, a body, and a conclusion.

The introduction should orient and entice the audience to read more. The body should contain the ideas, examples, and other types of support, including narratives, and the critical analysis should be woven through it. The conclusion wraps up the essay. The placement of the thesis is strategic and is not limited to just the introduction or conclusion.

CHAPTER 5

LANGUAGE CHOICES IN WRITING

Our language choices are crucial to our papers. While we use punctuation and other symbols for coherence, words constitute the bulk of our writing. Mark Twain once said that the difference between the right word and the nearly right word is the difference between lightning and a lightning bug. Language allows our audience to understand us or to miss—perhaps just slightly, but sometimes completely—what we mean.

Some students in a class I once taught suddenly made what I thought were peculiar language choices in their essays. One student, Marcus, seemed to have a large vocabulary but misused words frequently. For example, he used the word *talon* instead of *claw* in describing a cat's foot. His roommate, Craig, explained in one essay how he *arraigned* the guy down the hall of stealing from him; I thought *accused* fit the situation better. I was really thrown when yet a third student, Ding, described a goof-off in his high school as a *lotus-eater*. Since these three students usually sat together in class, I thought their strange language choices might be the product of their peer feedback to one another. So I sat with them during the next peer feedback session.

"When you guys look at each other's papers," I said, "pay close attention to the words you're choosing. It seems like you are trying to reach for larger words in your descriptions, and it confuses me when I am reading your papers."

"You mean you don't know the words?" Marcus smiled at me.

"It's not that," I said. "But I wonder if you are comfortable using these words. They don't sound like you."

Online Study Center

This icon will direct you to web links and additional resources on the website http://college.cengage.com/english/thelin/
114 writing_without_formulas/1e/student_home.html

"Well, we're writing," Craig said. "We're supposed to sound different."

"We want to sound like we belong in college," Marcus chimed in.

"But what makes you think that these words make you sound smarter?" I asked. "I mean, come on, Ding. In your last paper you said a guy in your class was a lotus-eater. Have you ever heard anyone use that expression before?"

Ding shook his head. The only woman in the group, Melissa, was laughing. "I told them they shouldn't do it," she said.

"Do what?" I asked.

"They said we should use a thesaurus," Melissa announced. "But I told them it was a bad idea."

The men in the group looked sheepish. "It's not like we were cheating or anything," Marcus said.

Marcus, Craig, and Ding were not cheating, but they were depriving themselves of understanding the richness of language. They were also communicating poorly because they did not appreciate how language functions. While a term like *lotus-eater* might sound exotic, it carries a meaning that goes beyond the synonym Ding found in the thesaurus. A lotus-eater is someone who indulges in luxury, ignoring the concerns of day-to-day living. The term is archaic, referring to the people in Homer's *Odyssey* who ate fruit coming from a plant called a lotus that produced a dazed state. Did Ding mean to employ this term as a metaphor to implicate the class clown in drug use? Was he implying that the guy was a rich kid who had it made and didn't bother studying? Ding was not aware of the associations of the term, and using it in this context sounded strange. An audience could have easily misinterpreted him or could have read inaccurate implications into his story.

Here is the draft in which Ding used the term *lotus-eater*. Notice the other places where the vocabulary usage sounds strained.

DING GUANG

Negative Cliques in Schools

You can look at all different schools in America and they will have the same types of cliques. Students gain status by becoming associated with others on a social hierarchy. Often they will abandon their anomalous characteristics to match the habits and quirks of pupils more popular than themselves. This tendency allows for negative behavior to impinge upon the learning of others.

An observation conducted at a high school in the San Fernando Valley supports the contention that cliques will endanger both the person and the students surrounding them. Many negative cliques exist, but the ones that confine themselves to after school activities are relatively harmless. Skiers, jocks, and heavy metal enthusiasts will permit their ideologies to filter into the classroom and cafeteria, but their main actions engage elsewhere. They simply associate with others like them. The dangers, as documented here, come from the group who do not really have any activities except loquaciousness and tomfoolery.

Every class in this particular high school contained individuals who were too lazy to do their homework and constantly caused mischief. The main lotus-eater was a student named Kyle. He reclined in the back of his classes, his legs extended onto another desk, and refused to participate intelligently. He would remark on the answers given by other pupils, trying to take the attention off of them and onto himself. In so doing, he relegated their learning to an inauspicious endeavor and substituted his needs for the needs of others. Instructors tried to be patient, but they even would laugh and consort to banter with him.

For example, he had not studied for a certain quiz in history. The students only had 15 minutes to complete this quiz, but they had been given sufficient notice of it. While they struggled to recall answers to questions, Kyle would shout out ridiculous statements to the more studious pupils like, "Let me use your cheat sheet when you're through, Benson." The teacher issued a warning to Kyle, but since he was going to fail the quiz anyway, the warnings went unheeded. He fidgeted, tried to replicate from the student in front of him, and noisily ate a snack. Some pupils had difficulty concentrating and were unable to recall answers or did not finish.

Other students would mimic Kyle's persona and make jokes during crucial times in class. It appeared they had no incentive to perform adequately in school. Any class where the loafers attended ended up being disrupted through puerile behavior. The formation of this cabal resulted in reduced education for others. Therefore, cliques can give youths identity but they can be destructive if not properly monitored and curtailed.

DISCUSSION

Do you think Ding's vocabulary was influenced by the audience he perceived for this paper? Discuss Ding's intended audience and try to find more appropriate vocabulary to substitute for words or terms in the paper that sound awkward. What other types of audiences might a student target for a topic such as Ding's, and how would the audiences affect the word choices?

Vocabulary growth comes about gradually through experience, reading, and interacting in society. No one can develop a new, stronger vocabulary overnight, and finding synonyms in a thesaurus will not cover up other deficiencies in a paper. As a writer, you need to be aware of the strength of language and of how it operates, not just within a paper, but in society also.

We must search for precision in our language choices and also realize that we cannot completely control the effect words will have on people. Words can carry different meanings for different audiences, so again the influence of the reader is important as we prepare any piece of writing.

DISCUSSION

Think of the many terms, especially slang expressions, you may use or have heard in reference to the following items: home, boyfriend or girlfriend, police officers, free time, quality (when something is good or bad, whatever that thing might be). Have one class member write all of the terms you come up with on the board.

When you are finished, look at the lists, and discuss what you think might be the origins of some of the terms. What happens when you hear someone use these terms, especially the slang expressions, in contexts that do not reflect their origins? Do the terms lose their power? Do they take on new meanings? Do they adjust comfortably into new settings? Talk about why and how this process occurs.

Language can entrance readers, evoke pity, secure cultural bonding, produce outrage, and affect society in many other ways. As writers, we should understand the way language functions and the ways in which we manipulate it and it manipulates us.

Mediating Experiences

The world exists outside our perception of it. The only way we can understand it is through language. Without language, we cannot give meaning to the sensory impressions that barrage us. Furthermore, we need language to communicate with others—to share what we experience. Language mediates among the writer, the audience, sensory impression, and even nonsensory events in forming what we know as experience or reality. While language takes many forms, such as bodily gestures and signs, we'll concentrate on the written word.

If words mediate our experience, choosing the best words possible becomes vitally important. Every time we delete one word in favor of another, we subtly change the reality of a situation. We are helping create reality as we go. How do we know, then, what is appropriate and what is not in word choice? What is the difference between fabrication and the selection of words that enhance an experience? The following three tips help answer these questions.

Consensus Building When you experience an event, your memory records the details that you found most striking. You may miss other details. Our brains are so remarkable that they often store data that passed under our radar. Some activities, such as brainstorming and freewriting (see Chapter 6), can help us recall details we missed. However, sometimes we must rely on the recollections of others to construct the best understanding of what happened. Unless something happened to you alone, other people will have seen it. The news media and others often employ audiovisual equipment to record events of social or political importance.

You do not want to surrender your personal vision of an event, but when writing about it, you need to verify your impressions with others involved or check the records if the event was recorded or otherwise documented. By putting together several accounts, you can build a consensus, even if just a localized one, about the truth or reality of a situation. Once you establish the truth, you can choose words that accurately convey the consensus and, thus, avoid misleading your audience.

People's memories vary, and some recollections conflict in key ways. When this happens, you can account for differing perspectives by giving both versions and then expressing what you believe to be the case. For example, let's suppose you heard opposing accounts of a friend's behavior while watching a play on campus. We'll call him Bert. One account had Bert yawning loudly and texting throughout the production. The other said he was bored but politely paid attention. Knowing Bert, you could write the following:

A classmate of Bert's was very disturbed by his behavior at last night's play. She claimed that Bert started yawning in an exaggerated way early during the play, even stretching out his arms at one point, and then stayed on his cellphone throughout the rest of the night, texting and viewing websites. Bert's friend, though, said that he did not notice Bert on his cellphone but that the play was boring, so he had no doubt that Burt quietly yawned once or twice. Bert did not want to attend the play and only did so for extra credit in his literature course. He is known for being disruptive when he is bored and does not mind being rude. I have seen him yawn in class before with that exaggerated stretch, so it would be in character for him to act that way during a play he did not like.

Both perspectives are given here, but you clearly state which one you believe to be true and why. We talk about solo experience in the "Describing and Shaping" section later in this chapter.

Naming the World   Use language that falls within the parameters of your vocabulary. A thesaurus may remind you of words you have forgotten, but you do not want to use the thesaurus the way Marcus, Craig, and Ding did in the opening example. You want to stretch your vocabulary by using appropriate words, and you want to acquire new words to build your vocabulary. However, always keep in mind the connection between reality and the language that mediates it.

Sometimes our minds search for a word to describe a situation, and we just do not feel right until we can remember what that word is. The reason for this feeling is the connection between language and experience. When we are not able to recall a particular word, we sense that we have not properly recaptured a moment or correctly expressed our feelings.

There are also times when we need new language in order to act, a process called "naming the world" by Brazilian educator Paulo Freire. In this process, individuals or groups empower themselves by utilizing terminology to cast a more appropriate light on a situation. At its best, naming the world allows for an understanding of forces that influence us in almost invisible ways. Feminists, for instance, use *patriarchy* to name the sense of oppression and dislocation women feel in a world dominated by men and male norms. Once a source of oppression can be named, action can be taken to correct the situation.

Figurative Language   Writers name their worlds in many ways, such as by using metaphors and similes. These words allow for comparisons among events and feelings that are not literally similar. They attempt to convey an attitude or perspective by encouraging readers to transfer their feelings about one event to another. A writer might say, "With a gazelle-like burst, the runner sprinted to victory." A gazelle has four legs and many other features completely unlike human features. By using *gazelle-like*, the writer wants the audience to associate this particular sprint with the amazing speed of the animal, conjuring an image assumed to be familiar to all.

When you use the word *like* in a description, as in the above example, you have created a simile. In contrast, a metaphor implies rather than states a relationship with something literally dissimilar. Metaphors often appear in the form of a verb, as in the sentence "The news of his death crushed me." The news is not literally squashing the person, but the use of *crushed* conveys the pain the writer feels.

In the following reading, does the figurative language suggest more than a concrete description would?

MARTIN LUTHER KING, JR.

I Have a Dream

This famous speech by Martin Luther King, Jr., employs figurative language. Isolate and list the figurative language, and discuss its effect in this speech. King also makes use of allusions, which are references to famous works of art and literature, or, at times, historical events or persons. Do you think King's Biblical allusions function the same way his figurative language does?

Five score years ago, a great American, in whose symbolic shadow we stand, signed the Emancipation Proclamation. This momentous decree came as a great beacon light of hope to millions of Negro slaves who had been seared in the flames of withering injustice. It came as a joyous daybreak to end the long night of captivity. But one hundred years later, we must face the tragic fact that the Negro is still not free.

One hundred years later, the life of the Negro is still sadly crippled by the manacles of segregation and the chains of discrimination. One hundred years later, the Negro lives on a lonely island of poverty in the midst of a vast ocean of material prosperity. One hundred years later, the Negro is still languishing in the corners of American society and finds himself an exile in his own land.

So we have come here today to dramatize an appalling condition. In a sense we have come to our nation's capital to cash a check. When the architects of our republic wrote the magnificent words of the Constitution and the Declaration of Independence, they were signing a promissory note to which every American was to fall heir.

This note was a promise that all men would be guaranteed the inalienable rights of life, liberty, and the pursuit of happiness. It is obvious today that America has defaulted on this promissory note insofar as her citizens of color are concerned. Instead of honoring this sacred obligation, America has given the Negro people a bad check which has come back marked "insufficient funds." But we refuse to believe that the bank of justice is bankrupt. We refuse to believe that there are insufficient funds in the great vaults of opportunity of this nation.

5   So we have come to cash this check—a check that will give us upon demand the riches of freedom and the security of justice. We have also come to this hallowed spot to remind America of the fierce urgency of now. This is no time to engage in the luxury of cooling off or to take the tranquilizing drug of gradualism. Now is the time to rise from the dark and desolate valley of segregation to the sunlit path of racial justice. Now is the time to open the doors of opportunity to all of God's children. Now is the time to lift our nation from the quicksands of racial injustice to the solid rock of brotherhood.

It would be fatal for the nation to overlook the urgency of the moment and to underestimate the determination of the Negro. This sweltering summer of the Negro's legitimate discontent will not pass until there is an invigorating autumn of freedom and equality. Nineteen sixty-three is not an end, but a beginning. Those who hope that the Negro needed to blow off steam and will now be content will have a rude awakening if the nation returns to business as usual. There will be neither rest nor tranquility in America until the Negro is granted his citizenship rights.

The whirlwinds of revolt will continue to shake the foundations of our nation until the bright day of justice emerges. But there is something that I must say to my people who stand on the warm threshold which leads into the palace of justice. In the process of gaining our rightful place we must not be guilty of wrongful deeds. Let us not seek to satisfy our thirst for freedom by drinking from the cup of bitterness and hatred.

We must forever conduct our struggle on the high plane of dignity and discipline. We must not allow our creative protest to degenerate into physical violence. Again and again we must rise to the majestic heights of meeting physical force with soul force.

The marvelous new militancy which has engulfed the Negro community must not lead us to distrust of all white people, for many of our white brothers, as evidenced by their presence here today, have come to realize that their destiny is tied up with our destiny and their freedom is inextricably bound to our freedom.

10   We cannot walk alone. And as we walk, we must make the pledge that we shall march ahead. We cannot turn back. There are those who are asking the devotees of civil rights, "When will you be satisfied?" We can never be

satisfied as long as our bodies, heavy with the fatigue of travel, cannot gain lodging in the motels of the highways and the hotels of the cities. We cannot be satisfied as long as the Negro's basic mobility is from a smaller ghetto to a larger one. We can never be satisfied as long as a Negro in Mississippi cannot vote and a Negro in New York believes he has nothing for which to vote. No, no, we are not satisfied, and we will not be satisfied until justice rolls down like waters and righteousness like a mighty stream.

I am not unmindful that some of you have come here out of great trials and tribulations. Some of you have come fresh from narrow cells. Some of you have come from areas where your quest for freedom left you battered by the storms of persecution and staggered by the winds of police brutality. You have been the veterans of creative suffering. Continue to work with the faith that unearned suffering is redemptive.

Go back to Mississippi, go back to Alabama, go back to Georgia, go back to Louisiana, go back to the slums and ghettos of our northern cities, knowing that somehow this situation can and will be changed. Let us not wallow in the valley of despair. I say to you today, my friends, that in spite of the difficulties and frustrations of the moment, I still have a dream. It is a dream deeply rooted in the American dream.

I have a dream that one day this nation will rise up and live out the true meaning of its creed: "We hold these truths to be self-evident: that all men are created equal." I have a dream that one day on the red hills of Georgia the sons of former slaves and the sons of former slaveowners will be able to sit down together at a table of brotherhood. I have a dream that one day even the state of Mississippi, a desert state, sweltering with the heat of injustice and oppression, will be transformed into an oasis of freedom and justice. I have a dream that my four children will one day live in a nation where they will not be judged by the color of their skin but by the content of their character. I have a dream today.

I have a dream that one day the state of Alabama, whose governor's lips are presently dripping with the words of interposition and nullification, will be transformed into a situation where little black boys and black girls will be able to join hands with little white boys and white girls and walk together as sisters and brothers. I have a dream today. I have a dream that one day every valley shall be exalted, every hill and mountain shall be made low, the rough places will be made plain, and the crooked places will be made straight, and the glory of the Lord shall be revealed, and all flesh shall see it together. This is our hope. This is the faith with which I return to the South. With this faith we will be able to hew out of the mountain of despair a stone of hope. With this faith we will be able to transform the jangling discords of our nation into a beautiful symphony of brotherhood. With this faith we will be able to work together, to pray together, to struggle together, to go to jail together, to stand up for freedom together, knowing that we will be free one day.

This will be the day when all of God's children will be able to sing with 15 a new meaning, "My country, 'tis of thee, sweet land of liberty, of thee I sing. Land where my fathers died, land of the pilgrim's pride, from every mountainside, let freedom ring." And if America is to be a great nation, this must become true. So let freedom ring from the prodigious hilltops of New Hampshire. Let freedom ring from the mighty mountains of New York. Let freedom ring from the heightening Alleghenies of Pennsylvania! Let freedom ring from the snowcapped Rockies of Colorado! Let freedom ring from the curvaceous peaks of California! But not only that; let freedom ring from Stone Mountain of Georgia! Let freedom ring from Lookout Mountain of Tennessee! Let freedom ring from every hill and every molehill of Mississippi. From every mountainside, let freedom ring.

When we let freedom ring, when we let it ring from every village and every hamlet, from every state and every city, we will be able to speed up that day when all of God's children, black men and white men, Jews and Gentiles, Protestants and Catholics, will be able to join hands and sing in the words of the old Negro spiritual, "Free at last, free at last; thank God Almighty, we are free at last!"

Building consensus and naming the world can serve many purposes. You can do it in numerous ways without having to use words that go beyond your vocabulary. Words you wield effectively can empower you. With that power, however, you have to be ethical. Figurative language can be misused, as we will see when we discuss euphemism and obfuscation later in this chapter. When you feel you have named the world accurately, you can feel confident that you have not fabricated and instead have enhanced your writing.

WRITING

Write a brief story about the very first memory you have. Describe the event or scene fully from your recollection, and try to find the right words to capture the sensation you remember. Do not settle for words that do not feel right. Feel free to use metaphors and similes.

When you are satisfied that you have recorded this event accurately, check with your parents or with other relatives who might have been there or might have seen what you remember. What can they add to your memory? Can you include their ideas to build a consensus that does not violate your sense of the event or scene?

When you discuss the stories in class, ask your fellow students if their memories take place before or after they were able to talk. With rare exceptions, you will find that first memories are of events or scenes from after they were able to use language. Otherwise, people struggle to remember what happened and have only vague impressions. They didn't have the language to interpret the events around them, so they cannot recollect those events now.

Describing and Shaping

Chapter 3 discussed the uses of specific and concrete words when writing about life experiences to appeal to the senses of readers. We mentioned that such words help readers relate to places and events that they have not experienced for themselves. When we describe situations, we are shaping the way readers will perceive these events.

When narrating a solo personal experience, you are your readers' only source about what transpired. The same is true when you summarize research from an obscure source or discuss world events not known to your audience, although ultimately this type of writing can be independently verified. While readers can judge the truthfulness of what you say through their sense of logic, probability, and common knowledge, they rely on you to give as accurate an account as possible and to keep them interested. The words you choose comprise their understanding of the event and re-create the person, place, or thing you describe. Be aware of the effects of your word choices.

Vague Words   Perfectly good words in the English language do not always convey enough information to allow a reader to envision a situation. The verb *to see*, for instance, carries multiple meanings through its various usages and can elicit many different responses from a reader. The writer needs to narrow the meaning by choosing words that are more specific. A thesaurus can be handy at these times, if it is used properly. The synonyms found in a thesaurus cannot casually be inserted into a paper; substituting one word for another alters the reader's impression, even if only slightly. But the changes that a different word brings about might shape the reader's impression to a much more accurate representation of a situation.

Think of the different images called up by some of the synonyms of *to see* in the sense of looking: spot, stare, glance, spy, detect, notice, leer, gape, observe, peer, and ogle. Each of these synonyms evokes much more from a reader. Inserting one of them for *see* shifts the image conveyed to the reader. If the new image captures the situation accurately, the word should be used. If the word creates an impression that confuses the situation or incorrectly represents an element in it, the word should not be used.

WRITING

Look through your current writing assignment, and circle words that are vague—words that convey only a general impression of the subject or the action. Consult a thesaurus to find synonyms, and determine whether any of the choices better represent what you are describing. Do not simply substitute a synonym for the word you already have, especially if you have never heard the synonym before.

Connotations   Words have common definitions that we call denotations. The denotations allow us to find synonyms for the words. But words that have essentially the same denotation hold further meanings that signal perspectives on a situation. These meanings, called connotations, are frequently subtle; they might be suggested by differing usages of the words in a subculture or in previous generations. Often, the dictionary alerts us to connotations through primary definitions or through secondary definitions.

For example, take two synonyms of *see*—*observe* and *spy*. Either word can be substituted in the sentence "I saw [observed/spied] a difference in her behavior." *Observe* implies close scrutiny; the person has studied and noticed a difference in behavior. Readers associate *spy* with a secretive type of seeing, as if the person were prying. The association comes from the noun form of the word *spy*, which conjures up images of espionage and secret agents. This association could cast a negative light on the person doing the seeing or make us wonder about the effect of the difference in behavior. The verb choice sets up an additional impression for the reader. The question is whether we want readers to have that impression.

We can convey much more with some words than with others. If our purpose involves displaying an attitude toward a certain act, understanding the connotations of words is important. Some connotations are fairly easy to apprehend, and the dictionary helps us. *Thin, slender,* and *skinny,* for instance, are synonyms, but the dictionary tells us that *skinny* means unappealingly thin, while *slender* implies attractively thin.

Sometimes we must rely on the audience's understanding of what a word connotes. For some audiences, the word *aggressive* connotes positive images. An aggressive ballplayer is someone we want playing on our team, and the term does not disturb most readers in this context. While we might want our doctor to exercise caution in diagnosing us, we also want him to seek a cure aggressively, and the description would give us confidence in the care we are receiving. But some audience members associate the term *aggressive* with violent, careless behavior, and they would react negatively to this description. These readers might see the aggressive ballplayer as confrontational or perceive the aggressive pursuit of a cure as reckless behavior by the doctor.

Peer readers, as discussed in Chapter 3, can be of great value to writers in gauging how a larger audience might react. If we direct peer readers to look for language choices, they can tell us which words or phrases produced an association, whether that association was positive or negative, and whether it was within our goals or outside of them. Our sentences can be greatly strengthened through the proper understanding of the connotations of words, but they can also mislead readers and leave an impression outside our intention if we casually insert words that connote more than we realize.

MIKE ROSE

from The Mind at Work

In this brief excerpt from the introduction of The Mind at Work: Valuing the Intelligence of the American Worker, *Mike Rose analyzes the term* skill *in relation to intelligence by relating its connotations to readers. Does this analysis put Rose into a position to rename* skill, *as discussed in the subsection on naming the world?*

Within the West there are powerful research traditions that yield other conceptions of intelligence and other means to assess it. In various ways, these traditions posit, for example, that there are multiple components to intelligence, or even multiple intelligences; that intelligence is variable and dynamic; that social context is crucial to its emergence and display; that creativity, emotion, aesthetic response, and the use of the body—removed from traditional psychometric definitions and tests of intelligence—must be considered as aspects of intelligent behavior. And, finally, it is very important to note that any discussion of intelligence is culture-bound. Some aspects of what we consider intelligence might well overlap with definitions from other cultures, but many cultures posit a range of further or different attributes to intelligence, for example, the ability to live in harmony with others.

It is undisputed that formal education will affect one's score on an intelligence test, since the tests tend to be heavy on verbal and numerical items. The big challenge to test designers, then, is to create at least a few components that, in theory, will not be affected by schooling, for example, identifying the missing element in a visual pattern. Though the success of this endeavor is (yet another) contested issue, it seems pretty clear that it is difficult—some say impossible—to tease out the effects of education (including a familiarity with and investment in tests like these) from the effect of "pure" intelligence. Here's what concerns me. . . . If one does well on an intelligence test, that clearly indicates some kind of cognitive competence. But if one doesn't do well—and, historically, poor performers would include low-income, working people—then the meaning of the score is much less clear. So, we have a measure that works only at the upper end of the scale. To do well tells us something about intelligence—and, usually, schooling—but not to do well provides much less information about intellectual capacity . . . though that poor performance may speak volumes about educational opportunity. My worry is the ease with which poor performance gets interpreted as an accurate measure of intelligence, and the effect that interpretation has on the test-taker, both personally and societally.

This is not a call for a simplified egalitarianism. I am not denying the obvious fact that people come to any pursuit with different interests, talents, knacks for things, motivations, capabilities. Nor am I claiming that all bodies of knowledge and expressions of mind are of the same level of cognitive complexity and social importance. All the cultures I'm familiar with make judgments about competence in the domains that matter to them. (Though ours is more obsessed than any I know with developing measures of the mind and schemes to rank them.) No, the distressing thing is that both in our institutional systems and in our informal talk we tend to label entire categories of work and the people associated with them in ways that generalize, erase cognitive variability, and diminish whole traditions of human activity. Attributions of merit and worth flow throughout the process. We order, we rank, we place at steps upon a ladder rather than appreciating an abundant and varied cognitive terrain.

Skill. Let's begin with the *American Heritage Dictionary.* Skill is "proficiency, facility, or dexterity that is acquired or developed through training or experience." In traditional usage, this proficiency would be related to the use of body or hand, though more recently, the word *skill* has come to apply to a wide range of activities. We talk, for example, of communication skills or general problem-solving skills.

5   It is important to remember, however, that what gets defined as a skill is historically and culturally determined, and this process is of special significance in labeling kinds of work. The politics and power plays by which particular interest groups get one kind of work categorized as "skilled" and another as "semiskilled" or "unskilled" have significant economic and social consequences. Another historical phenomenon to note here is the increasing role school has played over the past century in developing and certifying skills that, in previous eras, would have been developed within the job setting itself. The value that a skill has is also determined by time and place. In the rhetoric of the "new economy," for example, communication skills or general problem-solving skills or the ability to work in teams are privileged, while more specific mechanical skills—associated with conventional blue-collar work—tend to be perceived as less valuable. All of these processes of definition and the status they confer involve attributions of cognition and intelligence.

Charged Language

Writers must strive to act ethically. A writer who resorts to name-calling, tries to establish guilt by association, or uses evocative language to arouse readers' fears and doubts has gone outside accepted ethics. Such tricks with words, called charged language, often damage the writer's credibility. Much like the person who spreads gossip, the writer might gain momentary popularity but soon establishes a reputation of untrustworthiness. More important, the writer polarizes audience members and undermines any attempt she or he has made to utilize critical analysis.

Name-calling tends to be blatant and is easy to avoid. If a writer has strong feelings about a person and considers that person to be an insensitive lout, terms that clearly express such sentiments can be weeded out in the revising process. The more subtle moments of charged language, though, can slip by. Sometimes, for example, writers defending one interpretation of the Second Amendment refer to gun control advocates as "anti-gun people" or contend that the first action of third-world dictators is to remove all weapons from the citizenry. The term *anti-gun* can conjure up negative images because *anti-* emphasizes oppositional behavior (advocacy groups usually emphasize what they favor: pro-life and pro-choice, for example). The reference to dictators associates gun control with tyranny. Not only does this language misrepresent the position of gun control advocates, but it also creates images that make engaging in critical analysis difficult. Danger lurks when a writer does not monitor her or his writing for such language choices. Readers might be angry if they feel a writer has tried to manipulate them, and they probably will not consider the writer's perspective further.

Slang and Obscenity

Language serves many purposes. One of them is to unite groups. Another is to express the inexpressible. Slang and obscene words fulfill this purpose. Their place in writing, though, depends on a profound understanding of the context and audience. It can be argued that these words create a world of their own and, thus, shape reader perception better than more conventional word choices. A well-placed obscenity can perhaps make a description appear more real or down to earth. Similarly, slang shows membership in a group, conveying a sense of cool that might be compromised if replaced by other terminology.

Professional writers sometimes use slang and obscenity. You have probably read articles or web pages that use slang and obscenity extensively. However, the writers (and their editors) are aware of the possible consequences of such language choices. Much obscenity is linked to misogyny and racism. In other words, it degrades women and people of color. Slang tends to become out of date in popular culture and can be repetitious.

If you are quoting dialogue, it is fair and accurate to use the words that you heard. Narrative relies on a believable voice, something we discuss later in the chapter, and some writing situations call for the narrator to be trusted in the culture he or she describes. But the impression you convey matters. If your use of slang or obscenity deflects from your main point, you should edit it out.

Start by playing with the words that come to you immediately to see how they shape the reality you are creating for your reader, and test them on peer readers. Rather than reflexively self-editing language simply because some groups feel it is bad, think critically and carefully about your audience. If good reasons for change prevail—if, for example, you are not communicating effectively (some obscene words are used so frequently that they do not even work to intensify a situation) or if your audience feels insulted—revise accordingly.

RICK BASS

from The Lost Grizzlies

This excerpt comes from a firsthand account of searching for grizzly bears in the San Juan Mountains, where grizzlies are thought to be extinct. Rick Bass is describing the arrival of Doug Peacock to a preliminary meeting of an informal research group the two have organized. Decide how the use of obscenity shapes the reader's impression of Peacock in this passage, which is his first appearance in the book. Is something conveyed through the obscenity that could not have been conveyed through other words? How does it align with other characteristics revealed about Peacock shortly thereafter?

The next day, down in Colorado, when I reach Betty Feazel's ranch the aspens are as Doug had promised they'd be: in the full glory of autumn. I turn up the long gravel drive and see Peacock and Betty at the top. Peacock's walking around in shorts and hiking boots and a long flannel jacket. As usual, his wild thinning hair is askew. Dust still rises from the driveway; he's just arrived, too. He always reminds me of how good it feels to be alive. I get out of my truck and we shake hands, then hug.

"Wow," Peacock says, spreading his arms, "just look at this." Betty stands next to him, beaming, as if she'd planted these snow-crowned mountains herself. "Oh, shit," he says, and whirls around and stalks back to his Subaru. The tail end of the car nearly touches the ground under its load of bulging burlap sacks. "I forgot gifts. I was in Santa Fe last night. Jeez."

Empty beer cans, books on tape, canteens, and a pair of binoculars tumble out when he lifts the hatchback. He lunges, tries to catch each object as it falls.

"Aw, fuck it," he says, and crawls inside. The burlap sacks contain peppers, hundreds of big, red, spicy chili peppers. "Here," he says, wrestling one of the bags out. "To cook with. Where can I put this?"

5   Betty claps her hands, delighted. "In the basement," she says.

When I get within ten feet of Peacock's car, my eyes start to water and I sneeze.

"It was wonderful driving up here, breathing all that shit," he says, laboring beneath the bag. It looks like he's bought every pepper in Santa Fe. Just then Marty comes driving up in a dusty brown Volkswagen Rabbit. There is a big wolf-looking dog in the back seat of the car: his faithful, ancient Keetina.

We've come four thousand miles altogether, the three of us, and have arrived within ten minutes of one another. We go inside with Betty and Lucy and Bruce to reconnoiter—to look at photos and maps and listen to background information.

We'll only have a few days; I've got a grouse-hunting appointment with a friend back in Montana early the next week. This is mainly a trip to see and smell and feel the country, rather than to try to decide right away, yes or no, if there are any grizzlies left.

10   We sit like students at Betty's long dining room table. The farmhouse's windowpanes are wavy with age, bending the straw-colored sunlight that passes through them. Betty's energy is inspiring as she leans over the maps and points out areas where rumored sightings have occurred.

"Oh Jesus," Peacock says, looking at the topo maps. "Oh fuck, that's good country. Excuse me," he says to Betty, but she waves him off. "Oh fuck," he says again, "fuck yes."

The rumors are good. They're so similar to the rumors of the sixties and seventies that it seems certain a bear or bears are in there. A bear with a large hump was seen along Jo Jo Creek (most of the place names in the book have been changed to protect grizzly habitats). An outfitter saw what he believed were grizzly tracks—ten to twelve inches long, with big claws—along Blazo Creek in the summer of 1989. Sightings were reported along Wolf Creek Pass. The following year, Tony Povolitis, a senior scientist for the Humane Society, found a big track near Grizzly Creek and photographed it. We pass the photo around. It was taken in snow, and the track looks huge. We can tell where the claws landed. It's not conclusive, but it looks good.

Tom Beck is the biologist who headed the two-year Colorado Division of Wildlife study in the South San Juans in the wake of the Wiseman bear's "confirmation." Four trackers lived in tents from June to October, 1980 to 1982, and hunted for grizzly sign and set snares. Peacock bristles and huffs at this method; he's convinced that these bears won't be trapped and that all bears, especially grizzlies, know when they're being hunted.

Beck wrote, of that previous search, "Sometimes they'd trap a bear and really get excited because of its size, bleached tips on its brown fur, and the way it stood giving it a humped back, they'd swear they caught a grizzly." But all the trappers ever caught in their snares were black bears. Gary Gerhardt, a staff writer for the *Rocky Mountain News* who's been covering the rumors, wrote, "Beck said the division [of wildlife] assumes there aren't any grizzlies in Colorado, and it's going to take some strong documentation—such as a grizzly in a trap—for him to believe any are left in the San Juans."

One can imagine Peacock's terror at this philosophy. He's been trying 15 to round up money to put a couple of fieldworkers in the San Juans, but he believes that they should engage in lower-impact methods to document grizzlies, such as photography or making casts of a track, but no trapping.

We could, of course, solve the problem quickly and simply. We could find grizzly sign or photograph a grizzly. I've got my camera. We could end all this political foolishness, all these abstractions. It might happen.

Now, in late September, the grizzlies are up high, getting ready to den. We aim to investigate the north-facing sides of the San Juans, and other places. We plan to do a lot of bushwhacking, crawling around in jungle and heavy windfall—which is not where bears typically hang out. But Peacock has a theory that any remaining San Juan grizzlies are atypical. They're smarter, and over the last forty years the mothers have raised their cubs to be solitary and to avoid humans. He's certain that these bears will by now be active primarily at night.

Before we begin to look for sign of them, we'll camp for two or three days at twelve thousand feet, so as to thin our blood and ready ourselves for the long hikes and heavy packs.

The next morning we say goodbye to Betty, Lucy, and Bruce and set off in two cars. We can feel their hopes riding with us like a net, a thing of a certain density, a specific weight. Of course the odds are long that in this brief trip we'll see a grizzly or find any sign of one, but there's always the chance. That empty place in our hearts.

He knows the habits of wild grizzlies better perhaps than anyone else in 20 the country, and yet he abhors scientific meetings, academic conferences, and the like. He is an eloquent writer, and yet you absolutely cannot wring more than one or two sentences out of him concerning literature. He was a medic in Vietnam—a soldier, a warrior—and yet he dissolves into loving baby talk around children—around anyone under voting age.

For all of Peacock's complexity, however, he has basically two behavior patterns that I've observed. The first and most striking mode of behavior occurs when he's wired with an anxiety that leads to a mania reminiscent of the Bugs Bunny–Tasmanian Devil cartoons. When he's wound up that tight—twirling and blinking rapidly, owlishly, as if he can't believe how the world has turned against him—he'll invariably bolt, whether through a crowd of people or a heavy, tangled briar bush. Once spooked, he'll walk furiously away, his body seeking isobars of lower pressure—a calmer register of atmospheric conditions against his cells, is how I picture it. Peacock may be out of control, but it's nothing personal against the people who've spooked him. The second mode of behavior involves deep, unpretentious happiness, like the parody of a man in a beer commercial who takes a sip of fine brew, smacks his lips, and says "Ahhhhh!"

COLLABORATING

Your instructor will select two students who will go into the hall and then, one at a time, walk through the classroom door. As individuals, write down brief descriptions of what you saw. Compare notes with group members, looking at the words that you have used.

For each action verb in your description, such as *walk*, find three synonyms to describe the action. Do the same thing for each noun, then for any adjectives you used. Work with each other to avoid repetition. Does the description change through the use of the synonyms? Did the synonyms blur the situation or convey it more accurately? Discuss the effect of language on your descriptions, and decide what words best capture the situation.

Euphemisms

The previous section stresses the way language can shape a world for readers. While most writers want to be honest, some try to cover up the reality of a situation for their own purposes. As a reader, you want to be alert for euphemisms, expressions that make a painful or coarse situation seem less harsh. Euphemisms avoid bluntness. Instead of saying a woman is pregnant, some prefer to say she is "expecting" or use the archaic expression "in the family way."

Euphemisms present three problems. First, they can prevent clarity if the reader is not familiar with the expression that is substituted. Second, they can be used to mislead, as when a battlefield is called a "theater," thus equating killing with entertainment. And third, they tend to cover up natural experiences, thereby reinforcing ignorance and preserving a puritanical view, such as when "sins of the flesh" is substituted for direct reference to sexual acts.

Writers can drift toward these expressions if they grow overly concerned about audience reaction or want to sound more sophisticated or dignified. You do not want to sound prissy, though, and talk around your subject without ever naming it. Readers will think you are obfuscating your point, or trying to hide something. Furthermore, writing about the subject in direct terms will help in your critical analysis, as will studying the euphemisms society tries to substitute for concrete language.

DAVID CAY JOHNSTON

from Perfectly Legal

In this passage, David Cay Johnston shows how the manipulation of a term obfuscated an agenda and duped the public into supporting a tax break that benefited the extremely wealthy only.

Patricia Soldano owns Cymric Family Office Services in Costa Mesa, California, which takes the hassle out of everyday life for the rich extended families whose wealth it manages. Cymric creates budgets for family members, pays their personal bills, manages their investments, keeps track of all the paperwork and prepares their tax returns with a focus on paying as little as possible. The name Soldano gave her firm refers to an ancient breed of pussycat with a double coat of fur that requires special grooming.

A prim middle-aged MBA who maintains a laser focus on the problems and desires of her clients, Soldano decided one day in the early nineties that the best way to serve them better would be to get the estate tax repealed. When Soldano first raised the matter in her intensely private and wealthy circle in Orange County, she encountered doubt. "I was told it couldn't be done, that no one cared about the estate tax except the people paying it," Soldano said. It was at the time the conventional wisdom—no one cared about the estate tax except two groups. One was the very rich, or at least those among the very rich who hated it but figured they had no one with whom they could make common cause. The other group was wonks who believed it was critical to ensuring that America would be a meritocracy and not an aristocracy of inherited privilege and power. Soldano believed she could change that wisdom.

Soldano hired Patton Boggs, a Washington lobbying firm, and built alliances to wealthy families with privately held companies and a public history of hostility to taxes, notably the candy-making Mars and wine-making Gallo families. She founded the Center for the Study of Taxation. Despite its name there is nothing scholarly about the center. It publishes brochures opposing the estate tax, relying on anecdotes and witty quotes, not scholarship, to make its points. It is a pure marketing organization, no different from the big ad agencies except that it sells ideology instead of detergent.

She also hired Frank Luntz, the Republican pollster and idea man, to examine public attitudes toward the estate tax, along with pollster Peter Hart. Luntz believed that wording was crucial to shaping public opinion, that saying something the right way could sway voters and, if said the wrong way, could turn them off. That politicians did not seem to appreciate this and still got ahead fascinated him, as did the resistance of some of them to his ideas on the effective use of slogans.

"Classic example," Luntz said, "if you ask people, 'Would you be will- 5 ing to pay more taxes to improve law enforcement?,' 51 percent of Americans would say yes. If you ask people, 'Would you be prepared to pay more taxes to halt the rising crime rates?,' 68 percent say yes. Same thing. Law enforcement is the process. Rising crime rate is the result. Half will pay more for process but two thirds will pay more for results. The key to this is how to wrap the language . . . the difference between a tax cut and tax relief. *Tax cut* is a political term that politicians offer in every election cycle. Tax relief is what the American taxpayer is actually looking for. They want a break. They don't want a political promise. They want their elected officials to give them a break."

Luntz didn't really want to do the Soldano project because he assumed, like her clients, that the estate tax was just a tax for the rich. There'd be no way to sell an effort to repeal it, he said, except to make it the caboose at the end of the tax cut train he was helping assemble in Washington.

But there was one little thing that intrigued Luntz, the phrase *death tax.* That phrase is usually attributed to James Martin, a conservative leader of older Americans. Luntz did not know or care where it came from, only how it played in focus groups and surveys. "I went out and looked at the difference between the estate tax, the inheritance tax and the death tax. And even back in '96, about half of Americans would support a repeal of the estate tax and 58 percent would support repeal of the inheritance tax and about 65 percent would support repeal of the death tax," he said.

After concluding that *death tax* was language he could change attitudes with, Luntz started selling. "I took it to every politician, every journalist, started using it in my own interviews, and right now, the only people who still call it the estate tax are lawyers. Now when you talk about repeal of the death tax, support is somewhere in the mid-70s, because the definition has changed. The same tax, roughly the same rates, but the definition of the tax, the focus of the tax, is no longer on millionaires, it's now on dying and death."

The term *death tax* is a superb example of marketing triumphing over reasoned debate. So thoroughly has the phrase been infused into Washington that many journalists, like White House correspondent David Gregory of the General Electric–owned NBC network, employ this term of advocacy instead of the neutral, and correct, term *estate tax*, without rebuke by their superiors. Even the usually scrupulously straight Dow Jones news wires used the phrase without qualification or explanation.

10   So had Luntz been advising the Democrats, what advice would he have given them to keep the tax?

"Honestly? They should raise the exemption from $1.5 million, raise it to $10 million, lower the top rate to 25 percent. If you cut the percentage to 25 percent, people think, Well hey, you still get to keep 75 percent. And you raise the exemption to $10 million, because Americans like round numbers."

And, he said, he would have taught the Democrats to always refer to "the billionaire's tax" because that was a fortune beyond the dreams of nearly all Americans. "We all want to be millionaires, but how many of us will actually ever be worth $10 million?"

You will find all sorts of assumptions embedded in language. In fact, euphemisms appear frequently in writing because writing often reproduces the language of society. Your goal should be clarity and critical insight, so you need to avoid the following types of euphemisms.

Filler Words   Many writers have trouble breaking free of filler words. When we cannot figure out what to say, we will stall and claim that a dress is "nice," or that a book was "interesting," or that you consider a friend "special," or that the church service produced a "good" reaction from the parishioners. You might notice that these four words evaluate through summation; when used in writing, they fail to shape a situation or subject for a reader.

The harm of these filler words extends beyond evaluating for your audience. They are so vague and so overused that they have ceased to carry any meaning. In fact, we might mean something different from the dictionary definition of the words. Do we mean "pleasing" when we describe a blind date as "nice"? Does a counselor want "special" to be construed as "better than ordinary" when he or she talks about "a special case"? In both cases, the speakers are trying to avoid saying what they really mean. "Nice" might be a way of saying "not physically attractive but personable." "Special" might mean "troublesome." These types of euphemism, when written, produce a bland, blah feeling in readers, who sense that the writer is just filling up space. Filler words do not allow the writer to communicate sincere ideas and can mislead an audience.

Bureaucratese   Writers often want the audience to believe they have more confidence and authority than they actually do. They will turn to a form of euphemism we call "bureaucratese"—the language of a bureaucrat. Bureaucratese, just like filler words, lulls the audience to sleep and does not help establish credibility. It evokes the blustery speeches of a mayor or the gibberish of a company spokesperson who wants to evade the central issue behind a legal probe.

Bureaucratese about a possible supernatural occurrence (a topic discussed in Chapter 13) might sound something like this: "While genuine concerns have been extended by esteemed members of the county board and good people of our city, the events in question are being investigated by top experts in our department to determine whether an apparition can be confirmed to reside on the top floor of city hall or anywhere else within this locale in which claims have been made to ensure the safety and well-being of our populace." In this stuffy, long-winded sentence, the writer (let's assume he is a man and has a position within a city government) is simply stating that he has assigned someone to look into reports of a ghost. The rest is gibberish and deception. Outside of largely discredited paranormal investigators, who are not usually on the payroll of a city, what government worker would be considered an expert on this? What qualifications would the person have? Would the government have so many of such people on board that two or more could be considered "top experts"? If this ghost were to be confirmed, what exactly would the writer do about it? How would he ensure the safety of the populace? Notice the language. The writer inflates it unnecessarily, referring to a ghost as an "apparition," for instance, and resorts to flattery early on to appease his audience. Despite the assurances to the audience, the writer uses no personal pronouns to assert his responsibility for the actions he has taken. This haughty persona, then, has no substance. More than likely, very little, if anything, is being done to investigate the reports of a ghost. The sentence uses a lot of words to send an empty message.

Since bureaucratese is deceptive and ineffective, you might be wondering how to establish confidence and authority when you write. The next section, on voice, helps in this area. Ultimately, you can establish confidence and authority only if you first have them. Do research and know your subject as well as you can. If you do not have confidence and authority, though, do not pretend that you do. Depending on the writing task, do your best to convey your ideas in your natural voice. Some writing tasks might demand establishing an ethos with which you're not entirely comfortable, but quite often audiences will not mind if you explore a topic with them. A questioning novice voice is always preferable to bureaucratese.

Sanitizing   A dangerous type of euphemism occurs when writers sanitize events, policies, and positions for the audience. If an occasional euphemism displays a sense of delicacy in stressful situations—saying someone "passed away" rather than "died," for instance—sanitizing distorts to an unacceptable degree, trying to fool readers into believing that an event, a policy, or a position is not what it seems to be. The language used in sanitizing does not suggest a new perspective or a rosier way to view a situation. It constitutes a callous treatment of a subject and dodges responsibility. Calling a neutron bomb a "radiation enhancement device" does not change the destructive nature and devastating effects of the weapon. A temporary worker who has been told to "strengthen" her "relationship" with her employment agency will not feel better about being fired.

Writers use sanitizing to try to avoid a hostile audience reaction or to avert blame, figuring that readers are not intelligent enough to see through the obfuscation. Sanitizing often has the opposite effect, though. Instead of ameliorating a situation, it enrages people. Initial confusion evolves into anger. Citizens equate government euphemisms to lying and do not believe anything they hear. Former employees become upset by the deceptive way sanitizing hides a termination and accuse companies of unfair treatment, sometimes bringing lawsuits. As writers, we want to be careful to avoid confusing delicacy with duplicity. Some instances of sanitizing sound nice, and we might believe we are clever coming up with such colorful synonyms, but the effect will be reduced credibility.

WILLIAM LUTZ

Life Under the Chief Doublespeak Officer

William Lutz, a professor at Rutgers University, discusses sanitizing language that he calls "doublespeak" in this article. Some of his examples evoke the speech patterns of bureaucratese.

If there's one product American business can produce in large amounts, it's doublespeak. Doublespeak is language that only pretends to say something; it's language that hides, evades or misleads.

Doublespeak comes in many forms, from the popular buzzwords that everyone uses but no one really understands—"globalization," "competitive dynamics," "re-equitizing," and "empowerment"—to language that tries to hide meaning: "re-engineering," "synergy," "adjustment," "restructure," and "force management program."

With doublespeak, no truck driver is the worst driver, just the "least-best" driver, and bribes and kickbacks are called "rebates" or "fees for product testing." Even robbery can be magically transformed with doublespeak, as a bank in Texas did when it declared a robbery of an ATM to be an "unauthorized transaction." Willie Sutton would have loved to have heard that.

Automobile junkyards, junk and used car parts have become "auto dismantlers and recyclers" who sell "predismantled, previously owned parts." Don't want people to know you're in the business of disposing of radioactive and chemical wastes? Then call your company "U.S. Ecology Inc."

Wages may not be increasing, but the doublespeak of job titles sure has increased. These days, your job title has to have the word "chief" in it. How many kinds of "chiefs" are there? Try these titles on for size: Chief Nuclear Officer, Chief Procurement Officer, Chief Information Officer, Chief Learning Officer, Chief Transformation Officer, Chief Cultural Officer, Chief People Officer, Chief Ethics Officer, Chief Turnaround Officer, Chief Technology Officer, and Chief Creative Officer. After all the "operations improvement" corporations have undergone, you have to wonder who all those "chiefs" are leading. Never before have so few been led by so many.

These days, a travel agent may be called a "travel counselor," "vacation specialist," "destination counselor," or "reservation specialist." As part of their merger, Chase Manhattan Bank and Chemical Bank decided that the position of "Relationship Manager" would be divided between executives of both banks. What is a "Relationship Manager"? Once upon a time this person was called a salesman. And if you're late in paying your bill after buying something from one of these "Relationship Managers," you'll be called by the "Persistency Specialist," or bill collector. If you're "downsized," the "Outplacement Consultant" or unemployment counselor will help you with "re-employment engineering," or how to find another job.

With doublespeak, banks don't have "bad loans" or "bad debts"; they have "nonperforming assets" or "nonperforming credits" which are "rolled over" or "rescheduled." Corporations never lose money; they just experience "negative cash flow," "deficit enhancement," "net profit revenue deficiencies," or "negative contributions to profits."

No one gets fired these days, and no one gets laid off. If you're high enough in the corporate pecking order, you "resign for personal reasons." (And then you're never unemployed; you're just in an "orderly transition between career changes.") But even those far below the lofty heights of corporate power are not fired or laid off. Firing workers is such big business in these days of "re-engineering," "restructuring," and "downsizing" that there are companies whose business is helping other companies fire their workers. (Think about that for a minute.) These companies provide "termination and outplacement consulting" for corporations involved in "reduction activities." In other words, they teach companies how to fire or lay off workers. During these days of "cost rationalization," companies fire or lay off workers many different ways. How do I fire thee? Let me count the ways.

Companies make "workforce adjustments," "headcount reductions," "census reductions," or institute a program of "negative employee retention." Corporations offer workers "vocational relocation," "career assignment and relocation," a "career change opportunity," or "voluntary termination." Workers are "dehired," "deselected," "selected out," "repositioned," "surplussed," "rightsized," "correct sized," "excessed," or "uninstalled." Some companies "initiate operations improvements," "assign candidates to a mobility pool," "implement a skills mix adjustment," or "eliminate redundancies in the human resources area."

10   One company denied it was laying off 500 people at its headquarters. "We don't characterize it as a layoff," said the corporate doublespeaker (sometimes called a spin doctor). "We're managing our staff resources. Sometimes you manage them up, and sometimes you manage them down." Congratulations. You've just been managed down, you staff resource you.

An automobile company announced the closing of an entire assembly plant and the elimination of over 8,000 jobs by announcing "a volume-related production schedule adjustment." Not to be outdone by its rival, another car company "initiated a career alternative enhancement program" that enhanced over 5,000 workers out of their jobs. By calling the permanent shutdown of a steel plant an "indefinite idling," a corporation thought that it wouldn't have to pay severance or pension benefits to the workers who were left without jobs.

Doublespeak can pay for the company, but usually not for the workers who lose their jobs.

As Pogo said, "We have met the enemy, and he is us." Or maybe Dilbert got it better: "Do we really get paid for writing this stuff?"

DISCUSSION

When have you found it appropriate to use euphemisms? For instance, can a euphemism for a job title enhance the dignity of the job? Some companies call their low-wage workers "partners." When I worked in a hospital years ago, I preferred the title of "courier" for my job of delivering and picking up medical charts instead of the usual name of "runner." Some trash collectors are referred to as "sanitation engineers." We also use euphemisms in personal relationships. In refusing a date or romantic overture, many people have said "we don't have chemistry" instead of "I find you unattractive" or other words of rejection. What is the effect? Do euphemisms soften the blow or create other problems?

Finding Your Voice

Words are essential for creating what is known as a narrative voice. This voice conveys the tone of the writing, such as humorous, conciliatory, ironic, or thoughtful, and conjures up an image of the writer for the audience. We want the narrative voice to be lively in our writing, not dry or dull, even when assignments call for a formal approach to a paper or project. We also want the voice to be genuine, portraying our sensitivities and passion.

Combined with the perspective that emerges from your critical analysis, the words you choose will shape an impression for the audience of your values, experiences, and attitude—the concept of ethos discussed in Chapter 3. Some audiences even form a physical description of the writer in their minds. The person they imagine you to be, whether pleasant or mean, influences how they receive your ideas. You can see, then, how important a narrative voice can be.

Constructing a voice that you deem to be genuine presents you with a challenge. Our voices change as we mature, discard old beliefs, embrace new ones, and stretch the boundaries of our identities. What happens if our personalities can be abrasive, especially when we talk about certain subjects? How can we be genuine, critically analytic, and audience-friendly all at the same time? Finding one consistent voice that is appropriate might seem impossible.

Identity, though, is not fixed. While weaknesses in our personalities will emerge during writing, just as they do in normal social interaction, we can control more than we might think. As during social interactions, we want to put our best face forward and make adjustments depending on the situation. We are not compromising our integrity or necessarily being insincere when we change our tone and vocabulary to accommodate those around us. If we want to impress a potential employer during a job interview, we monitor our use of slang and obscenity, extend courtesy, use appropriately intelligent language, and show enthusiasm. We could not do these things if they were not a part of us. Even if we fail to be polite more frequently than we like, prefer modest vocabulary when talking to our friends, and fend off bouts of depression instead of demonstrating exuberance, our identities are not limited to one set of traits. Our subtle alterations to adjust to shifting social environments are the type of changes to make when constructing the right voice in our writing.

Writing also allows you to test the limits of acceptability and, through revision, to find an appealing voice that is lively, critical, sensitive, credible, and still genuine. You will not have the advantage of using inflections in your voice, gestures, eye contact, and physical appearance, as you do when speaking, but you have the chance to do it over should you make mistakes in your word choices or in the arrangement of those words. Here are some ways to guide your decisions when it comes to finding voice.

Choosing Your Words

While voice is more than the catch phrases we see represented in some television sitcoms, people develop a set of terms or phrases that they feel comfortable using. When they are able to incorporate these words in their writing, part of them is down on the paper. I have a friend, for instance, who uses copious and alarming frequently in conversation. The words add a spark to his writing and convey a genuine narrative voice. Do you envision a certain type of person from these sentences? "After copious observation of the two neighbors at the party, I detected an unmistakable bond. It became alarmingly apparent to all as the evening progressed that the two were involved in an affair." The words fit naturally into the voice he has established, and an audience probably sees someone who is astute and maintains an air of decorum.

Of course, you want to avoid comfortable words that are too vague or clichéd, but sometimes a slang term or common saying can achieve voice. When a writer describes a character with the words, "He wasn't the sharpest knife in the drawer, if you know what I mean," I hear a voice, even though the metaphor is not original. The writer has adopted a colloquial, humorous voice. Filling an essay with such phrases would lessen their effect, but one well-placed expression that a writer is comfortable with can work toward constructing this voice.

Types of Words   The words you select, especially the adjectives and verbs, help shape your voice. A writer who chooses a number of adjectives conveys an observant voice. A writer who understands distinctions, such as in color (the difference between mauve and purple, for instance) or in sound (a screech as compared to a scream), can construct a narrative voice that goes beyond being observant. The writer can display sensitivity and taste, for example, by describing details in the design of an old house that might escape the notice of a casual observer. A writer who uses action verbs throughout an essay and can distinguish between a car that is chugging down a street and a car that is creeping down a street constructs a voice that might be considered more pragmatic and subdued than the adjective-driven, observant voice but that is nonetheless dynamic and engaging. While no formulas exist for matching a voice to a subject or for creating a certain tone, attention to word types helps in a subtle way.

Active Sentence Constructions   Arrangement of the words is the final piece to the puzzle of voice. Overuse of passive sentences creates a dry voice that might be appropriate for scientific reports, where the narrative voice does not concern the audience, but that takes life away from writing centered on civic concerns, social matters, and persuasion. A passive sentence construction uses compound verbs and moves or removes the actual subject of the sentence, known as the actor, to emphasize what should be the object. Typical examples of passive constructions are "The ball was hit by the boy" and "The ball was hit." The active sentence construction is "The boy hit the ball," where the actor, the boy, takes the prominent place in the sentence and acts on the object, the ball. Notice that the passive sentence construction forces the writer to use the *to be* verb, which, although essential in many places, is the weakest verb in the English language. The active sentence construction conveys movement, while the passive sentence construction emphasizes stasis. Thus, revising passive sentences into active sentences restores vigor to what might appear to be lifeless prose.

Writers should also look for expletive sentences, those that begin with variations of *there is* or *it is*. If *to be* is the weakest verb in our language, the pronouns *there* and *it* rank among the most boring subjects for a sentence. A sentence using the two in combination starts as poorly as possible. Consider this sentence: "There was a dog in our neighborhood that barked all the time." A simple revision changes it to "A dog in our neighborhood barked all the time." The sentence loses no meaning in the revision, and you can see how it rolls off your tongue better than the expletive beginning. Be aware of the arrangement of the words in your sentences; it can determine how much life your voice has.

COLLABORATING

Have everyone in your group bring an editorial from a local newspaper to class. Read through the editorials, and write a description of the voices you hear. How was each voice constructed? What made you think the narrator seemed dry, witty, intelligent, angry, pompous, or any other description you wrote? As a group, rewrite one of the editorials to create a different voice, whether better or worse than the one in the editorial, focusing on word choices and sentence arrangement. Be prepared to explain the effect you think you have achieved and how the voice differs from the original.

Summary

When all is said and done, writing comes down to words. Writers need to pay special attention to the choices they make and should not rely on gimmicks, such as a word search through a thesaurus, to build vocabulary. Words have the potential to create a world or a mindset for an audience; they mediate experience and shape events. While writers cannot control every association a reader might make with a particular word, they need to be aware of possible reader reactions and strive for precision.

Words can also mislead and deceive, as when writers employ euphemisms to avoid impoliteness or to cover up something unpleasant. Writers do not want to lose credibility by resorting to these tactics. Instead, writers can build credibility by using language to construct a genuine, vigorous narrative voice that is appropriate to the subject matter and audience.

· PART II ·

CONFRONTING WRITING TASKS

Now that you have increased your awareness of the key concepts behind writing, you can look at other issues that might confront you while producing an essay, researched writing, or a report. One or more of the key concepts—reasons for writing, critical analysis, audience, organization, and language usage—will factor into nearly all the other decisions you need to make when writing, but the areas discussed in the following chapters deserve special attention.

Chapter 6 discusses the writing process. The steps of the writing process vary with each writer and help divide the work into manageable tasks. However, some steps in an individual's writing process might actually hinder progress; other steps might better be done at a different stage of the process. Therefore, Chapter 6 reviews ways to get started on a project and to see it through to completion, all within the framework of the successful parts of the process you have already developed. While the reasons for writing will dictate much of what you do during your process, this issue needs to be discussed separately.

Some writing tasks will require you to work with others. Chapter 7 focuses on times when writers collaborate. Since most writing involves much work with other people, *Writing Without Formulas* treats collaboration separately from the major concepts. Many students enjoy the prospect of a group project but fear that one or two people will end up doing most of the work. In Chapter 7, you will find ways to effectively combine your strengths as a writer with those of your peers and make sure that everyone contributes equally.

Chapter 8 analyzes difficulties students typically encounter with college-level reading. Reading is a form of interpretation that does not differ all that much from other kinds of literacy we have developed. By drawing parallels to other forms of literacy, Chapter 8 seeks to help you develop an effective reading process that will work beyond your academic reading needs.

Chapter 9 looks at the specific issue of writing with evidence. While the chapter builds on the knowledge that can be found in the discussions about critical analysis, audience, organization, and language, it dives deeper to discuss problems that arise when writers use evidence. Chapter 9 contains information on what constitutes evidence, how to use it, when to use it, and why it can be integrated in some ways but not others.

Picking up on this information, Chapter 10 discusses the task of researching during a writing project. While the issues involved in research tie into the previous discussions on critical analysis and language, much remains to be discovered about the particulars of finding and evaluating sources. Chapter 10 reviews locating critical knowledge, evaluating your sources, untangling conflicting sources, and citing sources in a paper.

The information in Part II takes you directly into the realities of writing. You might not need to use every chapter for this class. For example, your course might not involve writing with research, or your instructor might not assign a group project. Still, the activities and advice will prove valuable in all sorts of future situations involving writing. You could be collaborating with coworkers during your first experience in a professional setting away from college. Knowing how to use evidence and do responsible research will matter in other courses as well as in civic activities. The suggestions in these chapters will add to your understanding of the key concepts and allow you to develop further as a writer.

CHAPTER 6

DISCOVERING YOUR WRITING PROCESS

During my early years as an instructor of writing, I told students to follow a writing process that had discernible stages. I broke down every assignment into prewriting, drafting, revising, more revising, and editing. I demanded that students turn in their work at every stage so I could check for improvement and make suggestions about critical analysis, audience considerations, and language. Some students turned in perfunctory prewriting or partially completed drafts, or they started editing during the revision stage, or their revisions looked no different than the previous versions. I deducted points and chastised students, trying to get them to conform to what I called the writing process. I must have been a holy terror.

It dawned on me how wrong I was to teach this way only after some students complained about my odd formula. They said that trying to conform to it made writing mechanical. It wasn't that they did not want to follow my assignments; they couldn't. My realization started with a conference I had with a competent writer named Akil. As we reviewed his revision, Akil grew more and more fidgety, asking if he could smoke and not seeming to agree with my comments that he had not revised sufficiently.

"I'll get to that," he told me about a lack of detail in his introduction. "I'm not ready right now."

"But you're not going to have time for proofreading and editing if you have to do all of these revisions in the next stage as well," I said.

"I do that as I go along," he said.

"But I told you guys to wait on that," I replied. "You're going to mess up

Online Study Center

This icon will direct you to web links and additional resources on the website http://college.cengage.com/english/thelin/writing_without_formulas/1e/student_home.html

the process and not get everything done." I shook my head and leaned back in my chair.

Akil leaned forward. "Look, I know what you're saying, but I don't write that way. This process is your process, not mine. I don't want you to get mad at me, but I don't do these things. Can't you help me work with *my* process?"

So that's what I did. I asked Akil to explain how he composed essays and tried to figure out a way to make his process work with the assignment. After he left, I thought about his resistance to the formula I had constructed. I wondered how many other students were having similar problems.

I started the next class session by talking about the approaches students took to writing assignments and wondering what students really do when they compose. I welcomed them to critique my formula, which they did, almost wildly, and I tried to group together ideas they used to get through an assignment. Each student wrote a list of his or her general writing steps, and we discussed the lists as a whole class. Ideas came flooding forward so quickly that I had trouble writing them on the board. When I had finished, I counted five patterns of composing. Although nearly every student had some variation and no two patterns were identical, they followed one of these five models, not the formula I had forced on them.

Of course, some of these models contained approaches to writing tasks that were not productive. Procrastination crept into many processes, forcing students to crank out drafts of papers the night before they were due. Other students did not know how to get through writing blocks and stared blankly at lined paper or computer screens. A couple of students became so caught up in proofreading that they were reluctant to revise beyond their first drafts, except for further proofreading. Some habits, then, needed to be changed, especially if the students found writing frustrating. The question was how to distinguish a strong writing process from a weak one. I needed to figure out how to tweak the individual processes so they could work better.

The five models I ascertained are as follows.

1. Write a partial draft, get feedback, complete it, and proofread.
2. Write a full draft in one session, edit while rereading, and submit it.
3. Jot down initial ideas, start the draft one day, revise and edit that part of it, finish the rest of it the next day, get feedback, add additional details, and proofread.
4. Think about what to write, do an outline, determine the thesis, do a rough draft (in one or more sessions), edit while you go, get some feedback, and do a final revision.
5. Wait until the last second to start the writing task, put something together, get feedback or directives, revise, get more feedback, revise again, and proofread.

Does one of these models look similar to what you do? I'm sure some approaches to writing are not represented fully, but you probably recognize the basic traits and the ordering of activities of your own writing. I believe we can find value in all of the models and find ways to make them productive. Four of the five, though, rely on being able to turn in drafts and receive feedback from peers or the instructor. In writing for civic purposes or personal expression, you may have to arrange for other forms of collaboration and feedback. We want to create models that can be used for writing activities beyond the classroom.

DISCUSSION

Talk about the approaches you take to activities other than writing. When you have household chores to do, do you make a plan? What if you are giving a party? What about crafts you might enjoy? Compare the ways you go about doing these and other activities. Which methods enable you to complete these tasks most efficiently? Which methods cause delays or problems?

This chapter should help you refine what you do when you have a writing task in front of you. You will understand what it means to prewrite, draft, revise, edit, and proofread. For many writers, these components or steps overlap; other writers separate them into discrete stages. Perhaps you do not need or want to incorporate certain components. Uncover what you do, and inject what you feel is missing, if anything, into your process. No one formula produces good writing.

Seeing Your Own Patterns

Do you take the same approach to differing writing tasks? Or does the purpose behind your writing dictate your process? For instance, if you are responding to a friend's email about your plans for the evening, you might pound out a quick answer without much planning. But if your friend wants to know whether you saw her boyfriend with another woman, you might not want to respond right away, especially if you witnessed her boyfriend stepping out on her. You have to consider whether you should mind your own business, how to break the news if you decide to tell her, how to avoid a gossipy tone and whether to use a sad, sincere one, and whether you should give advice. The two email messages demand differing approaches to what you write, so the processes have to be different.

Within all the disparate purposes, you should be able to discover patterns of how you approach a writing task. In other words, despite the differences the tasks call for, you will notice consistent tendencies. For example, I usually spend a short period thinking about any kind of writing I am doing, envisioning both the structure and the desired effect of the piece. I compose part of it, and then reread, inserting and deleting as appropriate to improve flow, correctness, and meaning. I then continue to write. Once I am finished, I reread at least twice to check for tone and for clarity and to do further proofreading. I always make sure that my audience has enough previous knowledge to understand the context of my communication, and I fill in details just to be on the safe side. I also am keenly aware of thoroughness. I do not want to leave anything out.

Before I deliver the writing to its intended audience, I think once more of the effect on that audience. Assuming that the purpose of writing is not to repeat something I have stated before (some email messages and memos do have the purpose of recapping prior exchanges), I want to make sure that I have added something to previous knowledge and that I have analyzed my ideas critically. If I see a problem, it might mean doing a global revision, the type of rewrite that leads to a change of perspective, structural alterations, or the revamping of a thesis. I might have to enlist somebody else to read the writing to check the need for local revision—the need for another example, the use of more concrete words, a snappier introduction, or other concerns that involve only insertion and deletion.

Finding such patterns in your approaches to writing is not that difficult. Try one of the following two methods to uncover them.

Track Your Steps   The next few times you sit down to compose something, be aware of what you do when you write. Keep in mind your purposes and how they change your approach to writing. Look at your perception of quality. Do you tend to do your best writing in a journal you keep? How do you decide what and when to write in this journal? Perhaps you keep a blog. How do you go about conveying your ideas? Do you go back and edit, or do you edit while you are writing? Have you ever decided not to send something after having finished it? Why?

Don't forget classroom assignments. How do you prepare for an essay exam? How does that preparation differ from the way you prepare to write a longer paper? While it is not necessary to make a list of the persistent tendencies you note, you should get a sense of what components of your writing process keep reappearing and how the purpose changes what you do.

Note What You Do Not Do   What you do not do in approaching a writing task can also reveal much. Perhaps you are at a loss for words to describe patterns within your process. You know that you do the writing involved, but beyond understanding your inspiration, or looking at the assignment, or reading the email you received, you cannot articulate anything other than that you put together a finished piece of writing.

Later this chapter discusses the differences between prewriting, drafting, revising, editing, and proofreading; for now, it is not necessary to use these terms. When my students discussed their practices and I drew up the list of the five models, we never used the term *prewriting*, for example, although two of the models describe activities that align with prewriting. If you describe what you do rather than trying to classify your activities into categories, you might find the patterns you are looking for.

Still, it might be easier for you to make a list of approaches you do not take in a given writing task. Anything that you do not write down or circle is likely to be part of your process. By understanding what you do not do, the process you use will become clearer, and you will give yourself ideas about where you need to tinker with it.

COLLABORATING

Look at the five models described by my students. Which of these models most closely aligns to your writing processes? Are there parts of each model or one model in particular that seems to be the opposite of what you do? Discuss the processes you use, compare them to the five models, and determine which components seem to be mentioned most often. What parts of the processes help produce successful writing? What parts interfere? Keep these in mind as you read through this chapter so as to determine which parts of your model need to be adjusted and which parts should be left alone.

Breaking Through Writer's Block

Many of my students have wondered how to get started writing. They experience what is known as a writer's block, the inability to respond to a writing task and put words on paper. Even professional writers confront a writing block at times. To some extent, every writing task initially produces a block. This is especially true of classroom assignments because, as students, you might not know what to write or even have much interest in the topic. You might also feel anxiety about being graded or evaluated.

Most writing teachers look to prewriting strategies to help students break through writing blocks and get started. When determining which strategy to use, the reason for the block has to be considered. For example, one type of block has to do with the inability to generate ideas. In such cases, group brainstorming is ideal; students, colleagues, or citizens can bounce ideas off each other and collectively help individuals who are stuck. Other times, writers might have so many ideas that they cannot focus on one good way to start. To clarify thinking and find relevant connections between possibly conflicting ideas, these writers can construct outlines to get started. But many other times, nothing more than just starting to write without stopping is needed.

Writers adapt this strategy, called freewriting, to break through writer's block. Freewriting involves continuously writing on the computer or on paper for five to seven minutes, even if only nonsense comes out. The act of nonstop writing enables the writer to get started. Start with what is on your mind: "I don't know what to write" or "I'm blocked." You can repeat that until another idea or phrase joins it. Often, freewriting serves a double purpose, both breaking the block and uncovering a thought or issue that might prove important for your paper. This strategy should help you get started on a writing task. Many writers will even use it in the middle of their drafting or revising to generate fresh ideas if a section or paragraph seems to have gone stale.

If you experience writer's block on a regular basis, consider incorporating prewriting into your process. Look at the following techniques to see if one or more respond to the reasons you get blocked.

Discovering Why You Are Blocked   When a writing task confronts us, perhaps a paper for the classroom, perhaps a report for a business meeting, staring at the computer screen and hoping an idea will magically appear frustrates us and sometimes transforms a mild writing block into a severe one. Rather than trying ways to get started, many writers have success reflecting on the reasons for the block. In other words, they freewrite about the block, trying to figure out why they cannot find a way to begin. While this might sound like additional work that takes you away from the actual writing, it is not. You cannot write effectively until you understand why you're having problems. Trying to write without such understanding would be like running for office without knowing the identity and strategies of your opponent. Once you know the who and the what, you can respond.

Here is a checklist of questions designed to help you determine why you are blocked.

- Is the block caused by the particular task in front of you?
- What part of it can you single out as the primary problem?
- Are you worried that you do not have enough knowledge about the subject?
- Do you need more information on how to structure the writing?
- Do you have a clear idea of who your audience is?
- Are you worried about a negative evaluation from an instructor or manager?
- Do you feel that your writing does not express your thoughts well?
- Have you had trouble with sentence-level issues, and do you want to avoid making mistakes?

This list is not exhaustive, but the point is to ask yourself questions that will help you precisely nail down the issues you are facing. Once you can articulate the reason for your block, you will be one step closer to overcoming it. This reflection will allow you to figure out what you need to do next, whether it is to find out more information about the writing task, to do some reading to prepare you, to make time in your process for more editing and proofreading, or to use a specific prewriting strategy.

CHARLEY LAU, JR.

from Lau's Laws on Hitting

How is a writing block like other types of slumps? Read this excerpt about the hitting slumps of baseball players, and see if you can find similarities between the mental processes of hitting a baseball and of completing a writing assignment.

Ever notice when you get into a slump in any athletic endeavor the amount of people are eager to help you? Fall into a 1-for-25 slide in baseball and it seems everyone has a solution for you, from your teammates to your coach to your wife. Your head is pulling out. Your stance is all wrong. Your bat is too heavy. You name it: Everyone's identified the problem. The problem is, of course, that you can do more damage and prolong your slump by taking too much advice. Listening to everyone's suggestions often only clogs the mind. This is when the brain can get in the way of hitting. If the brain is trying to process too much information, the message it finally sends to the body is slowed. And hitting is all about timing and quick reactions. You want that message from the brain to the body to occur instantly. The point is this: When mired in a slump, be wary of taking in too much advice. Don't create an information overload.

Hey, the truth is, everyone goes into a slump. Everyone. Even the great hitters. In baseball, as with any other sport, you have to accept a certain degree of failure. As you've probably heard a million times, the best hitters in the game, the .300 hitters, fail seven out of 10 times. What keeps a great hitter great is his ability to fight through slumps. As I've pointed out before, there often is a mechanical reason for why a hitter isn't hitting well. Maybe he's not starting his swing soon enough. Maybe his top hand has become too dominant. But sometimes slumps occur simply because of your mental approach. You can't be successful at anything unless you first believe you can be successful. Yes, I believe in mind over matter. Your brain can do wonderful things if you let it and convince it to.

Focused Freewriting While much freewriting to generate ideas can be done on the spur of the moment, some of the most effective freewrites are focused around a central question, either a sticking point in a draft or a puzzling part of an assignment. A motivating question can arise from reflecting on why the writer has a block. If, for instance, you have narrowed down the problem to part of an assignment that asks for a summary of a difficult reading, a focused freewrite could start with the questions, "What do I understand about the reading? What don't I understand?" As with all freewrites, you must force words out of the keyboard or pen, even if just, "I don't know. I'm confused." You have the obligation to ask, "Why am I confused?" and to list specifics of what you already know and understand about a topic or assignment. Confronting the problem head-on is the start to breaking through the block.

A focused freewrite can also be beneficial in trying to understand what an audience needs in order to comprehend and consider your point of view. Freewriting in response to a simple question, such as "Who would disagree with my position?" will help you grasp and respond to the audience's perspectives as discussed in Chapter 3. Some blocks hit writers after they have received feedback from peers, teachers, or supervisors. Freewriting on a question such as "How can I restructure this paper to make it less confusing?" will generate possibilities for you to consider. Don't be afraid to do more than one focused freewrite, as many questions can be posed. A good freewrite will often generate questions that can be answered in another freewrite.

Starting with the Critical Analysis

Writer's block can occur when you find it difficult to attach significance to the task at hand or perhaps even to your first draft. Your draft may sound clichéd, or a peer group may have told you that a stronger thesis is needed. Chapter 2 discusses critical analysis as a strategy for gaining insight and developing ideas. What better way to find significance and gain momentum in the writing process than to immediately get beyond clichés that can bog you down and make you think your writing is ordinary?

While some of the suggestions for critical analysis in Chapter 2 will work best after you have developed some content, the ideas in the section "Investigating Assumptions" on pages 39–45 can be used when you already have a topic. By critically analyzing the stereotypes that exist about a given topic, you can make a list of the ways race, class, and gender might influence first impressions. You can unearth agendas by freewriting about the reasons you and others feel a certain way about a subject. Critical analysis can give you a clear direction and shatter the writing block.

Drawing a Tree

Visualizing your options in writing can help you to literally see the connections between seemingly disparate ideas. One visualizing strategy is to draw a tree about the broad topic of humor. The trunk represents the topic or assignment, and the branches represent major ideas. Each smaller branch can represent a new idea or connection. When you exhaust all ideas, go to another branch and begin to "grow" another idea. You can come back to any branch if necessary, but the idea is to see how all the branches grow from the same subject.

When you have drawn as many branches as possible, you might have a tree that looks something like the one on page 151. The main branch that is connected to the largest number of smaller branches probably has the most potential as a topic, but the connections can be clearly seen, too. For instance, one smaller branch is about the cruelty of humor. The even smaller branch that grows out of it, teasing an old softball mate, John, about his age, relates to

---

DISCUSSION

What other ways do members of your class break through writing blocks? In the writing models listed earlier in this chapter, students mentioned jotting down notes and outlining. In this section, we discuss group brainstorming and freewriting, as well as drawing a tree and critical analysis. Are there others? Or has everyone used only the techniques mentioned in this chapter? Talk about the positive and negative results of any strategies for breaking through writing blocks that you can think of. How should these strategies blend into your individual writing process?

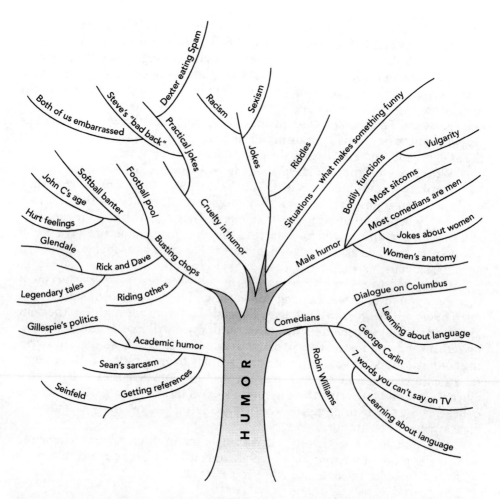

the main idea. You can easily see that the theory represented in a main branch can be supported by the specifics laid out in a smaller branch. Such visual aids can make a writer move through a writing block toward a well-organized draft.

Discovering Strategies for Drafting and Revision

Have you ever been required to put together a rough draft for a deadline? If so, what did it mean to you? People know that drafting involves writing, but many are not sure what a draft of an essay or a research project is supposed to look like. A useful description springs from an understanding of the differences from similar activities, such as revising, editing, and proofreading. Drafting implies writing that is ongoing and is in a stage of construction beyond just notes, outlines, or ideas. When writing is being revised, a finished rough draft is being overhauled to make structural alterations, add or expand important elements, or change the focus. Inserting or deleting elements, rearranging the order, and refining an otherwise finished product constitute editing. Proofreading means giving a finished piece one final look to catch mistakes.

A rough draft looks like an attempt at completing a task. It might be strong in one area and weak in another. It might have sentence-level errors, such as verb tense problems or sentence fragments. Critical analysis might have been attempted, or audience expectations might have been taken into consideration. The writer has spent time thinking about the writing task, has shaped some paragraphs containing ideas that meet the crucial elements of the assignment, and knows that the piece needs further work.

Writers have differing ideas about how a rough draft should function. Some writers like to break drafting into several stages. To ensure that they are heading in the right direction, they might seek feedback on the first part of an essay before attempting to write more. They might like to review and edit one part of an essay before starting the next part. Sometimes what you should turn in when asked for a rough draft is not as clear as it should be. You need to ask your instructor about her or his expectations.

Being told to revise can be confusing as well. Often, if we have spent time on a rough draft—reviewing and editing on our own, for instance—we resist revision. We feel that we have done all the work for nothing, that our ideas and style have been harshly judged, or that we will make the essay worse by rethinking and restructuring major areas. Revision helps a piece of writing conform to its purpose, whether narrowing a focus for space requirements for an editorial for a newspaper, making sense of a personal experience in a journal, or simply meeting the instructor's expectations for an assignment in college. Most of the important activities involving critical analysis and audience awareness occur during revision.

Revision is an opportunity, not an impediment. It gives you a chance to look at the piece of writing for a second time, allowing for perspective, feedback, and new ideas to enhance what you started.

JANE TOMPKINS

from "*Indians*": *Textualism, Morality, and the Problem of History*

This excerpt from Jane Tompkins's essay concerns the multiple ways of trying to arrive at the truth behind an historical event. In her exploration of the American Indians' relationship with Puritan culture, she has to revise and continue to revise her initial views of Indians as she reads source materials. By looking critically at representations of Indians, she comes to understand the complications involved in making judgments about the European–Indian encounter while also knowing the moral imperative to do so. Her willingness to take a second look at her subject led to critical insights.

When I was growing up in New York City, my parents used to take me to an event in Inwood Park at which Indians—real American Indians dressed in feathers and blankets—could be seen and touched by children like me. This event was always a disappointment. It was more fun to imagine that you *were* an Indian in one of the caves in Inwood Park than to shake the hand of an old man in a headdress who was not overwhelmed at the opportunity of meeting you. After staring at the Indians for a while, we would take a walk in the woods where the caves were, and once I asked my mother if the remains of a fire I had seen in one of them might have been left by the original inhabitants. After that, wandering up some stone steps cut into the side of the hill, I imagined I was a princess in a rude castle. My Indians, like my princesses, were creatures totally of the imagination, and I did not care to have any real exemplars interfering with what I already knew.

I already knew about Indians from having read about them in school. Over and over we were told the story of how Peter Minuit had bought Manhattan Island from the Indians for twenty-four dollars' worth of glass beads. And it was a story we didn't mind hearing because it gave us the rare pleasure of having someone to feel superior to, since the poor Indians had not known (as we eight-year-olds did) how valuable a piece of property Manhattan Island would become. Generally, much was made of the Indian presence in Manhattan; a poem in one of our readers began: "Where we walk to school today/ Indian children used to play," and we were encouraged to write poetry on this topic ourselves. So I had a fairly rich relationship with Indians before I ever met the unprepossessing people in Inwood Park. I felt that I had a lot in common with them. They, too, liked animals (they were often named after animals); they, too, made mistakes—they liked the brightly colored trinkets of little value that the white men were always offering them; they were handsome, warlike, and brave and had led an exciting, romantic life in the forest long ago, a life such as I dreamed of leading myself. I felt lucky to be living in one of the places where they had definitely been. Never mind where they were or what they were doing now.

My story stands for the relationship most non-Indians have to the people who first populated this continent, a relationship characterized by narcissistic fantasies of freedom and adventure, of a life lived closer to nature and to spirit than the life we lead now. As Vine Deloria, Jr., has pointed out, the American Indian Movement in the early seventies couldn't get people to pay attention to what was happening to Indians who were alive in the present, so powerful was this country's infatuation with people who wore loincloths, lived in tepees, and roamed the plains and forests long ago. The present essay, like these fantasies, doesn't have much to do with actual Indians, though its subject matter is the histories of European–Indian relations in seventeenth-century New England. In a sense, my encounter with Indians as an adult doing "research" replicates the childhood one, for while I started out to learn about Indians, I ended up preoccupied with a problem of my own.

This essay enacts a particular instance of the challenge poststructuralism poses to the study of history. In simpler language, it concerns the difference that point of view makes when people are giving accounts of events, whether at first or second hand. The problem is that if all accounts of events are determined through and through by the observer's frame of reference, then one will never know, in any given case, what really happened.

5   I encountered this problem in concrete terms while preparing to teach a course in colonial American literature. I'd set out to learn what I could about the Puritans' relations with American Indians. All I wanted was a general idea of what had happened between the English settlers and the natives in seventeenth-century New England; poststructuralism and its dilemmas were the furthest thing from my mind. I began, more or less automatically, with Perry Miller, who hardly mentions the Indians at all, then proceeded to the work of historians who had dealt exclusively with the European–Indian encounter. At first, it was a question of deciding which of these authors to believe, for it quickly became apparent that there was no unanimity on the subject. As I read on, however, I discovered that the problem was more complicated than deciding whose version of events was correct. Some of the conflicting accounts were not simply contradictory, they were completely incommensurable, in that their assumptions about what counted as a valid approach to the subject, and what the subject itself was, diverged in fundamental ways. Faced with an array of mutually irreconcilable points of view, points of view which determined what was being discussed as well as the terms of the discussion, I decided to turn to primary sources for clarification, only to discover that the primary sources reproduced the problem all over again. I found myself, in other words, in an epistemological quandary, not only unable to decide among conflicting versions of events but also unable to believe that any such decision could, in principle, be made. It was a moral quandary as well. Knowledge of what really happened when the Europeans and the Indians first met seemed particularly important, since the result of that encounter was virtual genocide. This was the kind of past "mistake" which, presumably, we studied history in order to avoid repeating. If studying history couldn't put us in touch with actual events and their causes, then what was to prevent such atrocities from happening again?

For a while, I remained at this impasse. But through analyzing the process by which I had reached it, I eventually arrived at an understanding which seemed to offer a way out.

COLLABORATING

Jane Tompkins suggests that looking at the process that leads to a decision can help in finding solutions to a problem. We might have experienced this feeling of enlightenment when we retraced our steps in a mathematical problem. Can you think of any other situations where you analyzed the process and discovered a solution? Talk with your group about whether members have had similar experiences in which probing the process allowed them to see a situation better.

You need to incorporate revision into your writing process in such a way that it seems like a natural step toward adding depth to your paper. Revision should not worry or derail you. The suggestions that follow should help you discover a drafting and revising strategy that works for you.

Focus on Revision   Some of the models discussed earlier broke the drafting of an essay into several parts. In other words, some writers don't crank out drafts in one sitting. If you work this way, you might think about utilizing the same process for revision. In fact, you should consider shifting the focus of your process to revision.

Revising a paper can seem daunting when you do it all at once. No wonder many students look at it as a chore. If the draft can become the preliminary step in which you test out ideas but do not worry about the shape of an essay, you can work through it much more quickly. The time you would normally put into drafting can be used for an extended revision period. You can do some of the revision on your own, and base some of it on feedback from others. Most important, you would not do the revising all in one sitting. You would be taking a crucial part of your own drafting process and applying it to your model of revision. By transferring your labor to the revision end of the process, you will be less likely to feel anxious about having to "redo" a paper. You will know in advance that you're going to make significant changes.

This method can accommodate the first-draft procrastinator as well. In many ways, there is nothing wrong with grinding out a draft at the last minute. Many of us work this way. We need to feel the pressure of an impending deadline to produce writing. The last-minute draft gets ideas on the paper in a presentable form. Unfortunately, if the writer also procrastinates on the revision process, the gains become losses. In other words, at some point revision must be thought out and suggestions implemented slowly. Time must also be budgeted for editing and proofreading.

Create Options   Even when faced with a draft marked up with comments and corrections from an instructor, an editor, or a supervisor, a writer sometimes has difficulty envisioning anything other than the original writing. Feeling that a draft is set the way it is—that the structure cannot be changed by significant revisions of content—makes writers sensitive to judgment and resistant to audience needs.

If you have felt this way when a paper was returned for revision, you might try creating options for yourself before turning in the draft. For shorter writing tasks, a writer may create a draft, put it away, and then write another draft without referring to the first one. No one fully memorizes writing that quickly, so there will be differences between the two drafts, some more significant than others. Having two separate first drafts creates options that facilitate the revision process. Questions your instructor wrote in the margins, for example, might have already been answered in the alternative draft.

While you might not always want to rewrite a full draft, you might try this technique on an area in the first draft that is causing difficulty. You can try a different analysis, rewrite a poignant part of a narrative, or summarize support for your main point a second time. After receiving feedback, or maybe just on your own, you can compare the two versions to see which more closely addresses the needs of your audience. From bits and pieces of both drafts, you might be able to weave together a stronger critical analysis than you had in either. You might see openings that show how to restructure or develop your thesis.

You can also do this with revisions. If you do not know where to take your writing after submitting a draft, revise a section or even the whole paper one way, put the revision aside, and produce another revision. Whether you intend it to or not, the revisions will differ. You will be giving yourself choices. Again, you can compare the two revisions, combine them as you see fit, or look for further options. Try this if your revision process seems to be hampered by indecision or resistance to change. While the technique might sound like more work, producing two options on your own will make you feel more in control and more able to readily revise.

Write Out of Order   During both drafting and revising, nothing compels you to proceed sequentially. As long as the version you show to others demonstrates order or structure, it does not matter how you arrived at it. Thus, you can break writing tasks into parts, starting with the easiest and moving gradually to the most difficult.

Many writers have difficulty writing introductions, for example. Writers often leave the introduction for last. They do not know what they want to introduce until the paper has a clear shape and purpose. If you have difficulty with introductions, try saving this part of your task until you have written other sections. Writers often leave the introduction for last, as discussed in Chapter 4.

As another example, some writers panic when confronted with too many revision suggestions. Perhaps a suggestion to add detail to an event you observed racks your brain; you cannot remember much more than what you have already recorded. Why not start with the revision of the critical analysis, even though it is interspersed throughout your paper? As long as you leave enough time to add to your description before the due date, the delay in addressing issues will not harm you.

Incorporating such techniques into your writing process allows for natural breaks in drafting and revising. The parts you finish first might give you hints about tackling the more difficult areas of the paper. Introductions do not magically appear, but a clear idea of your topic and thesis will make writing one less stressful. If you find that a critical analysis focuses on gender issues, it could lead you to remember details concerning male–female differences in an event you witnessed, for example. While your finished product should be organized coherently, your process needs to be logical only to you.

COLLABORATING

You might find this activity especially helpful if you are currently working on a draft. Make a list of what you do when you draft and revise. Share your list with your group. Refer to your draft to point out specific examples of techniques that seem to work, as well as those that cause procrastination, incomplete drafts, or poor revisions. Could any of the techniques in this section be integrated into your process? What modifications would you have to make? What obstacles would hinder you from making changes to the model you now use? Make sure each group member receives feedback and contributes ideas.

Editing and Proofreading

There is no right time to start editing and proofreading. Some of the students in my class incorporated editing early, but proofreading—when treated as a separate part of the process—always seems to be the last step a writer takes. As noted earlier in this chapter, revision is a chore when a writer has spent too much time proofreading a draft. No one wants to redo a paper that appears superficially polished and correct. The writer risks making more mistakes, and proofreading must be repeated.

Editing involves similar risks. A writer might have to delete a particularly clever phrase he or she spent time conceiving. Shuffling the order of ideas often means creating a new introduction. Choosing different words to avoid repetition, as Chapter 5 suggests, can create a perspective that you must take into consideration. The significant changes brought on by editing indicate why many writers do not wait for the end to engage in it. Editing can produce as much resistance as proofreading, so writers incorporate editing at different times in their processes to avoid the anguish of last-minute overhauls.

Although editing and proofreading differ from drafting and revising, making them completely separate stages is unnatural. We don't want editing and proofreading to interfere with the construction of a piece of writing. Getting sentences correct and paragraphs in the form you want takes time and can shut down creative and critical impulses of writers who focus on "making it right" early in the process. However, gradual editing and proofreading can help you avoid the anxieties associated with a full edit and full proofread of a writing assignment. The resistance at having to redo a seemingly finished draft or revision will be lessened because you will be used to inserting, deleting, or changing words, reordering, checking spelling, and looking for mistakes.

The following are suggestions on incorporating an ongoing process of editing and revision.

Weaving in Analysis   Except for scientific reports, essays generally are not divided into discrete sections. (See Chapter 4 for information on structuring an essay.) While we can usually identify the introduction, body, and conclusion of an essay, writers weave analysis and detail throughout the body instead of moving sequentially from thesis to content to analysis. "Four Stops on a Bigfoot Hunt" in Chapter 13 serves as one example of analysis woven into the body of an essay.

Allow time in your editing to integrate the critical analysis throughout the body. In reviewing the body of your essay, find the points of significance on which your critical analysis rests, and linger on them to let the audience know their importance to your thesis. For an essay that uses narration in the body, lingering means disrupting the story to alert the audience to key elements. If you are using facts and research in your body, lingering means tying these elements together, showing how one builds on another. Jeff Parker slows his narration of the Bigfoot hunt, for example, by talking about the disagreements among Bigfoot researchers on matters as mundane as whether the plural of *Bigfoot* is *Bigfeet* and on more important matters about theories of what Bigfoot eats. All this speculation feeds into his ambivalent feelings about the purpose of Bigfoot research.

If you are describing a scene or relating an observation, lingering means slowing down your description to start explaining why you have emphasized a particular detail. This type of editing can take place at almost any point in your process. Some writers prefer to construct separate sections during drafting. They then cut and paste the critical analysis material, inserting relevant parts into significant text within the body. There should be obvious correspondence.

Other writers like this phase of editing to occur while they draft, making the review discussed above unnecessary. Based on freewriting that starts with the critical analysis (as discussed in the section on breaking through writing blocks), editing is incorporated when the writer sees a point of significance occurring, such as a detail about race or gender. Such writers rarely write separate analysis sections (except for the ideas generated through the freewrite); analysis is woven into their process, so the body leads directly to a conclusion.

Writers can mix these two editing strategies together as well, inserting a little analysis but also writing a critical analysis and reviewing the body during the revision process to see where more analysis can be woven in. The important point is that leaving this type of weaving until the end of your process will not allow enough time to consider structural changes that might be needed as a result.

Word Choice and Sentence Variety Editing and proofreading sometimes overlap in this part of the process. Most writers find it difficult, for instance, to check that they have not used filler words and then to return to the same sentence later to make sure words respond grammatically to the structure of the sentence. Generally, writers subconsciously do the editing (word selection) and the proofreading (checking for correctness) at the same time. Yet, catching mistakes differs from experimenting with words and rewriting sentences. Your process needs to reflect this distinction.

Although you can and should edit and proofread throughout your writing process, a final edit for word choice and sentence variety will not add an undue burden. Simply read your essay aloud from beginning to end, stopping when you notice too many short sentences in a row or too many long ones. You can combine some sentences with common connector words, such as *and* or *but,* and break up longer ones by deleting the same type of words and starting new sentences. While doing this final read, look for repetition of words and areas where your voice could come through more clearly. You probably used this strategy while you drafted and revised, but one final read will let you see the essay as a whole and fine-tune problem areas. When you insert a different word or revise a sentence, restart your oral reading at the beginning of the paragraph in which the change occurred. You want to make sure your rewrite fits into the flow of the paragraph.

Proofreading   Writers stumble in proofreading because they do not know the rules. However, confusion caused by a lack of recognition of mistakes should not deter you from proofreading. The more you write, the more you will recognize what most writing teachers call patterns of error. Recognizing errors is the first step toward correcting them. For instance, if you know you have difficulty with comma placement, you will have spotted one such pattern. If you realize that the problems occur when you construct longer sentences, you will have a further understanding of the pattern. The more you narrow the pattern down, the closer you will be to finding the exact set of rules you need to understand and implement better.

Consult your teacher or see a writing center tutor to start working on the recognition of your errors. On your own, you can locate mistakes that you do recognize as well as other lapses, such as leaving out a word, by doing one more silent reading of your essay after your oral read for editing. For this final read, take each sentence out of context so that your mind does not play tricks on you. Because you as the writer know what you mean to say, you might subconsciously insert or delete words to match your prediction of what should be there.

We can often see the errors in other people's writing better than we can in our own because we do not know what to expect when we read their words, and we are aware of everything. Mistakes do not pass us by. To turn off the natural filter in your mind, you must stop reading for meaning. In the final read, look at the very last sentence in your paper. If it looks correct, go to the second-to-last sentence. If that seems all right, go to the third-to-last sentence. Follow this process until you have read your whole essay backwards, sentence by sentence. Make corrections when you see them, but do not read two sentences in a row or try to edit. By following this practice, you will slow down your reading and find mistakes that you previously failed to notice.

Using Spelling and Grammar Checkers   Using a computer gives you an advantage in finding certain types of mistakes, since every word-processing program comes with a spelling and grammar checker. The checker highlights words that it cannot locate in its dictionary and sentences that do not seem to conform to the standard rules of grammar.

While these checkers come in handy, you need to understand their limitations. First, the spelling checker does not know what word you meant to spell. It will make suggestions from a list of words that look something like the word you spelled. You should not just click Change or Change All to fix a mistake. So what should you do when you do not know how to spell the word? Your program probably also includes a thesaurus. Run the suggested spelling through the thesaurus. If the synonyms listed match the meaning you want, then the word given by the spelling checker is correct. If not, seek alternate spellings.

Spelling and grammar checkers do not recognize most mistakes made that involve homophones (words with different meanings and spelling that sound alike, such as *there* and *their*). Study your own patterns of error concerning homophones, and pay special attention to them when you are doing your final proofread.

While grammar checkers are wonderful in locating sentence fragments or subject-verb agreement problems, the technology is far from perfect. Sometimes, a grammar checker will flag a sentence that does not need correction because it is unable to understand how a sentence functions in context. Other times, it confuses stylistic choices with mistakes. Consider the points the grammar checker makes, but do not click Change every time it flags a problem. Click the appropriate icon to get an explanation of the problem. If the explanation does not make sense in relation to your sentence, do not change it.

Also ask your teacher or a tutor for further guidance. There might be a pattern of error that you need help to recognize. In this case, talking with someone best helps you learn. Do not rely on spelling and grammar checkers to do your thinking. Learn to use these programs as aids, not as substitutes for skill development.

COLLABORATING

Practice the editing and proofreading techniques on a current writing assignment. Choose the group member who is farthest along in the process, and have him or her bring in enough copies of his or her paper for every member of the group. Use the techniques for weaving critical analysis into the body of the text, then do editing for word choice and sentence variety—having the writer read the paper aloud—and finish with a proofreading session in which the group reads the essay sentence by sentence in reverse order. Make changes that you can all agree on, and place check marks next to the lines that you wonder about. Consult with your instructor about the marked items. When you are finished, discuss the effectiveness of this strategy and its applicability to your individual processes. Can you think of ways to modify or otherwise tweak these suggestions so they work for you?

Summary

Writing processes are highly individualized. As you write more, you will develop a process that keeps the strong elements of the model you now use while allowing for changes that will improve the finished product. Some practices will help you accomplish this task. Understanding your current model and isolating problem areas in it are important. You must learn to recognize what causes writer's block and find methods to break it to ensure that it does not derail your ability to complete a task. Differentiating between drafting and revision, giving yourself options, and reorganizing your time to focus more on revision will help conquer your resistance to the process. Finally, weave editing and proofreading into your process so that they do not hinder the important areas of content development and analysis, but also do not leave everything to the very end. Final readings of an essay using various strategies will help you find the right words, ensure sentence variety, and catch mistakes.

CHAPTER 7

USES OF COLLABORATION

"Can't we get in groups to talk about this?"

I have heard this refrain from students many times. Students genuinely like working together. They can talk more freely among themselves than they can in larger groups. There is less fear of saying the wrong thing, appearing uninformed, or even sounding too smart. As a student, you probably enjoy active tasks more than lectures, so groups keep you attentive and allow you to learn more. And, yes, I know: When no teacher is hovering over you, you are freer to laugh and to get off task without reprimand. Groups can be fun, and they allow you to get to know the other students.

Based on requests and students' generally positive attitude toward group work, I decided years ago to extend in-class group work to out-of-class group work. My research told me that students were already consulting each other about editing, assignments, and other matters. I figured that a group project would give students a chance to continue enjoying the process of collaboration. Boy, was I wrong!

"One person always gets stuck doing all the work," my student Natalie complained when I introduced the final writing project of the year, a collaborative venture in which students would research the origins of their favorite holiday and compare purposes and intent with modern-day celebrations.

"Do we all get the same grade?" Nguyen chipped in. "That's not fair if my part of the project is good but the overall paper is bad."

"We should be able to select our own partners," Mildred said.

"Can I just do it on my own?" Kassim asked.

Online Study Center

This icon will direct you to web links and additional resources on the website http://college.cengage.com/english/thelin/

It seemed that the thought of sharing responsibility for a grade, especially with students who might drag them down, frightened my students. They could not imagine producing a stronger final piece through collaboration. I wondered why and asked. The students' past experiences had apparently been mixed.

Natalie had been grouped with slackers but would have felt like a snitch explaining to the instructor that the others had not contributed. "I wanted to help them, but they did not want to help me," she said.

Mildred felt she had been punished for her group's lack of caution in an experiment she reproduced as part of an oral group presentation in a chemistry class. "I did everything like I was supposed to, but the experiment did not reproduce like it was supposed to," she told everyone.

"I just could not work with these guys," Nguyen said, recalling a research report he had done on abortion. "They would not consider any argument about women having the rights to their own body."

Kassim was short and to the point. "I get everything done quicker if I do it alone."

Each of them had a valid point; yet, I knew that groups compose most professional and government documents. Few individuals produce a piece of writing to which no one else adds or on which no one else comments at some point in the process. Shouldn't we be teaching students how to collaborate?

Then it dawned on me: Teaching students how to collaborate is what I needed to do in class. While outcomes like the one Mildred described might still occur, experiences like Natalie's and Nguyen's could turn out better with guidance. If students like Kassim could see an advantage to working with others, the time involved might seem less important. I decided then and there that, rather than imposing collaboration on students, I would show them the benefits of working together and make them want to collaborate.

DISCUSSION

What have you experienced when working with groups outside of school projects? Make a list of the attitudes, actions, and discussions that helped the group function well. Make a similar list of behaviors that hindered the group. Discuss the attributes of functional and dysfunctional groups, and figure out how to avoid dysfunction. Can these ideas work in an academic project as well? What can each individual do to prevent dysfunction?

This chapter will help you learn to work together in an effective group. While these ideas can transfer to other disciplines, writing relies on collaboration more than does any other subject. Groups allow your strengths as a writer to shine through. A group will make use of these strengths, and areas in which you are perhaps weaker will be assigned to somebody else. Your weaknesses are probably somebody else's strengths. Working together, you can produce a much better finished product and enhance your skills as a writer.

MARCUS LAFFEY

Inside Dope

Many occupations use collaborative techniques to ensure that a job is done properly. In the following essay, a New York City police officer writes about his experiences arresting dope users. Pay attention to the necessity of collaboration. One person acting alone could not accomplish the goal.

If there were ever a Super Bowl matchup of junkies versus crackheads, it would be hard to figure which team the odds would favor. Both sides would most likely disappear during halftime. The crackheads would believe that they had won, and the junkies wouldn't care. If they did manage to finish the game, the smartest money would invest in a pawnshop next to the stadium, and within hours the investors would own every Super Bowl ring, for pennies on the dollar. Winners and losers would again be indistinguishable.

The war on drugs is a game for me, no matter how urgent it is for poor neighborhoods or how grave the risks are for cops. We call dealers "players," and there are rules as in chess, percentages as in poker, and moves as in schoolyard ball. When I went from being a beat cop to working in narcotics, the change was refreshing. For one thing, you deal only with criminals. No more domestic disputes, barricaded schizophrenics, or D.O.A.s, the morass of negotiable and nonnegotiable difficulties people have with their neighbors or boyfriends or stepchildren. Patrol cops deal with the fluid whole of people's lives, but usually when the tide's going out: people who have the cops called on them aren't happy to see you; people who call the cops aren't calling when they're having a good time. Now all I do is catch sellers of crack and heroin, and catch their customers to show that they sold it. The parts of their lives unaffected by coca- or opium-based products are none of my business. Patrol is politics, but narcotics is pure technique.

My unit, which consists of half a dozen cops and a sergeant, makes arrests for "observation sales." One or two of us go to an observation post ("the OP," and if you're in it you're "doing OPs") on a rooftop or in a vacant apartment to watch a "set," or drug operation, and transmit information to the "catch car," the unmarked van used to pick up the perps. The set might be a lone teenager standing on a corner with one pocket full of crack and another full of cash. Or it might be an organization of such intricate subterfuge—with lookouts, managers, moneymen, steerers (to guide customers), and pitchers (for the hand-to-hand transactions)—that you'd think its purpose was to deliver Soviet microfilm to covert operatives instead of a ten-dollar bag of junk to a junkie. But we watch, and give descriptions of buyers for the catch team to pick up, a few blocks away. Sometimes the dealers send out phantom or dummy buyers—people who appear to have bought narcotics but haven't—to see if they're stopped; we wait until we have a handful of buyers, then move in on the set. Most of the spots that we hit are well established, visited by both customers and cops on a regular basis; others pop up and disappear. You might drive around to see who's out—the faces at the places, the traffic pattern of steady customers and usual suspects. Sometimes you feel like the man on the catwalks over the casino floor, scanning the tables for the sharps and card counters, looking out for luck that's too good to be true. Other times, you feel as if you were watching a nature program, some *National Geographic* special on the felony ecology of the streets.

You read the block, seeing who moves and who stands still, their reactions and relations to one another; you sift the players from the idlers, the buyers from the passersby. Most people occupy their environment blithely, with only a slack and occasional awareness of their surroundings. A store window or a noisy garbage truck might distract them in passing, and they might look around before crossing the street, but the ordinary pedestrian is a poster child for daydreams and tunnel vision. Not so in the narcotics trade, where the body language of buyer and seller alike signals a taut awareness of opportunity and threat. There are distinctive addict walks, such as that of the prowler, who might be new to the spot, or sussing out an operation that has shifted to a more favorable corner. He hovers, alert for the deal, floating like a flake of ash above a fire. The addict on a "mission walk" moves with double-quick footsteps, leaning forward, as if against a strong wind, so as not to waste an extra second of his already wasted life. A player, on the other hand, has a self-contained watchfulness, a false repose, like a cat sunning itself on a windowsill, eyes half-closed but ready to pounce.

Every street set operates through an odd combination of aggressive mar- 5 keting and strategic defense, needing simultaneously to broadcast and to deny its function. The young man on the park bench should look like a high-school senior from thirty yards away but has to show he's a merchant at three yards, and he has to have the drugs near enough for convenience but far enough away to be out of his "custody and control" should he be stopped. If he's holding the drugs, he has to have an escape route—through a hole in a fence, say, or into an alley, or into the building where his grandmother lives. The man on the bench is just a man on a bench, after all, until his context proves him otherwise. But, as you watch, figures emerge from the flow of street life like coördinates on a grid, like pins on a drug map.

Say you're doing OPs from a rooftop, looking down on a street that has three young guys on the corner by the bodega, a couple with a baby in a carriage by the stoop, and a group of old men with brown-bagged brandy bottles by the vacant lot. A man on a bicycle moves in a slow, lazy slalom, up and down the street. The corner boys are the obvious pick, but I have to wait. When a buyer comes, he is easier to recognize, and his arrival on the set sends a signal, a vibration, like a fly landing in the web. The buyer is the bellwether and the bait: he draws the players out and makes them work, prompts them into visible display.

The buyer walks past the old men at the lot, the family on the stoop, to the corner boys, as expected. One corner boy takes the buyer aside and palms his cash, the second stands still, watching up and down the block, and the third goes to the family on the stoop and has a word with the woman with the baby. The woman steps inside the lobby for a few seconds—Thank God, I think, it's not in the carriage—and when she returns she hands something to the third boy, who meets up with the first corner boy and the buyer and hands off the product. The buyer walks away, retracing his route. The man on the bicycle follows him slowly.

I put the buyer over the air: "Hispanic male; red cap; Tommy Hilfiger jacket, blue; bluejeans. South on Third. Be advised, you got a lookout on a bike—white T-shirt, bluejeans, black bike—tailing him to see if he gets picked up. Let him run a couple of blocks, if you can."

Now I have a three-player set, with Mama and corner boys Nos. 1 and 3 down cold. The buyer should be taken, and No. 2 only observed for now. Mama's short time in the building tells me that the stash is not in an apartment but either on her person or right in the lobby, in an unlocked mailbox or a crack in the wall. Corner boy No. 2 is the one to watch, to see if he's the manager or a lookout, up a rank from the others or down. His position will become clear as I watch the group dynamic of the trio—the choreography of who stands where, who talks and who listens, who tells the jokes and who laughs, who's the one that runs to the bodega for the chips and soda. Until he participates in the exchanges, taking money or product, he's legally safe from arrest for an observation sale. If he's a manager, he's the one we want; if he's a smart manager, touching neither cash nor stash, he's the one we're least likely to get. In a sense, everybody wants the spot to get busy: the players grow careless as they get greedy, bringing out more product, paying more heed to the customer and less to us. The manager might have to step in and lend an incriminating hand. When the spot is slow, both groups—the cops and the players—have to be patient.

10   Even when nothing happens, there is much to interpret. Are they out of product, and will they re-up within ten minutes or an hour? Are they "raised"—afraid we're around—and, if so, is it because they saw our van (unmarked but patently obvious) or saw one of us peering over the roofline, or is it because a patrol car raced by, to a robbery three blocks away? Did they turn away another customer because he wanted credit, or because they thought he was an undercover cop, and were they right? Is the next deal worth the wait?

The wait can be the most trying part of the operation. I've spent hours on tar rooftops, crouched down till my legs cramped, sweating, shivering, wiping the rain from my binoculars every ten seconds. There have been times when I've forgotten to look down before I knelt by the ledge, and settled in beside piles of shit, broken glass, or syringes. On one rooftop, there was an ornate Victorian birdcage, five feet tall, bell-shaped and made of brass, and chained to it, still on a rotten leather leash, was the skeleton of a pit bull. You walk up dirty stairs to a dirty roof to watch a dirty street. At night, even the light is dirty, the sodium-vapor street lights giving off a muddy yellow haze. But sometimes, when something finally does happen, you realize that your concentration is perfect: you feel the cool, neutral thrill of being completely submerged in your task. The objects of surveillance inhabit a living landscape, and you can be struck by the small, random graces of the scene even as you transmit a streak of facts over the radio: "Gray livery cab, buyer in back seat, passenger side, possible white with white sleeves, U-turning now to the left. . . ."

A soap bubble, then two, then dozens rise up in front of me, iridescent, shimmering in their uncertainty. There is a child two floors below me, as rapt with the view above as I am with the view below.

"Arright, we got one, he's beelining to the player, they just popped into the lobby. . . . Now he's out—that's fast, he must have the stash on him. Arright, buyer's walking off now—Hold on, he's just kind of idling across the street. It's not an I-got-my-rock walk. I don't think he got done. Stand by. . . ."

A man standing on another tenement roof whirls an orange flag, and makes it snap like a towel. His flock of pigeons takes flight from the coop with a whoosh like a gust of wind, spiralling out in broadening arcs—showing the smoky gray of their backs as they bank out, the silver-white of their bellies as they circle in—rising up all the while.

"Player's walking off, he sent the last two away, he's out, he's raised, 15 I don't know, but—Go! Go! Go! Hit the set!"

An incinerator chimney shoots out a lash of black smoke, which loops into a lariat before dissolving into the grimy sky.

At the other end of the OP is the catch car. You want a buyer's description, or "scrip," to have something distinctive about it—something beyond the "white T-shirt, bluejeans" of warm weather, "black jacket, bluejeans" of cold. You don't want "Male, walking three pit bulls." You're glad to hear about hot pink and lime green, or T-shirts with legible writing on them, or, even better, "Female in purple-and-yellow tracksuit, with a Cat-in-the-Hat hat, riding a tiny bicycle." For crackheads, as much as for any other species, protective coloration can be a successful evolutionary strategy.

Once you get the scrip and the buyer's direction of flight, you move in, allowing yourself some distance from the set, but not too much, or else the buyer will be home; in neighborhoods like this, people don't have to go far for hard drugs. Sometimes buyers run, and sometimes they fight, and sometimes they toss the drugs (though sometimes you can find those drugs later), and sometimes they eat them when they see you coming. There have been buyers who at the sight of me have reacted with a loss of bowel control, and control of the belly and the bladder as well. The truth is, I am the least of their problems: a night on a cell bench, with prison bologna sandwiches to eat, ranks fairly low amid the hazards of being at the bottom of the criminal food chain.

For crackheads, in particular, a stint as a model prisoner might be a career peak. While the street dealers at dope spots are often junkies themselves, crackheads can't be trusted with the stash—they can't even hold a job whose main requirements are to stand still and watch. The majority of them are figures from a famine: bone-thin and filthy. Months of that life take years from their lives, and thirty-year-olds can pass for fifty, burned out almost literally, with a red-hot core of desperation beneath a dead, charred surface. Junkies generally have a longer ride to the bottom, as the habit gradually slides from being a part of their lives to becoming the point of them. Heroin is purer now than it was in the past, and fewer than half the addicts I arrest have needles on them. They snort it instead of shooting it, which decreases the risk of disease and also seems to slow the forward momentum of addiction. But to me the terminal junkies are especially awful, because they have none of the trapped-rat frenzy of the crackhead; instead, they possess a fatal calm, as if they were keeping their eyes open while drowning. When you collar them, they can have a look of confirmed and somewhat contented self-hatred, as if the world were doing to them what they expect and deserve.

20   Addicts deserve pity, always, though often they inspire contempt. We collared one crackhead, bumping into him by accident as he stood in a project lobby counting out a handful of vials. He was a street peddler who sold clothing, and had about eighty dollars in his pocket. He had the shrink-wrapped look that crackheads get, as if his skin were two sizes too small. He moaned and wept for his infant child, who would starve, he said, without his support. Yes, he acknowledged, the baby lived with its mother, but he was the provider. The mother and child were only about ten blocks away, at a playground, so we drove to meet them. The mother was a pretty, well-dressed woman, though her soccer-mom wholesomeness may have been artificially heightened by the presence of her handcuffed mate. We called her over, and her look of mild confusion became one of mild dismay as she saw our back-seat passenger. She didn't look surprised, and didn't ask questions. He took out his wad of cash, peeled off four dollars, and handed it to me to give to her. "You gotta be kidding me," I said. "You give me all this father-of-the-year shit, just to throw her four bucks?"

"C'mon," he said. "When you get out of Central Booking, you're hungry, you want some real McDonald's or something."

I gave him back the four dollars and took the wad for the mother. "The Number Two Special, two cheeseburgers and fries, is three-twenty-nine," I told him. "It's what I get, and it's all you can afford." For an addict, the priorities are never unclear.

After you've collared the buyers, it's time to move in on the dealers. When you hit a set, there is always a charge of adrenaline, arising from the jungle-war vagaries of opponent and terrain. There are elusive adversaries, explosive ones, and lots of sitting ducks. Some dealers opt for a businesslike capitulation, aware that it's the way to go through the process with the least fuss. Others, especially lobby dealers with access to an apartment upstairs, tend to make a mad dash for freedom. The bust could be a surrender as slow and dignified as Lee's at Appomattox or it could be bedlam—roiling bodies and airborne stash. When you can't count the evidence at the scene, you have to at least control it—the hundreds of dollars in small bills, the fistfuls of crack slabs, the loose decks, the bundles of dope—so you jam it in your pockets like a handful of ball bearings, and all the while there may be a crowd screaming, or perps for whom the fight-or-flight reflex is not a simple either-or proposition.

The smarter dealers carry nothing on them, but you await information from the OP, sometimes with a distaste that verges on dread:

25   "It's in his sock."

"It's in the cast on his right hand—"

"It's in his cheek—sorry, guy, the other cheek. I mean, check between 'em, you copy?"

Stash can be hidden under a bottle cap or in a potato-chip bag, or strewn among heaps of noncriminal trash; it can be wedged in a light fixture in a hall or tucked inside the bumper of a car; it can be in a magnetic key case stuck to the iron bolt beneath a park bench; or it can be on a string taped to the wall and dangling down the garbage-disposal chute. A thorough search can lead to unexpected threats and rewards. Once, when I was rooting through a janitor's closet in a housing project after hitting a heroin set, I found a machine gun in the bottom of a bag of clothes. We continued to search the building and found more than a thousand dollars' worth of heroin, two more guns—a 9-mm. handgun and a .45 revolver—and also ammunition for another machine gun, an AK-47: copper-jacketed bullets more than two inches long, coming to a sharp, conical point like a dunce cap. An AK-47 can discharge bullets at a speed of more than two thousand feet per second, which would allow them to pass through my vest with barely a pause.

In the movies, there are a lot of drug-dealer villains, but those characters usually have to slap their girlfriends or kill a lot of cops to heighten the dramatic point of their bad-guyness. Because the victims of drug sales line up and pay, so to speak, for the privilege, the perpetrators don't have the forthright menace of violent felons. But most of the players I collar have a rap sheet that shows a more diversified criminal career—of earlier forays into robbery or theft—before they settled on the more lucrative and "less illegal" world of drug sales. And although some drug spots operate in a fairly quiet, orderly manner, as if a man were selling newspapers on the street, or a couple were running a catalogue business out of their apartment, most are established and maintained by means of assault, murder, and many subtler thefts of human dignity.

In New York, heroin dealers stamp brand names on the little wax-paper 30 envelopes in which the drug is packaged. This practice gives a glimpse not only of a corporate structure, when the same brands appear in different sites, but also of a corporate imagination, showing what they believe their product should mean to their customers. Some convey the blandly generic aspiration of quality—"First Class," "President," "Original"—that you might find on brands of cornflakes or of detergent in some discount supermarket. Others go for a racier allure, but the gimmick is so hackneyed in conventional advertising that the genuinely illicit thrill of "Knockout" or "No Limit" suggests the mock-illicit thrill of ads for perfume or fat-free ice cream. Topical references are common, from the flat-out copyright infringement of "DKNY" or "Ford" to the movie tagline "Show Me the Money." But the best brand names are the literal ones, which announce without apology the bad things to come: "911," "25 to Life," "Undertaker," "Fuck You." There is a suicidal candor to "Lethal Injection" and "Virus," a forthright finality to "O.D."—a truth in advertising here that few products can match.

Recently, I had a talk with one of my informants, a junkie with AIDS who sleeps in an alley. A few days before, I'd obtained a search warrant for a spot he visits several times a day, and he fervently wished me luck with the warrant's execution. That my success would cause him inconvenience in supplying his own habit was a mild irony that did not trouble him. He said, "I know you're a cop and I'm—" and there was a sliver of space before his next word, enough for me to wonder what term he might use for a shorthand self-portrait. And, knowing that there would be a measure of harsh truth in it, I was still surprised, and even felt sorry for him, when he said, "And I'm a fucking scumbag." But he was equally firm in his opinion of those who had benefitted from his self-destruction: "I done time, I'm no hero, but these people are blood-suckers. Them and rapists are as bad as people get. Those people are worse than rapists. Those dealers will suck you dry. I hope you get every last one of them."

Every day, we go out and hunt people. When we do well—picking off the customers with dispatch, swooping in on the dealers, taking trophies of their product and profit—we feel skilled and lucky at once, at the top of our game. We have shut down spots, reduced robberies and shootings, made whole blocks cleaner, safer, saner places. But other spots withstand daily assaults from us with negligible losses, and I've driven home after a twenty-hour day only to recognize, with the hallucinatory clarity of the sleep-deprived, the same man, on the same mission walk, that I'd collared the night before. Typically, buyers spend a night in jail and are sentenced to a few days of community service. Players might get less, odd as that may seem, if there weren't enough transactions in open view, or if no stash was recovered. We'll all meet again, soon enough. There are breaks and interruptions, retirements and replacements, but, no matter how often the whistle blows, the game is never over.

Beyond the In-Class Response Group

The most frequently used in-class collaborative task is a version of a peer response group. As discussed in Chapter 3, receiving feedback from readers allows a writer to ponder suggestions generated from actual responses and to use them in making decisions about revising. Outside of class, writers consult with people around them to get feedback. A writer contemplating the proper words in a note intended for a bereaved friend might share a version with someone who knows the person to make sure the note sounds sensitive without being sappy. A writer constructing a flyer to encourage people to come to a peace rally probably will let other organizers evaluate the strength of the appeal before printing several hundred copies. Peer response accompanies most writing endeavors.

Sometimes students shy away from organizing peer response groups outside of the classroom. You might feel comfortable having a family member or a roommate read an assignment you intend to submit to your instructor, but you do not look for advice from fellow students unless you have the opportunity during class time. You shut out the people who have the most knowledge about class lessons, teacher expectations, and assignment requirements. While the feedback you receive from others can be valuable, responses from your peers could be the difference between an A and a C on a final project.

You may have never considered forming peer response groups outside of class time, but you do not want to ignore this opportunity for important insights. Out-of-class response groups relieve some of the pressure of classroom tasks. They give you practice in the collaborating that will be fundamental in your professional and civic endeavors.

Response groups can meet at a time convenient for everyone. They can be done in conjunction with a potluck dinner or can take place during the first hour or so of a social outing. You can get together face-to-face or online. You can enjoy the time together as long as you attend to the writing part.

Face-to-Face Groups   Weekend nights carry expectations that might undermine a serious effort at an out-of-class peer response group. Some students work at weekend jobs or return home for family visits. Thus, face-to-face groups should try to meet during the week. Ideally, the meeting should occur after everyone has attended his or her last class for the day. You can meet at a coffee shop, a dorm room, or anywhere that will be quiet enough for you to read and talk. Try to avoid more formal settings, such as a library or a vacant classroom, where the aura of schooling and the expectation of silence will be present.

Limit the number of people in a group, keeping it below five. More will make the session last too long and could shortchange writers whose work is considered toward the end of the session, when respondents are tired. Choose students with whom you can communicate. Sometimes the most popular or attractive person does not make the best group member. Rather, focus on students who participate effectively during class, usually come prepared, and show interest in improving as writers.

Skill level should not factor in as much as you might think. If you stack your group with the best writers in the class, you must be prepared to give as well as take, since they will have no incentive to help you if you do not offer substantial feedback. As long as a student has a desire to learn, he or she can contribute effectively to a group, despite skills that might be weaker. Everyone has the innate ability to judge, at some level, how well a writer has communicated to a reader. Everybody can give feedback on the important concepts of critical analysis, audience considerations, organization, and language.

If a piece of writing confuses a reader, no matter how good or bad a writer that person might be, his or her reaction can be probed for its usefulness in revision. Sometimes weak writers understand certain issues of critical analysis, audience, organization, and language better than strong writers. In matters related to proofreading, however, consult a handbook to verify the accuracy of feedback; when in doubt, consult your instructor.

To differentiate the out-of-class response group from the dominant mode of education—correction of error—the group should concentrate on matters of content. Members should bring copies of their essays for the other members to read (even if the group decides to read the essays aloud). Talk about ideas; keep the assignment handy to make sure requirements have been met; and make genuine suggestions about how to make the essay more insightful and stimulating.

Whether you are working on a draft, trying to start a revision, or testing a revision to see how an audience reacts to your attempts at improvement, out-of-class response groups can help. You can meet as often as you like, but scheduling meetings at a regular time every other week or so can make those meetings part of your routine that you arrange the rest of your life around instead of an obligation added to a hectic day. Remember to make it fun. Laugh, plan to see a movie afterwards, eat while reading, and get to know your peers. Learning involves discipline, but within the confines of responsibility and proper preparation, there is plenty of time for enjoyment.

Online Groups   Online variations of out-of-class response groups include chat rooms and bulletin boards, such as those used in course management systems like Blackboard. Essays are posted so that peers in the group can review them. Responses can be sent as email messages or email attachments. Synchronous discussion of essays allows for dialogue and is therefore preferable to asynchronous postings.

Chat rooms can be established between pairs of students or the whole group, depending on members' preferences. Sometimes having too many respondents in a chat room makes following a strand of conversation difficult. One way to alleviate this problem is to establish rules. For instance, the writer could discuss the first peer reviewer's critique with that person only, while others listen. The other peers can voice agreement or disagreement with the first set of comments when it is their turn to critique.

Simple technology enables online discussions. For a course that uses Blackboard or another course management system, the instructor can allow the chat room capabilities to be used by the online group. Anyone who uses instant messaging can carry on a synchronous discussion. Arranging the online group is easier, too, by inviting classmates to join—perhaps by sending online invitations so as to weed out the technologically challenged—without having to find a place to meet or organizing transportation.

While the online option does not permit the socializing that face-to-face groups enjoy, contributors can instead establish different identities or play with text while engaging in the discussion. As is the case with the face-to-face groups, the group needs to focus on the important concepts of writing while resisting the temptation to proofread.

DISCUSSION

Talk about the strengths and the weaknesses of your first experience with in-class peer groups in this or other courses. What benefited you? What do you wish could have happened? Imagine that the peer group discussion had taken place in a location other than a classroom. What might have been different? How do the constraints or structure of the classroom hinder or help you in the task of responding to student writing? Discuss the structure that would make an out-of-class group utilize the strength of in-class groups while avoiding the problems that occur.

Assigning Tasks in Group Projects

Ideally, the group project assigned to you will have so many layers and require so much time that everyone will see the advantage of working with peers. But if the assignment is open-ended, the group must create tasks that will produce a final product above and beyond individual capabilities. Otherwise, you or another student might be tempted to take over the project should a problem emerge. If other members, particularly any who are inclined to be lazy, sense that one group member will pick up the slack, they may not work as hard. Furthermore, the instructor will expect more from a group of four or five students than from a single person. Match the teacher's expectations with a plan that will exceed what you could produce individually.

Assigning tasks to each member of the group is essential to the success of a group project. Collaboration starts with individual effort. As a member of a group, you must follow through on a specific part of the project that will link with the work turned in by the other students.

Selecting a Secretary
Instead of electing a leader, have one person function as the secretary. The secretary should be responsible for taking notes at group meetings, organizing the deadlines for each phase of the process, and distributing the schedule and a list of everyone's tasks. The group should agree on the details of the schedule and the allotment of tasks; the secretary merely arranges and records the decisions.

The importance of having a secretary rests in writing down the agreements and making the list available, perhaps through email or on a temporary website such as one offered by FreeWebs or another online provider. If there are disputes about what tasks were assigned and when, the secretary can refer to an official record. If technology is not available, the secretary can record the important information on paper and give copies to all members to prevent legitimate mistakes and strengthen each person's sense of responsibility. The secretary's work puts the agreements reached in words and acts as a contract of sorts for the group.

Strengths and Weaknesses
Tasks should utilize the best attributes of each member. If a project involves both library research and data gathering (Chapter 10 explains these elements of writing), the group members who best know the library databases should probably be assigned to this aspect. Members who are outgoing and who are comfortable approaching people might conduct interviews or collect questionnaires. Perhaps one member analyzes evidence well, so his or her task is to figure out the meaning of the results gathered in the data collection.

Tasks depend largely on the assignment. While writing should be done by everyone in the group, it may be easiest to have one person put together the whole first draft, to have two or three others work on the revision, and to have yet another do the final proofreading. In groups of four and five, you can also consider pairing a person strong in one area with a person who is weak in that area. The stronger person can teach the weaker person how to do something, and the weaker person can take the lead at some point. This type of task assignment helps everyone learn while completing the project. The strong person must not overstep boundaries so as not to compromise the learning and allow others to avoid doing any work.

Keep a Progress Log   Too often, groups meet to discuss progress but do not have written material to show each other. This allows members to hide poorly done work or even to fabricate their efforts. The group then dives into writing the report or paper without any text to start from.

Groups should require each member to keep a progress log. The log should include specifics about what the member did—and where, how, and when he or she did it—and summarize important information. It will provide a chronological narrative of the task and will be especially useful in evaluating the work. Posting the progress logs online will give other group members access. Members can review and comment on one another's logs before group meetings.

A group cannot allow a member to summarize too broadly or to give details of some work and skim over the rest by saying, "There's much more, so we're okay." This line is frequently used by someone who has done the work at the last minute. Online intervention can urge the member to explain exactly what he or she did and prevent a member from covering up lax work. If an individual's task was to conduct a poll, the progress log should explain what was on the poll, where he or she approached people to get information, how people were selected to be polled, and when the polling took place. If the task was an online search for recent information on a topic, the log should explain what search engines and websites were used, with what key words, and when the search was completed.

It is also a good idea to include how many hours each member put into his or her part of the task. Although members might fudge a bit, this information will give an indication of everyone's involvement outside of the classroom. If a person claims to have worked ten hours but has a skimpy progress log, other members can ask how the time was spent and suggest better ways to get the work done.

Following is an example of a week's progress log that a student typed up and distributed to his group during the exploratory parts of a large research project.

Jim's Progress Log

The assignment was to research a historical mystery, uncover the political and social agendas that surrounded the mystery, and come to a conclusion about the influence of those agendas in preventing the mystery from being solved. While Jim seems frustrated with his research at times and wants to concentrate on specific information that he finds, he is recording relevant observations about the political battles surrounding his group's topic, the Dead Sea Scrolls, that may find their way into a final paper. It might have been best for Jim to give more detail about the articles he did not understand, but in at least mentioning them, he is showing a pattern in the published information that his group might be able to use as they synthesize the materials.

October 7: I spent 2 hours in the library trying to find articles about the Dead Sea Scrolls. I used Ohio Link and tried to find printable articles. There are several articles on the subject, most of them coming from a journal, Biblical Archaeology Review. I couldn't understand the points these articles were making. They were a bit over my head, so I stopped reading after a while. In 1982, an article called "Essene Origins—Palestine or Babylonia" talked about the Dead Sea Scrolls, but it was referring to terms and people that did not seem to concern our project. I don't know who the Essenes are or why the Hellenization of Judaism matters. I think this article was meant for a different type of audience. We might be able to make use of "Is the Vatican Suppressing the Dead Sea Scrolls?" I read more of it and printed it out. It's confusing, but I think it is talking about people's fears that the Dead Sea Scrolls would undermine Christianity and Judaism. It says there were no Jews on the editing team until after about 40 years and that the Vatican limited accessibility to the scrolls to only a few people. The author, Hershel Shanks, says that the scrolls do not challenge anyone's faith and that the Vatican was not trying to cover up anything about its content. It's from 1991.

October 9: I found another journal called Bible Review in our libraries' collection that had article on the Dead Sea Scrolls by James C. Vanderkam. It was from the issue in December 1991/February 1992 and was titled "The Dead Sea Scrolls and Christianity." It mentioned stuff that I could understand, like John the Baptist. I didn't read all the way through it, but it shows what the Dead Sea Scrolls could mean and how some people have misinterpreted them. For example, some people have claimed that Paul and even Jesus were meant when the scrolls referred to a "wicked priest." I think it is saying that the scrolls show us about the culture of early Christianity, but even though I tried, I couldn't finish it. I spent over an hour reading this article, so I didn't look for any more in this journal.

October 11: There was a book in our library called Who Wrote the Dead Sea Scrolls? by Norman Golb. I think it will help us because it gives a lot of background. The book is long, so I only skimmed it. One chapter talked about the same stuff as the article I found from Bible Review. There's a big struggle over who has the right to translate, edit, and interpret the scrolls. There's also a chapter about their discovery, which might help us, but it looks like the author is more interested in ownership of the scrolls, I guess. The more I look into this, the more it seems like historians want to argue over who said what and why their interpretation is better than others. This book has chapters like "The Deepening Scrolls Controversy" and "The New York Conference and Some

Academic Intrigues." I do not think it is really answering its question about the author or how the scrolls fit into Judaic and Christian beliefs. But the good thing is that the book has a glossary of all the important terms. It will make the chapters easier to understand. I just don't think we can read all of the book by our deadline. Maybe we can divide up chapters or something.

October 13: I visited the exhibit in our museum on the scrolls. I should have done this first! It actually had some of the scrolls on display! They had note cards which were written in pretty plain English that explained what the scrolls were supposed to mean and why they are important. I didn't bring a notebook with me, but I think we should go back together. I know I will understand the articles better if we take notes from the display. I think we can see what the real controversy is. One display said that a reference to a dying Messiah in the scrolls would be the first time a pre-Christian text mentions Jesus as Messiah. This is the type of stuff we're looking for. It's really pretty exciting, but I just can't remember everything. We need to go to the display.

Instructor Intervention   What are your options if a group member is not contributing? You have three choices: Let that member's irresponsibility drag down the quality of the finished work; do the work and let the person receive credit for doing little or nothing; or arrange for intervention.

In the professional workplace, your employer is not going to accept excuses; a team member who does not carry his or her share has to be dealt with, not ignored. If a faulty product may be distributed to the public, you have to make someone aware. Ultimately, you will have to tell your employer that your group needs a replacement for the person. When raises and promotions are on the line, you want to get due credit. If you have been covering up for somebody, that person will reap the same rewards as you, perhaps even greater ones. Covering up enables the person to continue his or her unproductive ways. Since you have shown the ability to produce a good product while working with the person, you are bound to wind up on that team again, producing an ongoing cycle of unfair workloads. Clearly, you need to go to your manager and explain the unequal labor put into a task. Are these instances of ratting somebody out? Or are they responsible interventions?

The question is when to intervene when a classmate does not perform as required. The longer you wait, the worse the situation will become. To avert more negative consequences, speak to your instructor on the first missed due date or the second instance of sloppy work. Be sure to provide the group secretary's notes, materials from the group website, and relevant progress logs. The intervention should be done during conference time with the instructor in the presence of the less-productive team member, if possible. This allows the instructor to make recommendations to the student or the group, perhaps requiring the student to catch up quickly and turn in the work at the next class period. The instructor might replace the student with another student. Whatever the instructor's decision, group functioning probably will improve.

Asking the instructor to intervene also shows that you have been doing your part of the project. The instructor will likely continue to keep an eye on the group. Most important, intervention sends a message to the irresponsible student that you will not do his or her work and you will not put up with poor production.

While there could be initial social awkwardness if you travel in the same circles as the person, college functions differently from high school. Most college students understand the importance of doing good work and will not chastise a student doing a group project for making sure that everyone shares equally in the task.

COLLABORATING

Each group should select a topic from one of the Group Work sections in Chapters 11 through 16. Construct a plan for completing the project, including due dates and task assignments. Make sure your expectations are realistic and each member's task is clear. Assign a secretary to keep track of the group's meetings. When you have completed your assigned tasks, meet as a group, read each other's work, and discuss what else is needed. If you feel that each member has done his or her duty, follow the suggestions in the following section on synthesizing.

Synthesizing Ideas

Group projects usually involve tasks outside the classroom, such as observations, library research, experiments, data gathering, and analysis. If each member completes his or her task correctly, the group advances to the next step—synthesizing this information. Synthesizing means combining materials and drawing conclusions from the varying ideas presented in the group. For most projects, synthesis involves a written essay. If everyone has maintained a project log, you can start with the research summaries in putting together the first draft.

Some group members think they can just link the various contributions together to create a functional finished piece. This notion is mistaken. Every section must connect to the previous one, providing a smooth flow throughout the report. Group members must work together to ensure that the analysis is critical enough to produce an intriguing thesis, that the audience's needs are understood, that the best possible words have been chosen, and that the organizational strategy works well for the content. A final essay has to go beyond patching together pieces from sections.

However, the first draft should probably start with a rough connection of ideas. The member who has been assigned the task of assembling the first draft (it should be just one person to avoid too much confusion at this early stage) should put the sections together and propose a thesis statement, an introduction, and a conclusion. The initial draft should not go too far beyond this. The group member should email the draft to other members as an attachment or should post it to a website, so that the other group members may read and think about it.

Either electronically or face-to-face, group members must talk to one another, share critiques, and assess how the pieces fit together. Sometimes, even if each member was diligent in his or her research task, you might need more information. Some data and research raise questions that call for more data gathering and research. In the earlier example, Jim realized that the group had to do more than he initially accomplished alone. While we might fault Jim for not recording his visit to the museum appropriately, he intuitively realized that his group would profit by visiting the exhibit together. There's no shame in realizing that you need more information to produce coherence. Other times, you might have to rethink the thesis that the draft writer has produced.

Once you have the draft and one person's attempt at connecting together the sections, you are ready to proceed with real group synthesis. Following are some tips for synthesizing.

Critiquing Peers' Work   Nothing is more important at this stage in a group project than being able to talk honestly and openly with one another. If you want a high-quality finished product, you must be willing to criticize group members' work constructively as well as receive criticism about your own contributions.

When you are assembling the parts of a project to give an essay its initial shape, you will see sections that are stronger than others, missing links between sections, and inconsistencies in tone. Often, some sections need more attention than others, which can frustrate the group and hurt the feelings of the individual whose section has been targeted. Cutting examples or sentences can also bruise a writer's ego, especially if these parts are done well but just do not fit the overall theme. Critiquing properly requires showing sensitivity toward others.

Many cooperative strategies will allow you to communicate. Here is one technique. First have everyone critique his or her own section, pointing out at least one strength and one weakness. Then, have each member critique every section in the report or paper, listing at least one strength but focusing on the weak areas and the possibilities for revision. Revision might include reorganizing, analyzing in more depth, adding more information, deleting parts, finding a more logical thesis, or rewriting for stronger language, audience awareness, or correctness. The revisions might extend from individual contributions all the way to the choices the draft writer made in putting the sections together.

This method will let you see the agreements among the group as well as each person's reasoning, and it will let the group reach consensus through the majority's opinions. Some individuals might spot unrealized potential or problem areas that did not occur to other members, but the group can voice its approval or disapproval even if individuals had not thought of these ideas originally.

Revision or editing suggestions do not need to be initially presented by a majority in order for them to be understood and agreed on by the majority when the group reaches consensus. Vote on each suggestion to ensure the participation of all group members. The secretary must keep especially good notes at this time, since two or three group members will implement the actual changes based on the agreements that have been reached.

With this technique or similar cooperative strategies, everyone will have an equal chance to give his or her opinion, and everyone's section will be discussed. Group decisions still might strike some members as adversarial, but this method softens seemingly harsh blows and yields a productive outcome.

Weaving Sections Together   The two or three individuals who take responsibility for the revision of the essay should follow the guidelines set by the group. Yet, the group should not assume that they are robots who must merely follow instructions. Although specific suggestions will be made during the group critiques, transitioning from section to section involves initiative on the part of the writers. The analysis must be woven into the text. Each section must show awareness of the previous section, which calls for overlaps among sections as well as the use of transitions. The thesis must be introduced in a strategic area of the text. The only way to make such decisions is to try different approaches and see how they work. While you can implement many of the strategies suggested in previous chapters to make the strongest revision possible, transitioning from sections within a group project might involve some sticky issues. Frequently, the shift from one writer's research to the next disrupts the flow because of repetition or contradictions.

For example, if the topic is endangered species, the group might divide the tasks by having one member find information about specific species in danger of extinction, another find the history of laws designed to protect endangered species, and another look for conflicts between the economy and the survival of species. The first writer will probably uncover information about the grizzly bear and ranchers' complaints that not being allowed to shoot grizzlies who feed on livestock will run them out of business. In dutifully reporting this, the first writer has strayed into the territory of the other two, since the laws protecting grizzlies are the source of the ranchers' concerns about economic survival. Thus, the best of transitions will not link the two parts. Instead, the information has to be organized. You might choose to report on one animal at a time, including the information about laws and economics as they apply directly to that animal, or to separate the information into sections of general information (statistics about species size, descriptions, history), the laws (including specifics related to each animal), and the various economic effects. You will need to dissect information, placing some parts of a contributor's information here, other parts there.

When pieces of research contradict one another, you must account for these differences as well. Conflicts often emerge when one group member does library research and another does web-based research. In such cases, the revision writers must make decisions about the most reliable sources while still mentioning the other sources. For example, a revision about conflicting reports of bear attacks on cattle might read, "While online websites by ranchers paint a dire picture of their future cohabitating with grizzlies, current research by naturalists indicates that the financial losses caused by marauding bears are exaggerated." You would also have to document the sources.

Thus, weaving sections together involves much more than carrying out the instructions of the group. The revision writers play a key role in the success of the final paper or report.

Stabilizing the Voice   With so many different writers of project sections, prose styles and tones throughout your report or paper might conflict. Therefore, when the two or three revision writers present the revision to the larger group, one of your main functions will be to stabilize the voice in the paper.

Some areas are obvious. The group should not be referring to *I* or *me* in the paper. Sometimes, the use of *we* is inappropriate, such as in a personal experience used as an introduction or as an example. In cases like this, you should refer to the writer in the third person or introduce the experience with a phrase similar to this one: "One of our group members, Alan, reports on a personal encounter with an animal from an endangered species that adds support to our thesis. In Alan's words: . . ." You would then shift to a different font or block off the section to insert Alan's narrative. You could also continue with third-person reporting if it does not harm the flow of the narrative.

Some areas are not as obvious. All of us use expressions that are particular to ourselves. As discussed in Chapter 5, these expressions help establish our narrative voice. In a group project, however, the different voices might collide. Individuality must be assimilated into a group voice. Thus, the person responsible for the final proofreading and editing should eliminate places where such expressions give the impression that two different writers are speaking. The person should also make sure the diction is consistent throughout the essay. He or she will want to "revise upward" so that all sections match the best section in terms of vocabulary. As always, the person should make sure to avoid misusing words. Finally, combinations of sentences can reveal distinct styles and might give the sense of too many voices in a paper or report. Going through the sections to make sure all paragraphs use a variety of sentence lengths should solve such problems. Final editing and proofreading will not differ much from the editing and proofreading individuals do on a paper, but group work does demand stabilizing the voice.

COLLABORATING

To practice this type of synthesis, group members should agree on an episode of a television series, a movie, a concert, or an event that they all saw and write about it. One person should write about the beginning; the middle can be divided up among two or three members; and one person can write what happened at the end. After finishing these pieces, the group's job is to put it together as a coherent piece of writing. Go through all the steps in "Synthesizing Ideas," but do the synthesizing, weaving, and checking for voice as a group. Make note of the parts of the process that cause difficulties for your group. Also observe which members seem to be best suited for the various tasks.

Taking Responsibility

Groups function most efficiently when every member takes individual responsibility for the project's success. This is easier said than done. As an individual, you can monitor yourself, but what about the others? Who ensures that they take the proper responsibility? As pointed out earlier in this chapter, groups must take action when a member does not fulfill his or her commitment to the group.

Sometimes a problem emerges gradually. A member's work deteriorates as the project goes on. Perhaps a person suffers an illness that sets him or her back a week. Maybe the member breaks up with a boyfriend or girlfriend, or homework for another course takes up more time than a person expected. Enthusiasm for a project can wane as well. The group cannot readily replace somebody late in the project, and it is possible that the final product will be affected.

If each person takes responsibility for failure to meet deadlines or to produce satisfactory work, others will find it easier to pitch in. Humans tend to dislike excuses. However, they respond to admissions of neglect and to the willingness to suffer consequences. There are two ways for a group to rescue itself when problems arise late in the project. Both hinge on individual group members acknowledging their failure to do their share of the work.

Individual Evaluations   While you are functioning as a team, individual efforts must not be forgotten. When you submit your final paper or report, each group member should write to the instructor about his or her contribution to the project. Do not share the letters with other group members. If you have fulfilled your responsibility for all tasks assigned to you, you should be able to list them in specific terms and explain how well you did them. You should indicate which tasks you performed alone, which ones you did with one or two other group members, and which ones were a whole-group effort.

Take credit only for what you did. If two people take credit for the same task, or if one person fails to acknowledge a partner in a collaborative task, the contradictions will alert your instructor to problems. These letters should serve as a time for honesty and reflection.

Teamwork   A group must make every effort to produce the best essay possible, even when one or two individuals fade at the end. Sometimes swapping duties will help. In a recent collaborative project, the lead writer of our group produced a functional first draft of an article with the help of one other cowriter. The lead writer wanted me to look at structure and tone, but I was too busy at the time. I asked another writer to step in and look at the structure and agreed to contribute more heavily during the revision and final polishing of the paper. She reviewed the structure, and I performed the majority of the duties later on. No one complained, since everyone did his or her share.

As long as people are capable of doing the task at hand, there is nothing wrong with veering from the plan and trading with somebody else. The key is to take responsibility and to tell the group what you haven't done or what you will not be able to do. If you delay in alerting the group, the essay will be affected. If you miss a meeting or give feeble excuses for failing to turn in materials, your group is likely to be disgusted. But people pitch in when they realize that one person cannot carry his or her load, as long as the person concedes the point and accepts the consequences.

Being a team member is much like being an understudy in a play. The understudy is responsible for taking the lead role in some performances (matinees, for instance) and for filling in when the lead actor is unable to act. The performance could be in jeopardy if the lead actor does not inform anyone in advance and just fails to show up or shows up with a litany of excuses about why he or she cannot go on that night. Disaster would also ensue if the understudy had not learned the lines. Strong teamwork does not necessarily demand equal production or the same quality from each person, but it does rely on individual responsibility.

DISCUSSION

Should the evaluations discussed in this section involve a critique of other group members' contributions? To what extent? Can you talk about what you did or did not do without comparing it or placing it in the context of the work done around you? Discuss ways you can write about the collaborative process without blaming group members for not fulfilling their responsibilities.

Summary

Most writing projects for business or community action involve the contributions of others. Therefore, writers need to practice collaborating with groups in the classroom. However, many students have had negative experiences in groups, with one member doing all the work or with the contribution of one member diminishing the overall quality of the project.

To avoid conflict and develop collaborative skills, students must understand behaviors that help and hinder effective group work. Taking classroom activities, such as peer response groups, outside of the classroom is one way to practice collaboration.

When an instructor assigns groups to collaborate on a writing project, group members must establish deadlines for each stage of the project, keep records, and hand out tasks according to ability. At each stage, group members must provide a complete written record of their individual work. Keeping a progress log ensures consistent recording of each member's work. If a member does not meet early deadlines, the group must ask for instructor intervention so that the member's lack of work does not snowball into an incomplete or poor final essay.

Even when individuals have done good jobs on their individual tasks, the group must make sure that the final essay is more than just strung-together individual sections. Drafting, revising, and editing must all be attended to by group members working separately and together. Individuals must be held accountable for their inability to fulfill their responsibilities as well as being given credit for success.

CHAPTER 8

PURPOSES AND STRATEGIES FOR READING

To develop a process and collaborate effectively, writers must move outside their immediate experience and learn about the world around them. While direct observation yields many insights, reading the ideas of others, especially ideas supported by research and facts, can stimulate you when you hit a writing block and can ensure the credibility of a group project. Yet, some students are reluctant to read materials that appear at first to be daunting.

Recently, a student named Ben complained to me about an assigned reading, "Executive Pay in the U.S." by Jack Rasmus. The assignment, one the students had helped me create, involved investigating the careers they hoped to enter upon graduation. I found the article to be extremely relevant; the statistics cited in it would have bearing on the students' futures. Ben could not make sense of the article, saying that he did not understand the references to the Enron scandal, earned income, and SERPS. He also felt overwhelmed by the sheer number of statistics given.

I recited the tired lines used by many professors: "When you have trouble understanding a passage, you should make a note in the margin and come to class prepared to ask questions about it. You can't just give up on the reading."

"But who wants to read this stuff anyway?" Ben asked.

Writing instructors often fail to realize that everyone does not enjoy reading as much as they do. Instructors see reading as a vital step in obtaining knowledge and heightening critical thinking skills as well as a source of entertainment and pleasure. They believe that people miss out on a lot of life

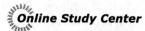
Online Study Center

This icon will direct you to web links and additional resources on the website http://college.cengage.com/english/thelin/ writing_without_formulas/1e/student_home.html

if they do not exercise their reading skills. They can become defensive, too, and say things they perhaps shouldn't, as I did.

"What's the difference between a person who can't read and a person who doesn't read?" I asked.

Ben took up my challenge. "Newspapers are written so that a seventh grader can understand them," he observed. "Why do we have to do more than that for this class?"

"Because we're several years removed from seventh grade, aren't we?" I responded. "Do you want to remain at a seventh grade educational level for the rest of your life?" Most professors would probably respond to Ben the way I did, and even students would have to admit, albeit grudgingly, that I had a point. But as they were to teach me that day, Ben's question resounded with validity. Couldn't complex ideas be captured in plain language?

Moira was the next student to speak up. "Just because I don't like to read books doesn't mean I don't read," she said. "I read instant messages, signs, advertisements, gaming instructions, and all sorts of labels every day."

"Okay," I granted. "But don't you think more exposure to reading will make you better able to understand subtle parts of advertisements? Some instructions for gaming are complicated. Practice in reading difficult material beyond the seventh grade level will help you understand, right?"

Ben had given up on me, collapsing into his seat with a sigh of frustration. This was Moira's battle now. "Instructions usually come with diagrams. I can always ask someone if I don't understand some washing instruction on a label. And I can see through ads. I know they try to manipulate us. There's always something visual that goes with reading that helps me understand. That's how I comprehend all sorts of complicated stuff."

Moira was making sense, so I had to think for a second. "Aren't you doing a type of reading when you look at pictures and charts and everything? We talk about trying to read somebody, like in a poker game when you're trying to read somebody's face to see if they are bluffing."

"Yeah, I guess so," Moira said. "So reading is a way of interpreting and understanding something, right?"

I agreed.

"Then good writing should be easy to interpret and understand."

Some students clapped in approval. "Not necessarily," I said.

"Hold on a second," a student named Jasmine piped up. "There's different types of movies you like that require thinking. I wouldn't want every movie I see to be Disney or something like that. I want to be challenged sometimes. My feelings aren't simple. For a movie or a song or anything to get me to feel, it has to match my complexity. Same thing for writing, I suppose."

Jasmine's insight led the class to a rich discussion about the many kinds of reading we do. Students were able to see that more difficult reading might have a purpose—not as practice for the future, but as a way to evoke complicated feelings and ideas within us.

JACK RASMUS

Executive Pay in the U.S.
CEOs still take the money and run

Here is an excerpt from the article I assigned. Do you think the reading is too difficult? Does it appropriately match the complexity of the subject matter?

The most fundamental and singular result of corporate policies of the past 25 years has been a massive shift in relative income from the roughly 105 million workers to the wealthiest 10 percent of non-working class households in the U.S. This enormous income transfer grew in scope and magnitude annually throughout the 1980s and Reagan years, continued to expand steadily during the Clinton years, accelerated during the first term of George W. Bush, and now promises to exceed more than $1 trillion per year during the rest of Bush's second term.

Few groups within the ranks of the U.S. corporate elite have gained more from this historic income shift than the CEOs and senior managers of corporate America. In 1978, according to the *Wall Street Journal*, typical U.S. CEOs earned approximately 35 times the pay of the average paid worker in their company. In recent years CEO total compensation has risen to more than 500 times the average worker's pay, according to the conservative global business source, Reuters.

Defining Executive Pay

The typical worker in the U.S. receives about 90 percent of their earned income from their paycheck whether earned as an hourly wage or weekly salary. Not so for the typical CEO and senior manager. Historically only 7–10 percent of their income is earned from a salary as such. Focusing only on CEO salaries, therefore, totally misses the point and statistics quoting CEO salaries as the sole indication of executive pay levels should be especially suspect. At times the term "direct compensation" is used as an alternative measurement of executive pay. But that too underestimates such pay, as it excludes hidden indirect forms of compensation.

A slightly better term is "total compensation." It includes direct and indirect forms of executive pay. CEO total compensation may include salaries, bonuses (cash or other forms), stock options, stock grants and awards, long term incentive pay, deferred pay of various kinds, regular and supplemental management pensions, below market rate mortgage loans to managers by the company, write offs of personal loans by corporate boards, innumerable forms of perks with direct dollar value, prepaid charitable donations, lifetime use of corporate jets, company payment of CEO tax obligations (called "gross up" compensation), and so on in a long list of forms of creative and hidden pay. These and other non-salary forms of executive pay account for 90 percent or more of CEO and senior managers' total compensation.

5   But even "total compensation" is an inadequate indicator of executive pay. With hearings on executive pay by the U.S. Securities and Exchange Commission (SEC) to begin this spring, it is clear that many other forms of executive compensation remain hidden by opaque corporate accounting and reporting practices, are not counted as part of "total compensation," and are never communicated to the IRS.

During the Reagan years average CEO pay rose from just over $1 million a year to roughly $2.5 million by 1989. By 1992, at the close of the George Bush senior administration, it nearly doubled again to $4.5 million—despite the recession of 1990–91 and falling corporate profit performance. It more than doubled again under Clinton to $11.1 million by 2000, for a 342 percent gain over two decades. Some estimates placed the pay of the average U.S. CEO as high as $14.4 million by 2001.

According to a just released study by professors Lucian Bebchuk of Harvard Law School and Yaniv Grinstein of Cornell University, based on interviews of CEOs and top managers at the 1,500 largest publicly traded corporations in the U.S., the group of 5 top managers at the corporations received collectively $122 billion in compensation between 1999–2003 compared to $68 billion for the same group during 1993–1997. On top of these 1999–2003 gains, the Harvard–Cornell study estimates another 39 percent increase in average executive compensation in 2004 for the surveyed group of the largest corporations.

But even the Harvard–Cornell figures are underestimations as they exclude the lucrative and fast-growing supplemental pensions for executives, called Supplemental Executive Retirement Plans (SERPS). Some sources estimate SERPs constitute as much as an additional one-third of total executive compensation. Were SERPS and other supplemental retirement plans included in the Harvard–Cornell study estimates, the nearly doubling of executive pay that was estimated between 1999–2003 would have been even higher.

As corporations over the past decade have been busy reducing pension benefits for workers, under-funding and even abandoning their pension plans for workers, SERPs were being added across the board by corporations in the U.S. Changes in the tax laws in 1994 provided a strong incentive for creating SERPs for senior executives as a way to shelter more of their total compensation from taxation. Less than half of senior executives had supplemental pension plans prior to 1995; today more than 90 percent have such plans. Thus billions more have been squirreled away for CEOs and senior managers of the largest public companies over the past decade.

10   For CEOs of the largest corporations that means at least another $60 billion in addition to the $122 billion of the Harvard–Cornell study. But that additional $60 billion still does not include the rest of the 90 percent of corporations—apart from the 1,522 surveyed by Harvard–Cornell—that have also established SERPs today for CEOs and senior managers.

One of the great scandals at Enron when it went bankrupt was that Enron executives froze workers' pensions and did not allow them to take their money out as the company began to default, while those same executives were cashing out their pensions in a separate, supplemental management pension plan.

Other measures of growth in executive compensation corroborate the above trends and figures for executive pay. The non-partisan research group the Corporate Library recently surveyed "median" as opposed to average CEO pay. It estimated that median CEO compensation for 2003 rose 15 percent in 2003, followed by another increase in median executive compensation of 30 percent in 2004. No doubt results for 2005 will show a continuing accelerating trend.

Trading Jobs for Executive Pay

CEOs who have been doing especially well under George W. Bush are those companies that have been involved in aggressive offshoring of jobs. Approximately eight million quality, high paying jobs have been lost due to "free" trade policies and offshoring since the 1980s and the number continues to rise rapidly. Free trade policies and offshoring reflect the radical restructuring of trade relations and foreign direct investment strategies implemented by corporate America since Ronald Reagan. More than a million jobs have been lost due to NAFTA in the last decade alone and another 2.5 million have resulted from the granting of special terms of trade with China in 2000.

For dismantling of a good part of the U.S. manufacturing base, CEOs and senior managers of U.S. corporations involved in offshoring of jobs have been generously compensated compared to their already well-paid corporate peers. For example, a *Business Week* survey in 2003 of CEOs at the 50 largest U.S. companies that outsource the most showed that their CEOs enjoyed an average increase in compensation of 46 percent between 2001–03, earning as a group a reported $2.2 billion while sending an estimated 200,000 jobs offshore.

CEOs and managers are now compensated at record levels, not for their 15 contribution to the corporate bottom line anymore, but for selling off the company, for leaving quietly, or for gross performance failure. Thus Carly Fiorina, ex-CEO of Hewlett-Packard, departed last year with a package of more than $40 million. David Pottruck of Schwab left with around $50 million, and Craig Conway of Peoplesoft exited with a total package of more than $60 million. Among the biggest winners of CEO departees, however, were Phillip Purcell of the investment bank, Morgan Stanley, who left with a reported $113 million, and James Kilts of Gillette who walked out the corporate door with $165 million. Even more amazing was Steven Crawford, recent co-president of Morgan Stanley, who left after only three months of employment with $32 million—or a rate of pay of more than $10 million a month. Crawford's gain was more than matched in terms of the bizarre, though, by Daniel Carp, still CEO of Blockbuster Video Corp., who in 2004 received more than $50 million in compensation even though the company recorded a loss of $1.25 billion that year.

Comparing Pay

As previously noted, executive pay between 1980 and 2000 climbed an astounding 342 percent, outpacing the rate of inflation over the period by at least 4 to 1. In contrast, the average hourly wage for more than 100 million workers, when measured in 2003 dollars, rose from $14.86 at the start of 1980 to only $14.95 at the end of 2000. That's a 9 cents an hour gain after 20 years.

Furthermore, the average hourly wage today for 105 million workers after adjustment for inflation is exactly the same at year end 2005 as it was in 2001, according to the U.S. Department of Labor's statistics. In 2004–2005 it has fallen steadily as inflation has begun to accelerate. For the 60 million at the medium wage level or below, inflation the past two years has been rising at twice the rate of their hourly wage.

To compensate for stagnant and declining real hourly wages and earnings, U.S. workers have had to resort to alternative means to try to maintain income levels and spending. These alternatives to wage gains fall into three categories.

First, more U.S. families have been having other family members enter the workforce to supplement family incomes and/or have had to take on second part time jobs in addition to their normal job. U.S. families have increased the number of hours worked by more than 500 a year since 1980. Americans now work by far the greatest number of hours per year than workers in any of the other industrialized countries—approximately 1,970 hours each per year out of 2,040, based on a normal 40 hour work week. The next closest is Canada where workers average about 1,800 hours. Workers in industrialized economies of Europe average fewer hours worked, 1,600–1,800 hours per year.

20   Second, they have had to take on record levels of consumer and installment debt, levels that have doubled from $4 trillion to more than $9 trillion since Bush II took office.

Third, workers fortunate enough to own their homes have been refinancing those homes and using the proceeds as discretionary income to pay for major purchases such as medical expenses, education, and large ticket items—in effect living off their assets.

All three solutions to the stagnation and decline of real wages over the past quarter century, however, have their finite limits and cannot continue long term as safety valve alternatives to declining real wages, earnings, and incomes for the 105 million.

Ben, Moira, and Jasmine argued that reading is the understanding of a complex system of signs and that literacy is our determination of a person's ability to decode that system of signs. But reading and literacy encompass many complementary and competing elements.

Trailblazers, longhunters, and scouts in the eighteenth and nineteenth centuries had to "read" such signs as paw prints and footprints in the sand, broken twigs, and scat to determine the path of a herd, the whereabouts of outlaws, or the proximity of war parties. Many of these adventurers were illiterate in the sense of being able to decipher meaning from sentences written in our alphabet. Yet, they possessed a complicated and effective literacy in their understanding of the nuances of the land and of movements on it. In our century, an effective starting quarterback in the NFL must be able to "read" a defense as he approaches the line of scrimmage and to audible if the play he initially called does not align well against what he sees. The opposing team disguises its defense, so the quarterback has to pick out subtleties in order to predict the best play. Quarterbacks must be extremely literate to read these signs correctly.

The key element in reading is prediction. When game was plentiful, a longhunter such as Daniel Boone or Davy Crockett had no difficulty finding deer or elk. It was easy to predict where to go. But when game was scarce, initial predictions would prove unreliable, so Boone and Crockett had to look for deeper, less obvious signs to determine the location of a pack of animals. The ability to succeed in youth, high school, and even college football rests on being able to interpret obvious defensive formations. But when a quarterback is drafted into the NFL, he has less time to react to the game's fast pace and the defense's clever strategies. He has to predict what the defense will do based on previous knowledge of the team's habits and anything he can read from the alignment he sees.

This type of reading can lead to the creation of informed texts for others to follow. The focus of this book is on writing, but do not overlook oral text construction. Daniel Boone told other settlers about the areas he explored. When those settlers saw the places themselves, Boone's oral description provided a context through which they interpreted their observations. A map is a written form of such a description. In the twenty-first century, good readers of situations around them inform others through many text-bound activities, such as blogs, collaborative websites called wikis, and editorials. Critically reading not just their own experiences but also the writing of others allows them to create purposeful critical writing.

In reading written texts that others have created, we also use prediction. The more familiar we are with a genre or subject, the easier it is to read. When we know how stories or articles generally will unfold, we can read stories and articles quickly. If we uncover something we were not able to predict—the identity of a murderer in a mystery or information about how a cosmetic might react on our skin in a pamphlet—we become genuinely intrigued, so our reading is still not disrupted. Understanding one unfamiliar element is not difficult in the context of what we already know.

When our first set of predictions fails to unravel a text, our reading slows down. This is the point at which reading becomes difficult. Every paragraph seems to contain something we cannot predict. How can we penetrate this seeming barrier?

DISCUSSION

Think about the different types of literacy you possess beyond the ability to read books and articles. What skills—from car mechanics to fashion sense—do you possess? Do you need to read situations that involve those skills? List the characteristics of your types of literacy, and then talk about them with the group. Are you able to predict certain situations? What do you do when you cannot predict a situation, when a snag or a problem occurs?

This chapter considers the many purposes for reading and then explores strategies for reading effectively. Reading (in the broad sense) is essential to the type of critical analysis needed for effective writing. The four main reasons to read are for knowledge, safety, and awareness as consumers; for social and civic engagement; for information retrieval; and for academic achievement.

When you cannot easily predict a text or are not interested in a subject, you must develop strategies to break through reading blocks and to motivate yourself. Understanding the strategies you use in other types of reading will help. While individuals get pleasure and entertainment from personal reading, the social purposes for text reading supply the necessary motivation for required reading.

Knowledge, Safety, and Awareness as Consumers

It might sound strange that a process associated with mental activity can protect us. The concept of safety makes more sense in relation to the many ways we use reading as consumers. Purchasing even small items compels us to read. Sometimes we need to consult a resource, such as *Consumer Reports*, before we shop to know which products will serve our needs best. For dieting purposes, we read the ingredients on food labels, checking on calories, carbohydrates, or protein. To repair household items, we read instruction manuals, or we read the small print etched on equipment to make sure to buy the proper replacement parts. Reading in this sense is as an active component of empowerment.

Warning Labels   Practically every product on the market comes with some sort of writing on its packaging that cautions consumers about proper and improper use. While we only scan this information if we have previously used the product or similar products, we look at the label closely if we are using it for the first time, especially if we perceive a possibility of danger. We have to be aware, for example, of the side effects of a medicine, and we have to avoid mixing it with other medication that might cause an adverse reaction.

Other types of warning labels protect us from improper usage of items we have purchased. We want to be able to wear clothes more than once, for instance, so we look at washing, drying, and ironing labels. Such labels rarely use full sentences, so a reader has to decipher the message. We usually do not give up when trying to understand warnings about line drying and using a cool iron. When we have invested money in a piece of clothing, we generally put in extra effort to achieve full comprehension.

Instructions   Product instructions can be the most frustrating types of text. Many consumer items require assembly at home, and we need to protect ourselves from numerous hazards. Poor construction can be dangerous—improper wiring can cause fires; faulty assembly of a weight-bearing product can cause it to collapse. Damaging a part when attempting to put it where it doesn't belong can void a warranty.

Some people who are good with their hands might be able to put a bicycle together or assemble an entertainment center after quickly reviewing the instructions. Others may be guided by the drawings in the manuals. The rest of us must read the text, step by step, to construct something that resembles the picture on the packaging. We can distinguish instructions that are clear and detailed from those that are vague and skimpy.

Recipes are also instructions. While some cooks learn by watching others and relying on instincts thereafter, most of us have to follow the processes outlined in cookbooks. Otherwise, our meals can taste bland, overly spicy, dry, undercooked, or otherwise unsavory.

To install programs on computers, we also have to follow instructions. The directions that pop up on the computer monitor tell us what to do and when to do it. Few of us can override these instructions to install software on our own. If we want to use the program, we have to read the instructions.

Most instructions for consumer purchases demand full comprehension, so we have to scrutinize ambiguous passages. Consumers spend a lot of time making sure to do the right thing. Misreading could render the investment of money and time worthless.

Contracts   Often, when we purchase items or make business agreements, we enter into contracts. While contracts usually concern payment plans, they also spell out our rights and responsibilities. Many include warranties or guarantees of which we need to be aware. Contracts with auto mechanics, carpenters, and repair people spell out the precise work they will do and our recourse if we are not satisfied.

Because of the importance of contracts, wise consumers read them, even when the contracts appear to be generic. While most businesses maintain honest standards, the old saying "let the buyer beware" applies. For example, many college students sign credit card deals with an average percentage rate (APR) of interest at 5.9 or 6.9 percent, only to find that the APR increases to 18.9 percent after a few months. While the advertisement says "fixed introductory rate," the rate is fixed, which means remains the same, only through the period the company deems to be "introductory." Everything purchased under that introductory agreement will be subject to the higher interest rate if it is not paid off completely before the introductory period ends. While such advertisements, though deceptive in this way, are legal, the contract must indicate the particulars of the agreement with the company. You might be willing to enter into the agreement if you need financing to buy some items, but the knowledge that comes with reading the contract will make you fully aware of the terms so that you can account for the payments in your budget.

Many students also enter into contracts for financial aid packages (student loans). Reading the contract makes you aware, for example, that you will never be able to default on the loan, even if you declare bankruptcy. You will also know the stipulations about the number of credit hours you must carry, about withdrawing from classes, and about extended illnesses or other emergencies that interfere with attending class. Awareness of the information in the contract can save you from serious financial problems later.

COLLABORATING

As a group, collect a warning label, a set of instructions, and a contract. Look at the language in each and determine its effectiveness. Does it appear to be consumer friendly? Opaque? Condescending? Unnecessary? Discuss the reasons for the language choices made by the writers of the label, instructions, and contract.

Social and Civic Engagement

Our responsibility as citizens is to ensure that our government responds to the needs of the people. We also have to do our part by engaging in socially responsible activities. To ensure that our local community and the nation prosper and offer all citizens freedom and opportunities for happiness, we need to do certain kinds of text reading. Not only must we be able to read documents that involve a higher level of prediction, but we must also examine them critically to uncover any manipulation of language. Chapter 5 discussed common misuses of language; this chapter focuses on the purposes for reading.

Voting   We often are encouraged to "get out and vote." But a vote cast in ignorance of the candidates and the issues does not help the cause of democracy. Voting responsibly demands reading with a critical eye.

While television news programs, talk radio, and even advertisements offer information, the brevity of the information and the agendas behind it prevent citizens from making informed decisions. Citizens develop critical awareness in their reading and listening by arming themselves with information from a variety of sources and testing out its validity. (Chapter 10 discusses how to test the credibility of online sources.) They can then determine what propositions or platforms best benefit them, their community, and society as a whole.

Casting uninformed votes has consequences. Voting choices can mean the difference between job creation and job loss, clean water and polluted water, the right to free speech and the suppression of speech, and even hope for a better future and limited future prospects. Knowing the facts can help you make the best choices possible on your ballot and can influence the people you talk to into doing the same.

Protesting   Protest can take a number of forms, including putting together petitions, forming advocacy groups, writing to government officials, and marching in the streets. Without doing the necessary reading, you are taking a chance when you raise your voice in protest. There are negative consequences to getting behind a cause and complaining, only to find out that you lacked accurate information.

For example, the American public supported the invasion of Iraq in 2003 under the impression that Iraq had weapons of mass destruction. Advocacy groups rallied in favor of the war to counter peace demonstrations that also took place across the nation. The public has since learned that the documents suggesting that Iraq had obtained uranium were falsified and that we were misled as to Iraq's capabilities of using weapons of mass destruction. That information had been available on the Internet and in alternative magazines before the invasion.

Critical awareness increases our chances of being aware that information is misleading or false. Basing our convictions on the most reliable information allows us to protest with knowledge and certainty.

FAIRNESS AND ACCURACY IN REPORTING

Smearing Anti-War Activists?: NY Times *Op-Ed Laments Anti-War Funeral Protests*

The watchdog group Fairness and Accuracy in Reporting (FAIR) advocates for ethical, informed news coverage. The following is an example of one of the Action Alerts in which the group documents distortions in major media outlets and demands better editorial oversight. Notice how a person who was not critically aware and who did not investigate could react inappropriately to the initial claim in the New York Times *article.*

A June 12 op-ed in the *New York Times* made a bold accusation: anti-war activists have targeted funerals of Iraq War soldiers with noisy protests. But evidence to back up that charge is nonexistent.

The author of the piece, writer Karen Spears Zacharias, recounted an interview with a war widow who said that "antiwar protesters . . . lined the streets across from the service . . . carried signs and . . . shouted as her husband's flag-draped coffin was carried past." Zacharias expanded on this claim when she wrote of the "hundreds of anti-war protestors who appear at military hospitals and funerals."

Following the op-ed's publication, several readers posted questions on Zacharias' website, asking if she could substantiate either the specific incident she had reported, or the broad claim that "hundreds" of anti-war activists have protested at multiple sites. The author responded by posting a link to a story on a conservative website about small vigils that were held at Walter Reed military hospital.

Many of the posts on Zacharias' website suggested that the funeral protests she was describing were more likely those organized by Fred Phelps' Westboro Baptist Church, a virulently homophobic group that celebrates U.S. military deaths as punishment for the military's "don't ask, don't tell" policy towards homosexuals. The Phelps group is by no reasonable definition anti-war.

5   In a response to one reader, Zacharias acknowledged that further research revealed that the widows she spoke with were all referring to Phelps' group.

Though the piece appeared on the *Times'* op-ed page, the paper has a responsibility to verify such claims—particularly when, as in this case, they serve as the premise of a column. Moreover, such anecdotes have the potential to smear an entire political movement, and live on long after they are published. Accounts of Vietnam vets being spit upon by anti-war protesters, for example, persist to this day *(Newsweek,* 6/12/06)—despite the fact that it is difficult to corroborate any of those alleged incidents (see *The Spitting Image: Myth, Memory, and the Legacy of Vietnam,* by Jerry Lembcke).

Action:

Contact the *New York Times* op-ed page and ask them to verify the claim that "hundreds of anti-war protestors" have demonstrated "at military hospitals and funerals." If they cannot, ask them to correct the record.

Public Interest   True social engagement must start with one's own family. Problems that begin in the home often spill into society. Manuals produced by government health agencies and reliable advocacy groups offer accurate information on common social problems. For example, pamphlets on AIDS and other sexually transmitted diseases distinguish fact from fiction and give advice on preventing infection. Drug and alcohol awareness groups produce literature on the effects of addiction and options for treatment. In both cases, nipping a problem in the bud can prevent harmful social consequences, such as spreading a disease or driving while intoxicated.

Sometimes we want to trust our instincts rather than read information, only to find out later that we have done the wrong thing. For example, people who live near mountains or woods may encounter young, seemingly abandoned animals and may want to care for them. However, public service bulletins explain that such animals are probably only temporarily separated from their mothers. Their best chance for survival is for people to keep their distance; the scent of a human will keep such an animal's mother from retrieving it. A young animal taken to a person's home likely will die. To maintain a thriving, diverse ecosystem, humans often must forego their maternal or paternal instincts. Interference can lead to wilderness destruction and species endangerment in small and large ways.

Of course, bringing up our own children is tremendously important for society. Children who are not raised well may commit crimes, destroy property, and cost taxpayers money. Child-care pamphlets and books not only help parents ensure their children's health, but also give advice based on research to guide parents toward enacting proper discipline, creating acceptable boundaries, and establishing nurturing environments. Reading to ensure responsible personal behavior affects society positively.

OHIO DEPARTMENT OF PUBLIC SAFETY

Where to Ride on the Road

The following advice on bicycling comes from a manual produced by the Ohio Department of Public Safety. Read the instructions and determine whether the guidelines offer information about bicycling that you did not know. What are the social costs of bicyclists' not following such guidelines?

We've all seen bicyclists who wander from left side to right, who go from the sidewalk to the street and who weave in and out between parked cars. From moment to moment, nobody can tell what these bicyclists are about to do. Pedestrians jump back, and car brakes squeal as such bicyclists approach.

On the other hand, we've seen bicyclists who seem to blend into the traffic flow smoothly and effortlessly. You always know where they are headed and what to do around them, whether you're on a bicycle, in a car or on foot. They make bicycling look easy—but aren't they taking a risk? Isn't it safer to avoid the traffic as much as possible?

Part of the Traffic Pattern

With very few exceptions, *the safest way to ride is as part of the traffic,* going with the flow of the normal traffic pattern. Bicyclists who ride this way get where they're going faster and, according to scientific crash studies, have about five times fewer crashes than bicyclists who make up their own rules (J. Forester, *Effective Cycling.* Cambridge, MA: MIT Press, 1993).

Generally, the more you follow the normal traffic pattern, the safer and more predictable you become: The rules of the road set up a pattern for every situation, telling which driver has the right of way. Sometimes you have to wait for other drivers—for example, at a stop sign—but sometimes they have to wait for you. Bicyclists have the same rights—and responsibilities—as motorists.

In this way, the rules of the road protect you by making it clear what 5 you're going to do next.

If you ride in violation of the traffic laws, you greatly increase your risk of a crash. You also may give up all of your rights. If you get into a crash, the courts will almost always find that it was your fault!

On a two-lane highway, be alert to drivers ahead of you pulling out to pass, especially if the lanes are narrow.

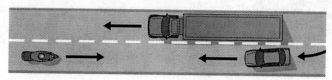

Understand that the law is on your side. The law gives you the right to use the road, the same as a motorist, and to make other traffic slow down for you sometimes. The driver approaching from the rear is always required to slow and follow if it's not possible to pass safely.

It may seem dangerous to make a motorist slow for you, but it's not. The usual reason that bicyclists feel unsafe on narrow roads is that they do not take control of the situation. Remember, the drivers behind you don't have room to pass you safely anyway. If you ride all the way over at the right, you're inviting them to pass you where the road is too narrow and, too often, you will get squeezed off the road. If you show clearly that it's not safe for drivers to pass you, they're unlikely to try.

Right

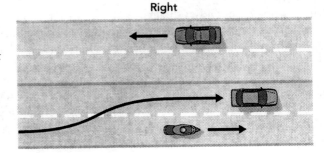

On a multilane road with a narrow right lane, ride in the middle of the right lane.

Wrong

If you hug the edge, you are likely to get squeezed out.

But be courteous. When it becomes safe for the car behind you to pass you, give the driver a wave-by signal. If you block traffic for more than a short time, common courtesy suggests, and the law normally requires, that you pull to the side and let the traffic by when you can safely do so.

10   On a road with two or more narrow lanes in your direction—like many city streets—you should ride in the middle of the right lane at all times. You need to send the message to drivers to move to the passing lane to pass you. If you ride all the way to the right, two cars may pass you at the same time, side by side, and squeeze you off the road.

> **WRITING**
>
> Look on the Internet or in local newspapers to find stories on tragedies or waste that involved behavior inconsistent with authoritative information that the people involved could have learned by reading. What type of knowledge guided the people involved? Were they acting on instinct or responding to false information? Could prior reading have altered their actions? Make sure to verify your knowledge on the subject before making assertions about what the people should have done.

Information Retrieval

Much reading involves information retrieval. A person, place, or event intrigues us, and we want to know more. Workplace responsibilities sometimes require us to use information retrieval skills, whether in a library or on the Internet. If you look at the way you find information for personal purposes, you will be better able to carry out these other responsibilities.

Competition   People compete in many ways. In American lore families often try to "keep up with the Joneses," meaning that when a family makes home improvements, their neighbors feel compelled to do something to their houses so as not to lag behind. Searching through magazines for ideas, finding regional trends on the Internet, and getting information on potential contractors from the Better Business Bureau will help them avoid costly mistakes.

As another example, many people play fantasy sports. Successful fantasy players read newspapers and surf the Internet for current information on athletes and teams. Reading about a coach's or manager's tendencies gives the fantasy player an advantage when deciding when to reserve or trade a player. Reading is the difference between winning and losing.

Still other people get hooked on trivia games. Perhaps they watch *Jeopardy* every night, play Trivial Pursuit with friends, or engage in electronically connected national rounds of Buzztime trivia in local taverns. Clearly, those who read and digest bits of information compete better than those who do not.

While competition sometimes serves negative purposes, it can also be fun. Reading can contribute to your enjoyment of the competition.

Hobbies   Keeping up with trends in your hobby means reading. Sometimes you need to know what's new, such as about current stamps produced by the U.S. Postal Service, and have to scan popular websites or magazines to find the information. You discover the potential value of a set and decide whether to purchase it.

Other times, you might be trying to solve a problem. For example, perhaps, like many backpackers, you tend to get blisters. A technological innovation in hiking boots might make your next expedition more pleasurable. You doubt the salesperson's rating of boots because he is trying to earn a commission from your purchase. You need a source that evaluates new equipment, such as *Backpacker* magazine, for an unbiased assessment of new boots.

There is also the joy of experiencing a gathering of people with similar interests. Sometimes hobby conventions advertise on television and radio, but Star Trek conventions, for instance, do not necessarily receive that type of publicity. The only way to know that such an event is coming to your area is to stay current with fanzines and websites that have information about conventions.

In these and many other cases, reading helps you attend to your hobbies. Chapter 12 further discusses the intricacies of hobbies and their effect on our culture.

Social Discourse   It's no fun to attend a social function and not be able to participate in the conversations. Whether your friends discuss celebrity gossip, music, current events, academics, or local happenings, you need to know something about contemporary culture to take part in the conversation. Reading serves this purpose better than any other medium. Not only does it keep you up to date on important local and national topics, but it can also give you information that is more precise and thorough than the sound bites others might have heard.

As mentioned earlier, we cannot completely trust the accuracy of television and radio sources. Respectable papers, magazines, and websites can keep us from succumbing to rumors and hate mongering. Sometimes, urban legends are spread at social functions because people do not have the proper information at their disposal. They enter into lively discourse without the context.

A student of mine once turned in an assignment detailing a "personal experience" of picking up a hitchhiker who later disappeared. According to his paper, an accident had occurred at the curve in the road where she vanished from his car. The student did not know that the legend of the vanishing hitchhiker is infamously just a myth. When confronted, the student claimed that the experience was not really his but a story he had overheard at a party that the storyteller claimed was true.

While we cannot be responsible for knowing about every subject, we can be held accountable for reading up on a subject before spreading a rumor. And, of course, no one should ever claim that an experience is his or hers just because it sounds like a good story! In any case, information gained through reading can prevent embarrassing social situations and can stop rumors from being circulated.

JAN HAROLD BRUNVAND

from The Vanishing Hitchhiker

In the following excerpt from The Vanishing Hitchhiker: American Urban Legends and Their Meanings, *Jan Harold Brunvand reviews variations of the same story, showing how features of the tale remain constant even when the details*

change. Think how stimulating it might be at a party to discuss the actual his-
tory and purpose of an urban legend rather than perpetuating the myth as a "true
experience."

Urban legends belong to the subclass of folk narratives, legends, that—unlike
fairy tales—are believed, or at least believable, and that—unlike myths—are
set in the recent past and involve normal human beings rather than ancient
gods or demigods. Legends are folk history, or rather quasi-history. As with
any folk legends, urban legends gain credibility from specific details of time
and place or from references to source authorities. For instance, a popular
western pioneer legend often begins something like, "My great-grandmother
had this strange experience when she was a young girl on a wagon train going
through Wyoming when an Indian chief wanted to adopt her . . ." Even though
hundreds of different great-grandmothers are supposed to have had the same
doubtful experience (being desired by the chief because of her beautiful long
blond hair), the fact seldom reaches legend-tellers; if it does, they assume that
the family lore has indeed spread far and wide. This particular popular tradition, known as "Goldilocks on the Oregon Trail," interests folklorists because of the racist implications of a dark Indian savage coveting a fair young
civilized woman—this legend is familiar in the *white* folklore only—and it is
of little concern that the story seems to be entirely apocryphal.

In the world of modern urban legends there is usually no geographical or
generational gap between teller and event. The story is *true;* it really occurred,
and recently, and always to someone else who is quite close to the narrator,
or at least "a friend of a friend." Urban legends are told both in the course of
casual conversations and in such special situations as campfires, slumber parties, and college dormitory bull sessions. The legends' physical settings are
often close by, real, and sometimes even locally renowned for other such happenings. Though the characters in the stories are usually nameless, they are
true-to-life examples of the kind of people the narrators and their audience
know firsthand.

One of the great mysteries of folklore research is where oral traditions
originate and who invents them. One might expect that at least in modern
folklore we could come up with answers to such questions, but this is seldom, if ever, the case. . . . [M]ost leads pointing to possible authors or original
events lying behind urban legends have simply evaporated. . . .

A prime example of the adaptability of older legends is "The Vanishing
Hitchhiker"—*the* classic automobile legend. This returning-ghost tale was
known by the turn of the century both in the United States and abroad. It
acquired the newer automobile motif by the period of the Great Depression,
and thereafter spawned a number of subtypes with greatly varied and oddly
interlocking details, some of which themselves stemmed from earlier folk
legends. Merely sampling some of the many "Vanishing Hitchhiker" variants that have been collected over a period of some forty years can help us
trace the legend's incredible development. Surely most readers already know a

local "true" account (or maybe two or three) similar to Example A, as told by a teenager in Toronto, Canada, in 1973:

A

5   Well, this happened to one of my girlfriend's best friends and her father. They were driving along a country road on their way home from the cottage when they saw a young girl hitchhiking. They stopped and picked her up and she got in the back seat. She told the girl and her father that she just lived in the house about five miles up the road. She didn't say anything after that but just turned to watch out the window. When the father saw the house, he drove up to it and turned around to tell the girl they had arrived—but she wasn't there! Both he and his daughter were really mystified and decided to knock on the door and tell the people what had happened. They told them that they had once had a daughter who answered the description of the girl they supposedly had picked up, but she had disappeared some years ago and had last been seen hitchhiking on this very road. Today would have been her birthday.

This version has the basic elements—not necessarily "original" ones—well known in oral tradition and occasionally reported in newspapers since the early 1930s. The stable story units have been labeled in brackets in the following text from South Carolina collected by workers of the South Carolina Writers' Project (Work Projects Administration) sometime between 1935 and 1941:

B

A traveling man [driver] who lived in Spartanburg [authentication] was on his way home one night [setting] when he saw a woman walking along the side of the road [hitchhiker]. He stopped his car and asked the woman if he could take her where she was going. She stated that she was on her way to visit her brother who lived about three miles further on the same road [her address]. He asked her to get in the car and sit by him, but she said she would sit in the back of the car [her choice of seat]. Conversation took place for a while as they rode along, but soon the woman grew quiet. The man drove on until he reached the home of the woman's brother, whom he knew [more authentication]; then stopped his car to let the woman alight. When he looked behind him, there was no one in the car [disappearance]. He thought that rather strange [curiosity or concern], so went into the house and informed the brother that a lady had gotten into his car to ride to see him, but when he arrived at the house the lady had disappeared. The brother was not alarmed at all and stated that the lady was his sister who had died two years before [identification]. He said that this traveling man was the seventh to pick up his sister on the road to visit him, but that she had never reached his house yet.

Variations on the basic story are endless, and trying to sort them out into any kind of possible chronological development is hampered by the fact that the date when a version happened to be collected and published bears little relationship to its possible age in tradition, and by the principle that legends become highly localized and rationalized with many circumstantial details whenever they are adopted into a particular context. For instance, the plot has several different twists and turns in this 1935 version (paraphrased by the collector) from Berkeley, California:

C

This story was heard in a Durant Avenue boarding house, told several times as a true story. It happened to a friend of the narrator. This friend was driving up Hearst Avenue one rainy night. As he came to North Gate (Hearst and Euclid avenues) he saw a girl, a student with books under her arm, waiting for the streetcar. Since these had stopped running, he offered her a ride. She lived up on Euclid. They drove out along Euclid quite a way with some conversation. As they were crossing an intersection, another car came down the steep hill and they would have crashed if the girl had not pulled on the emergency brake [a unique detail in the story]. The fellow was flabbergasted and sat looking at the other car, which pulled around him and went on. When he remembered his companion and looked over, she was gone. Since it was near her home, he assumed she had simply gotten out to walk the rest of the way; but she had left a book on the seat. The next day he went to return the book. He found her father, an English professor, at home. He said that the girl was his daughter, that she had been killed in an auto accident at the same corner one or two years ago that very day. But since the fellow had the book, the father took it into the library, to look on the shelves for it—he found the place where it should have been vacant.

A strictly urban setting for the story allows for more precise and thorough double-checking of factual details. In 1941 Rosalie Hankey of the University of California, who was gathering materials for a lengthy study of "The Vanishing Hitchhiker," tried to verify specific accident reports from Berkeley. In one version the automobile crash in which the girl was killed was supposed to have happened in 1935 or 1936 at the corner of College and Bancroft. But in checking the Berkeley city records from 1934 to 1937, Hankey found that only a single accident involving personal injury, non-fatal, had occurred at that corner during the five-year period. 10

The specific "proof" in the story of the hitchhiker's actual presence in the car and her status as the ghost of a particular individual is always a key motif. Besides the book she leaves behind in Example C, the object may be a purse, a suitcase, a blanket, a sweater, a scarf or some other item of clothing, or simply footprints or water spots in the car. The identification of her at the family's home may depend upon showing the object to her relatives, or upon the driver's description of her, the girl's name, or a photograph of her which is displayed on the piano or mantel and which often shows her wearing the same party dress in which her ghost appears. One group of variants which includes either the clothing (hers or something borrowed from the driver) or the portrait detail (sometimes both) moves the climax of the story to a cemetery.

DISCUSSION

List every type of reading you did yesterday or today in order to retrieve information. Think of everything from box scores in the morning paper to listings of movie times while deciding which to see at a theater. Include any nontext reading, such as road signs without words and anything else you had to interpret. Share your information, and compare the amount of time you spent reading to the time your classmates spent. Was it more than you thought? Did you consider it a burden? Discuss the different purposes served by your reading.

Academic Achievement

When you consider your investment of money and time, doing well in college courses is a legitimate goal. Reading assigned texts can be the difference between succeeding and failing in a class. In the example at the beginning of this chapter, Ben and some of the other students would have suffered had there been a quiz on the Rasmus article. The farther you go in your education, the more important it is to read materials and be able to apply them on a test or in a paper.

Academic Learning   Many students do acceptable work in colleges and universities by listening to lectures, viewing presentations, and preparing for quizzes and tests. Some distinguish themselves by learning more through in-depth reading. These students become critically aware of the context surrounding the subjects they study. They grasp the real-life application of theories and research sooner than other students. They spot connections among the courses they take and can readily and accurately use that knowledge. They turn the game of school into a learning experience.

Sometimes textbooks can be boring, but they give learners a background in the subject that a lecture or project can enhance. Students with awareness of the subject beforehand have a better sense of what is and is not relevant and can thus take more accurate notes. They can better predict the information that is coming, even if the professor is updating or augmenting facts and theories. Textbooks also let students check facts. If you're not sure that you recorded something correctly in your notes, you can look in your textbook to confirm the information. Textbook reading can often lead to interest in primary sources, which might give you information that will surprise your professor.

It feels good to know something that the teacher doesn't know, right? Critical awareness earns you respect and prestige.

Learning for Future Application   Information gained through text reading has real-life applications. The reading for courses in your major prepares you for your career. Naturally, you want to pay particular attention to assigned texts, and you probably will have sufficient motivation to get through them. But what about the other reading you must do? What application can it have to your life?

Instructors in general education and specialized courses often assign reading that has relevance to your civic and social responsibility. You do not have to be a psychology major to appreciate information you find in the pages of a psychology textbook. You might learn to reflect on your own behavior better and to understand and accept the peculiarities of other people. The novels, poems, and plays you read in literature classes will be useful throughout your life as shared cultural icons that add depth to conversations or provide clear examples of complicated subjects.

Knowledge gained from reading can create indelible memories. When my daughter Katrina was young, she and I looked at the stars in the night sky. She could identify the Milky Way and other constellations, and I talked about the myths surrounding their creation based on knowledge from courses about mythology and told her scientific facts about the Milky Way, checking my old astronomy textbook to be accurate. Katrina and I would then make up our own stories about constellations in the sky. Later, I bought her a telescope, and we spent many nights looking for planets and trying to identify what we saw. We couldn't have enjoyed ourselves more. The applications of academic reading can surprise you.

COLLABORATING

Jot down information from a high school or college course that you applied to a real-life situation. What you record does not have to be a completely successful application of the material or have produced positive results, but be specific about the situation and the information you knew. As a group, review these applications and ask whether information beyond what was in the textbook or assigned reading could have augmented what transpired. In retrospect, would it have been the worth the effort to have read more?

Developing Reading Strategies for College

You may not need further convincing about the empowering aspects of reading. Your question may now be how to navigate through all the reading in college. It may still seem daunting. If you recognize the purpose of reading, you have the first key toward developing a strategy, but what about the rest? How does a reader move from reading he or she sees as purposeful or enjoyable to reading that is difficult? Student Mandy Badar discusses her development as a reader in an essay tracing different stages of her growth.

MANDY BADAR

An Analysis of the Dietary Habits of a Known Bookworm

How do you produce a bookworm? By what means do you cultivate a creature that devours texts insatiably? How do you stoke its hunger without starving it? How much do you feed it without causing it to choke or gag? And, most importantly, how do you get it to acquire the taste for books in the first place?

The way to whet the appetite for books is the same method by which you develop any other appetite. By this I mean that eating is an inextricable element of everyone's world. To encourage someone to develop healthy eating habits you draw on natural propensities and create conducive circumstances. Eating is simply something one must do. It is a basic need around which we build social, family, and other structures. It is also something that can be shaped by the behavior of the people one is surrounded by. If a child grows up eating healthy foods or exotic dishes, the child will not think that eating healthy or exotic foods is remarkable. Similarly, it would never occur to anyone to force feed a child to stimulate her appetite. Furthermore, it would not make sense to surround a child with unappetizing, unpalatable, or even inedible foods. Instead, one would surround her with enticing dishes and let her exercise her own culinary discretion. Nurturing a natural inclination and satiating varying appetites when they arise will make a bon vivant of most people.

Of course, one will not die if one does not get a regular dose of literature, but reading is still a skill that promotes survival. It's something almost everyone has to do to some extent to survive in a nation like ours. Reading is also a basic thing around which a much greater structure is built; it can be part of family life, the basis of social gatherings and much more. Reading habits and affinities can be shaped and encouraged by those around us. For example, if the people we see every day make reading a part of their lives, we will take for granted that reading is part of life. It cannot be inculcated by force, just as a liking for brussel sprouts cannot be ingrained by a parent's will. If one is brought up in a world of literature, if it is part of the backdrop of one's existence, then it is simply a matter of culturing the palate, determining from the choices by which one is surrounded which dish is most amenable to the tongue.

This is how I was turned, very early in life, from a bouncing baby girl to a ravenous bookworm. I was surrounded by reading material and constantly exposed to other readers. I had only one of those plastic, inane baby books; the rest of my numerous books were actual storybooks. My playroom was dominated by a bookcase, the contents of which grew and changed as I matured. At a mere four years of age my mom took me to story hour at the local public library. During these trips I listened to stories, picked out books, and played with other kids. As I grew older I raided the bookshelves of various family members and picked up whatever books Mom left lying around. Books were part of the lives of everyone I grew up around, and I took it for granted that they would be part of my life too.

Even though reading was a commonplace activity for most of the adults in my life, no one ever forced me to interact with texts. All too often I hear that someone was turned off to reading because her parents or teachers became unrelenting taskmasters who force-fed her "appropriate" literature. As a small child I was given the option of reading with my mom, along with many other choices. I am told that I opted for coloring as often as reading. Later, when I was able to read in my own right, I chose to join summer reading programs and to read for enjoyment, but no one ever forced me to make reading a daily or regimented activity. This is largely because I come from a blue-collar family, the members of which are not overly concerned with formal education. I am first-generation college-educated. To my knowledge, no family member before me was an outstanding student, let alone valedictorian. My eagerness to learn was regarded as a pleasant surprise, not a mandatory attribute. Thus, no one ever made reading (or any other educational activity) unbearable by demanding that I meet certain quotas or choose materials of a certain caliber. There was never any pressure to read, to read well, to read certain things, or to share my reading with others.

I was motivated to learn to read anyway. Although no external pressure was applied, I ached for the day when the secret of reading would be revealed to me. For so long I had watched the adults in my life sample a buffet of delights of which I could not partake. I wanted to sit at the grownup table and gorge myself on the delights I knew were there. In first grade, after half a year of drilling with letter flashcards, I got my chance. We were presented with primary readers and left to puzzle them out for ourselves. I knew that sounding out one word at a time was not reading because when my mom read to me at home the sense was immediately evident, whereas, when I tried to read at school, I would have to figure out all the words, then go back and re-read the sentence to get the meaning. I distinctly remember the day when it all came together. In a rush of understanding, a moment of epiphany, the text I had been laboring over suddenly made sense. The key turned in the lock and I was reading. I was so excited I refused to come back to my desk for my snack break. It was just like learning to ride a bike and the knowledge was just as irreversible. After that day I can't remember a time when a book was beyond my grasp, at least not until I took up Shakespeare, Chaucer, and a minor in philosophy, respectively.

Certainly, as with eating, some texts or authors are acquired tastes. One does not usually become a connoisseur of coffee or wine after the first sip. Becoming acclimated to and appreciative of Shakespeare, Chaucer, and philosophical texts was, for me, a great deal like developing a taste for wine. At first wine is harsh to the senses. It is unfamiliar; it is not immediately pleasurable; it can leave you with a massive headache. Similarly, delving into Chaucer's Troilus and Criseyde or plumbing the depths of Alvin Plantinga's Does God Have a Nature? is not immediately pleasurable and can certainly leave one with a terrific headache. Frankly, as with wine consumption, such reading endeavors often start for elitist, status-based reasons. It is impressive to be able to confidently assess a restaurant's wine list, and it is awe-inspiring to be able to read, understand, and expound upon Shakespeare, Chaucer, or philosophy. As time goes on, as with wine, familiarity engenders a comfort level with and appreciation for the experience. The antiquated or intensely cerebral language becomes familiar and discernible enough that the content becomes the focal point. It is like reaching the point at which you can tell a sangiovese from a shiraz, you know what glass and temperature are appropriate for serving, and even a dry white won't make you grimace. This is something that one achieves with practice and patience, and not a little desire, but the payoff for having mastered the medium is well worth it, especially socially.

Mandy's wine metaphor is useful for understanding that students can acquire a taste for reading. Reading is not beyond your capabilities as a college student. But many students want practical tips. To begin to develop an effective reading strategy, start by recognizing your processes of reading and comprehension.

You might be familiar with the situation where your mind is elsewhere but your eyes are still going down the paragraph. You have been reading, but you do not remember what you read. Strangely, if you reread the paragraph, you will remember bits and pieces of it. This situation usually occurs because of distractions. In developing a reading strategy, you must first eliminate the physical and psychological barriers that keep you from your purpose. See what you do when you're engaged in nontext reading. Draw parallels so that you understand how the process of prediction is most readily enabled.

Short Spurts   When I take novices on backpacking trips, some tire quickly. The increase in altitude, the weight of the pack, and the number of miles in front of us often combine to make them want to quit. To keep them going, I usually devise short-term goals. I will point to a tree and say, "Let's reach that. We'll rest there." When we arrive, everyone feels a sense of accomplishment.

This makes my companions more willing to continue after resting. I repeat this process whenever spirits ebb and my companions think they cannot go on. By not conjuring images of all the land in front of us, I am able to get the group to keep pushing, and eventually we reach our destination.

A similar process works when you have required reading to do. Count the number of pages you have to read, and divide them into manageable units. For example, if you have to read fifty pages, break the assignment into five separate goals. If the class meets at the end of the week, read ten pages on Saturday, ten pages the next day, and so forth so that you are done by the day of the class. If on Monday you are assigned fifty pages to read by Wednesday, use the same system, but find two or three specific times during the day to squeeze in a reading of ten pages, such as before breakfast or during lunch. These chunks are manageable, and you can read more in a sitting if your interest increases.

The Right Spot   Finding a quiet spot to read can be especially challenging when you juggle school, work, and family responsibilities. Often, physical comfort is not as important as solitude when it comes to focused reading. You have to eliminate the parts of your life that act as distractions when you are reading.

If you need familiar surroundings to be comfortable, your dorm room or bedroom at home might be the best place. This allows you to fix a snack or to prop up your feet when you read. Perhaps you need space and cannot read if you are surrounded by clutter. The backyard or a balcony might be the best spot. Or getting out of a wooden chair into something soft that you can sink into is what matters most. The point is to make yourself comfortable and avoid distractions.

Turn off your cell phone. If the crowd noise from the ballgame on television is going to cause you to look away from your reading, turn off the game and put some music on. Don't be afraid to ask your roommates or family members to respect your study time and space. You will be amazed by the increase in your level of comprehension and the speed at which you read when you are in the right environment.

READING PLANNER

Compile a list of the reading you have to do for your courses for this week or next week. Follow these directions and fill in the chart on the next page.

- In the first column, list the course by its number or abbreviated title.
- In the second column, give an abbreviated title for each book from which reading has been assigned. Also list the titles of handouts or other assigned reading materials.
- In the third column, list the total number of pages you must read, such as "50 pages."

READING PLANNER

Course	Book	No. of Pages	Sun.	Mon.	Tues.	Wed.	Thurs.	Fri.	Sat.

- In the fourth through tenth columns, write the page numbers you will read from the text under the days of the week you will read them—for example, "pages 20–29." Make sure you divide the total number of pages from each book into equal and manageable units. Put a simple abbreviation next to the page numbers to indicate where you will do the reading (H for home, CS for coffee shop, L for library, and so on).
- On a given day, you might read from more than one book. Just make sure that the total number of pages does not exceed what you can realistically do, so as not to defeat the purpose of filling out the chart. Also make sure that you do not schedule the reading of two different books at the same time.
- Remember deadlines. If you have a quiz on reading materials on Wednesday, do not schedule reading from that book for Thursday or Friday. Prioritize your reading on the basis of the due dates your instructor gives you.
- Make sure to take into consideration the time you will be attending class, deadlines for reading, obligations to friends and family, work schedules, and other constraints, such as exercise routines and church services. Do not overlap reading with other commitments that will make adherence to the reading chart impossible.
- Do not designate a place for reading that your schedule will not allow. If you're going to try to read ten pages between classes, you will need to find a spot on campus that suits your needs, since you will not have time to get home to that favorite couch or chair.

Once you compile this chart, give it a trial run. If it helps you achieve your reading goals, constructing a chart every week will help you meet deadlines. If it does not seem to work, tweak it. Figure out what got in the way of following the schedule, and account for that in a new schedule. Unexpected occurrences may still get in the way, but the point is to use short spurts to accomplish your reading. A chart will aid you in avoiding destructive habits, such as procrastination. Work with it so that it becomes an effective tool for reading.

Comprehension

After you have eliminated the barriers to reading, you must make sure that you comprehend the material in front of you. You have to be able to understand what you read in order to apply it. In college, one of the purposes of reading is writing.

Textbooks generally help you in the process of comprehending for writing purposes by putting key terms in boldface or italic type. Textbooks usually are also broken into easily digestible sections in which the main point is stated in the first paragraph and summarized at the end. However, you might read primary sources in some courses, which are structured differently than textbooks.

Primary Sources	Secondary Sources
Material appeared in this form originally	Material reproduced in this form
Author conducted research and suggested a theory	Author summarizes research and repeats theories
Intended audience is made up of people knowledgeable about and/or interested in the topic	Intended audience is students or those who prefer more general information

For academic proficiency as well as for some civic responsibilities, you have to reach the same level of comprehension of primary sources as you do of textbooks. Here are some useful strategies.

Focused Freewriting   After you finish one of your short spurts—or perhaps after going through the whole reading task in front of you—write down what you think you have learned through the reading. At this point, your writing does not have to accurately summarize the reading you have done, but you should make an honest attempt at conveying what you learned. Such focused freewriting, discussed in Chapter 6, should help improve your comprehension.

Think of this step as part of your reading process. Budget it into the time you spend on reading. What ideas can you articulate without going back to the text and copying it? What were the main points? What happened? You will discover that you understood more than you realized at first. Remember the phenomenon of not recalling what you just read until you reread it? Your brain is functioning in ways that you might not understand. It can predict and fill in blanks even when you might not consciously realize that it is doing so. By writing, you are activating the same processes used in rereading.

When you do a focused freewrite, do not be afraid to take educated guesses—to predict, in other words—about what your mind tells you must have been a part of your reading. You can go back and check what you wrote to see if it captures the spirit of the text. You can cross out and insert paraphrases as necessary. This activity will enable you to start putting ideas in your own words so that you can later use them in a paper.

Molly Egan's Freewrite

Here is a student example of a focused freewrite based on the excerpt from The Vanishing Hitchhiker.

It seems like urban legends always happen to other people. I wonder if there are any first hand accounts of this story. What's weird about it is that they persist even when people come out and say that they are fake. The one person did research and proved that the accident could not have taken place as the story said. Just the fact that versions of the story have occurred at all these different times and places should clue people in. But I guess the point that Brunvand is getting at is that people keep telling the stories because it fulfills a need in our culture. I'm just not sure I understand what that need is. Perhaps we have to maintain a belief in the fantastic or the nearly unbelievable. I think he said that we prefer to tell stories of escaped lunatics, which could happen, rather than of aliens or monsters, which couldn't. But I don't know what the moral of the Vanishing Hitchhiker is. Maybe this legend confirms for people that there is an afterlife. I'm not sure what Brunvand thinks it does.

This student takes educated guesses when she does not exactly understand Brunvand's ideas. In so doing, she takes the opportunity to extend Brunvand's ideas for a possible writing assignment on the topic. This focused freewrite will also guide her rereading and highlighting when she looks for places where she does not exactly understand the author's point.

Highlighting   Underlining or highlighting text helps us concentrate on important or difficult sections and facilitates reviewing them. Be careful about highlighting or underlining too much; highlighting half the book defeats the purpose of the process and also slows down your reading.

Try highlighting after you have gone through one of your short spurts. Ten pages or so will be fresh in your memory, so you can easily go back and highlight important information. This makes referencing the text later that much easier. Highlight only key facts and theories. Often, examples are not as important as the main point, but sometimes it is difficult to tell an example from a fact or theory. Remember that an example is a specific instance of a larger point. Highlighting the key facts and theories will separate the important information that you can use later as evidence, as discussed in Chapter 9.

Check Marks in the Margins   Do not get bogged down by strange allusions or vocabulary. If a text uses an allusion or a word that you do not understand, place a check mark in the margin and move on (use pencil if you have borrowed the book from the library or a friend). Even if the word or reference seems essential for full comprehension, you do not need to stop reading to go to a dictionary or an encyclopedia. Doing so will frustrate you and distract you from your reading task. Much comprehension can be gained from understanding the context around the word or reference. If you are reading the text for a class, you can assemble a set of questions for the instructor or listen for the answers during the lecture. The good thing about this process is that it tends to stick with you. You increase your vocabulary and recognize allusions the next time around.

This passage from The Vanishing Hitchhiker *is an example of how to highlight important points and use check marks to identify strange words and references.*

Urban legends belong to the subclass of folk narratives, legends, that—unlike fairy tales—are believed, or at least believable, and that—unlike myths—are set in the recent past and involve normal human beings rather than ancient gods or demigods. Legends are folk history, or rather quasi-history. As with any folk legends, urban legends gain credibility from specific details of time and place or from references to source authorities. For instance, a popular western pioneer legend often begins something like, "My great-grandmother had this strange experience when she was a young girl on a wagon train going through Wyoming when an Indian chief wanted to adopt her. . . " Even though hundreds of different great-grandmothers are supposed to have had the same doubtful experience (being desired by the chief because of her beautiful long blond hair), the fact seldom reaches legend-tellers; if it does, they assume that the family lore has indeed spread far and wide. This particular popular tradition, known as "Goldilocks on the Oregon Trail," interests folklorists because of the racist implications of a dark Indian savage coveting a fair young civilized woman—this legend is familiar in the *white* folklore only—and it is of little concern that the story seems to be entirely apocryphal.

In the world of modern urban legends there is usually no geographical or generational gap between teller and event. The story is *true*; it really occurred, and recently, and always to someone else who is quite close to the narrator, or at least "a friend of a friend." Urban legends are told both in the course of casual conversations and in such special situations as camp-fires, slumber parties, and college dormitory bull sessions. The legends' physical settings are often close by, real, and sometimes even locally renowned for other such happenings. Though the characters in the stories are usually nameless, they are true-to-life examples of the kind of people the narrators and their audience know firsthand.

One of the great mysteries of folklore research is where oral traditions originate and who invents them. One might expect that at least in modern folklore we could come up with answers to such questions, but this is seldom, if ever, the case. . . . [M]ost leads pointing to possible authors or original events lying behind urban legends have simply evaporated. . . .

A prime example of the adaptability of older legends is "The Vanishing Hitchhiker"—*the* classic automobile legend. This returning-ghost tale was known by the turn of the century both in the United States and abroad. It acquired the newer automobile motif by the period of the Great Depression, and thereafter spawned a number of subtypes with greatly varied and oddly interlocking details, some of which themselves stemmed from earlier folk legends. Merely sampling some of the many "Vanishing Hitchhiker" variants that have been collected over a period of some forty years can help us trace the legend's incredible development. Surely most readers already know a local "true" account (or maybe two or three) similar to Example A, as told by a teenager in Toronto, Canada, in 1973:

A

Well, this happened to one of my girlfriend's best friends and her father. They were driving along a country road on their way home from the cottage when they saw a young girl hitchhiking. They stopped and picked her up and she got in the back seat. She told the girl and her father that she just lived in the house about five miles up the road. She didn't say anything after that but just turned to watch out the window. When the father saw the house, he drove up to it and turned around to tell the girl they had arrived—but she wasn't there! Both he and his daughter were really mystified and decided to knock on the door and tell the people what had happened. They told them that they had once had a daughter who answered the description of the girl they supposedly had picked up, but she had disappeared some years ago and had last been seen hitch-hiking on this very road. Today would have been her birthday.

This version has the basic elements—not necessarily "original" ones—well known in oral tradition and occasionally reported in newspapers since the early 1930s. The stable story units have been labeled in brackets in the following text from South Carolina collected by workers of the South Carolina Writers' Project (Work Projects Administration) sometime between 1935 and 1941:

B

A traveling man [driver] who lived in Spartanburg [authentication] was on his way home one night [setting] when he saw a woman walking along the side of the road [hitchhiker]. He stopped his car and asked the woman if he could take her where she was going. She stated that she was on her way to visit her brother who lived about three miles further on the same road [her address]. He asked her to get in the car and sit by him, but she said she would sit in the back of the car [her choice of seat]. Conversation took place for a while as they rode along, but soon the woman grew quiet. The man drove on until he reached the home of the woman's brother, whom he knew [more authentication]; then stopped his car to let the woman alight. When he looked behind him, there was no one in the car [disappearance]. He thought that rather strange [curiosity or concern], so went into the house and informed the brother that a lady had gotten into his car to ride to see him, but when he arrived at the house the lady had disappeared. The brother was not alarmed at all and stated that the lady was his sister who had died two years before [identification]. He said that this traveling man was the seventh to pick up his sister on the road to visit him, but that she had never reached his house yet.

Variations on the basic story are endless, and trying to sort them out into any kind of possible chronological development is hampered by the fact that the date when a version happened to be collected and published bears little relationship to its possible age in tradition, and by the principle that legends ✓ become highly localized and rationalized with many circumstantial details whenever they are adopted into a particular context.

COLLABORATING

Select one of the readings from Part III of this book to read as a group. On your own, read the selection and do a freewrite. As a group, compare freewrites and see which aspects of the essay appear in all of the freewrites. Use your findings as the basis of highlighting and check marking the text. Make sure to differentiate between facts and examples in highlighting, and do not highlight more of the text than is necessary.

As with all the strategies suggested in this book, find what works for you. Analyze what you do to make accurate predictions about nontext reading, and apply that to text reading. Reading can be bearable and even fun if you develop strategies that make you a critical reader and support you as a writer.

Summary

Even people who do not read many books or magazine articles engage in acts of interpretation that can form the basis of a strong reading process. As a reader, you unconsciously try to predict texts. Difficulty in reading arises when texts are not easily predictable, and you may give up on your reading at this juncture. You need to see the purpose for reading to get through such blocks. With motivation established, you can develop a reading strategy that will get you through the actual reading and enhance your comprehension. You must attempt different processes to find out what works best for you.

CHAPTER 9

WRITING WITH EVIDENCE

Recently, students in my class selected the sensitive subject of religion as an essay topic. I expected some awkward moments during our whole class workshops, where we would critique student work and make suggestions for improvement. Since religion is, by its very nature, a matter of faith, not of fact, many students wrote drafts that lacked evidence to support their contentions. I was not asking students to prove that God exists or to defend their personal faith. Rather, I was asking them to explain the beliefs in their religions, describe the religion's appeal for them (or, if students had turned away from their religions, they could explain that choice), and generalize through examples to arrive at a thesis. One discussion from the workshop has relevance to this chapter.

Julie volunteered to be in the first group of students whose drafts were critiqued. The other students and I read her essay and came to class prepared to comment. Julie had been raised a Baptist and liked her religion very much, but she did not like its prohibitions against premarital sex. She argued logically for her position. Her peers, however, spotted a problem with her reasoning.

JULIE SPRINGFIELD

Sex and Religion

I love my church and would never think of changing religions. Ever since I can remember, I was a Baptist and went to the Antioch Baptist Church. I liked the feeling of praying together and being

Online Study Center

This icon will direct you to web links and additional resources on the website http://college.cengage.com/english/thelin/ writing_without_formulas/1e/student_home.html

reminded to live a good life. We believe that Jesus is our savior and that he died for our sins. We believe in the truth of the Bible. We believe that the Ten Commandments are God's laws for us. We reject the devil and all he stands for. We believe everyone should try to be a good Christian and not to sin.

Despite this, I do not understand why premarital sex is wrong. I have heard people condemn it and talk about the deterioration of morals and values because couples will not wait until they get married to have sex. Some people in my church have formed coalitions against television shows which allude to sexual situations or where men's and women's bodies are not concealed by heavy layers of clothing. They also don't believe in giving out birth control because they think it encourages sex.

I respect that they want to follow God's law, but I do not see the sense in it. Sex is very natural. While one of its purposes is for reproduction, just like the church people say, I do not think God would have created urges in all of us if that was all it was for. People will say that if you wait until you find the right person and get married, you will experience sex in a better way than if you have multiple partners. But how would they know? If you only experience sex with one person, you cannot tell if there is anything better or worse.

I do not believe people should be sleeping around casually with each other. But I think if you're in a relationship and you are in love, you shouldn't have to get married to have sex. You want to be closer to your boyfriend, but you cannot really know how mature or caring he is if you keep him at a distance. If you marry him and then discover that he has trouble with intimacy or needs freaky things to make him satisfied, you are stuck in a marriage. It is better that you know as much as you can about a guy before marriage. If you find out that he is not the guy you want to marry, you can go your separate ways without having to go through a divorce or anything.

I do not understand who anyone is hurting by having premarital sex. As long as you are careful with your birth control and stick to one guy at a time, you are not going to get pregnant or catch a disease. It's really no one else's business. You are not breaking any laws or causing anyone else harm. You are just making a decision about a relationship that influences you and nobody else.

When I turned sixteen, I did not go to church as often as I used to. It seemed the sermons did not talk as much about what Jesus wanted from us as much as what he did not want. I wanted to do good things to keep my walk with Jesus strong, but I had to let people know how I felt about sex. Especially in Youth Group, where they kept telling us not to succumb to temptation, I had to make my feelings known. All of a sudden, Mrs. Jorgenson, who led the group, automatically thought that I was having sex, which I wasn't. She went from being a kindly second mother to me to being a cold, intolerant old lady. She would scoff at me, make comments about my activities, and say that Jesus did not care for my activities. I stopped going to Youth Group and only showed up for Sundays once in a while.

I missed going so last year, I talked to Mrs. Jorgenson and I practically apologized for thinking like I did. I told them I realized I was wrong and that I had drifted away from my walk. I started going back to church and tried not to think about this conflict. I feel good about my church and I want to be a good Christian. I believe what the Baptist religion tells me on most things. But I think its stance on premarital sex is wrong.

"Are you questioning what the Bible says?" Lester asked Julie.

"I don't think so," she said.

"Well, what does the Bible say about sex?" Lester continued.

"I guess it says it's bad," Julie replied with a shrug.

"How do you know that?" I asked.

"Well, people tell me that," she answered.

A student who was familiar with the Bible suggested that Christ's advice to the prostitute he saved from death to "sin no more" clearly indicated that sex was a sin. Julie said she would look for other places to support this point.

"That's not what I meant," Lester said. "If you're a Baptist, you should be taking the Bible literally, right?" Julie didn't know what he meant. "You can't pick and choose," he emphasized. "The Bible is the authority on these matters."

"I'm just saying that I don't see the logic behind not having premarital sex," Julie said. "I don't think it should be a sin."

"But that's not being a Baptist," Lester said. "If you choose to have premarital sex, you are choosing to defy God, right? Because it is in the Bible, and the Bible is God's word."

"Well, maybe not," Julie said, looking confused.

"That's my point," Lester said triumphantly. "By questioning this one rule, you are contradicting yourself. A Baptist believes that the Bible is God's word. Aren't I right, Dr. Thelin?"

"Did you look into the basis of your religion?" I suggested to Julie. "Do you know why John Smyth started the denomination? Do you know about the principles of your faith?"

"I don't," she said. "I was just stating what I believed in."

The mistake Julie made was to think that she could assert something without producing evidence. In this case, she needed to check her knowledge about her religion before asserting its beliefs. For that part of the assignment, she had listed information she thought she understood without verifying it. She simply repeated basic fundamentals of many Christian denominations without talking about the specifics of her denomination. Thus, she did not take the opportunity to critically explore her religion in a way that could have helped her better understand and convey the dilemma between her reasoning and the Bible.

Even though the subject of religion might touch on personal areas that some students find uncomfortable, in another section of the same course students wanted to invent a philosophy of life that would make the world a better place. We decided that critiquing the values they personally adhered to could make for interesting essays and discussions. The students were supposed to explore the principles that they felt their lives stood for and critically assess whether the world would be better or worse if everyone followed these principles. Brad, a student in this class, submitted a very short draft to the whole class workshop in which he asserted that people should not worry about rules and should follow their instincts instead.

BRAD TURNER

Instincts vs. Rules (draft)

I have worked ever since I turned sixteen years old. Not a summer went by that I didn't have to earn my keep, and even during school, I had chores to do before class and a job picking up scrap at construction sites after school ended. I work forty hours a week now and then make some spare cash working on folks' cars on weekends. I haven't had much time to worry about my principles or philosophies, as I think you just have to live.

People talk about rules you have to follow, but I won't have any of that. You should do your job, take care of yourself, and just follow your instincts about right and wrong. I don't need anyone telling me that I can't do this or I can't do that. There are things that aren't healthy for you, but you have to decide that. What people tell you is not always the truth, either. Some people mind your business better than they mind their own. You got to decide what you want to do, then do it.

So people have to just do what comes natural. I'm a good person by anyone's definition. Instincts can guide you toward right and wrong. You don't need to list principles or say that you're following some guidelines to end up in the right place. If people just stuck to this, the world would be a better place.

The class had all sorts of questions. "How can you call yourself a good person and talk about right and wrong if you don't have any values?" Roger asked Brad. Brad shrugged his shoulders and looked at me.

"Does Roger mean that right and wrong have to relate to some sort of code?" I asked the class. "Do good and bad have any meaning otherwise?"

"They can have different meanings," Patricia said.

"But it's got to come back to something," Desmond stated. He turned to Brad. "It's like you just want us to accept that you know right and wrong without telling us what they are."

"I'm just saying that it's inside all of us what's right and what's wrong," Brad answered. "You don't have to get all fancy about it."

"To make that claim," I said, "you must show how you know what most people believe about right and wrong. You would have to give examples to support your belief in instinct."

"But all I'm trying to say is that my life works for me," he responded.

"No," I replied. "You're suggesting through this paper that people in general—not just you—could live better if they did not burden themselves with rules. Am I right?"

"Yeah," Brad said. "What's wrong with that?"

"How do you know others could live better if you don't know how they're living?" Patricia asked.

"Right," Desmond said. "You're just dissing the values of others because you can't hang with them."

"And what evidence do you have that you're living better than you would?" Roger followed.

"But it's my opinion," Brad stated adamantly.

Like Julie, Brad had assumed that he did not need to support what he said because the assignment included a personal component. But even when writing tasks seem to call for your opinion, you must supply evidence. In academic papers and in most forms of public writing, you are making a claim, which can be defined as a position you hold or that you believe has validity for others. A mere opinion has little meaning for a reader if it is not supported by evidence.

You also cannot divorce your experiences from the larger context of the rest of the world. You have a perfect right to hold an opinion in your personal life that is not supported by evidence or to follow ideas that are inconsistent with the public beliefs with which you identify them. But in academic and professional writing, your ideas must be supported so that they make sense to an audience. You must transform these beliefs into claims for them to be worthy fodder for an essay and to keep your readers' interest. Just as if a narrative contained a feat that defied the known natural laws of this world, readers will scoff at explanations or opinions that show no understanding of the context in which crucial components of the argument take place.

Brad's initial resistance softened, and he produced a revision that supplied evidence for his claims.

BRAD TURNER

Instincts vs. Rules

I have worked ever since I turned sixteen years old. Not a summer went by that I didn't have to earn my keep, and even during school, I had chores to do before class and a job picking up scrap at construction sites after school ended. I work forty hours a week now and then make some spare cash working on folks' cars on weekends. I haven't had much time to worry about my principles or philosophies, as I think you just have to live. But my experiences working gave me a code that helped shape my instincts about right and wrong.

People talk about rules you have to follow, but I won't have any of that. The only rules a person should follow are the responsibilities that are laid out to them. Life is like a job. You hire on to do what is needed and you know what you're going to get for it. You know what you're supposed to do. You do it without whining. You get paid at the end. Beyond that, I don't need anyone telling me that I can't do this or I can't do that. For example, with my girl, I knew what it meant to commit. The codes behind getting into a relationship are no different than signing up for a job. I'm supposed to take her out and treat her good. I'm not supposed to mess with other girls. I'm supposed to help her out when she needs it. I'm not supposed to be rude or disrespectful. It doesn't take a philosophy in life to figure these things out.

In the same way, there are things that aren't healthy for you, and you have to decide what risks you want to take. If you want to party it up, that's okay, but you got to take responsibility for what you say and do. You can't make excuses the next day that you didn't know what you were saying or you didn't mean to start that brawl or whatever. If you're sick or your liver gives out or you get addicted to drugs and have to go to rehab, well, you knew what could happen when you started partying. No one's broken any promises. You got high, which is what you wanted, but you knew there was a limit and you got what you knew you would get when you went past it.

What people tell you is not always the truth, either. You have to be wise and let your instincts guide you. You know that if someone is offering something that seems too good to be true, it probably is. You don't need laws to protect you when your common sense will do just as well. Also, some people mind your business better than they mind their own. You got to decide what you want to do, then do it. Just like at the job, pay attention to what you're doing and make sure it's done right. Don't worry about what they're saying or doing.

People have to just do what comes natural. I'm a good person by most people's definition, and I think if people listened to me, they would live a better life. If people didn't try to get more than they deserve and made sure they deserve what they got, we would have a better world. This instinct can guide you toward right and wrong. You don't need to list principles or be reminded of rules or say that you're following some guidelines to end up in the right place. The world is a job. If you get it done right in the first place and don't try to cut corners, you don't have to go back and do it a second time.

COLLABORATING

Brad improved his essay by adding evidence to support his claim. What do you think of his point? As a group, decide if you agree with Brad's point, and write down evidence from your experiences or observations that could either support or refute his ideas.

WRITING

Think of a person who you think is the best at doing a particular activity. Write a short essay in which you state your opinion on this matter. You can write about a football player, a singer, a corporate leader, or anyone else. How do you support your contention that this person is the best? In other words, how is he or she better than the other persons in that category? Be specific, and make sure to give several different reasons for your opinion. Once you are done, ask yourself how much of what you claimed is supported by clear evidence. What other information would you have to obtain to support your point if all your claims aren't supported by clear evidence?

This chapter discusses the ways writers use different forms of evidence. Chapter 10 goes into more detail about the research process; this chapter covers what is necessary to transform an opinion, which is an unsubstantiated claim, into a supported position. It also examines the necessity of verifying your understandings of the world. Keep in mind that supporting a claim requires evidence. The most insightful critical analysis will fall flat if the body of your argument does not support it with evidence.

Examining Evidence

We must distinguish evidence from proof. Evidence consists of verifiable details that have relevance to a claim a writer makes. It suggests that a particular thesis, argument, or line of reasoning is valid. Proof, on the other hand, is undeniable evidence in support of the claim. When you have proof, you have established validity to the extent that the proof can be applied to your claim. In casual conversation, people use these terms interchangeably, but when you write—and when you evaluate claims made by other writers—you must be keenly aware of the distinction.

Our writing frequently deals with issues that contain much uncertainty. An audience would have little interest in reading about a position that has no reasonable counterargument. For instance, we have proof that Richard Ramirez, the infamous "Night Stalker," committed a string of serial killings in Los Angeles during the 1980s. He never seriously denied his guilt and has been convicted. Writing a paper to assert his guilt would be a ridiculous endeavor, since no reasonable person would disagree with it. Writers deal with subjects about which they feel passionate and about which reasonable counterclaims can be made.

Sometimes a topic has to be explored deeply to find an issue. For example, many students in my classes have written about smoking. The thesis that results from their research is that smoking is bad. Is there any reasonable counterargument to this? Medically speaking, there is not. Smoking seriously harms people, affecting their lungs and hearts and putting them at risk for cancer. An essay's thesis that claims that people should not smoke because of the medical evidence has merely stated the obvious. Scientific research has proven the point beyond any reasonable doubt. Yet, people still smoke. Thus, the claim could consider the reasons people smoke even though they have full knowledge of the dire consequences. Perhaps smoking can be seen as good psychologically, as it eases tension in a unique way. Maybe the rewards outweigh the risks for smokers. More compellingly, though, a writer could argue that advertising aimed at teenagers, who generally do not have as clear a sense of their mortality as adults, piques their spirit of rebellion. People will debate this point. It has not been proven. Thus, a writer can explore it and can supply evidence to support or refute the claim.

COLLABORATING

What sensibilities about smoking are represented in this vintage ad for Camel cigarettes and in the recent antismoking ad with Joe Chemo? Could looking into advertisements make an investigation into smoking worthwhile? As a group, reach a consensus on the type of evidence you would need to make a claim about the influence of cigarette and antismoking advertisements.

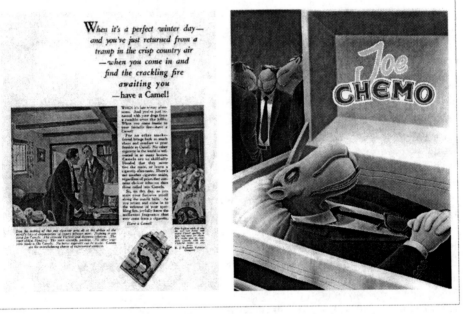

Some forms of evidence carry more weight than others. The more a writer relies on weaker forms of evidence, the more his or her claim has to suggest a conclusion rather than asserting it. Personal experiences, for instance, can help an audience relate to a claim, but they are the weakest type of evidence. When compiling evidence, you must examine each piece and understand what type of evidence you need to support your thesis.

Facts   The strongest type of evidence is a fact. Facts cannot be disputed. They span a range of disciplines. In history, for example, we cannot dispute that Abraham Lincoln was the president of the United States during the Civil War. Many scientific discoveries and theorems, such as the laws of gravity, can be considered facts, although new discoveries will displace some of them as scientists progress in understanding the natural world.

Facts are neutral. For example, the short article "Courthouse Camera Captures a Ghost" in Chapter 13 discusses a peculiar light that appeared in a Maryland courthouse. The most important fact was a surveillance tape that showed a light with no apparent source moving on a stairwell. No one could dispute that something was showing up on the tape. Some people tried to interpret the fact as evidence of a ghost, while others felt it was evidence of a malfunctioning camera. (You can read the follow-up article on page 393 to learn what the mysterious light actually was.) The point here is that it is important to understand the difference between facts and the way people try to interpret them. Facts have no bias and usually are the strongest type of evidence for a claim. The claim can be disproved, but the facts cannot.

Statistics   Statistics are the result of a formal study—an experiment, a survey, a protracted qualitative research project, a questionnaire, or a review of data. They strongly support claims when used. But the facts in statistics are limited by when the statistics were compiled, what sampling size was used, and other matters about how the researchers conducted the study.

The numbers produced from research come from interpretation of the information in the study. Interpretations can be and often are challenged, leading to follow-up studies that produce statistics that counter the previous study. The agenda of a research team, especially of its sponsor or financier, can call into question not just the interpretation of the results, but also the validity of the study itself. People can manipulate statistics to hide obvious points while highlighting less sustainable ones. The source of statistics, then, must be considered when using the statistics. Furthermore, statistics springing from surveys and questionnaires can be understood only in the historical moment. As evidence, they are limited to sentiment on a particular date and time and thus can support a claim only marginally.

Writers also need to avoid inadvertently implying the use of statistics. Even statements that start with "the majority feels" or "most people think" indicate statistical numbers, since both phrases are understood in relation to the marker of 50 percent. Writers must be careful about making such statements without support of a formal study. Qualifiers, such as "from my observation" or "I imagine" can be used when no statistical evidence is available, as can vague statements like "quite a few" or "many." Such phrases do not count as statistical evidence.

Witnesses   Writers use firsthand accounts as evidence. Although witness statements rely on subjective observation, making them a weaker type of evidence than facts or statistics, firsthand accounts can verify the initial observation of an event and lend it credibility. Readers tend to be suspicious of a single account of an episode. When several witnesses recount essentially the same event, readers believe that the episode unfolded the way the initial person claimed it did. In an essay, being able to cite more than one person who perceived the same thing aids in the acceptance of your thesis.

Even a witness who saw something similar helps verify a previous account. For example, I grew up near a mountainside in northern Glendale, just outside Los Angeles. Coyotes, deer, and rattlesnakes visited our neighborhood every year. One neighbor claimed to have seen a mountain lion, a very rare animal in that part of California. Nobody believed him, even after his dog was killed by a large animal that came down from the hills. Less than a year later, another neighbor spotted what he described as a bobcat. With two claims, the other neighbors started believing that some large feline was roaming around, even though they were not certain of the species. Both neighbors could have been mistaken about what they saw, so their witness statements are a far cry from facts, but they do support a basic claim that some sort of wildcat was prowling in the neighborhood. A letter to the newspaper editor or a flier circulated in the neighborhood could have used this evidence effectively in warning parents to be watchful when their children played in the area.

Personal Experiences and Observations   Our personal experiences and observations have a lot to do with shaping our view of the world. Yet, the narratives or examples we form from these experiences and observations are the least reliable type of evidence a writer can use. This statement puzzles many students, as some of our greatest lessons have come from learning from mistakes, growing through a tragic event, or succeeding when a challenge was put before us. The problem resides in the inability of an audience to verify the writer's personal experiences. Readers cannot simply believe everything a writer tells them. Many writers exaggerate experiences. Others remember details incorrectly. Still others leave out parts of a story that might complicate the point. Hard as it might be to believe, some writers simply lie about what happened or what they observed. For example, James Frey wrote a memoir in 2003 called *A Million Little Pieces* that he claimed was a completely true portrayal of his alcohol and drug addiction along with his criminal exploits. The book was selected for Oprah Winfrey's book club, and Frey became famous from his appearance on her television show. He even wrote a follow-up book, *My Friend Leonard.* In January 2006 The Smoking Gun, an investigative website, revealed that little in Frey's memoir actually happened.

Narratives or personal examples also tend to serve the interests of the person telling them. Their subjective nature leaves them vulnerable to opposing narratives. You might recount an experience about the hazards of bicycling at dusk, for instance. A reader might dismiss your account simply because he or she has ridden at dusk without incident on many occasions. One narrative cannot disprove the other, so you are left at a standstill.

Yet, narratives and personal examples can be used as evidence. Sometimes the body of a paper will be an extended personal example. You just have to temper your thesis statement, understanding that your personal examples can allow you to build a theory and share insights with an audience, but that your ideas need to be supported by more than just your experiences to gain validity. In "Face of the Spider" (Chapter 16), David Quammen narrates a story about his encounter with black widow spiders in his house. Rather than using the story as the sole piece of evidence for his theorizing, Quammen places his dilemma about whether to kill the spiders in the context of what other people think and feel about killing other forms of life, thereby giving his ultimate decision much more impact.

P. J. O'ROURKE

To Hell with Lipitor

P.J. O'Rourke supports his claim about Medicare with facts and projections about the national budget. Notice how he inserts his personal observations about senior citizens without relying on them as the sole means of evidence.

The Medicare Prescription Drug, Improvement, and Modernization Act of 2003 will—let's say—improve and modernize Medicare, mostly by giving old people money for drugs, at an expenditure of whatever, to be funded somehow. In his State of the Union address the President said the ten-year cost would be $400 billion. Medicare's chief actuary, Richard Foster, had informed the Administration that the cost would be more than $500 billion. He was told he'd lose his job if he let Congress know. Senator Trent Lott now estimates "closer to $600 or $800 billion." Good health is priceless. So are old people's votes.

Three quarters of seniors already had some prescription-drug coverage that cost Medicare nothing. The act "improves and modernizes" this, giving subsidies of $70 billion to employers and retirement plans that provide drug benefits.

Starting in 2006, Medicare recipients can enroll in government-approved private prescription-insurance plans (also subsidized) for about $35 a month. After a $250 deductible, 75 percent of drug costs will be covered up to $2,250; then no costs will be covered up to $5,100; then all costs will be covered except for five percent that won't be. Until 2006 government-approved private prescription-discount cards will furnish 15 to 25 percent savings (just in time, with wholesale prices for brand-name prescription drugs having risen 27.6 percent since 1999). Low-income beneficiaries will get $600 a year credited to these cards, which are free unless they use them. (There's a co-pay of five to 10 percent.)

Insert the phrases "a bewildering array of" and "until costs skyrocket" into each of the preceding sentences for a better understanding of new Medicare drug benefits.

These benefits were exhaustively explained in May, at a senior center in 5 Nashua, New Hampshire, by Congressman Charles Bass, by an AARP representative, by the House Energy and Commerce Committee's chief health counsel, and by the New England regional director of the Department of Health and Human Services. The audience's questions were acute: Preferred-drug lists and plan formularies? Benefit carry-overs? Calculation of income for assistance threshold? Multiple entitlement eligibilities?

Anyone who has experienced a Greatest Generation soliloquy on macaroni coupon rebates knows that this age cohort can shop. The HHS regional director, Brian Cresta, gave the audience his phone number: "Call me personally if you still don't understand the discount cards."

"I've given my number in dozens of meetings," Cresta said later. "I haven't gotten a call yet."

The old people weren't confused. And they weren't grateful. Tell kids they deserve a treat. Then give them 15 percent of a Snickers, or a little more if it's some generic candy bar. Tell them how, in two years, they can have candy free—if they pay for part of it and a bite has been taken out of the middle.

There must be a better way to give old people money for drugs—such as giving old people money for drugs. For Medicare recipients, average out-of-pocket spending on prescriptions in 2003 was $999. Pay them each $600 a year and the Prescription Drug Act's cost is slashed to $242.2 billion.

10   "How come," a man in the Nashua audience asked, "Canada can have the same drugs and pay less? [*applause*] Why don't they get some brain power down in Washington and lobby these drug companies down in price? [*applause*]"

The act in fact bans reimportation from Canada—devil take NAFTA principles—and forbids Medicare to bargain with pharmaceutical companies, although the Department of Veterans Affairs successfully does so.

But we might not want to cut drug prices too much. America is the last important free market for pharmaceuticals. Perhaps coincidentally, America produces two thirds of all "innovative drugs." Twenty years ago a more laissez-faire Europe produced two thirds of all innovative drugs, perhaps coincidentally. Anyway, drugs account for only 10.5 percent of health-care costs.

Which still leaves us wondering where to get that $242.2 billion or $400 or $500 or $600 or $800 billion, not to mention the $27.7 trillion in unfunded liability that Medicare's trustees say Medicare faces over the next seventy-five years. (Picture nonagenarian ravers demanding coverage for Ecstasy prescriptions.) Americans are now spending $1.55 trillion a year on health care. There's no way to cut these costs, because there's no way Dad's going to Dr. Bob's Cut-Rate Osteopath Shop.

We could raise taxes. (A lot. Medicare will consume half of all federal income-tax revenue by 2039 if current trends continue.) We could means-test fairly—by including the incomes of the people who owe everything to Medicare recipients: their kids. (That's me. Scratch that.) Or we could privatize Medicare. U.S. median household income is around $40,000. The federal Medicare tax is 2.9 percent. Invest that $1,160 a year, from age twenty-five to age sixty-five, at a six percent return, and you'd have $215,589. But that's in forty years.

15   Until then we have a choice: a realism about what Medicare can do, or a reality in which it can't do much. Perhaps the latter option isn't unthinkable.

At the Nashua senior center a Mr. Kim, who looked well into his seventies, addressed the audience. After apologizing for his English, he said, "To hell with Lipitor, a hundred and fifty dollars a month! I decided to hell with it. If I die, I die. I exercised. I lowered cholesterol level. Ran half marathon!"

DISCUSSION

Explore the following claim: "Corporal punishment serves to reinforce the use of violence as a solution to problems. Might becomes right, producing a child with limited self-discipline and a tendency to comply with authority out of fear." After mulling over this statement, explore its implications. If it was supported by facts, statistics, and witness statements, how would we negotiate our own experiences of discipline into the evidence, especially if the evidence conflicted with our experiences? Do we defend what we experienced no matter what the evidence? Do we deny our experiences in deference to the evidence? Find a strategy for dealing with such situations, and relate the strategy to writing tasks you have had.

Establishing Criteria for a Claim

Evidence for a claim makes sense only if it is compared or applied to an agreed-on standard by which it can be evaluated. The agreed-on standards by which we base claims are called criteria. Think of criteria as categories. Each category is an area needed in order to make a decision or form a thesis. The category headings are the criteria you have established. You will measure your evidence by how well it aligns with the categories.

In a writing activity earlier in this chapter (page 221), you were asked to make a claim about someone who is the best at doing an activity. In writing this essay, did you arrange evidence in categories so as to make comparisons to other people who do the same activity? If so, you established criteria by which to rank these people. When you determined criteria, you gave yourself a way to make clear decisions and to make your evidence better understood by your audience.

While a comparison uses criteria in an obvious way, an essay like Brad's also needs criteria. Brad's thesis was that people could live better lives if they followed their instincts instead of society's rules. Look back on your group writing about the evidence in Brad's claim on page 219. Did his evidence fit people's assumptions about a "better life"? In other words, did Brad anticipate audience needs and construct criteria about a better life? Were categories such as "personal responsibility" and "self-discipline" obvious, even if not stated explicitly in his text? For an essay to be effective, the writer's implied criteria should organize the essay and be clear to the audience.

Without the structure of criteria, your argument might haphazardly include information without showing its relevance. If you have anticipated audience needs well enough, your evidence should support your claims, even if audience members disagree with some of the criteria you used. When determining the criteria—something to think about early in your writing process—you should keep certain matters in mind.

Ensuring the Relationship to the Claim

Writers should fill the bodies of their papers with evidence that is relevant to the claims. Thus, the criteria they establish should directly bear on the claims. Writers can become distracted when they know a great deal about a subject. If research has been done, they sometimes desire to show what they know and forget that some of the information is irrelevant to supporting a suitable thesis.

For example, if you were assigned to show why a historical figure should be considered heroic and decided that Mother Jones, the famous labor agitator, would be a good subject, you might become captivated by her biography. Mother Jones traveled from Europe to Canada to the United States, personally heard Lincoln speak, and experienced the advent of the industrial age firsthand. These facts might not work toward a thesis about heroism. Mother Jones suffered personal tragedy during the Chicago fire of 1871 and in one week lost her husband and all four of her children to an outbreak of yellow fever. This information, though interesting, still might not be relevant to your paper; overcoming personal crisis does not necessarily make for heroism. More relevant information includes her sacrifices for coal miners, her advocacy of oppressed Mexican revolutionaries in the Southwest, and her work in founding unions and political parties for working people. In other words, these accomplishments comprise the most worthy set of criteria because they have more to do with standard definitions of heroism. While background information might set the stage for your evidence, establishing criteria to make that information sound like evidence would dilute your thesis.

Establishing Substantive Criteria

Criteria not only have to be relevant; they have to be substantive. Establishing superficial criteria does little except make the writer seem to be avoiding the real issues. Writers tend to succumb to superficiality when they worry about the validity of their theses. If establishing a criterion might jeopardize a point, some writers disregard that criterion and slip in something less deep.

Instead of establishing superficial criteria, try one of these two options. First, as was mentioned in earlier chapters, acknowledge the validity of opposing points of view. Explain that your point might seem weaker when viewed through this set of criteria, but establish why the criteria you chose more appropriately assess the situation. Second, rethink your thesis. If your point falls apart when serious criteria are applied, it probably has less value than you initially thought.

Look again at your writing about the person who is best at an activity to see whether other criteria might have been more appropriate for your claim.

Avoiding the Bandwagon Mentality

Some criteria seem valid but actually do little to supply evidence for a point. One common mistake writers make is to use popularity as evidence. On the surface, popularity appears to be a good method of persuading an audience. If one of your criteria is that many people should agree with a point of view for it to be worthy, supplying evidence that people do, indeed, support your point seems helpful in securing the acceptance of your claim by readers. But this criterion is flawed. As we all know, the majority can be wrong. Further, a genuine critical analysis does not kowtow to the status quo. Critical analysis seems fresh and astute for the very reason that it does not produce the most popular or obvious points of view. Therefore, stating that your claim is correct because it is popular constitutes a logical fallacy that undermines your credibility.

Do not jump on the bandwagon when you are considering evidence. The bandwagon mentality appeals to prejudicial ideological assumptions. While few writers intentionally establish a criterion that relies on racism or sexism, this type of appeal does slip in. If a person were writing a paper about John Stockton, who holds the NBA record for assists, and established a criterion that Stockton was one of the few white stars in basketball when he played, the argument could be interpreted as racist, even though the writer did not say anything negative about other races. When writers establish categories that connote civic pride, patriotism, manhood, or other ideological constructions, they are committing the logical fallacy of the bandwagon argument. If your claim is so weak that you need bandwagon criteria to categorize your evidence, you need to reexamine the claim.

COLLABORATING

As a group, collect several different reviews of the same recent movie. Determine the implicit criteria the critics used in evaluating the movie. A critic rarely states such criteria explicitly. For example, a review will not state that a good movie must contain convincing performances. However, if the critic mentions flawed acting during the review and has an overall unfavorable opinion of the movie, you can ascertain that one criterion is the acting ability of the cast. Note how the criteria are woven into the reviews, and decide how valid they are to the critic's final judgment.

Checking Information

Whether your writing task involves asserting a claim, suggesting a possibility, or weaving in another type of thesis, you need to critically examine the information you use to support your reasoning. Novice writers frequently consider themselves to be experts and do not bother to verify their facts. Other times, knowledge that has been passed down, perhaps by their families, proves to be incorrect or less broad in application than they anticipated.

In the draft presented at the beginning of this chapter, Julie assumed quite a bit about her religion and its relationship to the Bible. Julie's claim about premarital sex needed to be understood in the context of Baptist beliefs on the primacy of the Bible. During the process of revision, Julie researched Baptist doctrine. She never knew, apparently, about key tenets of the denomination, and she came to understand that she would have to equate her logic to the word of God in order to validate her argument for a Baptist audience. Julie had never thought of this. She and her friends had talked about the issue, and relying on logic had worked in other academic arguments she made. She assumed that her opinion always mattered because "that's the way it was." She further assumed that she completely understood the position of her faith on the issue, but she really knew a simplified version. This led her to make a claim that did not accurately convey the complexity of Baptist beliefs.

Julie was willing to check her information when confronted with the possibility that she was wrong. But when armed with the facts, she found that she did not have a claim to make. For some reason, however, she did not want to reconceive her paper, so she turned in a revised piece that still had the glaring inconsistency. If she had checked her information first, she could have detected the problem much sooner and have taken the paper in a different direction. Following are guidelines about what information to check, how much information to check, and where to check the information.

Beliefs, Histories, and Definitions   Writers should verify information about the beliefs of an institution or person, the history of a person, place, or institution, and the definition of key terms. Beliefs can be slippery, so you want to represent what somebody else feels in words that the person would see as accurate. As a citizen, for example, you might believe that your governor lacks commitment to cleaning up the environment. However, you would need to find a statement by your governor that supports your view, since you could be misinterpreting his or her actions. The governor might, in fact, believe wholeheartedly in cleaning up the environment but has not prioritized it. A more accurate statement would be that cleaning up the environment is not among his or her top priorities.

History is usually a matter of facts or of well-supported theories, although the perspectives and biases of those who narrate and interpret historical events have been questioned. For example, a student wrote in an essay that eight thousand people were killed in the September 11, 2001, attack on the World Trade Center. That figure was an estimate made at the time of the attack; the number was changed in subsequent days until the government arrived at the much lower tally of just over three thousand people. With some fact-checking, this student could have provided more accurate information. Any reference to past events, even recent ones, should be verified.

Confirming the definition of a key term can prevent embarrassing moments. Keep the advice about language in Chapter 5 in mind. An additional tip is to look up concepts that an instructor introduces in class. For example, the word *feminism* evokes many reactions. If you use the term, make sure you understand its meaning and the specific context in which it is used so as to not misuse it. In a recent class, a student essay talked about "feminism" when the student clearly meant "sexism." The two terms are not synonymous but are instead in opposition to each other.

The Straw Man Fallacy   The straw man fallacy is an argument that does not represent the opposing side in a substantial, truthful way. Sometimes writers who are passionate about a claim see the opposition as unreasonable, perhaps even ignorant and immoral. In writing about opposing arguments, they create a caricature of the actual evidence and claims. If you have written a very negative description of counterarguments to your claim or of the people making a counterargument, check your information carefully. Research the purpose of the opposition and the ways the opponents construct their arguments. Consider the logic behind their goals and the strong points in their claims. To do otherwise is to succumb to the straw man fallacy, which many audiences consider unethical.

Dictionaries, Encyclopedias, and Websites   Verify your information in reliable reference sources, both print and online, that provide concise and accurate information. In college-level writing, do not use a dictionary or an encyclopedia as a primary source of a paper that requires research. However, you can use such reference materials to check accuracy and to give you a starting point for more detailed research.

Dictionaries should be consulted for basic definitions. However, some concepts are better explained in extended form. For example, a philosophical movement, such as stoicism, existentialism, or postmodernism, needs more than a thumbnail sketch to be accurately represented. An encyclopedia or a website would supply more thorough information about these belief systems. The reference librarian at your campus library can direct you to the best sources for specific subjects.

For historical facts, encyclopedias or websites will give enough information to verify most information you might use. When using websites, confirm that they are legitimate. Keep the perspective of the person or organization running the website in mind. A pro-Palestinian website, for instance, will discuss the history of the West Bank much differently than a pro-Israeli website. Confirm controversial or sensitive information through several websites just to make sure. We discuss this issue more thoroughly in Chapter 10.

COLLABORATING

In your peer response group, share drafts of your current essays. Underline or highlight every sentence that states what a person or institution believes; that refers to the history of a person, place, or institution; and that uses a key concept. Figure out what the writer needs in order to verify this information. If you are working online, look together for reliable resources. If you come across a source that contradicts a claim in one of the drafts, how might the new information affect the essay's argument? Should the writer consider altering the claim?

Integrating Sources

You need to integrate evidence from sources into your essay as smoothly as possible. Plopping a quotation into the middle of an essay does not help the audience understand its context or relevance. You must take responsibility for clearly signaling that you understand the material and that you have a purpose for presenting it in the essay.

The key issue in integrating sources is for you to retain your own voice. An essay should not be an amalgamation of different sources but rather the coherent argument of a writer who uses different sources to support a claim. While using full quotations can be appropriate at times, this section suggests ways to locate key words within a quotation and to paraphrase so the voices in sources supplement rather than supplant your voice. Effective paraphrases extract evidence from source materials. Whether you are using ideas, facts, witness statements, or statistics, you need the information, not the words in which it is embedded.

The next chapter discusses how to use citation systems. The following ideas explain how to integrate evidence from sources into your writing.

Extricating the Information Often, writers simply need information from a source. In such cases, it makes no sense to retain the original words or sentence structures. Instead, you need to extricate the information. Claudia, a student in my class, discovered the story of Anne Bonny, an eighteenth-century pirate, while researching an essay about female outlaws. Claudia claimed that female criminals can be as brutal as male criminals, and Bonny's story supplied evidence. Consider this excerpt from Nancy Roberts's *Blackbeard and Other Pirates of the Atlantic Coast.*

NANCY ROBERTS

from *Blackbeard and Other Pirates of the Atlantic Coast*

Captain Rackham is the notorious pirate, "Calico" Jack Rackham. Bonny became attracted to him shortly after she married James Bonny, whom she grew to despise because he betrayed former mates for reward money. Rackham was hanged in November 1720, but not until Anne Bonny condemned him as a coward for not fighting hard enough in his last battle.

According to the law of the day the punishment for a woman who left her husband for another man was a public flogging. Though this punishment was seldom carried out, the governor threatened Anne with this treatment if she didn't return immediately to James Bonny. By this time Rackham was already plotting with Anne to steal a sloop and put to sea. When the governor's threat reached the pair, they accelerated their plans, and by dawn the next morning Rackham was sailing his new, ill-gotten ship with a new crew member on board—a woman.

Anne was faithful to her pirate captain. Writer Daniel Defoe says that a young crewman once made advances to Anne, and she beat him so badly that no one else tried to seduce her again. But she did give Rackham some jealous moments. After a time she became fast friends with a new pirate who had joined the crew, and the pair were constantly seen together, sometimes walking the deck arm-in-arm. This infuriated Captain Rackham.

"If I see you with that little fop again, I'll slit his throat!" he roared. In order to calm his rage, Anne asked that they have a private meeting with the new pirate in Rackham's cabin. He consented reluctantly, fingering the handle of his dagger and muttering, "I would rather solve the problem my way."

When the three were alone, Anne's pirate friend said in a soft voice, "I'm no threat to you, Captain Rackham." To Rackham's astonishment the pirate opened "his" shirt to partially reveal the breasts of a woman! The new crew member was a young widow named Mary Read, and she was the only woman friend Anne had ever known. Later Mary married one of the crewmen, and she and Anne remained close friends.

Then Anne began to have a much more serious problem. To her distress, 5 she noticed her agility lessening, her footing becoming unsteady, and her dagger thrusts finding their mark less often as she fought the crews of the vessels Rackham plundered. Sometimes, to her humiliation, her blows missed altogether. She was pregnant.

When Anne told Rackham, he suggested that they put aside piracy briefly and seek a more peaceful environment. They sailed for Cuba—a haven for pirate families, where husbands returned periodically for whatever semblance of home life pirates could have. Some women stayed there the year around, but not Anne, for she loved the sea. Scarcely risen from her childbed, she gave the baby up to another family in the pirate colony and was soon back on board ship, fighting at Rackham's side, capturing and plundering one ship after another.

During October of 1720, Rackham's ship *Curlew* attracted the interest of the governor of Jamaica. He had given the Brethren of the Sea offers of pardon if they would surrender, and many had done so. But some of the more stubborn had lacked gratitude for this generous treatment, and Rackham was one of them. This angered the governor, who sent an armed British sloop to attack the pirate captain's vessel.

The sloop took the *Curlew* by surprise. Soldiers and marines clambered over the side with swords drawn and revolvers firing. After running two Britishers through with her sword, Anne Bonny turned just in time to catch sight of most of her fellow pirates scrambling down the ladder to take refuge below deck. Captain Rackham, too, disappeared, and she and Mary Read, with the help of one man, found themselves holding off the attackers.

"Come up and fight, you sea scum!" Anne called out. Mary angrily fired her pistols into the hold to shame—perhaps rally—the crew, killing one pirate and wounding several others. "Fight, you cowards, or you'll hang!" Anne raged at them from the top of the ladder, but neither Rackham nor any of his crew emerged from the hold to defend themselves.

"Surrender! We don't want to kill women," a British marine shouted to Anne and Mary.

10   Then one of the soldiers closed in and began tearing at the beautiful red-haired pirate's clothing. Whirling, Anne jabbed him in the groin with a blow of her knee. "Get back! I'll die before you bloody scoundrels touch me."

"Let her alone!" shouted an officer, and he grasped her with a vise-like grip. "You wildcat!" he said with some respect as she continued to fight him. "Be still, and I'll make sure that you're not molested."

At the same time Anne glanced up to see the ominous black pirate flag of the *Curlew* lowered and the British Union Jack being raised in its stead. She ceased struggling. Everyone aboard was taken prisoner, and the two women, so that they would not be subjected to crude remarks, were led to the captain's cabin.

When the pirates were tried in Jamaica, spectators jammed the courtroom of St. Jago de la Vega. Crewmen who were able to prove they had been forced into piracy were soon acquitted, and Mary Read's husband was one of them. But there could be no plea of "being forced" for Anne Bonny and Mary Read. Both were still defiant, and the testimony of the crew members of the *Curlew* did not help them.

"No one was more ready to attack a ship and fight in hand-to-hand combat than these two women," the men testified. Their accounts of the women's ferocity horrified spectators and jury alike.

15   Anne Bonny, pregnant for the second time, entered the courtroom, striking even in tattered men's clothing.

"Look at that red-haired monster," women murmured as she passed. "To think she's going to be a mother!" The male spectators and even officers of the court regarded her warily, as if she were a tigress who might leap at them. But many found it impossible not to admire the proud way she held herself, staring straight before her, head high, oblivious to insulting remarks. There was a hush as she passed through the crowd, for she drew their attention like a magnet.

Claudia did not need to quote large extracts from Roberts's account of Bonny. Instead, she jotted down the facts in her own words: "Bonny beat with her fists any crewman who tried to seduce her; she plundered ships while pregnant; she shot and killed fellow pirates who would not fight when her ship was boarded." Claudia realized that she had to document where this information came from, but she knew that the facts could be effectively and accurately paraphrased. Roberts's purpose was to tell stories about different pirates. Claudia's purpose was to find women outlaws who were brutal. She wove the evidence from Roberts's biography into her own sentences, relying on her criteria for brutality as the frame for the information. Consider the following paragraph from Claudia's essay.

Extract from Claudia's Essay

Throughout history, women have performed acts as horrendous as men when put into unfortunate circumstances. For instance, Anne Bonny, an 18th century pirate, fought with her fists against men, plundered many ships, even when pregnant, and was not averse to killing her fellow crewman when they did not do as she demanded. Bonny seemed to excel at criminal acts at times when her crewmates were less inclined toward violence (Roberts 109–11). It is the greatest irony that she was released from her sentence of hanging because she was pregnant.

The voice in this excerpt is not the voice of Roberts, but of Claudia, using the facts for her purpose.

Paraphrasing

Effective paraphrasing extracts ideas and information from a source. Paraphrasing is not changing a word or two in a sentence and calling it your own. That kind of carelessness is plagiarism. Rather, paraphrasing involves summarizing the ideas of a source while still retaining the flavor by using key words or phrases. In college writing, many instructors prefer students to paraphrase rather than to quote, as paraphrasing shows that the students understand the source material.

In most cases, paraphrasing provides greater clarity and consistency of tone than does simple quotation. To paraphrase properly, you need to read the source carefully. You should not be rooting through it, looking for a good quotation, but instead you should be trying to comprehend the overall point. Once you have finished your reading, write down in your own words what you believe to be key pieces of information or the main points of the arguments. Next, look for words or phrases in the selection that might give your paraphrase more precision.

For example, the first chapter of Paul Shepard's book *The Tender Carnivore* explains his theory that the advent of agriculture brought crisis, not progress, to Earth.

PAUL SHEPARD

from The Tender Carnivore

Often considered to be the father of ecopsychology, Paul Shepard linked contemporary environmental problems to humanity's desire to separate itself from its natural habitat.

The destructive combination of hydraulic agriculture and theocratic state has been the major force in the creation of our over-dense society and apocalyptic culture. Outside the great valleys other combinations have been chewing at the earth's skin just as effectively though less dramatically. In Morocco, pastoral nomadism and other grazing, charcoal-making, wood-burning, and land-clearing by fire have combined to deforest a once verdant and shady country. It is difficult to overestimate the extent of the damage by that arch destroyer, the goat.

Historians have blamed the Moroccan demise on Arab nomads who hated trees, just as the Mongols were blamed for the collapse of the

Mesopotamian irrigation systems. Ideology has been used to explain ecological situations. It is as though there were some cultural block against recognizing the fatal mishandling of the natural environment by the agricultural society and its urban overlords.

In China men struggled to control the Yellow River for four thousand years, while at the same time other men ravaged the upper watershed, creating gullies 600 feet deep. The mud that came down settled in the river bed, gradually lifting it high above the surrounding flood plain, and the river was contained entirely by manmade dikes. Flooding runoff from the denuded slopes occasionally overtopped the dikes. The great flood of 1852 shifted the mouth of the river 400 miles and drowned hundreds of thousands of people. The Biblical Flood of the Old Testament, about fifty-five hundred years ago, which was probably the Tigris River, had the same basic cause. There is evidence that the early Sumerian civilizations did not know floods of the Tigris, and that flooding began with upper-watershed destruction. The soils that fathered the first domestic plants and animals were ripped off the earth by hooves and teeth and sent down the Tigris and Euphrates, forming a delta that advanced 180 miles into the Persian Gulf, as though the skin had been peeled from the whole land and heaped into the sea, making 35,000 square miles of salt marsh from the topsoil.

The destruction was not necessarily the result of poor agricultural practices. It was rather the nature of husbandry itself. The record of agriculture everywhere on the planet is that of a blind force extending sand dunes and other wind damage by excavation and burial, lowering water-tables, increasing flooding, altering the composition of plant and animal communities, and diminishing the nutritive quality and stability of ecosystems. The loss of certain substances from the soil reservoir—especially phosphates, nitrates, and calcium—decreases crop food value. Change in floral composition affects a complex, stable species by replacing it with a simpler, shifting association. A forest may remain a forest, or grassland remain grassland, yet be drastically altered in richness, productivity, resistance, and soil-building ability. Changes in composition are brought about directly by overgrazing and indirectly by the cultivation of surrounding lands; they are invisible to most people, even cattlemen and other pastoralists.

5   No other organisms are more intricately associated with civilization than the cereals—wheat, barley, rye, corn, rice: modified annual grasses on whom the masses of mankind depend. Ecologically, the cereals are takers, not makers of soil. By contrast, perennial wild grasses work as pumps; their deep roots bring fresh nutrient minerals to the surface and structure the soil. They live in conjunction with a wide variety of flowering legumes and composites, two groups of plants essential for good soil formation, which are dependent on insect pollinators for their continued existence and in turn support a rich animal life.

As men undertook the cultivation of vast fields of cereals, they turned away from an ancient relationship with the wild nectar- and pollen-seeking bees, flies, butterflies, and beetles. Such insects had made possible the arboreal life of early primates in flowering and fruit-making tropical forests.

Then they were instrumental in the evolution of prairies and savannas, which supported the first pre-human ground apes. Finally, pollinating insects supervised the evolution of the steppe and tundra flora, where the great herds of Pleistocene mammals fostered the final hunting phases of mankind.

The earliest subsistence agriculture did not abandon its dependence on flowering plants and their pollinators, but when men moved into the great river valleys and planted vast fields of grain they in part repudiated ancient connections with a host of tiny animals who compose the richest and most diverse fauna on our planet. The cereals are wind-pollinated annuals, shallow-rooted, ephemeral, without soil-forming virtues, and their association with flowering forms or pollinator insects is minimal. By supporting large, minimally nourished human populations and by their destructive effects in the environment when grown in cultivated uniformity, the cereals are truly the symbol and agent of agriculture's war against the planet.

A student named Sherry was developing a claim that explored the negative aspects of farming. She paraphrased Shepard's key ideas accurately, integrating his insights with her own voice.

Extract from Sherry's Essay

Paul Shepard, a professor of human ecology and an environmental activist, believes much of our current environmental crisis can be traced back to the advent of agriculture. He accuses aspects of nomadic life, such as the domestication of animals and the clearing of land, as "chewing at the earth's skin," and he gives examples of agricultural practices that alter ecosystems (23–24). He feels that the harvesting of grains, in particular, symbolizes farming's "war against the planet" because it disconnects humans from natural fauna (25).

Sherry used Shepard's exact words twice in this paragraph, but she did not merely rewrite his sentences. Instead, she integrated them through paraphrasing, being careful to use quotation marks to distinguish between Shepard's words and her own. She chose these words because they demonstrate Shepard's passion and give the reader a context in which to place his ideas. She documented the page number from which she took those precise words, and she succeeded in writing an accurate paraphrase of Shepard's ideas.

Tag Phrases When you use a quotation or a paraphrase, you must introduce the source and briefly establish the author's credibility. Employ tag phrases to attribute the quotations to their source. While tag phrases such as "he said," "she asked," "we replied," and so forth are common in narratives with dialogue, different tag phrases are used with evidence. They introduce the author you are citing and indicate why the source is important.

When writing about music, for example, you might state that music allows listeners to relax. In introducing your support, you would write, "According to Alan Wells, who conducted research into the relationship between moods and music," and work in the relevant statistics from Wells's piece. "According to" is a standard tag phrase, and the following clause gives the audience a sense of why you are referring to this author. Another tag phrase is "Alan Wells, a qualitative researcher, finds that music . . . ." Depending on the evidence you have extracted, you can use the terms *claims, asserts, suggests, questions, states, believes,* or *cites*. The relationship to the paper makes the tag phrase different than the tag phrases used in dialogue. Once you have introduced the author, however, you do not have to continue to explain who he or she is in subsequent paragraphs. You can simply write, "On this point, Wells asserts, . . . " and paraphrase or quote his ideas.

COLLABORATING

Read a magazine article on a topic of your choice, and write a one-paragraph paraphrase that includes a direct quotation from the author, as in Sherry's paraphrase. Under your paragraph, list facts you found in the article. In your group, exchange your paragraph with another person. Read that person's paragraph as well as the listed facts, and write your own paragraph based on what is in front of you. Feel free to incorporate one or two items from the list of facts if they seem appropriate. You can use the direct quotation as is, shorten it, or leave it out. Have each group member read the original paragraph and the second one. How do the second paragraphs compare with the originals? Did not having the article to work from harm your ability to paraphrase?

Summary

Writers need evidence to support their claims. Personal experience alone is not sufficient to support academic essays and arguments. When making a claim, be aware of the relative worth of certain types of evidence. Facts carry the most weight, followed by statistics, witnesses, and experiences. To be understood by an audience, evidence needs to be selected according to appropriate criteria. These criteria must relate to your claim, must have the necessary depth, and must not commit the bandwagon fallacy. When writing about subjects you know well, confirm the information, especially when discussing beliefs and historical facts or relying on the definition of a key concept. In all forms of writing, be aware of how to integrate evidence into an essay, argument, or other genre of academic, professional, or civic writing. Quotations are not always necessary; you often need the evidence from a source, not the exact words. When you do want to retain the flavor of a source, you can paraphrase, but you must still correctly cite and credit the original source.

CHAPTER 10

WRITERS AND RESEARCH

Students often become overwhelmed by the information now available at libraries. The many computers, audiovisual materials, journals, magazines, newspapers, and microfilm machines, as well as the stacks and stacks of books, can make a library intimidating. Although search engines and the Internet are said to have made research easier than it was in the past, more than ever students need to participate in library orientation, make use of the services of reference librarians, and ask questions of their instructors.

I once took a class to the library to conduct research on political parties. Virtually all the students knew something about Republicans and Democrats, but they did not know the origins of either party or much detail about party platforms. Some students also wondered about alternative parties, such as the Libertarians, the Green Party, and the Labor Party. They worked in groups to see what they could find, and I circulated among them, fielding questions. The students gravitated to sites about the alternative parties. Their questions about the process of investigation and the quality of information could apply to any topic.

"Where do we go from here?" Kevin asked. His group had found a website that listed political parties, www.Politics1.com. This website gave thumbnail sketches of all known American political parties.

"How do we find out more about this group?" Patty asked. Her group had stumbled across the Pansexual Peace Party, a Wicca-based group that desired to free Americans from sexual repression.

Online Study Center

This icon will direct you to web links and additional resources on the website http://college.cengage.com/english/thelin/ writing_without_formulas/1e/student_home.html

"Are these guys serious?" Pablo asked. He and Kevin were looking at the Constitutional Action Party, whose platform included banning abortion and doing away with the federal income tax.

Hilary's group felt that the Natural Law Party was on to something with its members' belief in transcendental meditation and yoga. Josh was amazed that the Nazis and the Ku Klux Klan had formal platforms. The many communist and socialist websites fascinated more than one group. Everyone wanted to know what to do with this information. How could they find out more? How could they be sure that they weren't being pulled into an elaborate joke? What type of people started and/or joined alternative parties?

All the groups logged into the first website Kevin's group had found, www.Politics1.com. It provided links to parties' web pages and to major figures, so students could see how party members viewed themselves and wanted others to perceive them. Students spent time reviewing platforms and statements of principles. Their explorations made some students curious to learn more about political parties that seemed to reflect their ideals.

"Why don't you send an email to the address provided?" I asked Hilary.

She stared at the screen. "Do you think it would be a good idea?" she asked. "I mean, couldn't I be hooking up with some crazies?"

"Yeah," Kevin joined in from a nearby terminal. "If these groups are so great, how come I never heard of them before?"

"People would be scared of this group," Patty said, fascinated by the platform of the Pansexual Peace Party. "People would be afraid that everyone would join. Students would join if these guys put more out there."

"So what is it you want to know?" I asked, as students in adjacent terminals looked at the sites others had found.

"Well," said Kevin, "how do we trust them? How can we tell if they're legit? Is it worth our time?"

"And what happens if we contact them directly, then get caught in something?" Pablo asked. "If we signed up, then they end up being traitors or something, we're like branded for life."

"So you guys don't trust what you're reading?" I asked.

"I don't believe nothing I read," Kevin responded. "I got to hear it from someone reliable."

"For a paper, the info's good, I guess," Patty mumbled.

"But for your life, it isn't?" I asked.

All of them stopped talking, some smiling awkwardly, others looking away. "I guess maybe if we don't trust it for life, we shouldn't trust it for school either," Pablo said slowly. "But what do we do? How do we find out?"

My students had identified a crucial problem of researching online. Like many people, students often too readily accept what they read on the Web. As long as the information seems pertinent to an assignment topic, they print it out or save it and use it indiscriminately. But for important decisions that may have a direct effect on their personal lives, they need more convincing. The verification they insist on before registering for a political party, paying membership dues to a club, moving to a new apartment, making sure a tattoo artist knows what he or she is doing, and other things does not carry over into their schoolwork.

Recognizing this inconsistent behavior is one thing. Changing it is another. As discussed in Chapter 1, students sometimes mistake the process of education for its substance, so they deem finding any source that seems to meet assignment requirements a success. Other students simply do not know where to go or what to do in working with sources for college assignments. They think they have to be let in on some secret or a magical formula for distinguishing legitimate from phony sources. As with so much in writing, though, the strategies students use in real life can be translated into academic researching methods.

DISCUSSION

What does a person have to do for you to trust him or her? When do you become skeptical of information a trustworthy friend gives you? Why does knowing the truth matter more in some types of situations? Make a list of the characteristics of a trustworthy person and another list of the type of situations that would make you doubt the information provided by a trustworthy friend. What characteristics or situations could you apply to your research for a paper? When does trusting the source matter?

While this chapter discusses specific research methods, you will find that most of the information parallels the strategies you use to make sound decisions in your daily life. Writing with research can frighten students, but armed with information, your task is not as daunting as you think.

Locating Critical Knowledge

Most instructors expect students to draw from a range of sources. They want you to avoid relying on superficial listings of facts and opinions, which will lead you to an analysis and a thesis that just repeat the same old thing. Beyond consulting some journals with small print runs and, of course, books, you can do most of your research from a computer terminal. You will run into the same problem whether you use paper or online sources: Which sources constitute merely surface knowledge, and which will give you an angle that can lead to a critical analysis?

Generally speaking, college-level papers, business reports, and documents constructed for citizen action should not use popular entertainment magazines. While *People, Us,* and others might relieve boredom while you are standing in line at the supermarket or waiting at the doctor's office, they do not have the depth or focus needed for serious research. Similarly, corporate websites and personal web pages generally do superficial analyses of products and issues, depending on their agendas. Blogs and wikis sometimes do excellent jobs of critically analyzing and debating current events, but contributors are not necessarily experts on the subjects they write about. Newsletters and fanzines are dedicated to a certain readership and can gloss over important information. You should be wary, too, of magazines or websites that propound extreme political views; they may distort the truth, despite coming up with fresh twists on issues. Following is a review of some sources that will help you critically analyze your subject and construct a sound thesis:

Mainstream Sources   Some instructors are critical of weekly news publications, such as *Time* and *Newsweek*, and online news sources, such as websites for CNN and Fox News. Their criticism stems from legitimate concerns about ideology and bias. Most mainstream sources do not question underlying assumptions about our culture, so they tend to operate under the auspices of patriotism and capitalism with lingering sentiments of sexism and racism. Since laws no longer prevent multiple ownership of media outlets, the same few people own most of the prominent American television and radio stations, newspapers, and magazines. Furthermore, pack journalism and embedded reporting, wherein reporters receive most of their information from government sources, seriously hamper investigative reporting for mainstream publications. So the same ideology is present in all mainstream sources.

This does not necessarily imply bias. People who rant and rave about the liberal slant of the news media, for instance, often simply are unhappy that mainstream sources show sensitivity to minority opinions, something the media must do to try to maintain objectivity. Mainstream sources are not and should not be conduits for either conservative or liberal platforms, although the lingering sentiments mentioned above are stronger or weaker depending on ownership of the media outlet. Once a reader gets beyond the legitimate concerns, he or she will see that these sources approach their subjects seriously, do the necessary background checks, and aggressively pursue stories within certain boundaries. The stories generally reflect important national and world concerns. The information found at these sources can serve as a start toward doing serious critical analysis.

Field-Specific Journals   Much prominent knowledge is generated by research from intellectuals. Mainstream media sometimes report on their findings. A substantial archeological discovery, for example, will likely be summarized in a newspaper article. The summaries often come from field-specific journals, and they are generally written on the day the journal publishes the article or the next day.

A field-specific journal is a serial publication that focuses on a particular subject matter. *College Composition and Communication,* for example, is published six times a year and focuses on the theories and experiences of teachers of writing. For the most part, field-specific journals have more rigorous standards than do mainstream publications. Many are published by universities or research institutes. Their goal is to disseminate higher levels of information than that found in mainstream publications. Their authors assume basic subject knowledge on the part of the readership and may use technical language and rhetorical forms in making their points. Since professors and professional researchers publish in these journals, the information generally is high quality. With little or no monetary profit at stake, the facts and theories distance themselves more freely from the ideology of mainstream publications.

Much critical knowledge is never summarized in mainstream publications because it is not accessible to or of interest to most people. However, with careful reading, you can extract much from field-specific journals that can be of help in your own writing.

Books   Knowledge found in nonfiction books is probably safe for use in your research with the exception, perhaps, of some trade nonfiction. While books may be beholden to the ideology of the publishing house, they are likely to provide more detailed, in-depth information simply because of the extended number of pages devoted to the subject. Libraries have vast collections, including books from academic and specialized publishers that might not be found in mall bookstores.

Books are reservoirs of cultural knowledge. Critical information compiled in books might have been common knowledge years ago, but now seems fresh and intriguing. When the background of a situation needs to be understood, a book may give the most detailed information.

Some books, called anthologies, bring together the ideas of many different authors, so that each chapter contains a separate point or worldview. Some students shy away from books because they don't have time to do that much reading. An anthology allows you to browse until you come on a chapter that reveals the information you need.

Not all books go through rigorous editing and fact-checking. Rush Limbaugh's *The Way Things Ought to Be,* for instance, contains glaring errors about history and scientific discovery. Though widely read, the book is not a legitimate source for a college-level paper. Academic presses publish the most credible books. In deciding what information to use, follow the same guidelines presented in the section on evaluating online sources later in this chapter.

Alternative Magazines   Many voices from the margins of society find homes in the multitude of alternative magazines available in paper form and online. Some students automatically dismiss such sources because the information seems too far removed from the mainstream. However, alternative magazines are among the best sources for critical knowledge. Since they challenge the cultural assumptions on which our society rests, they give many facts and viewpoints that will allow students to construct striking critical analyses.

People debate the distinguishing characteristics of alternative magazines. *The National Review,* for example, is hardly a mainstream publication, but its writers do not challenge dominant ideology as much as they expand on it. The magazine aligns its views with factions of the Republican Party and does not offer a fresh perspective. Its heavy funding further eliminates it from consideration. It can be best thought of as political commentary by conservatives and, as such, certainly offers facts and statistics that students can make use of, but it is not an alternative magazine.

Alternative magazines can have a conservative viewpoint, but most contain articles that lean left. *Z Magazine, The Progressive, UTNE,* and *The Nation* are examples of publications that are not in any way influenced by the Democratic Party, but that favor politics from the left. These magazines collect viewpoints from independent reporters around the world. Advertising revenues are limited, and they rely on reader subscriptions to stay in existence. Professors and instructors tend to take information in these magazines seriously because the reporting is not tainted by large media companies. Some stories that alternative magazines publish have been suppressed or censored by mainstream magazines because of the sensitivity of advertisers or the challenge to dominant ideology. While innuendo and shaky testimonials do find their way into the pages of these publications, most facts can be confirmed by experts. Readers can disagree with an analysis but still find value in the critical knowledge contained in it.

PETER PHILLIPS, TRISH BORETA, AND PROJECT CENSORED

The Top Censored News Stories of 2005–2006

Here are examples of censored stories compiled by writers from Spinwatch.org.

For 30 years, Sonoma State University's Project Censored has released an annual list of the most important news stories not covered by the corporate media in the United States. Here again are the Top 10 news stories that didn't make much news.

1. Net Neutrality

Throughout 2005 and this year, a largely underground debate has raged regarding the future of the Internet. More recently referred to as net neutrality, the issue has become a tug of war with cable companies on the one hand and consumers and Internet service providers (ISPs) on the other. Yet despite important legislative proposals and Supreme Court decisions throughout 2005, the issue was almost completely ignored in the headlines until 2006. And except for occasional coverage on CNBC's *Kudlow & Kramer,* mainstream television remains hands-off to this day.

Most coverage of the issue framed it as an argument over regulation, but the term "regulation" in this case is somewhat misleading. Groups advocating for net neutrality are not promoting regulation of Internet content. What they want is a legal mandate forcing cable companies to allow ISPs free access to their cable lines (called a "common carriage" agreement). This was the model used for dial-up Internet, and it is the way content providers want to keep it. They also want to make sure that cable companies cannot screen or interrupt Internet content without a court order.

Those in favor of net neutrality say that lack of government regulation simply means that cable lines will be regulated by the cable companies themselves. Internet service providers will have to pay a hefty service fee for the right to use cable lines (making Internet services more expensive). Those who could pay more would get better access; those who could not pay would be left behind. Cable companies could also decide to filter Internet content at will.

Source: "Web of Deceit: How Internet Freedom Got the Federal Ax, and Why Corporate News Censored the Story," by Elliot D. Cohen. Buzzflash.com, July 18, 2005.

2. Halliburton and Iran

According to journalist Jason Leopold, sources at Dick Cheney's former company, Halliburton, allege that as recently as January 2005, Halliburton sold key components for a nuclear reactor to an Iranian oil development company. Leopold says his Halliburton sources have intimate knowledge of the business dealings of both Halliburton and Oriental Oil Kish, one of Iran's largest private oil companies.

Halliburton has a long history of doing business in Iran, starting as early as 1995, when Vice President Cheney was chief executive of the company. In an attempt to curtail Halliburton and other U.S. companies from engaging in business dealings with rogue nations such as Libya, Iran, and Syria, an amendment was approved in the Senate on July 26, 2005. The amendment, sponsored by Sen. Susan Collins, R-Maine, would penalize companies that continue to skirt U.S. law by setting up offshore subsidiaries as a way to legally conduct business and avoid U.S. sanctions under the International Emergency Economic Powers Act.

A letter, drafted by trade groups representing corporate executives, vehemently objected to the amendment, saying it would lead to further hatred and perhaps incite terrorist attacks on the United States and "greatly strain relations with the United States' primary trading partners." The letter warned that "foreign governments view U.S. efforts to dictate their foreign and commercial policy as violations of sovereignty often leading them to adopt retaliatory measures more at odds with U.S goals."

According to Leopold, during a trip to the Middle East in March 1996, Dick Cheney told a group of mostly U.S. businessmen that Congress should ease sanctions in Iran and Libya to foster better relationships, a statement that, in hindsight, is completely hypocritical considering the Bush administration's foreign policy.

"Let me make a generalized statement about a trend I see in the U.S. Congress that I find disturbing, that applies not only with respect to the Iranian situation but a number of others as well," Cheney said. "I think we Americans sometimes make mistakes. . . . There seems to be an assumption that somehow we know what's best for everybody else and that we are going to use our economic clout to get everybody else to live the way we would like."

10   Cheney was the chief executive of Halliburton Corporation at the time he uttered those words. It was Cheney who directed Halliburton toward aggressive business dealings with Iran—in violation of U.S. law—in the mid-1990s, which continued through 2005 and is the reason Iran has the capability to enrich weapons-grade uranium.

It was Halliburton's secret sale of centrifuges to Iran that helped get the uranium enrichment program off the ground, according to a three-year investigation that includes interviews conducted with more than a dozen current and former Halliburton employees.

If the United States ends up engaged in a war with Iran in the future, Cheney and Halliburton will bear the brunt of the blame.

Source: "Halliburton Secretly Doing Business with Key Member of Iran's Nuclear Team," by Jason Leopold. GlobalResearch.ca, Aug. 5, 2005.

3. World Oceans in Extreme Danger

Oceanic problems once found on a local scale are now pandemic. Data from oceanography, marine biology, meteorology, fishery science, and glaciology reveal that the seas are changing in ominous ways. A vortex of cause and effect wrought by global environmental dilemmas is changing the ocean from a watery horizon with assorted regional troubles to a global system in alarming distress.

The oceans are one, say oceanographers, with currents linking the seas and regulating climate. Sea temperature and chemistry changes, along with contamination and reckless fishing practices, intertwine to imperil the world's largest communal life source.

15   In 2005, researchers from the Scripps Institution of Oceanography and the Lawrence Livermore National Laboratory found clear evidence that the ocean is quickly warming. They discovered that the top half-mile of the ocean has warmed dramatically in the past 40 years as a result of human-induced greenhouse gases.

One manifestation of this warming is the melting of the Arctic. A shrinking ratio of ice to water has set off a feedback loop, accelerating the increase in water surfaces that promote further warming and melting. With polar waters growing fresher and tropical seas saltier, the cycle of evaporation and precipitation has quickened, further invigorating the greenhouse effect. The ocean's currents are reacting to this freshening, causing a critical conveyor that carries warm upper waters into Europe's northern latitudes to slow by one-third since 1957, bolstering fears of a shut down and cataclysmic climate change. This accelerating cycle of cause and effect will be difficult, if not impossible, to reverse.

Atmospheric litter is also altering sea chemistry, as thousands of toxic compounds poison marine creatures and devastate propagation. The ocean has absorbed 118 billion metric tons of carbon dioxide since the onset of the

Industrial Revolution, with 20 to 25 tons being added to the atmosphere daily. Increasing acidity from rising levels of CO_2 is changing the ocean's pH balance. Studies indicate that the shells and skeletons possessed by everything from reef-building corals to mollusks and plankton will begin to dissolve within 48 hours of exposure to the acidity expected in the ocean by 2050. Coral reefs will almost certainly disappear and, even more worrisome, so will plankton. Phytoplankton absorb greenhouse gases, manufacture oxygen, and are the primary producers of the marine food web.

Mercury pollution enters the food web via coal and chemical industry waste, oxidizes in the atmosphere, and settles to the sea bottom. There it is consumed, delivering mercury to each subsequent link in the food chain, until predators such as tuna or whales carry levels of mercury as much as 1 million times that of the waters around them. The Gulf of Mexico has the highest mercury levels ever recorded, with an average of 10 tons of mercury coming down the Mississippi River every year, and another ton added by offshore drilling.

Along with mercury, the Mississippi delivers nitrogen, often from fertilizers. Nitrogen stimulates plant and bacterial growth in the water that consumes oxygen, creating a condition known as hypoxia, or dead zones. Dead zones occur wherever oceanic oxygen is depleted below the level necessary to sustain marine life. A sizable portion of the Gulf of Mexico has become a dead zone—the largest such area in the United States and the second largest on the planet, measuring nearly 8,000 square miles in 2001.

It is no coincidence that almost all of the nearly 150 (and counting) dead 20 zones on earth lie at the mouths of rivers. Nearly 50 fester off U.S. coasts. While most are caused by river-borne nitrogen, fossil-fuel-burning plants help create this condition, as does phosphorous from human sewage and nitrogen emissions from auto exhaust.

Meanwhile, since its peak in 2000, the global wild fish harvest has begun a sharp decline. Progress in seagoing technologies and intensified fishing have stimulated unprecedented decimation of sea life. Long-lining, in which a single boat sets line across 60 or more miles of ocean, each baited with up to 10,000 hooks, captures at least 25 percent unwanted catch. With an estimated 2 billion hooks set each year, as much as 88 billion pounds of life a year is thrown back to the ocean either dead or dying.

Additionally, trawlers drag nets across every square inch of the continental shelves every two years. Fishing the sea floor like a bulldozer, they level an area 150 times larger than all forest clear-cuts each year and destroy sea floor ecosystems.

Aquaculture is no better, since 3 pounds of wild fish are caught to feed every pound of farmed salmon. A 2003 study out of the University of Nova Scotia concluded, based on data dating from the 1950s, that in the wake of decades of such onslaught, only 10 percent of all large fish (tuna, swordfish) and ground fish (cod, hake, flounder) are left anywhere in the ocean.

Other sea nurseries are also threatened. Fifteen percent of sea grass beds have disappeared in the last 10 years, depriving juvenile fish, manatees, and sea turtles of critical habitats. Kelp beds are also dying at alarming rates. While at no other time in history has science taught more about how the earth's life-support systems work, the maelstrom of human assault on the seas still continues. If human failure in governance of the world's largest public domain is not reversed quickly, the ocean will soon and surely reach a point of no return.

Source: "The Fate of the Ocean," by Julia Whitty. Mother Jones, March/ April 2006.

4. Poverty Increasing in the United States

25 The number of hungry and homeless people in U.S. cities continued to grow in 2005 despite claims of an improved economy. Increased demand for vital services rose as needs of the most destitute went unmet, according to the annual U.S. Conference of Mayors Report, which has documented increasing need since its 1982 inception.

The study measures instances of emergency food and housing assistance in 24 U.S. cities and utilizes supplemental information from the U.S. Census and Department of Labor. More than three-quarters of cities surveyed reported increases in demand for food and housing, especially among families. Food-aid requests expanded by 12 percent in 2005, while aid center and food bank resources grew by only 7 percent. Service providers estimated 18 percent of requests went untended. Housing followed a similar trend, as a majority of cities reported an increase in demand for emergency shelter, often going unmet due to lack of resources.

President Bush's proposed budget for fiscal 2007, which begins October 2006, includes a Commerce Department plan to eliminate the Census Bureau's Survey of Income and Program Participation. The proposal marks at least the third White House attempt in as many years to do away with federal data collection on politically prickly economic issues.

Founded in 1984, the Census Bureau survey follows American families for a number of years and monitors their use of Temporary Assistance for Needy Families, Social Security, Medicaid, unemployment insurance, child care, and other health, social-service, and education programs.

Some 415 economists and social scientists signed a letter and sent it to Congress shortly after the February release of Bush's federal budget proposal, urging that the survey be fully funded as it "is the only large-scale survey explicitly designed to analyze the impact of a wide variety of government programs on the well-being of American families."

30 Supporters of the survey elimination say the program costs too much at $40 million per year. They would kill it in September and eventually replace it with a scaled-down version that would run to $9.2 million in development costs during the coming fiscal year. Actual data collection would begin in 2009.

Sources: "New Report Shows Increase in Urban Hunger, Homelessness," by Brendan Coyne. TheNewStandard.com, December 2005. "U.S. Plan to

Eliminate Survey of Needy Families Draws Fire," by Abid Aslam. OneWorld. net, March 2006.

5. High-Tech Genocide in Congo

The world's most neglected emergency, according to Jan Egeland, the U.N. Emergency Relief Coordinator, is the ongoing tragedy in the Congo, where 6 million to 7 million have died since 1996 as a consequence of invasions and wars sponsored by Western powers trying to gain control of the region's mineral wealth. At stake is control of natural resources that are sought by U.S. corporations: diamonds; tin; copper; gold; cobalt, an element essential to nuclear, chemical, aerospace, and defense industries; and, more significantly, coltan and niobium, two minerals necessary for production of cell phones and other high-tech electronics. Eighty percent of the world's coltan reserves are found in the Democratic Republic of Congo (DRC). Niobium is another high-tech mineral with a similar story.

The high-tech boom of the 1990s caused the price of coltan to skyrocket to nearly $300 per pound. In 1996, U.S.–sponsored Rwandan and Ugandan forces entered eastern DRC. By 1998, they had seized control and moved into strategic mining areas. The Rwandan army was soon making $20 million or more a month from coltan mining. Though the price of coltan has since fallen, Rwanda maintains its monopoly on coltan and the coltan trade in DRC. Reports of rampant human-rights abuses pour out of this mining region.

Coltan makes its way out of the mines to trading posts where foreign traders buy the mineral and ship it abroad, mostly through Rwanda. Firms with the capability turn coltan into the coveted tantalum powder, and then sell the magic powder to Nokia, Motorola, Compaq, Sony, and other manufacturers for use in cell phones and other products.

Yet as mining in the Congo by Western companies proceeds at an unprecedented rate—some $6 million in raw cobalt alone exiting DRC daily—multinational mining companies rarely get mentioned in human-rights reports.

Sources: "The World's Most Neglected Emergency: Phil Taylor Talks to Keith Harmon Snow," The Taylor Report, March 28, 2005. "High-Tech Genocide," by Sprocket. Earth First! Journal, August 2005. "Behind the Numbers: Untold Suffering in the Congo," by Keith Harmon Snow and David Barouski. Z Magazine, March 1, 2006.

6. Whistleblower Protection in Jeopardy

Special Counsel Scott Bloch, appointed by President Bush in 2004, is over- 35 seeing the virtual elimination of federal whistleblower rights in the U.S. government.

The U.S. Office of Special Counsel (OSC), the agency that is supposed to protect federal employees who blow the whistle on waste, fraud, and abuse, is dismissing hundreds of cases while advancing almost none. According to the Annual Report for 2004 (which was not released until the end of first quarter of the 2006 fiscal year), less than 1.5 percent of whistleblower claims were referred for investigation while more than 1,000 reports were closed before they were even opened. Only eight claims were found to be substantiated, and one of those included the theft of a desk, while another included attendance violations. Favorable outcomes have declined 24 percent overall, and this is all in the first year that Bloch has been in office.

Bloch, who has received numerous complaints since he took office, defends his first 13 months in office by pointing to a decline in backlogged cases. Public Employees for Environmental Responsibility executive director Jeff Ruch says, "Backlogs and delays are bad, but they are not as bad as simply dumping the cases altogether." According to figures released by Bloch in February 2005, more than 470 claims of retaliation were dismissed, and not once had he affirmatively represented a whistleblower.

In fact, in order to speed dismissals, Bloch instituted a rule forbidding his staff to contact whistleblowers if their disclosure was deemed incomplete or ambiguous. Instead, the OSC would dismiss the matter. As a result, hundreds of whistleblowers never had a chance to justify their cases. Ruch notes that these numbers are limited to only the backlogged cases and do not include new ones.

On March 3, 2005, OSC staff members, joined by a coalition of whistleblower protection and civil rights organizations, filed a complaint against Bloch. The complaint specifies instances of illegal gag orders, cronyism, invidious discrimination, and retaliation by forcing the resignation of one-fifth of the OSC headquarters legal and investigative staff. The complaint was filed with the President's Council on Integrity and Efficiency, which took no action on the case for seven months.

40   This is the third probe into Bloch's operation in less than two years in office. The Government Accountability Office and a U.S. Senate subcommittee both have ongoing investigations into mass dismissals of whistleblower cases, crony hires, and Bloch's targeting of gay employees for removal while refusing to investigate cases involving discrimination on the basis of sexual orientation. The case has since been supplemented with allegations of Bloch supplying Congress with misleading information and misusing his office to support a person espousing creationist views even though his office had no jurisdiction to do so.

The Department of Labor has also gotten on board in a behind-the-scenes maneuver to cancel whistleblower protections. If it succeeds, the Labor Department will dismiss claims by federal workers who report violations under the Clean Air Act and the Safe Drinking Water Act. Government Accountability Project general counsel Joanne Royce sums up major concerns: "We do not want public servants wondering whether they will lose their jobs for acting against pollution violations of politically well-connected interests."

Source: All stories by Jeff Ruch, Public Employees for Environmental Responsibility website. "Whistleblowers Get Help from Bush Administration," Dec. 5, 2005; "Long-Delayed Investigation of Special Counsel Finally Begins," Oct. 18, 2005; "Back Door Rollback of Federal Whistleblower Protections," Sept. 22, 2005.

7. U.S. Operatives Do Torture

The American Civil Liberties Union released documents of 44 autopsies held in Afghanistan and Iraq on Oct. 25, 2005. Twenty-one of those deaths were listed as homicides. The documents show that detainees died during and after interrogations by the Navy Seals, military intelligence, and other government agencies.

"These documents present irrefutable evidence that U.S. operatives tortured detainees to death during interrogation," said Amrit Singh, an attorney with the ACLU. "The public has a right to know who authorized the use of torture techniques and why these deaths have been covered up."

The Department of Defense released the autopsy reports in response to a Freedom of Information Act request filed by the ACLU, the Center for Constitutional Rights, Physicians for Human Rights, Veterans for Common Sense, and Veterans for Peace.

One of 44 U.S. military autopsy reports reads as follows: "[A] 27-year-old Iraqi male died while being interrogated by Navy Seals on April 5, 2004, in Mosul, Iraq. During his confinement, he was hooded, flex-cuffed, sleep-deprived, and subjected to hot and cold environmental conditions, including the use of cold water on his body and hood. The exact cause of death was 'undetermined,' although the autopsy stated that hypothermia may have contributed to his death." 45

An overwhelming majority of the so-called natural deaths covered in the autopsies were attributed to "arteriosclerotic cardiovascular disease" (heart attack).

The Associated Press carried the story of the ACLU charges on their wire service. However, a thorough check of LexisNexis and Proquest electronic data bases, using the keywords ACLU and autopsy, showed that at least 95 percent of the daily papers in the United States didn't pick up the story.

Sources: "*U.S. Operatives Killed Detainees During Interrogations in Afghanistan and Iraq,*" *American Civil Liberties Union website, Oct. 24, 2005. "Tracing the Trail of Torture: Embedding Torture as Policy from Guantánamo to Iraq," by Dahr Jamail. TomDispatch.com, March 5, 2006.*

8. Pentagon Exempt from FOIA

The Department of Defense has been granted exemption from the Freedom of Information Act (FOIA). In December 2005, Congress passed the 2006 Defense Authorization Act, which renders Defense Intelligence Agency (DIA) "operational files" fully immune to FOIA requests, the main mechanism by which watchdog groups, journalists, and individuals can access federal documents. Of particular concern to critics of the Defense Authorization Act is the DIA's new right to thwart access to files that may reveal human-rights violations tied to ongoing "counterterrorism" efforts.

The rule could, for instance, frustrate the work of the ACLU and other organizations that have relied on FOIA to uncover more than 30,000 documents on the U.S. military's involvement in the torture and mistreatment of foreign detainees in Afghanistan, Guantánamo Bay, and Iraq—including the Abu Ghraib scandal.

50 Several key documents that have surfaced in the advocacy organization's expansive research originate from DIA files, including a 2004 memorandum containing evidence that U.S. military interrogators brutalized detainees in Baghdad, as well as a report describing the abuse of Iraqi detainees as violations of international human rights law.

According to Jameel Jaffer, an ACLU attorney involved in the ongoing torture investigations, "If the Defense Intelligence Agency can rely on exception or exemption from the FOIA, then documents such as those that we obtained this last time around will not become public at all." The end result of such an exemption, he told TheNewStandard.com, is that "abuse is much more likely to take place, because there's not public oversight of Defense Intelligence Agency activity."

Jaffer added that because the DIA conducts investigations relating to other national-security-related agencies, documents covered by the exemption could contain critical evidence of how other parts of the military operate as well.

The Newspaper Association of America informs that due to lobbying efforts of the Sunshine in Government Initiative and other open-government advocates, congressional negotiators imposed an unprecedented two-year "sunset" date on the Pentagon's FOIA exemption, ending December 2007.

Source: "Pentagon Seeks Greater Immunity from Freedom of Information," by Michelle Chen. TheNewStandard.com, May 6, 2005.

9. World Bank Funds Israel-Palestine Wall

Despite the 2004 International Court of Justice (ICJ) decision that called for tearing down the Wall and compensating affected communities, construction of the Wall has accelerated. The route of the barrier runs deep into Palestinian territory, aiding the annexation of Israeli settlements and the breaking of Palestinian territorial continuity. The World Bank's vision of "economic development," however, evades any discussion of the Wall's illegality.

55 The World Bank has meanwhile outlined the framework for a Palestinian Middle East Free Trade Area (MEFTA) policy in its most recent report on Palestine published in December 2004: "Stagnation or Revival: Israeli Disengagement and Palestinian Economic Prospects."

Central to World Bank proposals is the construction of massive industrial zones to be financed by the World Bank and other donors and controlled by the Israeli occupation. Built on Palestinian land around the Wall, these industrial zones are envisaged as forming the basis of export-orientated economic development. Palestinians imprisoned by the Wall and dispossessed of land can be put to work for low wages.

The post-Wall MEFTA vision includes complete control over Palestinian movement. The report proposes high-tech military gates and checkpoints along the Wall, through which Palestinians and exports can be conveniently transported and controlled. A supplemental "transfer system" of walled roads and tunnels will allow Palestinian workers to be funneled to their jobs, while being simultaneously denied access to their land. Sweatshops will be one of very few possibilities of earning a living for Palestinians confined to disparate ghettos throughout the West Bank.

In breach of the ICJ ruling, the United States has already contributed $50 million to construct gates along the Wall to "help serve the needs of Palestinians."

Sources: "Cementing Israeli Apartheid: The Role of World Bank," by Jamal Juma. Left Turn, issue No. 18. 'U.S. Free Trade Agreements Split Arab Opinion,' by Linda Heard. Al-Jazeera, March 9, 2005.

10. Expanded Air War in Iraq

There is widespread speculation that President Bush, confronted by diminishing approval ratings and dissent within his own party, as well as within the military itself, will begin pulling American troops out of Iraq this year. A key element of the drawdown plans not mentioned in the president's public statements, or in mainstream media for that matter, is that the departing American troops will be replaced by American air power.

Writing in *The New Yorker* magazine, Seymour Hersh quotes Patrick Clawson, the deputy director of the Washington Institute, whose views often mirror those of Dick Cheney and Donald Rumsfeld, as saying, "We're not planning to diminish the war. We just want to change the mix of the forces doing the fighting—Iraqi infantry with American support and greater use of air power."

While battle fatigue increases among U.S. troops, the prospect of using air power as a substitute for American troops on the ground has caused great unease within the military. Air Force commanders in particular have deep-seated objections to the possibility that Iraqis will eventually be responsible for target selection. Hersh quotes a senior military planner now on assignment in the Pentagon as saying, "Will the Iraqis call in air strikes in order to snuff rivals or other warlords, or to snuff members of their own sect and blame someone else? Will some Iraqis be targeting on behalf of al Qaida or the insurgency or the Iranians?"

Visions of a frightful future in Iraq should not overshadow the devastation already caused by present levels of American air power loosed, in particular, on heavily populated urban areas of that country. The tactic of using massively powerful 500- and 1,000-pound bombs in urban areas to target small pockets of resistance fighters has, in fact, long been employed in Iraq. No intensification of the air war is necessary to make it a commonplace.

Sources: "Up in the Air," by Seymour M. Hersh. The New Yorker, Dec. 5, 2005. 'An Increasingly Aerial Occupation,' by Dahr Jamail. TomDispatch .com, December 2005.

COLLABORATING

Agree on a topic, perhaps one from Part III of this book, and have each group member find a source that in some way connects with the topic. Make sure that each type of source discussed in this section is represented. Separately, each group member should make a list of the facts or perspectives contained in the source (the person doing a book should cover just one chapter). As a group, compare what you found. Is information repeated from one source to another? What stands out as common knowledge? What stands out as not so well known? Prepare a brief statement explaining which source could give you the best insights for constructing a critical analysis.

Evaluating Online Sources

While all sources need to be scrutinized, writing instructors are especially suspicious of information from the Internet. Thus, in writing for an academic assignment, pay extra attention to the information you collect from the Web. Anyone can publish on the Internet. Home pages, websites, blogs, and listservs do not answer to any editor. While people monitor contributions and uphold standards for some online publications, the checking and double-checking of facts that ensues during publication of a print journal or magazine does not occur for most Internet sources.

As mentioned, many print sources are uploaded to the Internet, and the same information you find in a magazine or journal can be found online. These sources of information do not necessarily need to be scrutinized any more than print sources. However, be aware that some publishers try to lure potential subscribers to the online services of print products by putting abridged material on a website. Some tease you with an opening line, an article title, or the first page or two. Others delay online publication so as not to compete with the print product or deny general access to the product to give their online subscribers, who have passwords and have paid money, the advantage in securing information. You will not be getting a complete article if you download or print a teaser, a preview, or an abstract.

To evaluate other online sources, look for the following.

Author   If a website has an anonymous author or the writer uses a pseudonym, the source cannot generally be considered credible. But just because a person takes credit for a website does not instantly grant the site authority. You have to ask who the writer is. If the person claims expertise, you can check that claim in an online search of her or his name.

If the person has credentials—is an MD if the article concerns medicine, for instance—you can assume that the website has credibility up to a point. Sometimes people falsify credentials. You cannot be responsible for tracking down every possible case of fraud, though, so you have to grant credibility in such cases, unless you spot inconsistencies that make you suspicious or if the website fails to meet standards discussed below.

Citation of Sources   When an Internet source presents information, whether a theory supported by evidence or facts about a subject, you can gauge its reliability by seeing whether the author has cited his or her sources. When a site conveys information, in other words, the author will explain how he or she has come to know and believe the facts and perspectives presented.

    The most legitimate websites give enough information for you to find the original source (systems of citation are discussed in the last section of this chapter). The writer uses quotation marks when appropriate, announces clearly when material is paraphrased, and usually confirms the results of studies, statistical analyses, or other research by citing the places he or she found them. If words in a website appear in other places on the Web without attribution, someone has plagiarized. Be suspicious of information on a website if you discover that the writer has plagiarized any material. If no citations are given, question the credibility of the source.

Updates of Sites   Most legitimate Internet sources are consistently updated and post the dates of the most recent updates. If your online source has not been updated for a long time or includes many broken links, you should wonder about the information you collect from it. There's a good chance that the person or organization behind it is not reliable and therefore not credible.

    When my students conducted research on political parties, they had to search for dates to see how committed a group was. Josh discovered a political party that was compatible with his beliefs, but it seemed that the group's commitment did not extend beyond the last election, when it ran a candidate for a seat on a local council. All the information ended at the time of the election. The site did not even announce the results of the election. Thus, Josh had to wonder whether the site was a hoax or was run by people not committed to a party platform as much as they were interested in getting a particular person elected. The information about their beliefs and principles and the facts they presented in support of their platform had to be questioned.

    If a website does not indicate how often it is updated, question how much you can rely on the information. Look for contact information—an email address or phone number. If you cannot find the information or if it is no longer valid, factor this into your evaluation of the source.

Agenda   Is the website trying to sell you something? Has it been created to promote a product? If you answer "yes" to either question, be careful about the information you gather from the site. It is not always true that such websites cannot be trusted, but the agenda behind the persons or organization must be critically analyzed. The people in charge of the site want you to believe certain principles or facts so you will spend money on their product. When a website is blatant and leads you to a catalog and product descriptions, you know the agenda and can take it into consideration. If a site looks to be informational at first but then prompts you to buy a book or purchase a membership, you must question the credibility. The site is being run for profit and is not being upfront about it.

This does not automatically disqualify the site as a legitimate source of information. For instance, people get sports statistics from ESPN's website. The site is not a public service. Advertisers pay to promote their products there, and the site has links to let you purchase merchandise from ESPN. But the statistics can be trusted. It would be foolish to set the information aside in search of a nonprofit site. You do, however, have to be careful about ESPN's self-promotion; don't use ESPN's references to itself as the number-one sports network as evidence in a paper rating cable sports channels.

More subtle agendas also need to be unearthed. In the political websites my students found, the information had to be considered in its context. While the students could confidently state that the Green Party stood for environmental protection and could relate information about its platform without hesitation, they could not use the Green Party web page (or those of its local chapters) to confirm that its candidates did not compromise their principles, backed their words with actions, or had better qualifications than their opponents. The Green Party would have a strong incentive to state those things and would be disinclined to publish information that would undermine its candidates. This agenda would bring the information it publishes into question. This is not to cast aspersions on the Green Party, which is an admirable organization. Rather, it suggests that a smart reader looks for confirmation elsewhere for any information or perspectives gathered from a website that has an agenda. Consistent confirmation of information or perspectives first gathered from a site give the site credibility over time.

GREEN PARTY WEBSITE

2006 Green Party Candidate Spotlight

http://www.gp.org/

This screenshot from the Green Party's home page offers a critique of Howard Berman. Students wanting to use this information would need to confirm the assertions made here, as the Green Party has an agenda to paint Berman in an unfavorable light. Also, notice that the party is soliciting donations. While other links from this page give you more specific information about the election, all the information you could gather would come from a group with an agenda.

Fanatical Approach   Some websites, frankly, are run by kooks. For example, look at the number of websites that discuss alien abductions. While you should never discount something simply because it defies common assumptions, the sheer lack of evidence that any human has encountered an alien should alert you to the possibility that a person claiming to have alien implants or to have been surgically probed on a spaceship suffers from a delusion or trauma.

More worrisome are extremist groups that base beliefs on racism, sexism, and jingoism. If you come across a website that uses charged language repeatedly, makes claims that appeal to prejudices, and misrepresents the ideas of opponents, you should dismiss the facts or perspectives you find there. Such sites take a fact or a legitimate perspective and twist it until it serves their cause. The sources consist of materials written by people who think just like they do.

Conspiracy theorists are another type of fanatical group. While legitimate sites discuss conspiracy theories about the assassinations of John and Robert Kennedy in the 1960s, the Iran-Contra scandal in the 1980s, and the 2000 presidential election, illegitimate conspiracy theorists make numerous claims that cannot be supported. They're missing key pieces of evidence or speculating elaborately based on small pieces of evidence. They make connections that do not add up. Serious investigators of conspiracy can verify what they say. They might offer hypotheses, but they clearly separate conjecture from facts. If you see charged language, allegations of secret societies, or claims of destruction of evidence, be wary of using the information. If information is legitimate, you will be able to confirm it elsewhere.

WRITING

Find a website involving a supernatural occurrence—guardian angels, UFOs, Bigfoot, ghosts, or another such occurrence. Evaluate the site's credibility by checking out the author, the citation of sources, the updates to the site, the agenda, and whether the site takes a fanatical approach. Write a two-page analysis in which you show how your findings either validate the site or limit its credibility. Indicate the extent to which you find the site to be legitimate and whether your beliefs about the subject matter have changed at all due to your checking. Does anything else influence your evaluation of the source?

When Sources Collide

When you separate the legitimate sources of information from the illegitimate, you still will run into conflicting evidence and perspectives. If your topic has depth and intrigue, experts will weigh in with differing positions. The "facts" you hear from one side might contradict the "facts" you hear from another. You probably will wonder why, since facts by their nature are beyond dispute. Facts do not change unless new discoveries upend long-established knowledge.

To determine what sources to use or follow in your analysis, consider how facts are interpreted, how much a writer emphasizes them, and how much facts that do not fit the agenda of the writer have been dismissed. You may find some instances in which facts support two or more different understandings of an issue or event.

Since you want your thesis to be as original as possible, you probably do not want to simply accept reputable sources that favor a majority opinion. In other words, if three sources agree on an interpretation of an event and one source offers an alternative, you should not necessarily believe the three sources at the expense of the one. In challenging the status quo, professional writers often depart from the mainstream. Since the ideas they have formulated do not work to the advantage of powerful forces, those ideas do not get published as often. Lack of publicity or popularity does not make an idea less valid, as discussed regarding the bandwagon fallacy in Chapter 9.

To develop a critical analysis, consider marginalized ideas. Instead of dismissing the minority opinion, look at the other possibilities for resolving the problem when legitimate sources collide.

Which Follows the Pattern?

If a source too easily or obviously supports dominant ideology, consider the opposing alternative. The status quo operates on what looks to be common sense. As discussed about investigating assumptions in Chapter 2, society acknowledges some basic assumptions so readily that discussion rarely ensues about them. Other assumptions are repeatedly discussed.

For example, everyone has heard about the need for more personal responsibility. It appears to be obvious that we should take care of ourselves. Yet, politicians, the media, and corporations constantly repeat the need for citizens to take responsibility for their actions and indicate that people are slacking off or are blaming difficulties on others. When you read about lawsuits against corporations, it often seems like the complainant is trying to take advantage of the system by blaming a wealthy business or individual for something the complainant should have known not to do. The implication is that the complainant is refusing to take personal responsibility. If you use information about someone who sued because a cup of coffee was too hot or because he or she gained weight from eating too much fast food, your critique turns the issue into a matter of personal responsibility and aligns with the status quo.

An alternative look at lawsuits would show you that some corporations have been negligent in their treatment of workers, causing acute as well as chronic difficulties, and have not been willing to make things right unless faced with lawsuits. Your alternative look would show you the many times corporations have taken advantage of vulnerable populations—people who cannot afford lawyers—and have covered up their misdeeds with small hush payments. The majority opinion, then, cannot always be trusted, even though its position is supported by some facts. It might not serve your purposes to always believe the position or evidence you find most represented in sources.

How Do They Deal with the Other Side?

You might not always want to disavow the status quo. A thorough critical analysis might take you back to dominant ideology. One strategy is to see how opposing sources deal with one another's positions. If a source appears fair and rational when discussing tenets of opponents, the source probably has little to conceal and has arrived at its conclusion intelligently. If the source sounds condescending toward the other side or represents opponents as buffoons or villains, it might have something to hide.

This being said, authors who feel slighted by the mainstream or who have suffered injustice might be harsh in writing about the other side. For example, the writings of Leonard Peltier, a member of the American Indian Movement, use charged language and bitter accusations about opposing perspectives.

LEONARD PELTIER

Statement to Judge Paul Benson

Leonard Peltier, a Chippewa, made the FBI's 10 Most Wanted Fugitive List in the mid-1970s following his alleged involvement in a shootout on the Pine Ridge Indian Reservation. Peltier was eventually apprehended in Canada, extradited, and convicted of two murders. He is serving life imprisonment in a U.S. penitentiary but has always maintained his innocence.

There is no doubt in my mind or my peoples' minds you are going to sentence me to two consecutive life terms. You are, and have always been prejudiced against me and any Native Americans who have stood before you. You have openly favored the government all through this trial, and you are happy to do whatever the FBI would want you to do in this case.

I did not always believe this to be so! When I first saw you in the courtroom in Sioux Falls, your dignified appearance misled me into thinking that you were a fair-minded person who knew something of the law and who would act in accordance with the law! Which meant that you would be impartial and not favor one side or the other in this lawsuit. That has not been the case and I now firmly believe that you will impose consecutive life terms solely because that's what you think will avoid the displeasures of the FBI. Neither my people nor myself know why you would be so concerned about an organization that has brought so much shame to the American people. But you are! Your conduct during this trial leaves no doubt that you will do the bidding of the FBI without any hesitation!

You are about to perform an act which will close one more chapter in the history of the failure of the United States courts and the failure of the people of the United States to do justice in the case of a Native American. After centuries of murder of millions of my brothers and sisters by white racist America, could I have been wise in thinking that you would break that tradition and commit an act of justice? Obviously not! Because I should have realized that what I detected was only a very thin layer of dignity and surely not of fine character. If you think my accusations have been harsh and unfounded, I will explain why I have reached these conclusions and why I think my criticism has not been harsh enough:

First, each time my defense team tried to expose FBI misconduct in their investigation of this lawsuit and tried to present evidence of this you claimed it was irrelevant to this trial. But the prosecution was allowed to present their case with evidence that was in no way relevant to this lawsuit—for example, an automobile blowing up on a freeway in Wichita, Kansas; an attempted murder in Milwaukee, Wisconsin, for which I have not been found innocent or guilty; or a van loaded with legally-purchased firearms, and a policeman who claims someone fired at him in Oregon State. The Supreme Court of the United States tried to prevent convictions of this sort by passing into law that only past convictions may be presented as evidence if it is not prejudicial to the lawsuit, and only evidence of said case may be used. This court knows very well I have no prior convictions, nor am I even charged with some of these alleged crimes; therefore, they cannot be used as evidence in order to receive a conviction in this farce called a trial. This is why I strongly believe you will impose two life terms, running consecutively, on me.

Second, you could not make a reasonable decision about my sentence 5 because you suffer from at least one of three defects that prevent a rational conclusion: you plainly demonstrated this in your decision about the Jimmy Eagle and Myrtle Poor Bear aspects of this case. In Jimmy's case, for some unfounded reason that only a judge who consciously and openly ignores the law would call it irrelevant to my trial; in the mental torture of Myrtle Poor Bear you said her testimony would shock the conscience of the American people, if believed! But you decided what was to be believed and what was not to be believed—not the jury! Your conduct shocks the conscience of what the American legal system stands for—the *search for the truth* by a jury of citizens. What was it that made you so afraid to let that testimony in? Your own guilt of being part of a corrupted pre-planned trial to get a conviction no matter how your reputation would be tarnished? For these reasons, I strongly believe you will do the bidding of the FBI and give me two consecutive life terms.

Third, in my opinion, anyone who failed to see the relationship between the undisputed facts of these events surrounding the investigation used by the FBI in their interrogation of the Navajo youths: Wilford Draper, who was tied to a chair for three hours and denied access to his attorney; the outright threats to Norman Brown's life; the bodily harm threatened to Mike Anderson; and finally, the murder of Anna Mae Aquash, must be blind, stupid, or without human feelings so there is no doubt and little chance that you have the ability to avoid doing today what the FBI wants you to do—which is to sentence me to two life terms running consecutively.

Fourth, you do not have the ability to see that the conviction of an AIM activist helps to cover up what the government's own evidence showed: that large numbers of Indian people engaged in that fire fight on June 26, 1976.

You do not have the ability to see that the government must suppress the fact that there is a growing anger amongst Indian people and that Native Americans will resist any further encroachments by the military forces of the capitalistic Americans, which is evidenced by the large number of Pine Ridge residents who took up arms on June 27, 1975, to defend themselves. Therefore, you do not have the ability to carry out your responsibility towards me in an impartial way and will run my two life terms consecutively.

Fifth, I stand before you as a proud man; I feel no guilt! I have done nothing to feel guilty about! I have no regrets of being a Native American activist—thousands of people in the United States, Canada, and around the world have and will continue to support me to expose the injustices which have occurred in this courtroom. I do feel pity for your people that they must live under such an ugly system. Under your system, you are taught greed, racism, and corruption—and most serious of all, the destruction of Mother Earth. Under the Native American system, we are taught all people are brothers and sisters, to share the wealth with the poor and needy. But the most important of all is to respect and preserve the Earth, who we consider to be our Mother. We feed from her breast; our Mother gives us life from birth and when it's time to leave this world, who again takes us back into her womb. But the main thing we are taught is to preserve her for our children and our grandchildren, because they are the next who will live upon her.

10   No, I'm not the guilty one here; I'm not the one who should be called a criminal—white racist America is the criminal for the destruction of our lands and my people; to hide your guilt from the decent human beings in America and around the world, you will sentence me to two consecutive life terms without any hesitation.

Sixth, there are less than 400 federal judges for a population of over 200 million Americans. Therefore, you have a very powerful and important responsibility which should be carried out impartially. But you have never been impartial where I was concerned. You have the responsibility of protecting the constitutional rights and laws, but where I was concerned, you neglected to even consider mine, or Native Americans', constitutional rights. But, the most important of all—you neglected our human rights.

If you were impartial, you would have had an open mind on all the factual disputes in this case. But, you were unwilling to allow even the slightest possibility that a law enforcement officer would lie on the stand. Then, how could you possibly be impartial enough to let my lawyers prove how important it is to the FBI to convict a Native American activist in this case? You do not have the ability to see that such a conviction is an important part of the efforts to discredit those who are trying to alert their brothers and sisters to the new threat from the white man, and the attempt to destroy what little Indian land remains in the process of extracting our uranium, oil, and other minerals. Again, to cover up your part in this, you will call me a heartless, cold-blooded murderer who deserves two life sentences consecutively.

Seventh, I cannot expect a judge who has openly tolerated the conditions I have been jailed under to make an impartial decision on whether I should be sentenced to concurrent or consecutive life terms. You have been made aware of the following conditions which I had to endure at the Grand Forks County Jail, since the time of the verdict:

(1) I was denied access to a phone to call my attorneys concerning my appeal;

15   (2) I was locked in solitary confinement without shower facilities, soap, towels, sheets or pillow;

(3) the food was inedible, what little there was of it;

(4) my family—brothers, sisters, mother and father—who travelled long distances from the reservation, were denied visitation.

No human being should be subjected to such treatment; and while you parade around pretending to be decent, impartial, and law-abiding, you knowingly allowed your fascist chief deputy marshal to play stormtrooper. Again, the only conclusion that comes to mind is that you know and always knew that you would sentence me to two consecutive life terms.

Finally, I honestly believe that you made up your mind long ago that I was guilty and that you were going to sentence me to the maximum sentence permitted under the law. But this does not surprise me, because you are a high-ranking member of the white racist American establishment which has consistently said, "In God We Trust," while they went about the business of murdering my people and attempting to destroy our culture.

Should Peltier's ideas be dismissed because of his clear disregard for Judge Benson and the justice system? Hardly. Peltier believed his activism was the catalyst for prosecution, and the investigative process and trial did appear to be tainted by racism, obstruction of justice, and induced perjury. He is on Amnesty International's list of political prisoners. Another person admitted on 60 Minutes that he, not Peltier, committed the murders. Yet, Peltier still remains in prison. It should surprise no one, then, that Peltier comes off as a bit testy when trying to defend himself.

A side that supports the status quo has fewer legitimate reasons for reactive rhetoric than do oppressed proponents of an opposing position. The perspective supporting the status quo prospers because of it. Thus, if you see name-calling, dismissive attitudes, or misrepresentations from a source aligned with the status quo, you should wonder about the perspective, even if the source has solid evidence to back the claims. While supporters of the status quo might feel threatened by alternative perspectives, they should be able to show why an opposing idea has less merit than their own, and they should deal with the other side fairly.

Account for All Evidence   In understanding that sources should deal fairly with the other side, you should also see the necessity for a source to account for all evidence. A source that ignores pertinent evidence that you find in another source must be questioned.

A source that has nothing to hide will wrangle with counterevidence by refuting it, explaining how it might fit into a different interpretation, or acknowledging its validity while still maintaining that its side is correct. The evidence will not be misrepresented or dismissed. In shorter op-ed pieces where space is at a premium, writers might not discuss counter-information thoroughly, so they might generalize about opposing evidence instead of analyzing it. In such cases, use another source that does account for counterevidence to confirm the perspective. If all the sources you consult avoid serious discussion of opponents' evidence, you should probably ask why. The source that can best explore opposing perspectives often winds up being the best source.

WRITING

For your current research project, find two articles from legitimate sources that present opposing positions. Putting aside for the moment what you personally believe, analyze the two articles in the three ways listed above. Write one or two paragraphs about each article, making sure to cover their relationship to dominant patterns, their treatment of opposing positions, and their accounting for all evidence. Which source is most valid? Why?

Giving Credit Where It Is Due

A writer must indicate how and where sources were used in an essay or report. A responsible writer has to distinguish among quotations, paraphrases, references to statistics, facts not commonly known, and theories or ideas that she or he gained from research. All must be documented with enough information to make it possible for a reader to find the sources and locate the information.

Documentation systems have been designed to give academic writers—not just students—a common structure to use in citing sources. Unfortunately, this commonality has been complicated by the use of many different systems of documentation. At some time during your academic career, you will see or use such systems as MLA (Modern Language Association) style, APA (American Psychological Association) style, and one of the documentation styles from the *Chicago Manual of Style*. All are valid.

When writing with research, ask your instructor which system she or he prefers. In this section, you will not follow any particular system but instead learn about the basic information you need for any of these systems.

Some students complain about having to cite sources. They point out that newspapers and magazines do not have bibliographies or internal citation systems such as footnotes or parenthetical documentation. The difference is that professional publications have editors and fact-checkers who research and confirm facts. If reporters or publications falsify information, use sources inaccurately, or do not give credit for words or ideas garnered from others, they are subject to lawsuits and other sanctions. Consequences for these kinds of unethical behavior are severe as well as embarrassing.

Reporters often work with primary sources, so quotations come directly from people who are interviewed. When they work with facts and evidence, they refer to archival information, which has been researched and confirmed by others, or they explain who or where the information came from. Students, as well as researchers publishing in discipline-specific journals or books, use documentation systems to verify that their information is accurate, to place it in a context, to give credit to original sources, and to avoid accusations of plagiarism.

In the workplace, plagiarism or dishonest use of information can get a writer fired and an organization sued. Universities do not take issues of academic dishonesty lightly either. Every instructor hates to give a student an F on a paper or for an entire course because the student copied from sources without crediting the original author. A student who downloads a paper from an Internet source or cuts and pastes sections from several such papers intends to deceive and deserves punishment. What is unfortunate is when a student makes mistakes that can be misinterpreted as an attempt to cheat.

Your handbook or research guide has detailed information on citation styles. Here, based on my own students' concerns, are some additional strategies.

Include an Acknowledgement Page   In my courses I ask students to submit an acknowledgement page at the ends of their papers. In books and discipline-specific journals, authors give credit to all the people who helped them put together their work—from research assistants to peer reviewers to typists to babysitters. Everyone who deserves credit receives it.

For the acknowledgement pages in my class, students list the members of their peer groups, roommates who helped them proofread, friends who found websites for them, and television shows that gave them ideas for topics, anal-yses, or theses. They also list the books, websites, journals, and magazines they consulted to get information. I ask them to be specific about what they found, where they found it, and where in their papers they used it. So if one book gave a student all the facts needed for the paper, the student mentions the book, the library where it was found, and the section in the paper where its information appears. The student may also name the research librarian who helped her find the book. Perhaps an article gave a very specific example that another student used, so he tells me the article's name, where he found the journal or magazine, and the point in the paper he used the example. Maybe a website provided a summary of an event that proved helpful, so another student explains that her friend surfed the Internet one night and located the site, tells about the location, and shows where she used the information. Before you turn in a paper, construct an acknowledgement page of your own, whether or not your instructor asks you to include one.

The acknowledgement page does not take the place of a formal Works Cited (MLA) or References (APA) list, but it alerts you to problems in your documentation. You might realize, for example, that you would have had no way of knowing about a case study you used unless you had read it in a book that was neither listed in your bibliography nor referred to in your paper. You understand that you cannot borrow the case study without acknowledging its source. You might discover that you cited only one of two sources concerning an opposing position.

It also feels good to give credit to a parent or a significant other who helped you reword a few sentences or figure out an organizational strategy. On top of that, you can look back at how much work you did and be proud. Much like a journal entry, an acknowledgement page can be cathartic.

Author, Title, and Publication Information

For every college assignment that requires research, no matter what documentation system the instructor follows, you need the same information from your sources. You should note the name of the author, the title of the book or article, and the date of publication. With books, you also need to find the city of publication and the publisher's name. For journals, the city and publisher are not necessary, but you should include the name of the journal, the volume and issue numbers, and the page numbers on which the article appeared. Magazines are similar to journals in that you need to name the magazine title and note the page numbers, but you do not need the volume and issues numbers. For websites, locate the address, the title of the web page (if different from the article name), the date of publication, and the date you found the information. When you have this information, you will be able to construct a Works Cited or References page at the end of your essay and insert all necessary information in accordance with the documentation system you use.

In-Text Citations

All documentation systems require in-text citations to go with the Works Cited or References page. In-text citations are used in conjunction with the bibliographical information. You need to note the exact pages on which you found information you are quoting, paraphrasing, or otherwise using.

Note that you must use in-text citations for more than just quotations. You must give an in-text citation everyplace you relied on a source for information, even if you completely reworded the exact phrases. Some documentation systems require footnotes that include the author's last name, the title, and the page number.

Most in-text citations use a type of parenthetical reference. After a quotation, paraphrase, set of statistics, facts not commonly known, or ideas, you put a parenthesis, write the last name of the author, write the page number on which the information can be found, close the parenthesis, and add the end punctuation, usually a period. Some systems suggest putting in the year of publication. If you used two articles or books by the same author, you need to distinguish between them by including the year of publication or an abbreviated title. Check the rules of the documentation system you are using to make sure.

Distinctions Between Cited Materials   When using an exact quotation, put quotation marks around the entire quotation. As discussed in Chapter 9, quotations should be used sparingly. It is best to paraphrase or to weave facts into your sentences. Paraphrases sometimes rely on the use of a key word or two. You can put these in quotation marks, but place the parenthetical reference at the end of the sentence. Make sure you introduce the paraphrase with a tag phrase so that your instructor knows that you are giving credit to the source. For summaries that do not contain key words, you can put your parenthetical reference at the end of the paragraph.

Facts not commonly known and statistics indicate by their very nature that they were found through research. In other words, readers automatically know this type of information has come from a source. As long as you have not copied sentences or phrases exactly, you do not need quotation marks or tag phrases. Just make sure to put a parenthetical reference immediately after the information. It is often difficult to know when a fact constitutes common knowledge that does not need to be documented. A guideline to keep in mind is that if you learned the fact through your research, document it. You might find out later that the fact is a common one, but it is best to err on the side of caution when making these determinations.

COLLABORATING

As you move from class to class, you will be asked to use different documentation systems. To familiarize yourselves with the differences, take the one you are using for this class and one other that your teacher assigns to your group. The rules for using these systems can be found in your handbook or the documentation system's web pages. Your instructor might provide handouts. Using one group member as a secretary, record all the differences you find between the two systems. In what ways does the bibliography differ? What about the in-text citations? Discuss your findings with the class as a whole, and decide which system you like best and why.

Summary

Much library research is now done in front of a computer screen. With the increased ease of locating sources, however, it is more important than ever to learn how to critically evaluate potential sources. Many search indexes refer writers to research sources, such as discipline-specific journals, mainstream magazines, books, and alternative magazines. These sources can provide critical knowledge and usually do not have to be closely scrutinized to determine legitimacy.

Online sources can be just as valuable, but writers need to evaluate the credibility of the information, since websites and other online sources often do not benefit from checking and cross-checking of facts. Even when sources have been determined to be credible, they may contradict one another. You need to decide what perspectives to believe, keeping in mind that the most familiar or comfortable is not always the best when critically analyzing a subject.

Once you have determined which sources to use and how to work them into your paper, you must abide by the requirements of a documentation system for a bibliography and in-text citations. You must account for the places where quotes, paraphrases, statistics, facts not commonly known, and ideas have been used.

· PART III ·

TOPICS FOR WRITING

The following chapters will introduce you to a variety of topics that may be used for writing assignments. The topics spring from aspects of our culture, common emotions, and ideas and ideals often thought to be in conflict with one another. Each chapter pushes for understandings that critically analyze the familiar. In other words, the chapters encourage your pursuit of the type of critical analysis discussed in Chapter 2 by questioning societal assumptions, looking beyond obvious conclusions and interpretations, and perhaps making familiar topics a bit strange or unfamiliar.

Each chapter begins with an overview of the topic. The overviews discuss common beliefs and begin the process of critical analysis by raising questions about the topic. They give a perspective from which you, the writer, can start your analysis.

The overviews lead into sections called "Openings for Writers." They contain brainstorming and freewriting activities that will help you work through any writing blocks that might have developed. While your instructor—or perhaps your instructor and the class in tandem—may choose ideas from the overview or may construct writing assignments based on beliefs about holidays, honesty, animals, or the other topics, the "Openings for Writers" sections will point you to other possibilities.

The sections on language pick up on the issues discussed in Chapter 5. Instead of providing vocabulary quizzes or definitions, these sections ask you to scrutinize your understanding of keywords used in the overviews and to see how your examination extends or limits the ideas in the overview. This scrutiny can help you analyze the perspective offered in the overviews, extend into your understanding of the readings in each chapter, and give you practice in paying close attention to your own use of words.

The next part of each chapter consists of selected readings on the topic. Some of these readings present information that you can extract and use in your writing. Other times, they add to the process of critical analysis by pursuing issues brought up in the overviews or by offering a differing perspective. The readings are intended to make you pause and consider a particular angle on a subject, and they serve as the focus of some of the assignment options.

The "Assignment Ideas" that follow this first cluster of readings are not meant to limit your choices but rather to focus you on possibilities. The prompts remind you of the importance of audience considerations from Chapter 3 and ask you to utilize ideas you generated in your brainstorming or freewriting. The options consist of questions based on the readings, extensions of the overview, or ideas that spring from or draw parallels to key issues surrounding the topic.

"Group Work" ideas give your class the option to pursue a collaborative research project. The questions break down a pertinent issue drawn from the chapter and start the process of assigning tasks, as discussed in Chapter 7. The questions are not more complex than those under "Assignment Ideas," but they have been designed to be most easily completed in a group situation.

The final sections consist of additional readings that provide supplementary information and perspective on the topics. Some are personal experiences, while others offer facts to consider. They often narrow the broad topic heading, going from a general topic like the supernatural in Chapter 13 to specific looks at Bigfoot researchers and at psychic John Edward. All ground the issues presented in the overview and the first set of readings and give extra perspectives to ponder.

Do not be afraid to veer away from the perspectives offered in the overviews and readings. Critical analysis must come from you. It does not involve nodding your head in agreement with a perspective that seems to be challenging the status quo. These chapters are designed to help you reexperience the ordinary. In your writing, you can extend the ideas more or draw back to a place you find more reasonable. The point is to go through the process of critical analysis to develop your critical faculties.

Part III lets you implement the important concepts introduced in Part I while allowing you to experiment with your writing and reading processes, use of evidence and research, and collaboration as discussed in Part II. You will become a stronger writer and reader by thinking through your ideas in relation to the perspectives in the following chapters and by analyzing them to reach a thesis interesting to you and your audience.

CHAPTER 11

BEGINNINGS AND ENDINGS

Overview

Every composition teacher is familiar with what is known as the "Dead Grandmother" essay. It goes something like this. The student starts with an experience or series of experiences that demonstrate what a wonderful person his or her grandmother, grandfather, aunt, uncle, cousin, sibling, or other relative is. An experienced writing instructor knows right away that the poor person is doomed in the course of two to three pages. And, indeed, the essay will take a turn away from the good times and discuss an illness or an accident or just plain old age that has affected the student's beloved relative. And, unfortunately, the person dies. Students might talk about the funeral, but in general, they will conclude by saying how much the relative meant to them. These essays, sadly, tend to bother English instructors, as there is no way to grade them. It would be a heartless instructor who would allow her students to pour their feelings onto the page, only to reward the student with a "C." Yet, the essays seem so similar to English instructors, as there is not much for students to say about death that hasn't been said many times before. Even the strongest of prose cannot rescue an essay that resorts to the clichés about mourning and loss. Few students are able or eager to twist the cliché of this genre (see Chapter 2).

The same can be said of essays that talk about birth. Students often write about what a miracle it is, even though birth is extremely common. Even experienced writers have difficulty conveying much that has not already

Online Study Center

This icon will direct you to web links and additional resources on the website http://college.cengage.com/english/thelin/ writing_without_formulas/1e/student_home.html

been said over and over. And perhaps sometimes, such celebrations of birth or other matters are highly appropriate, as the repeated phrases and themes strike the right chord with the intended audience. But when writing, whether in response to a course assignment or in a personal way to gain perspective on what we are feeling, we have to interrogate the obvious themes and tease out meanings not at first apparent. It might be best, then, to put both birth and death into a larger context of beginnings and endings. In doing so, I want to argue here that the concepts of beginnings and endings are actually social constructs more than they are hard and set reality and that we lack the perspective to even classify them as such.

Beginnings and endings tend to be construed as momentous events in our lives. This explains why when instructors assign an essay that includes a personal experience component, students think of the death of a loved one or the birth of a niece or nephew—or maybe of their own children. The importance of these types of events seems self-evident and is supported by the attention our culture gives them. But, really, we have been conditioned to understand many other of our experiences as either starting points or ending points, too, some even as individual triumphs. If you look closely, our culture marks these occasions through celebrations, the law, and rituals, sometimes to the point of artificiality. This attention prevents us from seeing the cyclical nature of life, giving perhaps undo importance to common experiences and blinding us to the many conflicts and contradictions brimming below the surface of these occasions or the less remarkable but potentially more meaningful moments that occur between them.

Celebrations of these occasions appear everywhere in our culture, especially to mark beginnings. Most people celebrate birthdays, for example, to commemorate the day they were born. Some special birthdays are interpreted as a rite of passage. For older writers, this might be their 40th or 50th birthday, as these are seen as landmarks into middle age. For younger writers, the age 21 functions similarly because it signifies the legal right to drink alcohol. Earlier, the age of 16 was similarly epic because the law allows teenagers to apply for a driver's license then. Some ethnic cultures see this age as the debut of a child into the world of adulthood. The age of 18 is peculiar, as legally, minors become adults and are granted responsibilities and privileges, such as the right to vote. It misaligns, though, with the concept of being a teen, as until the age of 20, adults are still teenagers, and the term "teenager" connotes a transitory period between childhood and adulthood. Further, science now tells us that the brain does not fully form into maturity until much later, perhaps around 26 or 27, depending on the individual, so cognitively—and in many cases physiologically—18 year-olds are not yet adults. But whether natural or otherwise, all these birthdays tend to carry significance as points, sometimes as both a starting and an ending. When we turn 18, opportunities present themselves to us as adults that just the day before were unavailable. And we are also no longer children, so we bid goodbye to that chapter in our life.

While birthdays have a biological component that has relevance to our development, other celebrations of beginnings border on the ludicrous. With the American divorce rate still around 50% for first-time marriages and even higher for second or third marriages, we might better approach a wedding with some degree of caution and financial restraint. Yet, we still abide by many wedding customs that signify, as the old saying goes, "til death do us part," and ostentatious displays of wealth, especially on the part of celebrities, accompany many weddings. The purpose is to recognize the beginning of a life together, but outside of those couples in arranged marriages, the real beginning happened during courtship. The event of the wedding, then, is artificial.

How interesting it would be to look at the wedding as an ending instead! Both the bride and the groom leave behind the freedom of the single life, after all. The marriage symbolizes in much the same way as birthdays supposedly do the maturation of the individuals, so there is a loss of childhood, too. Responsibilities mount when married, particularly when children are involved, so the wedding heralds the end of independence and a carefree attitude, as well.

What would this do to our perception of divorce, then? The process of separating from a spouse, culminating in a legally-decreed divorce, involves much pain, as it symbolizes the end of a union. Yet, at least one person in the divorce wanted that ending—or perhaps, the chance at a new beginning. Reflective individuals can look at the mistakes they made in the relationship and learn from them when they attempt to enter into another. Some might realize that being married simply isn't for them at this juncture in their life. Whatever the reasons, life changes and people start over. Seeing divorce as an ending of a relationship, then, can be quite inaccurate. Many divorced couples still interact, especially when their union involved children, and some forge new relationships. Divorce is not merely an ending, therefore, except that our culture attaches notions of failure to it.

To a lesser extent, those in relationships experience the same perceptions. Nothing quite simulates the euphoria when we meet someone special initially. We think of her or him constantly. We rarely see flaws. But what is strange is that the strength of the relationship is often judged by its culmination into marriage. A culmination can be thought of as the climax signaling the end. So what, then, ends when marriage seemingly begins? And, of course, when two people break up, the relationship is at an end— though some endings take longer than others—and the relationship is thought of often enough as a failure. People give reasons as to what went "wrong." Sometimes, one or both partners tell mutual acquaintances what happened and what the other partner did, often exaggerated and sometimes fabricated. Some social circles become divided over the breakup, siding with one person or another. But what really ended? A formal commitment had not been made, unless the couple was engaged. Each person will now be spending his or her time alone or with others, perhaps, and we cannot deny the heartache that occurs when someone in our lives departs from it or takes a different role in it, but is this an ending? Or could it be a beginning?

This confusion about what really constitutes an ending is made manifest in our conception of graduation. Graduation marks the completion of a degree or a certificate. Many of you reading this book will recently have finished high school, so you have direct experience with graduation. It is the end of forced schooling. But another term for graduation is "commencement." Students generally go through "commencement exercises" when they graduate.

Ah

But "to commence" something is to start it. So in the very language of an ending, we find a beginning. Many famous graduation addresses have discussed the end of high school or college as a beginning. The emotions that go with it, not too surprisingly, are mixed. Students love the sense of accomplishment. Some are glad to have made it through and never want to attend another school again, ever. Others focus on how the degree is allowing them to attend college and start another period of their lives. Still others mourn the loss of the familiar surroundings of high school. They know that an ending has occurred to not only the routines of taking classes, but of the many friendships, rivalries, gossip, and antics that took place. These students feel sentimental about it. Some will always look back at high school—or maybe college in the sororities or fraternities—as the good ol' days. The reunions that occur every five or ten years after high school and college tell us that at some level, many others long for those good ol' days, too.

Is it possible that some of the heartache of endings—and the joy of beginnings—are related to expectations that directly connect to our constructed concept of those very beginnings and endings? To return to our original discussion of the passing of a relative, in some Wiccan traditions, death is seen like the melting of a snowflake. The departed have changed form and have been incorporated into other parts of the world, just like a snowflake becomes water in some other form. More snowflakes will fall, maybe not identical to the one that has melted, but fall nonetheless, perhaps with particles of that former snowflake in it. By the same token, people will continue to exist, perhaps influenced or nourished by the one who has passed. Death does not exist. The living just change forms.

Of course, many people from different religions have difficulty with this concept, as it is cyclical and denies a pristine form of individuality. Yet, even most Christian conceptions of death contain the notion of an afterlife where a person's soul lives on for eternity. So if not cyclical, certainly a continuum of sorts exists in this belief system that is infinite. If the continuum can extend out to infinity after death, surely we can question whether it actually starts at birth. We can also question the linearity of time, as many scientists currently do. This understanding might give us a perspective on births and deaths that could take some of the impact out of them and perhaps from other beginnings and endings, as well. They could become for us small parts of existence rather than momentous points in life. But how desirable would this be?

In our everyday life, we might not want to remove the highs and lows of emotions; it could weaken our humanity and our empathy for others. Whatever place beginnings and endings might have in creating, affirming, or exacerbating emotion, our conception of beginnings and endings will probably remain etched in our society. But asking these questions allows for the type of reflection that a writer needs when tackling such subjects. If he or she can take a step away from a beginning or an ending, our immediate reactions to such events might seem a bit strange. For example, the student writer Aaron DeBee in "No Dominion" (page 286) discusses how our burial rituals deny the reality of death. Using personal experiences, Joel Stein (page 290) finds humor in a ritual his wife wants to enact concerning the birth of their son.

They are not unemotional. Rather, they avoid clichéd uses of sentimental-ity and broaden the audience's understanding of their emotions. Other begin-nings and endings can be reimagined, too. Writing does not simply reflect back an event as we perceived it. Rather, writers probe such events, lingering on some aspects, trying to find answers, and ultimately seeing the situation in a larger context. The "Dead Grandmother" essay needs to be laid to rest. Complicating our understanding of endings—as well as beginnings—is, well, a starting point.

Openings for Writers

1. Endings and beginnings—Consider an event in your life that you've always clearly perceived as an ending. Now ask yourself in what ways was it also a beginning? Turn it around and try it the other way: How was a beginning also an ending?
2. Good and bad endings—What is the difference between a "good ending" and a "bad ending"? Is the deciding factor whether or not it was our choice? Do we sometimes resent an ending imposed by someone else even when we sort of agree it's for the best?
3. Fear of failure—Have you ever not begun something because you were afraid of how it might end? Can we avoid this type of thinking? Is it possi-ble to mentally allow notions of beginning and ending to fall away so that we can focus on what's "in the middle"? How might this sort of orientation improve/compromise/complicate our life experiences?
4. Cycle or continuum—Where do you weigh in concerning beginnings and endings? Is life more of a cyclical process or are we on a continuum with a starting and ending point? Think of the ways that nature indicates a cycle and discuss why a continuum might be more or less valid of a concept. What motivates us to believe in continuums?

Language

1. **Social construct** What does this term mean to you? Often, we are told that things are either natural or (hu)man-made. Does the term "social construct" connote artificiality? Can we view it as natural? See if you can come up with synonyms for this term.
2. **Cliches about mourning and loss** Make a list of clichés we use to describe beginnings and endings. For example, we say things like "All's well that ends well," or "Every day is a new beginning." But what do these sayings re-ally mean? Do they mean anything at all? Are they valid? Try re-writing them in ways that are more specific or nuanced.
3. **Commencement** Thinking about your own graduation—whether it's in the past or soon to occur—what does the word "commence" mean to you? Sometimes we give this word a specific object: we say we shall commence *with* a specific action or task. Other times we use it more abstractly, as in the notion of "commencing" from one phase of life to another. How are these two usages different, and what sort of implications does each have upon meaning?

Readings

This essay by Jennifer Glaser comes from the collection *20 Something Essays by 20 Something Writers*. Glaser discusses the loss of her lover, Neil, from leukemia. While she conveys her grief throughout the essay, she also celebrates life, especially her sexual relationship with Neil. She concludes that Neil's death was a "strange gift" in the world of "twentysomething dating."

JENNIFER GLASER

"Sex and the Sickbed"

In sex ed, they tell you all about normal sexual development. The trajectory of your sex life is supposed to be narrow and straight, passing through preordained landmarks – the prepuberty hormone spike that makes you rub eensy-weensy genitalia against bicycle banana seats, the first-time hand-on-thigh fumblings of teenagerdom, the early-adulthood serious relationship that careens from experimentation into mom-and-pop warmth and the necessary question of "Is this what my parents' sex life was like when they first met?" What they don't tell you about are the detours. Your lover might die. You might wake up to find him dead. Gone. And then there is just you and your libido and the question of what sex in the new world will look like.

Neil was twenty-seven and I was twenty-four when he was diagnosed with leukemia. As for most twentysomethings, mortality was a subject eternally deferred for us. But the weekend after the doctor put his hand on Neil's shoulder and bleated out his diagnosis, I met my boyfriend at a motel in his hometown on Long Island to exchange words only whispered at the Jewish family functions we regularly attended: [*pursed mouth*] "cancer," [*moue of distaste*] "chemo," and [*shhsh-ing finger to lips*] "treatment." It was not the first time we'd met at this anonymous motel near the Long Island Rail Road Station. We had been convening in a dun-colored room on the third floor every weekend since the doctors began to suggest that the swollen lymph nodes on Neil's neck and shoulders were not the sign of a local infection but of something far more, um, global, something insidious, circulating, buzzing. Neil had returned to his parents' nest to deal with the bad news, and every weekend I would visit him, the chug-chug of the train carrying me from the city into a territory of anxious conversation and too-tight hugs.

Often, he would get to the hotel before me and sit in an armchair by the window to wait for my arrival. When I entered the room, he would hold me at a distance and look at me for a moment before reaching out to take my hand and place it on his erection-distended zipper. "I am so glad you are here." He would squint through his glasses and touch my hand. "Look at what you do to me. It's been a long time since I've had one of these." I would fondle his pants and wonder why moments of randiness and vulgarity were so beautiful during this time of crisis. Having Neil's denim-cloaked erection in my hand felt like the opposite of the uncertainty of his disease, I guess. For the most part, erections are a sure thing – a gun introduced in the first act that's sure to go off in the third if you handle it right. It is shocking, I know, to speak of ejections and sexual interludes while death is looming. Cancer works very hard to make life unsexy. Freud was right. The only thing that can beat the sex drive is the specter of death. Every kiss or touch is undermined by the images a potentially terminal disease tattoos onto the surface of your mind. White blood cells strangulating your loved one. Cathodes distending his neck and chest like a modern-day Frankenstein. Hair loss. Emaciation. It is coming. And, well, for the time being, at least, you are not.

Leukemia carries with it particular visions of disaster. It was hard not to allow my imagination to take elephantine footsteps ahead of the situation when Neil took me into his arms. I would think about how leukemia makes your body produce blanks. White blood cells without the capacity to do what white blood cells do best. Red blood cells like mules, dead-end hybrids, unable to function. Wastes of space, they crowded out all green terrain in Neil's body. They siphoned off his strength and left vast lunar landscapes behind them. Sometimes I touched Neil and his skin felt cold and I imagined the Pluto that was his innards, the world inside his body that was orbiting so far from the sun.

The dehumanizing aspects of the treatment were even worse than the images that plagued me when I pictured what the future might bring. The first thing the doctor mentioned after handing out Neil's diagnosis was sperm. More precisely, she said that Neil might want to leave some sperm samples at a bank called Cryotex Labs as soon as possible, like this minute, like now. "Well, she said, "what we're about to blast you with kills a lot of things inside of your body, your reproductive capacity being one of the first entities to meet its demise." "La-Z-Boy comfort awaits the patrons of Cryotex Labs." That's what the brochure in the waiting area said, at least. The pamphlet also featured a small insert about the laboratory's prominence among professional athletes. "Groin injuries are part of the game for baseball players. They play it safe by leaving something behind at Cryotex Labs. Cryotex Labs, the first in safety." But, we didn't feel safe.

Neil told me that when he was led into one of the hidden masturbation rooms at Cryotex Labs' sperm bank, he felt like he was entering a bat cave. There were rooms it recalled: the secret room under the stairs where your two-headed brother would be kept; the S and M dungeon that a suburban couple maintains behind their fluorescent-lit den. The juxtaposition between the public and private spaces was perverse. The sperm bank's reception room, reeking of antiseptic and nervous men trying to mask what they were waiting to do in a cup backstage, versus the private depositories located off long hallways, the creepy closeness of those rooms where you do your business, seal the deal, wank – whatever you want to call the sperm-depositing process.

Antiques copies of *Hustler, Juggs,* and *Swank* littered the cupboards. The walls were tacked with pinups, spanning decades of titillation from subtle Betty Grable-esque poses to seventies cheesecake pix. Sexy photos so densely papered the place that they formed a kind of space-age wallpaper. Some of the posters were dog-eared and a bit stained, and Neil couldn't help but wonder if his battered immune system might be leaving him open to contracting whatever weird germs the weird men who had inhabited this room had left behind them. It was like the room of an adolescent boy who sleeps under photos of naked women as some kind of fort or bulwark against pimply loneliness. It was like the room of an adolescent boy who tried to touch at intimacy by rubbing his face against the pinups of nudie magazines until they begin to sweat and run with moisture. It was a sad-ugly room. → *disturbing*

It was a sad-ugly disease, depleted of glamour, whatever its well-meaning and beribboned denizens might suggest. When I visited Neil in the hospital after his chemotherapy had started, he scuffed his white-socked feet along the floor, searching blindly for his slippers. I pushed my feet under his hospital bed and kicked the slippers his way. I tried to be unobtrusive about getting the shoes, like I would be about letting an eight-year old kid win at checkers. Neil slid his feet into the slippers and then sat on the side of the bed looking at me. It was the first time our faces had been so close since his admission to the hospital. I looked at him. "Don't look at me like that. I want to kiss you when you look like that," he said as he turned his face away.

We couldn't kiss. We couldn't kiss because mouths are full of billions of microbes and critters and tiny breaks in gum lining. My mouth was no exception, and a kiss from me could communicate something far more than love and warmth to Neil. It could communicate something that would have left him hobbled and legs waving in bed, Kafka's Samsa-bug come to life.

Months later, though, after multiple chemos and a failed bone marrow transplant and family drama and Neil's death, it wasn't these dystopian postcards from the sickbed that I remembered most. It was the fact that during Neil's lengthy and wholly unsexy illness, he had never ceased to be sexy to me. We flirted, we canoodled, we talked about sex, and we had sex when Neil was sick because, well, sex wasn't death. It was the antithesis of death, and damn if it didn't feel good to forget for a while that nothing we could dream up could act as an effective talisman against the iceberg floating along the horizon into our sights. After Neil's diagnosis, we led an airless life filled with take-out Chinese food and a bed that dwarfed our shared existence, Alice-in-Wonderland style, growing and filling minds that should have been taken up with twentysomething concerns. Instead of thinking about Neil's illness, though, we thought about how not to leave the bed: how we could spend twelve hours touching and laughing and weeping and singing in a bed like a boat. A bed like a boat that was sinking.

We imagined mocking Neil's illness and its emasculating powers by making a jokey promotional video for Ara-C, the chemo compound Neil received daily during his inpatient treatments. Neil wrote the script.

[A closely shorn] Neil: Everybody tells you about the downside of being diagnosed with cancer.

[Camera pans back to show wide-angle shot of the hospital room with me sitting on the edge of Neil's bed]

[A *sotto voce*] Me: But, we'd like to tell you about some of the, ahem, benefits. Let us show you what chemo can do for your libido.

They were distancing mechanisms, now that I think of it, the playful commercials and the bed-soaked existence. Furtive embraces and black-humored jabs at Neil's illness and treatment were welcome existential breathers from thinking about death. For me, they had an added benefit. They allowed me the illusion that I would always be approaching Neil's prognosis as part of a dynamic duo, a twosome who could feint and jab together at this overwhelming new opponent, cancer. *Shift from this joking around to this!*

But then, Neil died. My friends treated me with the type of reverence usually reserved for South American shamans. "You have sipped from the River Styx and lived to tell about it." They were comfortable with the occasional teary jag or sentimental reminiscence about Neil's all-around loveliness, but nobody wanted to hear the truth: Neil was great in bed. When your lover dies, it is the body as much as those intangible qualities of the personality that you miss. I wanted to tell them and everyone that what I missed was sex with Neil, taking naughty baths and using fingers and tongues and toes to explore whatever pockets of the other we could reach. Eulogies praised Neil's imagination, his writing prowess, his generosity and warmth. I praised these qualities, too. But praise be the body, I told them. It is only in such praise that I could give Neil back what leukemia ended up taking from him, trace the contours of what he lost: his material form, with its capacity for messy emissions and spontaneous boners, parted lips, enveloping bear hugs and leg cramps, beautiful all.

I wanted to explain to my friends and family that it was only by praising Neil's body, his prowess as a lover, his unique hands and eyes and chest that I could hope to restore his particularity. Neil was a material boy. A boho Jewish gal's dreamboat, he was a man equally comfortable having sex all day and doling out stories and whitefish around my grandmother's kitchen table. He was of that elusive species hunted by urban ladies of a certain age, the aw-shucks writer boy who turned me on with his horizonless imagination, as much as with his self lacerating with and gorgeous prose. I used to call him my Proust, still churning out stories from his sickbed. That was part of it, too. Insisting upon Neil as embodied was an insistence on the realness of the sickbed, on the realness of his illness, the material reality of night shakes and nausea and pain that accompanied his many months of illness and treatment. Illness is supposed to be romantic and meaningful, right? That's what art tells us. The consumptive cousin making eyes at Isabel Archer in Henry James' *The Portrait of a Lady*. Or think of the opera. The divas are little more than a series of sexy terminal cases, women slo-mo-swooning to the ground in the last act like interlocked paper dolls. Talking about the body, the details of what happens to the human body during illness, is the quickest way to defetishize illness and its effects.

Of course, it's not entirely altruistic, my refusal to reduce Neil to the ether, my desire to resurrect him as an entity both embodied and real. After Neil's death, I experienced an extreme form of what long-distance lovers feel, the sense that they want to lick the phone, the closest thing they can get to a material incarnation of their mate. Like these lovers, separated by thousands of telephone polls and thruway exits, I felt the distance between Neil and me as a vastness that I wanted desperately to shrink. And so I praised Neil's body and all it had been to me. Without his body, there was only this liquid, aqueous longing.

Even more confusing than the physical experience of loss that accompanies the death of a partner, whatever one's age, were the expectations that came along with having lost Neil when I was only twenty-five years old. Where was a twenty-five-year old widow supposed to go? In what sort of community, dating or other, could such a person fit? As I saw it, I had few options. I could become a retirement community hottie, raising tents in pleated polyester pants from Boca to the Palms as I lowered the median age of Shady Meadows by forty years or so. My new boyfriend Sual-ie and I could hold each other companionably through the night and spend our days with heads bowed beneath photos of our lost beloveds, Esther and Neil, like they hadn't so much died as had the audacity to go off any marry goys. Another option: I could move to a war-rent nation where young women buried their lovers on a daily basis. I could wear a head scarf and ululate with anguish next to my global widowed sisters. Instead, I was foolish enough to remain in the twentysomething dating scene in the good old urban Northeast.

My first post-Neil man was not, ahem, a rousing success. The fact that I use the term "first post-Neil man" to describe him might explain the inscribed failure of that effort. I would look into this young man's face for signs of Neil-ness. He was sweet and intelligent, but I didn't care. He wasn't Neil, and no amount of caresses would transform him into my lost beloved. For a long time, I felt like I was waiting for Neil to return from travels unknown. Would he stage a homecoming? He might be Odysseus, I thought, but I was a terrible Penelope, impatient and angry, hopeful that my suitors might metamorphose into my absent sweetie over coffee.

Admittedly, I pushed myself to date far too quickly, thinking that if I had to mourn, it might help to have someone to cry alongside me. But whether I knew it or not, I was transmitting my disappointment and wish for Neil's return to every man unlucky enough to cross my path. So haunted were the men I casually dated by the thought of my idealized former love that they would discover traces of him throughout my apartment, mistaking framed antique postcards for photos of him and used ticket stubs for sacred relics of our shared past. I didn't help matters by conveying my loss to my paramours as early as possible in the relationship. A man with whom I had gone on three dates and with whom I'd just had a hearty bedroom make-out session confessed some problems he'd been having with his family. Seeing my chance, I blurted out, "Yeah, that sounds rough…Um, I had a rough time recently too… About a year ago, my boyfriend, the man I thought I'd spend my life with, died of leukemia."

"Wow … that was difficult, I'm sure," he said before awkwardly baring his teeth. "Huh." Silence. He looked longingly at his pillow, whether with the idea that it would make a good instrument to smother me or with the sense of "Why didn't I lapse into unconsciousness when I had the chance?" I couldn't' tell. But I could tell that he was not going to call me again. It was often difficult to constrain this Tourette's syndrome of the unconscious when meeting a potential suitor. After having told me about his most recent long-term relationship, one first date said, "Wouldn't it be funny if our exes ever started dating?"

I held my hand over my mouth, trying not to emit the words. "Our most recent exes would date only if your last gal pal was an inveterate necrophiliac."

It was hard not to emblazon my difference from those I was dating onto a placard that I held in front of my chest to advertise my loss and keep my distance. Later, I realized that this urge to confess might get me more than I had bargained for, namely the men who are turned on by female misery, the Superman sans capes. I am tough and demanding and snarky, a bossy Jewish girl with a bottomless sexual appetite. In other words, I make a really bad damsel in distress. It was often comical to see the newest superhero-in-training puff out his neurasthenic chest and encourage me to cry out my loss on him. It never worked, and it only made me long for Neil to untie me from the metaphorical railroad tracks and usher me back into the familiar.

A year plus later, though, I started to see something. In the messy world of twentysomething dating, Neil's death was a strange gift, something infinitely painful but instrumental, useful in that seeing how men respond to the story of his death is a finely honed barometer of compatibility, kindness, for-realness, intelligence, and unconventionality. And finding someone who gets that I need to appreciate my sex life with Neil as much as my sick life with him is awe-inspiring. If you find someone who can handle sex and death, well, I think anyone would agree you've got things covered. Early on in my relationship with my present beau, as is my wont, I told him about Neil. His response was radical. He didn't look away from me or blanch or hold out paternal arms in which to enfold me. He just listened to me and told me that he admired my strength and that he knew from death, and then he kissed me.

When I met my boyfriend's relatives at a family party, I knew I was home. He and his cousins kept a running tally of how many times death was mentioned by their parents: whether their parents were singing the praises of those who had died, were in the process of dying, or - please, God, no – might die if they weren't careful to watch their cholesterol or diabetes. The number came out to twelve, but I was told that twelve was a small number of deaths to be discussed at a family-wide party and that everyone had been on best behavior, trying to impress me by muzzling their morbidity and dark Irish humor.

On our fifth date, my boyfriend smelled my hair and said, " I love what you smell like."

"What do I smell like?"

"A combination of Secret antiperspirant and Home."

I smiled. He didn't realize what I was thinking at that moment. I'm sure we were thinking about different things at that moment. I imagine that he was thinking about the grandfather and aunt who died young and his miniature self afloat in a kiddie pool and the musty smell of his attic bedroom filled with indie-rock posters curling at the edges and a personality that was too big for that tiny room. I was thinking that it must have sunk down into my DNA, thick like silt, that comfort with endings and bottomless things, with sex and death. My comfort with those things once known as the private things, the behind-closed-door things, the best-swept-under-the-rug, kept-within-the-family things. The stuff my mother and grandmother and all the nurturing matriarchs in my family couldn't help plunging into up to their elbows, the unfortunate reality that comes of caring for and loving the bodies of others. My genetic material, soupy with loss and desire. He could smell it and he felt at home. And so did I.

The next article centers on the controversy regarding commencement addresses given at high schools and colleges. Ignited in part by David McCullough's recent address to Wellesley High School (you can find the speech at this link: http://www.youtube.com/watch?v=_lfxYhtf8o4), the tendency among some speakers is to be more blunt and critical than the celebratory speeches of past. Katie Roiphe reviews a few of these speeches and seeks to understand them.

KATIE ROIPHE

The Meanest Commencement Speeches

The world loves a hostile or challenging graduation speech, one that eschews the warmth and supportiveness and grand inspirational sweep of the usual thing. Take the recent, interestingly bitter graduation speech delivered by a Wellesley High School teacher, David McCullough, with his mild-mannered preppie demeanor, wire glasses, purple striped tie:

"None of you is special. You are not special. None of you is exceptional."

In one transcendent part of the speech, which on the whole flirts pleasingly with being entirely out of control, he says, "Across the country no fewer than 3.2 million seniors are graduating . . . that's 37,000 valedictorians . . . 340,000 swaggering jocks . . . 2,185,967 pairs of Uggs." Although he tries to end on a more uplifting note, and move the speech into more conventional territory of inspiration, and caring about other people, the true heat of the speech is in its critique of the emergent generation he believes is overly managed, overly protected, and exquisitely nurtured: "Yes, you've been pampered, cosseted, doted upon, helmeted, bubble-wrapped." (Though really, read carefully, this is a critique of their parents.)

McCullough's suggestion is that their confidence, their carefully bolstered self-esteem, might be unearned. He argues that they are operating under a false impression of their own centrality and vividness. (As he puts it, "hundreds gasp at delight with your every tweet") The speech could be read as very practical, useful advice for these students, an explicit, tough love exhortation to do something interesting, unusual, extraordinary, not just to think they are interesting, unusual, extraordinary. But it could also be read as a statement of finely wrought contempt.

Every time it happens that someone breaks out of the inspirational platitudes with a hostile or challenging commencement speech, people are ruffled and interested, and it seems like an anomaly or maybe a mistake. But these mini-nervous breakdowns in commencement speeches are a recognizable genre, borrowing heavily from the truth-telling ambience of a J.D. Salinger story or novel. The outward stance "I am not going to tell you the fake thing you think you are going to hear" is very common, though few achieve the authentic surprise, the true frisson of a graduation speech that shakes people up, and almost never does it get as good as "2,185,967 pairs of Uggs."

The temptation to tell the gathered students—all dressed up under their graduation gowns, in the heat, the smell of fresh mown grass, the watercolor-blue sky, celebratory cakes in boxes on counters at home—something they are not expecting must be hard to resist for a certain kind of charismatic, boundary-breaking educator or writer or other distinguished person. There is rarely such a rich, glimmering possibility for upending platitudes and an audience so primed, so emotionally wrought, so unusually open to listening, so uncharacteristically reflective.

At my own graduation, the headmistress of my girls' school gave an overtly hostile graduation speech enumerating in startling detail how difficult, theatrical, and irritatingly self-righteous the graduating class was. The rows of girls in white dresses felt extremely betrayed, along with their parents. She singled out the hypocrisy of a piece I had written for our underground newspaper, Samizdat, called "The Mystique of the Ivies" about how the school was pressuring students to go to Ivy League colleges, even though I myself, along with many of the other editors of this pretentiously subversive publication, was headed to an Ivy league college in the fall. She attacked us for our half-informed, rather-festive sit-in in the lobby against the school's investment in South Africa. Sometime later she stepped down from her position and left the school.* It was widely believed that she had suffered some form of nervous collapse: The bracing originality of her act or performance piece was not appreciated, in part because she lacked the panache of McCullough, if not the simmeringly channeled rage.

David Foster Wallace's famously excellent Kenyon commencement speech is not exactly hostile, but it is challenging (and if closely read, it is hostile to the complacency that McCullough is attacking, and to the future selves of the vast majority of the graduating seniors. Does that matter, though? Do any of them see clearly the settling, the mediocrity, the comfortableness they will embrace in coming years? Or do they all, down to every last "swaggering jock," think of themselves as Holdens, as outsiders, as possessing of singular integrity and unique alienation?)

Michael Lewis' recent charming, and mildly subversive, commencement speech at Princeton attributed his professional success to luck, specifically being seated next to the wife of someone who worked at Salomon Bros., at a dinner in his 20s. He then went on to discuss a psychological study about how people who were randomly assigned "leaders" in a group felt they were entitled to an extra cookie. In the most tactful way possible, he suggested to the gathered Princeton graduates that they had that extra cookie but should understand very clearly that they don't deserve it.

When my mother was in high school, one of her suitors with literary aspirations wrote to J.D. Salinger asking him to write a letter addressing the graduates in the Andover yearbook. Somewhat surprisingly, Salinger wrote back to him, and the boy showed my mother the letter to impress her. Salinger had written something that could also apply to commencement speakers: "On the train to New York at Christmas time walk through the cars until you see a smallish boy struggling to get his suitcase up on the rack. He is sitting alone. He seems to have a cold and his nose is running. He is the one who should write to your graduates. Ask him."

Assignment Ideas

This chapter is asking you to critically reconsider your understanding of beginnings and endings. Therefore, you might consider employing some of the techniques suggested in Chapter 2 regarding critical analysis. However, remember to keep your audience in mind. For subjects such as death, readers might have considerable sensitivity, especially if they have lost a loved one recently, so anticipate your readers' objections to the thesis you develop and make sure your language use is deferential. Avoid clichés and euphemisms, however, both discussed in Chapter 5.

1. Jennifer Glaser conveys much pain over the loss of her boyfriend in "Sex and the Sickbed." Yet, her essay successfully veers away from the staleness of the "Dead Grandmother" genre and moves to a complicated thesis that ties together two seemingly unrelated topics, sex and death. See if you can connect the loss of a loved one you might have experienced to another topic. Compare your feelings to what Glaser discovered about herself. Make sure to summarize her essay and discuss her main points to make the comparison clear. Does analyzing death in the context of something else help you to achieve better understanding or perhaps aid in the process of healing?

2. Choose a recent news story or cultural event of which there was extensive media coverage. It could be something good—a major athletic competition or a public celebration—or something bad—a school shooting or a natural disaster. Using transcripts, editorials, documentaries, etc., interrogate the ways in which the media engaged cultural values or norms associated with beginnings and endings. Do you find many clichés? In what ways did the media coverage serve to highlight certain elements while eclipsing others? For example, in the wake of the September 11th terrorist attacks, there emerged a renewed sense of patriotism and camaraderie in the U.S. People drew together to comfort and support one another; songs were written and performed in honor of those who died and survived and those who helped; makeshift memorials materialized and expanded at the sites of disaster. How do these things encompass ideas of beginnings and endings simultaneously? Who gets "left out" of these rituals? Is there an element of disrespect for those lost when we celebrate how much the loss has drawn us together as citizens? In writing to this assignment idea, ask these sort of questions in relation to the event you choose and write toward offering your audience a perspective of the event that may be different—or even more accurate—than they may have received from simply watching the news.

3. This chapter discusses some "big" beginnings and endings: birth, death, marriage, divorce, graduation. Choose an aspect of life that is not normally considered a momentous occasion—going to work on a Tuesday,

writing and turning in an essay, going to a party with friends, etc. Now imagine how that aspect of life would change if we suddenly attached a level of symbolic value to it that we do to the "big" stuff. Would this alter our consciousness in a way that could lead to greater mindfulness and meaning in smaller moments? Would it unnecessarily add drama to events that don't warrant it? Speculate on the opportunities such an orientation might facilitate and/or the consequences or complications it might imply.

4. Much debate has ensued over commencement addresses that break the mold, so to speak. How would you react to the type of speeches that Katie Roiphe reviews if you had received one as a graduate? Compare the ones she discusses (Follow this Link for McCullough's speech: http://www.youtube.com/watch?v=_lfxYhtf8o4) with more traditional ones you find during an Internet search. Compare it further with one you have experienced. What do you remember about it? If little or nothing, does that tell you anything? Ultimately, come to a thesis where you discuss the purpose of these addresses and, perhaps, what could or should be done.

Group Work

As a group, consider the traditions, rituals, and ceremonies with which we generally mark weddings or funerals. Do some research on the practices of cultures other than the status quo in the United States, perhaps looking at ancient cultures if you prefer. Using your understandings of how and why weddings or funerals are conducted, propose an entirely different way to acknowledge (or perhaps not acknowledge) these life transitions. You might look in the "Additional Readings" sections at "No Dominion" and "10 Wedding Reception Rituals We Wish Would Die Already" to get some ideas. How might a shift or re-visioning of a wedding or a funeral change our conception of marriage or death? What implications would that shift or re-visioning have upon the couple entering the marriage or the loved ones left behind?

Additional Readings

The selections that follow give additional information and insights into the five main themes of the chapter—death, birth, divorce, marriage, and graduation. "10 Wedding Reception Rituals We Wish Would Die Already," "No Dominion," and "Afterbirth: It's What's for Dinner" all discuss rituals in ways that might make us question society's motivations for engaging in them. "Divorce! It's Good for the Children!" rebuts many of the current arguments that divorce hurts families.

GALLAGHER FLINN

"10 Wedding Reception Rituals We Wish Would Die Already"

(Link: http://tlc.howstuffworks.com/weddings/10-wedding-reception-rituals.htm)

AARON DEBEE

No Dominion

Our perception of death is at the same time both defined and clouded by fear. The human sentience that allows us the awareness of our mortality is the same quality that makes love, religion, and humanity possible. Unfortunately, it also instills a sometimes superstitious reaction to the idea of our own inevitable ends. The uncertainty of the afterlife combined with the pain of losing loved ones has motivated us over the centuries to adopt extreme practices in the pursuit of comfort and consolation (King 3). But when our elaborate ceremonies have ended and the proverbial dust has settled on our graves, are we truly better as a people, as a society, and as individuals for our attempts to deny the inevitable and unvarnished truth that at some point all living things must pass from the earth?

What is perhaps the most disturbing and destructive aspect of our preoccupation with traditional casket burial is that it shifts our outlook from one of management and acceptance to one of fear, resentment and reluctance. Referred to by T.S. Eliot as "fear in a handful of dust", in-ground burial smacks of a reluctant sacrifice to a greedy god and supports a feeling of worried helplessness (4). Instead of helping us to cope with death in a constructive way, it promotes a lingering notion of defeat by a much more powerful and opposing force. Abandoning the practice of in-ground burial allows us to eliminate those feelings which prevent us from embracing death as a natural and acceptable part of life and which cause us to see ourselves as pitiful victims. As suggested by the poet Dylan Thomas, we should approach our transition to the afterlife not with self-deception and denial, but in a manner through which we insist that "death shall have no dominion" (49).

When it comes to dealing with death, the difference between healing and fearful avoidance may lie in the difference between funerals and the tradition of burying the dead in lavish coffins in the ground. Repetition has encouraged us to forget that the two are separate and independent activities. Where funerals satisfy a need to mourn, a need to remember and a need for closure, modern interment attempts to trick the mind out of mourning, to manipulate and marginalize memory, and to circumvent a need for true closure. Where funerals provide a socially and psychologically healthy method for coping with the death of a loved one and transitioning past this loss, in-ground burial displays an unhealthy lack of willingness to accept death as a natural and tolerable part of life.

Because this urge to escape the reality of our mortality is a difficult phenomenon to admit, a number of scholars and experts have defended the continued American preference for burial despite a global trend toward more practical means of corpse disposal. Former Harvard Professor Richard Gill has claimed that this is not the result of a fear of death but instead a reluctance to abandon a time-honored tradition. He cautioned that a willingness to cast aside this ritual signals a de-emphasis on belief and a devaluation of past social priorities (Gill). I would argue, however, that there exists a difference between thoughtlessly abandoning tradition and making a well-reasoned decision to cease practices which refined judgment tells us are wasteful or even harmful to us. The power of tradition is not housed within the practices themselves, but within that upon which they are based. The encasing of bodies in decorative and ornamental caskets is not the aspect of the tradition that deserves preservation. What we must instead ensure is the continuation of a tradition of respecting the lives, efforts and contributions of the generations preceding our own. The act of lowering a coffin into the ground and leaving it ignored there for decades is not in and of itself crucial to our society's positive views on aging and past generations as Gill would suggest. The same values and approach to aging and the deceased can be accomplished through the combination of funerals with alternative means of corpse disposal, thereby eliminating the waste and psychological blockading that inevitably accompany the act of interment.

Because less fortitude is required during this time of extreme vulnerability to treat the corpse as the person we loved, we mistakenly assume that the act of lowering the coffin into the ground provides a necessary psychological comfort and closure to the bereaved. Former theology professor and expert on the sociological effects of death, Douglas Davies points out that it is not difficult to understand that this is instead a form of wishful thinking that serves to defend a desired but ultimately harmful practice (Davies). True closure would be achieved and displayed by understanding that the person for whom we cared is no longer present within the corpse. The lowering of a body which has been decorated and positioned to mimic a person at peaceful rest inside a protective casing into the ground where it can be securely stored for decades speaks less of an acceptance of the loss of a loved one and more of a denial that the body no longer requires our comfort or protection. The only possible reason at the heart of our insistence that the body be temporarily maintained is the deeply held urge to see that our loved ones (or ourselves) are not harmed. This very idea that the person may suffer from harm to their corpse is a perfect example of the irrational fear that drives the preference for interment. It is a fear of confronting the reality that the person we knew and loved in life is now beyond the influence of our physical care. It is not a sign of a healthy acceptance of death as a natural part of life, but rather the empowerment of death to influence our abilities to effectively process negative emotions.

In addition to the very primal fear that accompanies the acknowledgement of our own mortality, burial is also a response to a looming fear of being forgotten. We would like to claim that we practice in-ground burial and the marking of graves in an attempt not to forget our loved ones. That's a difficult claim to support, however, when a rational look at interment seems to suggest the opposite. In fact, Davies argues that traditional burial serves as an escape from the inconvenience of being reminded of the dead as individuals (Davies).

We comfort ourselves by squirreling the dead away underground and amongst a sea of similar graves, so that we won't be reminded daily that they have passed. If we're so anxious to remember those who have passed, would it not be easier to actively keep them in our memories by creating memorials to them in our houses (as a number of other cultures do) where we can see them daily?

Gill also suggests that the increasing social trend away from in-ground burial is our attempt to avoid dealing with death. However, covering the dead with six feet of earth in impersonal locations that we rarely visit is arguably more of an attempt to avoid dealing with death than quickly and permanently disposing of a body. The real fear driving the continuation of in-ground burial is the fear that we will be forgotten ourselves. That sad truth is that eventually we all will be. The sadder truth is that instead of coming to terms with this idea, we choose to allow the avoidance of it to define our outlooks on life and death.

Another fear influencing our decision to opt for interment over its alternatives revolves around religion. Because of the nation's history of dominant western religions and their traditions of interment, along with the inherent spirituality involved in the ideas of death and the afterlife, Americans tend to assume that interment is fundamental to these religions (Cahill). This, however, is not true. While it is true that the Catholic Church did forbid cremation for hundreds of years, it is important to note that it did so at the behest of Charlemagne in his attempt to reform the Church to reflect the influence of his own empire (Harris 55). This edict stood within the American arms of the Catholic Church until 1963 when Church authorities lifted the ban, admitting that cremation itself was not inherently anti-Christian. However, even Charlemagne's reformed Catholic Church never declared that a body be protected within a vault or lined coffin for burial, so even adhering to these obsolete guidelines does not preclude burial alternatives outside of cremation (Harris 56).

It is not a fear of disobeying a religious institution that ultimately concerns us regarding the role of burial in spiritual matters. The real source of our discomfort is our uncertainty regarding the afterlife. "To sleep – perchance to dream. Aye, there lies the rub." William Shakespeare understood that beyond the idea of death exists an uncertainty that we find even more frightening. And so we package, protect and preserve our "mortal coils" to hedge our bets against the unknown circumstances of the afterlife.

What is perhaps most maddening about this discussion is that the one aspect of deciding a method for the disposal of corpses that should give rise to fear is the one that is generally the most summarily dismissed; the long-term environmental effects. Graves are often lined with metal or concrete which disrupt the natural processes of the soil for a long period of time. When they do eventually break down, they add materials to the soil that would not normally be present, possibly interfering with the area's natural ecology. In addition to the grave lining, there is the matter of the coffin and its materials and contents. Almost every step that we traditionally take to prepare a corpse for burial adds years to the time it will take for the earth to reclaim the materials and adds foreign and potentially harmful substances to the soil. Every coffin that is lowered into a grave that may or may not be lined with metal or concrete does more damage to our already ailing earth.

This damage is of course in addition to the increasing amount of space that we endlessly need to dedicate to cemeteries. As the living population threatens to overwhelm the earth and her natural resources, it only stands to reason that the exponentially growing number of graves will someday surpass our ability to conveniently or even capably store them in extravagant coffins and place them in the rapidly mounting number of public cemeteries we're setting aside. This is already a very serious problem in countries with longer histories and less space, but these two factors will eventually become significant in the United States. Our true fear regarding the management of the deceased should spring from the realization that as long as the human race survives, the dead will continue to accumulate, but the resources we are able to afford them are limited. It is a shift in perspective such as this which could transform our view of handling death and the disposal of bodies from one of passive victimization to one of active responsibility.

Admittedly, when surrounded by the pain and mourning that follows the loss of a loved one, it is often difficult to make rational and reasonable decisions. It seems almost natural to lean on tradition and convention as tools for guidance in these difficult times. Minds so flooded with swirling tempests of memories and fear have little room for considerations such as the greater societal effects of our customs, the psychological responses to the confrontation of our own mortality, and the possible environmental effects of our individual methods for managing such an emotional event. Outside of these trying times, however, it is imperative that we attempt to step back and focus on the bigger picture. It is crucial that we take the time while we are in good health to thoughtfully reflect on how we feel about the disposal of the bodies of the deceased and what our reasons are for espousing these beliefs. It is during these periods of clarity and calm that we must come to terms with the realization that we all must someday die, and that we have a duty to ensure that this is handled in the best and healthiest possible way. No longer can we rely on fear and avoidance to guide us through our encounters with death. For with acceptance and reason comes true peace, "and death shall have no dominion."

Works Cited

Cahill, Michael. "The Dead Should Be Buried." *At Issue: Disposal of the Dead.* Ed. Diane Andrews Henningfeld. Detroit: Greenhaven Press, 2009. *Opposing Viewpoints Resource Center.* Gale. University of Akron. 2 Mar. 2010.

Davies, Douglas. "Essay: Death, the Great Taboo." 48–49. Reed Business Information Limited (New Scientist), 2007. *Academic Search Complete.* EBSCO. Web. 2 Mar. 2010.

Eliot, T.S. *The Waste Land.* Ed. Valerie Eliot. Orlando, FL: Harvest, 1994. Print.

Gill, Richard T. "Whatever happened to the American Way of Death?." *Public Interest.* n123 (Spring 1996 n123): p105(13). *Opposing Viewpoints Resource Center.* Gale. University of Akron. 2 Mar. 2010.

Harris, Mark. *Grave Matters: A Journey Through the Modern Funeral Industry to a Natural Way of Burial.* New York: Scribner, 2007. Print.

King, Melanie. *The Dying Game: A Curious History of Death*. Oxford: Oneworld, 2008. Print.

Thomas, Dylan. *The Poems of Dylan Thomas*. Ed. Daniel Jones. New York: New Directions, 1971. Print.

JOEL STEIN

Afterbirth: It's What's For Dinner

There is so much you can't know about your spouse when you get married, like that one day she will want to eat her placenta. But there are two things you don't argue about with a pregnant woman: what she eats and that being full of life indeed looks sexy. So when Cassandra told me that for $275, a woman would come to our house, cook Cassandra's placenta, freeze-dry it and turn it into capsules to help ward off postpartum depression and increase milk supply, I said, "$275 is a bargain compared with the $20,000 I'll have to spend to tear out our kitchen immediately afterward."

Most mammals, Cassandra explained, eat their placentas, to which I countered that most dogs eat their poop. I stopped arguing there, figuring that like many of Cassandra's hippie ideas — the compost bin, rubbing lemon on her underarms instead of deodorant — she'd give up on this in a few weeks. Even as the due date approached and she was still set on eating her placenta, I couldn't imagine that she'd remember to request it from the doctor after the most physically draining experience of her life. This is a woman who, 9 times out of 10, forgets the bag of leftovers at the restaurant.

Though I am exceedingly squeamish, when my son was born, I was shocked that I saw only the beauty of childbirth. Until the placenta came out. There are many normal human reactions to seeing a placenta, ranging from screaming to vomiting to warding it off with a cross. For those of you who have never seen one, the placenta is to the baby what Stephen Baldwin is to Alec Baldwin. It's what your liver would look like if it got into an accident on the autobahn with one of those aliens from *Mars Attacks!* and their bloody carcasses threw jellyfish at each other.

When the placenta did come out, Cassandra, dazed from 21 hours of labor, somehow made sure the nurses delivered it to us in a flat plastic container, which I put into an ice-filled *Monsters vs Aliens* cooler I brought. When I asked if I could keep the placenta overnight in the refrigerator out in the hall, the nurses looked at me like I was crazy. When you gross out people who work at a hospital, you have accomplished something.

In a fog, I drove the placenta home, where I wrapped the container in a bag and wrapped that bag in a bag and wrapped that bag in every remaining bag we had in the house. I slept at the hospital that night, grateful that my son will never remember what his parents just did.

The next day I drove back to the house to meet the placenta lady, Sara Pereira. To my surprise, Sara did not look unkempt, frumpy, heavy or in any way like a Wiccan. She got into placenta-cooking after taking a Chinese-medicine course and has already prepared more than two dozen placentas this year — and orders are picking up rapidly. When I asked Sara if her parents were embarrassed by what she does, she told me that her father sells bull semen.

By law, Sara has to cook the placenta at the placenta owner's home. But to my great relief, she brought her own equipment, gloves, sponges and even more detergent than I'd hoped, scrubbing constantly as she worked. If I ever kill a man in my own home, I am totally calling the placenta lady.

As she steamed the placenta with some herbs, the kitchen got that iron-like smell of cooked organ meat, with vague undertones of a consciousness-raising group and a Betty Friedan rally. Sara said Cassandra had a particularly robust placenta, and she hoped to get 120 pills out of it. As she sliced the cooked organ and put it on parchment paper in a dehydrator, she told me that some people drink the placenta raw as a smoothie. "I do this for a living, and I couldn't do that," she said. The pills, she explained, were superior, since Cassandra could stretch their hormone-rich benefits much further, perhaps even freezing some for menopause. Sara did not understand that when Cassandra's looks fade in her 50s, there's no way I'm putting up with this crap.

I drove back to the hospital where, thanks to my experiences, the food looked good. When we got home the following day, Sara gave us a truly beautiful placentapill presentation: a pretty glass jar, a card, a CD of lullabies and a satin pouch. In which was part of my son's umbilical cord, fashioned into a heart. When I asked Sara what the hell I was supposed to do with that, she said people often use it to keep a baby's first tooth and lock of hair. That's when I realized that placenta-eating is really just the beginning of how gross we humans are. And I went to change my first diaper.

JANE SMILEY

Divorce! It's Good for the Children!

When I asked my older daughter what she thought of my divorce from her father (she is 32), she said, "Do you really think I wish we had remained in that suffocating little four-person family?" But my daughter is a pro-divorce radical. Even as a teenager, when she dated boys from nuclear families, she was open about how dull their lives were compared to ours-always the same few people sitting around after dinner, no step-brothers and sisters, half-brothers and sisters, foster brothers and sisters. Here we were with an extended family and none of the parents had had to defy the prescriptions of Zero Population Growth (she is strict about over-population). It was divorce that gave her the tribe of peers that she wanted, and she has never seen a downside.

I will say, though, that when I've defended divorce in the past-notably in an Op-Ed for the *New York Times*, the response has been outrage. In America, you are never supposed to treat divorce with anything but appalled lamentations. No type of family is better than an intact nuclear family, ever. That millions of Americans have voted with their feet for other types of families is just a sign of cultural failure, or personal failure (the personal failure of the divorced ones, of course-the married ones have at least kept it together, even if . . . well, I won't go into the cost of keeping it together. I come to bury divorce, not to praise it. Amen.)

So, let me not praise divorce. Let me just offer a few suggestions about how to make it good for the children.

1. No United Front.

People are quite frequently eccentric. Grown-ups quite frequently do not agree on basic issues like discipline of the children, the balance of power within the marriage, budgeting, running the household, sex, how the world works, etc. When they attempt to present a united front for the children, this can come to be, basically, a lie, as in "Daddy and I love each other very much, and we agree on everything, especially what is good for you." If the reality is that Daddy and I don't know what in the world we agree on or whether we actually love each other, then the dissonance between the presentation of the united front and what the child sees for him or herself can undermine the child's sense of reality. Once the parents are divorced, Mom and Dad are able to discuss with the children those things that they differ on. That doesn't mean either one can say, "Gee, your ___ is a full-fledged mindless jerk." A better approach: when the child says, "Why does ___ do that?", the parent says. "Well, here is how ___ sees it. Here are some reasons for that. It's possible to agree or disagree with that point of view, but I see it differently, and here's why." A steady diet of this, I think, allows the children not only to differentiate between the parents, but also to differentiate between lots of points of view, and to develop a point of view of his or her own. Most importantly, his or her sense of reality is not undermined by a determined effort on the part of the parents to deny reality.

2. More Siblings.

I was an only child. I've known only children. From this experience, I do believe that the children should outnumber the parents. Parents are powerful. Children need friends and allies as well as playmates and antagonists. They need a cohort of peers to liven the place up and counterbalance the parents' ideas. Combined families often get bad reviews, but the family my children got when they traded away "the suffocating four-person" nuclear one is one that has benefited all of them. My daughters got stepsiblings with whom they have lifelong relationships and a half-brother they love, and my son got an older step-brother who has been an excellent example for him, and a good friend. The only siblings I have are half-siblings. My nuclear family would have been an extra-suffocating threesome. Instead, I have an interesting brother and sister, in-laws, and darling nephews.

Not everyone in my children's cohort has a relationship with everyone else, but the relationships that do exist are important to them. However, you must let these relationships form independently of you. You can't force the kids to like each other, though you can insist that they be courteous to one another and you can forbid bullying. And why shouldn't you? You wouldn't let them bully school friends, would you?

3. Conflict Management.

It's good practice! Nuclear families tend to get into patterns of conflict that last for years and seem like normality. Step-families have to be more self-conscious about conflict management. My most important piece of advice is, the step-parent has to be the good cop and the parent has to be the bad cop, and both members of the couple have to do their jobs. This means that if there is some indulging to be done, the step-parent has to not only be willing to do it, but to do it sincerely. I mean, these are kids! They are not kids you gave birth to, but they are cute and they are inexperienced. They also can be won over with gifts and kindness. There is no reason to take a stand or operate by some authoritarian standard—as an intruder (in the eyes of the children), the step-parent does not have that option. If they behave badly, then the parent's job is to correct them, and the step-parent's job is to discuss this with the parent quietly and reasonably behind closed doors when no one is angry. Forewarned is forearmed-the step-parent has to know going into the family that these conflicts will come up and have a strategy for not losing his/her temper and for persuading the parent to deal with things. The parent has to know that the children and the step-parent have to learn to like each other. Chances are that members of a couple with step-children had plenty of conflict in the marriages they have left, so now's the time to gain some selfknowledge and some new techniques.

4. Love.

With luck, we learn more about love as we get more practice. Why divorce the father if we can't learn from it? I never saw an example of conjugal affection and compatibility until my mother married my step-father, and even though that marriage was cut short by his premature death eight years later, I knew what to emulate in my own adulthood. My partner and I offer a model of love that is kind, generous, affectionate, and fun. The children may or may not learn from it, but at least it is visible to them. Maybe, in fact, what it says to them is "if at first you don't succeed, try try again." Is that bad? I don't think so. I would be very sad if one of them got into a bad marriage and gave up.

5. Home.

Everyone agrees that home is good and instability is bad. The nuclear family is supposed to offer a domestic haven in a scary world, and maybe it does. And maybe this haven is to be purchased at all costs—this is an individual decision. But any person or two people or three people can make a home, they just have to be willing to do it. <u>When I was a child, my grandmother and grandfather made a part-time home for me, and now I would be sorry to have missed out on that, because they were vivid personalities and I loved them dearly.</u> The home my mother made was appealing, too—she could cook and clean and decorate and welcome my friends. My two homes had two different sets of playmates and two different sets of activities. Because my mother was willing and able, I never felt strange in our two-person home, and because my grandparents were loving and involved, I never felt strange in their (our) home, either. My children were reared by joint custody-sleeping at each parent's house an equal amount of time. That they would feel at home in both houses was our first priority, and, according to them, they did feel at home, and also liked the change of venue. In fact, some of their friends were envious—two rooms? Two sets of Christmas presents? As I said, children are materialistic. The heart is where the home is, but you have to make it welcoming and homey. At the same time, children who have to negotiate two homes can learn to operate with flexibility and imagination. I remember reading in the New York Times that the crop of soldiers and junior officers in Iraq were cannier than their by-the-book superiors. This was attributed to what they had learned from divorce. I kid you not.

Divorce is based on the idea that we marry for love; you can't have one without the other. In cultures where marriage is based on property (women as property, marriage as exchange of property) divorce is much less common and love, at least for men, doesn't have to be (isn't often) a part of marriage (ask your wealthy French uncle if this isn't true). Falling in love is an expression of freedom and so is divorce. Freedom is, as they are always telling us, a responsibility. If we have the freedom to divorce, then we have to use it wisely. So far be it from me to praise divorce. For that, you're going to have to go to my daughter. Or Newt Gingrich.

thesis:

support:
—notice she doesn't appologize we know
this is how she feels (doesn't mean
you have to agree)

CHAPTER 12

COURAGE AND COWARDICE

Overview

Most of us would like to maintain a self-image that includes bravery and honor. In the face of danger, we hope that we will behave in a way that defends our dignity, protects others, and confronts challenges. In our society, we mistake, I think, the posturing of daring do and pride for the many ways courage inserts itself in our lives. Thrillseekers, for instance, the type who show up on the news every once in a while for performing a stunt or who take dares designed by reality shows such as *Jackass* and *Fear Factor*, look to be quite bold. They risk life and limb demonstrating their ability to survive a dangerous leap, face down a nest of spiders, or simply behave recklessly. Ultimately, though, the danger involves personal injury, whether physical or emotional, and has no principle behind it. A principle takes risk beyond mere contrivance. What happens when the risks we take involve other people? What about the many people who endure persecution for social justice? While these people might not be great physical specimens, a different type of courage burns in their hearts.

Sometimes showing courage means standing up to peer pressure. While it is perhaps clichéd to talk about teens who have to say "No" to temptations to drink, smoke, use drugs, and have sex, many people have had their first test of courage come under these circumstances. Courage, in this respect, does not denote throwing punches to stop someone else's actions but rather maintaining a set of standards and sticking by them, being able to endure ridicule

Online Study Center

This icon will direct you to web links and additional resources on the website http://college.cengage.com/english/thelin/ writing_without_formulas/1e/student_home.html

295

or exclusion based on principle. It takes some guts to stand up to other people under these circumstances.

It also takes courage to risk losing something you have or want by not going along with behavior you think is wrong. When people have power over us, such as a supervisor, a coach, or even a parent, we can suffer the consequences of confronting them for actions that seem detrimental to others or to the overall project under consideration. Many people involve themselves in talking behind the backs of the person with power over them, which is often thought to be cowardly. For example, the coach of my high school's football team dressed down a lineman in front of others, humiliating him and destroying his self-esteem, for poor blocking on the field. When this happened, many players looked away and offered whispered comfort later, telling the lineman how wrong they thought the coach was for his actions. However, one player, Ben, met with the coach to tell him that the public berating was wrong, risking getting on the coach's bad side, even losing playing time. Yet, through this show of courage, he also earned the respect of the coach and his teammates.

In both of these types of courage, one person breaks from the crowd to establish a point. An action cannot really be considered courageous, after all, if everyone did or could do it. At what time, though, does courage become stubbornness or perhaps mask fear? Can courage prove to be disruptive? Or can it be self indulgent, embraced to satisfy personal ego at the expense of the needs of the larger group? Our lexicon is full of sayings such as, "Discretion is the better part of valor," or "Live to fight another day." Both, generally speaking, mean when odds appear insurmountable, self-sacrifice becomes meaningless for the overall cause. We deem it better to strategize and fight when we have a chance of winning. Thus, even within our ideological construct of courage, we acknowledge that the path of the hero might not always be wise or effective. Is there such a thing, then, as having the courage to walk away from a confrontation? Having the bravery to consider options that compromise our principles? Being heroic enough to accept what we cannot change? One of the readings that follows, an excerpt from the screenplay of the movie *Billy Jack*, confronts this issue. Going out with a fight appeals to the character, Billy, but he has to consider the emptiness of such a gesture and its ultimate cowardice, especially in light of what his girlfriend endured to prevent bloodshed. Certainly, one definition of courage could be to take the most difficult path, not the easiest, toward solving problems.

If there are times where heroism proves to be detrimental, perhaps we need to start thinking of the bravery within some acts otherwise deemed cowardice. Protesters of governmental policy face all sorts of denouncements for speaking their minds in public. In the past few years, our country has seen many anti-war demonstrations. The protesters questioned the Bush Administration's decision to make pre-emptive strikes on foreign nations. Derided as cowardly and unpatriotic, many people still worked feverishly to have their voices heard, as they saw a bigger picture of innocent people dying senselessly. While the image in American minds of a young soldier willing to face death in a foreign land to protect our freedom appeals to our sense of unselfish courage, the opposite image, that of the person resisting war and refusing to fight, does not necessarily equal cowardice. We can look at draft resisters or protesters as showing great courage. Not only are they standing on their convictions, whether grounded in pacifism or political dissent, they also are saying "No" to perhaps the most dominant type of peer pressure exerted on us—the call to patriotism. They paradoxically have the courage to be branded as cowards.

True courage must come from behaving in responsible ways when we are afraid. Environmental advocates who try to disrupt logging of old forests, toxic pollution, and out-of-control suburban sprawl face retribution. Some of what they do involves sneaking around and sabotaging operations of which they do not approve. Members of the Earth Liberation Front (ELF) have taken the environmental battle away from the forests and into the cities. They target mostly sport-utility vehicles, which they feel represent corporate America's and consumers' disdain for conservation efforts, and development sites that encroach upon wilderness areas. While avoiding harm to humans or animals, ELF uses arson and Molotov cocktails among other weapons to enact destruction. ELF has been denounced as craven. Yet, what else can environmentalists do? Legal routes have been upended by the influence of corporate money. Dispensing information for boycotts also means challenging the money behind corporate propaganda. Individually, ELF members could put up macho, one-on-one fights with each lumberjack or construction worker or SUV owner they encounter, but the effectiveness of such violence would be limited, especially if the environmentalists were to lose these fights. Thus, the only way to win is to take what often is deemed the "coward's way out," that is, fighting through trickery when the other party isn't looking. When confronted directly or caught in the middle of sabotage, the environmentalist might deny his or her actions to the point of ridiculousness, appearing quite cowardly. Doing nothing, though, and allowing for environmental damage to continue, would actually be the coward's way out. Claiming the problem is too big, many people ignore injustice. ELF members take responsibility for others in order to enact a greater good, often standing on their own to take the retribution for certain acts. ELF member Jensen Contrell, for example, faces 35 years in prison for his activities. He noted in a 2004 interview that he could have fled the country when he knew he was under suspicion. But as he said, "If you just run, nothing happens. This way, more attention gets drawn to the problems with the government and their environmental policy." He is afraid of prison, but he faced the consequences of his actions.

While the concept of cowardice typically generates images of people afraid of pain, maybe a more accurate conception of true cowardice would be someone fearful of balance and reflection. Maybe acts of bravado are cowardice. Anyone can endure a physical beating. It takes no toughness. Not everyone, though, can step back, analyze a situation, and act in such a way that promotes the best possible outcome for everyone involved. Relieving tension or anger through physical conflict or challenges might look courageous, but it can be a cowardly way of not facing up to weaknesses or other problems. Understanding the cause of tension or anger and using insights from reflection productively and selflessly might appear like backing down during a moment of confrontation, but the bravery behind it might yield far more responsible outcomes.

Openings for Writers

1. **Fear and courage** Must there always be an element of danger for an act to be considered courageous? Think about incidents you have observed where courage was involved and discover if they confirm, refute, or complicate the connection between fear and courage.

2. **Breaking from the crowd** If standing alone on principle marks an act of courage, wouldn't that suggest that cowardice dominates most social situations? In other words, wouldn't the majority of people who don't speak up to injustice or wrongdoing, whether politically or socially, be considered cowards if individuality is an important trait of courage? Write about this characterization in light of images of courage and cowardice you have seen on television or in movies.

3. **Gender and courage** Often, expressions like "Act like a man!" substitute for telling someone to act with courage. Focus on the connection between gender and courage, looking to see how women perceive bravery and cowardice. How does it differ from men's perceptions?

4. **Backing down** Are there good reasons to back away from confrontations? Can these reasons be correlated to courage? Think of the other values you might hold and how they might take precedence in a situation where courage is called for. Can you reconcile seemingly cowardly behavior such as backing down with prudent, mature behavior? Would you hesitate to associate backing down with bravery?

Language

1. **Courage** Compare this word to "integrity" and "dignity." Can the three words be used interchangeably? Think about how the use of "integrity" or "dignity" instead of "courage" throughout this Overview might have contributed to a different sense of the subject matter. What would the opposite of "integrity" or "dignity" be if not "cowardice"?

2. **Pride** What connotations do you attach to this word? Are they mostly positive or negative? See if your associations to the word "pride" match your associations to the word "courage." Is there a lack of pride in cowardly acts? Does looking closely at the word "pride" shed some light on the importance or unimportance of courage in your life?

3. **Convictions** This word has secondary meanings but primarily refers to something being definite or certain. Does "conviction" connote purity? Stubbornness? Criminality? Rationality? Can secondary meanings impinge upon the primary one when it is used?

FRANK AND TERESA CHRISTINA

The Surrender of Billy Jack

The movie Billy Jack was released in the early '70s and concerned a former green beret, Billy, and his role as protector of children who attend a progressive school on an American Indian reservation. The following scene taken from the climax of the movie depicts Billy willing to die rather than to surrender to local authorities. During the film, Billy has protected local American Indians at the school against racism from the townspeople, especially from Bernard, the son of a wealthy council member. After Bernard rapes Billy's girlfriend, Jean, then murders his friend Martin, Billy finds Bernard and kills him. Billy now is holed up in an old church on the reservation, armed and protecting a teenager, Barbara, who is running away from her abusive father. The excerpt from the screenplay that follows was written by the stars of the movie, Tom Laughlin and Delores Taylor, using the pseudonyms Frank and Teresa Christina.

CHURCH EXTERIOR DAY
The church is surrounded by police cars, troopers, deputies, the press, spectators, and youngsters from the school.

> **COLE**
> (over bullhorn)
> Billy! Billy Jack! Can you hear me? Jean is coming in to talk to you. It's no trick. No one will try to sneak up on you, she just wants to talk to you.

CHURCH INTERIOR DAY
A few moments later. Jean hasn't taken her eyes off Billy since she came into the church but doesn't know what to say.

> **JEAN**
> I don't suppose you care too much that you're bleeding to death.

> **BILLY**
> Everything they want from here on out they're going to have to take. You don't understand that, do you?

> **JEAN**
> No. I only know you can't solve everything by violence, Billy.

There is the sound of wailing sirens. Jean walks to the window, looks out, then turns back to Billy.

JEAN
(turns to Billy, weeping softly)
They'll kill you, Billy. I wish there was something I could say to change all that. I know I've never said it to you. . . but I think you know. . . I love you.

Without looking at Jean, Billy nods to indicate his feelings.

BILLY
I think you know too.

JEAN
(crying)
It just seems so insane that we have to go on living without you.
(tears choke her)
What about Barbara?

BILLY
It's up to her to decide.

JEAN
Barbara, will you go out with me?

BARBARA
No.

JEAN
May I ask why?

BARBARA
From the day I was born, to this moment, and every second in be-tween, life has just been one big shit brick. I just can't take it anymore. And the way things are going. . . well as the Indians say, "Today is as good as any to die."

JEAN
(to Billy)
You've taught her well.

BILLY
An Indian isn't afraid to die. Don't ever expect a white man to under-stand that.

JEAN
I understand it. It's good – for an Indian.

BILLY
Like the old man said, being an Indian is not a matter of blood, it's a way of life.

JEAN
I understand that too.
(anger clears the tears from Jean's voice)
But she's a fifteen-year-old child who worships the ground you walk on. And now she's going to die needlessly because you haven't got the guts to control your temper.

Billy doesn't respond. Jean knows she hasn't changed his mind – and can't.

JEAN
It's so easy for you to die dramatically. It's a hell of a lot tougher for those of us who have to keep on trying.

Jean walks out the door.

CHURCH EXTERIOR DAY
A helicopter lands with several officials—including Charlie and Jim from the Governor's office. Armed troopers and police swarm about. The size of the crowd has increased. Nearby, a television crew is setting up.

COLE
Hello, Charlie. How are you Jim!

CHARLIE
What's the situation!

COLE
He's barricaded himself in the church.

CHARLIE
We must make every attempt to take him alive.

COLE
No way.

CHARLIE
He's only one man, it shouldn't be too tough.

JIM
What do you mean no way! Why can't you just move on in there and take him with some cover fire, then bring him out with some tear gas. You've got a whole army here.

COLE
No way.

CHARLIE
Can you do it?

STATE TROOPER
We can do it.

REAR OF CHURCH EXTERIOR DAY
State troopers and policemen swarm about the church, armed with a variety of weapons. Silently, they take cover. At a prearranged signal they open fire, blanketing the church with a fusillade of rifle and small arms fire.

CHURCH INTERIOR DAY
As the bullets rip into the church, Billy slams Barbara to the floor behind a shield of tables and bunks he has built for her.

BILLY
Get down.

As Billy moves toward the window, Barbara moves to get up.

BARBARA
I want to help load.

BILLY
Stick your head up and I'll knock it off.

The firing outside grows heavier. Billy moves from one window to another, returning fire with the loaded rifles he placed at each position. He ducks as bullets shatter the glass, ricocheting off walls and splintering furniture. Then there is a momentary lull. Billy swivels into firing position and pulls the trigger.

CHURCH EXTERIOR DAY
A trooper, trying to move closer with tear gas, is hit and sprawls into the dirt.

CHARLIE
(over bullhorn)
Pull back! Pull back! Cease fire! Cease fire! Cease fire! Pull back!

CHURCH INTERIOR DAY

BILLY
Okay, you can come out now.

BARBARA
I don't think I can.

Billy rushes over to her. She has been shot in the leg, but smiles up at him through her pain.

BARBARA
This darn stuff's not all it's cracked up to be.

Billy admires her courage.

BILLY
Oh you crazy nut.

CHURCH INTERIOR DAY
Hospital aides are taking Barbara out on a stretcher. Billy's rifle follows them. Jean stands off to the side.

BARBARA
Don't let them take me.

Billy waves the aides aside with the muzzle of the rifle and comes over to Barbara.

BILLY
You don't even have a medicine bag, so how can it be your day to die? You're going. Period.

BARBARA
It's just that if you die, that'll kill Jean and the school and everything she lives for, and, if you love her, I don't see why you do that to her. That's all.

Billy hugs Barbara, holding her tightly as she kisses his cheek. He releases her and the aides step forward. They lift the stretcher and carry Barbara out.

CHURCH EXTERIOR NIGHT

CHARLIE
We've got to take him alive. Where's that girl?

STATE TROOPER
She's already been in there several times.

CHARLIE
Well, then send her in several more.

COLE
Maybe a couple of us ought to go in there with her this time.

CHURCH EXTERIOR NIGHT
A few moments later. Jean, the doctor and Cole approach the church door and stop.

COLE
(projecting)
Hey, Billy. We're not armed. No tricks, you have my word.

BILLY
Come ahead.

CHURCH INTERIOR NIGHT
Billy sits listening, but unconvinced.

DOCTOR
...but you will get a fair trial. Because the whole world will have reporters here watching it, and because a lot of politicians will realize it's in their selfish interests to at least go through the form of giving you a fair trial. But in the meantime you will have accomplished an awful lot of good.

BILLY
Like what?

DOCTOR
Like calling attention to the unbelievably horrible way that the Indians are cheated and forced to live in this country, and the stupid insensitivity of Washington and the whole Indian bureau.

COLE
For God sakes, Billy, if you get killed now, it's a headline in tomorrow's paper. But if you go to trial, millions of people will learn what's happening.

BILLY
(still skeptical)
Like you just said, not a damn thing will be done about it.

JEAN
(to the doctor)
What about the school? Could we get enough money and freedom to run it for the next five years without any interference?

DOCTOR
They'd give you that in a minute.

JEAN
In writing?

COLE
I'm sure they would.

BILLY
It's funny, isn't it? Only the white man wants everything put in writing and then only so he can use it against you in court. You know, among the Indians a promise is good enough. As far as I can tell, Washington entered into 3,500 treaties with the Indians to date and they've broken about 3,499 of them.

COLE
I agree with you, Billy, promises haven't meant very much. But this is one they'll keep. The important point is this, if you have to go out, you might as well make it count for something.
(beat)
Well, I can't think of anything else to say.

The room is silent, then:

BILLY
Tell them that I'll give them an answer in the morning.

Sheriff Cole and the doctor leave.

BILLY
(to Jean)
We're different, you and I. Your spirit is more calm and pacific in you than any person I've ever known. And mine has been in a violent rage from the day that I was born. And you know something, I didn't really want it that way.

JEAN
Billy, that's a bunch of crap. I'm no different than you. Do you think when Bernard was on top of me grunting and slobbering, I didn't hate? I hated more than anybody else on this earth ever hated and every time that picture pops into my mind. . . . (fights for control, then, without emotion)
I've never hated so much in my life. When I think of that, I dismember and mangle and I castrate Bernard over and over in my mind at least a million times a day. The bad part is even though he's dead I couldn't tell you: you could get your hate out. I had to keep mine in.
(they look at each other for a long time)
I knew what you would do. I knew how important it was to the kids, and I knew that their lives and their needs were more important

than any hate I had, were more important than killing Bernard. But maybe, maybe if I had told you, Martin might be alive now.
(beat)
I don't know. I don't know anymore.

Jean leaves.

CHURCH EXTERIOR DAY
Jean comes out of the church and faces Charlie.

JEAN
He wants these conditions. First, that the school be guaranteed to operate for the next ten years without any interference and that I be given a ten year contract as Directress. Second, that Barbara be put in my custody as her legal guardian.

CHARLIE
That all he wants?

JEAN
No. He also wants you to guarantee that someone from the governor's office will hold a press conference every year to announce the progress of the school.

CHARLIE
He's got it.
(to Jim)
Call Washington and make sure they'll honor their end of the bargain.

Jean turns back toward the church.

EVE ENSLER

Sisters in Sorrow and Strength
Contemporary women heroes

This article, published originally in O: The Oprah Magazine, compares the acts of women from our country shortly after 9/11 with women in Kosovo and Afghanistan who were living under terrifying conditions. The author Eve Ensler notes that the responses from women in the face of danger and destruction preserve dignity and seek justice, not revenge.

It is Saturday, four days after the terrorist attacks, and I am visiting some of the new zones in New York City where people come to claim their missing. At the New York State Armory on Lexington Avenue and 26th Street, families bring victims' toothbrushes and samples of their children's blood, so lost loved ones can be identified by their DNA. Those who still hope stand with photocopied images of their spouses, cousins, friends, and fiancés, happy pictures, pretty pictures, alive pictures.

A young Dominican woman holds a portrait of her sexy fearless best friend, Marlyn, who was 21. On the morning of September 11, Marlyn was thrilled to be working at her new job as a file clerk on the 101st floor of the World Trade Center's north tower. A Russian woman who came to America fleeing anti-Semitism clings to a photograph of her handsome executive son. He was addressing a group of colleagues on the top floor of the south tower.

At a fire station on 48th Street and Eighth Avenue, I talk with the wives of the 15 firefighters who have not yet returned. There are flowers heaped at the door and a sea of candles; everyone wears yellow ribbons. One woman, Rhonda, tells me her husband, Danny, had been working a shift that was to have finished at 9 A.M. on the morning of the attacks. At 8:59 the sirens called and he got on the truck that would bring him to the World Trade Center. As we speak, the station's siren shrieks. Rhonda flinches and begins to cry at the sound that took her husband away.

I scribble notes as I listen to these women. I hold their hands, rub their backs, cry with them. I think of all the Saturdays I have spent in war zones throughout the world. I remember a crowded refugee camp in Afghanistan, thick in mud, where a skinny baby surrounded by flies sucked at her mother's empty breast. I picture a family in Kosovo, sleeping on foam mattresses in the backyard behind their burned-out house. I recall refugees in Croatia, sitting in a circle sharing tears and chocolate outside the vast barn, once used for cows, that was now their home. For some reason, in all these memories, it is always hot the way it is today in New York. The humidity is always thick. I have smelled the worry and grief through the clothes of all the women who have told me their stories.

I think how difficult it has been to explain to people in America until now that Kosovo, Croatia, and Afghanistan were beautiful once, that they did not begin in rubble. I think how in one week, the city I grew up in and love has become a place people fear and flee.

I think how in every war zone, in every terrorized place I have been, the grieving women I have interviewed have sought justice, not vengeance. They have become healers. They have spent their energy rebuilding their societies and holding their families together, rather than hungering for more violence.

I think how the attacks on America have joined us, finally to the global community of women who grieve, who long for their voices to be heard, who perform heroic and noble acts that for the most part remain invisible, and if they were known might give us not only hope but concrete ways of transforming a violent world. I think how crisis and terror can either lead us to more crisis and terror, or awaken us to a more complex understanding of the world and our deepest missions in it.

I see Sheri Spero on the corner of Park Avenue and 30th Street, in high gear, directing and managing the unloading of trucks filled with supplies for the relief effort. She radiates a simple energy, a clarity and decisiveness I have seen before when crisis occurs and women awaken to their purpose. I stop to talk with her.

On the morning of September 11, Sheri, a freelance production manager for TV commercials who always sleeps with the TV on, awoke to *Live with Regis and Kelly*. Someone on the show was screaming about a fire at the World Trade Center. Sheri's niece and nephew, 9-year-old Hannah and 11-year-old Sonny, went to school less than a block away from the Twin Towers. Their mother, Sheri's sister-in-law, had died a month earlier and their father was working on Long Island. It was up to Sheri to secure their safety.

She threw on some clothes and skipped brushing her teeth. She'd recently been given a beautiful Raleigh bicycle, a prop for one of her commercials. Although she hadn't ridden for 20 years, she hopped on her new bike and pedaled furiously south through an enormous crowd evacuating in the opposite direction. "People tried to turn me away," she says. "There are two things not in my vocabulary: the word no and the word *hate*. I looked up and the second plane hit the tower. I kept going. I had to get to those children."

She reached Hannah first, then Sonny. They were both scared but safe, and threw their arms around their aunt before fleeing the building with her. Just as they got outside, they saw the first tower collapse. "There was smoke and debris everywhere. I told them the rule was not to look back," Sheri remembers. They ran with hundreds of others up the West Side Highway. When they finally made it to Sheri's apartment, they all wept. Sheri washed them and fed them and calmed them down.

The next morning she took herself to a place called the Olive Leaf, a women's health center. A group that had gathered there spontaneously decided to buy large quantities of peanut butter and jelly and meat and cheese to make sandwiches for the police and rescue workers.

Sheri posted fliers around the neighborhood, asking for volunteers and supplies. It took her two hours, and by the time she returned to the Olive Leaf, there were lines of people waiting to volunteer and so many canned goods piled up that she couldn't get in the door. There were women who knew how to heal, how to help people grieve, how to give massages. Sheri knew how to take charge. She set up a kitchen that made dinners for police officers and firefighters. She arranged for restaurants to deliver meals to precincts and morgues. She sorted out truckloads of products, ranging from bread to dog food, that were coming in from other cities for the workers at Ground Zero. She divided the volunteers into "preppers" and "schleppers"–some prepared the food, some delivered it. She worked tirelessly, barely eating, never sleeping. Before this, Sheri says, she had never volunteered for anything. She had never been a part of any group. She tells me it has been the most amazing five days of her life.

"I have been surrounded by so much love and compassion this week," she says. "Strangers asking me what they could do to help, everyone trying to find a way to make good come out of something so horrible. Every morning I wake up and I feel shattered and sad. But I feel like I have a purpose, and that gets me out of bed. I've never felt better about myself. This feels real to me. This is what I'd like my life to feel like all the time."

One of the things I've noticed in places of terror is the variety of vehicles women use to rescue their loved ones, or, in some cases, strangers. With Sheri, it was a prop bicycle. For Marta, it was a tractor.

In the fall of 1999, two weeks after the war ended in Kosovo, I went there to talk with Albanian women. I drove them home to their destroyed villages and sat with them in the liberated cafes of Pristina, the looted living rooms of Dakovica, the backyards of charred houses in Magura. There are stunning mountains in Kosovo and green, fairy-tale vistas filled with sunflowers, corn-fields, and cows. The roads of Kosovo were destroyed by shelling and the heavy traffic of NATO tanks. The red poppy fields were pocked by land mines.

Marta was the 32-year-old headmistress of a school in a village called Has. Short and fierce, she was the only woman headmistress in all of Kosovo. We spoke at a table in a small cafe, surrounded by a group of her women friends. "I feel happiness and sadness at the same time," she told me. "Happy to be back in Kosovo. Then sad when you see burned villages, find out about dead people. Most difficult part for me." The women at our table urged Marta to tell the story of Little Krushe. Marta was embarrassed, humble, but eager to talk.

"There was a village, *Krushe e Vogel*, Little Krushe. On the second day of the NATO bombing, the Serbs took everyone out of their houses in this village, separated men from women. They took the men, 120 in all, put them in four lines, and shot them. The women and children could hear the machine guns. Then they told the women, 'You have three choices: Go drown yourself in the river, go to Albania, or we shoot you here.' My village was on the other side of the river. I just happened to be looking out my window with binoculars. I saw hundreds of women and children at the bank of the river, screaming, waving frantically for help." Marta got her younger brother and the family's big tractor and went to the river. Marta's mother was shouting after her, "Why do you have to be the first one?"

"It was very dangerous," Marta said. "There was shelling all around. Women were screaming and crying. I cannot describe how much. It was dif-ficult to calm them down. I said, 'Don't lose your hope.' Everyone wanted to get on the tractor. Some cried, 'How can we get on? We don't know where our sons and our fathers are.' I said, 'Be patient. Don't be afraid. We will get every-one of you across the river. I promise.' The river was high. We made 15 trips. Most of the people in my village came down to help—they brought another tractor and took the women into our village.

"I was never afraid," Marta said. "It was very important to save the lives of the children. More important than my own life. In those moments you be-come strong. There is an old saying, A human is stronger than stone."

Marta took the fleeing women and children to her village's clinic. Two had been wounded by shells. Another had given birth just a few days before.

High blood pressure was rampant and most were suffering from severe trauma symptoms. The demands were enormous, yet Marta managed to give them the help they needed. "The people from villages all around came to me and said, 'What are we going to do?' They came to me for answers. I'm just a teacher, a headmistress.

"We kept the women in our village. Four days later the Serbs came and said we were harboring refugees. They threatened to kill us—so we said we were leaving, and we all walked miles and miles to a refugee camp in Albania.

"There was a young girl, Violetta. Her father had been with the men who were shot. She wanted to stay. She was very sad. I tried to stay very close to her. I kept saying maybe he was one of the survivors. We had heard four men had survived and stayed in the mountains. Then a few days later they appeared. When Violetta saw her father covered in mud and blood, it was too much to see him alive when she had prepared for his death. She couldn't bear to hug her father so she hugged me."

Her actual name sounds much fiercer and spicier, a warrior name. But let's call her Zeba. Using her real name would jeopardize her life. Less than two years ago, I traveled secretly with Zeba from Peshawar, Pakistan, into the broken world of Afghanistan.

Zeba was 23, with dark brown eyes. She was beautiful and graceful, and there was something completely focused about her, something definite, unrelenting. She took me into the world of RAWA (Revolutionary Association of the Women of Afghanistan), an underground network of thousands of Afghan women who operate in Pakistan and Afghanistan. Their mission is to educate, feed, rescue, and liberate the people of Afghanistan from the terrible fundamentalist regime of the Taliban.

Under the Taliban, which, as of this writing, controls 80 percent of the country, women's lives in Afghanistan have been virtually destroyed. Those who break the Taliban's repressive laws are subject to punishments that range from public verbal abuse to whipping, beating, imprisonment, or execution. The women of Afghanistan must wear a long, restrictive veil called a *burqa*, which covers them from head to toe. They cannot engage in any activity outside the home unless accompanied by a *mabram*, a close male relative such as a father, brother, or husband. They cannot work in a public setting. They cannot be treated by male doctors or study at schools. The list of prohibitions is endless. But the one that particularly bothers me, for some reason, is that women are not allowed to eat ice cream in public places.

Zeba told me her story without self-pity but her suffering was apparent in her shaking hands and quivering mouth. When she was 14, her parents and younger sister were killed by a rocket that hit their house in Kabul. "I loved my parents very much," she said. "Just their faces gave me pleasure, and my sister with her dark black eyes. She was so little, 3 years old, so innocent. I loved Kabul. I was born there. I remember the winter, the snow of Kabul. I loved the snow. Always I told my father, 'Please take me for a walk in the snow.' He would put me on his shoulders." As she spoke, she touched me constantly with her sweet, velvety hands.

Zeba's uncle brought her to a RAWA orphanage in Pakistan. She was lost in her own despair. The RAWA women told her she had to attend to the suffering of all the people, not just her own. RAWA became her new mother, teaching her to struggle against violence, to gain freedom for herself and her compatriots. Zeba is a true revolutionary. She earns no salary for her work. Her clothes, food, and transportation are supplied by the RAWA network. She lives in a community of RAWA members. She and the other women of RAWA have found ways to perform the most radical acts, such as teaching, reading, writing, healing, speaking—and by doing so, they each risk their lives on a daily basis.

Covered in burqas, we traveled to a clandestine school in Afghanistan where she was a teacher. She asked me not to reveal the location of this school. The school was clean and ordered. Somehow, in the middle of dust and poverty, Zeba and her RAWA associates had made things beautiful and safe. There were brightly colored cushions and pillows. A group of girls studied English, eager to learn. Zeba proudly showed me a single chalkboard, which RAWA managed to smuggle in. "To the Taliban, this chalkboard is worse than a machine gun. If they found it, we could be killed."

As we left the school in a ricksha taxi, she told me of a student who was recently caught by a patrol from the Ministry for the Fostering of Virtue and Suppression of Vice, who saw that she was carrying books on the street. "The girl was flogged," Zeba whispers. "We told her she was welcome to return to school, but she did not come back. She worried that she would be followed and the other students would be in danger."

Zeba has done many brave things since the death of her parents. She has fled her country and returned secretly. She has risked her life by teaching girls how to read. She has reached out to people like me, to educate us in the West and to plead for our help.

But what moved me most was what I saw that afternoon.

On our way downtown through intense heat, baking in our burqas, Zeba said she wanted to take me to meet some women. She had convinced a wonderful and brave Afghan man to serve ice cream to women in the back of his rundown restaurant. Of all the gifts Zeba brought to the women of Afghanistan, this was the sweetest.

We arrived at the restaurant and were immediately rushed to the back. There was a little room with four sheets hung around it. We entered and found a group of whispering women, waiting, their burqas pulled up and perched above their noses. The man served generous bowls of vanilla ice cream to each woman.

They paused, nervous, afraid to eat. Zeba, with true boldness, took her spoon and began, savoring the ice cream and encouraging the women to do the same.

As I watched those women eating ice cream, it occurred to me that in the midst of so much terror, Zeba had found a place where women could preserve their dignity and desire. I realized that it is in the simplest acts of courage and kindness that humanity stays alive.

Assignment Ideas

Approaching opposing concepts allows you to look at much fruitful terrain in the middle for your critical analyses. While you might adopt a hard line in your writing—perhaps a strict definition of a concept or a strong position on a topic—the complexity inherent in looking at courage and cowardice should keep you keenly aware of your audience's needs. Watch out for language that might alienate a reader or for beliefs you hold that need detailed explication.

1. In "The Surrender of Billy Jack," Jean tells Billy that she had to remain silent after being raped by Bernard because she knew Billy would take revenge. She felt her silence would better protect the children in the school from the inevitable retribution if Billy were to kill Bernard. Yet, it is Billy's refusal to back down and his ability to force a negotiation through violence that ultimately provides the school with the protection it needs. Analyze Jean's silence and Billy's surrender as possible forms of courage. Did they both act heroically? By succumbing to his anger, can we see Billy more as a coward? Use your analysis to discuss and generalize about the best codes of behavior we can adhere to when faced with potential or actual violence.

2. Examine your freewriting about gender and courage and apply your ideas to the actions of the women discussed in Eve Ensler's "Sisters in Sorrow and Strength." If these women were men, would their actions have been perceived as strong and dignified? Analyze why or why not, focusing on the language you might use if men were to act in this way. If these women had responded violently to the situations in front of them, would their actions have been perceived as strong and dignified? Analyze why or why not, again focusing on the language you might use to describe women using violence. Come to some conclusions about the impact of gender on our perceptions of violence and non-violence, perhaps using your own experiences/ observations or an outside source to support your contentions.

3. Who is the most courageous person you know of? What about the most cowardly? Describe these two people and compare them by giving an example of one's courage and the other's cowardice. Discuss how you feel about both of them and whether or not your perception of their courage affects those feelings. How important are our views of a person's courage in assessing his or her worth? While two personal examples will work fine, you might consider looking at two public figures—people you have not met—or comparing a public figure with a person of your acquaintance.

4. Have you ever had to pretend you felt more courage than you actually did? In other words, have you ever had to claim you were not afraid when you really were? What prompted you to fake it? Describe the situation and explain for the audience the difference between faking courage and showing courage. You might refer to your brainstorming or freewriting on the connection between fear and courage, but concentrate on whether courage is demonstrated through internal feelings or outward actions or whether a subtle relationship exists between the two that complicates our assessment of courage.

Group Work

Each group member should view a movie where a central character is either cast as a hero, a bully, or a coward. Give brief summaries of each movie and analyze the important situations in which the characters acted or failed to act in a courageous way. What patterns can you unearth? What characteristics or actions distinguish a hero, bully, and coward? Do these characteristics align with your group's experiences and observations? Come to some conclusions about the media's depictions of heroes, bullies, and cowards and suggest whether these depictions reflect reality or whether the media's ideas have imposed ideas onto our perceptions.

Additional Readings

In the previous chapters, additional readings have been supplied. However, the world of your generation contains many sites of conflict that might enrich our discussion about courage and cowardice. Find additional readings that represent your concerns, whether national situations, local ones, or even virtual or online circumstances. Share these with others in the classroom to complement or complicate the ideas presented so far in this book, in your writing, and in your class discussions.

CHAPTER 13

THE SUPERNATURAL

Overview

Many people have experienced phenomena that the status quo does not accept as existing within the realm of possibility. This realm consists of the natural and rational world, and it is supported by science, precedence, and logic. Anything that defies the known laws or facts within this realm is deemed "supernatural" or "paranormal," meaning that the event, sighting, or occurrence cannot be explained fully within our understanding of the world. The questions that persist concern just how all-encompassing this known world is. In other words, do we have full knowledge of every crevice on this planet? Do we completely comprehend mental processes and powers? Do we understand the worlds outside our physical limitations?

Many people react to a person's claim of seeing a ghost or encountering a UFO with skepticism, if not outright ridicule. Authority figures try to explain away these and other supernatural incidents by claiming that witnesses have overactive imaginations or did not really see or hear what they reported. Sometimes, of course, skeptics prove to be correct. A family of mice probably did cause the strange noise you heard in the old house you just moved into. A sheet fluttering in the wind only looked like an apparition to you when viewed from afar. The spiritualists at the party most likely did not read your mind but rather made educated guesses based on your body language and basic profile.

Online Study Center

This icon will direct you to web links and additional resources on the website http://college.cengage.com/english/thelin/

Yet, we have all either experienced something strange that has not been explained as an effect of natural causes or have heard a story from a person convinced that supernatural forces came into play in his or her life. The power of rational thinking and natural explanations wanes when it does not quite relieve the terror or satisfy the curiosity aroused by supernatural experiences.

As a young adult, I spent a night in a house that had been plagued by strange occurrences. Our coworkers Dominique and Patty had noticed strange events in their house. Doors slammed when they tried to put up a crucifix on the living room wall. They had an eerie feeling of being watched, as if a presence followed them. They were uncomfortable about staying alone. Several of us thought they were crazy and spent the night to prove that the house was harmless. Long after the last of us had gone to sleep, I awoke, sensing someone staring at me, and saw a large silhouette standing at the foot of my sleeping bag. Startled, I rubbed my eyes and shook my head, thinking it nothing more than a bad dream. But when I looked again, it was still there. I yelled and scrambled toward the person closest to me, but when she awoke and looked around, nothing was there.

The next morning I described the silhouette as we drank coffee. Patty's face turned white as I relayed my impressions. She wanted to know the color of his hair. "He was like a shadow," I said. "I have no idea what color his hair was. What does it matter?" Patty remained silent. "Because you described him," she finally said. She explained that before Dominique had moved in, she had shared the house with a male friend who, she said, had been using some sort of magic to try to seduce her. He had told her that he could project his presence from far away.

Had I seen this presence? Had this person somehow haunted or possessed the house? I don't know. Our other friends talked about weird feelings and bad dreams they had that evening, but no one claimed to have seen what I saw. Logical explanations can account for my sighting. I could have imagined it. Night vision combined with imagination fueled by the adventure of sleeping in a supposedly haunted house could have twisted my interpretation of a mere shadow. Having been made to look skittish, Patty could have invented the story about the male friend projecting his image. He might have looked nothing like the silhouette I saw. I also could have mistaken a real person for a silhouette. One of the other people spending the night could have been looking for a glass of water or sleepwalking. Less likely, an intruder could have entered the house and have been frightened off when I awoke.

None of these explanations has ever satisfied me. I know my sight had adjusted to the dark, and I saw the silhouette clearly. No one could remember getting up in the night, and we saw no signs of an intruder. Unless some sort of hoax was being perpetrated, the rational, natural explanations involved too much coincidence for me to believe them.

Other people with better proof of supernatural episodes also have to strive to be believed. Marc Dewerth, the leader of the Multi-State Bigfoot Research Roundtable, filmed what he believed to be Bigfoot in Coshocton

County in eastern Ohio. While the creature on the videotape initially looks like shadows in dense brush, subsequent movement shows a clear image of more than one primate. Dewerth took this tape to primate experts at the Cleveland Zoo, telling them that he had been on a trip, had caught the animal on film, and was wondering what it was. The experts assumed that Dewerth had been in Africa and had caught a glimpse of some relative of the mountain gorilla. When he told them the tape came from Ohio, they showed Dewerth other places in the video where the primates became visible. The experts could not identify the species.

Possible explanations? When a species that is not supposed to be in a part of the country appears suddenly, officials claim that the animal must have been somebody's pet that was released into the wild. Officials do not entertain the possibility that animals of the species escaped detection in that area all those years. So despite dung and fur samples, not to mention sightings from reliable witnesses, grizzly bears have been considered extinct in Colorado's San Juan Mountains for forty years. While alligators have been spotted in the Miami River through Ohio and Kentucky, a native population does not exist. In both cases, the escaped pet explanation follows the denials. Using this logic with Dewerth's experience, I suppose we should believe that the primates he caught on film were a family of mountain gorillas who used to be somebody's pets. That sounds too far-fetched for me, though. To read more about Dewerth and a different recounting of his sighting of Bigfoot, see "Four Stops on a Bigfoot Hunt" by Jeff Parker (page 326).

When people hear stories about the supernatural, they often deny that something exists outside our natural, logical world. No matter how convoluted a "rational" explanation becomes, no matter how many coincidences it relies on, people gravitate to it rather than embracing the possibility of supernatural forces. People who do accept the possibility of a supernatural explanation risk ridicule.

Yet, while we as a culture go to great lengths to deny the existence of the supernatural in cases like the ones above, we willingly give the supernatural credence in other places in our life. Popular talk shows feature mediums who claim to speak with, and for, the dead. The Catholic Church requires that miracles be attributed to individuals in order for them to be declared saints. Websites are devoted to people recounting their experiences with angels. While we do not want to confuse evidence of the existence of Bigfoot with our religious convictions, these beliefs nonetheless show a clear embrace of the supernatural, as do many aspects of our various faiths.

As a culture, we dare to explore by launching spacecraft, conducting experiments, and searching for the past. However, evidence of the natural extensions of these explorations seemingly panics us. We study psychology to gain understanding of the human condition but scoff at demonstrations of extrasensory perception (ESP). We land probes on Mars to look for signs of civilization but actively denounce accounts that suggest that our planet in turn has been visited by alien cultures. Fossils tell us that bipedal primates other than humans existed millions of years ago, but we greet signs of their present existence with skepticism. So while the supernatural fascinates many of us, it repels others and is dismissed as superstition and fancy. But what happens when the logical explanation seems less reasonable than the illogical one?

Openings for Writers

1. **Rational explanations** At what point do logical, natural explanations for a supernatural event falter? What type of evidence would persuade you that a supernatural event occurred? What evidence would you need to convince somebody else? Look for consistent features that arise when you reflect on these questions.

2. **Hoaxes** Hoaxes include Internet rumors that are spread through email and jokes friends play to fool or scare somebody. Why are they committed? What is the pleasure in deceiving others? Decide on the connection between harmless fun, fraud, and hoaxes.

3. **Wanting to believe** Sometimes we say that a person wants to believe in the supernatural as a way of explaining an apparition or a UFO they saw. Why would people desire to believe they had supernatural encounters? If they were ridiculed when they recounted something supernatural, what would cause them to wish or want it to be supernatural?

4. **Faith and the supernatural** What other beliefs does our culture accept that, like faith, fall under the category of the supernatural? Think about how these beliefs pervade our culture and what effect they have. Do they provide comfort? Do they release people from responsibility? Do they raise possibilities?

Language

1. **Imagination** People are offended when told they have let their imaginations run away with them. Why? Hasn't imagination allowed us to envision ideas that have let us progress? Think of the different meanings of *imagination* and the connotations that go with them.

2. **Coincidence** What is coincidence? How does it differ from the supernatural? Think of ways that the definition of *coincidence* might extend or limit the definition of supernatural.

3. **Bigfoot** Does the naming of a supernatural creature or event cause you to become skeptical before you have heard the evidence? *Bigfoot* can connote many images, as do *Loch Ness Monster*, *Martians*, and *phantoms*. Are the connotations of these words positive or negative? Why do you react to them the way you do?

4. **ESP and UFO** People use these acronyms more than they do the words they stand for. Do you know what the words are? Do you get a different sense from the acronym than from the words the letters represent? Describe what the acronyms and the words connote and whether the connotations predispose you toward the subject matter of the supernatural.

5. **Miracle** How do you use the word *miracle*? Does it always represent something supernatural? Think of miracles you have heard about. Do you have the same reactions to those stories as you do to stories about ghosts, alien abductions, telepathy, and other supernatural events? Why?

ROBERT ELLIS CAHILL

Whitman's Haunted Bed

The ghost story here is archetypal of those recounted in many books about local legends. This tale, taken from New England's Ghostly Haunts, *involves contemporary, innocent citizens experiencing strange happenings in their home attributed to an ancient curse or death. Typical of these stories, the people isolate a particular cause and take steps to rid themselves of the paranormal link. In this case, the cure seems to have worked. In other cases, the hauntings continue. While reading, think about what you would need to hear, see, or feel to grant this account credibility.*

David and Barbara English, with their year old son, moved to Whitman, Massachusetts, from Delaware, in the autumn of 1972. They moved into a quaint, 18th century Cape Cod cottage, on Temple Street, where they expected to live happily ever after. A few months after they had moved in, their good friends—a couple from Delaware—came to visit them. David and Barbara had little furniture and only one bed, but David remembered seeing an old bed folded into a corner crawl space in the attic of the old house. It was truly an antique with a carved headboard and intricately designed footboard. David pulled it out of the crawl space and set it up in a spare room. On the evening their guests arrived, the Englishes allowed them to use their room, and the hosts slept in the ancient bed in the guest room. David had a fitfull night and kept waking up with the feeling that someone was choking him. Barbara, on the other hand, slept soundly.

Next morning things began happening to Barbara. Her china teapot in the kitchen cabinet would not remain standing upright. As many times as she would stand it up in the cabinet, she would find it a moment later lying on its side. Then she stood there and watched after setting it on its base for the thirtieth time—she saw it rattle and tip over again. Also, all the coffee cups slid off their hooks in the cabinet. "I tried continuously slamming the doors of the cabinet for a long time one day," said Barbara, "just to see if the pot would fall over or the cups would fall off, but they didn't, because they couldn't." This convinced Barbara that there was either a ghost in the house, or some large truck kept traveling by the house and causing the pot and cups to tremble and fall.

David concluded, one evening, that Barbara's first guess was right, even though he didn't believe in ghosts. He found that the door to the attic crawl space, located near their bedroom, was always open—no matter how hard he tried to keep it closed. Barbara swore she hadn't been near the crawl space. Neither Barbara nor David could explain who or what could continuously pull back the latch and open the door to the crawl space; it certainly couldn't have opened by itself, and it was too high for their, now two year old, son to reach.

One evening, while Barbara was out bowling and David was puttering in the cellar, he heard footsteps upstairs. Thinking Barbara was home early, he went upstairs to greet her, but there was nobody there. This happened every Monday night in the English household, while Barbara was out bowling—footsteps, but no one there when David investigated.

The incident that stimulated David into action, and thoroughly fright- 5 ened him and Barbara, was when they invited a neighboring couple over one night to play cards. They played at the kitchen table, where David sat with his back to the upstairs stairway, while the other three could see it clearly. David's slippers were tucked between two posts of the stairway, where he could easily pick them up when he went to bed. Suddenly, the visiting couple and Barbara looked up in astonishment—the pair of slippers were floating in midair, and then they landed with a slap beside David's feet. One of their friends told them about a medium who lived in Brockton, who might help them rid the house of its ghost. David was somewhat embarrassed about asking a ghost chaser to come to their house, but when the Brockton spiritualist refused to come, David was angry.

His anger and fear increased a few days later, when he came home and found pieces of sandwich meat scattered over the kitchen floor. He shouted for Barbara, who was upstairs, and scolded her for messing up the kitchen. Barbara had left the slices of meat on the table only minutes before and it was too high for the baby to reach. David returned to Brockton and pleaded with the medium to come. The medium came, and, after sitting at the kitchen table for a few minutes, he asked Barbara and David to take him upstairs. He walked into the room where the old wooden bed which had been found in the attic stood, and he slapped the footboard with an open hand. Then he began mumbling. Soon, he was shouting, "You must go!" David then noted that the medium turned pale and looked as though he was going to faint. David and Barbara accompanied him back down to the kitchen where he told them what he heard and saw; although the Englishes had been standing beside him in the guest room they had neither seen nor heard anything unusual.

"The spirit is an old woman," said the medium, "who lived in this house over 100 years ago. She died in that old bed. Another old woman lived with her at the time," said the medium, "but did not aid your visitor while she was sick, and treated her quite brutally. She is very angry about this mistreatment, and, by the way," the medium added, "she does not like David."

The medium had insisted to the ghost that she leave the house and she, so he said, agreed. David and Barbara went to bed feeling a bit easier, but David did not sleep easy. Again, he felt that someone was choking him. Coughing and sweating profusely, he woke Barbara and they went downstairs. They sat at the kitchen table all night, and in the morning called the medium in Brockton. The medium was there at seven A.M., and, after going to the bedroom again, he told Barbara and David that the old woman's ghost had left, but returned during the night to choke David. The ghost intended to show David how she felt when she died in the bed by strangling on her own fluid, which filled her lungs. The medium suggested that the Englishes get rid of the bed, then the old woman was sure to leave.

That day, David sold the bed to a local antique shop, who, in turn, sold it to a ghost lover for over $100. David English, however, is happy to have the bed out of the house, and, although he now believes in ghosts, he sleeps soundly.

SUSAN MCCLELLAND AND JOHN BETTS

UFOs, Skepticism, and Belief

Many people who claim to have seen flying saucers or alien beings face ridicule and even sanctions when they persist in believing the paranormal or supernatural explanation. While authors Susan McClelland and John Betts sound almost whimsical in reviewing the controversies in the field of UFOlogy, the issues they touch on contain serious elements. A Harvard researcher has to defend his methodology in interviewing victims of alien abduction and still is scorned for granting credence to abductees' stories. An abductee frequently awakens with unexplained piercings and nosebleeds after being paralyzed for a night. A government investigating an unusual outer space phenomenon in 1967 has to classify its findings as a UFO incident. This article also alludes to profiteering, wherein a Canadian town cashes in on the history of UFO sightings. The conflict about whether to believe in supernatural events crystallizes in our views of possible extraterrestrial life, touching the boundaries that science keeps pushing.

To the first-time tourist, St. Paul, Alberta, could easily pass for a set from *The X-Files*. The billboard at the edge of the small farming community about 200 km northeast of Edmonton welcomes visitors to the world's first UFO landing pad—a circular cement deck attached to the Chamber of Commerce. The chamber itself looks like a spaceship. Businesses with names like Mama's Flying Saucer Pizza & Breakfast and the Galaxy Motel line the main street. Even the town's mascot, Zoot, is an extraterrestrial that looks like a large-eyed blue bug. The biggest surprise, though, may be just how long it's been since the townsfolk put out the alien welcome mat. "The landing pad was built during Canada's Centennial," explains Mayor John Trefanenko. "People wanted to create something that would be recognized around the world. Over the years, we kept building on that theme."

And build they have. UFO fervour has spawned an industry in the town of 5,000 that brings in some 30,000 visitors a year. Along the way, some townsfolk have developed otherworldly areas of interest. Fernand Belzil, for instance, a semi-retired cattle rancher, is one of Canada's few experts on a grisly type of animal mutilation in which all the blood has been drained and certain organs surgically removed. The lack of footprints surrounding the carcasses has led some to rule out natural predators and practitioners of satanic rituals. So that leaves, perhaps, creatures from outer space? "It's as if the body is dropped from the sky," says Belzil, who has investigated more than 60 mutilations, predominantly of cattle, in western Canada. "Six years ago, when the chamber got a call asking if they knew someone who could check out an animal, I went thinking no way. It wasn't killed by aliens. Now, well, I'm not going to come right out and say there are UFOs. But like a lot of people in town, I am a little more accepting of strange phenomena."

No joke, folks: turns out the residents of St. Paul aren't alone in believing the truth is out there. A 1996 Angus Reid poll found 70 percent of Canadians believe intelligent life exists elsewhere in the universe, and just over half of those sampled said they thought the planet had already been visited by extraterrestrials. Throughout the country, numerous UFO groups monitor alien encounters. They estimate as many as 10 percent of Canadians have seen unidentified flying objects—and reports of sightings are as numerous as ever. Last year, more than 500 people saw 263 UFOs—up 10 percent from 1989. "Am I surprised with the numbers of people who have these experiences?" says Errol Bruce-Knapp, host of *Strange Days . . . Indeed*, a radio program about UFOs on CFRB in Toronto. "No. From the moment our show begins, the phone lines are busy."

"They're letting us know we're not evolving," says [Dorothy Wilkinson] Izatt, who believes she's met many aliens, and whose movies have captured strange phenomena.

OK, but it's one thing to fess up to a little-green-men fixation when you're talking to an anonymous pollster or on the disembodied world of radio. What do you say to non-believers, who state categorically that flying saucers and creatures that drive them—and then abduct earthlings—do not, cannot, exist? These people cite reams of scientific data to prove their argument—and question the soundness of mind of the E.T. crowd. Groups like Heaven's Gate in San Diego and Quebec's Solar Temple, whose devotees committed suicide in the hopes their spirits would be taken by aliens, bolster the skeptics' contentions that only those on the lunatic fringe believe in UFOs.

Some reasonable souls, however, are troubled by the rigid orthodoxy of the two opposing camps. "The problem has been that you have the hard-nosed skeptics, who believe nothing, and the full believers, who see a light in the sky and are convinced it's a flying saucer," says Palmiro Campagna, an electromagnetics engineer and administrator with the Department of National Defence in Ottawa and author of 1997's *The UFO Files: The Canadian Connection Exposed*. "What is needed are investigators who take neither view, but just look at the facts." As it happens, an emerging breed of serious scholars is daring to do just that. And if, in the process, they answer the age-old question of whether humans are alone in the universe, so much the better.

One world-renowned figure who surprised his scientific colleagues by trying to take an open-minded look at the world of UFOs is Dr. John Mack, a professor of psychiatry at Harvard Medical School. Mack, an author of more than 150 scholarly articles, worked over the past decade with more than 100 people who claimed to have been abducted by aliens. He acknowledges he, too, was skeptical at first. "The psychiatrist in me is trained to distinguish mental states like when someone is hallucinating, having some kind of psychotic episode or confusion around a dream," he told *Maclean's*. "But the clinician in me said these people were talking about these encounters the way people talk about what is really happening to them."

"dangerous" to credibility

In 1994, Mack, who won a Pulitzer Prize for his 1976 biography of T. E. Lawrence, published *Abduction: Human Encounters with Aliens*. The book, which relates the experiences of 13 self-described abductees, went on to become a best-seller—and to irritate Harvard officials. They questioned his research methods, forcing Mack to vigorously defend his work before a university review board. The board accepted his methodology, but not before his reputation was sullied in a number of major U.S. newspapers.

People in high places, though, have long been curious about extraterrestrials. In the 1950s, alongside civilian groups, the Department of National Defence and the RCMP investigated reported sightings of UFOs. Ottawa also funded the work of Department of Transport Engineer Wilbert Smith, who was trying to figure out how they made it to Earth. "Smith was studying antigravity propulsion—if something was travelling through the stars, how would it be able to manipulate gravity," explains Campagna.

10   The research grant was small, and Smith was soon forced to wrap it up. Then in 1953, the federal government supported another one of his initiatives, providing Smith with a building at Shirleys Bay near Ottawa where he was developing an electronic device that could identify flying objects. Several months later, Smith reported his first detection of an "anomalous disturbance" to the media. But the resulting publicity spooked the federal agencies supporting Smith's work—they cut off his funding, and the engineer was forced to close shop.

Still, Defence continued to collect UFO reports until 1968, when it handed the task over to the National Research Council: after multiple changes at the NRC, it, too, got out of the UFO business. Since 1996, the task of investigating sightings has been left to nonprofit groups. Between 1989 and 2000, they checked into nearly 3,000 UFO reports. Most could be explained as aircraft or natural phenomena, including stars or meteors. But according to Chris Rutkowski, an astronomer who heads up one of the volunteer organizations, Ufology Research of Manitoba, about 5 percent can't be accounted for. This includes one outside Whitehorse, where in 1997 an object shaped like a satellite dish flew at tree-top level as it followed a mother and her three kids down the Klondike highway. "I know how unlikely it is for aliens to reach Earth," says Rutkowski. "But there is a certain percentage of cases that just can't be explained."

One of Canada's most famous—and still unexplained—incidents took place in Nova Scotia, on October 4, 1967. Hundreds witnessed an unidentified object fly erratically 300 km southwest along the coast from Dartmouth until it eventually crashed into Shag Harbour. "I saw this strange orange light tracing the shoreline," recalls Chris Styles, who was 12 at the time. "My first reaction was fear. I had never seen anything like this before."

And seeing, as they say, is believing. Styles and writer Don Ledger co-authored the 2001 book *Dark Object: The World's Only Government-Documented UFO Crash*.

In it, they interviewed RCMP and military officers who were involved in the official search for the UFO. Some recalled bringing odd-looking debris, including a yellow foam-like substance thought to be from the wreck, to the surface of the ocean. The authors discovered that RCMP records classified the incident as a UFO. "I know many people involved want an investigation," says Styles. "UFOs are a worldwide phenomenon and these few cases that are well corroborated should be looked into."

Others say they've had encounters of a much closer kind. Larry, a suc- 15 cessful 50-year-old Ontario businessman, appears to lead a normal life in every respect except one: from the age of 6, he's been visited by aliens. "I realized my experiences were abductions when I was in my late 30s after I watched a TV show about abductees," he says. "Until then, I didn't have a clue what it was. I just kept it all to myself. As it turned out, what I was experiencing was textbook abduction."

And, yes, there is such a textbook—or at least a fairly standard— abduction scenario. One was spelled out in the 1987 book *Communion*, in which American writer Whitley Strieber earnestly recounted his own abduction ordeals. The abductee is taken every few months, usually at night, feels paralyzed, has visions of bright lights, and afterward has a sense of lost time. Some recount having had sexual encounters with their abductors, while other abductees feel they've been prodded and poked with strange objects. In Larry's case, he frequently awakens the next day with unexplained nosebleeds and piercings on his body. He admits he has no idea why this happens to him.

Harvard's Mack has his own theories about what's going on. He maintains, for instance, that much of the UFO experience occurs during an altered state of consciousness. "Through near-death experiences or deep meditation, the psyche can be separated from the body and can connect to deeper forces of the universe," he says. Although some may liken this to a spiritual experience, abductions, notes Mack, are unique because they appear to cross from one dimension to another. "What is distinct about UFOs and aliens is that they appear to go beyond a spirit that has no substance and show up as a physical body in the material world," he explains. "This is a problem for our Western mind-set because we are so based on material evidence. If it comes from somewhere else, it is hard for us to accept."

Canadian author John Robert Colombo, who has written three books on UFOs, doesn't doubt that the experiences are genuine—that is, in the person's mind. He points to the work of Laurentian University psychologist Michael Persinger, who has refitted a motorcycle helmet to expose the wearers' brains to a rhythmic bombardment of low-intensity electromagnetic waves. Although the gadget was developed to help people suffering from ailments such as depression and chronic pain, Persinger discovered that the wearers also have unusual visual sensations, like seeing angels. He suggests these experiences may be nothing more than a neurological accident. Epileptics, for instance, tend to have mystical experiences during seizures. What people make of the presence before them, Persinger says, depends on their own beliefs. "Some people may have visions of Mary," adds Colombo. "Others might say it is an alien."

Don't try to tell that to Dorothy Izatt. The 78-year-old great-grandmother from Richmond, B.C., claims to have seen just about everything there is out there. Izatt has met numerous aliens—some are little grey creatures, others

[handwritten margin note: many different examples]

are fair-skinned blonds—since she first saw a spaceship in 1974. She's also made more than 500 home movies capturing strange phenomena, and photography experts who have viewed the films say they haven't been doctored. "She happens to have a highly sensitive antenna," explains Lee Pulos, a Vancouver-based clinical psychologist who knows Izatt. "She is still rooted in this reality, but somehow she is able to tune into these extraordinary frequencies that most of us don't even know exist."

20   Like many others keeping the UFO faith, Izatt thinks extraterrestrials are trying to tell us something: they're deeply concerned about mankind's future. "They're letting us know that we're not evolving," she says. "We have wars and then we forget so we have another war. We were put here to be guardians and keepers of the Earth, to look after it so that it will not die. So far we have failed." No argument there. But to true believers in visitors from the beyond, there's at least comfort in knowing they'll try, try again.

E.T., Check the History Books

[handwritten margin note: examples don't believe in this]

Nearly every civilization since the beginning of time has told tales of visitors from space. The ruins of Tiwanacu in Bolivia, for instance, reveal a city fortified by walls made of blocks weighing up to 100 tonnes each. According to some writers, pre-Incan folklore maintained bearded white giants from the stars we now call the Pleiades built the walls in just one night. In the Canaima region of Venezuela, some local indigenous people point to the tabletop mountains, known as tepuis, they believe once ascended to heaven; the mountains were cut off, trapping some aliens on Earth, and their descendants still walk among us.

Then there's an Egyptian creation myth about the age of Tep-Zepi. Long before the pyramids were built (some today believe that they, too, were built with help from the great beyond), sky gods in flying boats came to Earth and raised the land up from under mud and water. And sand paintings by the Dogon of Mali in West Africa reflect the tribe's beliefs that they were once visited by extraterrestrials from the star sign tolo, known today as Sirius. The evidence: although the Dogon had no telescopes or other astronomical equipment, they possessed arcane knowledge about some aspects of the stars and planets.

[handwritten margin note: thesis: people believe and have always done...]

In Canada, the first documented sighting of what is commonly considered a UFO was in the winter of 1792. David Thompson, a Hudson's Bay Company explorer, and a companion were camped out in an isolated area of what is now Thicket Portage, Manitoba, when they saw a large "mass of jelly" fly through the air and crash to Earth. As Thompson noted in his journal, they failed to find it. But several days later, he reported a second, similar sighting. Judging by the thousands of reported sightings since, the skies over Canada are a busy place.

Assignment Ideas

Reflecting on the ideas from Chapter 3 about audience will be important in responding to the following prompts. While the lure of writing about the supernatural stems from fun or childlike fancy, the topic lends itself to many serious discussions. Thus, you should realize that skepticism prevails in any investigation of the supernatural or paranormal. Do not assume that your audience will believe anything you say. Pay attention to detail, and be willing to scrutinize your own perceptions and desires.

1. Robert Ellis Cahill strongly suggests that the incident the Englishes experienced has supernatural origins. Compare the narrative of this story to something supernatural you might have experienced or a supernatural story a friend told you. Consider your prewriting about rational explanations. What makes more sense in the possible explanations of the Englishes's incident and the one you know about? Be specific about the criteria you used to reach your determination, and develop a thesis about the limits of belief.
2. St. Paul, Alberta, Canada, welcomes visitors and cheerfully makes connections to its history of UFO visitations. Many towns might not celebrate their connections to paranormal history. For instance, Danvers, Massachusetts, the town in which the Salem witch trials took place, has only scattered landmarks associated with the many historical and supernatural occurrences that took place in the seventeenth century. The town to its east, Salem, encourages tourism and a belief in its supernatural legacy. Using St. Paul, Salem, or any town that broadcasts connections to religious or other supernatural occurrences that you know of or can find in an Internet search, discuss the possible connection between marketing, profits, and belief. How do they feed into one another? At what point, if ever, is dignity compromised?
3. Do you distinguish between legends and folklore on one hand and the supernatural on the other hand? Why? Choose a legend, and compare it to a specific supernatural event. What characteristics do they have in common, and where do they differ? Theorize about a purpose for the propagation of this legend and the supernatural event. Why does belief persist in one or both, or in one but not the other? Does this shed any light on our culture's conformity to so-called established fact or anything that you pondered concerning the word *imagination*?
4. Do you hold religious beliefs? If so, how are they connected to aspects of the supernatural? Reflect on your freewriting about religion and the supernatural, and expand on your thoughts. Do you consider your religion more valid than a belief in supernatural phenomena? Why? Draw parallels between beliefs in the supernatural and your religion. How does such a comparison make you feel? Generate a thesis that explains or questions why we validate religious belief but remain skeptical about other supernatural phenomena. You might find it useful to consult one of the readings that follows, "Is God in Our Genes?" which investigates religious belief as a possible survival mechanism.

Group Work

Books, magazines, and Internet sources have multiple witness statements about differing types of supernatural occurrences ranging from the Loch Ness Monster to poltergeists. Focus on one supernatural phenomenon, and examine various narrative accounts of its appearance or activity. Establish reliable criteria for evaluating the observations in these published accounts, and scrutinize the claims made by the witness statements. "Scientific Investigation vs. Ghost Hunters" (pages 351–354) might give you some clues about how to scrutinize such claims. Speculate about possible alternative explanations for the supernatural phenomenon, remembering to apply critical analysis. Are you comfortable with the conclusion your group reaches? Make sure to include your feelings—your wish to believe or lack thereof—in assessing the materials you find.

Additional Readings

This section follows up on many of the issues discussed in this chapter. Look at the tone and language the writers use. How do the tone and language shape your attitude as a reader? Which writer seems to present his or her critique with the most balance? Why do you think this is the case?

JEFF PARKER

Four Stops on a Bigfoot Hunt

1

We are not two minutes into our hike, the monthly sojourn of the Tri-State Bigfoot Study Group, when travel coordinator Marc Dewerth stops and shushes us. "Listen," he whispers. And because the six mostly average-looking middle-aged white men I'm with take his command so seriously, I do too.

The sound is the wind blowing through the trees, quiet basically. Then an odd groan from somewhere in the hills. Everyone looks at each other. Their eyes grow and grow. They extricate cameras—each researcher carries at least two—from holsters and shirt pockets and point them up and around. Dewerth shushes us again, the noise of cameras distracting him. He doesn't move. You can tell by his squint he's a little annoyed the others don't hike, like him, with cameras at ready.

Nowadays Dewerth keeps his video camera in hand at all times so he doesn't miss the beast ever *again*. If you're near him when he stops like this, and if you're on a Bigfoot hunt, you stop too and try to see what he sees, hear what he hears.

The sound registers once more, clearer this time: a guttural roar. Dewerth's eyes tighten at the corners.

5   Admittedly I am a little freaked out by this, having not seriously expected to run across anything. I have done time in woods, and this I've not heard. So I rationalize: this must be a trick. The sound is that weird.

On the way out here, as our minivan trailed a caravan of two other vehicles—one bearing the license plate *Yeti 2*—into the boondocks, past a big red barn with *Sasquatch Valley* painted on the side, I asked Bruce where exactly we were heading.

Bruce is 55. He drives the six hours from Michigan to tromp around the woods outside of Newcomerstown, Ohio, researching Bigfoot. He is an avid reader of *Fate* magazine (a publication that chronicles UFOs and Yetis and Devil Monkeys, among other unexplained phenomena) and proudly boasts that he was born in the very year the magazine was first published. He is a model Bigfoot researcher. In the car he listens to CDs of "vocalization recordings." The creature sounds sometimes like a screaming banshee, sometimes like Yogi Bear. For no apparent reason Bruce is given to proselytize on Bigfoot-related topics, such as the possibility the creature moves through creekbeds: "They say gorillas and chimps are afraid of the water. I believe the Sasquatch is a better swimmer than the average man."

"I don't know where we're hiking today," Bruce replied. The locations of the hikes are always kept secret from him and the other hunters, "in case there's someone who'd try and throw down some bogus tracks or something." So—this is before I understand the true nature of their ritual—maybe they're hoaxing me. You don't bring up hoaxing, I figure, standing there amid this strange bleating, unless you hoax.

I'd met Marc Dewerth several months back at the annual Newcomerstown Bigfoot Conference. It's what makes Newcomerstown the Vatican City of Bigfoot research east of the Mississippi. This year it attracted 350 people from all over the world, the biggest gathering of Bigfoot aficionados anywhere. He invited me to come sometime on their monthly hikes, and maybe, just maybe, we'd run across something, he said. I couldn't help but thinking that these hikes were like their Sabbaths, and he was trying to convert me. 10

This realization excited me because I'd been doubting the concepts of belief and faith in general. I hadn't grown up in a religious household and found myself starting to feel something was missing from my life. I wanted to be converted. I wanted to believe. Not that there aren't certain things I do believe in. Love, for one, I suppose. But then again, love is a far more tactile thing than a Bigfoot. At least you know when love is there in the woods with you. As far as religious faith goes, that's more intimidating, something people work at all their lives. It made sense in a way, to start with something small. Or in this case big.

"What is it?" Bruce asks Dewerth, who is looked up to by researchers much older than him, being the only one in the present company who's actually seen it. In every Bigfoot outfit around the world there's a guy or two who's run into the thing. The Bigfoot researcher equivalent of a hajj pilgrimage to Mecca, but less spiritual; the slots player equivalent of hitting the jackpot, but more spiritual. In any case, he's seen it, so he's the deacon.

"To me that sounds like a coyote," Dewerth suggests. "It doesn't sound like a Bigfoot. It doesn't sound like a primate call."

The group pauses for a moment to consider this.

"Could be an engine," Bruce offers. "It's too regular."

"Well, let's see," Dewerth says, and just like that, with doubt cast, he 15 pushes on. Everyone gallops after him.

"Before you step in any soft mud, take a look," Bruce reminds us.

I witness a groundhog barreling through the brush away from us and point it out to Dewerth. "Look," I say. "Groundhog." They don't have groundhogs where I'm from, and they're something to see. Dewerth could not be less impressed. He is more interested in the ubiquitous volume of fresh deer and turkey tracks in the mud, and the fact that we have not and will not see a single deer or turkey today. He points out the density of the woods, how difficult it is to see anything in there. He emphasizes size. The toes on the turkey tracks, some of them—just the toes now—approaching three inches. Even the anthills are big as boulders. "There's all kinds of wildlife out here," he says. "Badgers, bald eagles, turkey vultures. And they grow huge. Some of the biggest deer taken from Ohio come from Coshocton and Muskingum Counties, monsters." Every now and then he mutters to himself about what in the hell that noise was.

2

"Stop!" Dewerth says, crouching slightly. "I just heard something running along that ridge away from us."

We stop and peer ahead.

20   There's an anxious silence. The leaves rustle again. "It's a blue jay," Bruce says.

A Bigfoot hunt is made up of moments like these. False stops. Just enough to get your heart racing, to make it exciting.

Dewerth divvies the group up, which increases the likelihood of a sighting. And when he splits off, I follow him. It's like Bigfootin' with a Steve Irwin, a Crocodile Hunter for Sasquatch. He talks the whole way. You imagine he'd even be talking (to it, to you, to the camera, to himself—just talking) if he ran across it again. *Now this here is a midwestern spotted Bigfoot. Look at him would you. Gorgeous, ain't he!*

He knows his field, though, and narrates with great flair while we search for this elusive of elusives. He explains why the wilds of Ohio are such a hot spot for the creatures, as opposed to the great Northwest and Canada, where they're normally assigned: those monster deer.

"One thing I used to wonder," he says, "is why Bigfoots . . . Bigfeet would live in Ohio. But after thinking about it, it's obvious. The deer aren't controlled naturally, and anything that needs to eat meat is going to come to where the pickings are thick."

25   There is disagreement among Bigfoot researchers on many aspects of their discipline. No one seems 100 percent confident as to how exactly to pluralize the name of their prey, and they switch often between Bigfoots and Bigfeet. Also, the fact that our journey today isn't a hunt in the true sense highlights a more telling schism. Dewerth and his minions only want to catch the creature on film, in hopes it will convince the mainstream scientific community to pursue it; many others believe the only way to accomplish this is to catch or kill one. In fact, most Bigfooters across the country have converted to the latter goal, partly because the biologists of the world, while they've come a long way the past

30 years in allowing for the possibility the beast exists, refuse to dedicate their research to it until the amateurs come up with a body. Even with a new documentary, Sasquatch, aired on Discovery this January detailing all the circumstantial evidence you could hope for (plaster casts of the animal's ass, footprints with nonhuman and nonprimate dermal ridges, blurry videos, petrified Bigfoot dung, indeterminate sound analysis on the spooky vocalizations), without a body or live capture there may never be bona fide scientific research into the Bigfoot phenomenon. Many Bigfooters nowadays carry guns instead of cameras in their holsters. The fact that Dewerth and his crew don't intend to haul the animal before the public puts them on the fringe of the fringe. Despite their claims, they know full well the evidence they're after is the same kind that's been refuted by scientists for years. What's one more footprint with impeccably sampled dermal ridges? What's one more low-resolution video with what could easily be a guy in a gorilla suit? It's as if they're after just enough to justify the continuation of their pilgrimage, just enough to keep alive the possibility. No more.

Dewerth has his Bigfoot Eats Deer Theory refined. The deer hunters have limits. They can only kill so many. The deer thus have no other natural predators, because coyote hunters *can* shoot all the coyotes they want, decimating that population. Also, this area is old mine country. Natural gas and sulfur. When the mining companies cleared out the land, they created meadows where the deer like to bed down. The old mine structures make for ready-made covert Bigfoot shelter.

We meet up with the rest of the group when two trails converge at a crossroads where hulking antique hinged structures grow from the hill, old mining equipment, a natural gas pump like a mini Texas oil well, and some other pumping apparatus with rusted steel doors aswing.

"You guys didn't hear any sounds?" Dewerth asks. "I wonder what the hell that sound was."

The woods out here smell of oil, and the bright orange sulfur water runs in small streams down to the river.

The crew shares granola bars and they talk about things like other peo- 30 ple in other groups, clubs you might say, talk about things pertaining to their club when they get together: Dewerth asks Bruce about recent sightings and investigations in Michigan. IRS busts out his Peterson's track guide and scrutinizes a small track in the mud. ("I never seen one with three pads before," he says.) They reminisce about the three-hundred-pound guy they took on a nine-mile Bigfoot hunt at the recent conference. ("He was sweating white foam," Bruce says, "like a horse.")

Rusty, a red-haired disciple of Dewerth's, inspects the steel doors around the pump, which howl as they blow in the wind. He wonders out loud if this could be the culprit, the odd noise we heard earlier.

"It's possible," Dewerth says, his statement setting them all to serious, deliberative nodding.

So we walk away again without any conclusion.

"Wouldn't it be great to employ one of those buzzards as your camera in the sky?" Dewerth says.

"Hey, anybody into falconing?" Bruce asks.   35

3

"Shshshshshhhhh," Dewerth says, stopping with his arms out at his sides, frozen in skanking position. He cocks his head. There's the sound again. And it's coming from behind us. "I think it's that pump."

There is a pause while his comment is again given its due consideration.

"It's something rhythmically turning, or blowing, like a windmill," Bruce adds.

Says Rusty, "It's those doors we saw—"

40   "Yep!" Dewerth cuts in. This is his careful Bigfoot researcher bit. "That's why I tell people, if you see or hear something unusual, it's just something unusual. We solved it. It's a pump. You'd get some people who'd say it had to be Bigfoot, had to be. And it's a pump."

He leads us on. No one acknowledges that six grown men—myself included— had mistook the sound of a rusty door blowing in the wind for that of a seven-foot man-ape until long after it should have been obvious. No one acknowledges that. We accept the setback and plow on.

"If we brought out a few bottles of Bigfoot testosterone we'd get him out here," IRS says.

IRS introduced himself to me just before the hike. He didn't say "Hello." Instead he stuck out his hand and said, "I'm an IRS agent." By this, he explained, after realizing I hadn't made the connection on my own, he meant that he's naturally suited to anything involving "research and discovery."

At first he seems like the wild-eyed crazy man you'd expect to see on an expedition like this. One minute he's tapping me on the shoulder to say: "I was just kidding about the testosterone by the way. You've seen those 'Animal Encounters' videos where the guy puts the female deer scent on him and the buck about tore his leg off. In 'Nam you couldn't wear any perfume, had to go *au natural*." Then I look at him to see if he's laughing (he's not), and he seems to recognize that I'm looking at him to see if he's laughing. So he qualifies. "I'm a CPA," he says. "I got my feet on the ground. I'm not out chasing ghosts. Got a buddy from high school into multidimensional beings. I don't go for that."

45   He even reveals that he's not out here today because he expects to see it; he suggests that none of them are. "The number of sightings go far apart, people and the animal just happen to cross paths, just for that fleeting moment. I'm out here because I enjoy being with people who believe in the animal, catching up on new discoveries or rehashing old ones. I have no hope at all of seeing it today . . . But it would be interesting, wouldn't it?"

Dewerth confirms this when he and I split off from the group again. It's more of a gathering prior to the Tri-State Bigfoot Study Group meeting later this evening. (He warns me that that's where I'll meet the real freaks: "They'll tell you the reason we're not finding carcasses is alien ships are beaming them up. *Nooooo*. The reason we don't find them is because nature takes care of its own. Why don't we find them dead? Well . . . cannibalism is common among animals. Food is scarce. If you're hungry you've got to eat what's available, even if it's your own mother. Maybe they bury their dead. Who knows?")

"This is a leisure day," he says.

"Not even a print?" I ask. Dewerth tells me especially not a print. The animal is clever and cunning. It's not going to step into any wet mud and just leave incontrovertible evidence for us. We're more likely to get a sighting than to find a usable print.

"It's just so smart," he says. "It may never get caught unless it wants to be."

Dewerth goes on Bigfoot hunts four times a month; once with the group, 50 by himself the other three. He came across the creature on one of these solo hikes in 1997. Most people, when they see it, happen to be alone. It was right in this area, Muskingum County. He was making his way up an incline and looked over at some *thing* with brown fur about thirty-five feet away.

At first he thought it was a bear, then it made its way up the steep hill in four humongous steps. He noticed the foliage shaking around it, as if it was keeping itself between him and something else—its family, he figures. He fumbled to get his camcorder out of his backpack and powered up just as it disappeared into the brush. He pursued it briefly, "until I came to my senses," he says.

The footage doesn't show much more than some shaking bushes. But this sighting is his street cred and also the saving grace of his Bigfoot researcher career. He was becoming disillusioned with the pursuit back then. All the reports coming in to the Eastern Ohio Bigfoot Investigation Center (EOBIC) were turning out to be hoaxes, or people calling—sometimes posing as Bigfoot—to make fun of him. The EOBIC follows up on sightings in eastern Ohio, checks them out, and if they're legitimate, posts them to its website. He criticizes other organizations for posting any reports that come in, no matter how unsubstantiated. He emphasizes that if a sighting is posted on the EOBIC site, someone of his ilk has been to the scene and done some poking around, has sought out the rational explanation, the swinging steel doors on the old pump say, if a rational explanation was to be found.

The sighting was his wake-up call, a renewal of his faith.

"Are you a religious man, Marc?" I ask him.

He has always been, he tells me, all his life. But recently his baby daugh- 55 ter died of sudden infant death syndrome, a tragedy that he's not yet come to terms with.

"So I'm at something of a standoff with God right now," he says.

After that we walk in silence awhile. The earlier excitability drains away.

Dewerth breaks the quiet with this word: "Coelacanth." Then he spells it—correctly my dictionary later attests—explaining that it's a fish thought to have been extinct for millions of years until a paleontologist glanced at a picture of two Chinese fisherman holding one. "Of course there's stuff out here we don't know about. Just cause you can't see it don't mean it's not there," he says.

4

There is this one point when Dewerth and I are way up ahead of the others. He walks faster than the rest of them. He says he's happy I'm there to keep up with him. He fancies himself extremely fit, a woodsman of sorts in his matching khaki shorts and tan 2001 Annual Bigfoot Conference tee. But I think it's just that, at thirty-three, he's about a decade younger than most of the other Bigfoot hunters behind us a ways.

60   Suddenly he stops and points his camcorder into the brush.

"Look at this, Jeff," he says. "Look at this shit. Look at it, would you."

I look briefly to the ground. Just moments ago we'd scrutinized a couple pieces of trail scat. We'd knelt to the ground, the two of us hunched over them. Knowing nothing of trail scat myself I looked to him for illumination. He moved them around with a stick and declared them definitely non-Bigfoot herbivore output. (He hadn't seemed to even notice a bright orange butterfly, the same fantastic orange as the sulfur streams, the orangest butterfly I ever saw, fanning its wings atop the output, fluttering away as he disturbed it.)

He's not being literal this time, though. We are looking at dense deciduous forest in the unglaciated foothills of eastern Ohio. He is turning in circles, his video camera in one of his outstretched palms. Dewerth's point being, best I can tell: we cannot see shit.

"For all we know a Bigfoot could have just squatted down somewhere out there and is right now wondering what these humans are up to," he says, his zoom lens whirring, the foliage obscuring the wild turkey and deer and whatever other creatures might be lurking in there at this very moment, aware of us while we're oblivious to them.

65   Then he goes and pees off a ravine. He does not even look down but keeps his eyes on the woods.

S.M.ELLIOTT

Psychic Detectives Part I

Some of the world's most famous psychics have dabbled in criminal investigation or searches for missing persons. Uri Geller, the Enemy of All Flatware, claimed he worked with the FBI, which has never been confirmed. Jeanne Dixon, arguably the world's most famous psychic next to Nostradamus and Edgar Cayce, claimed that she tried to warn the White House about the assassination of JFK and foresaw the death of RFK as well. But the notion of "psychic detectives" didn't really take hold until the 70s, and has never enjoyed the mainstream popularity it has today, thanks to a plethora of books, TV shows, and online material about the subject. Just a few of the offerings: *Medium* (inspired by psychic "profiler" Allison DuBois), *The Ghost Whisperer* (produced by psychic/medium James van Praagh), *Rescue Mediums*, the books of Sylvia Browne, and Tru TV's *Psychic Detectives*. If you had declared in the eighteenth century that you had a spirit guide who helped you solve crimes, you probably would have been shunned (if not prosecuted for sorcery). Today you stand a good chance of getting a TV contract, or at least long lineups at your local psychic fair.

Setting aside the mystery of how and why psychic phenomena seems to manifest spontaneously in ordinary people from time to time, we're going to look only at the claims of people who make their living as psychics and/or mediums. Are their abilities dependable enough to provide investigative leads that can't be obtained in any other way? Has any psychic detective actually solved a crime?

Even those who believe in the efficacy of psychic detection don't have any cogent explanations of how it works. Many mediums and psychics subscribe to a right brain theory: Their intuitive, creative right brains are more active than their logical, analytical left brains. There is absolutely no evidential basis for this explanation of psychic ability. If the phenomena was purely mental in nature, psychic detectives would have little need for the various tools and methods they use to focus or manifest their powers, which include psychometry (handling personal possessions to receive information about their owners), dowsing (using sticks, pendulums, or other objects to lead them to a missing person or thing), astrology, spirit guides, automatic writing (taking dictation from spirits or channeling spirits while in a trance state), and (in the case of Noreen Renier) heavy smoking and drinking.

Like other professional psychics and mediums, psychic detectives make extensive use of non-paranormal methods such as cold reading. Their apparent successes can often be attributed to retrofitting (subtly altering the details of a psychic reading to conform to facts that are discovered later), selective thinking (picking out accuracies while ignoring inaccuracies), and the Forer effect (the belief that a vague, widely applicable description applies specifically to one person).

Law enforcement agencies generally find psychics unhelpful, or a time- 5 wasting annoyance. However, in some cases psychics can actually damage a case, incite public hysteria (as with the warehouse excavations in the Beaumont case, discussed below), or further traumatize the loved ones of a missing person. For instance, in 1999 Audrey Sanderford of Saginaw, Texas stepped up to the dais during a taping of *Montel* and asked guest Sylvia Browne about her 6-year-old granddaughter, Opal Jennings, who had been abducted from the Sanderfords' front lawn one month earlier. Browne informed Mrs. Sanderford that Opal had been sold into white slavery and was still alive in "Kukouro or Kukoura", Japan (there is no such place). Mrs. Sanderford sat down with visible relief. In 2000, Richard Lee Franks, a sex offender with no known ties to white slavery or Japan, was convicted of kidnapping Opal. Three years later, the little girl's body was found roughly 13 miles from her grandparents' home. She had been murdered within hours of her abduction.

The media tends to be more credulous and laudatory than law enforcement when it comes to psychics, publishing amazing stories about psychic crime-solving that don't stand up to scrutiny. As this is where we get most of our information about crime, it's easy for some of us to believe that psychic detectives are a boon to law enforcement. Closer examination of the facts surrounding a few of the cases reportedly solved by psychics might lead us to a very different conclusion...

The Early Days

If you plumbed the depths of myth and history, you could probably dredge up countless instances of what we would consider psychic crime-solving. But the earliest modern example I can find is the ultra-weird case of the Coppin sisters and the Franklin Expedition, as described by Jeffrey Blair Latta in his bizarre book *The Franklin Conspiracy*. Numerous psychics and mediums tried to locate the missing crews of HMS *Erebus* and HMS *Terror*, but this is by far the strangest example (and, if the story can be believed, the most accurate).

In 1849, the three young children of Irish shipbuilder Captain William Coppin announced they were in communication with the spirit of their dead 3-year-old sister, Louisa ("Weasy"). Her spirit appeared to 10-year-old Anne Coppin as a blue glow and communicated with her by writing on walls. After Weasy accurately predicted the death of a family friend, an aunt instructed Annie to ask Weasy about the fate of the Franklin Expedition. Annie did so, and immediately received a psychic vision of an Arctic scene: two ships nearly covered in snow, and a channel leading to them. Anne drew a detailed chart of this scene. A more startling revelation came some three months later, when a message appeared on the wall in large letters: "Erebus and Terror. Sir John Franklin, Lancaster Sound, Prince Regent Inlet, Victory Point, Victoria Channel." Years later, searchers concluded that the survivors had abandoned the ships in the Victoria Strait off King William Island and crossed the ice to Victory Point.

This occurred in the early days of the Spiritualism craze that swept America and Europe in the mid-nineteenth century. Mediums and clairvoyants emerged from the shadows to hold court in the parlors of middle- and upper-class enthusiasts seeking communion with the dead, wisdom from the afterlife, or simply some cheap entertainment. Five years after the Coppin children entered into communication with their dead sibling, the family of Victor Hugo would enter into an intense two-year period of communication with some of history's most illustrious figures, via seances. So it's not surprising that the Coppins turned to a ghost in search of answers. As we'll see, psychic detectives tend to use the methods most popular in their own time and place.

10   Captain Coppin was an advisor to Lady Franklin for the numerous search expeditions, and he relayed his daughter's message to her. She tried without success to persuade both the searchers and the Navy to look in the Victory Point area for her husband's crew. William Kennedy, a fur trader who participated in the 1851 expedition, spent three days questioning Annie to glean as many details as possible. The family shied away from publicity, though; even Dickens, who was keenly interested in the Franklin expedition and wanted to write a book about Weasy, was turned away.

The story of Weasy Coppin is an intriguing historical footnote, but the directions given by a toddler's ghost in no way contributed to the discovery of the Franklin expedition. To this day, the remnants of the ships haven't been found.

At the end of the nineteenth century, there was British psychic Robert Lees, the man who supposedly learned the identity of Jack the Ripper via paranormal means. As legend is told in books like *The World's Strangest Mysteries* (author unknown), Lees (a psychic since his teen years) had a vivid psychic vision of the murder of Martha Turner in August, 1888. This was the first of the Ripper murders. After the third murder, Lees accompanied Scotland Yard investigators to the scene of the crime and followed an invisible trail all the way to a very posh house in the West End, which he declared the murderer's residence, The investigators knew this was the home of a well-respected doctor who wasn't likely to be a homicidal maniac, but they reluctantly questioned the man's wife anyway. To their surprise, she revealed that her husband was a brutal sadist who had nearly killed their little son. The detectives were left with little doubt they had their man. His reputation was so sterling, however, that Scotland Yard engineered a cover-up and swore Lees to secrecy.

Ripperologist Stephen Butt has traced the source of the Lees tale to an 1895 article in the *Chicago Sunday-Times Herald*, instigated by a local group called The Whitechapel Club. None of the information in that article has been corroborated by any other source, with the possible exception of Lees' own diary. Until his death in 1931, Lees claimed he had been a psychic confidante to Queen Victoria since the age of 19, and produced a single 1899 letter as proof. However, the letter is a simple thank-you note for a gift. Lees had no royal links whatsoever; he was a reporter and a little-known psychic medium who died in poverty.

Thirteen years after the Ripper murders, across the Atlantic, a Virginia psychic calling herself Madame Newman announced that she had solved the disappearance of 19-year-old Nell Cropsey. Nell had stepped onto the front porch of her family's home in Elizabeth City, North Carolina, to speak with a beau named Jim Wilcox on the night of November 20, 1901. She never returned to the house. According to Madame Newman, Wilcox and accomplice had knocked her out with chloroform, driven her into the countryside, and murdered her. Her body could be found in a well near an old house.

Nell's mother found her body floating in the Pasquotank River, which 15 ran only a few hundred yards from the Cropsey home, and no evidence implicated Wilcox in her murder aside from strange testimony given by Nell's older sister, Ollie. Nonetheless, public outrage against him ran high. At the conclusion of his second murder trial he was convicted, and served 15 years of his life in prison. He committed suicide shortly after his release.

This injustice soured Americans on the idea of psychic sleuthing for a while.

Though it doesn't involve any crime or missing persons, the story of archaeologist Frederick Bligh Bond's 1908 excavation of Glastonbury Abbey deserves mention here. Bligh Bond claimed that all of his decisions on where and how to dig came from the spirits of monks who had lived at the site centuries earlier, speaking to him through mediums. According to his 1918 book *The Gates of Remembrance*, he found all of their information to be wholly accurate.

Enter the Dutchmen

The first twentieth-century psychic detectives to gain international fame were Gerard Croiset and Peter Hurkos. Both were Dutch, both were Resistance fighters during WWII, and both realized their psychic powers in their

30s. Another thing they had in common: Their crime-solving skills were virtually nonexistent.

Croiset, a psychometrist and psychic healer, was renowned for pinpointing the spot at which Scottish teenager Pat McAdam was murdered in 1967, but her body has never been found. He also failed to find Australia's Beaumont children, or the two children of a Puerto Rican businessman. His only success came in 1976, when he claimed to have located the body of a missing Japanese girl. He said she would be found floating in a lake, and her body was found in a reservoir.

20   Croiset was brought into the Beaumont case by a friend of the family, his travel expenses paid for by Adelaide businessman Con Polites. The Beaumonts themselves didn't like the idea, and had no faith in this quirky little Dutchman's skills - a position that would be justified by subsequent events.

Croiset originally said the Beaumont children were buried in a cave within half a mile of the Glenelg beach where they vanished. They had not been murdered, they had been trapped by a cave-in while exploring. Later, he insisted the children were buried beneath the foundation of a warehouse that had been built about a week after their disappearance. Some Adelaide citizens were so convinced this could be true that they raised thousands of dollars to have the brand-new warehouse razed, and parts of its foundations torn up. Meanwhile, Croiset confided to journalist Jack Ayling and others that he actually believed the Beaumont children had fallen into a construction pit at the site of some newly-built flats near Glenelg.

In 1996 the warehouse was partially excavated again at the insistence of Con Polites. The Beaumont children were not found.

Croiset's son, Gerard Jr., followed in his footsteps. Though he reportedly described the Andes plane crash with some accuracy, he never solved a single missing person case.

Hurkos said he gained his psychic abilities after falling from a ladder in 1941. Despite his injury he joined the Resistance, and was imprisoned at the Belsen concentration camp. After the war he started a nightclub act, and in the '50s paranormal enthusiast Andrija Puharich brought him to the U.S. for extensive testing by parapsychologists. Rather than wowing scientists, he charmed Hollywood, befriending mystically inclined celebrities like Glenn Ford. Through his contacts and his shameless publicity-mongering, Hurkos became the first American psychic superstar of the twentieth century.

25   Though he claimed to have psychically solved dozens of murders and disappearances as well as the abduction of the Stone of Scone, the evidence is lacking. Scotland Yard flatly denied that he contributed in any way to the recovery of the Stone.

One of the men who financed Hurkos' immigration to America, department store magnate Henry Belk, turned to Hurkos when his 10-year-old daughter disappeared in 1957. Belle had been a patron of Hurkos, and even invested in a uranium mine on his say-so. Hurkos urged Belk not to worry; his daughter was safe. A short time later, she was found drowned in a pond on the family estate and the uranium mine went bust. Incidentally, these two events eerily echoed the fate of Belk's grandfather, Abel Belk, who had been drowned by Union soldiers when he refused to disclose the location of a gold mine.

Hired by a friend of Roman Polanski to solve the 1969 murders of Sharon Tate and her three friends, Hurkos stated that three men, friends of Sharon Tate, had slaughtered everyone in the house after ingesting huge quantities of LSD and performing a black magic ritual called "goona goona" (a faux-Balinese term for love potion, used as the title of a 1930s sexploitation flick). He claimed he knew the names of the men and had given them to the LAPD. Later he claimed that he had named one of the three as "Charlie", but even if that's true, Manson himself was not at the scene. Sharon Tate had glimpsed him briefly on just one occasion; she did not know any of the killers (three women, one man). And all of the killers have denied they were on drugs that night. Hurkos sold photos of the Tate crime scene to the press without consulting Polanski nor the Life photographer who took them. He also used his marginal participation in the case to advertise his L.A. stage show.

In the case of the murders of Michigan co-eds earlier that same year, Hurkos was spectacularly wrong. He said the killer was a "sick homosexual", a transvestite, a genius, and a motocyclist who belonged to a "blood cult" (like goona goona, he never actually explained what this was supposed to be). This killer was twentysomething, blonde, rather short, and baby-faced. He worked as a salesman but liked to hang around at garbage dumps. A short time later, he said the killer was dark-haired and tall. This second description applied to the killer, John Norman Collins. He drove motorcycles, but every other detail was wrong.

Hurkos was caught fishing for information while "investigating" the Boston Strangler case in the early '60s; he impersonated an FBI agent in order to interview people. Skeptics have documented his use of cold reading techniques (see James Randi's *Flim-Flam!*). He also perpetrated what appear to be gold- and uranium-mining scams, and made some truly bizarre statements that can't be verified (notably, that Hitler is still alive).

It's interesting to observe what happens when multiple psychics converge on a single case. For instance, the psychics who offered information on the Atlanta child murders came to dramatically different conclusions: Dorothy Allison (who will be discussed in the next post) declared that she had correctly identified the killer as "Williams", while other psychics claimed they had provided accurate physical descriptions of him. Texas psychic Karen Hufstetler, on the other hand, had intense visions of the murders but felt Wayne Williams was *not* the killer.

Dorothy Allison

Until her death in 1999, Allison enjoyed a fairly solid reputation as a psychic detective, despite her many exaggerated claims. This diminutive woman from New Jersey employed astrological charts and psychometry in her attempts to locate missing people, often over the phone, beginning in the late '60s. She claimed she assisted law enforcement in thousands of cases nationwide, that she led police to the place where Patty Hearst was held captive, that she predicted Son of Sam would be caught by a parking ticket, that she named the Atlanta child killer as Williams, and that she cracked the John Wayne Gacey case.

Allison's first case involved the 1967 of a teenaged boy in her hometown of Nutley, New Jersey. She approached police early the following year to report her psychic vision of the boy lying dead in a drainage ditch in a local park. Desperate for any clue, the police obligingly dug up a culvert in the park in search of a body. They didn't find one; the boy's body was later discovered in a pond. Even though this was a clear miss, word spread that Dorothy Allison had "found" a missing child.

In 1980, police in Paterson, New Jersey, consulted Allison on the whereabouts of another missing teenaged boy. She gave the exact location of an abandoned building, and said the boy's body would be found in the flooded basement. Police painstakingly drained the entire basement in search of remains, only to come up empty-handed. The boy's body was later found on the other side of the city, outdoors.

The Gacey murders were actually solved by police using ordinary methods; 15-year-old Robert Piest had disappeared right after Gacey offered him a job, and police found very incriminating evidence in his house, linking him to other missing boys. Confronted, Gacey confessed to killing one young man in self-defense and burying him in the crawlspace beneath his house, where investigators unearthed the remains of 28 other boys.

35   Allison had merely led police on numerous lengthy, costly wild goose chases in search of bodies.

In the case of the Atlanta child murders, "Williams" was just one of over 40 names provided by Allison.

Allison also claimed she saw the deaths of Paul and Karla Bernardo's victims before they occurred. What really happened: Police in Niagara Falls, Ontario supposedly consulted her concerning the March, 1991 disappearance of a teenage girl named Melanie Hall. I have been unable to locate any information about this disappearance. If it occurred in March, this was before Leslie Mahaffey (the Bernardos' first murder victim) was abducted. Allison described Melanie's body as being encased in cement.

Melanie Hall's body was not found, but in June Leslie's body was discovered (encased in cement) in Lake Gibson. Allison predicted that a second girl's body would be found soon (a very safe guess, as Melanie was still missing). The girl would be strangled and left in some bushes. In April 1992, the body of Kristen French (the Bernardos' second victim) was found in a culvert. She had been strangled.

Allison did not predict the death of either girl, did not identify the body of Leslie Mahaffey, and gave only partially correct details about the second body. She also didn't locate the girl she was originally enlisted to find. Nonetheless, Leslie Mahaffey's mother was impressed enough to recommend Allison to another Ontario woman one year later. Rose Lax wanted to know who killed her father, a Holocaust survivor and scrap-metal dealer named Morris Lax. Allison said his death was a revenge killing staged as a robbery, but her description of the killer was too vague to be of any use. His murder has never been solved.

Noreen Renier

Since the '80s, Noreen Renier has been the best-known and most highly 40 regarded "psychic detective" in the business, second only to Dorothy Allison. Former FBI agent and pioneering criminal profiler Robert K. Ressler has praised her accuracy, and pointed to her work as a showcase example of why law enforcement agencies shouldn't shy away from bringing psychics into criminal investigations. In 1981, Renier predicted the shooting of Ronald Reagan while delivering a talk to agents at the FBI Academy at Quantico, Virginia. She claims to have solved hundreds of cases.

In short, Renier has a lot of street cred. But do her psychic gifts actually solve cases, and is her accuracy as remarkable as it seems?

To answer that question, I'm going to turn first to the woman's own words: The second (2008) edition of her autobiography, *A Mind for Murder.* The book is written in a low-key style, giving the impression that Noreen was swept along her current path by forces far beyond her understanding. Smoking and gulping wine to steady her nerves, she simply goes wherever the spirit takes her. "Sure, why not? I'll try anything," is her mantra.

Noreen didn't know she was psychic until she was nearing middle age. In 1976 she was a divorced mom with two college-age daughters, working in PR at the Hyatt in Orlando, Florida. Then she and two friends decided to try group meditation, and on several occasions sat around a kitchen table to chant mantras. During one of these sessions, Noreen felt a sharp pain and spontaneously went into a trance. When she emerged from it, her friend tearfully informed her that she had been channeling the spirit of the woman's dead grandmother, talking of things only the two of them would know.

For the next several months, Noreen honed her powers by studying psychic phenomena, reading books on Edgar Cayce and the paranormal researcher J.B. Rhine, conducting more kitchen-table seances, and giving readings to hotel co-workers (this took up so much of her time that she was fired).

Noreen found she a particular knack for psychometry. She set up a 45 booth in a hotel, then a nightclub, then a home office, where she gave private readings. Through contacts in the paranormal research community, she gradually began working with police who were desperate for leads. She discovered she possesses the ability to see violent crimes through the eyes of both perpetrator and victim, enabling her to give detailed physical descriptions of the perpetrators. She also experiences a great deal of the fear and pain felt by the victims. After some time, Noreen found she no longer had to visit crime scenes to gain such impressions; she could give accurate readings over the phone, while holding a personal possession of the victim.

According to Noreen, though her information rarely contributed directly to the apprehension of the criminal, it always proved to be remarkably accurate. She was soon invited to speak at the FBI Academy. She also gave college and university courses in ESP, hosted a weekly call-in radio show (1980-85), and gave demonstrations in prisons.

In each chapter, Noreen recounts one of her notable cases:

Noreen's first murder case: In 1980, Noreen received a call from Chief Pat Minetti of Hampton County, Virginia (Noreen's home state, to which she returned in '79). He needed help solving the murder of "Sally". At the station, Noreen was given Sally's bloody dress, which so distressed her she asked for a glass of wine to calm her nerves (she smokes and drinks throughout most readings). The detectives gave her Scotch instead.

Noreen asked to be taken to the crime scene, a trailer. Seated on a blood-splattered sofa, she described the killer to a sketch artist and detailed how he stabbed Sally repeatedly before slashing her throat, then raping her post-mortem. The sketch revealed a boyish, browned-haired man in his early thirties. The detectives instantly recognized him as one of Sally's neighbors. He and a female neighbor had found the body two days earlier.

50 Later, Noreen was handed the wires that had been attached to this man when he took (and failed) a lie detector test. She had a clear vision of the curved hunting knife with an ornately carved handle that he had used to kill Sally. It was in his trailer, in a drawer-like box beneath his bed. It was at this point that Noreen learned the suspect was a police officer. The detectives asked her to pose as a secretary so that when he came to the station for another interview, she could speak to him directly and hopefully gain more info. She couldn't.

The box was found beneath the suspect's trailer, empty. But the man handed over a hunting knife that matched Noreen's description. It yielded no evidence. "The police were sure he had killed Sally, but were unable to produce any evidence. He was a professional – he knew that without evidence, there would be no case. Our suspect is a free man today."

Yes, he is. Because the killer of "Sally" (Dorothy White) was caught six years before the original (2005) edition of *A Mind for Murder* was published. DNA testing of crime scene samples identified a repeat offender named William Wilton Morisette III. Far from being a policeman, he did yardwork for Dorothy, her boyfriend, and others. He is serving a life sentence for the murder. Why doesn't Noreen Renier know this? She rarely receives updates on her cases, but it wouldn't have been difficult to find out if this one was solved.

Why did she call Dorothy White "Sally"? Is it because she wanted to conceal the identity of the suspect for legal reasons? Or because she didn't want her readers to know the crime was solved nine years earlier, and that her suspect wasn't the killer?

A 1984 plane crash in Massachusetts is Noreen's most controversial case, though I think the murder of Dorothy White is just as damaging to her credibility. It led to a 22-year legal dispute with a Florida skeptic that is still not fully resolved.

55 In early '84 Noreen was hired by Jessica Herbert to locate the small plane in which her 29-year-old brother, Arthur, and three others crashed somewhere near Gardner, Massachusetts, on the New Hampshire border.

In her vision of the crash, Noreen *became* the plane. She circled an isolated airstrip when bright lights blinded her, turned sharply to the left, and was sucked down into an area of wooded hills, gorges, and quicksand. Noreen sensed that a large city was a certain number of miles away, that nearby towns began with the letters G, T, and O (though in the 2005 edition of her book, as noted by skeptic Gary L. Posner, she gave the letters as H, D, and N), and that a dirt red led down the mountain to a gas station/store with a rusty Texaco sign, owned by old woman who had several barking dogs and no teeth.

Noreen also saw something truly amazing: *Arthur had survived the crash.* He had stumbled out of the wreckage with a broken leg, carrying something.

The Civil Air Patrol's lead investigator recognized the gas station. Jessica Herbert, her husband (FBI agent Mark Babyak), and FBI agent Jim Crouse rented a plane to survey the area. Bad weather stymied them, but a local man and his daughter, noticing the search plane, decided to conduct a snowmobile search on their own. They found the plane. Both would later attest that they searched this area not because they saw the search plane, but because it was well-known that the plane had gone down within half an hour's flying time from the Gardner airport. Authorities found the woman passenger decapitated and seated under a tree "as if someone had placed her there". Arthur's body was found "sitting on the side of a hill, his leg broken...It was clear to everyone that he had been alive when he left the plane."

Skeptic James Merrill pounced on Noreen's claim that she found the plane, when it was searchers who had done the hard work of slogging through woods and hills. Noreen hadn't even left her Virginia home. He accused her of making fraudulent claims.

Noreen went on the defensive, suing Merill for defamation and winning. 60 As part of the judgment, both parties signed an agreement to refrain from disparaging each other. But in 2005, Noreen's autobiography contained passages critical of Merrill. He sued for breach of contract, and won a large settlement. He has continued his criticism of Noreen's claims via a website. I find Merrill's work confusing and rather nitpicky, but he has made many significant points about the Herbert crash, notably this: Arthur Herbert did *not* survive the crash. All four passengers died on impact. Noreen's notion that Arthur walked away from the plane carrying the headless woman is a fantasy.

The murder of Debi Whitlock: This case contains a glaring inconsistency, even as recounted by Noreen herself. 32-year-old Debi Whitlock was stabbed to death in her Modesto, California home in 1988, while her little daughter slept. Her husband found her body a short time later. Noreen was hired by Debi's mom, Jacque McDonald, to conduct a phone session with Detective Ray Taylor of the Modesto Police Department. Taylor was "so impressed that he decided to fly all the way across the country to Orlando to pay me a visit in person and continue our conversation," He later told *America's Most Wanted* that Noreen gave "an eerily precise description of the murder" (Renier, 185).

In the session, filmed by *AMW*, Noreen described Debi receiving a phone call from her killer. He was stocky but very strong, "handsome and rugged". She spoke as both Debi and this man. As the man: "She's not gonna leave me and get away with it. She stays with me till I say it's over. I know she's in love with someone else." The impression we get is that Debi had a jealous lover – or was perhaps killed by her husband (police did suspect Harold Whitlock, and the public harrassed him until 1999). Noreen even quotes an investigator as saying Debi "might have been falling in love again."

However, in 1999 a former drug dealer named the killer as Scott Avery Frizzell, He was an 18-year-old drifter when he killed Debi in the course of a burglary. It's incredibly unlikely that he was her lover, yet Noreen does nothing to explain the contradiction between what she "experienced" and what really occurred. The worst-case scenario is that Noreen knew Harold Whitlock was the prime suspect when she did her reading, and tailored it to point the finger at him.

Not included in the book is Noreen's encounter with Lois Duncan, an author of young adult suspense and horror novels that I enjoyed as a kid. In 1989 Duncan's daughter, Kaitlyn Arquette, was murdered in what appeared to be a random drive-by shooting in Albuquerque. Noreen was able to "relive" Kaitlyn's last moments, but couldn't describe a perp. So Duncan turned to another psychic, Betty Muench. Muench used automatic writing to discover that Kaitlyn had been the victim of a contract killing because she knew too much about something dangerous. Duncan was deeply impressed by the wealth of detail in the psychic's descriptions, which were later confirmed for her by private investigators who suspected Kaitlyn's Vietnamese boyfriend had her killed to hide an insurance scam he and other Vietnamese men were perpetrating. Unfortunately, her detailed information wasn't any more helpful than Noreen's. The murder of Kaitlyn remains unsolved.

Sylvia Browne

65 I'm willing to give Noreen Renier the benefit of the doubt when it comes to honesty. Maybe she simply isn't as gifted as she thinks she is, and is sloppy when it comes to doing follow-ups. But Sylvia Browne won't be getting any such slack. She is a bald-faced liar and an utter fraud, the dagger-nailed embodiment of epic FAIL. I'll admit that her whiskey-and-cigs voice and deadpan delivery are weirdly endearing. She's like the lovably gruff white-trash aunt who sits in her trailer all day, knocking back black coffee while she waits for bingo. I'm not taken in by this, though. She can call people "honey" all she wants; this woman is *evil.*

Browne has been making her living as a psychic since the '70s, offering phone readings for hundreds of dollars and establishing the Nirvana Foundation for Psychic Research (now defunct). In the '90s she gained national fame as a regular guest on Montel Williams' TV talk show, *Montel.* She made weekly appearances until the show's cancellation in 2008. She steadily churns out books on reincarnation, heaven, psychic healing, and assorted New Agey topics. Her son, Chris, claims to be psychic too. Psychic ability often runs in families, as with the mother-and-son team of Bertie and John Catchings and the family of "lesbian psychic to the stars" Terry Iacuzzo. There have been psychics in Browne's family for the past three centuries. Don't worry if your family lacks the clairvoyance gene, though: Browne's Hypnosis Training Center offers classes on how to hypnotize your children and bring out their psychic abilities. Much of Browne's information about the afterlife comes from her spirit guide and co-author, Francine. No one knows just how Francine entered Browne's life, because she has given conflicting accounts of their first meeting.

She is also in contact with many different kinds of angels, as well as fairies and humanoid aliens, but insists there are no demons (as we'll see in a post about Ed and Lorraine Warren, other psychics vehemently disagree). After her psychical research outfit went bust, she founded a New Age/Christian church called the Society of Novus Spiritus.

In 1992, Browne and one of her many husbands, Kensil Dalzell Brown, pleaded no contest to several charges of investment fraud and grand larceny. They had been selling securities in a gold-mining venture under false pretenses, telling investors that their money would be used for operating costs when it actually went straight to their (now defunct) Nirvana Foundation for Psychic Research. Shades of Peter Hurkos.

Browne is cast firmly in the folksy New Age mold, but lately she's venturing into conspiracy theories and pop eschatology to attract an even wider audience. Her latest book, *Secret Societies*, deals with staples of conspiranoia culture: the Knights Templar, Freemasons, Catholics, and the New World Order.

I first realized that Browne was full of it when I watched her give a past-life reading on *Oprah*. A woman in the audience wanted to know why she had a phobia of leaving beverages unattended for even a few minutes, and Browne casually informed her that she had been poisoned in her former life as an Egyptian "high priestess". Then came the kicker: "I know because they poisoned me, too. I was the high priestess right before you were." How amazing, then, that they would end up in the same Illinois TV studio on the very same day! I wonder why Browne didn't pick her successor out of the audience right away to share some old times? "Hey, you, remember when we were both murdered in ancient Egypt? Wasn't that da bomb? Whatcha been doing lately?"

If I listed all of Browne's other false predictions, lies, and errors here, I'd have Carpal Tunnel before I was halfway done. So here are just a few of her "greatest misses":

- **She solved the 1993 World Trade Center bombing.** She actually was interviewed by the FBI, but the only suspect she could describe was "Salzeman", perhaps a reference to Emad Salem or Mohammad Salameh (if you're charitable). However, Salameh had been arrested 12 days prior to her interview.
- **Saddam Hussein wouldn't live to see his trial.**
- **She predicted 9/11.** She didn't, and the information she put on her website on 9/12 wasn't accurate either; it contained names of organizations and weapons that don't even exist.
- Clinton was falsely accused in the Lewinsky scandal.
- **Bill Bradley would win the 2000 presidential election.** He didn't even make it past the primaries.

- **Bush would bring the troops home in 2007.** Not one of the predictions she made in '06 was accurate; she actually advised people to buy property because it would be going up in value. Her predictions for '08 weren't any better; she said the auto industry would improve thanks to the introduction of new hybrids. At least she was smart enough to avoid making any stock market predictions.
- During one of several appearances on *Larry King Live*, Browne claimed to be working on numerous criminal cases, including one with Detective Stephen Xanthos of the Rumson, New Jersey, police department. She said she was getting ready to close the case. Xanthos turned out to be a *former* policeman and *former* P.I.
- **She cracked the case of a serial rapist in San Francisco in the '80s.** The extent of her participation was declaring the man's last name began with S.

When Browne is questioned about a missing or deceased loved one, she reacts almost instantaneously to whatever information is provided, as though her mind and the Great Beyond are in a neverending teleconference. This can't even be called cold reading; it's just wild-ass guessing. A woman says she has lost her mother and Sylvia automatically offers a statement that can't be refuted: "She was a beautiful woman." If she's wrong, is this woman going to admit on national television that her mother wasn't beautiful? Probably not. It's the safest possible statement Browne could utter. But sometimes this hairtrigger response doesn't work in her favour, and those occasions are very enlightening. During a taping of *Montel*, a tearful young woman with a New York accent rose to tell Sylvia that her boyfriends's body hadn't been found. Quick as a flash, Browne told her, "That's because he's in water...you can't find somebody in water". The woman looked puzzled, and for good reason: Her boyfriend died in the World Trade Center on 9/11. How did Browne get out of this one? She didn't. She continued to insist she could "see" the firefighter in water. "Is there any way he could have drowned? He says he couldn't breathe and he was filled with water." Finally she grasped at her last straw: Perhaps water from the fire hoses drowned him in the rubble.

Maybe this kind of mistake could be overlooked, if it hadn't happened *again and again* on *Montel* (and elsewhere). Just a few examples:

- The parents of a 17-year-old girl named Michelle asked Browne how she had died. "She was shot," Browne replied without hesitation.
The mother's brow furrowed. "But...she just collapsed in her room."
Again, Browne simply refused to admit any margin for error. She said *something* had hit Michelle in the chest. Told that the autopsy had revealed no external injuries, she snapped, "I don't care. Something hit her in the chest." I suspect she lost a few fans that day.
- In 2004 the mother of missing teenager Ryan Katcher was invited on *Montel* to consult Browne. 19-year-old Ryan vanished in 2000. A friend said he drove Ryan to his parents' Oakwood, Illinois home after a party and helped him lay down on the living room sofa, but by morning he was gone. His truck was also missing. Browne listened to the whole ac-

count of his disappearance, then explained that Ryan aspirated some of his vomit. Panicked, two friends dumped his body in "a metal shaft of some kind", somewhere across the state line (Linda Katcher had already told her they lived near a state border), A third friend took the truck.

In 2006, Ryan's truck was discovered at the bottom of Kickapoo State Park Pond. Apparently, he had driven himself to the area while still intoxicated and accidentally drove into the water. He drowned.

- The mother of 12-year-old Weyman Robbins asked Browne how her son died. He had been found dead in the backyard of his home in 2002, a bandana around his neck. Though the death was suspicious, investigators declared it a suicide, Browne declared that he had accidentally asphyxiated while playing the "choking game" with three other boys, and the boys didn't want to step forward.

In the end, private investigators hired by Misty Robbins found the killer: Her own brother, who had been living with her for seven years.

If there's anything worse than telling parents their child is dead, it's offering 75 false hope to people that their missing loved ones are alive. As mentioned in Part I,

- On a 2001 *Montel*, the daughters of Lynda McClelland asked Sylvia what happened to her. Lynda disappeared from her home in Forest Hills, Pennsylvania in 2000, shortly after visiting with her daughter Amanda and Amanda's husband, David. Browne instantly announced that Lynda was still alive, which sent Marcie into tears. Browne went on to say that Lynda had gone crazy, and was taken to Florida by a man with the initials M.J. She advised the young women to check all the mental health facilities in Orlando. Two years later, David Repaskey (Amanda's husband) told an acquaintance that he had been having an affair with his mother-in-law. When she threatened to tell Amanda about it, he strangled her and stomped on her throat until she was dead. He and friend Donald Wall, who were both involved in a burglary ring, then buried Lynda on a hillside close to the home of David's grandmother. She never had a chance to go to Florida,
- As mentioned in Part I, Browne told the grandmother of missing 6-year-old Opal Jennings that Opal had been sold into white slavery and was still alive in a nonexistent place called "Kukouro or Kukoura", Japan. One year later, Richard Lee Franks (a sex offender with no known ties to white slavery or Japan), was convicted of kidnapping Opal, Three years after that, the little girl's body was found roughly 13 miles from her grandparents' home. She had been murdered within hours of her abduction,
- In 1995, 23-year-old Holly Krewson went missing from La Mesa, California. In 2002, Brown told Gwendolyn Krewson that her daughter was working as a stripper in Hollywood, California. In 2006, the body of a Jane Doe found near Descanso in 1996 was finally identified as Holly's. Sadly, Gwendolyn had died three years earlier.

Knowing her track record, another of Browne's *Montel* guesses seems almost as unconscionable as her location of missing people. A woman (incidentally, the same one who was told her mother was "beautiful") asked Browne what her mother had been trying to tell her as she lay dying in hospital. "This is not easy to tell ya, but your father is not your father," Browne said. She didn't appear to find this difficult to say.

Despite all these disastrous errors, a few fans of Browne have tried to rehabilitate her public image by posting video clips of notable successes. In one instance, she supposedly helped a woman locate a ring owned by her late sister. She also guessed that Chandra Levy would be found in the park where she was last seen.

Browne's biggest mistake, from a PR point of view, involved the disappearance of Shawn Hornbeck. The boy's mother and stepdad, Pam and Craig Akers, turned to Sylvia Browne in their desperation. The 11-year-old had gone missing the previous year, en route to a friend's house, and there were no clues to his disappearance. On a 2003 *Montel*, Browne solemnly informed the Akers that their son had been murdered by a Hispanic-looking man with dredlocks. His body was in a wooded area about 20 miles southwest of their Missouri home, near two boulders. When she heard this news, Pam Akers lowered her head and began to sob. She had always held out hope that her son was alive. "Hearing that was one of the hardest things we've ever had to hear," Craig Akers said. Hornbeck was found three years later, living in the apartment of the man who abducted him. Michael J. Devlin is not Hispanic and never had dredlocks. This miss attracted a huge amount media attention, and may have been more damaging to Browne's image than any other colossal mistake of her career. Her days as a psychic detective are effectively over.

Still, she tried to save face. Asked by the producers of CNN's *360 with Anderson Cooper* to provide documentation that she had actually solved hundreds of cases, as she claims, Browne provided little more than two testimonial letters from people to whom she had given psychic readings over the phone. One was from Sharon James, a woman who paid $700 to ask for Browne's help in finding her missing son in 2003. She was assured that the young man was living in Tennessee, suffering schizophrenia. Two years after James wrote the letter, her son reappeared. He had not lived in Tennessee at any time, and had no mental illnesses.

80   The second most damaging error of Browne's career was made on the January 4-5, 2006 broadcast of the paranormal radio show *Coast to Coast AM*. Soon after rescuers reached the 13 men trapped in West Virginia's Sago mine and it was reported that 12 of them were alive, Browne informed host George Noory that she had known all of the miners would be found.

"That's what I said," Browne told Noory, without a hint of surprise in her voice. Noory accepts his guests' stories of alien abduction, time travel, and Bigfoot encounters, but even he couldn't let Browne's comments slide a short time later, when it was learned the reports had been in error: 12 men died, only one survived. He bluntly asked Browne to explain herself. Rather than give herself a graceful out by explaining that her powers are far from perfect, she actually tried to convince the listeners that she had correctly predicted the deaths. "I said they would be *found.* I didn't say dead or alive." Well, of course people trapped in a mine would be found. Who needs a psychic celebrity to tell them that?

How has Browne gotten away with this for so many years? For one thing, people are reluctant to criticize Browne because she cloaks her psychic ability in the language of religion, referring to it as a gift from God. Her publicist calls her a "spiritual teacher" and a humanitarian. It's far easier to criticize a psychic detective who says "I find stuff' than it is to criticize one who says, "I was sent by God to help you." Nonetheless, some brave souls have confronted Browne's nonsense over the years. Robert Lancaster started the website Stop Sylvia Browne, which contains many negative testimonials from people who paid for Browne's phone readings. James Randi urged her to take his Million Dollar Challenge to prove her psychic abilities (she initially agreed, then backed down with a long string of flimsy excuses).

As for law enforcement, conspiracy theorist Ted Gunderson (known for his outrageous and entirely insupportable statements about Satanic crime) is one of the only former law enforcement agents to provide a testimonial for Browne, calling her "probably one of the most accurate psychics in the country."

Sadly, he could be right.

Arthur Price Roberts

Roberts was one of America's first psychic detectives. Little is known about him, the main source of information being Frank Edwards' book *Strange People* (Lyle Stuart, 1986). Edwards reports that Roberts remained illiterate throughout his life because he feared that learning would dilute his gifts, which he used to predict disasters and identify criminals in the '30s. In 1935, Roberts warned Milwaukee police: "Going to be lots of bombings – dynamitings! I see two banks blown up and perhaps the city hall. Going to blow up police stations. Then there's going to be a big blowup south of the Menomonee river and it'll be all over." Edwards writes, "As Roberts was known for his predictions, extra precautions were taken. Eight days later the village hall was blasted to bits. Two people died and others were injured. The next day the dynamiters blew up two Milwaukee banks and two police stations. In spite of extra patrols, a sixth explosion took place. It was heard up to eight miles away. The garage where it had been centered was obliterated. Two young men, Hugh Rotkowski, and Paul Chovaonee, were inside when the fifty pounds of dynamite for their sixth bomb accidentally detonated." These bombings *did* occur, but Edwards got many of the details wrong. There is no indication that Milwaukee authorities were in any way prepared for the bombings, and the bombers were Isador "Idzi" Rutkowski and Paul "Shrimp" Chovenec. With information about Roberts being so scarce and unreliable, it would be foolish to declare the case an example of successful psychic detection. Likewise, Edwards' descriptions of Roberts' other cases are too vague for them to be identified and confirmed.

Chris Robinson

85 British psychic Chris Robinson, a former janitor, sees visions of future crimes and disasters in his dreams with 50% accuracy. He claims to have predicted several IRA attacks of the early '90s, 9/11, Chernobyl, deaths in his family, etc. All are unconfirmed. You'd think that years ago he would have started recording his dreams and secreting his predictions in a secure location in front of witnesses, to be confirmed later. Somehow he just never got around to doing that. Futurist and paranormal enthusiast John Peterson's Arlington Institute is attempting to do something similar with its online "Whether Map", but it's not operative yet. In the meantime, Robinson hopes that we'll take his word for it all.

Robinson calls himself a dream detective, and couches his abilities in Christian terms (though not as strongly as Sylvia Browne does). However, Chris openly admits that his gifts really aren't of much benefit to society yet. From his website: "At first I was accepted by Scotland Yard and other local police forces as being a credible source of information even though it was impossible most of the time to act in a meaningful way to prevent the crimes foreseen taking place. This proved to be very frustrating and after 10 years of the authorities monitoring and working with me there [sic] interest faded. The reason was that no academics in the UK or elsewhere seemed remotely interested in working with people like me on research into this subject." I think it's much simpler than that: Chris's tips weren't useful in preventing crime, and the tests he has undergone produced unimpressive results.

In 2001 Chris traveled to Arizona to be tested by University of Arizona professor Gary L. Schwartz, and produced what he considered decent results. But when Richard Wiseman and Dr Susan Blackmore tested him in controlled experiments, his performance was lackluster (and that's being generous). Chris seems to believe he was a success despite the poor results, and blames his failures on skeptics. One has to wonder why he bothers subjecting himself to tests at all, since he summarily rejects all scientific psi testing that does not support his own conclusions. For instance, on his website he promotes "the girl with X-ray eyes", who has also failed miserably at tests of her superpowers.

Allison DuBois

To be blunt, Allison DuBois is barely worth mentioning here. Her mediumistic experiences and her "internship" in the Homicide division of her local district attorney's office in Pheonix have been the subject of her three books, *Don't Kiss Them Good-bye*, *Secrets of the Monarch*, and the weirdly titled *We Are Their Heaven* (really? dead people have nothing better to do than watch us get on with our boring lives?), and Gary L. Schwartz vouches for her abilities as a psychic. She was the inspiration for the popular TV series *Medium*. But unlike Patricia Arquette's character, DuBois admits her information usually doesn't solve crimes. Some of the law enforcement agencies she claims to have worked with have declared she had no involvement with their cases, and others say she didn't provide any useful information. It's quite telling that Pheonix investigators never turn to her for help. Detective Alex Femenia denies she provided any useful information in one of her few claimed successes, the Baseline rapist case. Her insights into high-profile cases are less than astonishing (she told MSNBC she saw Natalee Holloway "near the water", which is an outrageously safe bet when someone disappears on an island). In short, her image as a psychic soccer mom and a "criminal profiler" doesn't seem earned.

Mary Ann Morgan

Morgan is a trim, middled-aged blonde best known for her involvement in the Laci Peterson case (the Petersons hired several psychics in an effort to find "the real killer", including Noreen Renier and a pet psychic who interviewed the only living witness in the case - Laci's dog). On an installment of *Psychic Detectives*, she was credited with locating the body of Loretta Bowersock in the Arizona desert, Bowersock's boyfriend, Taw Benderly, claimed that she vanished while they were passing through Pheonix en route to their home in California. There were some holes in his story, big enough to arouse suspicion, but his suicide took him out of the running as the prime suspect. The case remains officially unsolved.

Moore was brought into the case by Loretta's daughter, Terri. Though Terri gives some credit to several of the psychics she hired, including Morgan, her account of the case makes it clear that psychic Tammy Holmes was actually the one who contributed most to the discovery of Loretta's body. Holmes was in such close contact with the spirit of Ms. Bowersock that she was able to tell Terri a little of what to expect in heaven: free purses.

Morgan also inserted herself into the Natalee Holloway case, accompanying Texus EquuSearch to Aruba. She pinpointed an area of ocean in which Natalee's body had been dumped, and since her information dovetailed with the fact that a cage used by fisherman had been stolen around the time of Natalee's disappearance, divers from EquuSearch and the University of Florida scoured the spot. Nothing was found. Dave Holloway says some of the information Morgan provided about the night his daughter died seemed accurate, but notes, "the jury is out until she finds my daughter." (1)

Annette Martin

Once an opera singer, Martin promotes herself as a "medical intuitive", a psychic detective, *and* a ghostbuster. As a detective, she runs a psychic detective agency called Closure4U. Sgt.

Detective Richard Keaton of the Marin County Sheriffs Department vouches for her help in solving cases, notably the disappearance of an elderly former paratrooper named Dennis Prado. On a map, she circled a small area of a park in which he was believed to be, and he was found within that area, but as in so many "psychic detective" cases her reading did not actually lead to the discovery of Prado's body. Skeptic Joe Nickell pointed out to *48 Hours* that Martin was able to draw lots of useful information from the police prior to drawing her circle. As a medical intuitive, she channels the spirit of famed psychic healer Edgar Cayce. Martin has had a long string of claimed successes over the past three decades, and has been involved with a few high-profile cases in California. Information on her cases is extremely sparse, and like Chris Robinson she doesn't record any of her predictions for future confirmation. She claims she foresaw the death of John Denver in a plane crash 15 years before it happened, when he came to her for a reading, but has nothing to back up her story. She can't even prove he consulted her.

95   Perhaps the strangest moment in Martin's career: She became the first psychic to testify in a criminal trial when she testified for the defense in the Susan Polk murder trial. Polk, a deeply disturbed and delusional woman, was representing herself after her lawyer's wife was brutally murdered by a neighbor boy. She accused him of doing the deed himself. She also insisted that there was a conspiracy among friends and neighbors to frame her for Dr. Polk's murder; later, after her conviction, she admitted that she had stabbed him "in self-defense".

Martin came into the picture because Polk was trying to convince the jury she was psychic, and that Felix routinely drugged and hypnotized her in order to obtain accurate forecasts of world events. In this way, he found out about 9/11 in advance and told Israel's Mossad about it. You see, Susan insisted her husband was a Mossad agent even though he had no known connections to the intelligence agency, never worked in a government capacity, and had never even been to Israel. (I've written about some of Susan Polk's other delusions and allegations here.) Judge Laurel S. Brady called the psychic issue "tangentially relevant" to the case (2), but I think she was far too generous. Remember, Susan Polk was arguing that she had nothing whatsoever to do with her husband's death, so his alleged hypnosis sessions didn't have any bearing on Susan's guilt or innocence.

Martin's testimony consisted only of a rundown of her own work as a psychic detective; she was not allowed to weigh in on the reality of psychic phenomena. She said she had assisted in about 100 criminal cases and was successful in all of them, but didn't provide any specifics.

One-Time Psychics

There have been numerous instances of non-psychics receiving flashes of insight that enable them to find a body, solve a murder, or locate a missing person. These cases are far more baffling than those of psychic detectives, because the non-psychics involved typically don't continue to solve crimes after their experiences; they're one-off events. The strangest such case occurred in 1980, when Los Angeles nurse Melanie Uribe went missing. A woman named Etta Smith told investigators she "sensed" Melanie's body was in Lopez Canyon, but her information was ignored. So she went to the canyon on her own, and "felt" her way around until she discovered the body. Naturally, she was considered a suspect in the murder until three men were arrested and charged. In cases like this, it's entirely possible that the person has gained information about a crime through normal means, such as gossip, acquaintance with the criminal(s) or someone close to the crime, etc., and simply doesn't want to admit it. It's also possible that once in a while, out of the blue, someone receives a message from a place or a time we don't even know about yet.

JOE NICKELL

Scientific Investigation vs. Ghost Hunters

I have often crossed paths with The Atlantic Paranormal Society (T.A.P.S.), headed by Jason Hawes and Grant Wilson, stars of the popular Ghost Hunters series on Syfy (formerly the Sci-Fi Channel). On Saturday, July 26, 2008, my wife, Diana Harris, and I attended their presentation at Lily Dale, the spiritualist village in Western New York. Jason and Grant were kind enough to single me out—favorably—during their talk, and I accepted their invitation for a beer afterward. They graciously bestowed on me an autographed copy of their book Ghost Hunting: True Stories of Unexplained Phenomena from the Atlantic Paranormal Society, produced with, well, ghostwriter Michael Jan Friedman (Hawes and Wilson 2007). Interestingly, Friedman authors "science fiction and fantasy novels."

The book gave me a chance to compare notes with Hawes and Wilson. Because I had preceded them in examining several of the "haunted" places featured on the show, I was able to contrast my findings with theirs. Our mutual cases include The Myrtles Plantation (in St. Francisville, Louisiana), the Winchester Mystery House (San Jose, California), and the St. Augustine Lighthouse (on Florida's east coast).

The Myrtles

Located in the Louisiana bayou, The Myrtles Plantation is actively promoted by its owners as a haunted place. Indeed, says Jason, "Grant and I could barely contain ourselves. The Myrtles was known as one of the most haunted places in America. It was every paranormal investigator's dream to check the place out" (Hawes and Wilson 2007, 137). Well, I had been there, done that—courtesy of the Discovery Channel for a documentary.

In February 2005, the T.A.P.S. team got off to a good start at The Myrtles. They were shown a "ghost" photo, but it had been so enhanced by a "paranormal guy" that they promptly labeled it "tampered." But then came the incident with the lamp: In the plantation's "slave shack" (a structure of recent vintage that never held a slave), a lamp glided eerily across a table behind the pair while they were on camera. Although they conceded that "Grant might have snagged the lamp cord with his foot and dragged it without knowing it," the pair later decided to attribute this incident only to "a supernatural force" (Hawes and Wilson 2007, 146). Unfortunately, as reported by Television Week (Hibbard 2005, 19), "Upon close inspection, fans concluded the lamp was being pulled by its own cord. Even worse: a night-vision shot appears to show the cord extending from behind the table to Mr. Wilson's hand." Yet Grant maintained, "If we were looking for a sign that we were doing something worthwhile, we couldn't have asked for a better one than the lamp." The pair concluded, "The place was haunted" (Hawes and Wilson 2007, 146, 147).

In my own investigation at The Myrtles (including staying alone overnight there August 14–15, 2001), I had reached a very different conclusion about the place. Although its owners and staff hype the tale of a murderous slave named Chloe—a "legend" that Hawes and Wilson repeat in some detail—my research revealed Chloe to be fictitious and the tale not folklore but fakelore. Ghostly phenomena reported at the site can be explained without invoking the supernatural. For instance, a mysteriously swinging door was simply hung off center, and banging noises heard at night were attributable to a loose shutter (Nickell 2003).

[handwritten margin notes: "okay... but... why?" and "more here"]

Winchester Mystery House

San Jose's Winchester Mystery House is remarkable indeed. Even after the Gothic Victorian mansion was greatly reduced in size by the 1906 San Francisco earthquake, eccentric widow Sarah Winchester continued to add to the architectural wonder until her death in 1922. At that time it contained 160 rooms and included bizarre architectural details such as stairways that led nowhere. Legend holds that a Boston spirit medium had directed Mrs. Winchester to go West and build, without ceasing, a home for spirits. This was to halt an alleged curse on the Winchesters resulting from the "terrible weapon" (the repeating firearm) they had produced.

Jason and Grant retell the legend without skepticism, although the tale is unproved and exists in many contradictory versions. Neither is there any real evidence that Mrs. Winchester was herself a spiritualist. Indeed her close companion for years, Henrietta Severs, denied that she was (Rambo 1967, 8).

Visiting the mansion in July 2005, Hawes and Wilson (2007, 225–29) "didn't find anything of a supernatural origin"—and even concluded that "odd banging sounds" were probably "the result of a plumbing problem." Nevertheless, they and their T.A.P.S. team continued their pseudoscientific approach to ghost hunting (Hawes and Wilson 2007, 225–29). That is, they relied heavily on alleged ghost-detecting equipment that does not, in fact, detect ghosts. A reading on an electromagnetic field (EMF) meter, for instance, can be caused by faulty wiring, microwaves, solar activity, or any of a number of other non-ghostly sources. There is no credible scientific evidence that ghosts exist, let alone that they are electromagnetic—or radioactive: the T.A.P.S. team also on occasion uses a "portable Geiger counter" (Ghost 2006). Other ghost-hunting equipment is similarly useless, especially in the hands of non-scientists (Nickell 2006). I investigated the Winchester Mansion in 2001 (with colleague Vaughn Rees) and found that temperature variations, the settling of an old structure, and other similar characteristics accounted for cold spots, odd noises, and ghostly phenomena (Nickell 2002). I have learned that people's level of ghost experiences is approximately proportional to their psychological tendency to fantasize (Nickell 2000)—evidence for psychologist Robert A. Baker's wise saying that there are no haunted places, "only haunted people."

[handwritten margin note: "evidence"]

St. Augustine Lighthouse

Among the tallest such structures in the United States, the St. Augustine lighthouse is claimed to feature, in the keeper's dwelling, a girl in a red dress who suddenly vanishes and the lingering smell of cigar smoke. In the tower, various unexplained noises are often perceived (Elizabeth and Roberts 1999, 40–49).

Once again, the T.A.P.S. team lugged in the fancy equipment on which 10 their pseudoscientific approach to ghost hunting depends. They placed a wireless audio unit up in the tower; at the bottom, a thermal camera was positioned to shoot upward "just to see what we could pick up" (Hawes and Wilson 2007, 234–35). The team claims to have seen a shadowy figure and heard a woman's cry as they went up the stairs. Jason ran toward it but "couldn't catch more than a glimpse of the dark figure" as he gained the stairs (2007, 236). Afterward, their "video footage clearly showed a shadow at the top of the stairs. A moment later, we heard a female voice crying for help, and saw the shadow dart to the right" (2007, 238). They concluded that the St. Augustine Lighthouse was indeed haunted.

That lighthouse was one of several I investigated for my Skeptical Inquirer article "Lighthouse Specters" (Nickell 2008). (My wife and I even stayed as "assistant keepers" at a couple of remote sites.) On March 23, 2004, I climbed the 219 steps to check out the St. Augustine Lighthouse's tower and also explored the keeper's house. The occasional perception of cigar smoke in the latter may have a ready explanation. There is often confusion as to the true nature of the smoke (attributed alternately to cigars, cigarettes, burning wiring, etc.), and real smoke can drift inside or its smell be carried in on people's clothing (Nickell 2008, 24–25). The power of suggestion may be at work as well.

Apparitions at "haunted" sites are also explainable. For example, private citizens who rented the St. Augustine keeper's dwelling (after the light was automated in 1955) sometimes woke to see a young girl at their bedside (Elizabeth and Roberts 1999, 44). Such sightings are easily explained scientifically as "waking dreams," which occur in the state between sleep and wakefulness. Similarly, apparitions may occur when the percipient is in an altered mental state, such as daydreaming, and a mental image becomes superimposed on the visual scene (Nickell 2008, 22–23).

As to noises in the tower, there are a number of plausible explanations, beginning with the wind. Indeed, Hawes and Wilson themselves found one culprit in the form of a window "free to swing with the wind" (Hawes and Wilson 2007, 235). Temperature changes can also cause old steel to make noises as it expands and contracts (Thompson 1998, 73). One such screeching sound was interpreted as "a female voice crying for help" (Hawes and Wilson 2007, 238). (Another possibility is seagulls; the birds may "shriek" and "sound almost like humans screaming" [Vercillo 2008, 50].)

Glimpsed shadows might have an equally simple explanation. I studied the T.A.P.S. team's St. Augustine Lighthouse video episode (Ghost 2006) with two colleagues, Tim Binga and Tom Flynn, and all of us were underwhelmed. Flynn, CFI's video expert, summed up the evidence by stating: "These visual effects are so ambiguous that they may signify nothing at all." He added, "The observed effect might even be the shadows of the ghost hunters themselves as they moved about, several landings below" (Flynn 2009).

***

As this comparison of cases shows, the approach of so-called "ghost hunters" is simply one of mystery mongering. Like claims for the paranormal in general, their assertions that certain places are haunted are based on the logical fallacy of arguing from ignorance: "We don't know what caused such-and-such (a noise, say), so it must have been a ghost." In fact, one cannot draw a conclusion from a lack of knowledge. The problem is exacerbated by the pseudoscientific use of scientific equipment and by the distinct possibility that ghost hunters are actually causing—even if unintentionally—some of the very phenomena they are experiencing!

In contrast is the scientific investigator's approach: begin with the phenomenon in question, try to ascertain whether it in fact happened, develop hypotheses to explain it, and seek to find the most likely explanation—keeping in mind that one cannot explain one mystery by attributing it to another.

CHAPTER 14

HUMOR

Overview

Is laughter the best medicine? Certainly, we all love to laugh. Whether or not scientific evidence supports the healing effects of laughter, we seem to be cheerier and livelier after seeing a comedy act, recounting old stories with friends, or watching televised satires of the day's news. What produces laughter, though? What constitutes humor? We differentiate between funny and not-so-funny, between tired gags and fresh material, but have we ever stopped to think about how we make these distinctions?

As an undergraduate, I took several literature courses from a professor who used humor effectively. Dr. Lane combined sarcasm with clever observations about humanity, making his humor relevant to our reading. Yet, he was also sensitive to the plight of others and could make stinging critiques about sexism and war. I was never confused about when he meant to be funny and when he meant to be serious.

In the last course I took from Dr. Lane, a student in the back row tried to match wits with him. During every class, or so it seemed, this student cracked jokes or punned based on remarks Dr. Lane made. The student was not disruptive or disrespectful, but his attempts at humor never received more than some smiles or light chuckles. His jokes stunk. I consistently felt embarrassed for him and wanted to laugh just to relieve the tension. His sense of humor just did not match my own or, apparently, anyone else's. Dr. Lane started making jokes in response, trying to rescue some sort of humor

[handwritten margin note: things that resonate with us are funniest]

[handwritten annotation: circled "relevant"]

Online Study Center

This icon will direct you to web links and additional resources on the website http://college.cengage.com/english/thelin/writing_without_formulas/1e/student_home.html

355

in the student's failed witticisms, but other students started groaning at the exchanges. Dr. Lane eventually steered the class back to the original conversation and tried to avoid embarrassing the student. It seemed, though, that Dr. Lane called on the student less and less.

Toward the end of the semester, it occurred to me that the student's failed humor came not from a lack of cleverness but rather from a limited sense of his audience. In other words, the rest of us in the class did not share his viewpoints. In another context, he might have been very funny.

In one of Dr. Lane's classes, we discussed Carolyn Forché's prose poem, "The Colonel." Forché recounts the terror she felt at a Latin American colonel who showed her the severed ears of his human victims, shook one of the ears in Forché's face, and placed the ear in a glass of water—all while Forché sat at his table immediately after having dined with him. Hearing this, we were horrified and could feel her fear for her own safety. The student who thought he was funny quipped, as I remember the remark, "Bet she didn't have dinner there again." His words might have been greeted with laughter in a different context, but he had seriously misjudged his immediate audience's sympathy for Forché's situation. Forché was not a character or caricature we needed to laugh at to distance ourselves from the unpleasantness of the situation. The student, therefore, came across as being insensitive or worse.

An attempt at humor that extended the cruelty of the colonel to ridiculous extremes, or that understated his crudeness to the point of absurdity, or that cut him down in some way might have worked. In such a joke, we would have seen sensitivity toward a basic code of right and wrong, and it would have lightened a grim moment. We can see an attempt in the student's joke to intentionally misunderstand the situation to reveal how ludicrous the dinner table scene actually must have been. But Forché's persona in the poem did not lend itself to ridicule of her actions unless we had a viewpoint, as perhaps the student did, that she was naïve or foolish for having dinner with the colonel.

Humor does not have to have underlying sensitivity to succeed, but the audience must perceive the target of the joke as deserving of scorn or ridicule. Successful comedians understand dominant ideology. By this I mean that they understand assumptions that are shared by the majority of the audience members. When people accuse a comedian of telling "tasteless" jokes, that comedian has, essentially, misunderstood the audience's assumptions, as discussed in Chapter 3. Of course, some comedians thrive on offensive humor—but so do their particular audiences.

The dearth of comedy routines about the terrorist attacks in New York and Washington, D.C., on September 11, 2001, is an example of understanding assumptions. No comedians tried to lighten the mood with jokes about the victims, the firefighters and police officers who rescued victims or became victims themselves, or affected family members. Few audiences would have seen these people as deserving of scorn and ridicule. Instead, jokes revolved around what was going to happen to the perpetrators, around the ethnicity of the hijackers, and, eventually, around criticism of the government's handling of the situation. The ideology behind patriotism imposed limits on humor.

pause for discussion

If humor is linked to ideology, does humor reflect what society deems acceptable? How might humor reveal the dominant tensions in our culture? Many of us might not want to expose these hidden implications of humor. Yet, the connection exists. While juvenile bathroom humor reflects the tensions of adolescence, we can also see how natural functions of the body, such as flatulence and sexual stimulation, have been stigmatized in our culture so that they seem unnatural. In this type of humor, we can see the tension between appropriate societal behavior—not mentioning bodily functions—and what is apparent to every human being—how our bodies work. The tension produces the laughter. *→so similar to Mort. Nat.*

Comedians often make use of political tensions. Audiences seem to gain power from satire over dominant political discourse. Political comedians express publicly repressed angers and show the absurdity of decision making at the highest levels of government.

The Daily Show, for example, a parody of daily news shows, magnifies the inconsistencies in government leaders' speeches to poke fun at political figures as well as to make a point. In December 2006 there was much division in the government about withdrawing troops from Iraq. On December 4, Jon Stewart, the host of *The Daily Show*, engaged in a dialogue with the show's "senior foreign policy analyst," John Oliver, to supposedly interpret the president's strategy for the direction of the war. Oliver exaggerated the implications in President Bush's speeches by saying that Bush believed in fighting until the last possible second, "giving armed conflict every chance to succeed until all violent means have been utterly exhausted." Only then, according to Oliver, would Bush give "the grim task of talking" a chance. The segment was funny to those frustrated with the direction of the war and needing an outlet. *hyperbole ✓*

Many jokes that circulate on the Internet use gender and race. While the gender jokes sometimes center on crude sexual innuendo, many of them seek humor by exploiting gender stereotypes. Women forward lists of behaviors supposedly common to married men, such as leaving underwear everywhere but in the hamper. Men forward lists of the ten things married women do not need but stereotypically crave, such as twenty pairs of shoes. We seem to be able to laugh at ourselves in these caricatures. Do they suggest a truth or a conflict that we wrestle with? Race-based jokes, which often mock stereotypical attributes, evoke a different level of discomfort. An audience's involuntary laughter at such jokes shows an understanding of the stereotypes, but how much deeper does the understanding go? Does the audience unconsciously accept that a certain ethnic group is deserving of scorn or ridicule?

To analyze humor means to take a hard look at our beliefs and conduct. Why do some people find redneck jokes funny? Do the jokes not hinge on the poverty and struggles for dignity many working-class people endure? Jokes about blonde women should make us question why people need to see others as stupid. Gags about nerds should likewise make us wonder about our values and our need to conform to the standards of certain cliques. Humor based on obesity or other perceived physical defects could be a sign of how deeply media-generated images of beauty have corrupted our sensitivity to differing understandings of attractiveness. Perhaps we deflect some of our inner fears by targeting others.

No matter what conclusions we arrive at, humor cannot be considered innocent. While we need to laugh, our view of the world directs what we laugh at.

Openings for Writers

1. **Comedians** Identify comedians you find especially funny. Write about a routine by one of these comedians that exemplifies his or her humor. What was the subject matter in the routine? Can you identify a targeted group of people? If you saw the performance live or on film, how did the audience react?

2. **Puns** What is a pun? Do you ever find puns funny? Describe what a pun is, give examples of a few puns, and consider what makes them funny or unfunny. How does your reaction to puns reflect your sense of humor and even your worldview?

3. **Teaching and humor** Reflect on some of the best classroom experiences you can remember that involved humor. Do you distinguish between teachers who share humor with a class and teachers who use humor at the expense of students? Support your answer with specific examples. It might help to look at David Sedaris's "Me Talk Pretty One Day" (page 372) to see an example of a teacher who belittles her adult students with sarcasm.

4. **Humor and tragedy** Some people believe that the passing of time allows us to start laughing at incidents that were not funny when they occurred. At what point can you start making jokes about a painful or traumatic event? Have you had uncomfortable moments when you wanted to laugh at another person's misfortune? What happened, and how did both of you feel? Would your reactions have been more appropriate if they had come later?

Language

1. **Ridicule** What criteria do you associate with the term *ridicule*? Can you differentiate ridicule from humor? Are they related?

2. **Crudeness** What values do we as a community hold that allow us to designate some humor as crude and other humor as "clean"? In the overview's use of this term, do you sense any lines that a writer won't cross? If so, what are those lines, and how do they affect the writer's main ideas? If not, how does the designation of some humor as crude function in the other observations in the overview?

3. **Satire** Do you associate satire with political bias? Does it always function to critique or to undermine power? How does it differ from ridicule?

4. **Stereotypes** The word *stereotype* has negative connotations for most people. Describe these connotations. Can the word ever be viewed in a positive light? We all have seen connections between stereotypes and humor. What makes comedians' use of stereotypes acceptable and, at times, successful?

JOYCE CAROL OATES

Is Laughter Contagious?

This short story asks us to question the appropriateness and inappropriateness of certain types of social behavior, including laughter. Mrs. Delahunt tries to suppress giggling and chortles during a series of situations in which laughter might be seen as cruelty. Her lack of tact at the end and the readers' reaction raises issues about humor and its human targets.

Is laughter contagious? Driving on North Pearl Street, Franklin Village, Mrs. D. began suddenly to hear laughter on all sides, a wash of laughter gold-spangled like coins, just perceptibly louder issuing from the rear of her car, and she found herself smiling, her brooding thoughtful expression erased as if by force, on the verge of spontaneous laughter herself, for isn't there a natural buoyancy to the heart when we hear laughter? even, or particularly, the laughter of strangers? even an unexpected, inexplicable, mysterious laughter?—though Mrs. D. understood that the laughter surrounding her was in no way mysterious, at least its source was in no way mysterious, for, evidently, she had forgotten to switch off the car radio the last time she had driven the car, and the laughter was issuing from the radio's speakers, the most powerful of which was in the rear of the Mercedes.

What were they laughing about, these phantom radio-people?

Men's laughter?—and, here and there, the isolated sound of a woman's higher-pitched laughter?—delicious, cascading, like a sound of icicles touching?

Though laughing by this time herself, Mrs. D., who was a serious person, with a good deal on her mind—and most of it private, secret, not to be shared even with Mr. D.—switched the radio off, preferring silence.

There.

Christine Delahunt. Thirty-nine years old. Wife, mother. Recently re- 5 turned to work—a "career." A woman of moral scruples, but not prim, puritanical, dogmatic. Isn't that how Mrs. D. has defined herself to herself? Isn't Mrs. D., in so defining herself, one of us?—determined, for no reason we can understand, to define ourselves to—ourselves?

As if we doubt that anyone else is concerned?

Mrs. D. was to tell us, certain of her friendly acquaintances. Last Thursday it seemed to begin. Did others in Franklin Village notice—that afternoon, sometime before six o'clock? The time of suburban car-errands, family-tasks, last-minute shopping, and pickups at the dry cleaners and drugstore, the pace of the waning day quickening, yes and Thursday is the day-preceding-Friday, when the week itself notoriously quickens, a panic-sensation to it, as a river seemingly placid and navigable begins to accelerate, visibly, as it approaches a cataract—though there is, yet, no clear sign of danger? no reason for alarm?

10   Outbursts of laughter. Gay infectious laughter. In the Franklin Food Mart, our "quality" grocery store, at one of the checkout counters when the deaf-and-dumb packer wearing the badge FRITZ (pasty-skinned, in his fifties; the Franklin Food Mart is one of several area businesses that have "made it a policy" to employ the handicapped) spilled a bag of fresh produce onto the floor, and Washington State winesaps, bright-dyed Florida navel oranges, hairy-pungent little kiwi-fruit, several pygmy-heads of Boston lettuce, a dozen Idaho red potatoes, a single California melon—all went tumbling, rolling, startling yet comical as the deaf-and-dumb packer gaped and blinked, standing frozen in a kind of terror that for all its public expression seemed to us, witnessing, to be private, thus somehow funnier, and the very customer who had paid extravagant prices for these items laughed, if a bit angrily; and other customers, seeing, burst into laughter, too; and the checkout cashier, and other cashiers, and employees of the store, peering over, craning their necks to see what the commotion is, their laughter tentative at first since the look in poor Fritz's eyes *was* terror wasn't it?—then exploding forth, an honest, candid, gut-laughter, not malicious surely, but, yes, *loud!*

Mrs. D. was at an adjacent checkout counter, methodically making out a check to the Franklin Food Mart, a weekly custom this is, perhaps it might better be called a blood-sacrifice, this week's check for—how can it be? $328.98 for an unexceptional week's shopping? for a family of four? no supplies for a dinner party? no beer, wine, liquor? not even any seafood? making out the check with resigned fingers when she heard the strange laughter rising around her, rising, erupting, childlike raucous laughter, and turning, smiling, wanting to join in, Mrs. D. saw the cause—a bag of groceries had overturned, things were rolling on the floor, and that look on that poor man's face, it *was* amusing, but Mrs. D. suppressed laughter for, oh dear, really it *wasn't* amusing, not at all, that poor man backing off and staring at the produce on the floor, paralyzed as everyone laughed so cruelly, what are people thinking of? how can it be? in the Franklin Food Mart of all places?

Are the Delahunts neighbors of ours? Not exactly.

We don't have "neighbors," in the old sense of that word, in Franklin Village. Our houses are constructed on three- and four-acre lots, which means considerable distance between houses, and with our elaborate landscaping (trees of all varieties, shrubs, twelve-foot redwood fences, electrically charged wire-mesh "deer-deterrent" fences) it's possible for the residents of one house to be unable to glimpse even the facade of the house next door, certainly it's possible to go for years without glimpsing the faces of the people who live next door, unless, of course, and this is frequently the case, we encounter one another socially—on neutral territory, you might say. Nor have we sidewalks in residential Franklin Village. Nor have we streets, in the old sense of that word—we have "lanes," we have "drives," we have "passes," "circles," "courts," even "ways," but we do not have "streets."

Are Mr. and Mrs. Delahunt friends of ours? Not exactly.

15   We don't have "friends," in the old sense of that word, in Franklin Village. Most of us are relatively new here, and a number of us are scheduled to

move soon. Spring is the busiest time for moving! (Of course there are residents in this area who are known as "old-time." Who can recall, for instance, when the Franklin Hills Shopping Mall was nothing but an immense tract of open, wild, useless land, and when Main Street in the Village was residential from Pearl Street onward, and when Route 26 was a mere country highway!) Thus the majority of us make no claims to have (or to be) "friends"—but we *are* "friendly acquaintances" of one another and we *are* social. Very!

The Delahunts, Mr. and Mrs., became friendly acquaintances of ours within days of their arrival. They are highly respected, warmly regarded, attractive, energetic, invited almost immediately to join the Franklin Hills Golf Club and the yet more prestigious Franklin Hills Tennis Club. Mr. D. moved his family here three years ago from Greenwich, Connecticut—or was it Grosse Pointe, Michigan?—when he became sales director at W.W.C. & M., and Mrs. D. has recently begun public relations work part-time, for our Republican Congressman Gordon Frayne—Gordon's the man whom the papers so frequently chide, urging him to "upscale" his image. The Delahunts live in a six-bedroom French Normandy house on Fairway Circle, their fourteen-year-old daughter, Tracey, and their eleven-year-old son, Jamey, both attend Franklin Hills Day School. Mrs. D., like many of us, tries to participate in parent-teacher activities at the school, but—when on earth is there *time!*

"Upscaling" Gordon Frayne's image is a challenge, Mrs. D. laughingly, if somewhat worriedly, confesses. But Gordy Frayne—some folks even call him Gordo—wins elections. He's a big-hearted ruddy-faced shooting-from-the-hip character, often in the headlines and on television, one or another controversy, last year he was interviewed on network television and made a statement warning that "ethnic minorities" had better man their own oars "or the venerable Ship of State's gonna capsize and sink"—which naturally led to protests from certain quarters but a good deal of support from other quarters. Mrs. D., like other associates and friendly acquaintances of Gordon Frayne's, has learned to frown as she smiles at his witticisms, just slightly reprovingly, as Franklin Village women often do, she has unconsciously mastered this response, this facial expression, as adroitly as any professional actress—"Oh Gordy! Oh *really!*" It was at a party on Saturday night (the Saturday following the Thursday) that Gordy launched into one of his comical diatribes, the guy could have been a stand-up comedian for sure, cruel but ingenious mimicry of Jesse Jackson (an old routine, but a favorite), and the latest of his AIDS jokes . . . and most, though not all, of the company laughed, Mrs. D. among them, shocked, yes, but not wanting to be a prude, or to seem a prude; but smiling, shaking her head, avoiding the others' eyes as in a communal complicity, but thinking why, why, why, and what will come of this?

Five girls from the Franklin Hills Day School jogging on Park Ridge Road, Monday after school, pumping legs and arms, high-held heads, shorts and loose-fitting school T-shirts and identical expensive jogging shoes, and according to the girls' testimonies after the "vehicular assault" they were running single file, they were keeping to the left side of the road, facing oncoming traffic, careful to keep off the road itself and to run on the asphalt-paved

10 shoulder. As usual one of the girls was falling behind, there were three girls running close together, then, a few yards behind them, the fourth, and approximately twenty feet behind her the fifth, poor Bonnie, Bonnie S., fourteen years old, second year in the "upper form" at the Day School. Bonnie S. is a few pounds overweight, not fat, the most accurate word would be plump but who wants to be plump? who can bear to be plump? fourteen years old and plump in Franklin Village, New York?—poor Bonnie S., whom the other girls like well enough, feel sort of sorry for, she's sweet she tries so hard she's so generous but it's pathetic, Bonnie trying to keep up with the tall thin girls, the girls she envies, letting it be known at school that her problem isn't overeating it's glandular it's "genetic—like fate," and maybe that's true since none of Bonnie's classmates ever sees her eating anything other than apples, carrot sticks, narrow slices of honeydew melon, she'll devour fleshy-fruit and rind both—poor Bonnie S.! (But *is* her weight problem "glandular"? Maybe she binges?—in secret?—tries to stick her finger down her throat and vomit it up?—but can't quite *succeed?*—enough to make a difference?) In any case, there was Bonnie S. running fifth in the line of girls, breathless, clumsy, a sweaty sheen to her round flushed face, a glazed took to her damp brown eyes, and the carload of boys swerved around the curve, that curve just beyond Grouse Hill Lane, six older students from the Day School jammed together in a newly purchased white Acura. The girls could hear the radio blasting heavy-metal rock even before the car came into sight, they could hear the boys yelling and laughing as the car bore down upon them, they saw the faces of the boys in the front seat clearly, wide grins, gleeful, malicious eyes, a raised beer can or two, then the girls were screaming, scattering. It was Bonnie S. who was the target, poor Bonnie arousing male derision pumping away there twenty feet behind the others, poor plump sweaty Bonnie S. with her expression of incredulous shock and terror as the white car aimed for her, boyish-prankish braying laughter, she threw herself desperately to the left, the car skidded by, missing the screaming girl by perhaps a single inch, then righted itself, regained the road, on shrieking tires it sped away and there was Bonnie S., lying insensible in the shallow concrete drainage ditch like something tossed down, bleeding so profusely from a gash in her forehead that the first of her friends to reach her nearly fainted.

Tracey Delahunt tells her mother afterward, she'll confess to her mother solely, knowing her mother will understand, or, failing to understand—for who after all *can* understand?—will sympathize with the hungry wish to understand. "It happened so fast—oh God!—we looked back and there was Bonnie sort of *flying* off the road like something in a kid's cartoon—and it was horrible—it was just, just horrible, but—" lowering her teary eyes, thick-lashed tawny-green eyes Mrs. D. thinks are far more beautiful than her own, though closely resembling her own, "—sort of, in a way—oh God!—*comical* too."

20 Pressing her fingertips hard against her lips but unable to keep from bursting into a peal of hysterical laughter.

Three days later, the most upsetting incident of all.
Not that Mrs. D. allowed herself to think of it very much afterward.

Certainly not obsessively. She isn't that type of mother—the obsessive, neurotic mother. Fantasizing about her children, worrying, suspicious.

She'd entered the house from the rear, as usual. About to step into the kitchen when she'd overheard, coming up from the basement, the "family room" in the basement, the sound of juvenile laughter, boys' laughter, and ordinarily she would not have paused for a moment since Jamey and his friends often took over that room after school to watch videos, yes some of the videos the boys watched were questionable, yes Mrs. D. knew and, yes, she'd tried to exercise some restraint while at the same time she'd tried not to be, nor even to appear to be, censorious and interfering, but that day there was something chilling about the tone of the boys' laughter, and wasn't there, beneath it, another sound?—as of a creature *bleating?*—a queer high-pitched sound that worried Mrs. D. so she went to the door of the family room (which was shut) and pressed her ear against it, hearing the laughter, the giggling, more distinctly, and the other sound too, and carefully, almost timidly—she, Christine Delahunt, nearly forty years old, wife, mother, self-respecting surely?—self-determined surely?—opening a door timidly in her own house?—and saw there a sight that froze her in her tracks even as, in that instant, she was already shoving it from her, banishing it from her consciousness, denying its power to qualify her love for her son: for there were Jamey and several of his boy friends, eighth-graders at the Day School whose faces Mrs. D. knew well, Evan, Allen, Terry, red-haired impish Terry, and who was there with them? a girl? a stranger? and *strange?*—slightly older than the boys, with dull coarse features, eyes puckered at the corners, wet-dribbly mouth, no one Mrs. D. knew or had ever glimpsed before, and this girl was sprawled on her back on the braided "colonial"-style carpet in front of the fireplace, in the Delahunts' family room, her plump knees raised, and spread, naked from the waist down, and what was red-haired Terry doing?—poking something (too large to be a pencil, an object plastic and chunky, was it a child's play baseball bat?), or trying to poke something, into the girl's vagina?—while the other boys, as if transfixed, crouched in a circle, staring, blinking, grinning, giggling.

Mrs. D. cried, without thinking, "Oh what are you doing! Boys! Jamey! And you—you filthy, disgusting *girl!*"

Her voice was unlike any voice she'd ever heard springing from her. 25 Breathless, disbelieving, angry, wounded.

She slammed the door upon the children's startled-guilty-grinning faces and fled. Upstairs.

That evening, at dinner, not a word! not a word! not a word! to Jamey, who, frightened, subdued, ate his food almost shyly, and cast looks of appeal to Mrs. D., who behaved as—as usual?—knowing that the child *knew*.

"I'm so afraid."

Mrs. D. was sitting, yes in the family room, which Mr. D. preferred to call the "recreation" room, with a drink in her hand. Her voice was quiet, apologetic.

30   Mr. D. sipped his drink. Peered at the newspaper. Said, vague, but polite, "Yes?"

"Harry I'm so afraid."

"Well, all right."

Mr. D. was scanning the paper with increasing impatience.

"Christ, it's always the same! AIDS, crack, crime! 'Ghetto!'" He squinted at a photograph of several black youths being herded into a police van, he laughed harshly. "*I'm* a subscriber, for Christ's sake, d'you think these punks subscribe? Why the hell am I always reading about *them!*"

35   Upstairs a telephone rang. Tracey's private number.

Mrs. D. raised her glass to her lips but did not sip from it. She feared the taste of it—that first slip-sliding taste. She pressed her fingertips to her eyes and sat very still.

After a few minutes Mr. D. inquired, glancing in her direction even as his attention remained on the newspaper, "Chris—are you all right?"

"I'm so afraid."

"Cramps, eh? Migraine?"

40   "I'm *afraid*."

Mr. D. was scanning the editorial page. A sudden smile illuminated his face. He nodded, then, suddenly bored, let the newspaper fall. "Everyone has an *opinion*. 'Put your money where your mouth is' my father used to say."

Mr. D. rose—majestically. A solid figure, ham-thighed, with a faintly flushed face, quick eyes. At its edges Mr. D.'s face appeared to have eroded but his mouth was still that "sculpted" mouth which Mrs. D., a very long time ago, so long ago now as to seem laughable, like a scene in a low-budget science-fiction film, had once avidly, ravenously, *insatiably* kissed.

Mr. D. said, walking away, "Two Bufferin. That'll do it."

After dinner, rinsing dishes and setting them carefully into the dishwasher, Mrs. D. smiled tentatively at her reflection in the window above the sink. Why was she afraid? Wasn't she being a bit silly? Where, so often recently, she was thinking of what she was *not* thinking of, now, abruptly, she was *not* thinking of what she was *not* thinking of.

45   Elsewhere in the house, issuing from the family room, and from Tracey's room upstairs, laughter rippled, peaked—television laughter by the sound of it.

Simple boredom with the subject, maybe.

Which subject?

Mr. H., father of one of the girls who had been jogging on Park Ridge Road on the day of the infamous "vehicular assault," telephoned Mr. D. another time, and, another time, Mr. D. took the call in private, the door to his study firmly shut; and, as they were undressing for bed that night, when Mrs. D. asked cautiously what had been decided, Mr. D. replied affably, "We don't get involved."

Mrs. D. had understood from the very first, even as Tracey was sobbing in her arms, that, given the litigious character of Franklin Hills, this would be the wisest, as it was the most practical, course of action; she gathered too, as things developed, despite Tracey's protestations and bouts of tears, temper, and hysteria, that Tracey concurred, as her girl friends, apart from Bonnie, concurred, perhaps even before their worried parents advised them, yet she heard herself saying weakly, "Oh Harry—if Tracey *saw* those boys' faces, Tracey wants to *say*," and Mr. D., yawning, stretching, on his way into his bathroom, nodded vaguely in her direction and said, "Set the alarm for 6:15, hon, will you?—the limo's picking me up at 6:45."

Tracey no longer discusses the incident with Mr. and Mrs. D. *Ugly!— horrible!—nightmare!—never never forget!*—she restricts all discussions of it to her girl friends, as they restrict their discussions of it too.

That is, the girls who were witnesses to the incident, not Bonnie S., to whom it happened. Not pathetic Bonnie S., to whom they no longer speak, much, at all.

For weeks, red-haired Terry was banished from the Delahunts' house. Not that Mrs. D. spoke of such a banishment, or even suggested it to Jamey, who watched her cautiously, one might say shrewdly, his gaze shifting from her if she chanced to look at him.

No need to chastise and embarrass the poor child, Mrs. D. has begun to think. He's a good decent sensitive civilized child, he *knows* how much he has upset me.

Poor Mrs. K.!—poor "Vivvie"!

Since the start of her problem eighteen months ago, the first mastectomy, and the second mastectomy, and then the chemotherapy treatments, her circle of friendly acquaintances has shrunken; and those who visit her, primarily women, have had difficulties.

Yes it's so sad it's *so* sad.

Vivvie Kern of all women.

A few of us visited her at the hospital, some of us waited to visit her at home, it's awkward not knowing what to do or to say, it sometimes seems there isn't anything *to* do or to say, and there's the extra burden of having to exchange greetings with Mr. K., who appears almost resentful, reproachful, that's how men are sometimes in such cases, husbands of ex-prom-queen-type women, and Mrs. K. was, a bit boastfully, one of these. Of course it's wisest to avoid *the subject,* but how can you avoid *the subject* with that poor man staring at you unsmiling?—just *staring!*

But it's lovely in their new solarium, at least. So much to look at, outside and in, and you aren't forced to look at *her,* I mean exclusively at *her,* poor thing! chattering away so bravely!—and that gorgeous red-blond hair she'd been so vain about mostly fallen out now, the wig just sort of *perches* there on her head, and her eyebrows are drawn on so crudely, and with her eyelashes gone it's *naked eyes* you have to look at if you can't avoid it, but in such close quarters and with the woman leaning toward you sometimes even gripping your arm as if for dear life how can you avoid it?—except by not visiting poor Mrs. K. at all?

(Of course, some in our circle have stopped seeing her, and it's embarrassing, how painful, Mrs. K. joking to disguise her bitterness. Saying, "My God, it isn't as if I have AIDS after all, this isn't *contagious,* you know!")

Visiting Mrs. K. in late June, having procrastinated for weeks, Mrs. D. was nervously admiring the numerous hanging plants in the solarium, listening to Mrs. K. speaking animatedly of mutual acquaintances, complaining good-naturedly of the Hispanic cleaning woman she and Mrs. D. shared, perhaps half-listening was more accurate, not thinking of what she was not thinking but she *was* thinking of the ceremonies of grief, death, mourning, how brave of human beings yet how futile, how futile yet how brave, for here was a terminally ill woman now speaking aggressively of regaining her lost weight—"muscle tone" she called it—and returning to the Tennis Club, and Mrs. D. smiled at the woman's wide smiling mouth, a thin mouth now and the lips garishly crimson, yes but you must keep up the pretense, yes but you must be brave, and smile, and nod, and agree, for isn't it too terrible otherwise?

Sharp-eyed, Mrs. K. has noticed that Mrs. D. has another time glanced surreptitiously at her wristwatch, as a starving animal can sense the presence of food, however inaccessible, or even abstract, so does Mrs. K, sense her visitor's yearning to escape, thus she leans abruptly forward across the glass-topped table, nearly upsetting both their glasses of white wine, she seems about to bare her heart, *oh why does Vivvie do such things! with each of us, as if for the first and only time!* seizing Mrs. D.'s hand in her skeletal but strong fingers and speaking rapidly, intensely, naked bright-druggy eyes fixed upon Mrs. D.'s, thus holding her captive.

". . . *can't* bear to think of leaving them . . . abandoning them . . . poor Gene! poor Robbie! . . . devastated . . . unmoored . . . already Robbie's been having . . . only thirteen . . . the counselor he's been seeing . . . specializes in adolescent boys . . . says it's a particularly sensitive age . . . traumatic . . . for a boy to lose . . . a mother."

Mrs. D., though giving the impression of having been listening closely, and being deeply moved, has, in fact, not been listening to Mrs. K.'s passionate outburst very closely. She has been thinking of, no she has *not* been thinking of. What?

65 With a startled, gentle little laugh, Mrs. D. says, "Oh—do you really think so? *Really!*"

Frightened, Mrs. K. says, "Do I really think—what?"

Calmly and unflinching, Mrs. D. looks the doomed woman in the face for the first time.

"That your husband and son will be 'devastated' when you die? That they will even miss you, much? I mean, after the initial shock— the upset to their routines?"

70 A long moment.

A *very* long moment.

Mrs. K. is staring incredulously at Mrs. D. Slowly, her fingers relax their death-grip on Mrs. D.'s fingers. Her bright lips move, tremble—but no sound emerges.

It's as if, in this instant, the oxygen in the solarium is being sucked out. There's a sense of something, an invisible flame, a radiance, about to go *out*.

"Oh, my goodness!" Mrs. D. exclaims, rising. "I must leave, I still have shopping to do, it's after *six*."

She would tell us, confide in us, yes we'd had similar experiences lately, unsettling experiences, sudden laughter like sneezes, giggles like carbonated bubbles breaking the surface of something you'd believed was firm, solid, permanent, unbreakable, the way in her car that day, fleeing Mrs. K., Mrs. D. found herself driving like a drunken woman, dizzy-drunk, scary-drunk, but also *happy*-drunk as she never is in real life, she was hearing laughter in the Mercedes, washing tickling over her, so funny! so wild! you should have seen that woman's face! that bully! that bore! how dare she! intimidating us! touching us! like that! how dare! as if I wasn't, for once, telling the truth!

Hardly a five-minute drive from the Kerns' house on Juniper Way to the Delahunts' house on Fairway Circle, but Mrs. D. switched on the radio to keep her company.

There.

The Darwin Awards

The Darwin Awards website attracts many visitors. The website recounts how people end up accidentally killing themselves through actions that can only be labeled as stupid. Each story has been nominated for the annual Darwin Awards, which "commemorates those who improve our gene pool by removing themselves from it." The website investigates and verifies the stories before giving the posthumous award to the victims. The website's audience finds great humor in the stories even though each ends in the death of the key figure. The following is a sampling of recent nominations.

Shooting Blanks[1]

2003 Darwin Award Nominee Confirmed True by Darwin

(11 March 2003, Spain) Early one morning, police received a call warning that three robbers had invaded the bar of a Madrid brothel. The police dispatched several units, and confirmed that the call was true. Officers surrounded the building, and used a bullhorn to coax the offenders from the premises.

The robbers, understandably frightened, found themselves in an untenable situation inside a building surrounded by dozens of policemen. Their subsequent actions may have been influenced by the ready availability of alcohol. Instead of surrendering, they decided to go out in a blaze of glory, and tried to escape while shooting at everything in sight.

---

[1] Submitted by: Javier "RAM" Bringas, Mike Puchol. Reference: www.terra.es Terra Networks, South America

The policemen ducked, covered, and proceeded to shoot back at the running robbers. Two were fatally injured, and the third was wounded in his right leg.

Why was the gunfight over so quickly? The three robbers were carrying REAL guns loaded with FAKE ammunition. They were firing blanks, making enough sound and light to fool the police into shooting back, but not enough to actually help them escape.

What's That Sound?[2]

2002 Darwin Award Nominee Confirmed by Darwin

5 (2 August 2002, Kansas) Police said an Olathe man was struck and killed by a train after his vehicle broke down on Interstate 35. His attempts at repairing his car had failed, and he had stepped away from the busy freeway to call for help, when the train engineer spotted him standing on the tracks. The engineer said the man was holding a cell phone to one ear, and cupping his hand to the other ear to block the noise of the train.

> *Authorities are at a loss as to how to prevent train deaths. Long Island, New York, locomotive engineers recently formed a support group, as every year-plus veteran without exception has involuntarily killed someone in a grade crossing collision. The baffled engineers wonder how anyone could be so unaware of the laws of physics, which dictate that a train weighing hundreds of tons has too much inertia to stop on a dime—or even a football field.*

Depth of a Fisherman[3]

2002 Darwin Award Nominee Confirmed True by Darwin

(9 January 2002, New Zealand) A fisherman was swept away from the wild West Coast beaches of Auckland, pushed to sea by 12-foot swells encountered after ignoring warnings of the impending danger.

Onlookers could only look on in conditions too poor to allow for a rescue attempt. A Surf Lifesaver reported seeing the man standing and fishing as swells broke over his head in the wake of the oncoming gale.

His body was recovered not far from the rocks.

He is not the first fisherman to drown recently off the West Coast beach. Another man tied himself to the rocks to prevent being swept away, and was drowned by the incoming tide.

10   A story of yet another fisherman's odd capsize.

Mechanic Mayhem

2002 Darwin Award Nominee Confirmed True by Darwin

(15 January 2002, Washington) A 49-year-old Boeing worker was performing maintenance on a giant, computer-controlled machine that makes parts out

---

[2] Submitted by: Sharol. Reference: Kansas City Star & TV news
[3] Submitted by: Mike Peters. Reference: New Zealand Herald

of metal blocks using hydraulics to control its movement. The hydraulic lines are pressurized to 20,000 PSI even when the machine is shut off. Working on equipment such as this requires attention to detail, and a careless employee is liable to suffer dire consequences.

The potential for trouble should have been obvious to this sixteen-year member of the Machinists Union, and yet, despite redundant safety procedures, tags, warning signs, and a fearful co-worker, our Darwin Award hopeful began to remove a hydraulic line without relieving the pressure.

The bolts holding the line in place were so tight that he had to locate a 4-foot section of pipe to attach to his ratchet to give him enough leverage to loosen the bolt. For some, that would have been warning enough that the line was pressurized.

Four high-strength bolts attached the line to the machine. The soon-to-be-ex-employee had removed three, and loosened the fourth, when the over-stressed bolt snapped. A foot-long, 3″ diameter brass sleeve was inside the line to prevent the hose from kinking. It shot out and hit the mechanic in the forehead with such force that it knocked him back eight feet, ricocheted off his head, and hit a crane fifty feet overhead.

The maintenance worker never knew what hit him.

The details of this event come from eyewitness reports and a news release from Boeing. The precise details are disputed, but the story is written to take as many observations into account as possible. Eyewitnesses and knowledgeable parties are encouraged to step forward to confirm or dispute this account.

Think Before You Leap[4]

2001 Darwin Award Winner Confirmed True by Darwin

(21 July 2001, Idaho) When his brakes failed while driving down a steep mountain road, Marco bailed out on his eight passengers and leapt from his Dodge van. Too bad Marco didn't alert the others to the problem before he took flight so precipitously. Another passenger was able to bring the vehicle to a stop a short distance away. Marco struck his head on the pavement and died at the scene. No one else was injured.

Coke Is It![5]

2001 Darwin Award Nominee Confirmed True by Darwin

(12 December 1998, Canada) A man crushed beneath a vending machine while trying to shake loose a free soda? If you thought it happened only in Urban Legends, you're wrong!

Kevin, a 19-year-old Quebec student, killed himself at Bishop's University while shaking a 420-kilogram Coke machine. He had been celebrating the end of final exams with friends. He died beneath the soda machine, asphyxiated, with a blood alcohol level slightly over the legal driving limit.

---

[4] Submitted by: Sean Capps. Reference: South Idaho Press
[5] Submitted by: The Bitshipper, Dave Mann. Reference: The Canadian Press and Graeme Hamilton of the National Post

Kevin's last act was committed in vain. "Even as it fell over, the vending machine did not let out a single can," the coroner reported. Soda-holics take note! The report also states that toppled vending machines have caused at least 35 deaths and 140 injuries in the last twenty years.

20   For those with enquiring minds, I refer you to a website dedicated to the quest to clear Kevin's name. His family questions the official version on their website, aptly named cokemachineaccidents.com. They recently sued Coca-Cola, two related companies, and Bishop's University for "gross carelessness." Their website exposé proffers several explanations for why Kevin's death was not his own fault: shaking coke machines "was common practice at the University," and anyway, unknown persons might have crushed Kevin with the vending machine in a bizarre murder, as it "would be difficult for one person to move" the machine.

In response, a spokesperson for Coke said that Canadian machines are now labelled with a warning that "tipping or rocking may cause injury or death." They have also installed anti-theft devices in newer models to keep people from obtaining free drinks.

Blown Away[6]

2001 Darwin Award Winner Confirmed True by Darwin

(16 July, 2001, United States) An assistant plant manager for Blacklidge Emulsions died when he used an acetylene torch to cut a hole in a 10,000 gallon tank of asphalt emulsion. He was attempting to visually survey the amount of emulsion that remained in the tank, but "no safety precautions were taken before the cutting operation began," stated an OSHA representative. "[His] attention was twice called to a warning sign on the side of the structure which stated the contents were combustible. In complete disregard of safety procedures," the erstwhile manager "lit an acetylene torch and began cutting, causing an explosion that blew him 93 feet away."

Assignment Ideas

Writing about humorous events can be difficult for the very reason mentioned in the overview: your audience must share your viewpoint to be able to enjoy the humor. While you cannot control readers' sensibilities, you can be aware of their perspective and help them, through your language choices, clearly understand the situation you are discussing (review Chapter 3 about audience). Make sure to provide sufficient context for what you want your audience to find funny. The goal in these assignments is to analyze humor rather than to just get a laugh, but it will not hurt if you can make your readers smile!

---

[6] Submitted by: Jon Kade, Matt Newell, Gary Arbuckle, Chris Stockard, Dave. Reference: CCH Employment Safety & Health Guide Issue 1573, OSHA Regional News Release, Mississippi Sun Herald

1. Analyze differing forms of political humor. Describe some of the humor you read, heard, or saw, and explain why you found it funny or unfunny. Investigate whether your political sympathies make you enjoy the targeting of some political figures more than others. What does the nature of this targeting and your enjoyment say about you as a member of our society?

2. The Darwin Awards show a common tendency to laugh at stupidity, something that "Risible Law" (page 381) hints at. Find additional examples of this type of humor. Analyze the examples to uncover why some people find them humorous. Describe the consistent patterns that pervade humor focusing on stupidity. Contrast laughing at stupidity with another type of humor, perhaps pulling some ideas from your brainstorming or freewriting about comedians, puns, or tragedy. Try to isolate the key elements in both types of humor, and compare their functions in society other than simply making people laugh.

3. Does humor maintain dominant ideology, or does it undermine the privileged and the powerful? Take examples from several different sources. Look for the tension in the jokes, and spot patterns that align with race, gender, or sexuality. Some critics suggest that even the positioning of a person in a film, such as the sidekick or comic relief, aligns with racist thought. Don't forget to investigate the historical uses of humor by black, female, and Jewish comedians to support or complicate your argument.

4. Referring to your brainstorming or freewriting about humor and tragedy, analyze "Is Laughter Contagious?" (page 359) in light of an experience in which you had to hold in laughter, regretted having laughed, or burst into laughter in response to insensitivity. Does this type of laughter serve a purpose in times of tragedy or pain? Can such laughter be good medicine? Or is such laughter a reflection of inability to care about others? Make sure to answer these questions with support from Joyce Carol Oates's story and your own experiences.

Group Work

Obscenity and humor often go hand in hand, starting with the juvenile bathroom humor heard in junior high school and culminating with famous entertainers who earn remarkable livings using profanity and crudity in their routines. Explore the different uses of obscenity by celebrities such as Whoopi Goldberg, George Carlin, Dave Chappelle, Chris Rock, Roseanne Barr, and Howard Stern. Provide background details on their careers, and describe their humor through the use of explicit details. Theorize about why they turned to the use of obscenity in their comedy, and generalize about the place of such humor in our society. Does obscenity serve a purpose other than shock value? Does it deliver a serious message better than other types of humor? Be sure to discuss with your teacher and your peer review group the level of obscenity they will find acceptable in your paper, especially if you plan to quote directly from a comedian's more provocative material.

Additional Readings

The chapter from David Sedaris's book "Me Talk Pretty One Day" demonstrates what we might call observational humor. Do you find it funny or as funny as a good joke? "Divided We Laugh: Humor in a Time of Conflict" picks up on themes from the Overview about the way humor functions, extending it to times of crisis. Finally, F. H. Buckley's "Risible Law" discusses humor and nonsense, showing how humor exposes ridiculousness in the legal system.

DAVID SEDARIS

Me Talk Pretty One Day

At the age of forty-one, I am returning to school and have to think of myself as what my French textbook calls "a true debutant." After paying my tuition, I was issued a student ID, which allows me a discounted entry fee at movie theaters, puppet shows, and Festyland, a far-flung amusement park that advertises with billboards picturing a cartoon stegosaurus sitting in a canoe and eating what appears to be a ham sandwich.

I've moved to Paris with hopes of learning the language. My school is an easy ten-minute walk from my apartment, and on the first day of class I arrived early, watching as the returning students greeted one another in the school lobby. Vacations were recounted, and questions were raised concerning mutual friends with names like Kang and Vlatnya. Regardless of their nationalities, everyone spoke in what sounded to me like excellent French. Some accents were better than others, but the students exhibited an ease and confidence I found intimidating. As an added discomfort, they were all young, attractive, and well dressed, causing me to feel not unlike Pa Kettle trapped backstage after a fashion show.

The first day of class was nerve-racking because I knew I'd be expected to perform. That's the way they do it here—it's everybody into the language pool, sink or swim. The teacher marched in, deeply tanned from a recent vacation, and proceeded to rattle off a series of administrative announcements. I've spent quite a few summers in Normandy, and I took a monthlong French class before leaving New York. I'm not completely in the dark, yet I understood only half of what this woman was saying.

"If you have not *meimslsxp* or *lgpdmurct* by this time, then you should not be in this room. Has everyone *apzkiubjxow?* Everyone? Good, we shall begin." She spread out her lesson plan and sighed, saying, "All right, then, who knows the alphabet?"

5   It was startling because (a) I hadn't been asked that question in a while and (b) I realized, while laughing, that I myself did *not* know the alphabet. They're the same letters, but in France they're pronounced differently. I know the shape of the alphabet but had no idea what it actually sounded like.

"Ahh." The teacher went to the board and sketched the letter a. "Do we have anyone in the room whose first name commences with an *ahh?*"

Two Polish Annas raised their hands, and the teacher instructed them to present themselves by stating their names, nationalities, occupations, and a brief list of things they liked and disliked in this world. The first Anna hailed from an industrial town outside of Warsaw and had front teeth the size of tombstones. She worked as a seamstress, enjoyed quiet times with friends, and hated the mosquito.

"Oh, really," the teacher said. "How very interesting. I thought that everyone loved the mosquito, but here, in front of all the world, you claim to detest him. How is it that we've been blessed with someone as unique and original as you? Tell us, please."

The seamstress did not understand what was being said but knew that this was an occasion for shame. Her rabbity mouth huffed for breath, and she stared down at her lap as though the appropriate comeback were stitched somewhere alongside the zipper of her slacks.

The second Anna learned from the first and claimed to love sunshine 10 and detest lies. It sounded like a translation of one of those Playmate of the Month data sheets, the answers always written in the same loopy handwriting: "Turn-ons: Mom's famous five-alarm chili! Turnoffs: insecurity and guys who come on too strong!!!!"

The two Polish Annas surely had clear notions of what they loved and hated, but like the rest of us, they were limited in terms of vocabulary, and this made them appear less than sophisticated. The teacher forged on, and we learned that Carlos, the Argentine bandonion player, loved wine, music, and, in his words, "making sex with the womens of the world." Next came a beautiful young Yugoslav who identified herself as an optimist, saying that she loved everything that life had to offer.

The teacher licked her lips, revealing a hint of the saucebox we would later come to know. She crouched low for her attack, placed her hands on the young woman's desk, and leaned close, saying, "Oh yeah? And do you love your little war?"

While the optimist struggled to defend herself, I scrambled to think of an answer to what had obviously become a trick question. How often is one asked what he loves in this world? More to the point, how often is one asked and then publicly ridiculed for his answer? I recalled my mother, flushed with wine, pounding the tabletop late one night, saying, "Love? I love a good steak cooked rare. I love my cat, and I love . . ." My sisters and I leaned forward, waiting to hear our names. "Tums," our mother said. "I love Tums."

The teacher killed some time accusing the Yugoslavian girl of masterminding a program of genocide, and I jotted frantic notes in the margins of my pad. While I can honestly say that I love leafing through medical textbooks devoted to severe dermatological conditions, the hobby is beyond the reach of my French vocabulary, and acting it out would only have invited controversy.

When called upon, I delivered an effortless list of things that I detest: 15 blood sausage, intestinal pâtés, brain pudding. I'd learned these words the hard way. Having given it some thought, I then declared my love for IBM typewriters, the French word for *bruise,* and my electric floor waxer. It was a short list, but still I managed to mispronounce *IBM* and assign the wrong gender to both the floor waxer and the typewriter. The teacher's reaction led me to believe that these mistakes were capital crimes in the country of France.

"Were you always this *palicmkrexis!*" she asked. "Even a *fiuscrzsa ticiwelmun* knows that a typewriter is feminine."

I absorbed as much of her abuse as I could understand, thinking—but not saying—that I find it ridiculous to assign a gender to an inanimate object incapable of disrobing and making an occasional fool of itself. Why refer to crack pipe or Good Sir Dishrag when these things could never live up to all that their sex implied?

The teacher proceeded to belittle everyone from German Eva, who hated laziness, to Japanese Yukari, who loved paintbrushes and soap. Italian, Thai, Dutch, Korean, and Chinese—we all left class foolishly believing that the worst was over. She'd shaken us up a little, but surely that was just an act designed to weed out the deadweight. We didn't know it then, but the coming months would teach us what it was like to spend time in the presence of a wild animal, something completely unpredictable. Her temperament was not based on a series of good and bad days but, rather, good and bad moments. We soon learned to dodge chalk and protect our heads and stomachs whenever she approached us with a question. She hadn't yet punched anyone, but it seemed wise to protect ourselves against the inevitable.

Though we were forbidden to speak anything but French, the teacher would occasionally use us to practice any of her five fluent languages.

20   "I hate you," she said to me one afternoon. Her English was flawless. "I really, really hate you." Call me sensitive, but I couldn't help but take it personally.

After being singled out as a lazy *kfdtinvfm*, I took to spending four hours a night on my homework, putting in even more time whenever we were assigned an essay. I suppose I could have gotten by with less, but I was determined to create some sort of identity for myself: David the hard worker, David the cut-up. We'd have one of those "complete this sentence" exercises, and I'd fool with the thing for hours, invariably settling on something like "A quick run around the lake? I'd love to! Just give me a moment while I strap on my wooden leg." The teacher, through word and action, conveyed the message that if this was my idea of an identity, she wanted nothing to do with it.

My fear and discomfort crept beyond the borders of the classroom and accompanied me out onto the wide boulevards. Stopping for a coffee, asking directions, depositing money in my bank account: these things were out of the question, as they involved having to speak. Before beginning school, there'd been no shutting me up, but now I was convinced that everything I said was wrong. When the phone rang, I ignored it. If someone asked me a question, I pretended to be deaf. I knew my fear was getting the best of me when I started wondering why they don't sell cuts of meat in vending machines.

My only comfort was the knowledge that I was not alone. Huddled in the hallways and making the most of our pathetic French, my fellow students and I engaged in the sort of conversation commonly overheard in refugee camps.

"Sometime me cry alone at night."

"That be common for I, also, but be more strong, you. Much work and someday you talk pretty. People start love you soon. Maybe tomorrow, okay." 25

Unlike the French class I had taken in New York, here there was no sense of competition. When the teacher poked a shy Korean in the eyelid with a freshly sharpened pencil, we took no comfort in the fact that, unlike Hye-yoon Cho, we all knew the irregular past tense of the verb *to defeat*. In all fairness, the teacher hadn't meant to stab the girl, but neither did she spend much time apologizing, saying only, "Well, you should have been *vkkdyo* more *kdeynfulh*."

Over time it became impossible to believe that any of us would ever improve. Fall arrived and it rained every day, meaning we would now be scolded for the water dripping from our coats and umbrellas. It was mid-October when the teacher singled me out, saying, "Every day spent with you is like having a cesarean section." And it struck me that, for the first time since arriving in France, I could understand every word that someone was saying.

Understanding doesn't mean that you can suddenly speak the language. Far from it. It's a small step, nothing more, yet its rewards are intoxicating and deceptive. The teacher continued her diatribe and I settled back, bathing in the subtle beauty of each new curse and insult.

"You exhaust me with your foolishness and reward my efforts with nothing but pain, do you understand me?"

The world opened up, and it was with great joy that I responded, "I know the thing that you speak exact now. Talk me more, you, plus, please, plus." 30

PAUL LEWIS

Divided We Laugh: Humor In a Time of Conflict

Imagine for a moment that you're a member of an improv comedy troupe performing a skit called "185: Blanks" and someone in the audience has shouted out "terrorists" as the subject for the improv. Your mind is racing to come up with a punch line in an instant. Once the subject is chosen, the setup goes like this: "185 terrorists go into a bar and the bartender says, "Sorry, we don't serve terrorists in here.' And the terrorists say..." This is your part: what could they say? Well, they could say something like: "Guessed we bombed out tonight," or "Knock me over with an airplane," or "Sheesh, and all we wanted were Bloody Marys." In the post-9/11 world, an improv artist working with this material faces multiple challenges. In addition to finding a word or phase with more than one meaning to build a joke around, she needs to worry about audience responses to this no doubt explosive subject: how easy it would be to cross a line and offend members of the audience. Say the wrong thing and "I was only kidding" might just not do the trick.

Or imagine that you're a small fifteen-year-old-girl—a young woman really, though you don't look it—in for a major operation at a hospital that specializes in children's diseases. Though the surgery is likely to be successful, there will be a long period of recovery, with some pain. The afternoon before the operation you're lying in bed, contemplating your own mortality, the chance that you might not survive, that if you do, which seems probable after all, you may not be quite as active, as athletic, as independent as you were prior to the operation. Reaching into your self for whatever you have in the way of faith, anger, and grit, you're interrupted, surprised to find that a clown in a doctor's suit has come to Patch Adams you up: make you laugh about your situation. "Hey, little girl," he begins, smiling but also pushing a button that leaves you thinking, "Get this guy out of here"!

Or imagine that you're a politician in the early weeks of a race for election to a high office, say, senator. Your advisers are trying to come up with a strategy for dealing with a weakness or vulnerability in your past life or public work that just broke as a news story. Perhaps you were caught inflating your achievements; perhaps you used to do drugs or drink to excess; perhaps one of your best friends is a corrupt corporate executive who has just been indicted. You can't simply deny or disown the matter because (unfortunately) it's true and (even worse) everyone who follows these things knows it. The obvious alternative is humor: craft a joke or two about the issue to show that you concede the point, think it's a problem but not that serious, and are big enough to laugh at yourself. If the strategy works, the issue will shrink in importance. Impressed by your seeming wit and modesty, your supporters will be heartily amused. When your detractors point out that what you've displayed is not the ability to criticize and reform yourself but to manage public opinion through a performance as pat as that of any stand-up comic, their point, you hope, will be drowned out in laughter.

The paradox of American humor since 1980 appears in just such moments of conflict or perplexity: during years in which the country has been drawn together in ever larger audiences via new technologies of communication, the jokes we've told and our responses to them suggest that we are deeply divided. We think about humor in contradictory ways. Split into subgroups, we are delighted and outraged by the comic treatment of different ideas. Like Tonto in the old joke about the time when he and the Lone Ranger were surrounded by "Indians," the fractious quality of humor appreciation in our time leads us to question the existence of a unified American audience, asking along with the scout, "What you mean, *we*?"

Divided responses to the particular attempts to amuse above, the distance that can open up between joke tellers and listeners, suggest something
5 else about U.S. humor today: that much of our joking has serious objectives that can elicit acquiescence or resistance. For the most part, when jokes are exchanged around the stereotypical water cooler, when friends share jokes they remember over drinks, no lasting impact is desired. It may be, as early humor theorists noted, that these situations allow tellers to take fleeting pleasure in a sense of superiority (Thomas Hobbes); the venting of hostile impulses or in-

sinuation of sexual images into discussions (Sigmund Freud); the ridiculing of deviations from established norms (Henri Bergson); or puzzling incongruities and problem solving (James Beattie, Arthur Koestler). Still, since the experience of joke sharing tends to be brief and transitory, the images, ideas, or emotions jokes evoke often fade even before the laughter dies down.

But then there are jokes that linger, joke tellers who intend to do more than amuse or who find that, without intending to, they have done more, sometimes to their peril. Increasingly over the past thirty years, strains of U.S. humor have achieved a range of effects, becoming more purposive while also working at cross purposes. At one end of our intentional humor spectrum we find a New Age movement devoted to bringing mirth and laughter into our schools, hospitals, workplaces, and homes—not just to amuse but to improve learning, healing, working, and living in general. At the other end we find killing jokes that not only amuse but also affect anxiety levels through the excitation or relaxation of fear. A common element uniting these caring and cruel humor clusters with much joking in between is a sense of purpose beyond the momentary flash of amusement, a sense that joking can have serious and lasting consequences.

The purposive and embattled state of American humor comes into focus as soon as we attend to conflicts between the attempt to amuse and resistance to it—between ridicule and resentment, satire and outrage—rife in the land. By way of preliminary examples, consider a few such controversies that erupted during a six-month period beginning in the autumn of 2003. One concerned unamused executives at Fox News who in late October revealed a less-than cool affinity to Queen Victoria by taking umbrage over an episode of the animated *Simpsons* TV show called "Krusty for Congress" that featured a political debate on Fox News. According to *Simpsons* creator Matt Groening, Fox News threatened to sue in an effort to force him to cut out the segment. The real Fox News apparently objected less to being called "your voice for evil" than to the parodic "news crawl" at the bottom of the screen during the debate that read: "Do Democrats cause cancer? Find out at Foxnews.com... Rupert Murdoch: Terrific Dancer.... Dow down 5000 points.... Study: 92 percent of Democrats are gay.... JFK posthumously joins Republican Party.... Oil slicks found to keep seals young, supple.... Dan Quayle: Awesome." What added spice to this conflict was the fact that these antagonists—the *Simpsons* and Fox News—are products of the same network that in effect was chasing its own tail by threatening to sue itself.

In early November, within a week of when the Fox-*Simpsons* story broke, another controversy made news. When the Merriam-Webster Dictionary included the word "McJob" and defined it as "low paying, dead-end work," McDonald's CEO Jim Cantalupo was far from amused. In a letter to the lexicographers, he insisted that the term was "an inaccurate description of restaurant employment" and "a slap in the face to the 12 million men and women" who work in the restaurant industry. Of course, as a variation on the company name and an allusion to its mascot Ronald McDonald, the word McJob expresses a tendentious point directed not at undercompensated employees but at a corporation that serves billions and billions of hamburgers while maintaining high profit margins and low product cost. Cantalupo's protest, no doubt to his frustration, had the inevitable effect of publicizing the very word he deplored, "the kind of corporate strategy," observed, Jan Freeman, the *Boston Globe's* language columnist, "you'd expect from the clown, not the CEO."

Also around this time, similarly outraged senses of humor were on display in the Republican-controlled Senate Judiciary Committee where frustrated members of the majority were trying to advance the confirmation of Janice Brown, a conservative nominated by President Bush to the DC Court of Appeals. As a frequent dissenter during her time as a California state judge and a fierce opponent of affirmative action, Brown, though an African American, raised the ire of organizations like the NAACP for, in the words of Democratic New York Senator Charles Schumer, wanting "to turn back the clock.... by a century or more." In addition to defending Judge Brown, who, according to detractor Representative Diane Watson (D-CA), made "Clarence Thomas look like Thurgood Marshall," Republican senators railed against a cartoon (fig. I) drawn by Khalil Bendib and distributed by the on-line progressive Web page, www.BlackCommentator.com.

10   Waving, the cartoon during a hearing, Chairman Orrin Hatch (R-UT) declared, "It's.... filled with bigotry that maligns not only Justice Brown but others as well: Justice Thomas, Colin Powell and Condoleezza Rice. It's the utmost in bigotry.... I hope that everyone here considers that cartoon offensive and despicable." Although Democratic senators were quick to deplore the cartoon, an editorial posted on BlackCommentator argued that "the Republican's purpose in making a fetish of the cartoon was to disrupt the hearing, itself. Orrin Hatch staged an utterly cynical, perverse assault on a nomination process that occasionally frustrates the GOP's relentless packing of the judiciary with Hard Right lawyers."

The most conspicuous feature of these examples is not just that they are political but that they come from the political right and look very much like similar moves associated with earlier left-of-center politically correct critiques of joke cycles deemed insensitive and harmful in their treatment of racial, ethnic, or gender-based materials. Although political correctness was put down in the late 1980s and early 1990s by a backlash based to some extent on the charge that its critiques revealed a lack of humor (as in, "Hey, lighten up. It's only a joke!"), in its wake partisans on all sides of the culture wars are likely to cry foul when a particularly pointed or edgy joke crosses what they see as a line of good taste by conjuring painful associations that reveal raw emotions and beliefs.

When the 2004 Super Bowl half-time show featured not only the "malfunctioning" of Janet Jackson's costume but also ads for Bud Light that showed 5 flatulent horses, a crotch-biting dog, and a talking chimpanzee flirting with his owner's girlfriend, responses varied. While media blogs and college student newspapers offered varying rankings of the best and worst ads, and MSNBC media writer Jane Weaver opined that, though tacky, "there were no [2004] embarrassing candidates for the Super Bowl commercial hall of shame," George Konig, writing on his Christian Internet Forum, was outraged: "As bad as that [nipplegate] may be, some of the Super Bowl commercials were actually worse, especially the suggestion of bestiality in a beer commercial, where a monkey asks a human woman to go upstairs and have sex with him. Another beer commercial has a horse passing gas in a woman's face. Now in a short period of time during the Super Bowl, women have been degraded at least three times, with the monkey, the horse, and Jackson's peep show." Similar humor controversies bubbled through the run-up to the presidential campaign. For reminding the audience at a John Kerry fund-raising event of the association between the president's name and female genital hair in May 2004, Whoopie Goldberg lost her lucrative role in Slim-Fast advertising. Similarly, Teresa Heinz's jokes about the president ("George Bush is like Forrest Gump with an attitude") and his supporters (who seemed to be voting for "four more years of hell") drew predictably partisan responses divided between "You go, girl" and "She's Howard Dean in a dress." We have reached a point where the edgy-jokes-lead-to-angry-criticism-and-countering-defensive-moves dance has become a ritual of public discourse, where careers rise and fall on a celebrity's use of humor, where dueling political insult books (for instance, Al Franken's *Rush Limbaugh Is a Big Fat Idiot* and David T. Hardy and Jason Clark's *Michael Moore Is a Big Fat Stupid White Man;* Ann Coulter's *Treason: Liberal Treachery from the Cold War to the War on Terrorism* and Clint Willis's *The I Hate Ann Coulter, Bill O'Reilly, Rush Limbaugh, Michael Savage, Sean Hannity .... Reader;* Rush Limbaugh's *The Way Things Ought to Be* and Steven Rendall, Jim Naureckas, and Jeff Cohen's *The Way Things Aren't*) and radio talk networks (Limbaugh's Excellence in Broadcasting Network vs. George Sorros's Air America) struggle to shape public perception of individuals and issues.

The eagerness to provoke and be provoked operative in these exchanges suggest that they are rooted in sharp disagreements over the specific issues involved, with the jokers highlighting the inadequacies of some butt and the objectors insisting that the butt targeted is unfairly being seen as inadequate. In the cases considered above, the focus is on the objectivity of Fox News's reporting and analysis, the quality of work at McDonald's, the qualifications of a judicial nominee, the morality of humorous TV ads, and the appropriateness of comments about political figures. And each side has its own take on the underlying issues: fair and balanced reporting versus propaganda disguised as news; the poor quality of an increasing number of jobs in the United States versus opportunities in the service sector; the far-right opinions of a judge versus unfair or racist attacks on legitimate organizations and individuals; the use of what can be seen as comic and/or cruel images in advertising; and the limits of political mockery. The language of derisive humor—including put-*down* and send-*up* suggests the directional energy of these butt wars: how jokes can seek to achieve or contribute to a butt shift, defined as (1) a change in how seriously a person or idea is taken, and (2) the successful attachment of a negative trait to an individual or idea through comic association. The accumulation of examples from the past twenty-five or thirty years to be discussed here will suggest that butt wars- intentional humor and resistance to it—have become habitual.

To see the fault lines in our humor culture, to locate and evaluate intentional humor, we need to move beyond the predictable and safe joking of the most widely consumed comic genres: network sitcoms, romantic comedies, the nightly monologues, and most standup routines. By establishing a static situation around a set group of family members, coworkers, or friends, and by sustaining it up to the series finales at which point real changes can occur, sitcoms provide multiple variations on familiar themes, security through repetition. By snuggling up to taboo violation but never making a commitment to it, romantic comedies seek to draw large audiences by providing easy affirmation. By exploiting only the most widely shared knowledge (familiar news stories and celebrity character traits) and by steering clear of provocative, unexpected ideas, the monologists reassure audiences, preparing them for slumber. What's new in recent humor is discernible at the margins where one is more likely to be surprised, shocked or offended: in our response to national disasters and embarrassments; in stories about humor controversies and laughter clubs; in the deliberate use of humor in political conflicts; in on-line jokes and parodies; in gross-out horror films and TV reality shows; in the rants of Internet blog masters and talk show hosts.

F. H. BUCKLEY

Risible Law

Judges seldom show any signs of appreciating how risible American law may be. There are exceptions, to be sure. Judge Scalia once began an opinion with "I join the opinion of the Court except that portion which takes seriously, and thus encourages in the future, an argument that should be laughed out of court." Several other members of the bench, such as Judges Alex Kozinski, Frank Easterbrook, and Danny Boggs, are true wits as well.

There is much to be said for a sober-minded bench. The effort to seem witty might easily become tiresome, when the case is serious and the sally is issued from on high. Yet much of the law is highly amusing, and the failure to notice its comedic possibilities sometimes leaves us the poorer. Not only do we miss the diversion of comedy, but nonsensical legal doctrines survive because we have lost the knack of laughter.

There is a great store of harmless nonsense in the common law, to one who knows how to extract it. A.P. Herbert's satires were masterpieces of the genre. Herbert wrote up mock accounts of court decisions, recounting the efforts of an obstreperous layman, Alfred Haddock, to exercise an Englishman's rights and privileges just as often as he could. In *R. v Haddock*, the accused was charged with leading "a large white cow of malevolent aspect" through the City of London to the offices of the Collector of Taxes. In his defense, Haddock argued that the cow was tendered as delivery of his taxes, since he had signed the cow and endorsed it "Pay to the Collector of Taxes, who is no gentleman, or Order, the sum of fifty-seven pounds (and may he rot!)."

The court held that the personal comments were simply an honest man's understandable reaction to paying taxes, and did not deprive the cow of its status as an unconditional promise of payment, as required by the Bills of Exchange Act. The method of payment was somewhat unconventional, to be sure, but nothing in the statute required promissory notes to be written on paper. The charge was therefore dismissed, since the accused had lawfully paid his taxes with a negotiable cow.

My introduction to statutory interpretation came in the form of an apocryphal case, *R.v. Bird*, a parody written by Toronto lawyer Hart Pomerantz, which Canadian law students passed around in samizdat fashion. The case, a decision of Mr. Justice Blue, turned on whether a defense for cattle trespass (the tort of letting one's cattle stray across a neighbor's field) lay under the Migratory Birds Convention. After due consideration of the legislation and the mischief it sought to prevent, Blue J. concluded that for the purpose of the statute, a cow was a bird.

Such satires succeed because they contain a kernel of truth. Let us therefore look for the risible amongst real, not imagined, decisions, where the joke is unintentional.

1. An administrative agency regulates springs in one's backyard under a grant of authority derived from a statue that deals with navigable waters and adjacent wetlands.
2. An FBI agent was fired for embezzling $2,000 from the government to feed his gambling habit. He was reinstated after a court ruled that his passion for gambling was a "handicap" and that the government had wrongly discriminated against him.
3. Drew P. was a child in rural Georgia who suffered from infantile autism and severe mental retardation. The school board offered Drew an extensive educational program, including an expert on autism, but his parents were dissatisfied. They wanted a special school out of town, and a court agreed with them. The out-of-town school happened to be in Tokyo.
4. Chaya Amiad brought her dog to a Seattle clothing store and was asked to leave. Amiad was not blind, but afterward claimed that she had an emotional dependence on the dog and sued under the Americans with Disabilities Act. A psychologist treating Amiad for depression said the dog was a mental health service animal. The Seattle Office of Civil Rights agreed, ordering the storekeeper to pay Amiad $250 and attend sensitivity training.
5. As a final case, consider *Wickard v. Filburn*, which so expanded the scope of Washington's power over the states that American federalism began to look like a legal fiction. For many years, Filburn owned and operated a small farm on which he kept a herd of dairy cattle and some poultry. To feed his animals, he also raised winter wheat. Any wheat left over one year was used in the following year for reseeding. In planting and harvesting his wheat he exceeded the acreage limits of the Agricultural Adjustment Act of 1938, arguing that, under the interstate commerce power, the federal restrictions were inapplicable [5]

since the wheat never left his farm. However, the Supreme Court upheld the restriction: If Filburn had not grown his own wheat, he would have purchased it on the market, and such wheat might have come from out-of-state.

Now, how is it that such cases have escaped our laughter? They are not parodies, like *R. v. Bird*, but that should not matter. The best laughter is often reserved for the unintentionally comic. Yet, we do not laugh. The expansion of victim rights and the extensions of federal power are defended by liberals and opposed by conservatives with the same heavy seriousness. But in throwing away the self-correcting powers of laughter, they have conspired to produce the most comic jurisprudence.

Kreimer v. Morristown

Consider that most Swiftian of decisions, *Kreimer v. Town of Morristown*. Kreimer was sympathetically described by Judge Lee Sarokin as one "whose access to showers and laundry facilities [was] severely curtailed by his homeless status." It was more than a matter of personal hygiene, however. "Dressed in soiled and sweat-soaked clothes, the homeless man spent his days stalking, staring down, and speaking loudly and belligerently to library staff and patrons. Kreimer's foul smell and anti-social behavior literally drove people from the facility, a fact many witnesses observed." The lack of access to showers no doubt explains his nickname: Smelly Bum. And so the library patrons of Morristown, N.J., complained when he chose to spend much of his day in their company. The library responded with a set of admission guidelines which, not surprisingly, excluded Kreimer. His thirst for knowledge denied, Kreimer sued, the American Civil Liberties Union harrumphed, and the library policies were stuck down at trial as unconstitutionally vague and restrictive. That might bother some people, wrote Judge Sarokin, but *tant pis*.

No one can dispute that matters of personal appearance and hygiene can reach a point where they interfere with the enjoyment of the facility by others. But one person's hay-fever is another person's ambrosia.

Is this a deliberate satire? The giveaways are all there, in the clever parody of official legalese: the strident tone that dwindles to nothing ("No one can dispute"), the preference for the Romance word over the Germanic ("interfere with the enjoyment" instead of "bother"), the false opposition between hay-fever and ambrosia. Surely all doubt is removed when we come to the high flatulence of the peroration:

> No matter how laudable and understandable the goals of the library may be, we cannot—we dare not—cross the threshold of barring persons from entering because of how they appear based upon the unfettered discretion of another.

No, no, a thousand times no! And finally the bathetic conclusion, its author laughing up his sleeve.

The greatness of our country lies in tolerating speech with which we do not agree; that same toleration must extend to people, particularly where the cause of revulsion may be of our own making.

The learned to judge compares public policy analysis to excrement, and criticizes those who prefer one to the other! Did Gulliver ever visit a place so mad? Was there really a judge named Sarokin? Or was the name a pseudonym behind which a clever conservative hid his identity and exposed his savage indignation? A growing number of academics now believe that the opinion's true author is Judge Alex Kozinski, who lampoons the civil liberties invented last week in California as the "MTV Constitution." Say farewell to the Founders, and hello to trendy slogans and mushy, feel-good liberalism. Never mind the loss of property rights, says Judge Kozinski. Think instead of what you will gain when courts uphold euthanasia: the Right to Die!

Judge Kozinski's satire succeeded beyond his expectations, however, when gullible White House staffers had a "Judge Lee Sarokin" appointed to the Third Circuit Court of Appeals. Wholly lacking a sense of irony, they read the decision and thought they had found just the man for their employer. In every law school, academics wagered that the wittiest of judges had at last overstepped the bounds. But when the time came for him to be sworn in, a heavily disguised "Judge Sarokin" took his place with the other judges. For almost a year the farce continued, and Kozinski-Sarokin commuted back and forth between California and the East Coast, until an exhausted "Judge Sarokin" took early retirement, bringing an end to the most successful imposture since Gladstone adopted a false beard to bowl for England as "W. G. Grace." (Judge Kozinski denies all this—but that is just what one would expect him to do.)   10

The Sick Chickens Case

In the past, a case as ridiculous as *Kreimer* would never have seen the light of day, for then the wit (more than Shelley's pet) was the unacknowledged legislator of the world. He could repeal a ridiculous law through laughter, and that is just what happened in the "Sick Chickens" case—*Schechter v. U.S.*—which struck down a National Recovery Administration code as an unconstitutional attempt by Congress to regulate intrastate commerce. The National Industrial Recovery Act, a piece of extravagant socialism, had authorized the president to approve "codes of fair competition" that trade associations or groups had submitted to him. The codes sought to reduce "cutthroat" competition through highly detailed restrictions on industry practices. This harmed consumers by stifling competition, and for this reason industry groups supported the codes: they permitted merchants to organize a cartel and sell their goods at monopolistic prices.

One such code was New York's "Live Poultry Code," which regulated the poultry business in mind—numbing detail. For example, it mandated "straight killing," under which customers were barred from choosing the chickens they bought, and instead had to accept the luck of the draw. Otherwise, consumers would pick the best chickens and leave over the scrawny chickens that were worth less than the inflated monopolistic price. Merchants would then be stuck with unsold inventory unless they lowered their prices. The example wonderfully shows how difficult it is to police cartel-breaking, and how the grant of a monopoly means little unless every possibility of defection is bricked up. The only effective form of state capitalism is a Peronism that stifles the economy by prescribing rules through and through and absolutely.

Now, in the Sick Chickens case, the defendants operated a kosher poultry slaughterhouse in Brooklyn, where they purchased live poultry from commission men for slaughter and resale to retail poultry dealers and butchers. They were rule breakers, who sought to attract clients by chipping away at the Live Poultry Code. Their competitors took notice, and in due course they were charged and convicted with a variety of offenses under the code, including "selective killing," under which customers were permitted to pick their chickens, in violation of "straight killing" requirements.

On its facts, the case was trivial in the extreme. Yet the fate of the First Roosevelt New Deal hung in balance, and when the case reached the Supreme Court local counsel had been elbowed aside by more eminent litigators. Solicitor-General (subsequently Justice) Stanley Reed argued that the nation's economic recovery would be jeopardized if the impugned legislation was not upheld. Selective killing would shake up the price structure by depressing the price for good poultry rejected by the earliest purchase by the defendants, and that the federal government lacked the constitutional authority to pass the National Recovery Act. Given the court's previous rulings, however, the issue was a toss-up, and what won the case for the defendants was an exchange during the oral argument by Joseph Heller, the defendant's less than tony, original lawyer.

In the midst of Heller's rambling argument, Justice McReynolds asked for a definition of "straight-killing." The learned judge was one of the "Four Horsemen" (with Justices Butler, Sutherland, and Van Devanter), a group of conservative jurists who opposed early New Deal legislation so effectively that liberals saw Apocalyptic parallels. He could therefore be expected to sympathize with the defendant, but Heller wasn't biting.

> MR. JUSTICE MCREYNOLDS: What do you understand that provision amounts to?
15
> MR. HELLER: Which provision is that? (*Hunh?*)
> MR. JUSTICE MCREYNOLDS: The one that you are just speaking of, the "straight-killing" provision.

Heller was obviously confused. The Supreme Court wanted to be instructed on the selection of chickens?

> MR. HELLER: The straight-killing provision is in this Code.

But the learned justice was not put off so easily.

> MR. JUSTICE MCREYNOLDS: Yes. But the practice, what is it?
> MR. HELLER (*stalling now*): That is, of the "straight-killing"?

MR. JUSTICE MCREYNOLDS: Yes.

MR. HELLER: Do you want me to explain "straight-killing"? (*Amazing! You never know with these people.*)

MR. JUSTICE MCREYNOLDS (*despairing*): Well, never mind.

For a moment it seemed that the Court had lost interest in Brooklyn chicken-buying habits. But now another of the Four Horsemen began to smell blood.

MR. JUSTICE VAN DEVANTER: Explain what the clause requires.

MR. HELLER: (*stubbornly*): It is set out in the code.

MR. JUSTICE MCREYNOLDS (*catching on at last*): If I understand this correctly, these chickens are brought into New York by the carload, and then they are taken out and put in coops?

MR. HELLER: Yes, sir. They are put in coops by the commission merchant. (*Have these guys ever bought a chicken?*)

MR. JUSTICE MCREYNOLDS: How many are there in a coop?

MR. HELLER: From 30 to 40, according to their size. (*Or fought over one in Brooklyn?*)

MR. JUSTICE MCREYNOLDS: Then, when the commission man delivers them to the slaughterhouse, they are in coops?

MR. HELLER: They are in coops.

MR. JUSTICE MCREYNOLDS: And, if he undertakes to sell them, he must have straight-killing?

MR. HELLER: He must have straight-killing. (*But now the penny finally drops.*) In other words, his customer is not permitted to select the ones he wants. He must put his hand into the coop when he buys from the slaughterhouse and take the first chicken that comes to hand. He has to take that. 10

At this point, the transcript notes that most deadly of responses:

[Laughter]

Now, why was there laughter? Heller was not a wit. He was more than a little plodding. But, prodded by Mr. Justice McReynolds, he had brought home the absurd reach of the impugned regulations. The tension and ennui of economic crisis and *arcana juridical* were forgotten, as justices and spectators pictured a crowded, jostling butcher shop, and a regulator saying "Madam! Unhand that chicken!" After all the fine oratory, the statute and NRA codes were simply machine law, and ridiculous.

MR. JUSTICE MCREYNOLDS: Irrespective of the quality of the chicken?

[Laughter.]

MR. HELLER: Irrepsective of the quality or the price of the chicken.

MR. JUSTICE MCREYNOLDS (*warming to his audience*): Suppose it is a sick chicken?

MR. HELLER: Well, he could reject a sick chicken.

> MR. JUSTICE MCREYNOLDS: Now can he break up those coops
> and sell them, half a dozen chickens to one man, and half a
> dozen to another man?
> MR. HELLER: (*gleefully*): He cannot. He can sell a whole coop, or
> one-half of a coop.
> MR. JUSTICE MCREYNOLDS: And that is all?
> MR. HELLER: That is all. And when he sells five, or six, or two,
> or three, he cannot permit the purchaser any selection of the
> chickens in the coop.

Now the laughter becomes general, and everyone wants in.

> MR. JUSTICE STONE: Do you mean there cannot be a selection if
> he buys one-half of the coop?
> MR. HELLER: No. You just break the box into two halves.

> [Laugher].

> MR. HELLER: There is not selection in the case.
> MR. JUSTICE SUTHERLAND: Well suppose, however, that all the
> chickens

Have gone over to one end of the coop?

> [Laugher].

When the laughter had died away, President Roosevelt's first New Deal was dead.

What are the special characteristics of risible law? Of all the theories of comedy, Bergson's best explains which laws attract our laughter. We laugh at machine law, as we do at the machine man. We laugh at rigid laws, sensible enough when their scope is limited, but ridiculous when unbounded and seen as ends in themselves. Bergson gives an example of such law, in the customs inspector who narrowly saves the shipwrecked passenger from drowning and then asks if he has anything to declare. In the same way, constitutional liberties are risible when high-sounding mobility rights are employed to permit a vagrant to smell up a library, when a regulation is absurdly overextended, and when a whiner is awarded millions for bruised feelings.

What machine law lacks is the complexity and suppleness of a human legal system. Machine law absurdly takes a simple and modest rule to be a supreme and overriding principle, and thereby parodies itself. It sacrifices human happiness to no useful or admirable end, and forgets that the Sabbath was made for man and not for the Sabbath. It is like the man who elevates economy into avarice, temperance into abstemiousness, prudence into cowardice. What it lacks, more than anything, is a sense of humanity, of what it means to live well, and of the kind of life to which we should aspire.

The result is risible law, when we possess the detachment to ignore the human costs of nonsensical rules. With a stronger sense of pathos, the result is anything but comic, and this was the message of one of the best legal books in the last ten years. Phillip Howard's *The Death of Common Sense* described in human terms the blight of wasteful rules, such as those which prevented Mother Teresa from opening a homeless shelter in South Bronx. The nuns spent two years in navigating bureaucratic regulations, which mandated 20 household appliances their order had banned. Given their vows of poverty, the nuns did not want a washing machine—they preferred to wash clothes by hand, as they did in India. In the end they were defeated by a requirement that a $100,000 elevator be built in their four-story building. This was simply too much. The nuns thought that the money could be better spent on the poor in their other missions. They left New York, but not before sending a polite letter to the city expressing their regrets and noting that they had learned a useful lesson about the law and its many complexities. Howard described the absurd extension of rights, the explosion of litigation, and the mind-numbing regulations. The book had an enormous impact on the lay reader. So far as the legal profession was concerned, however, it might have fallen stillborn from the press. Evidently, what was needed was ridicule.

CHAPTER 15

HONESTY AND DECEPTION

Overview

In many cultures honesty is one of the most appreciated qualities. People do not like to be deceived. Even so-called white lies taint our impressions of others. We ask ourselves, "Why couldn't she have told me the truth?" having discovered after treating a friend to an expensive lobster dinner, for instance, that she does not share our fondness for seafood. Or we might confront a friend who told us that we looked fine before we attended a party wearing an outfit that proved inappropriate by stating, "You could have saved me a lot of embarrassment if you had just spoken the truth." These small lies can lead us to mistrust others and make us doubt their judgment in the future.

Ethics implore us to be honest. Philosopher Martin Buber (1878–1965) suggested that ethical treatment involves maintaining relationships that do not objectify another person's humanity. Lying treats other people as objects. We do not bestow on those people the dignity of being told the truth. We act as if we know what they can handle or understand better than they do.

Since violating ethical standards by deceiving others and the consequences of deception often outweigh the minor hurt feelings that might occur if we are honest, it seems advantageous to always tell the truth. So why do we lie? Nobody I know can claim to have never deceived somebody, but most would claim to be honest overall.

If we distance ourselves from pathological embezzlers or frauds who make a living deceiving others—who lie to conceal wrongdoing from authorities—we might be able to see lying in a different light. Deception may serve a purpose that is not as nefarious as we have been taught to believe.

For one, people have a right to their privacy. Sometimes, we simply do not wish to reveal details about our lives when people ask us questions. We have comfort zones regarding our personal lives, so we set up invisible barriers between public and private knowledge that are impermeable to strangers and acquaintances. Most of us, for instance, do not open our dalliances to public inspection. We also prefer to keep information about some illnesses between our doctors and ourselves. Many people believe that household finances—especially if the family is struggling financially—are no one else's business.

The difficulty arises from people's curiosity. Often, maybe inadvertently, we ask about things that others consider to be private. For example, you might ask a classmate, "How did you do on that exam?" Whether the person received a passing or failing grade, the classmate might feel that grades do not constitute an open competition and that the information should remain strictly between herself or himself and the professor. The person should be able to say, "I'm sorry, I like to keep those things to myself." But this answer strikes most listeners as evasive, if not overly protective, and we start assuming that the person failed the exam.

Perhaps media, with their intrusive questions about public figures' lives, have led us to believe that if there is no shame to hide, people should give answers. This forces people to lie to protect the boundaries of the personal and private. The more personal the information others seek from us, the more likely we are to defuse the situation with a lie. The most innocent person will look guilty if he answers "Are you having an extramarital affair?" with "That's none of your business." The latter answer functions as an admission of guilt. Therefore, the answer always must be, "No, of course not."

Whether we want to cloak incidents that deviate from standard morality, conceal unruly desires that might reveal character weaknesses, keep unpopular opinions to ourselves, or simply keep a secret, we deceive others for privacy's sake. Our belief in the privacy of our lives outweighs our belief in honesty. For an honest society to exist, people would have to quash their curiosity and not ask questions that might intrude on other's privacy. Since the boundaries are so different among individuals and between subcultures, lying becomes the best available option.

The irrationality of others also forces us into protective lying. A rational person, by most people's definition, does not prod someone unduly or enter into confrontations when his or her agenda meets resistance. Unreasonable people intrude on private matters, and they also act aggressively in public or in the course of their jobs, perhaps trying to coerce us to do something we do not want to do. Not being able to articulate our doubts or not caring to fully share our reasoning, we invent lies that will satisfy these people and avoid further confrontation.

Experiences with some salespeople epitomize the need for this type of lying. We often have to choose between being rude or lying to free ourselves from sales pitches we have no interest in hearing. I cannot count the number of times I have said, "No, I am not interested in a free vacation" and "No, I have no interest in being a millionaire." Such lies end the conversation; the salesperson has nothing left with which to lure me. Similarly, I lie to people wanting me to donate to charities or to support their religious affiliations. Of course, I want to feed starving children, comfort leukemia sufferers, and aid earthquake victims, but I do not want to have to explain my priorities and reasoning to people who try to make me feel guilty through insistence. Thus, I fabricate stories about balloon payments on my house or flooding in my basement. Though I am actually fascinated by any type of religious discussion, when people preach their convictions at me, I feel forced to tell them lies to preclude possible confrontations.

Rational people can become irrational in certain sensitive areas—such as about sports teams, politics, and work-related matters—and cannot accept disagreement. To keep confrontations from escalating into physical violence, other reasonable people lie. We step out of such a situation, in other words, by feigning agreement or pretending that the person's points have made us think differently. In our relationships, we also find ourselves telling these types of lies to avoid heated exchanges or other forms of stress.

Another type of deception comes from wanting to draw attention to ourselves. Few of us want to be taken for granted or ignored. We want to believe that events in our lives have significance and that we influence these events to some degree. Few of us actually live action-packed lives full of excitement and relevance. We are far more likely to feel like cogs in machines. Thus, when someone tells an exciting story, we might be jealous or want to chip in, perhaps to take the spotlight away, perhaps to create an affinity with other listeners. Therefore, we exaggerate our involvement in a similar story or fabricate details of a conflict to make ourselves look heroic or victorious.

Exaggerated stories can be the source of amusement at a party or get-together. Many cultures have long traditions of telling tall tales to bring a sense of magic or mystery or to relieve boredom. We can teach children cautious behavior by pulling their legs with stories meant to illustrate the dangerous outcomes of activities they might otherwise pursue. Generally, though, such lies function as entertainment and give the teller an identity that denies the tedium or dreariness in his or her life and establishes some importance that, however illusory, grants privilege or status in a group setting. If people did not try to call attention to themselves, we might not enjoy get-togethers as much as we do. So lies can function in a positive way for both teller and listener.

A much more complicated form of deception comes from a conflict between larger truth and mere honesty. While the actual evidence and details of a situation might point to our blame, we might not feel that we did anything wrong. We might embrace such values as personal responsibility, sincerity, and fairness that conflict with how we felt we were treated. An honest retelling of the events might obscure the larger truth we find in these values.

One day, when I was a teenager, I waved and yelled hello to my friend George, who was driving by. George turned toward me and started shouting a question about whether I needed a ride. As he was doing this, another car pulled out of a parking space, and the front end of George's car crashed into the driver's side of the other car. Its driver, an older man, got out and started blaming George for the accident, saying that he wasn't looking where he was going. George had not been looking at the road; however, he had the right of way and could not have avoided the accident even if he had been looking. I was the only witness. If I had said that George had turned to look at me a second before the accident, the credibility of the experienced driver, as compared to the lack of credibility of seventeen-year-old George, would have persuaded insurance companies and even courts to believe his account of the story, which was that his car had been stationary, waiting for George to pass, when George swerved into him. So I lied, saying that I saw George traveling down the road, looking straight ahead, when the other car pulled out in front of him.

Some might see such a lie as merely protecting a friend, but to me it served the purpose of justice. It might have been best if we all admitted our roles in the accident. I had distracted George; he hadn't brought his car to a complete stop to ask me about a ride; and the older man had pulled out into traffic instead of first letting George pass. But if the other driver had used my honesty to escape responsibility, a larger deception would have emerged. Most of us, I think, do not want to allow such injustices, so we lie to try to bring about fairer conclusions to incidents like this one.

Ultimately, we feel compelled toward honesty, and we never want to present ourselves as liars to people we want to favorably impress. We anguish over our own transgressions of ethics. But situations demand that we lie. We cannot get around it. The question, then, is our personal code: How many of our lies spring from selfishness? How many will hurt others? How much worse will a situation be if we lie? The only way to judge the value of honesty and deception, it seems, is to understand them in the context of our other values.

Openings for Writers

1. **Privacy** How much privacy should a person have? What social or political circumstances might make people lie to maintain their privacy? Is there always something to hide? Why might a person lie about something about which she or he feels no particular shame but just thinks is none of anybody else's business?

2. **Embezzlers and frauds** What does a person have to do to be called an embezzler and/or fraud? What distinguishes embezzlement and fraud from other types of lies? Are there ways in which our culture—through movies, public endorsements, or political chicanery—validates embezzlers and frauds? If so, why would we do that? If not, what values separate their activities and those of other people who deceive?

3. **Prioritizing values** Make a list of the values you hold, starting from the most important and ending with the least important. Where does honesty rank? Why did you put other values above or below it?

4. **Tall tales** Think of stories told in your family that you believe stretched the truth (at least at some level). Were there purposes to the stories? Write about the way you feel when you hear the stories and whether different feelings crop up now. If you can't think of any, analyze "The Lightning Struck Lost Mine" (page 408), which serves as a typical tale of a lost treasure that might be seen as fanciful when scrutinized.

Language

1. **Stretching the truth** Is the expression "stretching the truth" a euphemism (discussed in Chapter 5)? Compare it with other terms used for deception, and decide how the words you choose to describe lies shape the perception of a person or incident.
2. **Justice** Is justice predicated on honesty? Compare it to other concepts such as revenge, vengeance, and retribution. Do the differences shed light on the point the overview makes about larger truth?
3. **Honesty** How is honesty related to truth? What definition you can come up with, and what understandings of key terms must a person have for your definition to be acceptable?

STEPHEN L. CARTER

The Insufficiency of Honesty

In this 1996 article published in the Atlantic Monthly, *Stephen Carter argues that honesty does not require the ethical consideration that integrity does. He feels that people can use honesty as an excuse for performing the bare minimum under an agreement or for being forthright about beliefs without exercising proper judgment. His views about honesty complicate the understandings put forward in the overview.*

> *Honesty is not synonymous with integrity—and integrity is what we need*

A couple of years ago I began a university commencement address by telling the audience that I was going to talk about integrity. The crowd broke into applause. Applause! Just because they had heard the word "integrity": that's how starved for it they were. They had no idea how I was using the word, or what I was going to say about integrity, or, indeed, whether I was for it or against it. But they knew they liked the idea of talking about it.

Very well, let us consider this word "integrity." Integrity is like the weather: everybody talks about it but nobody knows what to do about it. Integrity is that stuff that we always want more of. Some say that we need to return to the good old days when we had a lot more of it. Others say that we as a nation have never really had enough of it. Hardly anybody stops to explain exactly what we mean by it, or how we know it is a good thing, or why everybody needs to have the same amount of it. Indeed, the only trouble with integrity is that everybody who uses the word seems to mean something slightly different.

For instance, when I refer to integrity, do I mean simply "honesty"? The answer is no; although honesty is a virtue of importance, it is a different virtue from integrity. Let us, for simplicity, think of honesty as not lying; and let us further accept Sissela Bok's definition of a lie: "any intentionally deceptive message which is *stated*." Plainly, one cannot have integrity without being honest (although, as we shall see, the matter gets complicated), but one can certainly be honest and yet have little integrity.

When I refer to integrity, I have something very specific in mind. Integrity, as I will use the term, requires three steps: discerning what is right and what is wrong; acting on what you have discerned, even at personal cost; and saying openly that you are acting on your understanding of right and wrong. The first criterion captures the idea that integrity requires a degree of moral reflectiveness. The second brings in the ideal of a person of integrity as steadfast, a quality that includes keeping one's commitments. The third reminds us that a person of integrity can be trusted.

The first point to understand about the difference between honesty and 5
integrity is that a person may be entirely honest without ever engaging in the hard work of discernment that integrity requires: she may tell us quite truthfully what she believes without ever taking the time to figure out whether what she believes is good and right and true. The problem may be as simple as someone's foolishly saying something that hurts a friend's feelings; a few moments of thought would have revealed the likelihood of the hurt and the lack of necessity for the comment. Or the problem may be more complex, as when a man who was raised from birth in a society that preaches racism states his belief in one race's inferiority as a fact, without ever really considering that perhaps this deeply held view is wrong. Certainly the racist is being honest—he is telling us what he actually thinks—but his honesty does not add up to integrity.

Telling Everything You Know

A wonderful epigram sometimes attributed to the filmmaker Sam Goldwyn goes like this: "The most important thing in acting is honesty; once you learn to fake that, you're in." The point is that honesty can be something one *seems* to have. Without integrity, what passes for honesty often is nothing of the kind; it is fake honesty—or it is honest but irrelevant and perhaps even immoral.

Consider an example. A man who has been married for fifty years confesses to his wife on his deathbed that he was unfaithful thirty-five years earlier. The dishonesty was killing his spirit, he says. Now he has cleared his conscience and is able to die in peace.

The husband has been honest—sort of. He has certainly unburdened himself. And he has probably made his wife (soon to be his widow) quite miserable in the process, because even if she forgives him, she will not be able to remember him with quite the vivid image of love and loyalty that she had hoped for. Arranging his own emotional affairs to ease his transition to death, he has shifted to his wife the burden of confusion and pain, perhaps for the rest of her life. Moreover, he has attempted his honesty at the one time in his life when it carries no risk; acting in accordance with what you think is right and risking no loss in the process is a rather thin and unadmirable form of honesty.

Besides, even though the husband has been honest in a sense, he has now twice been unfaithful to his wife: once thirty-five years ago, when he had his affair, and again when, nearing death, he decided that his own peace of mind was more important than hers. In trying to be honest he has violated his marriage vow by acting toward his wife not with love but with naked and perhaps even cruel self-interest.

10   As my mother used to say, you don't have to tell people everything you know. Lying and nondisclosure, as the law often recognizes, are not the same thing. Sometimes it is actually illegal to tell what you know, as, for example, in the disclosure of certain financial information by market insiders. Or it may be unethical, as when a lawyer reveals a confidence entrusted to her by a client. It may be simple bad manners, as in the case of a gratuitous comment to a colleague on his or her attire. And it may be subject to religious punishment, as when a Roman Catholic priest breaks the seal of the confessional—an offense that carries automatic excommunication.

In all the cases just mentioned, the problem with telling everything you know is that somebody else is harmed. Harm may not be the intention, but it is certainly the effect. Honesty is most laudable when we risk harm to ourselves; it becomes a good deal less so if we instead risk harm to others when there is no gain to anyone other than ourselves. Integrity may counsel keeping our secrets in order to spare the feelings of others. Sometimes, as in the example of the wayward husband, the reason we want to tell what we know is precisely to shift our pain onto somebody else—a course of action dictated less by integrity than by self-interest. Fortunately, integrity and self-interest often coincide, as when a politician of integrity is rewarded with our votes. But often they do not, and it is at those moments that our integrity is truly tested.

Error

Another reason that honesty alone is no substitute for integrity is that if forthrightness is not preceded by discernment, it may result in the expression of an incorrect moral judgment. In other words, I may be honest about what I believe, but if I have never tested my beliefs, I may be wrong. And here I mean "wrong" in a particular sense: the proposition in question is wrong if I would change my mind about it after hard moral reflection.

Consider this example. Having been taught all his life that women are not as smart as men, a manager gives the women on his staff less-challenging assignments than he gives the men. He does this, he believes, for their own benefit: he does not want them to fail, and he believes that they will if he gives them tougher assignments. Moreover, when one of the women on his staff does poor work, he does not berate her as harshly as he would a man, because he expects nothing more. And he claims to be acting with integrity because he is acting according to his own deepest beliefs.

The manager fails the most basic test of integrity. The question is not whether his actions are consistent with what he most deeply believes but whether he has done the hard work of discerning whether what he most deeply believes is right. The manager has not taken this harder step.

15   Moreover, even within the universe that the manager has constructed for himself, he is not acting with integrity. Although he is obviously wrong

to think that the women on his staff are not as good as the men, even were he right, that would not justify applying different standards to their work. By so doing he betrays both his obligation to the institution that employs him and his duty as a manager to evaluate his employees.

The problem that the manager faces is an enormous one in our practical politics, where having the dialogue that makes democracy work can seem impossible because of our tendency to cling to our views even when we have not examined them. As Jean Bethke Elshtain has said, borrowing from John Courtney Murray, our politics are so fractured and contentious that we often cannot even reach *disagreement*. Our refusal to look closely at our own most cherished principles is surely a large part of the reason. Socrates thought the unexamined life not worth living. But the unhappy truth is that few of us actually have the time for constant reflection on our views—on public or private morality. Examine them we must, however, or we will never know whether we might be wrong.

None of this should be taken to mean that integrity as I have described it presupposes a single correct truth. If, for example, your integrity-guided search tells you that affirmative action is wrong, and my integrity-guided search tells me that affirmative action is right, we need not conclude that one of us lacks integrity. As it happens, I believe—both as a Christian and as a secular citizen who struggles toward moral understanding—that we *can* find true and sound answers to our moral questions. But I do not pretend to have found very many of them, nor is an exposition of them my purpose here.

It is the case not that there aren't any right answers but that, given human fallibility, we need to be careful in assuming that we have found them. However, today's political talk about how it is wrong for the government to impose one person's morality on somebody else is just mindless chatter. *Every* law imposes one person's morality on somebody else, because law has only two functions: to tell people to do what they would rather not or to forbid them to do what they would.

And if the surveys can be believed, there is far more moral agreement in America than we sometimes allow ourselves to think. One of the reasons that character education for young people makes so much sense to so many people is precisely that there seems to be a core set of moral understandings—we might call them the American Core—that most of us accept. Some of the virtues in this American Core are, one hopes, relatively noncontroversial. About 500 American communities have signed on to Michael Josephson's program to emphasize the "six pillars" of good character: trustworthiness, respect, responsibility, caring, fairness, and citizenship. These virtues might lead to a similarly noncontroversial set of political values: having an honest regard for ourselves and others, protecting freedom of thought and religious belief, and refusing to steal or murder.

Honesty and Competing Responsibilities

A further problem with too great an exaltation of honesty is that it may allow 20 us to escape responsibilities that morality bids us bear. If honesty is substituted for integrity, one might think that if I say I am not planning to fulfill a duty, I need not fulfill it. But it would be a peculiar morality indeed that granted us the right to avoid our moral responsibilities simply by stating our intention to ignore them. Integrity does not permit such an easy escape.

10   Consider an example. Before engaging in sex with a woman, her lover tells her that if she gets pregnant, it is her problem, not his. She says that she understands. In due course she does wind up pregnant. If we believe, as I hope we do, that the man would ordinarily have a moral responsibility toward both the child he will have helped to bring into the world and the child's mother, then his honest statement of what he intends does not spare him that responsibility.

     This vision of responsibility assumes that not all moral obligations stem from consent or from a stated intention. The linking of obligations to promises is a rather modern and perhaps uniquely Western way of looking at life, and perhaps a luxury that only the well-to-do can afford. As Fred and Shulamit Korn (a philosopher and an anthropologist) have pointed out, "If one looks at ethnographic accounts of other societies, one finds that, while obligations everywhere play a crucial role in social life, promising is not preeminent among the sources of obligation and is not even mentioned by most anthropologists." The Korns have made a study of Tonga, where promises are virtually unknown but the social order is remarkably stable. If life without any promises seems extreme, we Americans sometimes go too far the other way, parsing not only our contracts but even our marriage vows in order to discover the absolute minimum obligation that we have to others as a result of our promises.

     That some societies in the world have worked out evidently functional structures of obligation without the need for promise or consent does not tell us what *we* should do. But it serves as a reminder of the basic proposition that our existence in civil society creates a set of mutual responsibilities that philosophers used to capture in the fiction of the social contract. Nowadays, here in America, people seem to spend their time thinking of even cleverer ways to avoid their obligations, instead of doing what integrity commands and fulfilling them. And all too often honesty is their excuse.

AL FRANKEN

I'm a Bad Liar

In this chapter from Lies and the Lying Liars Who Tell Them, *Saturday Night Live alumnus Al Franken recounts duping people at Bob Jones University into believing that a young man accompanying him on a visit was interested in attending the conservative Christian college. Franken's ruse exposes some of the extremes of the mission of Bob Jones University, but it also raises questions about the ethics behind deception and gags. What was Franken hoping to accomplish with this*
15 *gag, and at whose expense?*

I never lie. That is, unless it's absolutely necessary. So the story I'm about to tell you is a little embarrassing.

It starts two and a half years ago. My son, Joe, a junior in a very high-powered, expensive New York City private high school, was beginning his college search. We started to put together a list of schools to visit during spring break. The boy wants to be an engineer, so M.I.T., Michigan, Washington University, and Princeton were early contenders.

My wife, who, I have to tell you, is not usually funny, had a hilarious idea. Why don't I take Joe down to Bob Jones University as a prospective student (which, technically, he was) and have fun at their expense?

Great idea, honey! Hilarious! We could ask them all kinds of snarky questions in the information session. Like about their interracial dating policy. Because of bad publicity, Bob Jones had changed the policy since Bush's visit. Now, according to news reports, they were allowing kids to date interracially *with their parents' permission.* "Yeah, um, I understand the students need their parents' permission to date other races. I was wondering. My wife is fine with Joe dating a black girl. But I'm against it. How would that work out?"

Or "Yeah, um, on your interracial dating policy, I have a theoretical ques- 5 tion. Tiger Woods? Could he date *anyone?* Or *no one?* Could he even go out by himself?" Oddly enough, the answer to that last question, I would learn, was no, unless Tiger was leaving campus either to go home or on a mission.

Excited about all the comic possibilities, I immediately asked my assistant Liz to call BJU, which is what they call themselves. Find out when they have information sessions and tours. Liz called, and found the people in the BJU admissions office to be incredibly friendly. I mention this because it will become a leitmotif for the rest of this chapter.

Of course, there were plenty of information sessions and tours! Come down anytime! We'd love to get to know Joe! What's he interested in? Liz did her best—the boy's into history. Great!

That afternoon, when Joe got back from his fancy, two-thirds-Jewish high school, I told him the good news. We were going to go on a little comedy adventure. Joe—and in retrospect, this is to the boy's credit—was *absolutely appalled.* "No!"

"What?" I said incredulously. This was my son, who grew up in a comedy household. Didn't he recognize a great idea?

"Leave these people alone!" he said angrily. "What did they do to you?" 10

"Well, they're racist and nuts, and—"

"Dad, they just have a different belief system. Leave them alone."

And that, I thought, was that. What I didn't understand was that when you contact an evangelical organization, they will not stop mailing you shit. Did you know that BJU has quite a history department? Did you know that the BJU cheerleaders wear skirts down to their ankles? It's in their brochure.

And then there were the calls.

"Hi! Is Joe there?"

"Um, who may I say is calling?"   15

"Josie Martin from Bob Jones University."

"Oh. Joe's not here now."

"When will he be back?"

20   "Um, hmmm, I . . . don't know."

This happened a lot. A lot. And because I'm a busy man and my wife wasn't vigilant enough, Joe actually answered a few times, getting angrier and angrier at me because he was now being forced to lie. Something we Frankens don't do. Unless it's absolutely necessary.

The last straw was the call from a junior at BJU who was from Manhattan. "Where," he asked Joe, "do you go to church?"

"I don't go to church," Joe answered reflexively. On the other end of the phone, he heard a shocked GASP.

". . . in Manhattan," he quickly recovered. "I go to church on Long Island."

25   "Oh," said the very nice young man whom my son was lying to.

Joe charged out of his room and confronted me. "This has got to stop! I don't like lying to people!" He told me to call Bob Jones and tell them he had decided to go to a secular college. Which was, of course, entirely true.

So the next day, I had Liz call and tell BJU the bad news. They were disappointed, but understood. And were extremely nice about it.

Cut to: TeamFranken. Present day. A good idea never dies. I needed a kid without Joe's integrity. Fortunately, I was at Harvard. Among the fourteen members of TeamFranken, I had fourteen volunteers, including Owen Kane, a thirty-eight-year-old mid-career Kennedy School grad student.

But to maximize the chances of our little scheme working, it was important that my "son" or "daughter" be able to pass for a high school junior. Owen was out.

Andrew Barr was in. A sophomore at the college, Andrew was perfect. Fresh-faced, eager, he could easily pass for seventeen. Valedictorian at Boston Latin, the top public school in Boston, Andrew was razor sharp and quick on his feet. Only one problem. The Jewish thing. Neither Andrew nor I knew jack about Christianity, particularly the weird, freakish kind practiced by these incredibly nice people at Bob Jones University.

30   We decided to do our homework. Learning about Christianity would be too difficult and time-consuming. Also, boring. Instead, we checked out BJU's website, hoping not just to learn enough to pull off our scam, but also to find stuff to make fun of.

Unfortunately, we discovered that the interracial dating policy had been discarded altogether. Shit. There went the Tiger Woods joke.

But not to worry. There was plenty of other fodder. First of all, the "university" is not accredited. That's right. They have the same degree-granting power as Schlotsky's Deli. *They* claim it's because they don't *want* to be accredited. We think it's because they don't believe in *science*. You see, they stand without apology for the absolute authority of the Bible. God created the Earth in six days. And He didn't put gays in it, either.

Then, there's the BJU policy on student use of the Internet, which is "a source of much content antagonistic to Godliness." No argument there.

Chat rooms, instant messaging, and web-based email accounts are banned. Students are not allowed to access websites with "Biblically offensive material." In addition to the usual pornography and violence, this includes "crude, vulgar language or gestures, tasteless humor (excretory functions, etc.), and graphic medical photos." Fortunately, BJU has an automatic filter, updated *daily*, to block these websites. And since nobody's perfect (i.e., we're all sinners), if the filter picks up a student attempting to access one of these websites, the "incident" is logged for an Internet administrator. In fact, all Internet use is constantly monitored by the "university," giving parents real peace of mind. Like the incredible friendliness, "constant monitoring" would also become a theme of life at BJU.

And speaking of parents, Andrew and I found the linchpin for what would become "our elaborate ruse." On the BJU website is a letter telling parents that it is their "God-given responsibility" not to allow their children to choose their own college. The consequences of that are made clear in the vivid and terrifying stories of the "Three College Shipwrecks," written by Bob Jones, Sr., the founder of the "university."

The first two "shipwrecks," known as "His Only Daughter" and "The 35 Pride of His Mother," come to alarmingly similar ends. In each, a promising, God-fearing student is allowed to go off to a secular university. After returning from their freshman years, both have lost their way, their faith shattered. The Only Daughter "rushed upstairs, stood in front of a mirror, took a gun, and blew out her brains." Whereas the Pride of His Mother, having contracted "an unspeakable disease," announces his intention to "buy a gun and blow out my brains."

The third shipwreck, "The Son of an Aged Minister," is less violent, though certainly just as tragic. He had been "a great boy, bright, clean, obedient, Christian." Unfortunately, although the boy makes the life-saving decision to attend a Christian school, it isn't BJU. "A skeptic had got in the Science Department" of the less-Christian Christian school, and when the boy returns home, he has lost his faith and becomes "a drunken, atheistic bum."

So. Parents could save their kids from suicide, alcoholism, and the clap by forcing them to go to BJU. Excellent. This was our key. Since neither Andrew nor I could pull off being devout evangelical Christians, it would be Andrew's *mother* who desperately wanted him to go to Bob Jones. Instead of being Andrew's father, I would be a friend of the family—in fact, the best friend of Andrew's father, who had died tragically of brain cancer—no wait, boating accident—three years ago. Andrew's mom had sunk into a deep depression, then miraculously found Christ.

It was perfect. Neither Andrew nor I would have to know anything. But why wasn't Mom there? Sick? No. Threw out her back carrying boxes of blood at a blood drive. At church. As you can see, we started putting *way* too much thought into the back story, and way too little into the fact that I have been on television for nearly thirty years.

Seeing as how we did spend the time on the back story, you really should hear it. Because it's pretty good. Andrew's father, Hank, my college roommate and financial advisor, ran an incredibly successful hedge fund. Andrew's mother, Ellen, therefore, was not just a stunningly beautiful widow—she looks like Naomi Judd—but also fabulously wealthy. Now for the delicious spin. I was more than just a family friend. I had my eye on the Widow Barr, and seeing to it that young Andrew would agree to attend Bob Jones would be a feather in my cap.

40   Andrew's part was equally delicious. Eager to please his mother, he had happily agreed to visit what he thought was just a typical, fun-in-the-sun Christian school. Our plan, as you can clearly see, was brilliant. Neither of us would have to know anything about either Christianity or Bob Jones University. We had thought of everything.

And, yes, I considered the possibility that I would be recognized. A disguise? Nah. I'd just cut my hair extra short. Yeah, that would do it.

"Hi, Mr. Franken! Big fan!" "Good to see you, Mr. Franken!" "Loved you on SNL!" These were the security guards at La Guardia. Nothing to worry about. We were still in New York. Didn't mean the haircut wasn't working.

We arrived in Greenville. The Hertz rent-a-car gal, also a big fan. That's good, I explained to Andrew. It's good to have a fan base. But this Hertz woman, she wasn't a nutcase evangelical. She watched secular TV. Don't worry.

So we got there around 11 A.M. Drove through the gates. Didn't set off the Jew alarm. We're in.

45   Took a look around. Not an unattractive campus. Buildings, grass—nice day. But the place was eerily devoid of human activity. We'd soon learn that everyone was at chapel, this being a weekday. Out of the car and into the Administration Building. At the desk, an extremely friendly, well-scrubbed, wide-eyed young man greeted us and sent us along into the admissions office, where we were met by an extremely friendly, well-scrubbed, wide-eyed female staffer. Like every woman at BJU, she wore a skirt that covered not just her upper thigh, but her lower thigh, and her knee, and her calf, and her either well-turned or not well-turned ankle. No real way of knowing. But she was *really* nice and showed us the official admissions video, which featured two miniature pirates who introduced themselves as "your guardians." At BJU, they told us, you're never alone. Remember I said "constant monitoring" would be a theme? The creepy mini-pirates weren't kidding.

We scheduled a 1 P.M. interview with "Gerald"[1] and decided to grab some lunch, joining the mass of students pouring out of chapel and into the dining commons. There were thousands of them, young men in shirts and ties and khakis, young women in their ankle-length skirts. You could say we stood out. We were about to face our first test.

His name was Doug, an intense, though extremely nice, finance major. In an effort to appear as if I had nothing to hide, I said hi. Doug squinted, looked me over skeptically, and decided to keep an eye on us. Very nicely, he offered to help us get lunch and sit with us, and then asked us lots and lots of questions about who we were and why we were there.

I took this as an opportunity to take our elaborate ruse out for a little test drive. Andrew's dad, dead. Mom, depressed. Mom finds Jesus. Wants Andrew at BJU. Throws out back carrying boxes of blood. Doug asked if Andrew wanted to go there. Andrew didn't know, but I pointed out that his mother really, *really* wanted him to. Doug said that Andrew shouldn't go unless he really wanted to. Hadn't Doug read "The Three Shipwrecks"?

Then things started getting sticky. Doug was asking *me* questions. Like, what did I do for a living? And why did I look familiar? I told him I was a writer, which is true, by the way. Remember, I lie only when it's absolutely necessary.

To get us off a potentially incognito-blowing line of questioning, I clev- 50 erly changed the subject to creationism. You really believe it? Doug said he did, and so did all his friends sitting around us. According to Doug, evolution made no sense at all. No mutation, he insisted, had ever been beneficial. I looked at my thumb, but said nothing, as I used it to hold my fork and shove the worst lunch I've ever had into my mouth. It was some kind of creamed broccoli on a bun. But then again, you don't go to Bob Jones for the food!

Doug told us that the chances of protoplasm evolving into a human being were infinitesimally small: one over ten to the 256th, or something like that. Duane, an intense, but extremely nice, business administration major, came up with a vivid analogy. "The chances," Duane said, "of protoplasm turning into a fully formed human being are worse than the chances of an explosion in a junkyard yielding an intact Boeing 747."

Doug could tell that I wasn't buying. "So, Alan," he said. Oh, I forgot. I had changed my name to "Alan" as part of our undercover operation. My name really is Alan—remember, only when absolutely necessary. "So, Alan," he said, "why do you believe in evolution?"

"Well, Doug, I'm not a scientist. But it seems that every scientist in this field at an accredited university [heh, heh] believes in evolution. You know, at M.I.T., Stanford, Wisconsin, Arizona State, Wake Forest, you know, everywhere."

Doug had a good answer. "So, just because everyone believes something, you think it's true. Well, remember, the Catholic Church taught for hundreds of years that the sun revolved around the Earth. Then they persecuted Galileo for saying the opposite."

"I think you're making my point, Doug. The Church based their conclu- 55 sions on faith, just as you are. Galileo was an empiricist, like all those scientists at the accredited universities."

Andrew was growing more and more uncomfortable. Though he was thirty-two years my junior, he felt that I was exhibiting poor judgment by questioning the fundamental belief of the entire institution while attempting to remain inconspicuous. After a lot of eye contact between the two of us, we decided it was time to bail.

We told Doug and his friends that we had an appointment with an admissions officer, which again was true. Doug offered to walk us to the admissions office, but we told him that first we had to pick up something at a pharmacy, which while not true, was a necessary lie. We had to ditch Doug. Otherwise, our cover would be blown.

On the way to the "pharmacy," I was recognized by several students, some of whom yelled out, "Al Franken!" I waved. And gave out some autographs. The kids were very nice.

---

[1] All names have been changed to protect me.

There was still thirty minutes until our appointment, so we did the only thing that made sense. We hid.

60   At 1 P.M. sharp, we slipped into the Administration Building for our appointment with Gerald Fortenberry. We were praying that Gerald hadn't been alerted to the presence of a liberal satirist on campus. It was our only hope.

We were unbelievably lucky. Gerald had no idea who I was. Clearly a recent graduate of the university, he was a sweet, almost innocent young man. A perfect patsy. He bought our elaborate ruse hook, line, and sinker.

Moved by the story of young Andrew's father's death (boating accident), he understood totally Mom's depression and subsequent salvation. "It sounds like your mother's life has been transformed."

"Yes," Andrew said. "And now she wants me to come here."

"Well, you're the one who really should want this."

65   Hadn't *anyone* read "The Three Shipwrecks"?! Even in the *Admissions* Department?

"Well," Andrew replied, "I'm not into the whole religion thing as much as my mother."

"That would be impossible," I offered. "She's very beautiful. She looks like Naomi Judd."

Gerald nodded.

"But I'm okay with it," Andrew continued. "I haven't really developed my own personal relationship with Christ, but I think it would be good to work on that. Plus, I'm really pumped about going off to college. I have a friend at Syracuse, and he's having a blast."

70   Gerald moved past the blast at Syracuse and came back to Mom. "She sounds like she's happier than she's ever been."

"Yeah," Andrew nodded. "Well, at least since Dad died."

I had a couple questions. Andrew was interested in premed. "I know you teach creationism as opposed to evolution. How does that work out with medical schools?"

"Oh, it's no problem," Gerald reassured. "In fact, we have a higher percentage of students accepted to medical school than the national average."

"Really? And what would that percentage be?" I wanted to know.

75   "I don't have that offhand," Gerald replied. "Perhaps I can get it for you."

Then Andrew pounced. At the airport in New York, we had picked up a *U.S. News & World Report Guide to the 1400 Top Colleges and Universities.* "Maybe it's in here," Andrew suggested innocently, pulling it out of his backpack.

Gerald blanched, knowing, as we did, that Bob Jones was not listed among the one thousand, four hundred top colleges and universities in the United States. Andrew flipped to South Carolina. "Hmmm . . . maybe it's under J."

"Give me that." I took the book and examined it thoroughly, as Gerald looked on uncomfortably. "It's . . . it's not here."

"No," said Gerald. "A lot of colleges pay to get in that thing."

80   "Really?" I asked.

"Yes." He nodded authoritatively.

Andrew understood. "So it's like an advertisement?"

"Yeah."

That was quite a relief for me. Until that moment, I had been feeling more and more guilty. But now that Gerald was lying about the college guide, I felt a lot better. Putting the book aside, I smiled at Gerald. "Well, at least we know Bob Jones is an accredited university."

"Uh . . . no."

"No?"

85

"No. Actually, we *choose* not to be accredited. I can give you a pamphlet on that."

Assured that the pamphlet would explain everything, we moved on. Andrew expressed an interest in theater. Gerald got very excited. Every year Bob Jones's theater department presents what Gerald called a "Shakespeare-play." Gerald told us that before he came to BJU, "I wasn't much for operas and Shakespeare-plays."

One concern. Mom, the one that looks like Naomi Judd, was worried about a certain element that Andrew might be exposed to in the Drama Department. Did Gerald understand what I was getting at? To make it even clearer, I used the magic phrase, "alternative lifestyle." Any of that here at BJU?

"Oh, no, no, no, no." Gerald shook his head. "No, no, no, no. No." None of that here. We could be absolutely certain of that.

90

Good, good. Because Andrew was looking forward in particular to the heterosexual experience of college life.

"Yeah, my mom doesn't like me dating, because of, you know . . . but college is the time that, you know . . ."

"Oh, yes. We want you to meet girls here," Gerald smiled. "We encourage that."

"So, the dating scene," I asked on behalf of the boy, "what's that like?"

Before Gerald could respond, Andrew expressed some mild concern. "Yeah, I was talking to some guys outside and they said there were some . . . rules."

95

"Yes," Gerald nodded. "You cannot leave campus with someone of the opposite sex, unless you are accompanied by a chaperone."

Andrew raised his eyebrows. Then, looking for a ray of hope, "But on campus, you know . . ."

"We have a snack shop. You can sit and have a snack together."

Andrew and I looked at each other. How to put this?

I took it upon myself. "In terms of, um, you know, um—how far can he go?"

100

Gerald understood. "Well, obviously, there's absolutely no physical contact."

A numbed silence from the two of us.

"None?" finally came out of Andrew's gaping mouth.

"That's right. No holding hands, hugging, kissing, anything like that."

"Backrubs?" Andrew asked for clarification.

105

"No."

"Oh, you mean in public? Well, that's understandable," Andrew conceded.

"No. No physical contact anywhere. At all."

Andrew slumped.

110   Maybe Gerald had seen this reaction before. He knew just what to say. "Because, Andrew, you know what hand-holding leads to."

Andrew took a wild stab. "Sin?"

"That's right. You see, our rules are like guardrails that keep you on the path of Christ."

So far, our plan was working beautifully. Young Andrew, who at first seemed amenable to, even excited about, pleasing his mother, was now reeling. It was time to set up the kill.

"You know, Gerald, Andrew's mother really wants him to come here. I read that you have to be in the dorms by ten-twenty for the ten-thirty prayer group, and then lights out at eleven. But how about weekends?"

115   Andrew perked up. "Yeah, how far is it to Atlanta? Because my mom might let me bring my car, and a lot of the bands I like don't play here in Greenville."

"Well, you can have a car on campus, but you can only use it on weekends to go home or if you're going on a mission," Gerald explained helpfully.

"Oh, I see." Andrew nodded. "I guess it wouldn't be so bad to take the bus. Because Weezer didn't play in Greenville last time out."

"No, no. We don't want you going to rock concerts. There's no rock and roll."

"No rock 'n' roll?" I asked.

120   "No, we don't endorse that, obviously."

"What if I don't play it too loud?" Andrew said, becoming upset.

"No. We don't allow it in the dorms at all."

"I could use headphones," Andrew suggested.

"No."

125   Things were getting a little tense. "How about country music? That's good clean fun," I winked.

"No."

"*Christian* rock?" I tried. Certainly they must allow *Christian* rock. Gerald shook his head. "We don't endorse that."

By now, Andrew was visibly shaken. No hand-holding. No road trips. No tunes. Lots and lots of prayer.

130   That's when I spoke up. "Gerald, could I have a word with you alone?"

"Sure, Alan."

I nodded to Andrew, who excused himself and stepped into the nearby men's room. I waited for the door to close, then turned to Gerald, suddenly in his face.

"Listen. This kid's mother is *extremely* wealthy. She has *tons* of money. She wants him to come here. If he comes here, I'm talking another *building*. Okay?! And you're blowing it!"

Gerald recoiled. His eyes opened wide. It was as if he had seen Satan himself.

135   I was pleading. "Don't tell him everything. You said before 'nobody's perfect.' Certainly there are kids who do stuff here."

"Well, I said that because we're all sinners. And the rules are guardrails to keep you on the path of Christ. I can't withhold anything from Andrew. That would defeat the whole purpose. Which is to live a life in Christ."

Aw, hell. Gerald was absolutely, totally, without question incorruptible. Screw it.

We had our story. The place was weird, but the people extremely nice. A good honest day's work done, lying to God-fearing people. We'd sleep well tonight. But we decided to poke around a little more since we had some time to kill. Off to the museum, where BJU houses the largest collection of sacred art in the Western Hemisphere.

And let me tell you, it's a lot of sacred art: Botticelli, Granacci, Tintoretto, 140 Dolci, Rembrandt, Ribera, Rubens, Van Dyck. Twenty-seven rooms full. A priceless collection. Donated by wealthy alums? Not quite. Most of it was purchased by Bob Jones, Jr., himself, the second of the three Bob Joneses.

You see, Dr. Bob II had spent some summers in the 1930s as a tour guide in Rome, Paris, and Vienna, and had acquired a taste for fine art. Luckily, when he returned to Europe in the late forties, he was able acquire quite a bit of it at very reasonable prices. Hmmm, I thought. What do you suppose would be the chances of a white supremacist who came to Europe in the thirties knowing someone who knew someone who had recently come across some "misplaced" art in the late 1940s? In fact, I thought I recognized a couple pieces that used to belong to my grandfather, who was a big collector of sacred Christian art before he was hauled off to Buchenwald. Nah. Maybe I was jumping to conclusions.

Still with some time to kill, we decided to hop on the three o'clock tour with a delightful Christian family of four. We had a lovely time, even had some laughs, until we got to the theater, where our bluff was finally called. On the stage were several gigantic crosses, scenery for what they call "The Living Gallery." This involves recreating great works of sacred art using real people in tableaux. I was very excited about getting Andrew to take a picture of me hanging from one of the crosses. Then we met R.J. From the public liaison's office.

"I'll take them from here," R.J. told our tour guide. We didn't like the way he said that. Nor the way he said, "Let me tell you a little about the theater. The floor is from Rockefeller Center. But it's no *Saturday Night Live*."

The jig was up.

"Can I just ask what you're down here looking for?" he inquired 145 pointedly.

"Well, it's a long story," I said, willing, but not really eager, to go into the whole boating-accident-depression-salvation-boxes-of-blood thing again.

"Uh-huh. Look. We've had enough of being made fun of," R.J. said with more than a touch of bitterness. Then turning to Andrew, he added, "I hope this isn't awkward for you."

"Oh no," said Andrew cheerfully. "We've been getting this all day." Actually, we hadn't. But I thought it was a nice touch.

R.J. continued. "If you're legit, I'd be happy to show you anything you want to see. But we're not going to put our heads on the chopping block again." I had to admire his directness and his willingness to call us on what should have been obvious to everyone all day. And yet he had the manners to leave open the remote possibility that we were, as he put it, "legit." And even while being hostile, he was extremely nice about it.

150   Accompanied by R.J., we made a show of being interested in the alumni building, the least interesting building on campus, and then were walked to our car.

And as we bid farewell to old BJU, we realized that we had learned something, not just about Bob Jones University, but about ourselves. We'd come to Bob Jones expecting to encounter racist, intolerant homophobes. Instead, we found people who were welcoming, friendly, and extremely nice. A little weird, yes. And no doubt homophobic. But well-meaning. Kind of.

More important, we learned that while we were happy that we had successfully executed our ruse and relieved it had worked on Gerald, it was not something we were particularly proud of. Yes, we got a good story out of it. But while there's a certain subversive thrill in deceiving people, it also left us with an unsettled feeling in our stomachs that a trip to the Waffle House only exacerbated. It made us wonder what kind of person can lie like that every day of his life. How do the lying liars do it?

In a way, I was glad that R.J. had cut short our tour before I got up on one of those giant crosses. (Although if he hadn't, you'd be looking at a pretty cool picture right now.) I don't begrudge them their religion. Hell, I admire it. No, I don't. But it's their right to have it. Just as it's my inherent right to invade their privacy under false pretenses. No, it isn't.

Doug, Duane, R.J., and especially Gerald, when you finally read this— we're very sorry. Also, we stole some stuff from the gift shop. No, we didn't.

155   Yes, we did.

No, we didn't. We're not crooks.

Assignment Ideas

Moving away from clichés toward more profound insights about honesty and deception is the key to successfully responding to the assignment options below. While you might ultimately settle on a fairly standard view of the topic you choose, the method in which you explain your thinking must demonstrate sufficient complication. Reviewing methods of critical analysis in Chapter 2 will help you explore the topic and relate your decisions to your audience.

1. Summarize Stephen L. Carter's ideas from "The Insufficiency of Honesty" so that you convey a firm grasp of his concerns. Extend, limit, confirm, or negate his views by giving other examples, whether personal or public, that show the tension between honesty and integrity. Try to find a word or virtue of your own—perhaps from the list of values you brainstormed—to replace Carter's reliance on *integrity*. Look at the way Eric Dezenhall uses the term *hypocrisy* in "We Like Our Bad Guys to Be Honest About It" (page 410).

2. Compare two incidents in which you told lies, exploring the reasons that made you choose to deceive. Were the lies completely self-serving and no better than those told by embezzlers and frauds? Or can you categorize them into one of the four groups discussed in the overview? Explore

the effects of your lies. See if your reasons for telling lies were better than reasons you can think of for telling the truth, and reach a conclusion based on your analysis of whether some situations are better handled by lying.

3. Franken had difficulty sustaining his charade; after being exposed he asks how people can lie like that every day. He is alluding to politicians, but the question has application to people who continually lie in their social circles. In an essay, describe a person you know who tells a lot of stories or makes a number of claims that you don't believe or have found to be untrue. Recount some of the lies, and theorize about why the person continually deceives others, using your analysis as a generalization about lying and honesty in our culture.

4. Research con games, keeping in mind your brainstorming or freewriting about embezzlers and frauds. Describe some of the deception that goes into typical con games, such as pyramid schemes, bait and switch, and desert land schemes. Draw a parallel to Franken's prank. Since Franken profits from his deception by generating material for his comedy routine, how are his motives different from those of people who face imprisonment should they be caught? Is misrepresentation harmless? Think about ways you can supplement this parallel with examples from your own involvement in a practical joke or scheme. Do the justifications outweigh the harm of the deception?

Group Work

Deception and basic dishonesty have cost taxpayers billions of dollars, have bilked innocent people out of retirement funds, and have even caused the deaths of thousands. Each group member should investigate an example of large-scale deception. One deception should have been perpetuated by politicians, another by corporate executives, and a third by an ordinary individual. Look into the motives of the people involved. What did they stand to gain? Why did the possible gain matter more than the consequences of the deception? Place each incident in a context that shows the American reaction to it, including the punishment of the people involved, and use this to build a thesis about our cultural response to deception. Do we tolerate it? Do we make excuses for it? Does who is involved matter more than what he or she did? Do we hold individuals accountable to the extent that we should?

Additional Readings

The selections that follow build on our understanding of honesty and deception, looking at the tensions between the two. "The Lightning Struck Lost Mine" reminds us of tall tales that somebody believes and acts on, looking for hidden riches and losing more money, even his or her life, in the pursuit of the treasure. In "Radically Honest Online Dating," Sasha Cagen examines the reasons why people lie in their profiles on sites designed to help them find a desirable partner for a relationship. She questions the outcome of people not living up to their billing, so to speak, but then wonders how much honesty is really appropriate for such sites. "Is the Whole Truth Attainable?" gives some historical background on the topic of truth, and as its title suggests, debates whether complete truth on any matter is possible. The last article, "We Like Our Bad Guys to Be Honest About It," compares the dishonesty of mobsters to the dishonesty of the Enron executives who swindled millions from investors and employees.

ROGER HENN

The Lightning Struck Lost Mine

Great ranches now spread across the valley of Cow Creek: Sleeping Ute, Chimney Rock, and others. Some have their own private jet landing strips. Their ranch houses are pretentious, spreading to tens of thousands of square feet. Cow Creek and its valley is greatly different from what it was like in the nineteenth century.

One early map calls Cow Creek, Bache Creek, which was the Spanish word for buffalo. It is also a term for cow. Could it have been possible that early Spanish explorers found the valley filled with grazing buffalo? There is one old, old building in Cow Creek that has a buffalo skull mounted over the door. Could it be that the skull might have been found nearby? The Spanish name suggests that Cow Creek was known to their trappers, miners, or explorers far earlier than we have acknowledged. We do know that the Escalante explorers reached the Uncompahgre at about the present-day location of Colona in 1776.

When the Ute reservation was moved to Colona, Cow Creek became the grazing grounds for the Ute cattle herds. Chief Ouray and his key sub chiefs were working to change the Utes from hunters to cattle raisers—a change Ouray recognized would be necessary if the Utes were to survive in the white man's world. If the Utes had another ten years in the Uncompahgre Valley before their expulsion, they might well have become successful agrarians.

My story of the lost mine of this Cow Creek country must begin with the first white man we have record of exploring it. Charlie Hall came to the San Juans with the ill-fated Baker parties. Having no success in finding placer gold in Baker's Park near present-day Silverton, Hall and two companions left to look at the Uncompahgre Valley in 1861. In the bowl that is today Ouray they found no gold in their panning so they proceeded down the stream, panning as they went. Like others of the Baker parties they watched where their feet walked looking for evidence of free gold; if they had raised their eyes, they would have seen gold and silver veins all around them. Free gold, which can be collected by panning, is almost non-existent in the San Juans. Going downstream they encountered the recently abandoned camp of the Doc Arnold party that had spent the winter of 1860–61 a mile south of present-day Ridgway. The Arnold party was headed for Baker's Park and the hubbub there but got lost and ended up in the Uncompahgre Valley trapped for the winter by heavy snow. Although they did find some gold, when spring came they left to travel on to the exciting Baker camp which had always been their goal.

Charlie and his two friends continued down the river to the junction with 5 Cow Creek. Running out of food they headed up Cow Creek hoping to find a shortcut back to Baker's Park. Thus they became the first white men of record to have entered Cow Creek. Starving, they were so anxious to get back that they did no prospecting. In the years that followed Cow Creek remained unprospected.

And so we turn to our tale of the lost mine. First, however, much confusion exists in histories of Ouray as to two men named Long. As one of these is the center of our story we need to clarify this confusion. Robert F. Long was one of the group of thirteen men to first winter in Ouray. Long is first recorded as coming into the San Juans in early spring of 1875. With his small party he brought a number of wagons from Del Norte and started up Stony Pass, but the remaining heavy snow made it impossible to bring wagons over the pass. The wagons and supplies were left at Lost Trail Camp with a packer named Frank Blackledge who used Lost Trail as his headquarters. Long and his associates struggled up through the snow and then down to Cunningham Gulch and Howardsville. When the snow melted Long returned to Lost Trail, but to his dismay found the wagons burned and the valuable supplies missing. Blackledge had a number of conflicting stories, but Long never recovered the missing supplies.

Long worked his way up to Mineral Point (which with grandiose ideas was calling itself Mineral City) and joined a party of men setting out to explore the Uncompahgre. . . . Long helped stake out the town site of Uncompahgre and with the Cutler brothers built the third of three cabins that were to constitute the entire community that first winter. Long's cabin was selected by the La Plata County Commissioners to be the polling place for all of the sparsely settled Uncompahgre country. The La Plata Commissioners recognized the new community as Uncompahgre, but the post office designated it as Ouray. It was at Long's cabin that he cooked the famous Christmas dinner for the thirteen men wintering in Ouray. In celebrating the men drank from a gallon jug of vinegar. The hill where the cabin was located is still called Vinegar Hill. Long was petitioner for the 1875 application for the Town of Uncompahgre, was elected Trustee at the first town meeting of Ouray in 1876, and County Judge when Ouray County was formed.

Treatment of ore to free gold and silver was a real problem in the San Juans. The first ore from the Wheel of Fortune had to be packed on burros over the ridge of Imogene Basin, down to Silverton then over Cinnamon Pass to Lake City. To pay for that very long trip took very high ore values so ore was carefully sorted and the less valuable left on the dump. In 1877 it cost twenty-five dollars a ton to pack ore from Ouray to Silverton for treatment and then the result had to be carried by wagon to Pueblo for smelting. One mine was reported using 270 burros for that haul.

Long went back to Silverton, bought the equipment and works of the Brown, Epley & Company smelting plant, and hauled it to Ouray. He bought other equipment from outside the San Juans and placed in operation the mill and smelter named San Juan & St. Louis Smelting Company, a name suggesting his ties to St. Louis. The plant was located just short of four miles north of Ouray.

Unfortunately for Ouray, enterprising Robert F. Long died in 1882 at age 10 forty-one. He was a veteran of the Civil War, his wife a New Orleans belle.

Their eleven-year-old son died in St. Louis a month later. So it was not Robert Long who found the mine in Cow Creek which has been lost for so many years. It was Alfred E. Long who made the discovery. A. E. Long must have come into the San Juans before 1876 because he was well known enough to run for county clerk of the new San Juan County in that year. He lost in a three man race for the position. He was still involved in Silverton in 1879 when he was one of three men who incorporated a Silverton, Ophir, and Rico Toll Road Company which never turned a spade of rock.

By this time A. E. Long's interest had been transferred to Ouray and he ran again for county clerk, but this time for newly formed Ouray County, and he was elected. He held public office on and off for many years. In 1891 he founded the *San Juan Silverite*, a newspaper largely dedicated to his political aspirations. The short-lived paper was described as "a political paper with no party and a religious paper with no church."

Almost twenty years after his experiment of prospecting in the Animas country, Long decided to go gold hunting again. Most all the mountains deemed worthy of prospecting had been thoroughly covered and staked with mining cliams. But Long knew of one area that had been largely overlooked. He enlisted an acquaintance to go with him.

The two set out to prospect in Cow Creek country. Finding some promising float (rock that had rolled from higher up) led them to climb a high stony ridge leaving their horses below. There on the top of this bare ridge they found a six inch vein of quartz carrying good gold values. A heavy thunderstorm came up, and as there was no place on that barren ridge to seek shelter, the two men just continued to work at extracting gold-bearing quartz. A lightning bolt struck knocking Long's companion unconscious. When he recovered he found the bolt had killed Long. He packed Long's body across the back of a horse and led the animal with its burden back to Ouray.

15   Severely shocked, he told his story, climbed aboard the first train leaving Ouray, and was never heard from again. He left behind the story of a rich gold mine and some ore to prove it, but no direction as to how to find it. The Cow Creek drainage is immense, but somewhere in that vastness, on a rocky ridge, is a rich lost gold mine.

ERIC DEZENHALL

We Like Our Bad Guys to Be Honest About It

When I watched Enron's former chief executive, Jeffrey K. Skilling, testify recently before Congress, it sparked a decades-old memory of—don't laugh — the televised testimony of a very different kind of honcho, my hometown mob boss, Philadelphia's Nicodemo "Little Nicky" Scarfo.

As a kid, I used to see Nicky and his boys talking on the beach in Margate, N.J., and thought I was pretty cool when I got an acknowledgment, a

"Yo, kid," from Nicky or one of his killers. Years later, in the mid-1980s, I was a former White House aide still gaga over the political process, and I couldn't wait to see how Nicky defended his corner in a congressional hearing about racketeering. The highlight of Nicky's testimony was when he was asked if he swore to tell the truth. Nicky — visibly ticked, his South Philly pompadour bouncing — glanced at his lawyer for a little help. The lawyer urgently nodded a yes. In Nicky's business, lying was currency, and he appeared, well, betrayed, by the very pretense that the proceedings would be on the level. In contrast, Enron's Skilling, when questioned, conveyed an earnest, helpful demeanor and stayed "on message" in the spirit of a true wise guy: Wasn't me.

Lots of people have said they don't believe Skilling, and one of my friends even huffed that the ex-CEO was "worse than a gangster." I don't agree; I have always been amazed by how our culture grades corruption on a curve of moral relativism. Most scandals are called "Watergates," military conflicts become "Vietnams" and human rights horrors "Holocausts" when they're not.

Nor do I believe, in any legal or moral sense, that an accused corporate huckster is comparable to a convicted psychopath like Nicky Scarfo. Nevertheless, the Scarfo and Skilling testimonies point to an interesting cultural distinction. Everybody I've talked to seems to want the Enron guys to do hard time. I can't remember the last time I heard the same dark wishes expressed about the Mafia.

On the contrary, American culture often romanticizes the wiseguys of organized crime. *The Sopranos* became a TV show beloved both by cable viewers and the Emmy judges. Mobsters preen in beer commercials, asking "How ya doin'?" Successful films such as *Analyze This* and *O Brother, Where Art Thou?* portray professional killers as comic, even heroic characters.   5

The simultaneous vilification of Enron and glorification of organized crime makes me wonder what kind of bad guys America wants? Answer: honest ones. A thief pointing a gun at your head makes no pretense about his intentions, but a thief armed with a laptop and a smile is out to fool you, and Americans absolutely hate to be fooled.

The real sin of the Enron executives is their hypocrisy. They portrayed themselves as model corporate citizens, society's pillars, deeply concerned about their community. Meanwhile, it has been alleged, they were helping themselves to millions of dollars at the expense of their employees and shareholders. Murderous Little Nicky and his Mafia cronies have never tried to pretend to be anything other than what they are: wiseguys.

I suspect there's another reason we go easy on street-corner buccaneers, one tied more deeply to the roots of American culture. We like the Mafia because it is cheating the system from the outside. It's no coincidence that Butch and Sundance are lionized just as Don Corleone's Godfather is—though all are violent criminals.

Often the glorification is tinged with nostalgia. Last month, the front page of the *New York Daily News* revealed that prosecutors say mob boss Vincent "the Chin" Gigante—who for years roamed Greenwich Village in his bathrobe, feigning insanity to dodge the clink—is still running the Genovese Crime Family from prison. And when aging mobster Raymond "Long John" Martorano was mortally shot while driving on a busy street in Philadelphia, the newspaper articles reported the grisly details—but also reminisced that he was one of the last of the old-timers, whose killers didn't appreciate the power he once held. Ah, the old days, when grown men dispatched one another more discreetly. In the past year, barely a week has gone by when the networks haven't reported a "death watch" at the bedside of cancer-stricken mob boss, John Gotti, as if we were all waiting for puffs of white smoke to waft from the Vatican.

10   Chronicling the toughs is less a cry for justice than a spectator sport. Friends who know I write about the mob, including a priest and several rabbis, no less, contact me from time to time, thirsty for old yarns and gossip about South Philly rogues such as "Al Pajamas" (in prison), "Chicken Man" (blown up on his front porch with a nail bomb), Harry "the Hunchback" (recently died in prison), and "Nicky Crow" (in the witness protection program).

Despite the steady cavalcade of Mafia coverage, there are no letters to the editor asking that prosecutors take action. No demands to "Lynch the Chin." There's no public outcry, because most readers would just as soon write to the producers of *General Hospital* to complain about loose morals. Sensational behavior is the whole point of the show. But where Enron is concerned, the outraged public, understandably, wants blood. As for mobsters, dare I suggest that many of us do want their crimes to pay?

Maybe that's because of some warped spinoff of the American Dream, the idea that one can accomplish anything on rogue instinct and back-alley cunning. After all, isn't that our perception of the Founding Fathers themselves: hell-raising outsiders who took what was theirs? We somehow see thieves who operate outside the system as being more, well, honest than thieves who operate from within. Many of us love the mob because it beats the system; we hate Enron because it bought the system.

Americans have a long track record of celebrating wily subversives. What was vaudeville, after all, but shtick after shtick of immigrants slamming bluebloods in the face with a pie? What of National Lampoon's *Animal House,* where the piggish Deltas cheat the system by trawling through Faber College's trash for the exam answers (and flunk out anyway), while the priggish Omegas become "outstanding campus leaders" by doing Dean Wormer's dirty work? Is it lost on anyone that in the epilogue, the film's writers reward the Deltas' John Belushi, who resembles a Mafia thug, with a U.S. Senate seat, and punish the preppy Omega house honcho by revealing that he becomes a Nixon White House aide who is later "raped in prison"?

In the end, even if the Enron honchos are proven to have swindled anything resembling the mob's booty, there was something chillingly respectable about how they did it, which is the part, I think, that provokes our most furious wrath. I think I've got a good business sense, but like most investors I was reluctant to question the imperious, blue-chip facade of "limited partnerships" and "audited balance sheets." As a kid who grew up around green felt and velour beach wear, who was I to ask?

15   We'll see what happens to the Boys of Enron, who made fortunes, perhaps legally, without spilling a drop of blood. As for Little Nicky, he's doing life in Marion for directing a reign of terror that left dozens dead, including "Frankie Flowers," who was a friend of my family. Nicky swears he's innocent. His associates—the guys I saw hugging him on the beach—ratted him

out and are living under assumed names, trying to blend into the yellow prairies and small towns of rural America. The lawyer who advised a reluctant Nicky to tell the truth at the congressional hearing did some time himself for racketeering. John Gotti, who was caught on tape, apoplectic, saying that the FBI was persecuting him, will soon be gone. On one hand, I'm thinking, good riddance. On the other, I am very much a part of the phenomenon that I'm judging, not because I admire the bad guys, but because I miss the days on the boardwalk when we all knew who the bad guys were.

You got a problem with that?

SASHA CAGEN

Radically Honest Online Dating

Welcome to the online candy store of love, our dystopic world of disposable dating. Internet dating can become an exercise in ego stroking and gratification, getting emails and winks about how wonderful you are. It can be a perpetual dip into window shopping for love, rather than a means to an end of actually meeting someone and patiently getting to know them. Find a flaw, and it's on to the next person.

In cities such as San Francisco, Los Angeles, and New York, where online dating has been destigmatized, it's easy to meet someone new for drinks, but much harder to build a relationship that spans longer than four dates. So perhaps the answer is not to shy away from online dating, but to transform it.

Perhaps one solution is Radically Honest Online Dating (RHOD).

Forget doing a public relations job on yourself and selectively presenting your best headshots. Post neutral to unflattering photos. Don't brag about your achievements. Talk about your self-doubts on the way to achieving them. Whatever you have to offer, and where you need support. Unlike most people, who either lie or present a stream of bland clichés, the radically honest ad is an exercise in being very bravely honest in an ad, or maybe, in a document that wouldn't be publicly available to everyone, but that could be shared with people who seem interesting.

We're all dying to be accepted as we are, so why not just put it out there from the very beginning?

The idea originated in a conversation with my friend Rod, a biologist from 5 Colorado. He told me about his yoga teacher Chad who teaches his students about "radical integrity." Radical integrity means discovering and accepting yourself, presenting yourself to the world as your really are rather than selectively sharing the charming details. In essence, it's about getting comfortable with your angels and demons, and being transparent about all of them.

Rod explained, "There are always places life challenges us where we have no talent. His point is that these places can be admitted or hidden. Dating his way, we are looking for someone who says, 'Wow that's tough, but I can handle it and maybe even support you here.' In the absence of openness, that person will not be found."

To prove his point, Chad posted an online dating ad. He posted photos of himself entering a room, taken spontaneously at random angles—nothing flattering or glamorous. He talked about qualities he enjoyed about himself and posted eight weaknesses expressed through difficult periods: gambling and drug addiction and depression.

Three hundred people viewed his ad. Fifteen people wrote him. Most called him sick; a couple tried to get him banned from the site. Others offered advice on how to take better pictures or to emphasize his redeeming qualities. He ignored them. Rod explained, "Smoothing out his profile prevents him from meeting his goal: seeing where he does fit in. Ad if nowhere and with no one, then so be it."

10   Two women contacted him with interest. The most notable was a translator from Mongolia. The first time they spoke, Chad burned through 750 minutes on an international calling card. From Rod's point of view, their call was proof that a deep connection with a woman was possible. Or was she just looking for a way out of Mongolia? Was Chad even looking for a partner?

Rod accused Chad of doing a "social experiment." Chad denied it, saying his effort at meeting a partner was real. If he wasn't sincere in his search, he would not have used his real name and picture.

Rod threw his story down like a challenge. Would I ever write a radically honest personal ad? The idea thrilled and terrified me. The radically honest personal ad stands so in contrast to our marketing-based approach to online dating, which I can't say has been terribly effective. Bragging or outright lying is the natural inclination for most people when writing an ad. A Cornell study showed that over 80% of participants lie about their height, age, or weight. Authentic details are hard to come by when you read match.com profiles, which all seem to be advertising the same fun-loving, laid-back, good-hearted guy.

But what would you actually write? It's hard to imagine radically honest details that wouldn't be repellant. Would I comb through my journal for low moments in past relationships and post excerpts from my journal, describing sensitivity to criticism or talk about being 36 and not having a baby daddy? Or my tendency to leave just one dirty dish in the sink, never wanting to completely finish the dishes? Aren't these admissions intimate, and isn't intimacy earned through trust? Wouldn't it destroy the mystery in getting to know someone to put everything out there in an ad?

To be so naked on a public dating site, I don't know if I could handle that. I can reveal a few intimate things in this essay, but all I am seeking is to accurately express an idea. Doing it in a personal ad is scarier, because the idea is that we're going to meet, and then, you already know all this stuff about me. (Theoretically everyone knows everything about everyone now if we express ourselves online using our real names, but 15 that's another story.)

When you post an ad, you are necessarily objectified, a piece of entertainment, consumed, then click, on to the next human being baring her soul. Immediately I thought of all the people who could see a revealing ad: colleagues, potential future employers, exes, and friends. Isn't a radically honest ad potential career suicide? Online dating can feel like a spectator sport in sociology, studying how people market themselves. We all have to be careful about what we put out there.

Yet, there's something about the idea of radically honest online dating that I love. I'm so over the clichéd way we market ourselves online and return each other so quickly. Kind of like Zappos—it's really easy to try on those shoes and send them back in a box. It's so easy to lie, too. You would theoretically get fewer responses but perhaps more people who really get you. It only takes one.

I don't know that you would fall in love with someone by reading about his or her flaws. Maybe you would just be looking for the problems of a former partner for a re-do, or someone with the opposite problems to try something new. But it would be more authentic. I'd be more interested in checking out that site than trolling match.com.

Maybe instead of "who I am" and "what I'm looking for" we would be prompted to write our strengths and weaknesses.

The radically honest personal ad is a way of showing that you are a work in progress. Radically honest online dating could make us treat people less disposably; being honest reminds us that we're all human, not just consumer objects to be tried out for a glass of wine or a make-out session and then so quickly forgotten. We might meet fewer people, but treat them more humanely because they are more human.

Radically honest online dating probably appeals to only a self-selecting group. Self-examination is not for everyone. 20

Radically honest online dating reminds me of a book that my writer friend Andrew Boyd wrote called Daily Afflictions: The Agony of Being Connected to Everything in the Universe. One of my favorite daily afflictions is "Loving the Wrong Person."

Andrew writes, "We're all seeking that special person who is right for us. But if you've been through enough relationships, you begin to suspect there's no right person, just different flavors of wrong. . . it takes a lot of living to grow fully into your own wrongness. It isn't until you finally run up against your deepest demons, your unsolvable problems—the ones that make you truly who you are—that you're ready to fine a life-long mate. Only then do you finally know what you are looking for. You're looking for the wrong person. But not just any wrong person: the right wrong person—someone you can gaze lovingly upon, and think, 'This is the problem I want to have.'"

P.S. Rod is going to post a Radically Honest Online Dating ad. In a follow-up I'll let you know whether he finds the right wrong person for him. Let me know if you use this technique and how it works for you.

SISSELA BOK

Is the "Whole Truth" Attainable?

"Truth" – no concept intimidates and yet draws thinkers so powerfully. From the beginnings of human speculation about the world, the questions of what truth is and whether we can attain it have loomed large. Every philosopher has had to grapple with them. Every religion seeks to answer them.

One pre-Socratic Greek tradition saw truth – *aletheia* – as encompassing all that we remember: singled out through memory from everything that is destined for Lethe, "the river of forgetfulness." The oral tradition required that information be memorized and repeated, often in song, so as not to be forgotten. Everything thus memorized – stories about the creation of the world, genealogies of gods and heroes, advice about health – all partook of truth, even if in another sense completely fabricated or erroneous. In this early tradition, repeating the songs meant keeping the material alive and thus "true," just as creating works of art could be thought of as making an object true, bringing it to life.

Only gradually did the opposition between truth and error come to be thought central to philosophy, and the nature of verification itself spotlighted. The immense preoccupation with epistemology took hold with Plato and has never diminished since. In logic, in epistemology, in theology, and in metaphysics, the topic of "truth" has continued to absorb almost limitless energies.And since the strands And since the strands from these diverse disciplines are not always disentangled, a great many references to "truth" remain of unsurpassed vagueness.

Truth and Truthfulness

In all such speculation, there is a great risk of a conceptual muddle, of not seeing the crucial differences between two domains: the *moral* domain of intended truthfulness and deception, and the much vaster domain of truth and falsity in general. The moral question of whether you are lying or not is not *settled* by establishing the truth or falsity of what you say. In order to settle this question, we must know whether you *intend your statement to mislead*.

5   The two domains often overlap, and up to a point each is indispensable to the other. But truth and truthfulness are not identical, any more than falsity and falsehood. Until the differences are seen, and the areas of overlap and confusion spotlighted, little progress can be made in coping with the moral quandaries of lying.

The two domains are sometimes taken to be identical. This can happen whenever some believe that they have access to a truth so complete that all else must pale by comparison. Many religious documents or revelations claim to convey what is true. Those who do not accept such a belief are thought to live in error, in ignorance, even in blindness. At times, the refusal of nonbelievers to accept the dogma or truth revealed to the faithful is called, not merely an error, but a lie. The battle is seen as one between upholders of the faith and the forces of deception and guile. Thus Bonhoeffer writes that:

> Jesus calls Satan "the father of the lie." (John 8.44) The lie is primarily the denial of God as He has evidenced Himself to the world. "Who is a liar but he that denieth that Jesus is the Christ?" (I John 2.22)

Convinced that they know the truth – whether in religion or in politics – enthusiasts may regard lies for the sake of this truth as justifiable. They may perpetrate so-called pious frauds to convert the unbelieving or strengthen the conviction of the faithful. They see nothing wrong in telling untruths for what they regard as a much "higher" truth.

In the history of human thought, we find again and again such a confusion of the two domains. It is not unrelated to the traditions which claim that truth exists, that it can be revealed, that one can hope to come face to face with it. Even Nietzsche, at war with such traditions, perpetuates the confusion:

> There is only *one* world, and that world is false, cruel, contradictory, misleading, senseless. [...] We need lies to vanquish this reality, this "truth," we need lies in order to live [...] That lying is a necessity of life is itself a part of the terrifying and problematic character of existence.

The several meanings of the word "false" only add to the ease of confusing the two domains. For whereas "false" normally has the larger sense which includes all that is wrong or incorrect, it takes on the narrower, moral sense when applied to persons. A false person is not one merely wrong or mistaken or incorrect; it is one who is intentionally deceitful or treacherous or disloyal. Compare, to see the difference, a "false note" and a "false friend"; a "false economy" and a "false witness."

Any number of appearances and words can mislead us; but only a fraction 10 of them are *intended* to do so. A mirage may deceive us, through no one's fault. Our eyes deceive us all the time. We are beset by self-delusion and bias of every kind. Yet we often know when we mean to be honest or dishonest. Whatever the essence of truth and falsity, and whatever the sources of error in our lives, *one* such source is surely the human agent, receiving and giving out information, intentionally deflecting, withholding, even distorting it at times. Human beings, after all, provide for each other the most ingenious obstacles to what partial knowledge and minimal rationality they can hope to command.

We must single out, therefore, from the countless ways in which we blunder misinformed through life, that which is done with the *intention to mislead*; and from the countless partial stabs at truth, those which are intended to be truthful. Only if this distinction is clear will it be possible to ask the moral question with rigor. And it is to this question alone – the intentional manipulation of information – that the court addresses itself in its request for "the truth, the whole truth, and nothing by the truth."

But one obstacle remains. Even after the two domains of the ethical and the epistemological are set apart, some argue that the latter should have priority. It is useless to be overly concerned with truthfulness, they claim, so long as one cannot know whether human beings are capable of knowing and conveying truth in the first place. Such a claim, if taken seriously, would obviously make the study of truth-telling and deception seem pointless and flat. Once again, the exalted and all-absorbing preoccupation with "truth" then comes to boorish the reluctance to confront falsehood.

Skeptics have questioned the easy certitudes of their fellows from the earliest times. The most extreme among them have held that nothing can be known at all; sometimes they have gone very far in living out such a belief. Cratylus, a contemporary of Socrates, is said to have refused discussion of any kind. He held that the speakers and the words in any conversation would be changing and uncertain. He therefore merely wiggled his finger in response to any words to show that he head heard them but that reply would be pointless. And Pyrrho, in the third century B.D., denied that anything could be known and concluded that nothing could therefore be said to be honorable or dishonorable, just or unjust.

For these radical skeptics, just as for those who believe that complete and absolute truth can be theirs, ethical matters of truth-telling and deception melt into insignificance by comparison with the illumination of truth and the dark void of its absence. As a result, both groups largely ignore the distinctions between truthfulness and falsehood in their intense quest for certainty regarding truth.

15   But the example of Cratylus shows how difficult it is to live up to thoroughgoing skepticism. Most thinkers who confuse intentional deception and falsity nevertheless manage to distinguish between the two in their ordinary lives. And those who consider the study of "truth" to be prior to any use of information put such concerns aside in their daily routines. They make informed choices of books in libraries; of subway connections and tools and food; they take some messages to be more truthful than others, and some persons as more worthy of their trust than others.

Ordinary decisions can no doubt be made in spite of theoretical beliefs which confuse truth and truth-telling, or which set epistemological certainty ahead of ethical analysis. But the fact remains that moral choice is often harmed thereby; for to the extent that one has radical doubts about the reliability of all knowledge, to that extent the moral aspects of how human beings treat one another, how they act, and what they say to each other, may lose importance. Worst of all, this loss is especially likely to afflict one's own moral choices. For whereas it is only prudent to support morality in others, we are more hospitable to doubts about the possibility of moral choice when it comes to our own decisions.

The most important reason why philosophers have done so little to analyze the problems of deception goes beyond particular views about truth and truthfulness, and is more general. In most fields, theory is congenial, less frustrating, than application. Ethics is no different. Many hesitate to grapple with concrete ethical problems, intertwined as they are with psychological and political strands rendering choice so difficult. Why tackle such choice when there are so many abstract questions of meaning and definition, of classification and structure, which remain to challenge the imagination?

As philosophy has become an increasingly academic and specialized enterprise, this hesitation has grown. But it was always there. Thus Epictetus, in the first century A.D., refers to it as follows, using the "principle not to speak falsely" as his example:

> The primary and most necessary part of philosophy is the application of principles, as for instance the principle not to speak falsely.
> The second part is that of the arguments, as in "Wherefore ought one not to speak falsely?"
> The third confirms these, and distinguishes between them, as in "Wherefore is that an argument?" For what is an argument, what a consequence, what a contradiction [conflict], what truth, what falsehood?
> Therefore, the third part is necessary because of the second, and the second because of the first; while the first is the most necessary, and is where we ought to remain. But we do the reverse; we squander our time in the third part, and to it goes all our zeal, while we utterly neglect the first. And thus we do lie, but are ready with the arguments which prove that one ought not to lie.

Applied ethics, then, has seemed uncongenial and lacking in theoretical challenge to many moral philosophers even apart from any belief in epistemological priority and from muddles about the meaning of "truth." As a result, practical moral choice comes to be given short shift, and never more so than in the case of lies. To be sure, many do make some mention of lying. It is often used as an example, or ruled out in some summary manner. But such analysis cannot help but seem inadequate to those confronting difficult problems in their lives – wondering, perhaps, whether to lie to protect a client's confidences, or to keep shattering news from a sick man.

For all these reasons, deception commands little notice. This absence of 20 real analysis is reflected also in teaching and in codes of professional ethics. As a result, those who confront difficult moral choices between truthfulness and deception often make up their own rules. They think up their own excuses and evaluate their own arguments. I shall take these up in the chapters to come. But one deserves mention here, for it results from a misuse of skepticism by those who wish to justify their lies, giving rise to a clear fallacious argument. It holds that since we can never know truth or falsity of anything anyway, it does not matter whether or not we lie when we have a good reason for doing so. Some have used this argument to explain why they and their entire profession must regretfully forego the virtue of veracity in dealing with clients. Such a view is stated, for example, by an eminent physician in an article frequently referred to in medical literature:

> Above all, remember that it is meaningless to speak of telling the truth, the whole truth, and nothing but the truth to a patient. It is meaningless because it is impossible—a sheer impossibility [...] Since

telling the truth is impossible, there can be no sharp distinction between what is true and what is false.

[...] Far older than the precept, "the truth, the whole truth, and nothing but the truth," is another that originates within our profession, that has always been the guide of the best physicians, and, if I may venture a prophecy, will always remain so: So far as possible, do no harm. You can do harm by the process that is quaintly called telling the truth. You can do harm by lying. [...] But try to do as little harm as possible.

The same argument is often used by biomedical investigators who claim that asking subjects for their informed consent to be used in research is meaningless because it is impossible to obtain a *genuinely* informed consent. It is used by government officials who decide not to inform citizens of a planned war or emergency measure. And very often, it is then supplemented by a second argument: Since there is an infinite gradation between what is truthful and what is deceitful, no lines can be drawn and one must do what one considers best on other grounds.

Such arguments draw on our concerns with the adequacy of information to reach a completely unwarranted conclusion: one that gives *carte blanche* to what those who lie take to be well-meant lies. The difference in perspectives is striking. These arguments are made by the liar but never by those lied to. One has only to imagine how the professionals who argue in this way would respond if their dentists, their lawyers, or their insurance agents used similar arguments for deceiving *them*. As dupes we know what as liars we tend to blur – that information can be more or less adequate; that even where no clear lines are drawn, rules and distinction may, in fact, be made; and are drawn, rules and distinctions may, in fact, be made; and that truthfulness can be required even where full truth is out of reach.

The fact that the "whole truth" can never be reached in its entirety should not, therefore, be a stumbling block in the much more limited inquiry into questions of truth-telling and falsehood. It *is* possible to go beyond the notion that epistemology is somehow prior to ethics. The two nourish one another, but neither can claim priority. It is equally possible to avoid the fallacies which arise from the confusion of "truth" and "truthfulness," and to draw distinctions with respect to the adequacy and relevance of the information reaching us. It is therefore legitimate to go on to define deception and lying and to analyze the moral dilemmas it raises.

CHAPTER 16

PETS, PESTS, AND BEASTS

Overview

The animal kingdom often fills us with wonder. Few people do not admire the beauty, grace, or physical abilities of at least some type of animal. Some individuals feel affinity with a certain animal group; the worship of animals, especially predators, can be traced to virtually all early human cultures.

Human cultures distinguish among animals, having domesticated certain breeds, controlled or destroyed others as pests, and forced still others to keep their distance from us. Based on these groupings, we have endowed animals with certain rights and have determined a moral code by which to judge their behavior. In this code, we can see some self-defeating beliefs that might make us look more closely at our own actions.

The animals known as pets or companion animals reflect a relationship to the animal kingdom that sees humans as the supreme beings on Earth. No other animal owns another species, nor does any other animal try to change the eating habits of another species. It is true that animals try to deter other species from eating them, but they do not exert a concerted effort to prevent scavengers from scavenging, hunters from hunting, and grazers from grazing. No animal other than the human tries to control the breeding habits of other species, nor does any other animal cage, chain, or fence in other species. Only humans try to train other species to respond to commands and groom them to please human perceptions of beauty.

Online Study Center

This icon will direct you to web links and additional resources on the website http://college.cengage.com/english/thelin/writing_without_formulas/1e/student_home.html

While we clearly love our pets, we cannot deny that our actions represent a belief in our innate superiority and the right to dominance. While some pet owners might refer to themselves as "mommy" or "daddy" when interacting with pets, especially kittens or puppies, the term often heard is "master," as in a dog should obey its master. Where there is a master, there must be a slave.

The most obedient members of the animal kingdom garner the greatest rewards in this system of domestication. The less wild an animal is, the more likely it is to receive bountiful meals, medical attention, and regular exercise. The more the animal performs services—as a watchdog, for instance, or a racehorse—the more acclaim it receives. On the opposite end of the spectrum, domesticated animals unable to learn tricks or lackadaisical in their duties earn scorn. They are derided as stupid, do not receive treats, and sometimes are even abandoned or given away. The many incidents of neglect and ill-treatment of pets have led to the establishment of animal welfare laws, demonstrating that when some pet owners transgress the boundaries of humane treatment, other people respond protectively.

While many different types of animals can be owned as pets, we tend to grant fewer rights to smaller animals. The less they resemble us and the less we can project personalities onto them, the more we feel free to respond whimsically to our dominance. So while some people keep rabbits, snakes, and frogs as pets, other people treat these animals as unworthy of concern. Teenagers use rabbits for target practice with BB guns and .22s. Children capture frogs in jars, suffocating or dehydrating them, sometime unintentionally, sometimes not. Because of superstitions and phobias about snakes, some people automatically kill them, even if the snakes are nonpoisonous and present no danger.

Many cultures believe that animals exist for the benefit of humans. The use of lab animals in the developed world evinces this point. Scientists experiment on animals to find cures for human diseases more than to find cures for animal diseases. Animal rights activists receive support when they protest against pain inflicted in testing perfume or cosmetics on animals, but the public is much more tolerant of cruelty to animals when the testing is for diseases. That is, when the results might alleviate human suffering from cancer or bacteria, the animals' suffering is seen as necessary.

Animals that get in the way of progress, pose imagined or real threats, or interfere with our comfort are considered pests. Their very right to life is secondary. Some legitimate reasons for killing pests exist. Mosquitoes can carry disease. The bite of a brown recluse or a black widow spider contains enough poison to cause considerable swelling and discomfort in a fully grown human. A fly invades our personal space. Mice and rats invade food supplies, and the feces and other possible contaminating agents they leave are unsanitary. Bats or other creatures that fly can disrupt and foul a household, and they are difficult to remove without force. These smaller creatures, then, constitute a nuisance that we take proactive measures to stop. We feel little moral remorse in eradicating them.

On the opposite end of the spectrum are the animals that leave us alone, basically, but that we nonetheless consider threats. While they have mammalian characteristics, their size, strength, and ferocity frighten us, and we want to remove them if they get too close. While humans are not the natural prey of any animal, certain animals will stalk and kill humans given the opportunity. One in every hundred tigers is a man-eater. Polar bears, due to the sparse availability of food in their domain, hunt human travelers within the region. Great white sharks do not distinguish between human and other types of prey, even though their reputation far exceeds the number of human kills attributed to them. These predators, like most animals, also protect their young and attack when they perceive danger. Outside of, perhaps, the unpredictable behavior of the North American grizzly bear, though, the reaction of most larger animals to human presence is flight. They do not seek confrontations with us.

Despite the overwhelming documentation of this fact, human predation has caused the number of very large animals to dwindle, and many species will not survive to the twenty-second century. Big-game hunting accounts for part of this, as does poaching for treasures like ivory, but these activities alone would not doom a species. Rather, ever-increasing human encroachment on the terrain of wild animals poses the worst threat. We place our comfort above the existence of other species, refusing to curtail our expansion of settlements, to place limits on growth, or to modify our use of the land. And when human development of a wilderness area brings humans and animals in closer proximity, the animal that accidentally or deliberately kills a human will be hunted down and killed, as will many others of its kind in preemptive strikes against perceived dangers (see Scott McMillon's "Treat It Right" on page 435 for an example).

Humans, indeed, might have been ordained the caretakers of the world long ago by a higher being. Our actions could be the subconscious recognition of our destiny. But if so, our treatment of animals shows abuse, not stewardship. We need animals, from the smallest to the biggest and surliest of beasts, to survive. Their complex world must be understood beyond the immediate comforts and needs of humans. How do we reverse trends and scale back our expansion to allow ecosystems full of large and small animals to flourish? Must we suffer the inconveniences of pests when we head outdoors to ensure that an ecosystem persists? Should we allow predators such as cougars and alligators to enter our domain? Do we need to question elements of our relationships with domesticated animals? The questions outweigh the practical solutions, but perhaps the first step is to look at the moral code we enact on the animal world and spot the inconsistencies that, if not rectified, will lead to our doom as well.

Openings for Writers

1. **Relationships with pets** How would you describe your interactions with your pets? Have you ever given priority to the pet's needs? Judge your own actions regarding pets in light of the overview's claims of a relationship based on dominance.
2. **Animal rights** While the animal rights movement mostly seeks to protect animals from the fur trade and laboratory experimentation, its boundaries can be expanded to the right to live. Do species have an innate right to exist freely in the world as dictated by their instincts? What other rights

should they have? What should be done to strengthen the chances of survival of threatened species?

3. **Human destiny** Are humans superior to other life forms? Is it possible that animals know about life in ways that elude us? Think about the basis on which we grant ourselves an elevated position in the animal kingdom, and consider the possibility that we might be wrong. What changes would we have to make if we considered ourselves equal to members of the animal kingdom? You might want to consult Edward Abbey's "The Snake" (page 432) for a different perspective.

4. **Dealing with pests** How do you try to deter insects and rodents from creating a nuisance in and around your house or apartment? Have you ever felt guilty about killing pests? Why?

Language

1. **Master and owner** Do you use the term *master* when talking about a pet, or are you more comfortable with *owner*? What words do you associate with these terms? Are there any opposites other than *slave* and *laborer*? Develop complex definitions of *master* and *owner* that investigate positive and negative connotations of the words, and see whether a deeper understanding of the terms reveals anything about the topic of pets, pests, and beasts.

2. **Obedience and disobedience** Do the terms *obedience* and *disobedience* have meaning outside of a hierarchical relationship? What do they connote to you? Does *obedience* always have positive associations and *disobedience* negative ones?

DAVID QUAMMEN

Face of a Spider

This article extends the question of dealing with pests by putting actions into a philosophical context. Quammen tries to develop a guideline on when to act violently against another species. Although Quammen claims to have squandered his opportunity for moral growth, his reflections demonstrate a keen mind that does not accept easy answers.

One evening a few years ago I walked back into my office after dinner and found roughly a hundred black widow spiders frolicking on my desk. I am not speaking metaphorically and I am not making this up: a hundred black widows. It was a vision of ghastly, breathtaking beauty, and it brought on me a wave of nausea. It also brought on a small moral crisis—one that I dealt with briskly, maybe rashly, in the dizziness of the moment, and that I've been turning back over in my mind ever since. I won't say I'm *haunted* by those hundred black widows, but I do remember them vividly. To me, they stand for something. They stand, in their small synecdochical way, for a large and important question.

The question is, How should a human behave toward the members of other living species?

A hundred black widows probably sounds like a lot. It is—even for Tucson, Arizona, where I was living then, a habitat in which black widows breed like rabbits and prosper like cockroaches, the females of the species growing plump as huckleberries and stringing their ragged webs in every free corner of every old shed and basement window. In Tucson, during the height of the season, a person can always on short notice round up eight or ten big, robust black widows, if that's what a person wants to do. But a hundred in one room? So all right, yes, there was a catch: These in my office were newborn babies.

A hundred scuttering bambinos, each one no bigger than a poppyseed. Too small still for red hourglasses, too small even for red egg timers. They had the aesthetic virtue of being so tiny that even a person of good eyesight and patient disposition could not make out their hideous little faces.

Their mother had sneaked in when the rains began and set up a web in 5 the corner beside my desk. I knew she was there—I got a reminder every time I dropped a pencil and went groping for it, jerking my hand back at the first touch of that distinctive, dry, high-strength web. But I hadn't made the necessary decision about dealing with her. I knew she would have to be either murdered or else captured adroitly in a pickle jar for relocation to the wild, and I didn't especially want to do either. (I had already squashed scores of black widows during those Tucson years but by this time, I guess, I was going soft.) In the meantime, she had gotten pregnant. She had laid her eggs into a silken egg sac the size of a Milk Dud and then protected that sac vigilantly, keeping it warm, fending off any threats, as black widow mothers do. While she was waiting for the eggs to come to term, she would have been particularly edgy, particularly unforgiving, and my hand would have been in particular danger each time I reached for a fallen pencil. Then the great day arrived. The spiderlings hatched from their individual eggs, chewed their way out of the sac, and started crawling, brothers and sisters together, up toward the orange tensor lamp that was giving off heat and light on the desk of the nitwit who was their landlord.

By the time I stumbled in, fifty or sixty of them had reached the lampshade and rappelled back down on dainty silk lines, leaving a net of gossamer rigging between the lamp and the Darwin book (it happened to be an old edition of *Insectivorous Plants*, with marbled endpapers) that sat on the desk. Some dozen others had already managed dispersal flights, letting out strands of buoyant silk and ballooning away on rising air, as spiderlings do—in this case dispersing as far as the bookshelves. It was too late for one man to face one spider with just a pickle jar and an index card and his two shaky hands. By now I was proprietor of a highly successful black widow hatchery.

And the question was, How should a human behave toward the members of other living species?

The Jain religion of India has a strong teaching on that question. The Sanskrit word is *ahimsa*, generally rendered in English as "noninjury" or the imperative "do no harm." *Ahimsa* is the ethical centerpiece of Jainism, an absolute stricture against the killing of living beings—*any* living beings—and it led the traditional Jains to some extreme forms of observance. A rigorously devout Jain would burn no candles or lights, for instance, if there was danger a moth might fly into them. The Jain would light no fire for heating or cooking, again because it might cause the death of insects. He would cover his mouth and nose with a cloth mask, so as not to inhale any gnats. He would refrain from cutting his hair, on grounds that the lice hiding in there might be gruesomely injured by the scissors. He could not plow a field, for fear of mutilating worms. He could not work as a carpenter or a mason, with all that dangerous sawing and crunching, nor could he engage in most types of industrial production. Consequently the traditional Jains formed a distinct socioeconomic class, composed almost entirely of monks and merchants. Their ethical canon was not without what you and I might take to be glaring contradictions (vegetarianism was sanctioned, plants as usual getting dismissive treatment in the matter of rights to life), but at least they took it seriously. They lived by it. They tried their best to do no harm.

And this in a country, remember, where 10,000 humans died every year from snakebite, almost a million more from malaria carried in the bites of mosquitoes. The black widow spider, compared to those fellow creatures, seems a harmless and innocent beast.

10   But personally I hold no brief for *ahimsa*, because I don't delude myself that it's even theoretically (let alone practically) possible. The basic processes of animal life, human or otherwise, do necessarily entail a fair bit of ruthless squashing and gobbling. Plants can sustain themselves on no more than sunlight and beauty and a hydroponic diet—but not we animals. I've only mentioned this Jainist ideal to suggest the range of possible viewpoints.

Modern philosophers of the "animal liberation" movement, most notably Peter Singer and Tom Regan, have proposed some other interesting answers to the same question. So have writers like Barry Lopez and Eugene Linden, and (by their example, as well as by their work) scientists like Jane Goodall and John Lilly and Dian Fossey. Most of the attention of each of these thinkers, though, has been devoted to what is popularly (but not necessarily by the thinkers themselves) considered the "upper" end of the "ladder" of life. To my mind, the question of appropriate relations is more tricky and intriguing—also more crucial in the long run, since this group accounts for most of the planet's species—as applied to the "lower" end, down there among the mosquitoes and worms and black widow spiders.

These are the extreme test cases. These are the alien species who experience human malice, or indifference, or tolerance, at its most automatic and elemental. To squash or not to squash? Mohandas Gandhi, whose own ethic of nonviolence owed much to *ahimsa*, was once asked about the propriety of an antimalaria campaign that involved killing mosquitoes with DDT, and he was careful to give no simple, presumptuous answer. These are the creatures whose treatment, by each of us, illuminates not just the strength of emotional affinity but the strength, if any, of principle.

But what is the principle? Pure *ahimsa*, as even Gandhi admitted, is unworkable. Vegetarianism is invidious. Anthropocentrism, conscious or otherwise, is smug and ruinously myopic. What else? Well, I have my own little notion of one measure that might usefully be applied in our relations with other species, and I offer it here seriously despite the fact that it will probably sound godawful stupid.

Eye contact.

Make eye contact with the beast, the Other, before you decide upon ac- 15 tion. No kidding, now, I mean get down on your hands and knees right there in the vegetable garden, and look that snail in the face. Lock eyes with that bull snake. Trade stares with the carp. Gaze for a moment into the many-faceted eyes—the windows to its soul—of the house fly, as it licks its way innocently across your kitchen counter. Look for signs of embarrassment or rancor or guilt. Repeat the following formula silently, like a mantra: "This is some mother's darling, this is some mother's child." *Then* kill if you will, or if it seems you must.

I've been experimenting with the eye-contact approach for some time myself. I don't claim that it has made me gentle or holy or put me in tune with the cosmic hum, but definitely it has been interesting. The hardest cases—and therefore I think the most telling—are the spiders.

The face of a spider is unlike anything else a human will ever see. The word "ugly" doesn't even begin to serve. "Grotesque" and "menacing" are too mild. The only adequate way of communicating the effect of a spiderly countenance is to warn that it is "very different," and then offer a photograph. This trick should not be pulled on loved ones just before bedtime or when trying to persuade them to accompany you to the Amazon.

The special repugnant power of the spider physiognomy derives, I think, from fangs and eyes. The former are too big and the latter are too many. But the fangs (actually the fangs are only terminal barbs on the *chelicerae*, as the real jaw limbs are called) need to be large, because all spiders are predators yet they have no pincers like a lobster or a scorpion, no talons like an eagle, no social behavior like a pack of wolves. Large clasping fangs armed with poison glands are just their required equipment for earning a living. And what about those eight eyes—big ones and little ones, arranged in two rows, all bugged-out and pointing everywhichway? (My wife the biologist offers a theory here: "They have an eye for each leg, like us—so they don't *step* in anything.") Well, a predator does need good eyesight, binocular focus, peripheral vision. Sensory perception is crucial to any animal that lives by the hunt and, unlike insects, arachnids possess no antennae. Beyond that, I don't know. I don't *know* why a spider has eight eyes.

I only know that, when I make eye contact with one, I feel a deep physical shudder of revulsion, and of fear, and of fascination; and I am reminded that the human style of face is only one accidental pattern among many, some of the others being quite drastically different. I remember that we aren't alone. I remember that we are the norm of goodness and comeliness only to ourselves. I wonder about how ugly I look to the spider.

The hundred baby black widows on my desk were too tiny for eye contact. They were too numerous, it seemed, to be gathered one by one into a 20 pickle jar and carried to freedom in the backyard. I killed them all with a can of Raid. I confess to that slaughter with more resignation than shame, the jostling struggle for life and space being what it is. I can't swear I would do differently today. But there is this lingering suspicion that I squandered an opportunity for some sort of moral growth.

I still keep their dead and dried mother, and their vacated egg sac, in a plastic vial on an office shelf. It is supposed to remind me of something or other.

And the question continues to puzzle me: How should a human behave toward the members of other living species?

Last week I tried to make eye contact with a tarantula. This was a huge specimen, all hairy and handsomely colored, with a body as big as a hamster and legs the size of Bic pens. I ogled it through a sheet of plate glass. I smiled and winked. But the animal hid its face in distrust.

JANE GANAHL

Women Like Men Who Like Cats

Western culture tends to associate men with dogs and women with cats. A common stereotype suggests that men who own cats tend toward effeminacy. In a light-hearted article from the San Francisco Chronicle, *Jane Ganahl challenges this stereotype and proposes that men who own cats appeal to women because they demonstrate a certain sensitivity. Does the ability of our culture to shift away from the gender stereotypes associated with cats and dogs offer some hope for changing other ideas about animals in our lives?*

It seems as if single men are discovering what single women have known since ancient Egyptian times: Cats are worthy of worship.

At least unmarried British men say so, in a recent survey conducted by Cats Protection, a leading animal welfare society in the United Kingdom. And judging by the delirious worship that single men I know lavish on their kitties, I'd like to think American men—those brave enough to stand up and be counted— feel the same way.

The survey showed that 85 percent of men, and 94 percent of women, don't think it's wimpy or needy for a man to love his cat. In addition, just as many single men as single women said they enjoy "lavishing care" on their cat.

And yet there are still gender differences in how we view the often puzzling feline species. Given their choice of characterizing their cat as a good friend, a child, a baby or a partner, men chose good friend (aww), while women said they considered their cats either a child or a baby. And men chose a cat's "independent spirit" as the animal's most desirable trait, while women thought that trait was a cat's least desirable trait.

5   More than anything, the survey showed that unmarried laddies go as delightfully off the deep end over their pets as women have been teased for

doing for centuries. Single male cat owners are more likely than their female counterparts to have made, or consider making, a sacrifice for their cat, including giving up a vacation and going into debt. Three-quarters of male respondents say their cats fulfill their cuddle requirements, and single men are also almost as likely as single women to consider choosing their cat over their partner.

It's long been said by women that cats are excellent guy-o-meters—capable of spotting a bad one with a sniff. I always found the converse to be true: Men who were good to my cats—and not in a manipulative, let's-impress-her-with-my-sensitivity kind of way—were going to be good to me.

Noodge has always been easy to like. A bulldozer of a Maine coon cat, he is like a dog in cat's clothing. He's fearless, assertive, funny and loud. He possesses, as his vet said recently, more attitude than any other 16-year-old cat she'd seen. I've never looked to him to be an impartial judge on the men in my life; he liked anyone who would feed him and stay out of his chair.

But Bunny was harder to warm up to. She came to us in 1991, on the day of the Oakland hills fire—a tiny, ragged survivor of a brood most likely born in the field nearby. Terrified but plucky, she hung out behind the water heater in the garage for two days before she finally allowed my daughter to hold her. I came home from work and Erin was doing her homework on the concrete garage floor, beaming and ecstatic at the gray fur ball curled up in her lap.

Although we were able to tame her feral nature, Bunny (named for the rabbitlike way she would nestle under your chin, purring loudly) bonded only with the two of us, and was terrified of everyone and everything else—from the UPS man to the vacuum cleaner. Only a few boyfriends in the past 13 years have been patient and loving enough to coax her out of her hiding places with sweet words and smiles. Those were good men indeed.

Bunny loved her food—OK, OK, she was a bit of a porker. Erin would 10 admonish me when she came home from college for letting her get fat, while I would argue back that Bunny was merely big-boned. She loved Erin fiercely and even if they didn't see each other for months, the cat would recognize her instantly and burrow under her chin, relieved and happy.

After watching Bunny slow down in recent months, I should not have been surprised that she timed her collapse for the night Erin came home for Christmas. She knew the wagons were circled; she knew we'd be able to go through this together. At the vet hospital the next day, Dr. Heidi McClain noted that with a kitty this fat ("She's just big-boned!" I mouthed to Erin to keep her from crying), it was hard to get a sense of what had gone wrong inside. But it soon became apparent: kidney failure.

After five days of Christmas-week back-and-forth visits to the hospital, which saw her improve to the point of almost coming home, Bunny's heart unexpectedly gave out. I held her still body and called Erin. Through the tears we knew Bunny was better off without the tubes and the monitors, and all the scary things that had daunted her.

It's been two weeks and Noodge is confused and alarmed that his mate is gone. I watch him closely to see if his tough attitude softens and he starts to die, too. At that point, I will find him a new friend.

In the meantime, if a new man comes into my life, I guess I'll have to suss him out the old-fashioned way. And hope that any new kitty I get will be as difficult to love as Bunny was.

15   There is a moral to this story. Men, if you want many good things in life, get a cat. Why? So many reasons. There is the unconditional-love thing, the way science has proved that stress levels come down drastically when one is stroking a pet, etc. But here's additional incentive: They are babe magnets.

Yes, according to this same British survey, women love men with cats. Ninety percent of single women surveyed thought men who like cats are "nicer"—i.e., more caring and sensitive—than those who don't. A quick poll of my cat-loving single girlfriends bears this out.

Additional points were awarded to those who adopted mature felines from shelters, rather than adorable kittens that have a much easier time finding homes. I suspect I shall find myself doing that very thing quite soon.

More than anything, I'm pleased to find that single men might just be warming to the notion of single-with-cat as a worthy lifestyle. It might help deflect the endless guff single women with cats have taken over the centuries. And it will certainly be good for cats.

And rightly so. They rock. Even when they break your heart.

Assignment Ideas

Writing a critical analysis of issues related to animals will push you toward examining some of your most basic beliefs about hierarchy and moral behavior. You might assume that an animal's rights are secondary to human rights based on unquestioned views of human intelligence, progress, and religious beliefs. As a writer, be careful not to dismiss any position too quickly, and try some of the suggestions for analysis from Chapter 2. Also practice your critical reading skills when you peruse the selections in this chapter to help you avoid clichés and produce a relevant thesis.

1. Have you ever been in a situation, like David Quammen's, where the threat from an animal or insect was not imminent, but you considered preemptive action to prevent future problems? Describe the situation. Through a comparison with Quammen's experience, develop a thesis about animal (or insect) rights that outlines specific ethical measures humans can use in behaving toward members of other species.

2. Write about an animal on the endangered species list, which can be found on the Internet at http://endangered.fws.gov/wildlife.html. Describe the animal, providing background information about its physiology, habits, and distinctive features. Have humans associated any qualities with this animal that strike you as either accurate or inaccurate? Do legends surround the animal? How and why were its numbers reduced? Talk about specific ways that the species could recover that take some people's belief in human destiny into account.

3. Are you a "dog person" or a "cat person"? The study cited by Jane Ganahl suggests that men and women find different characteristics of cats appealing, making gender an important criterion for understanding how we grow an affinity for certain animals. Using your personal experiences or observations, develop this and other generalizations about the differences between dog and cat people and discuss the human traits that attract or draw certain types of people to particular pets. Do we really know something about a person by the type of pets he or she has? Do we know anything more about the pet?

4. Ecosystems can be delicate, and slight disruptions produce chain reactions that cause the depletion of species. We also have an emotional reaction when an old-growth forest is cut down or a river is dammed. Talk about an experience you had when nature and human needs collided, causing the destruction of part of an ecosystem. Did this destruction produce a chain reaction? Did you notice fewer animals than before? Look at Thomas McNamee's "Drainage Ditch" (page 448) to see how he describes the before and after as well as his reaction to the changes.

Group Work

Cartoon depictions of different animal species can tell us much about the qualities we associate with animals. They also can reveal our fears and, often, our sense of superiority. Study different television cartoons or animated movies that have talking animal characters. Describe the traits attributed to these animals. Can you find patterns that reveal conflicts in our culture's relationship with animals? For instance, do we admire a particular animal for strength and guile but still hunt it beyond what the species can sustain? Do we associate innocence with certain herbivores and castigate carnivores? Develop a thesis that takes a position on human relationships with the rest of the animal kingdom.

Additional Readings

This cluster demonstrates our broad view of different animals. The first two selections offer perspectives on domestication. "The Real Reason We Love Dogs" reviews theories that dogs manipulate child-parent instincts pet owners might have. "The Snake" suggests our anthropomorphism when we see animals enter our lives. The third selection takes a decidedly different view of animals in its recounting of a grizzly bear attack and the subsequent reaction of Glacier National Park officials. In "Drainage Ditch," Thomas McNamee reminisces about the old creek he used to play in and what happened to the ecosystem as a result of progress. Think about the ways these perspectives, from the concern that an evolutionary trick is the reason dogs respond to humans to the destruction of wildlife for resources, reflect our relationship with animals.

EDWARD ABBEY

The Snake

As mentioned before, I share the housetrailer with a number of mice. I don't know how many but apparently only a few, perhaps a single family. They don't disturb me and are welcome to my crumbs and leavings. Where they came from, how they got into the trailer, how they survived before my arrival (for the trailer had been locked up for six months), these are puzzling matters I am not prepared to resolve. My only reservation concerning the mice is that they do attract rattlesnakes.

I'm sitting on my doorstep early one morning, facing the sun as usual, drinking coffee, when I happen to look down and see almost between my bare feet, only a couple of inches to the rear of my heels, the very thing I had in mind. No mistaking that wedgelike head, that tip of horny segmented tail peeping out of the coils. He's under the doorstep and in the shade where the ground and air remain very cold. In his sluggish condition he's not likely to strike unless I rouse him by some careless move of my own.

There's a revolver inside the trailer, a huge British Webley .45, loaded, but it's out of reach. Even if I had it in my hands I'd hesitate to blast a fellow creature at such close range, shooting between my own legs at a living target flat on solid rock thirty inches away. It would be like murder; and where would I set my coffee? My cherrywood walking stick leans against the trailerhouse wall only a few feet away but I'm afraid that in leaning over for it I might stir up the rattler or spill some hot coffee on his scales.

Other considerations come to mind. Arches National Monument is meant to be among other things a sanctuary for wildlife—for all forms of wildlife. It is my duty as a park ranger to protect, preserve and defend all living things within the park boundaries, making no exceptions. Even if this were not the case I have personal convictions to uphold. Ideals, you might say. I prefer not to kill animals. I'm a humanist; I'd rather kill a *man* than a snake.

5   What to do. I drink some more coffee and study the dormant reptile at my heels. It is not after all the mighty diamondback, *Crotalus atrox*, I'm confronted with but a smaller species known locally as the horny rattler or more precisely as the Faded Midget. An insulting name for a rattlesnake, which may explain the Faded Midget's alleged bad temper. But the name is apt: he is small and dusty-looking, with a little knob above each eye—the horns. His bite though temporarily disabling would not likely kill a full-grown man in normal health. Even so I don't really want him around. Am I to be compelled to put on boots or shoes every time I wish to step outside? The scorpions, tarantulas, centipedes, and black widows are nuisance enough.

I finish my coffee, lean back and swing my feet up and inside the doorway of the trailer. At once there is a buzzing sound from below and the rattler lifts his head from his coils, eyes brightening, and extends his narrow black tongue to test the air.

After thawing out my boots over the gas flame I pull them on and come back to the doorway. My visitor is still waiting beneath the doorstep, basking in the sun, fully alert. The trailerhouse has two doors. I leave by the other and get a long-handled spade out of the bed of the government pickup. With this tool I scoop the snake into the open. He strikes; I can hear the click of the fangs against steel, see the strain of venom. He wants to stand and fight, but I am patient; I insist on herding him well away from the trailer. On guard, head aloft—that evil slit-eyed weaving head shaped like the ace of spades—tail whirring, the rattler slithers sideways, retreating slowly before me until he reaches the shelter of a sandstone slab. He backs under it.

You better stay there, cousin, I warn him; if I catch you around the trailer again I'll chop your head off.

A week later he comes back. If not him, his twin brother. I spot him one morning under the trailer near the kitchen drain, waiting for a mouse. I have to keep my promise.

This won't do. If there are midget rattlers in the area there may be dia- 10 mondbacks too—five, six or seven feet long, thick as a man's wrist, dangerous. I don't want *them* camping under my home. It looks as though I'll have to trap the mice.

However, before being forced to take that step I am lucky enough to capture a gopher snake. Burning garbage one morning at the park dump, I see a long slender yellow-brown snake emerge from a mound of old tin cans and plastic picnic plates and take off down the sandy bed of a gulch. There is a burlap sack in the cab of the truck which I carry when plucking Kleenex flowers from the brush and cactus along the road; I grab that and my stick, run after the snake and corner it beneath the exposed roots of a bush. Making sure it's a gopher snake and not something less useful, I open the neck of the sack and with a great deal of coaxing and prodding get the snake into it. The gopher snake, *Drymarchon corais couperi*, or bull snake, has a reputation as the enemy of rattlesnakes, destroying or driving them away whenever encountered.

Hoping to domesticate this sleek, handsome and docile reptile, I release him inside the trailerhouse and keep him there for several days. Should I attempt to feed him? I decide against it—let him eat mice. What little water he may need can also be extracted from the flesh of his prey.

The gopher snake and I get along nicely. During the day he curls up like a cat in the warm corner behind the heater and at night he goes about his business. The mice, singularly quiet for a change, make themselves scarce. The snake is passive, apparently contented, and makes no resistance when I pick him up with my hands and drape him over an arm or around my neck. When I take him outside into the wind and sunshine his favorite place seems to be inside my shirt, where he wraps himself around my waist and rests on my belt. In this position he sometimes sticks his head out between shirt buttons for a survey of the weather, astonishing and delighting any tourists who may happen to be with me at the time. The scales of a snake are dry and smooth, quite pleasant to the touch. Being a cold-blooded creature, of course, he takes his temperature from that of the immediate environment—in this case my body.

We are compatible. From my point of view, friends. After a week of close association I turn him loose on the warm sandstone at my doorstep and leave for patrol of the park. At noon when I return he is gone. I search everywhere beneath, nearby and inside the trailerhouse, but my companion has disappeared. Has he left the area entirely or is he hiding somewhere close by? At any rate I am troubled no more by rattlesnakes under the door.

15   The snake story is not yet ended.

In the middle of May, about a month after the gopher snake's disappearance, in the evening of a very hot day, with all the rosy desert cooling like a griddle with the fire turned off, he reappears. This time with a mate.

I'm in the stifling heat of the trailer opening a can of beer, barefooted, about to go outside and relax after a hard day watching cloud formations. I happen to glance out the little window near the refrigerator and see two gopher snakes on my verandah engaged in what seems to be a kind of ritual dance. Like a living caduceus they wind and unwind about each other in undulant, graceful, perpetual motion, moving slowly across a dome of sandstone. Invisible but tangible as music is the passion which joins them—sexual? combative? both? A shameless *voyeur*, I stare at the lovers, and then to get a closer view run outside and around the trailer to the back. There I get down on hands and knees and creep toward the dancing snakes, not wanting to frighten or disturb them. I crawl to within six feet of them and stop, flat on my belly, watching from the snake's-eye level. Obsessed with their ballet, the serpents seem unaware of my presence.

The two gopher snakes are nearly identical in length and coloring; I cannot be certain that either is actually my former household pet. I cannot even be sure that they are male and female, though their performance resembles so strongly a *pas de deux* by formal lovers. They intertwine and separate, glide side by side in perfect congruence, turn like mirror images of each other and glide back again, wind and unwind again. This is the basic pattern but there is a variation: at regular intervals the snakes elevate their heads, facing one another, as high as they can go, as if each is trying to outreach or overawe the other. Their heads and bodies rise, higher and higher, then topple together and the rite goes on.

I crawl after them, determined to see the whole thing. Suddenly and simultaneously they discover me, prone on my belly a few feet away. The dance stops. After a moment's pause the two snakes come straight toward me, still in flawless unison, straight toward my face, the forked tongues flickering, their intense wild yellow eyes staring directly into my eyes. For an instant I am paralyzed by wonder; then, stung by a fear too ancient and powerful to overcome I scramble back, rising to my knees. The snakes veer and turn and race away from me in parallel motion, their lean elegant bodies making a soft hissing noise as they slide over the sand and stone. I follow them for a short distance, still plagued by curiosity, before remembering my place and the requirements of common courtesy. For godsake let them go in peace, I tell myself. Wish them luck and (if lovers) innumerable offspring, a life of happily ever after. Not for their sake alone but for your own.

20   In the long hot days and cool evenings to come I will not see the gopher snakes again. Nevertheless I will feel their presence watching over me like

totemic deities, keeping the rattlesnakes far back in the brush where I like them best, cropping off the surplus mouse population, maintaining useful connections with the primeval. Sympathy, mutual aid, symbiosis, continuity.

How can I descend to such anthropomorphism? Easily—but is it, in this case entirely false? Perhaps not. I am not attributing human motives to my snake and bird acquaintances. I recognize that when and where they serve purposes of mine they do so for beautifully selfish reasons of their own. Which is exactly the way it should be. I suggest, however, that it's a foolish, simple-minded rationalism which denies any form of emotion to all animals but man and his dog. This is no more justified than the Moslems are in denying souls to women. It seems to me possible, even probable, that many of the nonhuman undomesticated animals experience emotions unknown to us. What do the coyotes mean when they yodel at the moon? What are the dolphins trying so patiently to tell us? Precisely what did those two enraptured gopher snakes have in mind when they came gliding toward my eyes over the naked sandstone? If I had been as capable of trust as I am susceptible to fear I might have learned something new or some truth so very old we have all forgotten it.

> They do not sweat and whine about their condition,
> They do not lie awake in the dark and weep for their sins. . . .

All men are brothers, we like to say, half-wishing sometimes in secret it were not true. But perhaps it is true. And is the evolutionary line from protozoan to Spinoza any less certain? That also may be true. We are obliged, therefore, to spread the news, painful and bitter though it may be for some to hear, that all living things on earth are kindred.

SCOTT McMILLION

Treat It Right

Put yourself in Buck Wilde's shoes. You're hiking alone in Glacier National Park in Montana when you find a blue hat lying in a trail. Then you spot a camera on a tripod, laid carefully down, the tripod legs neatly folded, the lens cap on. There's a small red backpack there, too, and this makes you suspicious and curious and you start to pay some serious attention. You move thirty feet or so back the way you came and there about three feet into the brush you spot the bad news: a pool of blood, a foot or more wide and still fresh.

Then you notice more blood, spots of it leading down the trail, and you see some grizzly bear tracks, claw marks scratched into the hard-packed ground. You follow them, making plenty of noise and moving downhill very slowly for about five hundred feet, until you find a bunch of scuff marks on the trail, a place where something heavy has been swept back and forth a few times. You keep going and you find more blood, then little pieces of what must be human flesh. You find some coins, you find a bootlace, you find more blood. Puddles of it, and a blood trail leading into the woods. You have spent a lot of time around bears and you know how dangerous they can be, but you also know they rarely kill people. Somebody is hurt very badly and the blood trail is there and you have only a can of pepper spray with you and you know somebody will surely die if you don't help so you go into the brush where you find more coins and a wristwatch and a boot and then you find a man lying on his left side.

The man is bitten and clawed from head to toe and the bear has eaten the meat from one arm and one buttock but his body is warm and he might still be alive even though you can't find a pulse and still there is nobody here but you and this dead or dying man. Surely you can do something so you hustle back to the red backpack only a few hundred feet and get a coat to cover him and keep him warm and when you get back to him after maybe five minutes the man is gone.

Not just dead. Gone.

5   Smears of blood tell you the bear has come back, probably after watching you follow its tracks, and has taken the man away, so you follow this grisly trail for a few steps and you see that it leads into a patch of timber really thick where you can't see anything at all.

Put yourself in Buck Wilde's shoes.

What are you going to do?

"That's when I knew I had really been more foolish than I thought I was being," Wilde recalls of that day, the third of October, 1992, a sunny Saturday in the high country. "I had the pepper spray in my hand the whole time, with the safety off. I was scared shitless. That was the point when I made the decision that I was in over my head and I had to get out. It was time to think about myself and other people, who I knew were alive."

Wilde was just off the Loop Trail, a vigorous four-mile hike that leads from the Going-to-the-Sun Road to the Granite Park Chalet, a popular back-country destination. But it was late in the season—the first days of October can be the early part of winter in some years—and as far as Wilde knew, there wasn't another person around for miles. Still, it was a pleasant Saturday, only about noon, and there was a good chance that other hikers would arrive soon and walk into an ugly situation. So Wilde backtracked to the trail, walked downhill a quarter-mile, and pinned a note to the middle of the trail with a small rock.

10   "A man has been attacked by a bear," the note said. "Turn around and go back to the highway. Shout and make noise every hundred feet or so. Don't run, but move fast. Send help."

Wilde left his bear spray with the note and gave instructions on how to use it. Then he moved back up trail to the chalet, closed at the time, and met some other hikers who had just arrived. He sent them back to Logan Pass, a relatively flat eight-mile hike away, but a place with lots of traffic and a visitor center, the quickest source of help. He gave them a note for park rangers.

"Help," it said. "Discovered signs of bear mauling about a quarter to a half a mile downhill from chalet backcountry campsite. Followed another quarter-mile and found body. He was in bad shape but alive. Went back to get coat to cover him and body was gone.

"Met these people at chalet. I plan to stay here for two reasons.

1. To turn people back toward Logan Pass visitor center.

2. To take National Park Service personnel to site I last saw victim."

He signed the note "seriously, Buck Wilde" and asked the hikers to turn back anybody they met coming toward the chalet.

After the messengers left, Wilde left another note at a second trail intersection, then climbed to the chalet's second-story deck to settle in and wait, scanning the area with his binoculars, looking for bears and watching for any hikers who might be coming in. At one point, he heard a scream somewhere down on the Loop Trail. He didn't investigate. He had already spent an hour or more too close to a grizzly bear's fresh kill. He'd already pushed his luck. Enough was enough.

Wilde is an unusual man. Forty-three years old at the time, he had given 15 himself his name when, at the age of forty, he gave up a lucrative career as an electrical engineer and launched a new one in wildlife photography. He spends several months a year in the wild, moving between places like Yellowstone National Park and Alaska, Florida and Southeast Asia, with periodic stays in his hometown of Julian, Pennsylvania. It's a tough way to make a living but he's been successful, publishing ten photo books. He lives a lifestyle he readily describes as "eccentric," one that often brings him into close contact with grizzly bears. He's been charged a few times but never attacked.

Wilde had walked into the Granite Park area the previous afternoon and spent the night in the backcountry campground. There were no other campers. He hoisted his food high into the air on the food pole there, then went to bed early and slept late. He walked around the area for an hour or so after he got up in the morning, then went back to the campground to fix breakfast in the designated cooking area, which is separate from the sleeping area to keep from attracting bears to the tents.

Sometime during the meal of hot cereal and tea, he caught a quick glimpse of a small grizzly bear. He heard a woof, probably from the cub's mother, and the little bear took off running toward the Loop Trail. Wilde hastily cleaned up his breakfast and raised his gear back up on the food pole. He found fresh grizzly tracks, small ones, covering the footprints he had left less than an hour earlier, grabbed his camera, and took off in the direction he had seen the bear going. It was about half past eleven in the morning.

By then, the bears probably had already attacked John Petranyi, a forty-year-old jazz buff from Madison, Wisconsin, who had hiked up the Loop Trail that morning.

"It was no more than five minutes to put the food up the pole, plus another ten to fifteen minutes to get to the point of the attack," Wilde says. "That's how quickly things unfolded there.

20   "In my mind, what happened was, the bears came in and saw me and smelled my food. They were looking at it, but did the good bear thing and split when mama saw one of the cubs getting too close to me and took off running down towards that trail."

Wilde knows a lot about bears, knows that grizzlies will almost always avoid an encounter with people if they have a chance. He had spent the previous summer guiding photographers to places in Alaska where they could watch, up close, as grizzlies fished for salmon. Less than a year earlier, a sow had bluff-charged him on Kodiak Island after he inadvertently came between her and one of her three cubs. She came close enough, charging from a hundred feet away, that he could feel her hot breath, and she got there fast enough that he never even had time to reach for the shotgun on the ground at his feet. That's when he decided guns weren't much good in a bear encounter, and he hasn't carried one since. He studies bear behavior, is a fanatic about keeping a clean camp, and is a self-professed "pain-in-the-ass person to go into bear country with."

"You've got to read the bear safety books. You've got to convince me you've read the books. You've got to obey the rules. And pay attention. Any time you're not, I'm giving you shit about it."

He was paying close attention as he walked toward the Loop Trail that morning, mostly because he was hoping for a good photograph. But he wasn't paying much attention to the trail itself. Rather, he was watching and listening for bears.

That's when he stumbled across Petranyi's cap, then the blood and the other grim evidence of bad trouble. That point in the trail is a narrow corridor between thickish stands of pine trees, a place where visibility reduces to twenty feet in some places. It's also where Wilde started paying even more attention.

25   He had walked right past the big pool of blood just off the trail, the largest amount of blood he would find, even when he finally located Petranyi. "It was pretty much his life in that pool of blood."

After that, he noticed the small spots of blood leading down the trail. Then he got to the bootlace, the coins, the place where it looked like the bear had taken the two-hundred-pound man in its mouth and shaken him, leaving the scuff marks in the trail.

Following the evidence was not something he had to force himself to do, he later said. But it wasn't easy either, and it got even harder when the blood and other sign pulled him off the trail and into the woods.

"I was spooked out of my mind, but I had every reason to believe I was alone in that situation and that this guy's life was on the line. It was a weird thing, but all my senses were heightened to the nth degree. I was hearing four times better than I normally do. And I was seeing and smelling four times better than I normally do. So I just set on the logical track and tried to do things as logically as I could. I mean I took my time.

"It wasn't like I had to force myself, it was like what had to be done. But I didn't just go whistling in there either. I mean I was scared. I looked. I observed everything. I heard everything. I continuously rotated in 360 degrees to make sure I wasn't missing something, and I made noise all the time. I expected the guy was, if not dead, then on his way to dying from the evidence I was seeing. But you don't know. I still don't know if he was actually dead when I found him."

Wilde could find no pulse, no breath. The blood around the man's wounds 30 was turning dark when he left to get the coat.

Moving the 750 feet—rangers would later measure the distance—between the backpack and where the bear first left Petranyi's body took about fifteen minutes the first time, Wilde said, because he was moving so carefully. But he made the round-trip from Petranyi to the pack and back in about five minutes, goaded by the faint hope of trying to keep somebody alive. Moving fifteen hundred feet in five minutes is no sprint, but it's no dawdle either, especially when there's a grizzly in the area.

When he returned to the spot where the body had disappeared, there was no doubt in Wilde's mind that he was in the right place. The blood, his own tracks, and other evidence were too clear to be mistaken. Petranyi had been lying under a small tree, the only one in the area, and now he was gone.

That meant the chances of him still clutching to life were even smaller, and Wilde knew what he had to do then: Back off, warn other people, and wait for help.

The help arrived at 5:02 P.M. in the form of a helicopter bearing two rangers armed with 12-gauge shotguns, loaded with heavy slugs. A pair of hikers had found Wilde's note on the Loop Trail (they were probably the source of the scream he had heard earlier) and hustled back to the trailhead to call rangers. The lead man in the helicopter was Charlie Logan, a Glacier veteran with long experience in managing grizzly bears.

But the rangers weren't the first ones on the scene. As Wilde waited at 35 the chalet, scanning the hillsides and trying to control his tension, a group of four hikers arrived. They had walked in on the Highline Trail, ignoring the warnings from the people Wilde had sent that way with another note.

"They came in, like, 'Hey, let's go see that bear that killed that guy.'

"When they got in there I was irate," Wilde recalls. "I lectured them like I probably shouldn't have. I was all over them and they came right back at me. They said they were from Montana and live with this kind of thing all the time and wanted to see it."

The rangers were almost as disgusted with the people as Wilde was. The hikers no longer were having much fun either. They got to thinking about the bear they had seen on the hike to the chalet, and one of them asked for a ride out on the helicopter. They were in the air within moments.

It took about thirty minutes for Logan to interview Wilde and organize gear. Then the two of them, along with ranger Curt Frain, hit the trail, hoping to find Petranyi's body before the approaching darkness fell. Stopping to inspect and photograph evidence along the way, it took them twenty-four minutes to reach the body. Wilde had found Petranyi's body 175 feet from the trail. The bear had moved it another 500 feet by the time the three men found it the second time. If Wilde hadn't been there, it would have taken the rangers a lot longer to find it.

40 "After seeing what he had seen, it was remarkable that he offered to go back," Logan says. "It took a lot of courage."

Logan's reports described the brief trip as "challenging tracking while watching our flanks." The bear carrying Petranyi's body changed course a couple of times. Along its trail they found Petranyi's sock and bits of his shirt, but Logan, a trained medic, found no evidence of life in Petranyi. The body was cold, the eyes glazed, the injuries massive.

Considering all of this and "that a real danger to us (including civilian Buck Wilde) still existed at this late hour, I decided that we quickly document and mark the scene and exit the area," Logan wrote in his reports of the incident.

Frain flagged the area and took notes while Logan stood guard, shotgun at the ready. Very fresh sign indicated the bear or bears were probably still close at hand. At this point, nobody knew for sure how many or what kind of bears were involved, but dirt had been shoved on the body, indicating the bear had claimed it as its own and was protecting it from scavengers.

The men then backtracked, continuing to photograph and document evidence, moving back to Petranyi's backpack, which they checked for food. They looked for identification, and they wanted to know if Petranyi's lunch had lured the bear. But there was no food in the pack.

45 That's when the bears charged.

Frain was searching the backpack "when I heard heavy, rapid pounding of feet on the trail section below us, followed by repeated woofing sounds," Logan wrote in his report. "I could not see what was running up the trail at us but guessed it was a bear so began yelling 'back bear.' Within a moment a grizzly appeared at the bend in the trail below us and stopped. I caught a glimpse of a smaller bear just behind but did not take my eyes off the larger bear, now squarely in the sights of my shotgun."

The adult bear bounced back and forth on its front paws several times, a sign of stress and agitation, looked back at its offspring, and "woofed" a few times. It was fifty feet away, later measurements would show, and Logan said later that if the bear had taken one more step he would have pulled the trigger. He did not believe the bear had run upon the men by surprise, he says. It was charging.

The charge "looked like a pretty deliberate deal on the bear's part," Logan says. "But there were three of us there and we were yelling at her. I think she sized us up and decided we were too much."

Then the bears took off, but the men could still hear them, woofing and crashing in the nearby brush, tearing through the area where they had first attacked Petranyi, moving around the men in a quarter-circle. By then, it was getting dark fast.

50 Logan later would call the incident one of the biggest scares of his life, but his report is written in the deadpan style of official documents. Wilde remembers the charge a little more vividly. He says he doesn't believe that guns do much good in bear encounters, that attacks almost always happen

too fast for most people to draw a weapon. But in this case, Logan and Frain were ready and probably could have killed at least the sow, had they chosen to.

"We heard the bears before we saw them," Wilde says. "It was like a freight train coming up that Loop Trail, coming on full speed.

"Charlie is on the left and [Frain] is on the right. I'm in the middle and we're standing right on the trail. And Charlie says, safety off, one up in the chamber. Bead down. Start yelling."

So the men started yelling. "Stop bear, stop bear." And the bears turned away.

"I don't know Charlie much outside this situation," says Wilde. "But the judgment he used right there, to not shoot those bears, I thought was very commendable. Most people would have been throwing lead. Trust me, I mean those bears were close and coming fast. But he gave them more than a fair chance and they did enough to avoid getting shot."

Logan says he didn't shoot for a couple of reasons. First, the bear stopped 55 when he started yelling at it. Second, he had no idea if these bears were the ones that killed Petranyi.

"I certainly didn't want to kill the wrong bear, especially one with cubs."

The men then decided, as Wilde had earlier in the day, that enough was enough. They left the pack and tripod where they lay and "cautiously retreated" to the chalet area, where Wilde broke down his camp in the increasing darkness as the rangers stood guard, shotguns at the ready.

They took Wilde to a nearby backcountry ranger station with them—he had been ready to catch what sleep he could on the second-story deck of the chalet—and spent a long, long night filling out reports, reliving the day, and trying to figure out what had happened to Petranyi. About four in the morning, they caught a couple hours of sleep.

John Petranyi had lived a quiet life in Madison, Wisconsin, where he was a supervisor of custodians for the city government and shared a home with his father, a Hungarian immigrant. He loved jazz music, fine beers, good books, and riding his bicycle, commuting on it the six miles to his job in all kinds of weather.

But his greatest passion was getting out into wild country, according to 60 his brother, Mark. Every year, he spent his three-week vacation in the wild country of the West: climbing volcanic peaks in Oregon, exploring Alaska, mountain biking in the canyons of Utah. In 1992, he took an auto tour of the Canadian Rockies, visiting Banff, Jasper, and other national parks, camping and hiking. Glacier was the last stop on his itinerary. Had he survived the day hike to Granite Park, he would have turned toward home the next day.

"That's what he worked all year for," Mark Petranyi says. "His three-week journey into the woods."

Stocky and strong, his five-foot-eleven-inch frame carried almost two hundred pounds. Bicycling, jogging, and cross-country skiing kept him in good shape. He was the oldest of three sons and his death was not the first sadness in the family: A brother had died in an accident in 1974 and his mother passed away in 1990. He was a bachelor, childless.

The evening after the day he died, a Sunday, a police chaplain came to the home of his father, also named John, and delivered the heartbreaking news. The next day, as Mark and John senior were preparing to fly to Montana to retrieve the body, a postcard arrived at Mark's house. It was postmarked from Kalispell, just outside Glacier.

"He said he hadn't seen any bears yet but had heard they were around," Mark says. "My wife almost didn't give me the card. It was a hard one to read."

65   John Petranyi liked to take pictures, but he wasn't an avid wildlife photographer. Almost all of his photographs were of landscapes, Mark says, a statement backed up by the film in John's camera, developed later by rangers. The pictures were all of the jagged peaks and cliffs that make Glacier so famous. No bears were on the film.

Mark says neither he nor his father blame the bears for John's death.

"He was just in the wrong place at the wrong time," Mark says. "It's unfortunate but he was in their home. You really can't blame the bears."

He and his father flew to Montana, where John's remains were cremated, and drove the dead man's car back to Wisconsin.

It was, as Mark recalls, a long drive.

70   Back in Glacier, Charlie Logan was getting ready to pull some long shifts himself.

As the bad news circulated around the park that Sunday morning, Logan, Frain, and Wilde rose in the ranger cabin to find the weather had gone to hell. Plans had called for a helicopter to arrive at first light and carry the body to park headquarters, but fog had cut the visibility to about one hundred feet when the sun rose at a little after seven. By half past eight, the temperature had fallen ten degrees, the wind had picked up, and snow was coming down in big round flakes. It wasn't until half past eleven that the weather cleared enough to bring a helicopter into the alpine bowl. On the way in, rangers spotted the bears on Petranyi's body. The sow had a distinctive marking—a light-colored collar around her neck and descending onto her chest.

More armed rangers came in on that flight, and Buck Wilde rode the helicopter back to park headquarters. His role was over, but the rangers' work had hardly started.

It took a couple of hours to get the six rangers and helicopter pilot Jim Kruger organized and a strategy worked out. Five rangers would walk to Petranyi's body. One would fly in the helicopter with Kruger, to observe the operation from the air. The ground crew arrived at the site at 2:15 and found Petranyi's body had been moved another seventy-five feet, where the bears had eaten more of it.

Pilot Kruger found the bear family—a sow and two cubs—still near the body. The bears didn't want to leave and kept trying to get closer, so he started hazing them with the helicopter, trying to keep them away from the body and the ground crew. "He'd get her going one way and then she would come back another way," Logan says. All this information was traveling to the ground crew via radio, but it was still hard to pinpoint the bear's exact location. It took only twenty minutes to load the body in the airship—four men carrying and one standing guard, keeping a close eye on the bushes—but it was a long twenty minutes. Then the ground crew continued documenting all the evidence they could find, working under a constant guard. With the helicopter gone, nobody knew where the bears were. As they back-tracked to the site of the backpack and camera and fanned out to search some more, the crew found Petranyi's wallet in the woods, a dozen steps from his backpack.

The wallet allowed the rangers to positively identify him and also pro- 75 vided a crucial piece of evidence. It had been torn by bear teeth, gouged deep enough to puncture the plastic credit cards inside it. There were a few traces of blood on the wallet and a little more blood on a nearby tree. That was enough to indicate that Petranyi had initially been attacked there and had then moved closer to the trail, where Wilde had found the pool of blood. Probably he had rested there, bleeding, and then moved down the trail the way he had come, hoping to find help.

Buck Wilde believes Petranyi met the bears in a surprise encounter, that the bears were running from the cooking area of the campground (tracks showed one bear had come within fifteen yards of him while he ate breakfast) and that, when they ran into Petranyi, the mother attacked to defend her cubs.

Rangers, who had more time to investigate, came up with a handful of possible scenarios.

Since the pack and camera appeared to have been laid carefully down, and because Petranyi's pants and underwear were around his ankles when he was found, they said it was possible that he had placed his things beside the trail and moved into the woods for a bowel movement or to urinate. That's where the bear hit him first. Then, either she let him go or he escaped and moved back to the trail, where he stopped long enough to leave the pool of blood before moving downhill, back toward his car and the only source of help he knew about.

It's also possible that he saw the bears on the trail and set his gear down before running into the woods, where the bears caught up with him. Under this scenario, they may have charged before or after he started running.

Maybe he saw the bears and put his things down, preparing to photo- 80 graph them, and they attacked.

Or he could have heard a noise and moved into the woods, leaving his gear behind, to investigate.

The bowel movement theory seems likely, but is not conclusive. The only evidence backing it up is that his pants were down around his ankles. But being dragged by a bear shredded his shirt and pulled a boot off his foot. It could easily have pulled his pants down, too. Plus, if he had stepped into the woods to relieve himself, why would he leave his hat in the trail? Unless, of course, he dropped the hat after being attacked, as he stumbled back to the trail. Rangers found his glasses and some other items in the woods, indicating considerable movement in a small area.

It's clear that the initial assault didn't kill him.

The blood spots that Wilde followed down the Loop Trail were round, indicating Petranyi probably walked down the trail under his own power. If the bear had dragged him down the trail, the blood would have been smeared.

Also, the bear left claw marks on the trail but no pad marks, indicating the bear was up on its toes, running.

85 Less than six hundred feet from the pack and camera, the bear caught Petranyi again, causing the "thrashing" marks in the trail. That's probably where he died. Then it dragged him down the trail a few steps and into the woods, where Wilde would find him.

It's possible that the bear chased Petranyi down the trail, but "he probably bumped into the bear again there," Logan says.

It is those last six hundred feet of his brother's travels that bother Mark Petranyi the most.

"Apparently he attempted to get away," Mark says. "Maybe that was the wrong thing to do. We'll never know. But that time from the first attack until she finally got him . . . it must have been sheer terror. Why didn't the bear go away? I've asked myself that question a thousand times."

Rangers asked themselves the same question. A grizzly bear had killed and eaten a man. It was an incredibly rare situation. In the ninety-year history of Glacier Park, where thousands upon thousands of people walk through grizzly country every year, Petranyi was only the ninth person to be killed by a grizzly bear. And in most of those cases, the bear left the body alone after the attack. During the same period, forty-eight people drowned in the park, twenty-three fell to their deaths from cliffs, and twenty-six died in car wrecks. Clearly, grizzly bears are only one of many perils in the park.

90 "In all my other cases, the bear attacks, neutralizes the threat, and leaves," Logan says.

The National Park Service met Monday morning to discuss the situation. Logan and the other rangers flew to park headquarters to participate. Chief Ranger Steve Frye called some outside bear experts for advice. After a few hours, the group of rangers and administrators decided the bears must die.

A combination of circumstances led to that decision. The initial attack on Petranyi may have been a defensive reaction by a surprised bear, and that is not normally a death sentence for a bear in Glacier National Park. But it quickly turned into a "predatory" situation when she started eating him. Add the bear's aggression on the trail, the way she had tried to buck the helicopter to get back to the corpse, and the way she had partially buried the body. Then add public and political perceptions.

"By removing that bear we perhaps saved many bears," Logan says.

That sounds like stilted logic at first, but it makes sense in the highly charged political debates over grizzly bears and their place in the modern world. If the bear had been allowed to live, "then," says Logan, "every attack after that would have been the man-killing grizzly" in the public mind.

95 "We're trying to have an atmosphere where people and bears can coexist," he says. But having a bear around that has earned a food reward by killing a person "is not consistent with what we want to achieve here. It was terrible to have to remove that grizzly bear, but I never had any second thoughts about it."

Logan and several other rangers packed up their weapons and flew back to the chalet at Granite Park.

The rangers searched from the air for as long as the weather held out that day but couldn't find the bears they were looking for. A family group was spotted a few miles away, but they were the wrong bears.

That night, snow fell, and by the next morning—day four of the incident—a couple of inches of fresh dust coated the high country.

Kruger flew in part of a rancid deer carcass to use as bait, carrying it in a 100 sling beneath his helicopter. Rangers on the ground had to adjust the bait, manipulating the smelly carcass and knowing there were hungry grizzlies in the area. Later that afternoon, a large, chocolate-colored grizzly came in, sniffed the bait, and disappeared with the whole bundle in less than five seconds as rangers watched through binoculars. Bait would be staked to the ground in the future.

The hunt was marked with frustration. Several snares were set and baited with more deer carcasses but they didn't do the job. The rangers caught a grizzly one day, but he was the wrong animal, a subadult male, so they let him go. Bear biologists with the Montana Department of Fish, Wildlife and Parks flew in to help. Bear sign was everywhere. Rangers on foot patrol found tracks of the bear family in one of the places where Petranyi's body had lain, along the trail where he had been dragged, and in nearby meadows. They found places where bears had "rototilled" their previous day's footsteps as they dug up roots. Rangers spotted the bears a couple of times over the next several days, but nobody could get a shot at them.

It wasn't until October 11, day nine of the incident, that they were finally killed. Kruger had spotted them while shuttling rangers in and out of the chalet area. But there was a problem. Another family of bears was in the same area. The rangers had to make sure they were shooting the right bears, so Logan and ranger Regi Altop climbed in the helicopter and buzzed over the bears several times until Logan saw what he was looking for: that light-colored collar around the sow's neck.

Kruger dropped the two rangers off about two hundred yards from the bears, and they crept closer while the helicopter hovered overhead. The bears paid little attention to the noisy chopper and focused on digging up roots, a testament to the single-minded quest for food that grizzlies display in the fall.

When the rangers approached within one hundred yards, they took careful aim at the feeding sow with their. 300 H&H Magnum rifles. Logan started counting. When he hit three, both men fired. The sow took a couple of steps and fell dead. Then they opened fire on the cubs. One dropped and the other took off into the woods, wounded but still scampering.

More rangers arrived to help Logan and Altop search for the wounded 105 animal, and after about an hour Kruger spotted it from the helicopter. The four rangers spread out and went after it, walking uphill.

That's when the second bear family showed up.

Kruger had to take his eyes off the cub and haze the second family away with his helicopter, trying to keep them away from the rangers, trying to keep a bad situation from getting worse fast. It worked, but the men lost the cub.

Kruger, always sharp-eyed, spotted the cub later in the day with a spotting scope that was set up at the chalet. It had come back to the area where its mother had died, wounded and alone. Kruger flew Steve Frye and another ranger to the area. It was almost dark by then, but they walked into a thick stand of trees and finished the animal off with a final shot.

At 6:43 P.M, on the eleventh day of October, 1992, after nine bloody and grueling days, Kruger loaded the cub in his helicopter and lifted off for the last time. The whole unpleasant business was finally over.

110   The three bear carcasses were shipped to the Montana Department of Fish, Wildlife and Parks diagnostic laboratory in Bozeman, Montana, where veteran biologist Keith Aune performed a necropsy, an autopsy for animals.

The National Park Service wanted to know if there was any evidence of Petranyi inside the bears, any hair or flesh or fiber. Bear scat collected near Petranyi's body contained human remains and two different types of cloth. But when Aune examined the bears, he found nothing unusual. Not that he had expected much. The bears had been passing huge amounts of food through their bodies in the days since Petranyi died. Each of them had a belly full of roots when it died.

Rangers singled these bears out for death working on the best possible evidence. They had seen these bears near the body and trying to get closer. There was no other family group in the area with cubs that size. But had they killed Petranyi? The rangers were sure, but they wanted scientific evidence, something to remove absolutely all doubt about whether they had killed the right bears. Aune couldn't give it to them.

"There was no evidence in the stomach or gastrointestinal tract which can confirm the presence" of the bears at the scene of Petranyi's death.

A niggling doubt would remain forever, and that's the kind of thing that can bother a park ranger. People don't sign up to be rangers because they enjoy killing grizzly bears.

115   "It's beyond a reasonable doubt," says Glacier spokeswoman Amy Vanderbilt, whose husband, Gary Moses, helped investigate the incident. "But we'll never be able to absolutely verify it."

Aune did, however, provide some information about the bears. The sow was at least fifteen years old, in good general health, and weighed 251 pounds. She harbored a normal load of parasites, was seventy-four inches long, and carried a layer of fat an inch thick along her back, indicating she was only in moderate shape. Bears often have two to four inches of fat along their backs at that time of year. Her two cubs, both females, weighed thirty-nine pounds and fifty pounds.

The sow's left front foot had been injured recently, which could have caused an attitude problem, but the most interesting thing Aune found was in her mouth: deep cavities in her molars.

"They had to be very painful," Aune says. Plus, one of her front teeth had rotted away almost entirely.

Did a constant and severe toothache make the bear more cantankerous? Aune, who has studied grizzlies for decades, thinks it probably did.

But why did she run away from Buck Wilde as he ate breakfast, then at- 120
tack Petranyi twice and feed on him? Seeing Wilde was probably no surprise
to her. She knew the area, knew that people were often seen in the campground and cooking area. Whether she first saw Petranyi on the trail or in
the woods, it likely was a surprise encounter, which triggered an instinct to
protect her cubs. The toothache probably reduced her tolerance level at least
a little. That, combined with her intense focus on calories prior to denning
for the winter, could have triggered some kind of switch that made her see
Petranyi as food rather than as a nuisance or a threat, made her attack a second time and begin to eat him.

Buck Wilde says it took him five years before he could talk about the
incident with any comfort.

When the helicopter took him to park headquarters, rangers interviewed
him again and then repeated Logan's earlier advice to get some psychological
counseling, "to make sure from a shrink point of view that everything was
sort of okay," is the way Wilde puts it.

He declined. Rather, he shouldered his backpack and slipped out the
back door of the headquarters building, dodging the reporters waiting for him
at the front door. Then he walked to the highway, stuck out his thumb, and
caught a ride with a couple he had met two days earlier while hiking in to
Granite Park. He told them the story, and the man bought him a bottle of
Wild Turkey whiskey ("It's one of my poisons, especially in high-stress situations") before dropping him at a trailhead on the east side of the park.

Wilde was seeking his own mental therapy.

"I decided I was going back into bear country." 125

It was an area new to him, the Triple Divide Pass, where waters run to
the Atlantic, the Pacific, and Hudson Bay.

"I wasn't just scared, I was scared to death. I had been shaken, funda-
mentally, to the core. I wanted to handle my shakiness in a way that would be
constructive, and I thought the most constructive thing to do, for my psyche,
was to get back in bear country. Fear management, I guess you'd call it."

He's had other big scares since then. A couple more charges by grizzlies
and a canoe wreck that left him stranded on an island in the raging North
Fork of the Flathead River for six days.

He doesn't like to talk about that one much either, for the same reason
he's avoided talking much about the Petranyi incident.

"It's taken me five years to get to the point where I'm ready to do that. 130
You get kind of weird when you spend as much time in the woods as I do. I
understand firsthand what is meant by the word 'taboo'. Taboos are things
that the Native Americans dealt with in special terms, by whispering or
whatever."

He's still a little uncomfortable talking about it. It brings things back,
he says, and he wants to treat the situation with respect for the bears and for
Petranyi's family. And there is another matter. Call it practical spirituality.
Long-term physical survival in the wilderness depends on having the right attitude, Wilde believes.

"I felt that if I didn't give this situation enough respect, spiritually, and with all the time I spend in bear country, that the bears would get me. That sounds pretty weird, but it's really the way I look at it. One thing you should get is that I was scared shitless. It scared me enough to make it very special."

He says he doesn't expect people to understand him, but he believes what he believes. It's important to him.

The trip into Triple Divide Pass lasted five days. He saw lots of bear sign, tracks, and evidence of fresh digging. But he didn't see a bear during the whole trip, and today he's comfortable in the woods.

135   Put yourself in Buck Wilde's shoes.

What would you have done?

THOMAS McNAMEE

Drainage Ditch

When my family moved to Whitehaven, Tennessee, in 1954, it was an unincorporated hamlet of a few thousand people, and just beginning to serve as a suburb of Memphis, several miles to the north. We were surrounded by country.

To the south lay the Mississippi Delta, destination of the early-morning busloads of black children turned out of their schools each spring to chop cotton and each fall to pick it while we white children stayed at our desks. The Delta was my daddy's ancestral home, and his kin all still lived there. When we drove down to see them, Highway 61 would plunge from the wide bright cottonfields into dark bayou bottoms, and the windshield would be so spattered with bugs that we had to stop to scrape them off. Dead deer and snakes and owls and opossums lay sprawled on the bridge sides. Ospreys nested in the cypress tops, and there were alligators in the mud.

To the east of my home rose the scrub-and-clay uplands of Fayette County, Tennessee's poorest county, pig country, Klan country, buzzard country. West was the river, too huge and too strong to be quite real to a boy of seven.

What was real was closer to home. A big Hereford bull lived across the road, a chaser of children. Down our side of Oakwood Drive there was a row of seven new houses, and beyond its dead end a deep forest began, with swamps and lakes and mysteries in it. Spring nights, the frog chorus there sang loud. In an abandoned barn pulled half down by honeysuckle vines, mud daubers built their terrible castles, tube on tube of wasp-brick. Because I was allergic, my mama said, one sting could kill me. I grew to dread all insects—June bugs, yellowjackets, bumblebees, dragonflies—alike.

5   The hedge, the lawn, the big hollow sweetgum in the front yard, the maples and dogwoods and pines, even the scruffy bushes that screened our garbage cans were wildlife habitat. Hundreds of songbirds squabbled at my mother's feeders. A family of rabbits every spring, shuffling quails and burbling doves, and countless reptiles and amphibians all thrived around our house. At lightning-bug time,

my friends and I had toadfrog-catching contests. You could catch three dozen of those warty, poison-peeing monsters in an hour, some of them fat as a softball. Terrariums, their glass walls slimed with the leavings of mudpuppies, skinks, snails, and prize toads, were my pride. I also tried to keep box tortoises and various snakes, but they always escaped, often inside the house.

Behind our house was a sharecropper's shack, with a friendly old retired workhorse. Later, when the shack had given way to the grounds of a grandiose white-columned pseudo-mansion, there came a fancier horse, who would eat my father's Chesterfield cigarettes from my hand. At the bottom of the pasture, a little creek had its source.

I cannot remember when I first began to follow that creek downstream. It flowed slowly and opaquely along the bottom of a deep winding gouge cut through layers of the wind-deposited silt called loess. Loess is a very fine and viscid stuff, and it makes one hell of a mud. Where the water backed up, the muck could be waist-deep on a boy.

Miraculously, there were at least a dozen boys within a year of my age all living on one sparsely settled square-quarter-mile quadrangle of roads (and only one girl). I was small, and bad at sports—nearly always last to be chosen for a team—but in the swamp I often led our expeditions, and was usually first to test the footing. My mother always said I was the muddiest boy of all when we came trudging home at suppertime.

Above a pool perhaps a mile downstream, we would swing on grapevines and do cannonballs into water the color of coffee with cream, where the bottom was a bottomless ooze. Snakes swam there, including the dread cottonmouth. Kingfishers laughed in the willows and tall tulip trees. Catfish took hooked bits of hot dog we dangled from cane poles on lines bobbered with porcupine quills. Once, a gang of us blundered on a hobo camp so freshly abandoned that a half can of beans was still warm on the coals.

As we grew older, I often went into the swamp by myself. I was a melancholy boy, sometimes lonely even among my friends. My solitary wanderings began, I think, as flights, from games in which I could not excel, from an uncomprehended restlessness, from the sweat and tumble and perplexity of social boyhood; but before long my long after-school afternoons alone in the woods had grown into pilgrimages, my weekends and summers rhapsodic quests: I felt that I was seeking something, and sometimes, I know, I found it, though I still could not tell you what it was. 10

Beyond the tangled muscadine and honeysuckle jungles, beyond the canebrakes in which whole chattering flocks of birds could hide, beyond the old overgrown fields snarled with blackberries and cocklebur, there came an even, easy, open floor of dead leaves and low, soft plants, pillared with trees of awesome girth and height. The canopy was far above, punctured only intermittently by the sun. I believe that this forest had never been logged, although, like some of these others, that memory may be colored by desire. I remember the air as very humid, very hot, very still. I remember the buzzing of wasps in that air, and, in response, the beating of my fretful heart.

My little creek (did it have a name? I never wondered) fed a larger one that fed Nonconnah Creek, which in turn fed the Mississippi River. Nonconnah was occasionally so audacious as to flood its own flood plain, and the Army Corps of Engineers dealt severely with such impertinence. Their chosen instrument of correction was the dragline, a great toothed scoop on a crane. It could rip out a ton of root-riddled earth in one bite. The messy, inefficient eccentricities of Nonconnah Creek—the oxbows, the riffles and pools, the braided channels, the islanded swamps, the tupelo bottoms—were chastened into an orderly, straight-running ditch. The rate of flow was thus increased, and flooding prevented, and development of previously unusable land made possible. That thousands of such acts of discipline would bring on anarchy downstream was not particularly a worry, for quelling the Mississippi's rebellion farther south would mean more contracts for the contractors, one of whom was the father of one of my neighborhood pals. Racing ever faster, full of the sediment that the old flood bottoms and swamps used to retain, the Mississippi today wants to crash through its banks down near Natchez and pour into the Atchafalaya basin—and leave New Orleans sitting on a mudflat. To prevent this will require one of the most expensive public-works projects in the history of the United States.

The dragline first came when the old one-lane wooden bridge at Mill Branch Road was to be replaced. Growling and grunting, it chewed out the bridge pool and left on the bank two alps of mud. They were the only steep hills we ever had, and they made a splendid place for dirt-clod fights—just the kind of thing my friends loved and I hated. In that deeper water the fishing improved, but where once a boy could sit all day undisturbed but by an occasional truckload of cotton banging over the planks toward the gin, now there was constant traffic: workers and materials for the tract-house subdivisions springing up to the south. I took my cane pole farther now, to the lakes.

My prey was mostly smaller here than the catfish of the creek, but better eating—bream, and crappies, and once in a while a largemouth bass. No matter how early I might come or how late stay, the best fishing spots always seemed to be occupied by an elderly black man or woman with little to say to a white child. I wonder now, did they fear that I might be the landowner's son? And who did own that land? The thought never crossed my mind. They would nod, and keep on fishing, catching ten fish to my one. For them, of course, it was not sport.

15　　There was a place on the creek we called the rapids—it was just a gravelly riffle, really—and there, one day, my best friend, Bobby Towery, and I came upon the most stupendous animal we had ever met outside the zoo. I knew at once, from my avid reading in field guides, that this was the mighty *alligator snapping turtle*—you could tell by the three mountainous keels on his carapace—the largest species of freshwater turtle in the world, sometimes surpassing two hundred pounds. He was very far from his home, which was supposed to be the Mississippi River.

Snappers are swimmers, not walkers, and this one seemed to have run aground. A gingerly probe with a stick elicited only a slight drawing-in of his huge plated head. We agreed that there was only one thing to be done: we had to capture the turtle. With my trusty Boy Scout hatchet we cut down a small tree and laid the trunk, about two inches thick, across the gravel shallows to block him from escaping into the opaque pool below. While Towery stood guard, I ran home for my green coaster wagon. When I got back, the turtle had not moved a muscle.

We had the idea that if we could get him to bite the pole he would not let go, and then we might haul him to land. How to get him into the wagon we would worry about later. But even with some pretty rowdy poking at his great hooked beak, the snapper could not be tempted to do more than flinch.

We sat on the bank and considered waiting him out. How hideous, how beautiful, how fierce, how still he was! How primitive, how ancient. What was time to a creature like this? Two boys could never outwait such a turtle.

We decided we would try to flip him onto his back. And then what? We'd see. At least he would be immobilized. Prying and pushing and sweating and slipping—and terrified that one slip would tumble us in on top of him—we got our pole beneath him, and the alligator snapping turtle came to life. He whirled—I know, turtles aren't supposed to whirl, but this one did—and bit our two-inch pole in half, and clawed his way into deep water and was gone.

Corpses of frogs, fish, snakes, and crawdads were ranged along my bed- 20 room bookshelves in jars of denatured alcohol. Then my wild bachelor uncle from the Delta, to my mother's horror, gave me a BB gun. No songbird was safe. The first shot usually only knocked it senseless from its perch, and I would seek it out in the brush to administer the coup de grâce to the brain. I made no pretense of collecting them; I left my victims where they lay. My favorite target was the mockingbird, the Tennessee state bird, illegal to kill. What could have possessed me? Remembering this makes my throat clench with shame.

The pursuit of Eagle Scouthood led me to gentler concerns. To take casts of animal tracks for my nature merit badge, I traveled deeper into the old forest than I had ever gone. There were mysteries at every step. Why did the mother raccoon and her family stop here? What made the heron take flight? Fox prints at the edge of the water: did the fox swim, or leap? Hence, slowly, my rage to possess wild creatures was displaced by empathy.

In a little pasture far back in the woods I found a dead calf. The head was twisted half around, the eyes staring into the sky. The skin was peeled back from the rib cage, which was crawling with flies. One leg had been eaten down to the bone. The day was hot, but the flesh had not yet begun to stink, so the kill must have been very recent, and the predator nearby. Crows called. A sharp hind edge of cloud-shade swept across the grass, and in the sudden brightness there was a clarity that I had never seen before, as if a veil had been lifted from the face of the world.

I looked for tracks, found one, and took its cast. It was big, three inches across. My field guide said, unbelievably, cougar! Mountain lion! *Panther.*

Not until years later, when the cast was long lost, did I realize what a find that may have been. *Felis concolor* is extinct now in the Mississippi valley. Indeed the cougar may be gone everywhere east of the Rockies, except for the minuscule and dwindling population of the Florida panther subspecies. Could this have been one of the last eastern cougars? Or was it, as a wildlife biologist suggested to me recently, the hybrid of a calf-killing dog and a boy's eager imagination?

25   The old-growth forest was cut down, and not even for lumber: the great trees were bulldozed into piles and burned. Most of the topsoil washed away, and the red clay beneath it required laborious cultivation to sustain the newly unrolled swaths of zoysia and Bermuda grass sod. Saplings were planted, and wired upright. The lakes were drained, and the black people moved out. The last hobo known to have visited Whitehaven was found dead beneath a hedge. We got a shopping center, and an interstate highway. Fluoridation of our drinking water was fought, thought to be a Communist plot to curb the birth rate. I had my first summer job as a carpenter's helper, putting up drywall in new houses.

Improved pesticides came onto the market, and it was possible now to drive through the Delta bottoms with no more than an occasional sweep of the windshield wipers. My wild uncle, who kept bongos and a conga drum in his den closet, got married. The ospreys disappeared from the cypresstop nests, the alligators from the bayous. The only lake left was appropriated by tough teenagers as a beer-drinking hideout; they raped a girl there. Quails no longer shuffled in the leaves on the lawn.

What had been done to Nonconnah Creek was done now to its tributaries. New sewers leaked into the stagnant trench that was all that remained of my creek's headwaters. Our grapevine-draped swimming hole and the alligator snapping turtle's riffle lasted longer, but we could get there on bicycles now, on smooth blacktop. Often I didn't make it that far, having stopped off to chew gum and laugh in Mary Scott Moyers's or Joellen Krayer's yard and lost track of time. When the last of my creek was ditched out, I believe I did not notice.

Twenty years later, home one Christmas from New York, I saw a dragline working in the parking lot of the cabana apartments that stand where my old creek went under the old wooden bridge. I was astonished to see that there was still some life in what the people there now called the drainage ditch: each time the great machine took a bite, the muddy water boiled with creatures forced downstream before it. The V-shaped ditch was being made into a box-shaped one. A chain-link fence was being built along both sides, to keep children safely out. The walls and floor of the drainage ditch were being lined with concrete.

JON KATZ

Why People Love Dogs

My friend and fellow dog lover Edie, an occupational therapist in Massachusetts, has been looking for a mate for nearly 10 years. She finally thought she'd found one in Jeff, a nice guy, generous and funny, who teaches high school. They dated for several months, and just as there was talk about a future, it occurred to Edie that Jeff hadn't really bonded with her yellow Lab, Sophie. In fact, as she thought more about it, she wasn't sure Jeff was a dog guy at all.

She confronted him about this at dinner one night, and he confessed, in some anguish, that he didn't love Sophie, didn't love dogs in general, never had.

They broke up the next week. More accurately, she dumped him. "What can I say?" Edie told me, somewhat defensively. "Sophie has been there for me, day in and day out, for years. I can't say the same of men. She's my girl, my baby. Sooner or later, it would have ended."

Having just spent two months on a book tour talking to dog lovers 5 across the country, I can testify that this story isn't unusual. The lesson Edie gleaned, she says, was that she should have asked about Sophie first, not last.

In America, we love our dogs. A lot. So much that we rarely wonder why anymore.

This, perhaps, is why God created academics.

John Archer, a psychologist at the University of Central Lancashire, has been puzzling for some time over why people love their pets. In evolutionary terms, love for dogs and other pets "poses a problem," he writes. Being attached to animals is not, strictly speaking, necessary for human health and welfare. True, studies show that people with pets live a bit longer and have better blood pressure than benighted nonowners, but in the literal sense, we don't really need all those dogs and cats to survive.

Archer's alternative Darwinian theory: Pets manipulate the same instincts and responses that have evolved to facilitate human relationships, "primarily (but not exclusively) those between parent and child."

No wonder Edie ditched Jeff. She was about to marry the evil stepfather, 10 somebody who wasn't crazy about her true child.

Or, to look at it from the opposite direction, Archer suggests, "consider the possibility that pets are, in evolutionary terms, manipulating human responses, that they are the equivalent of social parasites." Social parasites inject themselves into the social systems of other species and thrive there. Dogs are masters at that. They show a range of emotions—love, anxiety, curiosity—and thus trick us into thinking they possess the full range of human feelings.

They dance with joy when we come home, put their heads on our knees and stare longingly into our eyes. Ah, we think, at last, the love and loyalty we so richly deserve and so rarely receive. Over thousands of years of living with humans, dogs have become wily and transfixing sidekicks with the particularly appealing characteristic of being unable to speak. We are therefore free to fill in the blanks with what we need to hear. (What the dog may really be telling us, much of the time, is, "Feed me.")

As Archer dryly puts it, "Continuing features of the interaction with the pet prove satisfying for the owner."

It's a good deal for the pets, too, since we respond by spending lavishly on organic treats and high-quality health care.

Psychologist Brian Hare of Harvard has also studied the human-animal 15 bond and reports that dogs are astonishingly skilled at reading humans' patterns of social behavior, especially behaviors related to food and care. They figure out our moods and what makes us happy, what moves us. Then they act accordingly, and we tell ourselves that they're crazy about us.

"It appears that dogs have evolved specialized skills for reading human social and communicative behavior," Hare concludes, which is why dogs live so much better than moles.

These are interesting theories. Raccoons and squirrels don't show recognizable human emotions, nor do they trigger our nurturing ("She's my baby") impulses. So, they don't (usually) move into our houses, get their photos taken with Santa, or even get names. Thousands of rescue workers aren't standing by to move them lovingly from one home to another.

If the dog's love is just an evolutionary trick, does that diminish it? I don't think so. Dogs have figured out how to insinuate themselves into human society in ways that benefit us both. We get affection and attention. They get the same, plus food, shelter, and protection. To grasp this exchange doesn't trivialize our love, it explains it.

I'm enveloped by dog love, myself. Izzy, a border collie who spent the first four years of his life running along a small square of fencing on a nearby farm, is lying under my desk at the moment, his head resting on my boot.

20 Rose, my working dog, is curled into a tight ball in the crate to my left. Emma, the newcomer who spent six years inside the same fence as Izzy, prefers the newly re-upholstered antique chair. Plagued with health problems, she likes to be near the wood stove in the winter.

When I stir to make tea, answer the door, or stretch my legs, all three dogs move with me. I see them peering out from behind the kitchen table or pantry door, awaiting instructions, as border collies do. If I return to the computer, they resume their previous positions, with stealth and agility. If I analyzed it coldly, I would admit that they're probably alert to see if an outdoor romp is in the offing, or some sheepherding, or some beef jerky. But I'd rather think they can't bear to let me out of their sight.

CHAPTER 17

DEPRESSION AND HOPE

Overview

Most people experience rough times in their lives that produce heartache, loneliness, and ultimately despair. Generally, something shakes us out of it—a new romantic interest, for example, or positive recognition at school or work. We might think of such extended periods of feeling bad, whether several days or several weeks, as slumps, just stretches where circumstances didn't work in our favor, leaving us glum rather than content or happy. We recognize these slumps as deviations from our normal state. On any given day, we can get angry, feel frustrated, succumb to sadness, experience elation, or just go about our daily routines in a satisfied manner. A broad range of emotions governs our conduct without one particular feeling dominating our thoughts and behaviors.

Yet, some people do experience acute and chronic states of clinical depression that cripple their ability to function in appropriate, healthy ways. More than just a slump, depression binds certain people to a pessimistic, self-defeating outlook on life and raises serious concerns among family and friends. It's not only a person's mood that is affected, either. Clinical depression produces noticeable physiological effects, such as sleeping disorders, weight loss or gain, and an inability to concentrate. Seventeen million Americans suffer from clinical depression. The medical profession has recognized depression as a health risk, and approximately 25 million people a year seek treatment for depression, twice as many as fifteen years prior.

Online Study Center

This icon will direct you to web links and additional resources on the website http://college.cengage.com/english/thelin/ writing_without_formulas/1e/student_home.html

What has happened to make the number of people diagnosed and treated for depression skyrocket? Focusing on individual accounts of depression might yield some results, but we risk losing sight of the bigger picture if we confine ourselves to the causes of angst and blues among individuals. A pattern may certainly emerge, but we might need to dig deeper to uncover the causes that make depression so pervasive. It's possible that among teenagers and young adults, many episodes of depression occur due to emerging identities conflicting with parental expectations or societal norms. Yet, isolating such conflicts as a significant cause of depression would not answer why the rate of depression has increased now. After all, the struggles people endure in discovering who they are and in finding a place amongst family, friends, and society are nothing new. Teenagers and young adults of every generation have faced the challenges posed by sexuality, fitting in among peers, career goals, and negotiating parental issues.

We might have a better sense of the causes if we start with the language surrounding depression. In Chapter 5, we discussed the concept of "naming our world." While the word "depression" precedes us and has been in use for a long time, has it always been a label? Linguists have studied a phenomenon known as "nominalization" wherein people transform verbs into nouns to create an effect of permanence. You will see nominalization, for example, by looking at the difference between the phrases "Bill lied to me" and "Bill is a liar." One implies a specific instance of mendacity while the other suggests a character trait that we can assume will apply to instances in the future. This seemingly simple distinction in language carries much weight in how we perceive the situation and the subject. Could the same be true of depression? Does it make a difference if we say that "Bill is depressed" as opposed to "Bill suffers from depression"? The one phrase talks about a mood that is transitory. The other names a condition, giving it substance and power beyond the immediate situation.

If we can conceive for a moment that we as a society have participated in naming our world and, thus, in creating a condition called depression, we have to ask why and wonder whether depression empowers us in some way. But a depressed person lacks hope. He or she cannot see a reasonably positive future to embrace when setbacks occur. There would appear to be little empowerment in depression. So if not empowerment, then, is there something appealing in the image of a depressed person? Many creative people know the icon of the "tortured artist," someone who produces her or his best work as a result, apparently, of being depressed. The poet Sylvia Plath, who committed suicide, was considered a tortured artist. Further, countless movies and books have recounted tales of lovelorn individuals, miserable because their one true love spurned them or even died. We admire how much they cherish the object of their affection, and the image they have created endures, whether it is walking the streets alone at night, staring into nothingness, or engaging in acts of self-destruction like excessive drinking. It's hard to determine the actual appeal of these images of torment, but perhaps we cannot too readily dismiss the notion that a depressed person curls up into a ball of self-absorption that is consistent with the current generation's focus on the self (for more on this, see the excerpt from Jean Twenge on page 459).

However, few people want constant unhappiness, and in thinking of the role that language might play in the creation of depression, we also would not want to discount the chemical imbalances in some people that produce debilitating depression. But if we look at depression as a word that connotes much more than just the feelings of wretchedness, it becomes more manageable. We can see what is tied to depression and relate it to dominant ideologies in our culture, which would enable action against depression. Perhaps one purpose in naming it is to give us a better chance to combat it and find both individual and social happiness. For our purposes here, let's define depression as the absence of Hope and see if we can understand its purposes and causes better.

Hope guides us through difficult times and offers an alternative to otherwise bleak circumstances. In the well-known fable of "Pandora's Box," the spirit of Hope is locked away in a chest with evils disguised as stinging insects, and after Pandora is tricked into releasing these evils into the world, Hope works to heal the damage done by disease, cruelty, hunger, and others (see the tale on page 473). While some critics have asked why the spirit of Hope was included in the box, suggesting that hope is a delusion and might merely be just another evil, hope does not delude people when a realistic vision encompasses it. Hope differs from wishful thinking, just as legitimate aspirations differ from dreams. Hope requires action toward a particular goal. People who hope for something understand that the ultimate decision or outcome of any given situation might be outside of their control, but they give their best effort and lessen the odds against them. In this sense, hope combats depression.

So why, then have Americans in the last fifteen years seem to have lost hope?

Bruce Levine in his article on page 476 isolates consumerism as a cause of not just depression but of many maladjustments. While you can disagree with his analysis of capitalist culture and the effect on individuals, you might have a harder time denying the societal and world problems that surround us and that can subconsciously influence our outlook. Far too many nuclear weapons are unaccounted for or in the hands of unstable regimes. Leaders around the world still have not agreed to a comprehensive plan to battle global warming, much less enacted one. Diseases such as AIDS and Alzheimer's do not yet have a cure. Ethnic and religious intolerance, not to mention the continuing fallout from imperialistic practices, have led to armed conflict around the globe. People have more difficulty now than ever before in securing satisfying employment that allows for a comfortable standard of living. For an individual to remain cheerful under such circumstances would seem almost counter-intuitive. How can a person maintain hope when the world appears to be crumbling? Our individual outlooks and the smaller things that appear to trigger episodes of depression might simply be manifestations of a larger disease.

If we grant any credence to the possibility that the world around us has influenced the surge in the number of depressed people, what do we do? These massive societal and political problems seem too huge for any one person to conquer, so depressed individuals have looked for other ways to feel better, mostly through the use of anti-depressants and therapy. However, medication alleviates symptoms but does not cure the illness. And while therapy has many benefits, it focuses on individual behavioral modification, so it, too, might overlook the root social and political sources of depression. The focus on individual cures for depression seems to have deflected attention away from depression as a social problem. Such a diversion is consistent with our culture's embrace of individualism. Yet, the helplessness and cynicism many of us feel when we try to confront large political and social problems prevent us from doing much else except returning to ourselves and wondering what we can do to make our personal lives better. However, this focus on our individual lives and personal happiness might be the exact reason that so many people have abandoned hope and continue to be depressed.

Jean Twenge, a professor of psychology at San Diego State University, has traced much despair in the current generation to a lack of stable, close relationships and the loss of a sense of community. She feels that individuals focus too much on their own wants and expectations, leaving them cynical toward making change. It follows, then, that one way to create hope would be to place less emphasis on individualism. By the time an individual has hit the state of clinical depression, it might be too late, but hope, as Louise Danielle Palmer discusses on page 469, can be learned so that otherwise healthy people can avoid depressive episodes. While Palmer focuses on the character traits of hopeful people, the process of nurturing hope to fruition might start by individuals reaching out to others in meaningful ways and creating communal bonds. With hope comes strength, and combined with a social network, perhaps the strength needed to address some of the ills of society, as true hope encompasses action. Maybe in moving from an individual perspective to a more social one, we can also grow more empathetic toward those in foreign lands and gain perspective on our own lives. Maybe we can become involved in the struggles to save our environment. Maybe we can form organizations and let our voices be heard on both local and national issues. People banding together for a good cause produces hope. Through this type of collective action, we can then confront the causes of depression and work to change those gigantic problems that an individual cannot change. This process will take time, of course, and might work best as a preventative to depression than as an actual cure. But when all is said and done, a world less frightening and more hopeful presents us with our best chance to counter the rise in the number of depressed people.

Openings for Writers

1.   **Action as part of hope**—Brainstorm a list of your own wants and think about the action required to achieve the ends you desire. Based on this, think about which of these wants, if any, are merely wishful thinking, and, in contrast, which are hopes that you can work toward. What action have you taken to increase your chances of success?

2.   **Depression as a privilege**—Some people claim that generations past simply did not have time to be depressed because the demands of work and family kept them constantly busy. Is the amount of leisure time a

person has a possible source of depression? Do citizens in countries less privileged than the United States suffer through depression as much as Americans?

3. **Creating depression**—What part do you think the naming of depression has contributed to the increase in the number of reported cases of it? Can you think of other behaviors or perhaps societal trends that seem to gain power once a word has been attached to it? Look to see what insights such a comparison yields.

4. **Connection to political and social events**—Analyze the contention that the lack of hope stems from large political and social events. In other aspects of our life, can we be unaware of what is affecting our mood and behavior? If so, does this make the connection between lack of hope and world events more plausible?

Language

1. **Depression**—Do you agree with the definition given in the Overview? How else can you define the word? Talk about the ways in which the use of a different definition might produce a competing conversation about depression.

2. **Label**—Does this word carry any connotations? If you put "label" into its gerund form, "labeling," does its meaning change? List synonyms for "label" and "labeling" and ask yourself if describing depression as a label is accurate.

3. **Clinical**—How does the use of "clinical" before the word "depression" extend its meaning? Think of words that might substitute for "clinical" and determine if any might be more descriptive of the difference between "slumps" and the medical condition associated with depression.

JEAN M. TWENGE

The Age of Anxiety (and Depression and Loneliness): Generation Stressed

Jean Twenge has studied patterns of belief and conduct among generations through exhaustive research. She has found striking differences between the Baby Boomers and the generation that follows, which she calls "Generation Me." Twenge isolates several characteristics of Generation Me, but her general thesis is that those born from about 1970–1990 emphasize individual satisfaction over communal duties and rules, which sets up unrealistic expectations and leads to cynicism. In the following excerpt from her 2006 book Generation Me: Why Today's Young Americans Are More Confident, Assertive, Entitled—and More Miserable Than Ever Before, *Twenge discusses the rise of depression among young Americans and suggests the focus on the self deprives them of the communal network needed to get through difficult times.*

In most ways, Kim looks like a well-adjusted college student. She dates her high school sweetheart and is studying psychology at a university in the Midwest. For the past five years, however, Kim has struggled with severe depression. When it was at its worst, she could not force herself to get out of bed to go to class. After hours of therapy and courses of antidepressant drugs, Kim was stable and ready to graduate; then she had a relapse. Now it will take her another year to finish college as she tries to manage her depression. Jason, 22, appeared from the outside to have everything: he had just graduated with honors from an Ivy League university and was starting his first job at a leading investment banking firm. But he soon found that his job was not what he had imagined—the bosses doled out constant criticism and expected sixteen-hour days. The work itself was boring. Jason hated it, so after three months, he quit. Suddenly uncertain about what he wanted to do with his life, he sank into depression. He was devastated that a lifetime of achieving his goals had not brought him happiness. Beth, 19, became severely depressed in high school and seriously considered suicide. "My parents thought I was just a grumpy teenager," she says. "They didn't realize there were demons inside my head that screamed at me and ripped my life apart." Although her parents were opposed to the idea, she eventually saw a therapist and began to take antidepressant medication. "I have so many more opportunities now that I can control the depression and the crippling panic attacks," she says.

Being young has not always carried such a high risk of being anxious, depressed, suicidal, or medicated. Only 1% to 2% of Americans born before 1915 experienced a major depressive episode during their lifetimes, even though they lived through the Great Depression and two world wars. Today, the lifetime rate of major depression is ten times higher—between 15% and 20%. Some studies put the figure closer to 50%. In one 1990s study, 21% of teens aged 15 to 17 had already experienced major depression. Although some of this trend might be due to more frequent reporting of mental illness, researchers have concluded that the change is too large and too consistent across studies to be explained solely by a reporting bias. In addition, these studies use a fairly strict definition, counting only depression severe enough to warrant medication or long-term therapy. If more mild depression were included, the vast majority of young people would raise their hands in recognition.

Depression is oddly commonplace in today's society. In a ubiquitous TV commercial, a frowning, oval-shaped blob becomes happy and smiling after taking the antidepressant medication Zoloft. Panic attacks are the subject of cocktail party conversation and episodes of HBO's *The Sopranos*. Almost every high school and college student knows someone who committed suicide or tried. In past generations, suicide and depression were considered afflictions of middle age, as it was unusual for a young person to be depressed, but for Generation Me, these problems are a rite of passage through adolescence and young adulthood. Karen, 23, became depressed during college, as did her brother. One thing that helped, she said, was realizing that for young people, "going through a time of depression is normal."

It wasn't always "normal," but it is certainly heading in that direction. The number of people being treated for depression more than tripled in the

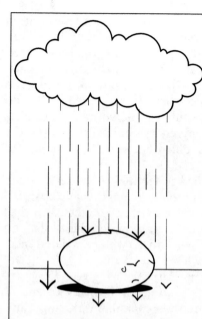

You know when you feel the weight of sadness.

You may feel exhausted, hopeless, and anxious.

Whatever you do, you feel lonely and don't enjoy the things you once loved.

Things just don't feel like they used to.

These are some symptoms of depression. They must last each day for at least two weeks and interface with your daily life. Depression is a serious medical condition. It affects over 20 million Americans. While the cause is not known, depression may be related to an imbalance of natural chemicals between nerve calls in the brain.

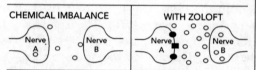

| CHEMICAL IMBALANCE | WITH ZOLOFT |

Prescription ZOLOFT works to correct this imbalance.

Only your doctor can diagnose depression. ZOLOFT is not for everyone. It is approved for adults 18 and over. People taking MAOIs or pimozide shouldn't take ZOLOFT. Side effects may include dry mouth, Insomnia, several side effects, diarrhea, nausea, and sleepiness. Please see the following page for additional information about ZOLOFT 25mg, 50mg and 100mg tablets.

Talk to your doctor about ZOLOFT, the prescribed brand of its land.

Call 1-800-6-ZOLOFT or visit www.ZOLOFT.com for more information.

Zoloft
(sertraline HCl)

When you know more about what's wrong, you can help make it right.™

The ubiquitous sad blob of Zoloft. Correct your chemical imbalances
and you might become a happy blob.

ten-year period from 1987 to 1997, jumping from 1.8 million to 6.3 million. During 2002 alone, 8.5% of Americans took an antidepressant at some time, up from 5.6% just five years before in 1997.

Depression now arrives at younger and younger ages. The number of chil- 5 dren on mood-altering drugs tripled between 1987 and 1996. A recent cover of *Time* magazine featured a picture of Jamari, 8, who is taking medication for a mood disorder. The article described numerous cases of children suffering from anxiety disorders, depression, and obsessive-compulsive disorder. A 2003 government survey asked high school students if, during the past year, they ever "felt so sad and hopeless almost every day for two weeks or more in a row that they stopped doing some usual activities" (an accepted definition of depression). A stunning 29% of teenagers said yes, including 36% of girls (more than 1 out of 3). At the Kansas State University counseling center, the number of students treated for depression doubled between 1988 and 2001, and the number who were suicidal tripled.

I wanted to find out if this trend extended to feelings of anxiety, which often lead to depression as well as to intestinal problems, relationship dysfunction, and low life satisfaction. If anxiety had increased, this would truly be bad news for young people. As part of my doctoral dissertation, I gathered data on 40,192 college students and 12,056 children aged 9 to 17 who completed measures of anxiety between the 1950s and the 1990s. I was stunned by the size of the changes I found. Anxiety increased so much that the average college student in the 1990s was more anxious than 85% of students in the 1950s and 71 % of students in the 1970s. The trend for children was even more striking: Children as young as 9 years old were markedly more anxious than kids had been in the 1950s. The change was so large that "normal" schoolchildren in the 1980s reported higher levels of anxiety than child psychiatric patients in the 1950s.

This study had another surprising finding: *when* you were born has more influence on your anxiety level than your individual family environment. Previous research found that family environment explains only about 5% of variations in anxiety (much of the rest is a combination of genetics, peer influence, and unknown factors). Generational differences explained about 20% of the variation in anxiety—thus four times more than family environment. So even if you come from a stable, loving family, growing up amidst the stress of recent times might be enough to make you anxious.

Other studies have confirmed that younger generations experience more anxiety and stress. Twice as many people reported symptoms of panic attacks in 1995 compared to 1980, and 40% more people said they'd felt an impending nervous breakdown in 1996 than had in 1957. The number of teens aged 14 to 16 who agreed that "Life is a strain for me much of the time" quadrupled between the early 1950s and 1989. A 2001 poll found that almost 75% of teenagers said they felt nervous or stressed at least some of the time; half said they often felt this way. One out of three college freshmen reported feeling "frequently overwhelmed" in 2001, twice as many as in the 1980s.

I know this trend toward depression and anxiety firsthand. Among my ten closest friends (most in their early thirties, and living across the country), seven have been in therapy at least once, two suffer from panic attacks, one is manic-depressive, and another recently had a nervous breakdown. These are college-educated, successful, and usually well-adjusted people, but loneliness, relationship breakups, and career pressures have taken their toll.

10   Many young people shared their stories of depression and anxiety with me through my website. Several confessed to being suicidal in their early

teens. Clarissa, now 20, became depressed when she was 11. At 13, she locked herself in her room for a week and refused to speak to anyone. She took apart a plastic razor, thinking "about slicing my wrist open and watching the life drain away, taking the pain and loneliness with it." Fortunately, she realized what she was doing, and soon began counseling. Matt, 28, stood at the top of a rock quarry when he was 13 and thought of "ending it all by jumping." He didn't, but only because he wondered what the future would bring; "even though that day and the preceding days basically sucked, tomorrow may suck in a novel way." Debbie, 20, says that when she was 13, "I became unable to see that people around me cared. I was confused and unsure of how to get through the transition of child to young adult. I contemplated suicide, but when it came to it, I couldn't actually cut my flesh because I thought about my family and how awful they would feel if they buried me."

Someone commits suicide every eighteen minutes in the United States. While the suicide rate for middle-aged people has declined steeply since 1950, the suicide rate for young people has more than doubled (though it has, fortunately, declined since its peak in the early 1990s). The suicide rate for children under age 14 has doubled just since 1980. Suicide is the third leading cause of death for people aged 15 to 24. In 2003, 16.9% of high school students admitted that they had seriously considered attempting suicide during the past year, and most of those said they had made a plan about exactly how they would kill themselves. These suicidal thoughts are often brought on by depression. Miranda, an 18-year-old from the Midwest, tried to commit suicide by overdosing on drugs. "Depression tends to grab people and suck them in," she says.

The year before I moved into my college dorm at the University of Chicago, a freshman from Ohio named Jay lived on the first floor. When no one had seen Jay for a while, the resident head opened the door to his room, calling his name. After a brief glance in, the resident head quickly shut the door, blocking the view of the other students huddled behind him: Jay had hanged himself on his closet door with a belt. He had been dead for two days.

In 2003, three students committed suicide at NYU within a month of each other, two by jumping off a balcony at the campus library. Three more, NYU suicides followed in 2004. In *What Really Happened* to *the Class of '93*, Chris Colin describes his high school classmate Sean Bryant, a Rhodes scholar nominee whose goal was to become governor of Virginia. In an incident eerily similar to that in my dorm, the resident head and a friend opened Sean's door when no one answered repeated knocks. As Colin describes it, "The two stepped in and then stepped back out. Sean was hanging over his bed, from a belt looped to his bicycle hook. He was twenty-one years old."

BUT SHOULDN'T WE BE HAPPIER NOW?

At first, it seems paradoxical that GenMe feels so much anxiety and pain. After all, the lives of people born from the 1970s to the 1990s have been remarkably free of traumatic historical events. Except for a few recessions here and there, economic prosperity has reigned. There have been no world wars, and since the early 1990s, no real worries of nuclear war. (The threat of terrorism did not emerge until after the rise in depression was well established.) GenMe has never been drafted. Advances in health care and safety mean that more kids live longer and better lives. More students graduate from high school, and fewer are involved in crime than were so in the early 1990s. Teen pregnancy rates have also declined markedly over the last decade.

15   In many ways, there's no better time to be alive than right now. Think of all of the advantages we have that earlier generations did not: television, cell phones, better medical care, computers, more education, less physical labor, the freedom to make our own choices, the ability to move to a more desirable city. These last two, however, begin to hint at the underlying problem. Our growing tendency to put the self first leads to unparalleled freedom, but it also creates an enormous amount of pressure on us to stand alone. This is the downside of the focus on the self—when we are fiercely independent and self-sufficient, our disappointments loom large because we have nothing else to focus on. But it's not just us: Generation Me has been taught to expect more out of life at the very time when good jobs and nice houses are increasingly difficult to obtain. All too often, the result is crippling anxiety and crushing depression.

LONELINESS AND ISOLATION

My friend Peter moved to an apartment on the North Side of Chicago after graduating from college. He did not seem happy when I visited him that fall. He had several hellish stories about going out on dates through personal ads, including one woman who told him outright that he was not good-looking enough. His friends from college were either still living near campus or had scattered to graduate schools around the country. In his apartment, he showed me the feature on his cable TV that allowed him to buy movies. "This is what I do most weekends," he said, a sad smile on his face.

He's not the only one. More than four times as many Americans describe themselves as lonely now than in 1957. In *Bowling Alone,* Robert Putnam documents the steep decline in all kinds of social connections: we're less likely to belong to clubs and community organizations, less likely to have friends over for dinner, and less likely to visit our neighbors. Our social contacts are slight compared to those enjoyed by earlier generations.

It's almost as if we are starving for affection. "There is a kind of famine of warm interpersonal relations, of easy-to-reach neighbors, of encircling, inclusive memberships, and of solid family life," argues political scientist Robert Lane. To take the analogy a little further, we're malnourished from eating a junk-food diet of instant messages, e-mail, and phone calls, rather than the healthy food of live, in-person interaction.

It helps explain a new kind of get-together that's popping up in cities around the country: cuddle parties. It's a deliberately nonsexual (though usually coed) gathering where pajama-clad people can enjoy the hugs and touch of others, overseen by a "cuddle lifeguard on duty" who keeps things friendly and nonthreatening. One 26-year-old participant called it "rehab for lonely people." As the official website (www. cuddleparty.com, of course) explains,

"In today's world, many of us aren't getting our Recommended Daily Allowance of Welcomed Touch." Most cuddle party participants are young and single. As the website notes, "It's okay to touch the one you're dating or married to ... but what about the single people? ... We are touch-and-snuggle deprived."

For many in GenMe, the instability in close relationships began at an early age with their parents' divorce. In *Prozac Nation,* her memoir of adolescent depression, Elizabeth Wertzel describes her father's departure from her life and her mother's subsequent struggle to raise her. When Wertzel told her therapists about her background, they would say, "No wonder you're so depressed." She was not as sure. "They react as if my family situation was particularly alarming and troublesome," she writes, "as opposed to what it actually is in this day and age perfectly normal." And she's right: almost half of GenMe has seen their parents divorce, or have never known their father at all. This has a clear link to the rise in depression, as children of divorce are more likely to be anxious and depressed. Beyond the statistics, the personal stories of children of divorce—painted in books such as *The Unexpected Legacy of Divorce*—vividly illustrate the lifetime of pain, cynicism, and uncertainty that divorce can create among young people. Ashley, 24, attended a group counseling session at her elementary school, unofficially known as the "divorce club," where she and the other kids would "share our feelings of anger, sadness and confusion and listen to our peers who were sharing the same."

GenMe's own romantic relationships often don't go much better. Although a little extreme, the situations faced by the four characters on *Sex and the City* are right on the mark; the young women I know describe similar dating pitfalls of strange behavior and dashed hopes. Even when the date goes well and becomes a relationship, there is no guarantee it will last. The cycle of meeting someone, falling in love, and breaking up is a formula for anxiety and depression. This often begins in high school. Maggie, now 20, broke up with her boyfriend of a year and a half when she was 17. "I honestly thought I loved him, and I wasn't sure how I would get through the pain and loneliness," she says. In college, many people find that their romantic relationships are a lifeline in an otherwise lonely place—until the relationship ends. Leslie, 20, went through a breakup a month ago. "He was basically my whole life besides school and family," she says. "Now I am very lonely and depressed because I don't have many friends and the friends I do have are all away at their colleges."

The situation is so dire that some young people think there has to be a better way. One day in a graduate class on cultural differences, I was surprised when the students—almost all Americans from the Midwest and West—expressed their approval of arranged marriage. Two women in their mid-thirties were particularly adamant: they hated dating, living alone sucked, and they wanted to settle down. The men in the class agreed. Arranged marriage is probably not the solution, but the students' attraction to the idea is telling—young people clearly feel that something is missing in the current dating scene. The Broadway musical *Avenue Q* includes a song that sums up dating in the modern era pretty well: "There's a fine, fine line between love—and a waste of time."

Dating websites are one recent development that has made it easier to meet people, though they, too, can often lead to anxiety. You write a profile, post your picture, and wait. About half the time, no one e-mails you; often the people who do e-mail are not your type. If you e-mail other people, most of them don't write back—some as a passive form of rejection, but many others because they have let their accounts lapse. My own two months of Internet dating were fraught with worry about what I must be doing wrong and will-he-write-me-back-please-let-him-write-me-back high anxiety. I have never checked my e-mail so obsessively in my life. Fortunately, my story has a happy ending: the man who would become my husband e-mailed me on match.com (asking me, in a particularly deft generational move, what my favorite John Hughes movie was). We went out on our first date two weeks later, and married two years after that. A month later, his best friend married a woman he had met on eharmony.com.

Typical for our generation, both men were in their early thirties by this time. GenMe marries later than any other previous generation. Though later marriage has some advantages, it also means that many in GenMe spend their twenties (and sometimes thirties) in pointless dating, uncertain relationships, and painful breakups. Many relationships last several years and/or involve living together, so the breakups resemble divorces rather than run-of-the-mill heartbreak (as if there were such a thing). By the age of 24, my friend June had been involved in five serious relationships. All had lasted more than a year, and all resulted in a wrenching breakup (often because she or her boyfriend was moving to a new city for college, graduate school, or a career). I have other friends who dated or lived with someone for seven years or more before breaking up. Divorce after only a few years of marriage has become so common that Pamela Paul wrote a book called *The Starter Marriage.* It is the rare member of GenMe who has not experienced the breakup of a serious romantic relationship (or two, or five, or ten).

25 Many people think of single women when they imagine lonely young people. Watch a TV show about single women, such as *Ally McBeal,* and the enormous wave of anxiety will practically knock you out of your chair. On *Sex and the City,* Carrie compares the Catholic Church to "a desperate 36-year-old single woman, willing to settle for anything it can get." (Let's hear it for a statement that manages to insult both the Catholic Church and single women in the same breath.) Yet there is a grain of truth in the media hype. The deadline for having children—somewhere between 35 and 40—makes life extremely anxious for many single women. They constantly perform the calculation I call "woman math": "If we get married next year, I'll be 32; we'll want a year or two to be married without kids and it might take a year to get pregnant, so I'll be 34 or 35 before I'm pregnant and probably 36 when the child is born. Then if we wait until the first kid is two years old before we try for another one, I'll be trying to get pregnant at 38. Crap."

Even—or especially—women who are living with their boyfriends hear the loud ticking of the biological clock as years go by and no proposal is imminent. The new equation of premarital sex and living together before marriage might be liberating, but it has major downsides. Waiting for a guy to pop the question can be almost as anxiety-producing as being alone. Laurie, interviewed in *Emerging Adulthood,* says that during the five years she lived with the man she eventually married, "I was really stressed, because I didn't know exactly whether or not I was going to be with him or if I was wasting that much time in my life." Another couple described in the book has been living together for eighteen months. Jean, 26, wants to be engaged by Christmas. When the author interviews her boyfriend Trey, 28, however, "It becomes clear that Jean can forget about getting engaged by Christmas .... Trey says he might get married—'possibly someday ... I'm not ready to settle down yet.'" Men have the advantage of a biological clock set at a later time. As Jake puts it, "I could be 35 and marry someone who's 23. I mean, I've got all the time in the world." (Women have a word for guys like this, and it ends with hole.)

But there are plenty of lonely guys out there, too. There are actually thousands more single young men than women—between the ages of 25 and 39, for every 1 unmarried woman there are 1.2 unmarried men. Even when you look only between the ages of 35 and 39, there are thousands more unmarried men. I can hear women immediately yelling that all of the good ones are taken, but the truth is that it's single men who should be anxious and complaining. Men get lonely too, though we rarely see that addressed on TV or in the movies. For a noteworthy exception, check out the great movie *Swingers,* which features a fairly realistic look at young men talking about loneliness and their anxiety around dating. For GenMe, loneliness is an equal-opportunity experience.

As a result of modern dating, later marriage, and the higher divorce rate, a lot of people spend a great deal of time living alone. Twice as many 15-to-24-year-olds are in one-person households now compared to 1970, as are almost three times more 25-to-34-year-olds. More than 1 out of 3 people aged 25 to 29 lives alone or with roommates. A recent in-depth study found that Chicago residents, on average, spend half of their adult lives single. Being single does not have to be lonely, but for many people it often is, especially if they have been moving around and don't have friends who live close to them.

That's the other sad reality: not only is GenMe single for longer, but we often don't stay in one place long enough to make friends. More than 1 out of 4 people aged 25 to 29 moved between 2002 and 2003. It is shocking to consider the number of professions that require frequent moves for advancement. This is definitely true in academia: I have lived in six states, my friend Kathleen has lived in all four North American time zones, and few of my friends live within 500 miles of where they grew up. Doctors must move to medical school and to a residency before looking for a city in which to practice. The economic downturn in Silicon Valley in 2000 and 2001 sent many young technology employees looking for work in other cities. Even professions that don't require an advanced degree often involve frequent moves. I recently met a group of people who work in sales for a hotel chain. All had worked at more than four locations, requiring them to move every few years. Author Chris Colin, 28, sums it up: "Since high school I've had five lines of work, ... eight street addresses, two bad trips, and one cat. I had a lousy breakup with doors slamming—house doors, car doors. I lived in New York and California and Chile.... I worry, but really I'm happy, though I worry."

30   Even if you stay in the same place, just having *time* to date and make friends is difficult. With the workweek expanding from relatively sane 9-to-5 hours into countless evenings and weekends, it's often impossible to find the time and energy to be with other people. "A decade after high school, that which most impacts my classmates' love lives might be busy-ness," says Colin. Seventy-five percent of women aged 25 to 35 say that their work lives interfere with their personal lives, and 35% say that the conflict is extreme. This goes for men as well—my brother works so many hours that it's no coincidence he met both his first New York girlfriend and his wife at work. When I visited him when he was single, he spent so many hours at work that his refrigerator contained nothing but a bottle of water ("I bought that for you," he said helpfully). I started to make a grocery list and then stopped short, wondering if I needed to buy more than food. "Do you even have any bowls?" I asked. "I have *bowl*," he quipped, opening the cabinet to reveal his lone dish.

Friends of mine who are lawyers and accountants often find it difficult to spare the time for a movie, a phone call to a long-distance friend, or a casual chat with a neighbor. In *The Costs of Living*, Barry Schwartz describes a former student who says his friendships "were not that *close*. Everyone was too busy. He thought twice about burdening friends with his life and his problems because he knew how consumed they were with their own, and what a sacrifice it would entail for them to spend the time required to listen to him and to help him out." I put a Post-it note on that page and wrote, "This is a very familiar story."

Isolation and loneliness readily lead to anxiety and depression. A mountain of scientific evidence links loneliness (and being alone) with negative mental health outcomes. Single and divorced people are significantly more likely to become depressed or suffer other mental health problems. Even people in unhappy marriages are happier than those who divorce. Of course, in many situations divorce is necessary and best in the long run, but even then it is painful and can lead to depression. When you consider the loneliness felt by many young people today, it's surprising that more of us aren't depressed. I often feel that many of us are one breakup or one move away from depression—our roots are not deep enough, our support systems too shallow.

The sadness of being alone is often the flip side of freedom and putting ourselves first. When we pursue our own dreams and make our own choices, that pursuit often takes us away from friends and family. An independence-minded society such as ours would never accept rules that encouraged arranged marriage or multigenerational households. Even marriage before a certain age—these days, around 25—is viewed as unwise and overly restricting. There is nothing wrong with individual freedom, of course; this is the advantage of the social change of the last few decades. But there are consequences, and loneliness is often one of them. Janis Joplin captured the GenMe dilemma with her famous line "Freedom's just another word for nothing left to lose."

One of the strangest things about modern life is the expectation that we will stand alone, negotiating breakups, moves, divorces, and all manner of heartbreak that previous generations were careful to avoid. This may be the key to the low rate of depression among older generations: despite all the deprivation and war they experienced, they could always count on each other. People had strong feelings of community; they knew the same people all their lives; and they married young and stayed married. It may not have been exciting, and it stymied the dreams of many, but it was a stable life that avoided the melancholy that is so common now.

LOUISE DANIELLE PALMER

Growing Hope

In this blog entry, Louise Palmer summarizes work done by Anthony Scioli, who has developed a hope scale. Palmer connects hope to good health and, following Scioli, theorizes that a strong belief system is essential in forming hope and protecting us against misfortune. Further, Palmer shows that hope is a skill that can be acquired.

We all know that hope is a good thing, even an essential thing: there is no life without hope, or so the saying goes. Psychologists believe hope might be the most important feeling state or emotion we can experience. Their studies show that hope is key to good health, the best predictor of a meaningful existence, and an indicator of academic and athletic performance. Yet we tend to think of hope as something you either have or you don't, something you're born with, or born into, through perfect parenting or perfect circumstances.

Now cutting-edge psychological research, spearheaded by Anthony Scioli, Ph.D., a professor of psychology at Keene State College in New Hampshire, shows that hope is a skill you can acquire. It is active—you can cultivate and nourish it. It is multifaceted--there are 14 distinct aspects, according to Scioli. It is self-perpetuating—hopeful people tend to be more resilient, more trusting, more open, and more motivated than those less hopeful, so they are likely to receive more from the world, which in turn makes them more hopeful— which is why it's so important.

Hope is, in essence, a way of being.

TOWARD A PSYCHOLOGY OF HOPE

While theorists, psychiatrists, and physicians have touted hope as a primary agent of healing for more than four decades, it did not emerge as a popular subject of psychological inquiry until the nineties, when C. S. Snyder published *The Psychology of Hope: You Can Get There from Here.* Snyder, a pioneering researcher in the field who died last year, defined hope as a "motivational construct" that allows one to believe in positive outcomes, conceive of goals, develop strategies, and muster the motivation to implement them.

In his last presentation to the American Psychological Association (APA) 5 in 2005, Snyder laid out the results of studies conducted over a decade using the "Hope Scale," a measuring tool and test he created. "Low hope" individuals, he found, have ambiguous goals and work toward them one at a time, whereas "high hope" individuals often pursue five or six clear goals simultaneously. Hopeful people had preferred routes to achievement and alternate pathways in case of obstacles. Low scorers didn't.

Other prominent researchers also have argued that hope is essential to aging well and performing well. Their work shows that hopeful people have more self-esteem, take better physical care of themselves, and can better tolerate pain. Hopeful people provide "social benefit," because they use a "me/we" way of thinking and help others succeed. Outlining the results of one study in which depressed elderly people were taught to think hopefully, Snyder said, "As they became more hopeful, they became more grateful ... and more likely to experience joy." They learned to "accentuate the positive," and to laugh at themselves and others. "If you haven't learned how to laugh at yourself," he concluded, "you've missed the biggest joke of all!"

THE NEW "HOPE THEORY"

With a new body of research and his own Hope Scale which took six years to develop, Scioli has expanded the conventional psychological approach to hope. His new theory captures the complexity of hope with its roots in the "deeper" self, its foundation in relationships, and its spiritual core. The kind of hope Scioli is concerned with is not about small wishes but big dreams. Hope sustains our intimate bonds, gives life purpose and meaning, and determines our prospects for survival and health.

Hope, Scioli theorizes, has a strong spiritual (and transpersonal) dimension. It is associated with virtues such as patience, gratitude, charity, and faith. "Faith is the building block of hope," he says. Above all, it is based on relationships, on a collaborative connection with people as well as a higher power, as distinct from optimism, which is connected to self-confidence. True hope also differs from denial, which is really false hope, an avoidance of reality that narrows one's field of focus. (For a look at your "hope foundation," see page 44.)

OUR MOST POWERFUL PREDICTOR OF WELL-BEING

Scioli recently studied the relative importance of hope, age, and gratitude as predictors of well-being. Based on his sample of 75 people between 18 and 65, using three different scales, he consistently found that a high level of hope was the most powerful predictor of well-being—a finding that surprised even him.

10   Hope also appears to buffer anxiety about death and dying. In another study, using his Comprehensive Hope Scale, Scioli showed a group of young adults a 10-minute clip from the movie *Philadelphia*, in which Tom Hanks plays a man dying of AIDS. Scioli then gave them a questionnaire to measure their fear of dying and death. The results showed that anxiety about death did not spike in people who scored high in hope, but did spike in low scorers.

Scioli believes that hope ultimately reflects the depth of the mind/body connection. Last year, he conducted a study of 12 thyroid cancer patients and found that the hopeful ones reported better health and less distress and worry about their health. Because the sample was small, Scioli added HIV-positive people to the study and got the same results: HIV-positive patients with high hope reported better health and less worry than those with low hope. Interestingly, they also exhibited less denial about their condition.

He corroborated their claims by examining their immune cell (CD4) count, as well as interviewing each individual's case manager. The CD4 count and case manager reports were a check against the chicken-and-egg question (did the patients feel more hopeful because they were physically healthier or were they in better health because they had hope?). His early findings strongly suggest that hope affects our immune systems and general health.

THE KEY TO A HEALTHY INTERNAL ENVIRONMENT

"Hope represents an adaptive 'middle ground' between the over-activated 'stress response' and the disengaged 'giving-up complex:'" Scioli writes in his forthcoming book. "At the physiological level, hopefulness can help to impart a balance of sympathetic and parasympathetic activity while assuring appropriate levels of neurotransmitters, hormones, lymphocytes, and other critical health-related substances. Equally important, a hopeful attitude may permit an individual to sustain this healthy 'internal environment' in the presence of enormous adversity."

Common sense tells us, and research shows, that harboring an open and "eternal" perspective lessens the impact of both minor stresses and major existential challenges. It brings light into times of darkness and uncertainty. If you are hopeful, you will be supported from within by your beliefs and values, and from without by a caring network of loved ones. Both systems of support protect you in misfortune, including serious illness. But Scioli's expansive view of this valuable resource and complex emotion reminds us that we can't rely on hope alone in challenging times. Rather, we need to have a belief system that gives us "a hope for every season."

Assignment Ideas

In writing your essay, keep in mind the importance of language in understanding this subject. Be careful not to use inappropriate synonyms for "hope" and "depression" that might connote meanings different than what you have in mind. The arrangement or organization of your essay will also be key, especially if you have a provocative thesis, as you may need to prepare your audience for understandings that might deviate from societal norms or expectations. Many people have suffered through depressive episodes and have strong feelings on the subject, so structuring your essay in a way that such readers can immediately relate to you will grant you credibility and make them more willing and eager to continue reading.

1. Twenge sets up a contrast between following individual pursuits with the concomitant excitement of possible success and allowing goals to be stymied in order to create stability and avoid depression. Locate the basis

of her ideas through a summary of the excerpt from her book and compare it to experiences or observations you may have had with depression. Further, talk to a relative or friend who was born before 1970 to see how depression was perceived and experienced. Relate what you find and see if it confirms, extends, limits, or denies Twenge's contentions. What part, ultimately, does individualism play in depression? You may refer to the Overview and any of your pre-writing about the effect of language in coming to a conclusion.

2. Palmer makes many claims about the effects of hope, suggesting that hope has a spiritual dimension and can strengthen our immune system while increasing our general health. Research more about hope theory. Palmer mentions C. S. Snyder and Anthony Scioli, so their work would be good places to begin. However, locate sources that might complicate, extend, or dispute Snyder's and Scioli's findings. Relate what you find and reach a conclusion about the place of hope in combating depression.

3. Can depression lead to insights or otherwise be helpful in forming character? The Overview suggests that our culture is full of images of brooding individuals that carry an appeal for many people, so there are associations between creativity, reflective, and other desirable character traits and depression. Use your experiences or observations to support your answer to the question, making sure to give plentiful detail of a specific instance that responds to the question, and consult outside sources to lend further credibility to your ideas. You might use Susanna Kaysen's "One Cheer for Melancholy" (page 479) as one source and perhaps information or writings from a tortured artist who interests you as another.

4. Using your brainstorming on the connection between the lack of hope and political and social events and/or your lists concerning hope and action, write an essay where you confirm, extend, limit, or deny the claim that hope can be formed through collective, political action. Have you ever participated in a protest, joined a political action group, attended a "beautify the city" or a similar community-based gathering or volunteered for programs or projects designed to help a particular segment of the population? How does that make you feel? Was it better doing it in groups or doing it alone? If you have never done anything collectively to confront a problem, why not? Do you think the lack of involvement affects your mood? Reach a conclusion where you use your experiences and feelings as specific examples and generalize about the connection between hope and collective action.

Group Work

Self-help books often give advice on how to improve your life and increase your happiness. As such, we can interpret them as attempts to combat depression and cynicism. Yet, do their methods work? Do they advocate individualism through their rhetoric? Do they suggest ways to help individuals become more social and communal? What are the assumptions behind them? Each group member should read and analyze one such self-help book, answer the above questions, and find other patterns and features of the book. As a group, compare your findings and write a paper that generalizes about the rhetoric and efficacy of these books, comparing the dominant patterns to either those in the Overview or those represented in any of the readings in this chapter. Do these books give realistic, helpful advice that could improve people's lives if followed? Be careful not to select a text that looks like a self-help book, but is really concerned with diets, do-it-yourself-repairs, or proselytizing.

Additional Readings

The following selections are designed to supplement the ideas and assignments already discussed. "Epimetheus and Pandora" represents one reading of the well-known Greek myth, "Pandora's Box." Bruce Levine's "Fundamentalist Consumerism and an Insane Society" suggests that consumerism is one of the main problems driving some citizens to medication and others toward what can best be described as insane acts. "One Cheer for Melancholy" comes from the collection Unholy Ghost: Writers on Depression and explore depression in unusual ways.

Epimetheus and Pandora

The first mortals lived on earth in a state of perfect innocence and bliss. The air was pure and balmy; the sun shone brightly all the year; the earth brought forth delicious fruit in abundance; and beautiful, fragrant flowers bloomed everywhere. Man was content. Extreme cold, hunger, sickness, and death were unknown. Jupiter, who justly ascribed a good part of this beatific condition to the gift conferred by Prometheus, was greatly displeased, and tried to devise some means to punish mankind for the acceptance of the heavenly fire.

With this purpose in view, he assembled the gods on Mount Olympus, where, in solemn council, they decided to create woman; and as soon as she had been artfully fashioned, each one endowed her with some special charm, to make her more attractive.

> "The crippled artist-god,
> Illustriol moulded from the yeilding clay
> A bashful virgin's image, as advis'd
> Saturnian Jove.

> . . .

> "But now when the fair mischief, seeming good,
> His hand had perfected, he led her forth

> Exulting in her grac'd attire, the gift
> Of Pallas, in the midst of gods and men.
> On men and gods in that same moment seiz'd
> The ravishment of wonder, when they saw
> The deep deceit, th' inextricable snare."
>
> *Hesiod (Elton's tr.).*

Their united efforts were crowned with the utmost, success. Nothing was lacking, except a name for the peerless creature; and the gods, after due consideration, decreed she should he called Pandora. They then bade Mercury take her to Prometheus as a gift from heaven; but he, knowing only too well that nothing good would come to him from the gods, refused to accept her, and cautioned his brother Epimetheus to follow his example. Unfortunately Epimetheus was of a confiding disposition, and when he beheld the maiden he exclaimed, "Surely so beautiful and gentle a being can bring no evil!" and accepted her most joyfully.

The first days of their union were spent in blissful wanderings, hand in hand, under the cool forest shade; in weaving garlands of fragrant flowers; and in refreshing themselves with the luscious fruit, which hung so temptingly within reach.

5   One lovely evening, while dancing on the green, they saw Mercury. Jupiter's messenger, coming towards them. His step was slow and weary, his garments dusty and travel-stained, and he seemed almost to stagger beneath the weight of a huge box which rested upon his shoulders. Pandora immediately ceased dancing, to speculate with feminine curiosity upon the contents of the chest. In a whisper she begged Epimetheus to ask Mercury what brought him thither. Epimetheus complied with her request; but Mercury evaded the question, asked permission to deposit his burden in their dwelling for safe-keeping, professing himself too weary to convey it to its destination that day, and promised to call for it shortly. The permission was promptly granted. Mercury, with a sigh of relief, placed the box in one corner, and then departed, refusing all hospitable offers of rest and refreshment.

He had scarcely crossed the threshold, when Pandora expressed a strong desire to have a peep at the contents of the mysterious box; but Epimetheus, surprised and shocked, told her that her curiosity was unseemly, and then, to dispel the frown and pout seen for the first time on the fair face of his beloved, he entreated her to come out into the fresh air and join in the merry games of their companions. For the first time, also, Pandora refused to comply with his request. Dismayed, and very much discouraged, Epimetheus sauntered out alone, thinking she would soon join him, and perhaps by some caress atone for her present wilfulness.

Left alone with the mysterious casket, Pandora became more and more inquisitive. Stealthily she drew near and examined it with great interest, for it was curiously wrought of dark wood, and surmounted by a delicately carved head, of such fine workmanship that it seemed to smile and encourage her. Around the box a glittering golden cord was wound and fastened on top in an intricate knot. Pandora, who prided herself specially on her deft fingers, felt sure she could unfasten it, and, reasoning that it would not be indiscreet to untie it if she did not raise the lid, she set to work. Long she strove, but all in vain. Ever and anon the laughing voices of Epimetheus and his companions, playing in the luxuriant shade, were wafted in on the summer breeze. Repeatedly she heard them call and beseech her to join them; yet she persisted in her attempt. She was just on the point of giving up in despair, when suddenly the refractory knot yielded to her fumbling fingers, and the cord, unrolling, dropped on the floor.

Pandora had repeatedly fancied that sounds like whispers issued from the box. The noise now seemed to increase, and she breathlessly applied her ear to the lid to ascertain whether it really proceeded from within. Imagine, therefore, her surprise when she distinctly heard these words, uttered in the most pitiful accents: "Pandora, dear Pandora, have pity upon us! Free us from this gloomy prison! Open, open, we beseech you!"

Pandora's heart beat so fast and loud, that it seemed for a moment to drown all other sounds. Should she open the box? Just then a familiar step outside made her start guiltily. Epimetheus was coming, and she knew he would urge her again to come out, and would prevent the gratification of her curiosity. Precipitately, therefore, she raised the lid to have one little peep before he came in.

Now, Jupiter had malignantly crammed into this box all the diseases, 10 sorrows, vices, and crimes that afflict poor humanity; and the box was no sooner opened, than all these ills flew out, in the guise of horrid little brown-winged creatures, closely resembling moths. These little insects fluttered about, alighting, some upon Epimetheus, who had just entered, and some upon Pandora, pricking and stinging them most unmercifully. They then flew out through the open door and windows, and fastened upon the merry-makers without, whose shouts of joy were soon changed into wails of pain and anguish.

Epimetheus and Pandora had never before experienced the faintest sensation of pain or anger; but, as soon as these winged evil spirits had stung them, they began to weep, and, alas! quarrelled for the first time in their lives. Epimetheus reproached his wife in bitterest terms for her thoughtless action; but in the very midst of his vituperation he suddenly heard a sweet little voice entreat for freedom. The sound proceeded from the unfortunate box, whose cover Pandora had dropped again, in the first moment of her surprise and pain. "Open, open, and I will heal your wounds! Please let me out!" it pleaded.

The tearful couple viewed each other inquiringly, and listened again. Once more they heard the same pitiful accents; and Epimetheus bade his wife open the box and set the speaker free, adding very amiably, that she had already done so much harm by her ill-fated curiosity, that it would be difficult to add materially to its evil consequences, and that, perchance, the box contained some good spirit whose ministrations might prove beneficial.

It was well for Pandora that she opened the box a second time, for the gods with a sudden impulse of compassion had concealed among the evil spirits one kindly creature, Hope, whose mission was to heal the wounds inflicted by her fellow prisoners.

"Hope sole remain'd within, nor took her flight,
Beneath the vessel's verge conceal'd from light."

Hesiod (Elton's tr.).

15   Lightly fluttering hither and thither on her snowy pinions, Hope touched the wounded places on Pandora's and Epimetheus' creamy skin, and relieved their suffering, then quickly flew out of the open window, to perform the same gentle office for the other victims, and to cheer their downcast spirits.

Thus, according to the ancients, evil entered into the world, bringing untold misery; but Hope followed closely in its footsteps, to aid struggling humanity, and point to a happier future.

"Hope rules a land for ever green :
All powers that serve the bright-eyed Queen
Are confident and gay;
Clouds at her bidding disappear;
Points to aught ?—the bliss draws near,
And Faney smooths the way."

Wordsworth.

BRUCE E. LEVINE

Fundamentalist Consumerism and an Insane Society

At a giant Ikea store in Saudi Arabia in 2004, three people were killed by a stampede of shoppers fighting for one of a limited number of $150 credit vouchers. Similarly, in November 2008, a worker at a New York Wal-Mart was trampled to death by shoppers intent on buying one of a limited number of 50-inch plasma HDTVs.

Jdiniytai Damour, a temporary maintenance worker was killed on "Black Friday." In the predawn darkness, approximately 2,000 shoppers waited impatiently outside Wal-Mart, chanting, "Push the doors in." According to Damour's fellow worker Jimmy Overby, "He was bum-rushed by 200 people. They took the doors off the hinges. He was trampled and killed in front of me." Witnesses reported that Damour, 34 years old, gasped for air as shoppers continued to surge over him. When police instructed shoppers to leave the store after Damour's death, many refused, some yelling, "I've been in line since yesterday morning."

The mainstream press covering Damour's death focused on the mob of crazed shoppers and, to a lesser extent, irresponsible Wal-Mart executives who failed to provide security. However, absent in the corporate press was anything about a consumer culture and an insane society in which marketers, advertisers, and media promote the worship of cheap stuff.

Along with journalists, my fellow mental health professionals have also covered up societal insanity. An exception is the democratic-socialist psychoanalyst Erich Fromm (1900–1980). Fromm, in *The Sane Society* (1955), wrote: "Yet many psychiatrists and psychologists refuse to entertain the idea that society as a whole may be lacking in sanity. They hold that the problem of mental health in a society is only that of the number of 'unadjusted' individuals, and not of a possible unadjustment of the culture itself."

While people can resist the cheap-stuff propaganda and not worship at 5 Wal-Mart, Ikea, and other big-box cathedrals—and stay out of the path of a mob of fundamentalist consumers—it is difficult to protect oneself from the slow death caused by consumer culture. Human beings are every day and in numerous ways psychologically, socially, and spiritually assaulted by a culture which:

- creates increasing material expectations
- devalues human connectedness
- socializes people to be self-absorbed
- obliterates self-reliance
- alienates people from normal human emotional reactions
- sells false hope that creates more pain

Increasing material expectations.   These expectations often go unmet and create pain, which fuels emotional difficulties and destructive behaviors. In a now classic 1998 study examining changes in the mental health of Mexican immigrants who came to the United States, public policy researcher William Vega found that assimilation to U.S. society meant three times the rate of depressive episodes for these immigrants. Vega also found major increases in substance abuse and other harmful behaviors. Many of these immigrants found themselves with the pain of increased material expectations that went dissatisfied and they also reported the pain of diminished social support.

Devaluing of human connectedness.   A 2006 study in the *American Sociological Review* noted that the percentage of Americans who reported being without a single close friend to confide in rose in the last 20 years from 10 percent to almost 25 percent. Social isolation is highly associated with depression and other emotional problems. Increasing loneliness, however, is good news for a consumer economy that thrives on increasing numbers of "buying units"—lonely people means selling more televisions, DVDs, psychiatric drugs, etc.

Promotes selfishness.   Self-absorption is one of many reasons for U.S. skyrocketing rates of depression and other emotional difficulties—and self-absorption is exactly what a consumer culture demands. The Buddha, 2,500 years ago, recognized the relationship between selfish craving and emotional difficulties, and many observers of human beings, from Spinoza to Erich Fromm, have come to similar conclusions.

Obliterates self-reliance.   The loss of self-reliance can create painful anxiety, which fuels depression and other problematic behaviors. In modern society, an increasing number of people—women as well as men—cannot cook a simple meal. They will never know the anti-anxiety effects of being secure in their ability to prepare their own food, grow their own vegetables, hunt, fish or gather food for survival. In a consumer culture, such self-reliance makes no sense. At some level, people know that should they lose their incomes—not impossibilities these days—they have no ability to survive.

10 **Alienation from humanity.**   The priests of consumer culture—advertisers and marketers—know that fundamentalist consumers will buy more if they are alienated from such normal reactions as boredom, frustration, sadness, and anxiety. If these priests can convince us that a given emotional state is shameful or evidence of a disease, then we will be more likely to buy not only psychiatric drugs, but also all kinds of products to make ourselves feel better. When we become frightened and alienated from a natural human reaction, this "pain over pain" creates more fuel for depression and other self-destructive behaviors and harmful actions.

Pain of false hope.   The false hope of fundamentalist consumerism is that we will one day discover a product that can predictably manipulate moods without any downsides. Modern psychiatry is a full member of consumer culture. Its "Holy Grail" is a search for the antidepressant that can take away the pain of despair, but not destroy life. In the late 19th century, Freud thought he had found it with cocaine. In the middle of the 20th century, psychiatrists thought they had found it with amphetamines, and later with tricyclic antidepressants like Tofranil and Elavil. At the end of the 20th century, there were the SSRIs, such as Prozac, Paxil, and Zoloft, which were ultimately found to create dependency and painful withdrawal and to be no more effective than placebos. Whatever the antidepressant drug, it is introduced as taking away depression without destroying life. Time after time, it is then discovered that when one tinkers with neurotransmitters, there is—as there is with electroshock and psycho-surgery—damage to life.

Fundamentalists reject both reason and experience. Fundamentalists are attached to dogma and if their dogma fails, they don't give it up, but instead resolve to deepen their faith and double down on their dogma.

Erich Fromm, 54 years ago, concluded: "Man [sic] today is confronted with the most fundamental choice; not that between Capitalism or Communism, but that between robotism (of both the capitalist and the communist variety), or Humanistic Communitarian Socialism. Most facts seem to indicate that he is choosing robotism and that means, in the long run, insanity and destruction. But all these facts are not strong enough to destroy faith in man's reason, good will, and sanity. As long as we can think of other alternatives, we are not lost."

Breaking free of fundamentalist consumerism means thinking of alternatives and it also means an active defiance: choosing to experience the various dimensions of life that have been excluded by the dogma.

SUSANNA KAYSEN

One Cheer for Melancholy

Sadness or gloom, says the dictionary, from the Greek "black bile." Definition two is, Pensive reflection or contemplation. Keats wrote an ode to it; Robert Burton wrote an anatomy of it; Freud wrote a major essay about it. Before somebody rechristened it depression, it was common, and commonly accepted as part of life.

That's all over now—the commonly accepted part, anyhow. Commonly complained about is more like it, to judge from the flood of memoirs and preventive manuals. I'm guilty of contributing to that flood. Consider this a sandbag.

I think melancholy is useful. In its aspect of pensive reflection or contemplation, it's the source of many books (even those complaining about it) and paintings, much scientific insight, the resolution of many fights between couples and friends, and the process known as becoming mature.

Here are the characteristic feelings: It's all wrong. I did it wrong. I'm no good at this. This idea stinks. That paragraph doesn't mean anything. These data don't add up to squat. We always end up yelling about the same two things. I can't ever seem to bring anything I start to completion.

Next step: Why bother?

Some people stop there. Some people get stuck there for months or years. Some people move to, But suppose I did it this way? Half the time, "this way" leads back to, It's all wrong. Even when it doesn't, It's all wrong might turn up at any moment.

Those feelings are unpleasant, but they spur change. What would we be without self-doubt and despair?

More energetic, more productive, and happier, say the depressophobes. In my continuing argument with them (which occurs only in my melancholic mind) I object that though we would probably be more energetic, we wouldn't necessarily be more productive. There's no certainty that our products would be better because there were more of them, anyhow. I'm not even convinced that we'd be happier.

A couple of my friends are chronic optimists. They are often disappointed because things didn't work out as well as they have expected. I have never had such a feeling because I'm a pessimist. I get my disappointment over with beforehand. If things don't work out, I'm smug because I predicted it. If they do, I'm pleasantly surprised. Any psychiatrist can tell you this is a standard defense mechanism against disappointment and loss. But so is optimism—and optimism is a lousy defense mechanism because more than half the time it leaves you feeling bad.

My main objection to optimism is that it's incorrect. Things are somewhat more likely to turn out badly. Taking the long view, things are definitely going to turn out badly, since we all die at the end. I once read about a study

5

10

of "depressives" and "normal people" predicting outcomes in real-life situations. The depressives' predictions were more often right. The pessimistic outlook is actually the realistic one.

If the price of being happier is an occluded worldview, I don't want to pay it. I'd rather see things clearly. Seeing things clearly, for me, is a sort of happiness, even if what I see is banal or sad. Does one of my friends turn on me every time I get depressed? Does another get pleasure from putting me down? Do the idiotic events of history continue to repeat themselves, with tragic consequences? Yes, yes, and yes—but at least I know what I'm up against.

I also know that I am supposed to say that there are serious drawbacks to the melancholic temperament. Deep depression is debilitating. As doctors and drug manufacturers like to remind us, depression can be fatal. Public health officials talk about all the time "wasted" by being depressed. And yet, it's not all uncommon activity, wasting time in this way. If the depressive and manic-depressive constitutions are such a liability, why are they rather prevalent in the human population?

One answer may be balance. I've learned this from my optimistic friends. I rely on them and their cheerful attitudes. Together, we make a complete picture. My doom and gloom may be more often right, but they aren't the whole story. My optimistic friends are more likely to take a risk than I am. They don't think it's risky, since they think things will work out well. They can prod me to try something I'd talk myself out of on my own. On the other hand, I've pulled them back from the brink of a few big messes, which they'd convinced themselves were going to be fabulous.

Extrapolate this to the general population and you have an American Constitution situation in which nobody gets too carried away. Checks and balances: not a bad arrangement.

15   Let's suppose this is true, that there is a species benefit to having a majority of can-do types mixed with a significant minority of worriers and brooders. Most people would rather be part of the optimist group than the pessimist group, at least in modern America, where optimism is highly valued and irony, pessimism, and sadness are seen as "negative thinking."

Americans are saddled with the idea that we can and should be happy. It's as if we've misread the Declaration of Independence and think it guarantees us the right not to pursue happiness but to achieve it. We have a low pain threshold for sadness, which inevitably means we complain a lot about it—especially when decades of prosperity have given the middle classes more time to ruminate on whether we feel good or bad.

The consensus seems to be that we feel bad. On talk shows and in support groups, in memoirs and collections of essays, we reveal that we've been abused, thwarted and disappointed, and are now depressed. Misery has come out of the closet. Now it's like a hyperactive jack-in-the-box that won't go back in.

It's telling that I wrote the word "hyperactive" there. Things that used to be adjectives are now diseases. Kids who were wriggly and irritable fifteen years ago have Attention Deficit Disorder nowadays. I won't even bother with the Love/Gambling/ Credit Addiction stuff. The general climate is a pathologizing one, and it's not hard to see why. Extraordinary leaps in medicine have raised extraordinary expectations for the cure (or at least mitigation) of ailments that have plagued people for millennia. Combine those expectations with our equally unreasonable expectations for happiness, and you get a lot of people clamoring to label themselves diseased in the hope that they can be cured. This faith in science is ill-advised. Despite Prozac and her daughters, there's no cure for sadness.

I can hear the objections. Sadness isn't depression! Depression kills! Depression, in its severity and duration, is different from what Freud called common misery. That's true, but I'm not convinced most people can tell the difference these days. People are often attracted by the idea that they have something really bad.

Here's an anecdote. When my book was having its moment of success, 20 I was part of a group of "experts" on a TV talk show about (what else?) Prozac, though I'd explained to several people connected with the show that I'd never taken it and knew nothing about it. The discussion was heated. I got into a wrangle with a woman in the studio audience whose dog had died. "I couldn't function," she said. "I *had* to take Prozac." When I pointed out that grief was a normal, healthy response to the death of her dog, she became furious. "You've never been really depressed," she told me. I didn't want to get into a competition about who'd been more depressed, so I repeated my idea that some things in life were truly sad and worth feeling depressed about. She just wasn't having any. "You don't understand clinical depression," she said. I gave up.

The important word was "clinical." She'd latched onto that, though I wasn't sure why. Maybe naming her feelings and labeling them a disease relieved the guilt and shame that often accompany depression. Maybe it helped her stop punishing herself for a failure of will.

The Failure of Will theory is equally popular with people who are not depressed. Get out and take your mind off yourself, they say. You're too self-absorbed. This is just about the stupidest thing you can say to a depressed person, and it is said *every* day to depressed people all over this country. And if it isn't that, it's, Shut up and take your Prozac.

These attitudes are contradictory. Conquer Your Depression and Everything Can Be Fixed by the Miracle of Science presuppose opposite explanations for the problem. One blames character, the other neurotransmitters. They are often thrown at the sufferer in sequence: Get out and do something, and if that doesn't work, take pills. Sometimes they're used simultaneously: You won't take those pills because you don't WANT to do anything about your depression, i.e., Failure of Will.

The one thing these attitudes share is the idea that sadness is bad and must be eliminated.

I don't think it's so bad. I think depression and despair are reasonable 25 reactions to the nature of life. Life has its ups and downs. It is unreliable and conditional and provisional. It can be, as we used to say in my youth, a real bummer. Failure, disease, death; standard life events. Is it any surprise if some of the time, some of us feel like hell?

The worst thing about depression—the thing that makes people phobic about it—is that it's a foretaste of death. It's a trip to the country of nothingness. Reality loses its substance and becomes ghostly, transparent, unbelievable. This perception of what's outside infects the perception of the self, which explains why depressed people feel they aren't "there."

This tells us something important about what it means to *be* "there." It means believing the evidence of our senses, believing in heat and cold and hunger and smoothness and sexual desire. What philosophers the melancholics are, positing a world in which the tree doesn't make a noise even when it falls right in front of your face!

When I'm feeling good, I sometimes think of feeling depressed, the sliminess of it, when what I see has a shimmer of not-thereness and what I feel has a slippery way of falling off after a minute, so that I can't sustain the sensation of being alive. But it's far away at that moment—as far as vivacity is when I'm depressed.

I know they are both real.

30   The melancholic temperament is equipped to perceive and, more important, to tolerate the fundamental ambiguities of life. The transient nature of happiness, beauty, success, and health may come as a shock to the upbeat person but it's old hat to the depressive. And, I think depressive people have more fun. Human nature being what it is, we enjoy more whatever is hard to get and in short supply. Happiness is certainly both, and nobody knows that better than someone who spends half the time sunk in gloom.

"Ay, in the very temple of Delight / Veil'd Melancholy has her sovran shrine," said Keats. He was right: everything passes, everything can become its opposite at a moment's notice. Read it and weep—or laugh, if you're a melancholic sort.

· CREDITS ·

· INDEX ·